GOVERNMENTS AND POLITICS

OF SOUTHEAST ASIA

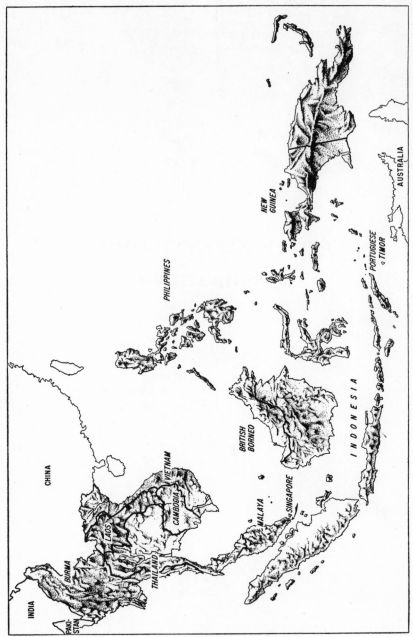

Southeast Asia

Governments and Politics
of Southeast Asia

EDITED BY GEORGE McTURNAN KAHIN

——————— CONTRIBUTORS ———————

David A. Wilson, Josef Silverstein,

Herbert Feith, J. Norman Parmer,

Wells C. Klein, Marjorie Weiner,

and David Wurfel

PUBLISHED UNDER THE AUSPICES OF THE
SOUTHEAST ASIA PROGRAM, CORNELL UNIVERSITY

CORNELL UNIVERSITY PRESS

Ithaca, New York

This work has been brought to publication with the assistance of a grant from the Ford Foundation.

© *1959 by Cornell University*

CORNELL UNIVERSITY PRESS

First published 1959
Second printing 1961
Third printing 1962

PRINTED IN THE UNITED STATES OF AMERICA

Preface

SOUTHEAST ASIA is not an area of great political homogeneity. Politically as well as culturally its component states are more varied than those of Europe. Differences in their traditional cultures and in their colonial and postcolonial histories have produced substantially dissimilar results, and any close scrutiny of their contemporary governments and politics will disclose at least as many important differences as similarities. Insofar as Southeast Asia is a unit, it is one largely because of the geographical propinquity of the countries it incorporates, because of a rough similarity in their economies and many of their economic problems, and perhaps also because in varying degrees all of them are aware of being flanked by the two colossi of Asia—China and India. And if the states of Southeast Asia are referred to as neighbors, they must be regarded as one does dwellers of adjacent apartments in an upper Fifth Avenue Manhattan apartment house—though they live next to one another, they have little common social intercourse, and their closest acquaintances are elsewhere. Originally, of course, this was not the case, this characteristic being primarily a consequence of dissimilar patterns of colonial rule by four different colonial powers. It has been only during the last few years that intercourse between the countries of Southeast Asia has shown promise of becoming once again significant; and even today their relations with countries outside the area—in Europe, in America, and elsewhere in Asia—are of considerably more importance.

There is now rather widespread agreement that the study of government and politics of Western states has reached a level making possible an appreciable amount of scholarly comparison and some generalizations based thereon. Although there are those who are impatient to do the same with such countries as are covered in this book, we have come to the conclusion in preparing the volume that, because of insufficient fundamental monographic material, an attempt at this stage to form broad generalizations about the political systems of the states of Southeast Asia would be premature. We have, however, made considerable effort to organize and analyze our data concerning the countries which we cover in order to provide for as much similarity of treatment as we believe is consistent with the differences in their cultural and political orders. By casting the six sections in a broadly uniform pattern of organization and applying approximately similar analyses to the political development and current political processes of each country, we have sought to make our materials more understandable, especially for those having little or no background concerning the area. At the same time we have tried to present these materials in such a way as to be of help to those desiring to go farther than we have in the drawing of comparisons.

In attempting to work out a system of organization and analysis which could be effectively applied to all the countries covered, the contributors and I met together regularly at Cornell University for several months before the first drafts were begun. We tried to confront the problem with a fresh eye and to avoid approaches worked out for the study of Western societies where they did not seem to be genuinely applicable. Upon completion of the several drafts we successively re-evaluated our initial findings. In view of the substantial effort we made, the results presented here will no doubt appear rather modest, but we are convinced that to have attempted any greater uniformity of treatment would have been arbitrary and have led to artificiality. We believe that we could have gone appreciably farther only by neglecting peculiar and vitally important attributes of government and politics in some of the countries covered, achieving then a consistency and balance which would have been spurious. Consequently we have limited our efforts and have sought to provide for a latitude and flexibility sufficient to do justice to the many differing characteristics displayed.

This book is limited to the six largest states of Southeast Asia—
Thailand, Burma, Indonesia, Malaya (plus Singapore), Vietnam, and
the Philippines. (The order in which they are presented may seem
arbitrary, but we believe it has a certain logic.) Cambodia, Laos, the
colonies of British Borneo, and Portuguese Timor are not covered. We
do not consider that Cambodia, for instance, is unimportant because
its population happens to be smaller than that of any of the six countries about which we write. It is important, and had it been possible
we would have included coverage of it as well as Laos and the few
still extant colonial areas. The fact that we have not is indicative of the
lack of competent specialists, not only at Cornell but in the United
States as a whole. Fortunately this situation is changing, and perhaps in
a future edition of this book it will be possible to include these omitted
countries.

It is likely that the six countries which we treat are strange to many
of our readers. Because of this and because like other states their
present courses are much influenced by their pasts, we have felt the
need to provide considerable historical background—the first chapter
in each section. In every case this is followed by a chapter describing
the contemporary social and economic setting insofar as this is necessary for understanding recent and current developments in government and politics. The generally more substantial third chapter of
each section is devoted to a description and analysis of governmental
organization and the political process. In the fourth and final chapter
of the several sections the outstanding problems presently confronting
the various governments are discussed. In the case of Vietnam a fifth
chapter is devoted to the Communist regime in the northern half of
the country. In each coverage the final chapter is followed by a critical
annotated bibliography of readings (limited almost exclusively to materials in English) designed to provide guidance to those readers who
wish to look more deeply into particular aspects of the subjects treated.

The contributors have several qualities in common. Each has spent
from one to four years in the country about which he writes. Nearly
all of them have already published scholarly monographs or articles
based on their research in these countries. Each is at present or was
until recently a graduate fellow in the Cornell Southeast Asia Program.
The academic discipline of five of them, and of the editor, is political
science; the other two have been trained primarily in history and in
anthropology but have substantial background in political science as
well. In addition, the several drafts of each writer's section have been

read critically by all, or nearly all, of the other contributors as well as by the editor.

Herbert Feith worked for four years (1951–1953 and 1954–1956) in the Ministry of Information of the Republic of Indonesia as a member of the Australian Volunteer Graduate Scheme for Indonesia. In 1956 he was appointed a research associate in political science of the Cornell Modern Indonesia Project. He spent another three months in Indonesia in mid-1957.

Wells C. Klein, who is trained as an anthropologist, served as director of the CARE operation in Vietnam from July 1954 to December 1955. He was a fellow of the Ford Foundation Foreign Area Training Program at Cornell from 1957 to 1959.

J. Norman Parmer, assistant professor of history at the University of Maryland, carried out research in Malaya from November 1952 to March 1955 under the auspices of the New York State School of Industrial and Labor Relations at Cornell University.

Josef Silverstein, instructor in government at Wesleyan University, undertook a year's research in Burma in 1955–1956 as a fellow jointly of the Ford Foundation Foreign Area Training Program and the Fulbright Program.

Marjorie Weiner, trained as a political scientist, served in Vietnam from June 1955 to August 1957 with the Education Division of the United States Operations Mission (ICA).

David A. Wilson, lecturer in political science at the University of California (Los Angeles), was in Thailand from 1952 to 1954 as a Fulbright teacher and lecturer at Čhulalongkǫn University and during 1956–1958 as a fellow of the Ford Foundation Foreign Area Training Program.

David Wurfel, instructor in political science at the International Christian University, Tokyo, studied at the University of the Philippines in 1947 and 1948 and carried out research in the Philippines during 1955–1956 as a fellow of the Ford Foundation Foreign Area Training Program.

A number of people gave generously of their time in critically reading through drafts of particular sections. Their comments and suggestions have been very helpful, and we wish to express jointly our sincere gratitude to them. Space does not permit mention of all those to whom we are so indebted, but we would especially like to express our thanks to U Aung Chan Tha, John S. Carroll, Boyd R. Compton, Idrus N. Djajadiningrat, Bernard Fall, Benjamin Higgins, Roy Jumper,

Thomas McHale, J. A. C. Mackie, Gerald S. Maryanov, David H. Penny, Herbert Phillips, Milton Sachs, Hans O. Schmitt, Lauriston Sharp, John R. W. Smail, Robert B. Textor, Ambassador U Thant, K. D. Thomas, and George Weightman. To Mr. Robert Dockendorff we wish to express our appreciation for his excellent work in preparing the maps and charts. Mr. Feith, Mr. Parmer, Mr. Silverstein, and Mr. Wilson wish to record their indebtedness to their respective wives, Betty, Bess, Lynn, and Marie, for their encouragement and their suggestions. Finally, I wish to express my gratitude to David Wilson for his valuable assistance in the final stages of editing and production of this book following my departure from Ithaca.

We do, of course, wish to make clear that we ourselves, the seven contributors and the editor, are exclusively responsible for the data and interpretations presented in this book.

GEORGE McT. KAHIN

Djakarta
February 1959

Contents

Part Four: MALAYA and SINGAPORE
By J. Norman Parmer

Part Five: VIETNAM *By Wells C. Klein and Marjorie Weiner*

Contents

Maps and Charts

PART ONE : THAILAND

By David A. Wilson

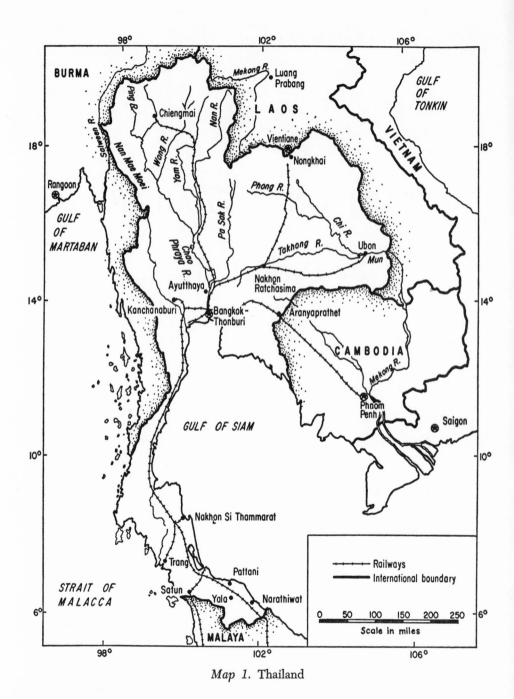

Map 1. Thailand

· I ·

The Historical Background

THAI kingdoms have for centuries played an important role in the politics of Southeast Asia. Located at Sukhothai (13th–14th century), at Ayutthaya (1350–1767), and at the present capital, Bangkok (since 1782), the essentially city-states of the Thai held sway at different times from Singapore to the border of China and from the mouth of the Irrawaddy to the lower reaches of the Mekong River. The Čhao Phraya River Basin draining the central portion of the Southeast Asia peninsula is admirably suited to wet rice agriculture. Therefore, this domain could provide the resources of men and food necessary to maintain the intricate system of plunder, threat, conquest, and elaborate ceremonial which was traditional kingship—the political form of much of ancient Southeast Asia particularly in Burma, Laos, Cambodia, Malaya, and Indonesia as well as Thailand. The lower Mekong, running through the Laos plateau and having its mouth in Cambodia and Vietnam; the Shan uplands of Burma, China, and northern Thailand; and the Kra Isthmus, leading to Malaya— all are readily accessible from the Čhao Phraya plain. During many centuries these regions, with the exception of the mouth of the Mekong, have come to be inhabited by Thai-speaking people: the Shan, the Lao, and the Siamese proper.[1]

[1] The terms Thailand, Siam, Thai, and Siamese may cause some confusion. Thai (or Tai) is a language and culture group living in Thailand, Laos, northern Vietnam,

3

Thailand of the present day is in the center of the Southeast Asia peninsula between the 5th and 21st north parallels and the 97th and 106th east meridians. It has an area of about 200,000 square miles and a population of about 23 million people. The climate ranges from semitropical to tropical, and seasons are determined by the monsoon winds. Four topographically distinct regions are generally recognized within Thailand's borders. The northeastern plateau is a semiarid table which is drained by the sluggish Mun River into the Mekong. The watershed of the Čhao Phraya River, which is entirely in Thailand, makes up two regions—first, the northern highlands which are constituted by the valleys of the Ping, Wang, Yom, and Nan rivers, the major tributaries of the Čhao Phraya, and, second, the central region, a broad alluvial plain and delta. The southern isthmus, essentially north-south mountain ridges drained by short rivers into the Gulf of Siam and the Indian Ocean, connects the mainland of Asia with the Malay Peninsula. Thailand is bordered by Cambodia on the east, Laos on the east and north, Burma on the north and west, and Malaya on the south.

The present dynasty of Thailand (of which King Phumiphon Adunyadet is the ninth reigning monarch) was established in 1782 with its capital in Bangkok.[2] Its early monarchs sought to reconstruct the traditions of the ancient Ayutthaya kingdom which was sacked and burned by the Burmese in 1767.[3] Splendor and majesty were the

southwest China, and northern Burma. These people are severally known as Thai, Shan, Lao, and, in the case of those living in the Čhao Phraya Valley, Siamese. The official name for the present kingdom of Thailand was Siam until 1939 and also from 1946 to 1949. In 1939 and again in 1949 it was changed to Thailand, a name which carries a certain note of nationalism and irredentism.

[2] The dynasty is known by the dynastic name Čhakkri and by an honorific name for Bangkok, Rathanakosin. Although the king is styled by an elaborate set of honorifics, it is customary to refer to each as Rama followed by a Roman numeral (as Rama I). Names of other people in Thai history are unfortunately not so simple. Thai names are usually preceded by a title which implies rank. It is convenient to refer to members of the royal family as Prince (e.g., Prince Damrong), and nonroyal officials under the absolute monarchy had one of the following titles, arranged in descending order—Čhao Phraya, Phraya, Phra, Luang, and Khun. Under the constitutional system no further titles have been conferred, and it has become customary to use either the title Nai, meaning mister, or a military rank. Older men still use their pre-1932 titles, however. Following the title is the given name and then the family name. People are usually referred to by their title plus the given name rather than the family name (as Nai Khuang or, more fully, Nai Khuang Aphaiwong).

[3] Prince Dhani Niwat, "The Reconstruction of Rama I," *Journal of the Siam Society*, XLIII, pt. 1 (Aug. 1955), 21–47.

primary qualities of traditional kingship. Without an appreciation of these qualities it is impossible to understand the working of monarchy or the system of government. The pomp and ceremony which filled the life of the distant and superhuman royal being were sufficient to fill the popular mind with awe and wonder. Thai society has no tradition of sweeping philosophical inquiry, and the ideal basis for royal splendor was spared that destructive intellectual criticism suffered by monarchy in Europe. It was not until European political and social ideas penetrated Thailand in the wake of imperialist merchants and soldiers that its kings were required to modify the extremes of their position. In the course of events these European ideas had reached the throne before the subjects, and the monarchy was able by a process of self-modification to forestall public disillusionment for a long time.

In premodern Thailand the king lived in his glittering palace in the center of the city. The high white walls surrounding it and soaring spires of bright colors were almost all the public knew of the king. He rarely ventured out. When he did, it was in a stately progress by land or water, and he was surrounded and protected by swarms of soldiers and officials. He met only his highest officials, his pages, and his wives, and all such meetings were ordered by ceremony. The royal styles by which the king was known and the language by which he was addressed were rich with elaborate terminology borrowed largely from Cambodian and Indian languages. These words were sonorous to the ear but unintelligible to the mind of the ordinary man. Consider the following title of King Čhulalongkǫn, who reigned until 1910.

Most excellent royal foot which is a glorious decoration for our hair; king wearing the great crown of the angel; royal descendant of the sun who shines like the finest jewel, most excellent of lineage, monarch as supreme as the greatest emperor of the worlds; greatest sovereign of righteousness, supreme king of men, King Čhom Klao the second, lord of Siam including the north, the south, and all the lands nearby which are Lao, Malaya, Karen, and many others.[4]

Kingship was also buttressed with a philosophical view which included the idea of the *devaraja* or god-king. According to this view, which is common to the Hindu and Buddhist traditions, the cosmos is a single moral universe in which all elements are related. At the center of the great cosmos is the holy mountain Meru, surrounded by

[4] Royal Order Establishing Ministries and Ministers, April 1, 1892, *Annual Collection of Laws*, XIII, 93–98 (in Thai).

oceans and continents, one of which is the dwelling place of men. Meru is the dwelling of the gods ranked in ordered levels of virtue and power. From this cosmology is derived the concept of the state or empire as a symbol and replica of the great cosmos. In the state the center of the capital is the holy mountain, and the king is the surrogate god. His wives and officials, the palace, the city, and the state are organized according to astrological and numerological systems so that they may be properly related to the larger cosmos.[5] Springing from this conception of the cosmos and the state as a great moral unity is the attitude, common in much of Southeast Asia, that persons of high rank are not only more powerful but also better.

Although this splendid esoteric mystery was the basis of popular acceptance of the monarchy, it was, of course, necessary to maintain it with policy and organization. In terms of power the king in the traditional system was conceived as the final arbiter of life and property within the framework of the ancient Hindu-Buddhist law, the *Phra Thammasat* or Code of Manu.[6] The conception of the political-judicial role of kingship is similar to the Hindu and in fact came to Thailand from India through Cambodia.[7] But the absoluteness of the Thai king may well have been greater than elsewhere because Thai society seems not to have included any independently powerful group such as the Brahmans in India or the barons of feudal Europe whose role was to see that the king lived by the law.

The king was encompassed by an elaborate bureaucratic structure of which he formed the articulating element. But the rigidity of this structure served to limit the sway of his personal will. His kingdom was surrounded by other states large and small with which he might be related by marriage, tribute, and fealty or not, but which were a perpetual potential threat. His city and fields were also surrounded by jungle and undeveloped land which provided possible sanctuary for the dissatisfied. These elements—his bureaucracy, his rivals, and the natural setting—severely restricted his power. He was enjoined thereby to some semblance of justice even if he was not impressed by the ideological strictures of the law.

[5] Robert Heine-Geldern, *Conceptions of State and Kingship in Southeast Asia* (Southeast Asia Program, Cornell University, Data Paper no. 18; Ithaca, N.Y., 1956), *passim.*

[6] Phra Woraphak Phibun, *History of Thai Law* (Bangkok, 1953), pp. 8–9 (in Thai).

[7] *Ibid.*

The Thai ruling class was made up of three groups—members of the royal family who were officials, members of the royal family who were not officials, and officials of nonroyal origin. All of these were graded in delicate steps of rank and privilege and carried elaborate titles [8] and other badges of authority. They were considered to be bearers of a portion of the king's majesty and lived and acted with similar pomp on a smaller scale. The senior officials were the two ministers of the north and the south who served as viceroys of those areas of the kingdom. After them were the four ministers of the palace, the capital, the fields, and the treasury.

These six made up the Council of Ministers who advised with the king daily and were responsible for general administration. Another group of senior officials comprised the judges who heard appeal cases in the king's name in the capital. Together the senior officials might serve as a council of general advisers on political matters.[9] Each of these officials presided over a department which carried on the king's business. Over time the departments acquired a variety of functions, both civil and military, and tended to take on a definite territorial rather than functional responsibility. The territory of the kingdom was organized in concentric rings with the palace at the center. This was both an ideological [10] and administrative device. The direct power of the king diminished with distance, and outlying provinces were organized like petty kingdoms under appointed governors or, at great distances, under hereditary lords.[11]

Below the ruling class were the people who, then as now, were rice farmers. They were divided into freemen and slaves, the latter being at times as much as one-third of the population. But the distinction was largely a matter of obligations rather than a way of life, for Siamese slaves (made up of prisoners of war, debt slaves, and persons born in slavery) were generally no worse off than freemen. Thai society traditionally, as well as at present, was hierarchical in conception and involved strong obligations on the part of the lower to the higher. A freeman's principal obligation to the government was

[8] Mary R. Haas, "The Declining Descent Rule for Rank in Thailand," *American Anthropologist,* LIII (Oct.–Dec. 1951), 585–587.

[9] Düan Bunnak and Phairot Chaiyanam, *Explanation of the Constitution Together with the Law on Election* (Bangkok, 1935), p. 9 (in Thai).

[10] Heine-Geldern, *op. cit.*

[11] Walter Vella, *Impact of the West on Government in Thailand* (Berkeley: University of California Press, 1955), pp. 326–327.

generally in the form of labor, although there were some persons
who had other forms of duty. The labor obligation could be, and
apparently often was, onerous. Each freeman was attached to a department of the bureaucracy and was under the patronage of the
department's head. The patron's function was to maintain peace
among his clients, to protect their interests legally, and to organize
and muster them for their *corvée* obligations. He was expected to
manage his department in such a way as to provide himself a living
as well as to meet royal demands. Officials received no salaries.

Government's business under this system was to maintain and protect the monarchy. It was in language and in fact the king's business.
The king was the state, or, put another way, the state was the king's
property. All land was the property of the king, and those who lived
on it had right of use only. No distinction was known between public and private funds. Trade was a royal prerogative, the king having
a monopoly of exports and the right of first refusal on all imports. Religion was under royal patronage, and the king controlled the loose
hierarchy of the Buddhist clergy. All men were slaves of the king;
he was under no obligation but to live like a king, to administer the
law, and to fulfill the ten virtues of the ruler.[12]

Foreign affairs were, of course, a major activity of the Crown. The
whole of mainland Southeast Asia was an interrelated system of
monarchies and princely states of the Thai, Burmese, Mon, Malayan,
Cambodian, and Annamese peoples. The system required constant
attention to diplomacy and war. In the second and third reigns of the
Bangkok kingdom a new diplomatic factor appeared in the form of
European, particularly British, merchant-diplomats whose movement
and resources were freed after the settlement of the Napoleonic
wars. The initial contacts and negotiations in the 1820s were cordial,
and in 1825 in the second year of Rama III's reign a treaty between
the British East India Company and Siam was signed. Among other
things it opened the port of Bangkok for limited British trade.[13]

During the last years of Rama III's reign the British and other
European powers became insistent upon renegotiation of treaties to
establish free trade principles, but the king was opposed to this. In
the last years of his reign he refused even to see the British emissary,
Sir James Brooke, and it is said that the two countries were on the

[12] *Ibid.*, pp. 317–320.
[13] Walter Vella, *Siam under Rama III* (Locust Valley, N.Y.: J. J. Augustin,
Inc., 1957), pp. 117–121.

verge of war.[14] The king, however, died in 1851, and the situation changed with the accession of King Mongkut, Rama IV.

The Beginning of Modern Thailand

Thailand's good fortune in mastering the threat of imperialism was in part luck, in part geography, but also a matter of successful government. Rising again after the end of disastrous wars with Burma in the eighteenth century in which the old Siamese capital of Ayutthaya had been destroyed, the kingdom was in a state of splendid vitality. The Bangkok dynasty, founded by a general hardened in the wars of liberation, was powerful and flexible enough to meet the challenge of the West with considerable vigor. Thailand's successful response to the West was in large measure the accomplishment of three kings— Mongkut (Rama IV), 1851–1868; Chulalongkǫn (Rama V), 1868–1910; and Wachirawut (Rama VI), 1910–1925. These three monarchs had the wit to understand the kingdom's changing place in a Southeast Asia that was increasingly dominated by the economic, intellectual, technical, and armed power of the West. They had also the will to act as was necessary to meet the situation. The great question which they faced was how to save the kingdom's independence. The response was a policy of yielding where necessary and of consolidating and reorganizing what remained. The implementation of this policy, in itself a remarkable political feat, created the modern state of Thailand.

Rama IV came to the throne in 1851 at the age of 46. Up to that time he had spent most of his adult years as a Buddhist monk engaged in scholarly pursuits in European languages and science as well as in the traditional culture of Thailand. In the late years of Rama III's reign he was the center of a pro-European group at court which after his enthronement became the nucleus of his administration.[15] This group seems to have grasped the implications of Western expansion and concluded that Thailand could no longer exclude European power.[16] Under Rama IV the kingdom was embarked on the course which it still follows today, that of adjusting itself willingly to the world as defined by the Great Powers.

[14] Prince Dhani Niwat, review of *The Fame of King Mongkut,* in *Journal of the Siam Society,* XLV, pt. II (Oct. 1957), 110.

[15] Prince Damrong Rachanuphap, *Lives of Important People* (Bangkok, 1953), p. 115 (in Thai).

[16] Prince Damrong Rachanuphap, "The Introduction of Western Culture in Siam." *Journal of the Siam Society,* XX (Oct. 1926), 89–100.

Rama IV's first action under this policy was to negotiate treaties with the envoys of European states seeking to open Thailand fully to their trade. By establishing principles of free trade these treaties laid the foundation for new elements in the economy—foreign trade on a large scale and the need for cash in public finance. Because certain elements of extraterritoriality were included, it became necessary to convince the West of the validity and justice of Thai law and procedure.

Education by Western teachers was also introduced in the fourth reign. Although among the royal princes only the heir to the throne reached any degree of fluency in a European language during Rama IV's lifetime,[17] a pattern was established and thereafter continued. Princes and later sons of officials were educated in English and given some conception of the world outside Thailand. It is evident, however, that Rama IV was fundamentally of traditional Thailand and was prepared neither to comprehend nor to accept the political and social implications of Westernization.[18] During his reign few fundamental changes were made within the country, but the king and his immediate group did turn the face of the Thai ruling class toward the West.

Although it may be said that Rama IV was father to modern Thailand, Rama V presided at the birth and nurtured the infant until it reached a state of secure health. He inherited a traditional Southeast Asian kingdom with its intricate web of bureaucratic and feudal relationships, its ancient ceremonies and symbols, and at his death he left a modern state with a rapidly developing system of communications, a sound fiscal position, and the general outlines of an effective administration and army.

Rama V also infused the monarchy with a new spirit more in keeping with the liberal age of the nineteenth and twentieth centuries. His intention in this matter was made clear at the time of his second coronation in 1873 when he decreed that the ancient custom of "crouching, crawling, and prostration" before the king and high officials would be abolished as an earnest of his intention of ending oppression.[19] Before his death Rama V had succeeded in ending slavery and *corvée* obligations and in general replacing the ancient personal obligations with the more impersonal relationships of wages, rent, public conscription, and taxes.

[17] Prince Damrong, "Western Culture," *loc. cit.*
[18] Vella, *Impact of the West*, p. 334.   [19] Vella, *Impact of the West*, p. 336.

During the reign of Rama V, Thailand passed through the most perilous period of European imperialism, and the king was forced to make some heartbreaking concessions. Both Britain and France were pushing out to protect their colonies and gain new territory. The British were on the Thai borders in the north and on the Malay Peninsula. The French were pressing westward from Annam into Laos and Cambodia. At the beginning of the reign Thailand claimed suzerainty over its present territory as well as four Malay states, Kedah, Perlis, Kelantan, and Trengganu; the Lao areas of Sipsǫng Čhuthai, Luang Phrabang, and Vientiane; and several Cambodian provinces. By 1909 these had been yielded to Britain or France.

The loss of territories, to which the Thai claim was of varying degrees of validity, took the form of a series of diplomatic dramas in which Britain, France, and Siam played the major roles.[20] The interests of each party were different, of course. Britain sought to protect its Indian and Malayan empire by assuming control of the most important Malay states and also by assuring that Thailand, particularly the isthmus, would not fall into the hands of a hostile European power. Within Thailand proper Britain was satisfied to protect the commercial interests of British subjects through extraterritoriality and limits upon tariffs. The French were interested primarily in acquiring control of territory, particularly on Thailand's eastern marches. In their persistent endeavors toward this objective they were countered not only by the relatively weak Thai kingdom but also by Britain. The climax (but not the end) of this struggle was the Anglo-French agreement of 1896 which guaranteed the neutrality of the Čhao Phraya Valley and thereby assured the continued existence of the Thai state. It was no doubt because of the rivalry of Britain and France that the kingdom never fell into the condition of a protectorate as had the Malay states, the Lao kingdom, and Cambodia.

Since the world situation as it came to bear upon Thailand was far beyond the control of the king and his councilors, Thailand's external policy could hardly have any dynamic qualities. By the policy of negotiation and partial yielding, however, time was bought to carry forward the inner reforms, consolidation, and reorganization required to put the kingdom on a secure footing from which to face the modern

[20] B. S. N. Murti in "Anglo-French Relations with Siam, 1876–1904" (University of London thesis, 1952) gives a careful account of the European side of this period. Luang Vichitr Vadakarn in *Thailand's Case* (Bangkok, 1941) presents a heavily biased Thai version.

world. There were three related aspects to the political changes of the reign of Rama V. The first was the transformation of the kingship from a semidivine mystery to an exalted administrative presidency of the government. The second was the reorganization of the administration to strengthen the central government and "rationalize" offices in terms of function. The third was the beginning of legal reform and codification mainly aimed at making law and procedure understandable and acceptable to the West.

In addition to ending the custom of prostration, Rama V in the first year of his full power established two councils of advisers on legislation and administration. He announced:

At this time it is our opinion that the benefits which are to come and the correction of the many confusions that persist from the past cannot be accomplished by the king alone. If there are many minds working together, the ancient confusions will be eliminated little by little and prosperity will surely arise in the country. Therefore we shall select some wise officials and establish them as advisers to the king.[21]

In a later statement to the council he said that it

must have the power to delay the king; for example, in matters in which the king presents an opinion which is not just and by which the people will be disturbed, ranging from such matters as extracting money from the people of the country to small things such as market fees.[22]

How effective such statements were in changing the minds of the Thai about the king is questionable, but Rama V did not stop trying. In 1892 he said:

There is no law which specifies the royal power in Siam because it is believed to be beyond the law, that there is no rule, thing, or person which can regulate or prevent it. But in truth any act of the king must be appropriate and just. For this reason we have no objection to a law which specifies royal power.[23]

The king waited until 1892 to make his sweeping administrative reorganization. During the preceding years, however, a variety of lesser changes were undertaken; among the most important was the

[21] "Notification about a Council and Legislation," *Annual Collection of Laws,* VIII, 155–156 (in Thai).

[22] "Notification on the Work of Advising the Government," *ibid.,* pp. 269–270.

[23] *Speech of Rama V Explaining Improvements of the Government,* printed by order of the king (Rama VII) on the anniversary of the death of Rama V, October 23, 2470 [1927] (Bangkok, 1927), p. 62 (in Thai).

establishment of royal governers over the more distant regions of the kingdom.[24] This was the first act in the creation of administrative uniformity throughout the country to replace the various traditional forms. In 1892 the king issued the great proclamation of reorganization which ended the six ancient departments of the North, South, Palace, City, Fields, and Treasury and established twelve ministries with heads of equal rank and privilege. These ministries were: Interior, Defense, Foreign Affairs, Treasury, Palace, City, Agriculture and Commerce, Justice, Public Works, Religion and Education, Royal Secretariat, and Military Affairs.[25] Within the ministries existing departments were grouped on the basis of function, and responsibilities were redistributed so that there would be some equivalence at the various levels. The result was the administrative unification of interior rule, armed services, finance, and justice, all of which previously had been dispersed through various departments. This functional grouping had the effect of greatly strengthening the control by the throne of the administration of the kingdom. To reinforce this effort the traditional system, whereby officials supported themselves through their own exactions on clientele, was replaced by a system of regular salaries which put control in the hands of the paymaster. At one and the same time the monarchy was strengthened administratively and weakened psychologically.

The problem of law was a central one in the relationships with European powers. The effort to end extraterritoriality involved complete revolution in the administration of justice and the law itself. In 1897 a commission was appointed to study the problem of revision of the law in order to bring it into conformity with standards acceptable to the powers and thereby lay a basis for the end of consular courts. In 1908 the first of the law codes, the criminal code, was issued, and the following year Britain recognized the principle of the end of extraterritoriality, although it persisted for almost thirty years.[26]

The reign of Rama V was long and eventful. His greatest accomplishment was the preservation of the kingdom's independence. In reorganizing his government and making acceptable the idea that Thailand should hasten to adapt and adopt the methods of the West, he set in motion a course of events which led eventually to the

[24] Reginald LeMay, *An Asian Arcady* (Cambridge, Eng.: W. Heffer & Son, 1926), pp. 123–129.

[25] Phra Woraphak, *Thai Law*, pp. 122–125.

[26] René Guyon, *The Work of Codification in Siam* (Paris: Imprimerie Nationale, 1919), pp. 9–16.

first limit of royal power by a constitution, a result which perhaps would not have disappointed him.

Rama V was succeeded by his vivacious son Wachirawut (Rama VI, 1910–1925), who in turn was succeeded by his younger brother Prachathipok (Rama VII, 1925–1935). During the reigns of these two kings the implications of the reforms and policies begun by Rama V were worked out. A national consciousness arose in the governing class, the bureaucracy became infused with a spirit of professionalism, the nation reached a state of complete legal equality in the world, and a constitutional system was established.

Rama VI was the first Thai king to be educated abroad. His reign was a colorful period in which the select of Bangkok society were introduced to many social aspects of the West, such as Western dress and cotillions. In addition, the king was in effect the founder of intellectual nationalism among the educated Thai. He wrote a number of articles in the press under various pen names on the subject of love of nation and also attacked the developing separateness of the Chinese community in the country.[27] From this period forward the Chinese became an issue and a problem in Thailand.

The king also addressed himself to the primary problem of regaining full legal autonomy for the nation. He pressed forward the work of legal codification which was substantially completed in his reign.[28] The First World War, which had effectively ended European imperial expansion, presented an opportunity to demonstrate Thailand's potential role in the world. The general sentiments in the country were by no means entirely with the Allied powers, since the memory of the recent indignities suffered at the hands of Britain and France was still fresh. The king, however, had been educated in England and personally felt close ties of affection with the British. Over strong objection among his advisers, he put Thailand into the war on the side of the Allies, and a small expeditionary force and flying corps were sent to France.

The position taken gave the Thai delegation a base from which to operate at the Versailles peace conference. A course of negotiations was there set in motion which by 1925 had resulted in the signing of new treaties with all powers. These treaties established a final date for the abandonment of legal and fiscal limitations on the nation.[29]

[27] G. William Skinner, *Chinese Society in Thailand* (Ithaca, N.Y.: Cornell University Press, 1957), pp. 164–165.

[28] Guyon, *op. cit.*, p. 16.

[29] Francis B. Sayre, "Siam's Fight for Sovereignty," *Atlantic Monthly,* CXL (Nov. 1927), 674–689.

Rama VI died in 1925 without a male heir and was succeeded by his youngest brother Prachathipok (Rama VII), who had never expected to come to the throne because he was the youngest son in his line. There was considerable contrast between the reigns of Rama VI and VII which can be explained in part by the personalities of the kings. Rama VI was a strong-minded man with his own ideas and great energy. He believed in absolutism probably as much by temperament as a matter of theory and ran the government largely by himself. He did not utilize the training of his royal relatives as fully as either his predecessor or successor and was not entirely popular with the more powerful among them. With the enthronement of Rama VII, however, this attitude was reversed, and top positions as well as high policy came almost completely under the control of a small group of high princes working with the king. Where Rama VI had been extravagant and colorful, Rama VII was careful and, apparently, rather shy.[30]

It is generally believed that Rama VII was personally interested in granting a constitution to the country as a crowning touch to the liberalization and modernization that had been the policy of the dynasty. This plan is said, however, to have met strong resistance among his advisers, and nothing was done before the revolution of 1932.

The Revolution of 1932

In 1932 a group of middle-level officials in the military and civil services organized a *coup d'état* which ended the control of the royal family over the government and established a quasi-parliamentary constitution. The origins of this event lie in at least three concurrent factors. First was the diminution of the psychological power of monarchy. This process was a result of democratic ideas from the West, the softening of the more extravagant claims by the dynasty itself, and the diffident personality of Rama VII. The second factor was the development of an attitude of professional expertise among officials—especially those educated in Europe—who resented the tendency to royal monopoly of power. Third were the financial difficulties in which the government found itself as a result of its previous extravagance and the developing world depression.

There were several groups among the promoters of the coup which over subsequent years have divided, re-formed, and in manifold ways struggled in the political arena. The main division in the early years was

[30] Vella, *Impact of the West*, pp. 351–360.

between older army officers and younger military and civil officials who
in large measure provided the driving zeal. Colonel Phraya Phahon
Phonphayuhasena is representative of the older generation. He had
received advanced military education in Germany and had risen to
a position of importance. But he found himself bumping against the top
level dominated by the royal family. Phraya Phahon, who was the senior
military man of the coup group and subsequently became Prime
Minister, explained in later years that although he felt himself well
qualified in technical matters the prince in command of the army
did not see fit to consider his advice. This hardened his heart against
the royal family and led him to join the coup.[31] The younger revolutionaries from among whom three men subsequently became Prime
Minister—Field Marshal Phibunsongkhram, Nai Pridi Phanomyong,
and Nai Khuang Aphaiwong—centered in a group which had studied
in France in the 1920s. It was divided into two segments, the military
and civilians. These younger men were moved both by the same frus-
trations as the older group and also by a certain ideological conviction.
In France they had had an opportunity to observe and study the
politics of Europe and had absorbed some of the ideas upon which
such politics are based. It is not surprising that the ideological leader
of the coup group as a whole was Nai Pridi, a Doctor of Law from
the University of Paris.[32]

During the years before the coup the government had been suffering from financial difficulties. Inheriting a chaotic state of affairs from
the proceding reign, the government of Rama VII found itself short of
funds. An effort to effect savings was made by reducing the payroll and
also by cutting expenses from the royal court downward. This course of
action created some uneasiness and dissatisfaction in the services,
particularly, it seems, in the army.[33] The coup was a likely result of
such a situation.

Absolutism served the Thai well in the centuries when society was
static. While the purely peasant culture was self-contained, affairs
of state were simple and the power of the government was limited.
It performed the needed ceremonials and fought the inevitable wars
and little more. But from the beginning of the age of international
commerce this simplicity was doomed. So long as the monarchy pro-

[31] Kulab Saipradit, *Behind the Revolution of 2475* (Bangkok, 1947), pp. 110–
116 (in Thai).
[32] Düan Bunnak, *Mr. Pridi, Elder Statesman* (Bangkok, 1958), pp. 1–18 (in
Thai).
[33] Vella, *Impact of the West*, pp. 356–360.

vided dynamic leadership for the necessary adjustments, its apparent position was strengthened. Its foundations were weakened, however, and the effective ability to control the bureaucracy was lost with the development of a rationally organized and technically expert state structure. When the monarchy faltered in its leadership, the internal dynamic of this great organization threw it off.

On June 24, 1932, at dawn the troops which were under the command of the coup group moved to seize certain key positions in the city of Bangkok and various high officials of the government. The end of the absolute monarchy was proclaimed, and the king was invited to rule under a constitution. Within a few days the matter was settled. The king accepted a provisional constitution; the coup group, organized under the name People's Party, appointed itself as provisional parliament, and a government acceptable to both the king and the People's Party was formed. This regime was to set the pattern for postcoup governments. The Prime Minister was a conservative judge who had not participated in the coup but was adequately sympathetic with its more moderate objectives. His cabinet included key figures in the coup.[34]

Drafting a permanent constitution was the first task which the new government set for itself. This work was accomplished in short order, and the constitution was proclaimed by the king on December 10, 1932. The structure of government as outlined in the constitution was of the classic parliamentary type with a single legislative house and a royal cabinet responsible to it. All power of independent action was taken from the king. A peculiarity of the constitution was the provision for a period of tutelage before the introduction of full democracy. During this initial period half of the parliament was to be appointed by the government. The parliament was to be so formed either for ten years or until one-half the eligible voters had completed four years of school, whichever came first. Such a provision ensured effective executive control of the government, a continuation of the pattern of the monarchy which has persisted to the present. The executive power is disposed to brook no nonsense from parliament.

Since the *coup d'état* of 1932, internal politics of Thailand has been in large measure a matter of factional infighting. The end of the monarchical principle and of the king's domination of the group

[34] Kenneth P. Landon, *Siam in Transition* (Chicago: University of Chicago Press, 1939), p. 17.

which controlled government and policy left something of a void. There has been no unanimity of opinion about who should have power or about the proper method of acquiring power.

The first five years of the constitutional period were filled with a number of significant events which amounted to a shaking down of the regime. The first was the *cause célèbre* of Pridi Phanomyong's Economic Plan of 1933. The People's Party at the time of its seizure of power had issued a manifesto which set forth a six-point program:

1. Freedom and equality of the people in politics, law, courts, and business
2. Internal peace and order
3. Economic well-being and work for all by means of economic planning
4. Equality of privileges
5. Freedom and liberty not conflicting with the foregoing
6. Education for all [35]

Nai Pridi took point three as a mandate to draft a general and rather elaborate Economic Plan for the nation.[36] The core of this plan was a radical statism which would have nationalized virtually all natural and industrial resources including land. The people, with some minor exceptions, were to become state employees. The plan immediately met strong opposition and was labeled, with perhaps some indelicacy of term but also with practical justification, as bolshevism. Rifts appeared in the People's Party between Pridi's civilian reformers and the more conservative army group. The compromise Premier seized the opportunity to close parliament and rule by decree. A broad law against communism was proclaimed, and Pridi was personally urged to go abroad. It looked briefly as if the People's Party had been shattered. With the settlement of the Communist issue, however, the army group again recaptured power and set the party up as the government.

Within a few months the new regime was threatened by a rebellion of provincial army and civil officials led by Prince Bǫwǫradet, a former Minister of Defense. The intentions of the rebels are still somewhat obscure, but it is clear that they threatened the monopoly of power held by the People's Party. The rebel army reached the outskirts of the capital where it was then defeated and dispersed by the firm resistance of the government troops and the quashing of

[35] Vella, *Impact of the West,* p. 371.
[36] Landon, *op. cit.,* pp. 29–31 and pp. 260–323 for a translation of the plan and related documents.

treachery among armed units in the city. Although the king denounced this rebellion at the time and later, he was seriously compromised in the minds of the People's Party leaders. Thereafter the place of royalty sank to its lowest in Thailand. Many high princes were in exile, and many of their supporters were in prison. Within two years of the failure of this rebellion, Rama VII went into exile in Britain and abdicated the throne. The People's Party leaders presented the crown to King Čhulalongkǫn's sixteen-year-old grandson, Prince Anan Mahidon, who was in school in Switzerland.

In international affairs, Thailand's long struggle for complete autonomy was finally achieved in 1935, when Nai Pridi, recalled and officially cleared of charges of communism, negotiated new treaties with all powers. These agreements fulfilled the promises of the treaties of 1925 and gave Thailand control over all legal and fiscal aspects of its administration. But by this time the world situation had changed. Thailand was bound up now with the fatal struggle impending in East Asia between Japan and Britain and the United States. The objectives of foreign policy were the same—continued independence—but the problems were new.

The period of rising international tension coincided with the emergence of the figure of Colonel (later Field Marshal) Phibunsongkhram as the dominant personality in Thai politics. This man, coming from rather obscure origins and rising in the army by a combination of ambition and ability, a promoter of the coup in 1932, the officer who suppressed the rebellion of the princes, had through various vicissitudes come to personal control of the army. Since 1934 he had been Minister of Defense, and in 1938, when Phraya Phahon chose to retire, Phibun became Prime Minister.

Although the general tone of the political attitude of the People's Party had been moderately nationalistic from 1932, the first Phibun era from 1938 to 1943 was one of extreme nationalism on the lines made popular in Italy, Germany, and Japan. In the years before the beginning of the Far Eastern war, Phibun and Pridi worked closely and enthusiastically to press a policy which aimed to glorify the Thai nation, first at the expense of the Chinese minority within the country [37] and subsequently at the expense of France in Indochina.[38] In a characteristic acceptance and adaptation of foreign models, the government issued a series of acts, decrees, and pronouncements

[37] Skinner, *Chinese Society,* pp. 261–272.
[38] Luang Vichitr, *op. cit., passim.*

which produced many of the trappings if not the substance of fascism in the Thai setting.[39]

The approaching war in the Far East began to have direct effect in Thailand with the expansion of Japan's interest south from China.[40] Japan's relations with Thailand were characterized by a cordiality cultivated on both sides. But the Thai government was as surprised at the speed and vigor of the Japanese attack throughout the Pacific as were the British and Americans. At dawn on December 8, 1941, Japanese troops landed at a number of points on the Gulf of Siam without forewarning, and the Japanese ambassador in Bangkok presented the cabinet with the alternatives of permitting passage of the troops on their way to Burma and Malaya or of fighting. The situation was complex. The ideas of Asia for the Asiatics and of a Japanese-led Asian co-prosperity sphere were not without their supporters in Thailand, as in other countries of Asia. At the same time the immediate prospect on December 8 was co-operation or the martyrdom of an independence which had been preserved through the worst European imperialism. Although the impulse to resist was clearly present, the wherewithal was deficient. It was decided to accept the best terms possible from Japan and preserve some freedom of movement.[41]

Japanese troops were stationed in Thailand not as an occupation force but as friendly allies. Thailand signed a treaty of friendship and co-operation with Japan and subsequently declared war on Japan's enemies, Great Britain and the United States. Such a status permitted the government considerable control of affairs within its borders. The broad policy line of the nation was well summarized by Field Marshal Phibunsongkhram in speaking to his chief of staff in 1942: "Which side do you think will be defeated in this war? That side is our enemy." [42]

Pridi Phanomyong, the second most prominent man in the kingdom, left the cabinet immediately after the Japanese invasion to act as a regent of the young king. During the war he became the rallying point for the anti-Japanese underground which was in contact

[39] Vella, *Impact of the West*, pp. 382–386.
[40] John L. Christian and Nobutaka Ike, "Thailand in Japan's Foreign Relations," *Pacific Affairs*, XV (1942), 195–221.
[41] Nicol Smith and Blake Clark, *Into Siam* (New York: Bobbs-Merrill Co., 1946), pp. 261–266.
[42] Net Khemayothin, *The Underground Work of Colonel Yothi* (Bangkok, 1957), p. 1 (in Thai).

with China, the United States, and Britain. Phibunsongkhram himself made some effort at underground contacts late in the war, but it was his role to play the villain for the Allies in the postwar years. The effect of this development of a two-pronged approach toward the war situation was to resound in postwar politics. Although the details have not been revealed, it is clear that the war broke up the unity of purpose of the People's Party, a breach that never healed.[43]

By 1944 it had become sufficiently clear to many politicians that Phibunsongkhram would have to go. He was, of course, completely unacceptable to the Allied powers which, it seemed apparent, would drive Japan out of Southeast Asia. At the same time he had also lost the confidence of the Japanese through his schemes of duplicity. Because of the deprivation and hardship which had resulted from the general breakdown of the economy of Southeast Asia, the popularity of Phibun in the country had ebbed. Pridi was able to engineer the parliamentary overthrow of the government, and Phibun was replaced by Nai Khuang Aphaiwong, who was well known in the country but generally uncommitted on foreign policy. Khuang held the office of Premier until the defeat of Japan.[44]

Thailand was better prepared for Japan's defeat than for its initial victories. The kingdom's major problem was to avoid treatment as a defeated enemy. The Free Thai underground was the national ace in the hole. Thailand's ambassador to the United States, Seni Pramoj, had from the very beginning of the war declared his Free Thai status and had built good relations with the United States government. Pridi had also worked through the OSS organization, with which he had been co-operating in the last years of the war. The United States government was inclined to be lenient. Seni Pramoj was rushed back to the country to take over as Premier under the aegis of Pridi and assumed charge of the negotiation of a postwar settlement. By the beginning of 1946 he had signed a treaty with the less sympathetic British, and Thailand was accepted back into international society.

Postwar Thailand

The war shattered the People's Party. In getting the nation out of the conflict it was necessary to drop Phibunsongkhram and also to

---

[43] *Ibid.*, p. 45; Khuang Aphaiwong, *My Struggle* (Bangkok, reissued, 1958), pp. 67–79 (in Thai).

[44] Khuang, *op. cit.*, pp. 83–239.

allow the re-entry of royalist sympathizers on the political scene. Postwar politics has been largely a matter of struggle by three groups for dominance. One is the military group, personified in Field Marshal Phibunsongkhram and based in the army. The second group, at first centering on the figure of Pridi Phanomyong, is rooted in parliament and the civil service. The third group, considerably smaller but full of prestige, is traditionalist and royalist in character. Khuang Aphaiwong and Seni Pramoj are its public leaders.

Because of the overthrow of the Phibun dictatorship and the extrication of Thailand from its position of international embarrassment at the war's end, Pridi Phanomyong was, in 1946, in a position of great prestige and, for the moment, unchallenged dominance. His prospects, however, were not enviable. He faced a turbulent political situation with not only the parliament but also the military and civil services divided by wartime sentiments and ambitions for the future. The economic situation was precarious as well. Inflation was under way, and the country's major exportable commodity—rice—was tied up by agreements with Great Britain. Perhaps most serious of all problems was the growth of widespread corruption in the government, a result at least in part of a breakdown of morale and discipline in the services and of the varieties of opportunity for illegal profit available in the chaotic conditions of the postwar years.[45]

On the international scene, Pridi also faced a number of difficulties. Although Thailand had avoided for the most part treatment as an enemy by the Allied powers, the need remained to rebuild its prestige in the world, to settle relations with neighboring lands which were in a turbulent state, and to seek admittance to the organization of the United Nations.[46]

Early in 1946, the parliamentary situation was crystallized by a general election and the promulgation of a new constitution. Parliament was changed from a single house with half the members appointed by the government to a bicameral form. The upper house was elected by the fully elected lower house. For the first time parties began to play a role. Two groups—the Constitution Front and the Co-operation Party—which combined to make a substantial majority supported Pridi and packed the Senate with his followers. The op-

[45] W. D. Reeve, *Public Administration in Siam* (London and New York: Royal Institute of International Affairs, 1951), pp. 69–77.

[46] Russell H. Fifield, *The Diplomacy of Southeast Asia, 1945–58* (New York: Harper and Brothers, 1958), pp. 237–243.

position formed around Khuang Aphaiwong and the Democrat Party. The complexities of the situation also forced Pridi to come down from his position of eminence as regent and elder statesman to accept the premiership himself. Here he was vulnerable to a vigorous attack by the nation's highly skilled slanderers and rumormongers as well as to more restrained critics.

Whether or not Pridi might have weathered the perils of this office under more or less normal conditions will never be known. His first two months of office were occupied by the promulgation of the new constitution and the election of the upper house which took place on May 24, 1946. On June 9 the young king, Anan Mahidon (Rama VIII), who had returned to the country after spending the war years in school in Switzerland, was found shot in his bed. The circumstances surrounding this unfortunate event were obscure and mysterious; and the government was unable or unwilling to make a conclusive and credible explanation of the shooting. Thereafter the burden of criticism against Pridi turned from corruption and partisanship to regicide. Within two months Pridi had voluntarily resigned the Premier's office in favor of his own choice, Luang Thamrong Nawasawat, a fairly conservative and independent follower.

The general decline of prestige and power of the Pridi-dominated Thamrong government, which continued as a result of corruption and economic difficulties as well as the king's death, caused its enemies to take heart. One aspect of the overthrow of Phibunsongkhram in 1944 had been the dismantling of his control clique within the army and a strong attempt to prevent the development of any new group of army politicians. Such an effort was widely resented among the officers, however. In the autumn of 1947 a broad conspiracy of troop commanders was organized around the figures of two retired high officers. In this conspiracy Field Marshal Phibunsongkhram, living in semiretirement, was no doubt indirectly involved, and the memory of his services to the army was a persuasive tool. On the night of November 8, 1947, the group moved to seize complete power and set aside the constitution. Pridi fled the country, and Luang Thamrong and other Pridi followers went into hiding to avoid arrest.

Fearing difficulty both internally and in diplomatic relations if they were overly bold, the promoters of the *coup d'état* asked Nai Khuang Aphaiwong, leader of the Democrat Party, to form a caretaker government until a new election could be held in January 1948.

After the election he was able to form a government on the basis of an unstable majority in parliament.

The status of the government having been regularized by the election and, soon thereafter, by foreign recognition, Nai Khuang settled down to solve some of the immediate problems of the country. But the army was impatient to show its hand, and on April 6, 1948, less than two months after the formation of the government, Khuang was forced out at gun point.[47] Field Marshal Phibunsongkhram succeeded him as Prime Minister.

The period from 1948 to the end of 1951 was one of extraordinary instability even for Thailand. A variety of groups and cliques were maneuvering for advantage. The supporters of the fugitive Pridi were driven out of politics. The conservative Democrat Party group, under Khuang, had been given some substance and reputation by its role in the governments between November 1947 and April 1948. This group, strongly represented in parliament, was rather resentful about the ouster of its leader by force. Nor was there unity within the military. The navy and marines were not in sympathy with the coup group. Top naval leaders were intimates of both Luang Thamrong, the last Premier before the coup, and of Khuang. On the whole the navy was antagonistic to Field Marshal Phibun and other army men. Within the army, younger professionals were not easily persuaded that the old officers, who had been discredited in wartime, should re-establish their hold. The coup group was divided against itself in the effort to take complete charge of the army and other government organizations. Field Marshal Phibun played his own game, gathering around him supporters from the wartime period; and other leaders began fighting among themselves.

The period was marked by three serious showdowns. On October 1, 1948, several Army General Staff officers were arrested and later were convicted of revolt. They were the most aggressive leaders of the anticoup-group faction in the army. In February 1949 a revolt broke out in the middle of Bangkok in which it is understood that the marines were supporting a comeback by Pridi. The revolt failed and was followed by a purge, of a type never before seen in Thailand. A number of officials and politicians were shot under mysterious circumstances.

In 1950 one of the two senior coup leaders was forced into exile

[47] John Coast, *Some Aspects of Siamese Politics* (New York: Institute of Pacific Relations, 1953), pp. 44–46.

under vague charges of rebellion. In June 1951 the navy and marines showed their hand again by kidnaping Field Marshal Phibun and going into revolt. The uprising was suppressed by the army and air force after three days of heavy fighting.[48] At this point two younger men emerged as dominant figures. They were General Phao Sriyanon, an intimate associate of Phibun since 1933 and son-in-law of the remaining senior coup leader, and General Sarit Thanarat, a junior coup leader and professional army man. General Phao was director-general of police and General Sarit commander of the Bangkok army. Field Marshal Phibun, still Premier, was a captive of circumstances in which he stood as chief between the two.

In the same period the parliamentary situation had gone through some radical changes. At the time of the coup the constitution of 1946 was set aside in favor of a provisional constitution. One of the important acts of the Khuang government was to appoint an assembly of members of parliament and experts to draft a new permanent constitution. Their work was finished by the end of 1948, and a new form of parliament was established which added to the troubles of the military. It was a bicameral assembly of which the lower house was elected by universal adult franchise. The new provision for an upper house was a departure from the long effort to exclude the throne from politics and marked the beginning of a resurgence of royal authority. The members of the upper house were appointed by the king upon the countersignature of the President of his Privy Council, whom he appointed with the countersignature of the President of parliament. For the first time in the experience of the military the selection of parliament was completely free of direct control by the government. The military leaders were thrown into a position of dependence upon elected members of parliament. The constitution put other irritating limitations upon the military as well.

This constitution lasted three years, from January 1949 to November 1951. During that time Khuang's Democrat Party held a number of seats in both houses. Although the Democrats never attempted to exert their parliamentary power, presumably recognizing the ultimate futility of such an effort, they were a potential threat. At the end of 1951, after the emergence of the Phao-Sarit combination, the military moved to eliminate this irritant. Early in the morning of November 30 a radio statement of the government declared the end of the 1949 constitution and the return to the 1932 law,

[48] *Ibid.*, pp. 52–54, 57–58.

which provided for a half-appointed parliament. The list of 123 appointed members included only a tiny sprinkling of nonmilitary men.

In subsequent years anticommunism became a keystone of the government's policy both domestically and abroad. Within the country it was directed against certain Chinese and also some opposition politicians. Among these there were doubtless some Communists. The anti-Communist drive culminated at the end of 1952 in a wide roundup of suspects in what was reputed to be a Communist plot. Those arrested and later tried included writers, intellectuals, young military officers, and Chinese who were associated with leftist thought. At the same time an anti-Communist act was rushed through parliament granting broad powers to convict on charges of Communist conspiracy.

It is a temptation to say that the breakup of the Phibun-Phao-Sarit group was inevitable. The triangular structure in which Phibun had to balance the one against the other was inherently unstable. The elements were unequal and the difficulties evidently too great. Phao and Sarit, who are both about 50, were in natural competition for the succession to Phibun. It is not possible to say whether this competition was personal, but in the course of events both Phao and Sarit became the heads of separate clique structures based in different institutions, the fates of which were bound to the success of their leaders. Phao as director of police and secretary-general of the government's parliamentary organization led a complex group which was free of and opposed to the dominance of the army under Sarit. This division was behind the tension leading to the coup of September 16, 1957.

The dramatic turning point seems to have been Field Marshal Phibun's tour of the United States and Great Britain in 1955. Upon his return it was announced that a new era of democracy had arrived. Several royal acts were passed to give emphasis to this idea. An act for the registration of political parties, the first in history, and an act for decentralization of power to local governments were particularly important. At the same time the Prime Minister set up two institutions of public information which developed rapidly. They were the regular press conference of the Prime Minister and the so-called "Hyde Park." The Hyde Park scheme gave opportunity to politicians to discuss politics publicly in the central park of Bangkok.

The motive for this sudden lifting of political repression is difficult to show clearly. Apparently Phibun was impressed during his travels in the United States and Britain by the relatively untroubled position of power enjoyed by popularly elected leaders such as President Eisenhower and Winston Churchill. Being himself in a difficult, not to say shaky, position between two strong men, he may well have thought of this as a way out. Anticipating the general election scheduled for early 1957, he may have decided to build himself a base of power in the general public. It is also possible that, having been impressed by the general strength and wealth of democratic countries, he made a simple equation in his mind. It is fully consistent with his conception of himself as the founder of the modern Thai nation that he decided to leave full democracy as the crowning achievement of his long career.

In any event, the political changes in 1955 opened the way to one of the most colorful and active years in Thai politics. A number of political parties were registered, and the elements in the coming struggle began to shape up quickly. The parties, of which ultimately there were more than twenty-five, can be sorted into four groups. The pivotal group was represented in a single party, the massive official government organization, Seri Manangkhasila, with the government's parliamentary supporters as its core. General Phao was its secretary-general and organizing genius. The second group included a number of parties which supported individuals in the government but not the government as such. The most interesting of these were the Thammathipat, which supported Phibun, and the National Democratic Party, which supported Sarit. In the course of events neither of these came to anything. The next group was also one party, the Democrats, with Khuang Aphaiwong as head. This group of conservatives made up the only party of any continuity of tradition. The final group comprised a number of leftist parties. The two most important of these, the Free Democrat and the Economist, were built around members of parliament from northeast Thailand. This group, which subsequently united with smaller parties to form the Socialist Front, led the fight against the government's foreign policy.

The second and perhaps more important political development of 1956 was the sudden outburst of public discussion. After years of repression the public of Bangkok was given carte blanche to discuss politics. This "great debate" was led, one might almost say monopolized, by the press and the Hyde Park speakers who vied with each other in the violence and audacity with which they attacked the government and all it stood for. The government found it difficult to get a sympathetic hearing for its views, and one might suspect that the public was somewhat skeptical about its democratic tendencies.

As the election campaign developed, it became apparent that Phibun and Phao were going all out for popular support whereas Sarit was staying in the background. Phao poured everything available into the Seri Manangkhasila Party. It was reported that at least 20 million baht (1 baht = US$.05) was spent by the party, ten times as much as any other organization.[49] The civil service was dragooned into party work. Although no other party succeeded in putting candidates up for all 160 seats, the Seri Manangkhasila endorsed no less than 230 candidates.[50] Phibun, who was head of the party, chose to lead a slate of candidates in the Bangkok district against the most popular opposition leader, Nai Khuang.

Tension was high on election day. The results of the polling were a moral defeat for Seri Manangkhasila. Actual accusations of corruption of the polls began the day before election when a follower of Field Marshal Sarit demanded an explanation for falsified ballot papers which he claimed to have discovered marked with Seri Manangkhasila numbers. From then on the press and the streets of Bangkok were clamorous with readily accepted stories of ballot-box stuffing, double voting, intimidation, and falsification of returns. Because Seri Manangkhasila had returned a bare majority and at least half its incumbent members had been defeated, any hope for a popular triumph or gain in prestige was shattered.

The election appears to have opened another period of political instability for the country comparable in degree to 1932–1935 and 1947–1951. Field Marshal Sarit and his associates in the army and other military services have moved to seize power completely and have been trying to stabilize their control. Public dissatisfaction with the conduct of the election in February 1957, which was vigorously expressed in the press and among students, caused the government to declare a national emergency. Sarit, who had successfully disassociated himself from the Seri Manangkhasila Party, was appointed commander in chief of all the forces. In public statements he proclaimed the elections to have been filthy on all sides and assumed responsibility for cleaning up the mess. In spite of his dominant position, Sarit made no immediate move against the Phao faction. His administration of the emergency served to dissipate public outrage, albeit in a manner which did little to revive public respect for General Phao or the Seri Manangkhasila.

Phibun Songkhram was able to form a government in March after

[49] *Bangkok World*, Feb. 25, 1957.   [50] *Ibid.*, Feb. 26, 1957.

considerable difficulty in conciliating the various factions in the party and military groups. Although General Phao received the powerful Ministry of the Interior, Sarit and his followers together held the stronger cabinet position. After a series of events in parliament and the cabinet Sarit broke openly with Phibun and Phao, and on September 16 tanks rolled, the constitution was suspended, and parliament was dissolved. Phibun fled the country, and a few days later Phao was permitted to go into exile.

New elections, administered by a caretaker government appointed by the military group which had seized power, were conducted in December. They were carried out in a quiet atmosphere, and public interest was focused on the manner in which they were conducted rather than on political issues. The dominance of the military was a foregone conclusion. A new Unionist Party, which had appeared before the coup with the tacit support of Sarit, ran against the Democrats and the Socialist Front. After the election Sarit announced the formation of a new combine, to be called the National Socialist Party, which was intended to amalgamate the Unionists, appointed members of parliament, and any others who would support the new government. General Thanom Kittikačhọn, Sarit's immediate deputy in the army, took over the office of Premier. Sarit, who was in a perilous state of health, left the country almost immediately for extended medical treatment in the United States.

Thanom's government was faced with a number of difficulties which weakened its grip on power. The more fundamental of these were fiscal, a result of falling revenues which presented obstacles to the drafting of a budget satisfactory to the bureaucracy, and political, a result of the disparate elements in the government's military and parliamentary support. The conflicting claims and demands of these elements, exacerbated by opposition politicians and newspapers, prevented the government from taking decisive action toward possible solutions. The situation moved from one minor crisis to another until October 1958, when Field Marshal Sarit suddenly returned to the country and, in another bloodless coup, overthrew the entire system and established himself as a military dictator. His dictatorship, said to be temporary, meant that the country again faced the problem of finding a system of government which might reconcile aspirations for both stability and democracy.

· II ·

The Contemporary Setting

THAILAND is dominated by one city, the Bangkok-Thonburi metropolitan area with a population of over one million. After Bangkok, urban centers are no more than large towns of some regional importance. The pre-eminent position of Bangkok is best understood in geopolitical terms. Located astride the Čhao Phraya River near its mouth, the capital is in a position to control the prime gateway to international trade. This natural control has been reinforced by the convergence at Bangkok of railways from all regions. The development of commerce in the past century and the strategic control which the government has over it in the capital city have greatly simplified the problem of revenues and to a significant extent lightened the direct burden of government on the country at large.[1] This strategic factor has also permitted the government to mitigate and moderate the impact of the commercial revolution on the agricultural population, and to a large extent social upheaval has been forestalled.

In natural resources Thailand is rich in relation to its population. The products which enter into international trade and provide a base for commerce and revenues are extracted from the earth, fields,

[1] James C. Ingram. *Economic Change in Thailand since 1850* (Stanford: Stanford University Press, 1955), pp. 182–188.

30

and forests. Tin and wolfram are mined in the isthmus and western hills and exported in ore form. The forests of the north produce quantities of valuable timber, the most important of which is teak. In the southern provinces Thailand joins the rubber-producing area of Malaya, and many small holders produce rubber for export in crude form. Although these products are important in international trade and contribute substantially to foreign exchange revenues and to the total national product, the industries and the people engaged in them are sociologically of minor importance, perhaps 1 or 2 per cent of the population.

The Economy

At least 80 per cent of the population is engaged in agricultural pursuits. The overwhelming majority cultivate wet rice. Rice is the largest single item in the economy of the country as well as the largest item in its foreign trade. The annual surplus available for export is between a million and a million and a half metric tons, which provide substantial sums of foreign exchange as well as revenue.[2] Although rice predominates, other products are cultivated, such as fruits, beans, and tobacco, and animal husbandry for meat and draft animals is significant. The waters of the rivers and the Gulf of Siam also produce large quantities of fish, which together with rice make up the bulk of the national diet.

The stability and security of rural life in Thailand are conditions essential to the make-up of the nation's present social and economic situation and underlie certain characteristics of its contemporary government and politics. The representative Thai farmer is a small holder operating his farm on a family basis. As a general rule he owns in clear title the bulk of his land, although rented land and tenantry are not by any means unknown. Renting practices are reasonable throughout the kingdom, the most common method being that of fixed rent usually paid in kind.[3] Substantial indebtedness is extremely uncommon, and responsible economists have pointed to sound farmer's credit as an unexploited source of investment capital.[4]

Subsistence is still the basis of rural household economy after a hundred years of commercial revolution. The primary crop of the

[2] Kamol O. Janlekha, *A Study of the Economy of a Rice-Growing Village in Central Thailand* (Bangkok: Ministry of Agriculture, 1957), p. 1.

[3] *Ibid.*, pp. 61–68.

[4] John C. Kassebaum, *Thailand: Economic Farm Survey, 1953* (Bangkok: Ministry of Agriculture, 1955), p. 251.

representative farmer is rice which at the same time is the staple
of his family's diet. Rice is also the main cash crop of agricultural
Thailand so that the relative importance of cash in the household
economy varies with the amount of surplus rice available for sale.
The tendency in areas of substantial rice surplus, particularly in the
central region, is for the household to live on its own rice supplemented by fish and vegetables gathered from the rich environs. Any
other goods, such as cloth, meat, tools, animals, and luxuries, are
bought for cash on the proceeds of the sale of surplus rice.[5] The
amount of bought in contrast to home-produced goods may be reduced to nothing in more remote regions, and it is certain that many
families in the nation are still virtually self-contained economic units.
Abounding in luxury is not the proper description of rural life in
Thailand, but it is a land of sturdy peasants. Suffering and fear do
not dominate any significant part of the population, although hardship is not unknown.

This comparatively happy situation is a result of natural blessing
to a great extent. The nation has plenty of rich land in proportion
to its population, and its climate and geography are such that fish
fill the streams and canals and many fruits and vegetables grow without cultivation. But the policies of a government whose interest has
lain in stability have contributed to the security of the rural population. The state has been extremely conservative. On the one hand it
has prevented any rapacious commercial exploitation of the land
which might undermine fundamental subsistence. On the other hand
it has increased police services to the end of greater domestic peace
and also pursued an enlightened land policy which has in fact
strengthened the cultivator's title and secured his status.[6]

Urban life is based on commerce, which in the case of Bangkok
is largely foreign trade. Government itself and also manufacturing
are to a large extent bound up with and dependent upon the export
of the country's natural products—rice, ore, timber, rubber, and a
variety of minor items. Fuel, with the exception of wood and rice
straw, and most cloth and manufactured goods are imported. Cement
is the only domestic heavy industry; most of the remaining industrial activity is in the processing of food (rice and sugar) or timber
and light consumer goods. A striking fact of urban life in Thailand is
the lack of large-scale enterprise.[7]

[5] Janlekha, *op. cit.*, p. 132.   [6] Ingram, *op. cit.*, pp. 75–87.
[7] *Ibid.*, pp. 132–148.

The Social Setting and Political Forces

The peasantry as a political force is latent material. Forming the basic productive force and constituting 80 per cent of the population, it is the foundation of the social structure. But the peasantry's inarticulate acquiesence to government and indifference to national politics are fundamental to the political system. A tolerable economic situation which provides a stable subsistence without encouraging any great hope for quick improvement is no doubt the background of this political inaction. In the foreground is a real freedom from political and social pressures. Relatively secure in his property rights and usually safe from bandits and plunderers, the Thai farmer may go about his vital activities in security. Although he may fear the intimidation of maverick policemen, or his son may get caught in the draft and spend two years in hard military service, usually if the farmer looks to the government for anything—and this he rarely does—it is for assistance. In his view the government should (and often does) provide a school for his children. If there is a road to town, the government has built it. If his canal is deepened, the government will help. If there is hardship, the government may provide emergency rice. Because government revenues are for the most part levied indirectly, all this does not seem to cost much. The peasant is free to pursue the activities that are important to him—the cultivation of his fields, the promotion of his religion, and the enjoyment of leisure.

The effect of religion and piety in the Thai countryside is very great. Thai Buddhism is derived from the austere Southern school of Ceylon, variously styled Hinayana or Therevada Buddhism. Philosophically it proclaims the virtue of gentleness and suppression of desire. The principal activity of its adherents is to support monastic life for men who seek enlightenment, that is, control over their desires and escape from the endless round of birth and death. In Thai Buddhism this abstract system has been simplified on the one hand and enriched with a multitude of magical practices and propitiation of endless numbers of spirits on the other. The temple or monastery is generally the principal institution of a village, and its support is an important responsibility of the villagers. The abbot and other venerable monks of the temple are often community leaders whose influence is usually directed toward peace and harmony. The government's attitude toward religion is one of benign support coupled with a loose control. It is both law and tradition that monks have no place in politics, and the clergy is excluded from the role of an organized national political force.[8]

Thailand's one substantial religious minority is its Muslims. These people constitute perhaps 3 per cent of the population. But the fact that three-quarters of the Muslims in the country are concentrated in the four southern provinces of Satun, Yala, Narathiwat, and Pattani and are actually a linguistic and cultural as well as religious entity makes them a problem of some significance. The government, though following a policy of complete religious tolerance, has attempted to impose Thai culture on its Malay population through education. This policy has met with little success, and in recent years a number of concessions have been made to the Malays.[9]

Overseas Chinese are the most important minority in the country socially, economically, and politically. This group, which is distinct culturally and linguistically from the Thai, has been immigrating to Thailand for centuries from the regions of Southeast China. The total number of ethnic Chinese—that is, people who speak a dialect of Chinese as their first language and maintain certain well-defined cultural characteristics—is estimated by Skinner at about 2,315,000.[10] The great flood of immigration occurred in the first three decades of the twentieth century.[11]

In Southeast Asia the Chinese are in general notorious for their powerful commercial position, and Thailand is no exception. Encouraged to come first as wage labor in such constructions as canal and railway building, the enterprising and mobile Chinese proletarian was quick to exploit the trading possibilities in a developing commercial economy. As the quantity of rice which was entering the world market increased at an explosive rate, the opportunity for middlemen and milling operators expanded accordingly. The Thai peasant population directed its enterprise into expanded production, and the Thai upper class was absorbed increasingly into administrative and political work, leaving the area of commerce to the Chinese.[12]

Initially Chinese immigration was almost entirely male, and those who chose to settle in Thailand were apparently assimilated to the

[8] Lauriston Sharp, ed., *Thailand* (New Haven: Human Relations Area Files, Inc., 1956), pp. 338–375.

[9] *Ibid.*, pp. 105–110.

[10] G. William Skinner, *Chinese Society in Thailand* (Ithaca, N.Y.: Cornell University Press, 1957), p. 212.

[11] *Ibid.*, pp. 63, 175.

[12] Ingram, *op. cit.*, pp. 71–74; Richard Coughlin, "The Chinese in Bangkok," *American Sociological Review*, XX (1955), 311–316.

Thai population fairly readily. Around 1910, however, Chinese women began coming in great numbers, and the basis was laid for the growth of a distinct social community. Chinese education was begun, and Chinese community organizations were founded to provide social and welfare services to the Chinese. The Thai elite became quickly aware of this new development, and as early as 1914 the "Chinese problem" was proclaimed, more or less officially. Since the revolution of 1932 control of the Chinese economic and political menace has been an implicit policy of all governments. The political side of the problem has been from time to time exacerbated by domestic Chinese politics as well. During the Japanese attempt to conquer China the Chinese in Thailand were openly anti-Japanese, and the Thai government for both domestic and international reasons embarked on a campaign to cut off immigration, break the Chinese domination of internal commerce, and end Chinese education. In the late 1940s a similar campaign coincided with the course of the Chinese revolution. In more recent years a somewhat intimidated Chinese community, split within itself over the political situation in China, has been seeking a *modus vivendi* with Thai political leadership.[13]

Bangkok has a much more complex social situation than rural Thailand. Bangkok society may be conveniently divided into four classes, which, because the Chinese are essentially urban, are divided on ethnic lines as well. The upper class is made up of top government officials and politicians and the most powerful commercial leaders. The upper middle class includes white-collar workers in government and business, and the lower middle class is comprised of petty shop-keepers and skilled workmen. The lower class includes the bulk of unskilled labor in factories, workshops, and service. Such class distinctions are arbitrary, and a fact of particular importance in understanding Thai society is that social movement is easy. The criteria for class status are various—money, family background, education, type of work, and general way of life—and it is not difficult to move up or down the scale. On the other hand, Thai society is very status-conscious, and equalitarianism is virtually incomprehensible to a Thai. Every social relationship is understood in terms of superior-inferior, and the very syntax of the language requires recognition of this fact.[14]

Urban workers are, like the peasants of the nation, but a latent

[13] G. William Skinner, "Chinese Assimilation and Thai Politics," *Journal of Asian Studies*, XVI (Feb. 1957), 237–250.
[14] Sharp, *Thailand*, pp. 165–170.

political force. Numerically they are still relatively few, but more importantly labor organizations are undeveloped. The ethnic division between Chinese and Thai workers has retarded the growth of a labor movement because of politically inspired competitiveness and because of great difference in organizing skill between the two groups. The Chinese, coming from a society in which the tradition of private social organizations is strong, have for years tended to band together in speech groups, benevolent societies, and secret societies for their own welfare and to exclude the Thai. Thai society has no tradition of private organizations, however, and only in recent years has the beginning of a trade union movement appeared. At present trade unions of various degrees of strength do exist in large industrial establishments such as oil-company installations, in the state railways, and in the state tobacco monopoly. These unions are in turn loosely grouped in labor federations inspired by government leaders and having little function other than observation and propaganda. There are three such federations at present—the Thai National Trade Union Congress, the United Thai Federation of Labor, and the Free Workman's Association. But the bulk of urban workers are employed in small shops of less than ten workers which operate on a quasi-family basis and make organization difficult if not impossible.[15]

The ruling class in Thailand may be divided into a three-tiered pyramid. The top level includes perhaps ten to fifteen persons who do or could dominate the ruling class and the country as a whole by a manipulation of the various political forces. This group includes senior military commanders, a few men of great reputation gained in the revolution of 1932 or in the interplay of politics since, and perhaps two or three men around the throne. At any given time there have never been more than six or eight such men in power. The second level of the pyramid is made up of perhaps a thousand persons including military officers of the rank of colonel or general, special-grade civil servants, prominent members of parliament, some princes, and perhaps some particularly powerful businessmen. Although the top group dominates, it is only through their manipulation and control of the second group that they gain, hold, and use power. The base of the ruling-class structure is what may be called the political public. It is made up of educated and articulate citizens in Bangkok and the provincial towns who interest themselves in the details of political activity. For the most part high school and uni-

[15] *Ibid.*, pp. 431–435.

versity graduates, they are largely in the bureaucracy but also include professional people, journalists and other writers, and Thai members of the commercial white-collar group. It may be estimated that the ruling class as described is between 1 and 2 per cent of the total adult population of the country.

The organizing institutions of this group are predominantly bureaucratic in the broadest sense of the word. They are, in approximate order of importance, the military—army, police, air force, and navy —the parliament, the throne, the civil service, and the business community. Public opinion as expressed by the press and the universities is also a major political force.

The military establishment, since 1932 and more particularly since 1947, has taken upon itself the mission of political mentor of the nation. By means of successful coups it has staked a claim to political dominance which it has enhanced by giving to the Ministry of Defense large budget appropriations and by keeping the allocation of these funds as well as their auditing within the ministry and therefore generally free from outside control. The services maintain their own educational institutions—the military academies. Administrative officials within the ministry are officers under discipline, and political control has always been in the hands of a military officer of high rank. The final and perhaps most important element in the organization of the military for political purposes is the fact that a substantial portion of the armed forces is based in the capital, where they are readily available at times of coups and elections.

Parliament has become the institutional base for provincial politicians. Because of the heavy and dominating hand of the executive backed by the military and the civil service, elected members of parliament have developed a certain *esprit* of their own. Members who depend on their election skills and position in their constituency have a common outlook which contrasts with the professional bureaucrats. They seek to further their common interests even though they are divided into voting groups and inchoate political parties. These parties have little or no extraparliamentary organization. In general each member must get elected through his own efforts in his own province. Party labels are incidental. From time to time government leaders have pressured officials of the civil service into the role of party workers in support of government party candidates. This practice has provided no permanent substance to party organization. Parties have never represented substantial social forces but only cliques and individuals within the top level of the ruling class. Because the governing group must bargain for parliamentary support while members of parliament must compete with military and civil bureaucrats for position and influence, parliament has tended to take on the character of a separate political force and institution within the political process.

The position of the throne and the use of its prestige in politics is rather obscure. Until 1932 the king and his close advisers were the dominant political force, and the revolution was aimed at the throne's power. Although it was preserved as a symbol of national unity, the royal power sank to almost nothing with the abdication of Rama VII in 1935. Since the breakup of the revolutionary group during the Second World War, however, it is clear that the throne is gaining in power and prestige. Beginning in 1950 the throne has been occupied by an adult [16] who is able, if cautiously, to exert a growing influence.

The civil service as a whole is docile. Organized on functional lines in the 60-odd departments grouped in about 12 ministries of the government, it lacks the unity and hierarchy of the military services which would be necessary for it to take a dynamic part in politics as a single organization. Within the civil service sphere it is possible for a man to rise to a position of prominence and power from which he may be drawn into the top group. At the same time, because the co-operation of the civil service is vital to the ruling clique and because civil servants have a fairly homogeneous social and economic outlook, the civil service forms a crucial public. In order for the ruling clique to press any novel course of action, it is necessary that the groundwork be laid in this group.

The Bangkok and national business community, like business communities everywhere, deals in politics on the level of influence. Because of the general conception of the businessman as alien, that is, Chinese or European, this community enters politics at something of a psychological disadvantage. For the European this is to a large extent offset by diplomatic support, but for the overseas Chinese it is necessary to work out an accommodation. From the point of view of the Thai political leadership the problem is one of regulation with a double motivation. On the one hand, since the state revenues rest substantially on commercial activity—customs, premiums on exports, and business taxes—careful regulation is vital to the state's stability.

[16] King Phumiphon was 31 years old in 1958.

At the same time the need of the businessman, particularly the Chinese, for some protection in the face of heavy regulation makes political influence a premium qualification for business management. The opportunities of enrichment for political and personal uses have not been overlooked by Thai political leaders.[17] As the prime source of ready cash the business community is a political factor of substance; but its relative weakness, having no guns and few votes, makes it manageable.

Public opinion is a political force of some consequence. But politics has a limited if highly interested public of perhaps no more than 2 per cent of the population. The major means of formal communication for this public is the Bangkok press and publishing industry. Because the articulate public is heavily concentrated in the metropolitan area, the informal network of rumor and gossip is also important. Radio and, increasingly, television are also widespread. In general, however, broadcasting does not involve itself in the struggle within the ruling class. But the press of Bangkok is exceedingly political and partisan. Each clique and major leader has a paper, and the public is assaulted daily and weekly by hundreds of thousands of words of political comment and opinion. Unfortunately this verbiage is not accompanied by any substantial amount of factual reporting. The general level of journalistic ethics is low, and the pervasiveness of venality and open corruption among the newspapers is proverbial.

Political Ideas

There is a deep consistency of political outlook throughout the Thai ruling class which has an overlay of various more or less alien ideologies to be manipulated in the power struggle. Four slogans or catchwords in common use in the Thai political vocabulary sum up the fundamental attitudes. They are king, Buddhism, nation, and democracy.

The king, or the monarchy, is a symbol of political conservatism. The Thai ruling class takes pride in the bloodless revolution which preserved king and national unity. They take satisfaction from the fact that the government form was brought "up to date" without shaking their position or disturbing the long and venerable tradition of good government.

Buddhism is a symbol of cultural conservatism and unity. It binds the highest and lowest in what is seen as a just and natural scale

[17] Skinner, "Chinese Assimilation," pp. 248–249.

of status and right. Bound up with religion is the fundamental ethic
of doing good for the sake of one's fate and also of seeking after
one's own good fate before all else. It reinforces the social virtues
of mercy, compassion, diffidence, and respect for one's betters upon
which society rests. It encourages a certain love of enjoyment, cool-
ness in the face of trouble, and indifference to disappointment,
which make life easier and suffering bearable. These concepts, all of
which are a part of Thai social and religious attitudes, are vital in
the ruling class. But more importantly they are vital in the nation
as a whole and serve to unify the classes in outlook.

Although monarchy and religion are symbols of universal meaning
among all Thai, nationalism is most lively in the ruling class. Several decades of national education and widespread military service,
however, have made symbols and slogans of nationalism current at all
social levels. Thai nationalism is for the most part unmilitant. Its
historical background is the long diplomatic struggle to maintain independence. Thailand succeeded in this struggle through a process
of adapting itself to the ways of the imperialist powers and de-em-
phasizing the differences. Because of this history, Thai nationalism is
unlike other Southeast Asian forms. Culturally, it is not traditionalist
but assimilative. Politically, it is not revolutionary but conservative,
often taking the form of appeals for peace and tranquility for the
sake of the nation. An important theme of this nationalism is the idea
that Thailand is one of the "civilized" nations, "up to date," able to
handle its own affairs, and the equal of all nations; in addition there
is a strong element of anti-Chinese sentiment.

Democracy is also a slogan generally accepted by the ruling class.
It symbolizes a combination of a sense of duty, of *noblesse oblige*,
on the one hand and the end of special legal privileges on the other.
When reduced to specifics democracy is found to mean a fully elected
parliament controlling the government, the purpose of which is the
people's happiness and prosperity. These ends are an ancient objective of Thai government. The idea appears in inscriptions of the
thirteenth century. The late Čhakkri kings adopted it as their objective and rationale; the constitutional government has taken it over
as their own. The objective is congruent with the Buddhist virtue of
benevolence which conditions the popular attitude toward government. The ordinary Thai ideally expects benevolence from his superiors, and government is understood as a web of superiors. But
in seeking benefit from the government, he does not approach it as

an institution with procedures practicable for him. His approach is more likely to be to an individual of power with whom he can establish a personal relationship of obligation. Such a relationship may be family, friendship, or, more often, a matter of "reasonable" financial persuasion. One developing trend is the use of the vote as a method of obligating the successful candidate to his constituent.

Democracy also carries the meaning of freedom. The Thai of all classes resists regimentation, systematization, and routine. Although the social system requires respect for authority, it also permits room to move. Religion ordains that a man's fate is his own responsibility, and his position is a matter of his personal relationships with other individuals. Broad legal restraints on individual autonomy are resented and evaded. For the love of this kind of freedom, democracy is a useful symbol.

Although built upon a foundation of broad unity of thought, the ruling class is divided on the matter of emphasis. There are three ideological groupings. The first, which is mostly made up of members of the older, more traditional elements of the ruling class, emphasizes respect for the king and religion but at the same time, because it has been at a political disadvantage since 1932, also emphasizes legal, political, and economic freedom. The second group, in the main the military, is strongly nationalist. It claims precedence for national defense with resultant increases in military budgets and privilege for soldiers. This group also has a fondness for appointing members to parliament for the sake of national stability. The third group, largely civilian politicians and elected members of parliament, tends to put heavy emphasis upon free elections, strong parliamentary control, and more economic benefit for the voters. Members of this group have often characterized themselves as socialists.

· III ·

The Political Process

THERE is broad, virtually universal agreement among politically conscious Thai citizens that their kingdom should have a constitution. Although Thailand has been governed under the constitutional regime for only a quarter of a century, any significant resistance to the idea has disappeared. But there is considerable disagreement on the detailed provisions which ought to be included.

In law the king granted the constitution to his people, and in fact the development of the government under the monarchy was clearly toward the idea of a constitution. The words of Rama V as far back as 1892 (see Chapter I) revealed the seed of the idea of limitation on arbitrary power. The elaborate structure of legislation of the fifth, sixth, and seventh reigns was constitutional in effect. On the other hand, the written constitutions since 1932 derive from the revolutionary tradition and are therefore imposed on the throne. The tradition and fact of absolute monarchy have been broken.

The written document receives none of the veneration which is accorded to the American constitution. It has been introduced into a prior and vital political system with a fully developed body of legislation, a powerful structure of government, and a vigorous bureaucratic tradition. The introduction of the document was itself revolutionary and contrary to the concept of orderly constitutional procedures. In such a setting, it is to be expected, perhaps, that the document's force is not dominant.

Chart 1. The structure of government in Thailand in 1958 *

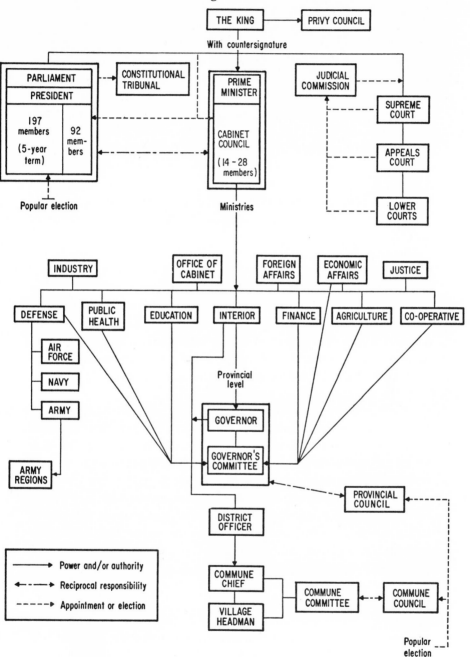

* Set forth in the constitution of 1932 as amended in 1952 and by statute.

During the past quarter century, Thailand has had six forms of written constitution, two provisional and four so-called permanent versions.[1] The king granted the first provisional constitution three days after the *coup d'état* of June 24, 1932. This was superseded on December 10, 1932, by the permanent version. Following the Second World War a commission undertook to revise the permanent constitution in order to eliminate the so-called transitional provisions. The commission presented a draft which was enacted as a new constitution on May 9, 1946. This document was replaced by a provisional constitution in November 1947 in connection with the *coup d'état* of that month. A new commission then set to work and produced a new permanent constitution on March 23, 1949, which lasted until November 1951. It was then set aside in favor of an amended form of the constitution of December 10, 1932, which was in force until 1958.[2]

There are broad areas of agreement in the various versions of the constitution. The king as head of state exercises the sovereign power of the people through three branches of government—the executive, in a cabinet of royal ministers; the legislative, through a parliament at least in part representative of the people; and the judicial, through a legally constructed system of courts. (See Chart 1.) Civil rights are protected from arbitrary executive action. Certain broad policies of social welfare are set forward as guides to the state.

Parliament and Legislation

It is in the form of parliament that the various constitutions differ most. This is not surprising because the essential effect of the constitutional revolution was to take the power for legislation and over-all direction of the state's policy from the throne and in law give it to parliament. At the time, however, parliament was little more than an idea. There was no traditional basis for it other than the various feeble councils which from time to time the throne had appointed.[3] Approaches to parliament have been, therefore, rather ambivalent in

[1] Adequately translated texts of all but the provisional constitution of 1932 are available from International Translation Service, Bangkok. The provisional constitution of 1932 is translated into English in Luang Pracherd Aksorluksna, *La Constitution siamoise de 1932* (Paris: Les Editions Domat-Montchrestien, 1933), pp. 163–172.

[2] Phairot Chaiyanam, *Explanation of Comparative Constitutional Law* (Bangkok, 1952), vol. II, *passim* (in Thai).

[3] Düan Bunnak and Phairot Chaiyanam, *Explanation of the Constitution Together with the Law on Election* (Bangkok, 1935), pp. 9 ff. (in Thai).

concept. First of all the bureaucratic background of the revolutionary group produced an inclination toward strong executive government and a suspicion of the unpredictable nature of a body of undisciplined men each having his own personal sources of power. From this it is perhaps natural to expect a concept of parliament as a group of wise but gentle elders which would express the consensus of the nation for the guidance of the government. Such a concept is fully in the historical tradition. But there was also the more doctrinaire view of the nature of a parliament as watchdog of the public interest against the more ruthless and exploitive tendencies of government. This concept, initially imported from Europe and without any traditional institutional basis, rapidly came to be shared by men who were themselves in parliament through election by the newly enfranchised people.

An admixture of these tendencies may be seen in the four forms of parliament which appear in the Thai constitutions. The most radical form, which is set forward in the constitution of December 1932 and in the amended version of 1952, is the unicameral body fully elected on the basis of universal adult suffrage. The government is required to maintain the confidence of parliament and present its every act for approval. In fact such a parliament has never existed. These constitutions provide for a transitional period in which half of the seats are filled by executive appointment. The government is thereby free of any serious threat from parliament so long as the governing group hangs together. The country has to date been ruled for twenty years under this regime (1932–1946, 1952–1958).

The other two forms of parliament are bicameral. In the constitution of 1946 an upper house was created. The members of this house had special qualifications of age and education. It was planned that this house would eventually be elected by an electoral college meeting in the capital for that purpose. In its initial and only election in 1946, however, the then existing lower house served as electors. The other bicameral form (1949–1951) provided for royal appointment of "senators" who in the view of the king had special qualifications. This power was exercised by the king in his own right rather than through the cabinet. In both of these bicameral arrangements the lower house was fully elected and had greater power than the upper, but in general both houses fully shared the parliamentary power.

Although its constitutional position is powerful, parliament has never succeeded in developing its potential authority. There are a number of reasons for the continuing weakness of parliament. First of all parliament is a new institution, and there is no agreement on its actual role in the political process. In addition to being only twenty-five years old, parliament has suffered various indignities during that period which include being shut up, being dissolved, and being reorganized at periodic intervals. At the same time the constitutional provisions discussed above have implicitly indicated a distrust on the part of national leaders of the good sense and wisdom of elected members. In all, parliament has no tradition of dignity. Secondly, parliamentary groups have little strength outside of parliament. Party organization is feeble and lacks any substantial popular base. Individual members may be strong within their constituency, but there are no national organizations to impose discipline within parliament. These factors contribute to the overwhelming dominance of the government over parliament. Bearing the immense prestige of the king's government and of the bureaucracy in general and military backing in particular, the cabinet generally is able to rule the house firmly. Using fear, persuasion, corruption, and patronage, in addition to the power to appoint members itself, the government has, with rare exceptions, imposed an iron discipline on its majority.

Under the constitution of 1932 as amended in 1952,[4] parliament is made up of one house called the House of the People's Representatives. Under the provisions of Section 115, members are to be divided into two categories for a period of ten years (until 1962). The first category of members is elected. The second category is appointed by the government. For the first five years (until 1957) these two categories were equal in number (123 each). At the time of the general election of February 1957 the number of elected members was increased to 160 on the basis of a larger population, and the government planned to appoint additional members to the second category as well. In a suit brought after the election, however, it was ruled by the Supreme Court that the constitution did not provide for increasing the size of the appointed category.[5] For various political reasons the government accepted this ruling, and the membership stood at 160 elected and 123 appointed members.[6]

The constitution (Sections 116 and 117) also makes provision for

[4] The specific constitutional provisions discussed hereafter are those of the constitution of 1932 as amended in 1952. Although this constitution was set aside in October 1958, the references serve to illustrate the intricacies and problems of Thailand's constitutional practice.

[5] *Bangkok Post,* July 10, 1957.   [6] *Ibid.,* July 11 and 16, 1957.

replacement of some of the government-appointed members by elected representatives during the second five years (1957–1962) of the transitional period. The established procedure is that a province wherein more than half the eligible voters have finished primary education gains the right to elect additional representatives equal in number to its representatives as determined by population. The same number of government-appointed members will thereupon be retired. On March 30, 1958, the first such by-election was held for 26 members from five provinces.[7] Thereafter the composition of parliament became 186 elected members and 97 appointed members.

Members of parliament are elected for a five-year term (barring executive dissolution under Section 65) from provincial constituencies. The number of members for each province is determined by its population. The rate is at present one member for each 150,000 population, with at least one member in each province. Provincial representation in the general elections of 1957 ranged from one to nine seats. Voting procedures are simple. Each candidate has a number, and the voter is given a set of numbers for all candidates. He selects the numbers of his choices up to the total number of seats and pastes them on the ballot. The candidate (or candidates) with the most votes wins.

The political parties of Thailand are no more than parliamentary groups. The nature of party organization is greatly influenced by the fact of extreme executive dominance in the house. The group which supports the government is necessarily built around the core of government-appointed members. To these are added the elected members who for whatever reason are willing to support the government. Their reasons are various, and the group is inevitably heterogeneous. At least three categories of motives for supporting the government are apparent. The first is respect for the leaders of the government. The second is attraction to power and the hope for preferment. The third is response to direct payment. All these motivations have been utilized by the government in power to build up firm parliamentary support. Since the government has all the facilities for attracting the opportunists, the opposition tends to form into small, more homogeneous groups. In recent years there have been two of these: a rather conservative group, the Democrats, and a leftist group, the Socialist Front. The overriding quality of party activity is instability,

[7] *Royal Thai Government Gazette,* vol. LXXV, Feb. 21, 1958 (International Translation Service, Bangkok).

however. With each shift of the political wind, groups are reorganized. Within the postwar period it is possible to count at least ten parliamentary groups of substance at different moments, but only one has persisted—the Democrats.

At election time the individual candidate is the basic unit. No party has a national organization, and there are only a few provincial party clubs. Candidacy is open to any qualified voter who can put up the deposit. The candidate's party affiliation is a matter of accommodation between himself and the central committee of the party. It varies in each case and is dependent upon the candidate's strength in his province, upon his compatibility with the party leadership in terms of personal relationship, reliability, and general ideological tone, and upon various monetary considerations. In any individual case the candidate may be wooed by one or several parties, or he may have to petition party leadership to give their endorsement. Although ballots make no reference to party and in most cases it may be assumed that party affiliation makes little difference to the voter, association with the prestige of well-known party leaders may be in some cases of considerable benefit in campaigning.

The dominance of the executive is clear in the process of legislation. According to the constitution (Section 2) sovereignty is exercised by the king. In fact the constitutional system of Thailand has found its model in the British system, and therefore the actual power of the monarch is completely circumscribed by the provision for countersignature of his public actions. In law this means that the responsibility for all acts of the government rests with the minister or other official who countersigns the royal act. In practice it means that, with the exception of whatever personal influence the king may be able to exert upon his officials and this is generally slight (although perhaps increasing), public action is taken by politicians and officials. As long as the constitution is in force, the legislative power is exercised "by and with the advice and consent of" parliament (Section 7). In concept this is similar to the role of the United States Senate in treaty making and often works out in that way, although members of parliament have certain powers of initiative. The general body of law is included in the codes—penal, civil, commercial, and procedural—which for the most part historically predate the constitution. The government, that is, the cabinet and parliament acting in the name of the king, has the authority to legislate through several procedures.

Two such procedures are provided by the royal act and the royal ordinance (sometimes called the royal decree-law). These must receive the consent of parliament. An act is presented to parliament in the form of a bill, and after debate it is passed or defeated by a majority vote. An ordinance may be enacted by the cabinet under Sections 88 and 89 either to authorize emergency action, "when there is urgent necessity to maintain public safety or to avert public calamity" at such time as parliament is not in session, or to enact such programs as taxes and currency regulations which would be damaged by prior publicity. An ordinance must be approved by parliament as promptly as circumstances permit or it is void.[8] This device is rarely resorted to in normal times (there have been six issued since 1946), but it was relied on heavily during wartime. Section 95 of the constitution grants broad mandate to the executive by providing that it may issue royal decrees "not in conflict with law." Such decrees, which are of course initiated by the cabinet, need no parliamentary approval. In fact, however, parliament often grants broad authority within an act to issue implementing decrees. In the period from 1946 to the middle of 1957 the government issued 782 royal decrees as compared with 468 royal acts passed by parliament.

Legislation in general takes the form of the delegation of certain authority to officials in terms of the most general objectives. To a great extent the development and implementation of policy are left to the bureaucrat. Many departments of the government have no specification of their powers and functions other than the act which created them and the conditions incorporated in the granting of their annual budget. Beyond that the specific role of the department is defined by the ministerial regulations, orders, notifications, and so forth which are developed under the authority implicit in its existence.

The budget is, of course, a most vital and effective form of control of the government and the bureaucracy. Under the constitution (Section 68) the budget must be enacted as a royal act with the approval of parliament. Parliamentary control is hedged, however, by the government's power to make emergency expenditures in advance of parliamentary approval (Section 69) and by the provision

[8] An ordinance enacted to meet an emergency while parliament is not in session must be "forthwith submitted to the Assembly at its following session," whereas an ordinance on taxes and the like enacted while parliament is in session must be submitted within two days following its publication in the Government Gazette.

to extend the previous year's budget if the new act is not passed in time (Section 68). Money bills may be introduced in parliament only by the government or with the approval of the Prime Minister. Although the constitution declares that no state monies may be spent unless sanctioned by the law governing the budget, there are in fact substantial funds available to government departments which are not accounted for in the budget. This situation arises from the fact that each department of the government has the status of a juristic person and as such can own property and enter into business. The profits of such activities are then available to the department for its own uses.

The Executive

The executive power of the government is made up of the Prime Minister, the cabinet, and the civil and military bureaucracy. Although the power to make policy is diffused and dispersed widely in the administrative structure, the ultimate power of appointment, investigation, and review rests with the Prime Minister. Not only does he have the power to form his cabinet which has political supervision over the ministries, but he also exercises the royal power to appoint and dismiss civil servants who are permanent undersecretaries and heads of departments (Section 96). He is thereby able to command the personal loyalty of the key bureaucrats. Moreover, the Prime Minister has personal charge of the elaborate Office of the Council of Ministers.

The Office of the Council of Ministers, though including secretariats for the cabinet and the Prime Minister, has developed duties more far-reaching than the purely secretarial. Within it there are three organizations of investigation and control of the bureaucracy, namely, the Civil Service Commission, the Administrative Inspection Department, and the Office of the State Audit Council. It is problematical how thorough or systematic the control of the bureaucracy is in fact, but there is little question that the necessary authority is available. In addition to organizations for control, the Prime Minister has available to him in the Office of the Council of Ministers the facilities of the Public Relations Department which operates the National Radio and handles press relations of the government. Also under this office is the Department of Public Works, which supervises government construction. Three organizations with the function of providing information and advice are under the Office of the

Council of Ministers as well: the Central Information Department, an intelligence agency; the National Economic Council, a fact-finding and advisory body with its own secretariat; and the Legislative Council,. which provides expert legal advice and service. The Prime Minister's secretariat, which is a part of this organizational structure, has in recent years had the power to spend certain unbudgeted funds available from the national lottery and special welfare revenues.[9]

Assessment of the Office of the Council of Ministers is difficult because no full study of its activities has been made, but that it provides the Prime Minister with an administrative tool of great power seems clear. The broad range of authority covered in such activities as public information, intelligence, and construction combines in the hands of the Prime Minister a number of political and administrative weapons of persuasion and control which can be used to maintain his authority over the government. If he can maintain himself in office, the Prime Minister has control over much government power.

The Cabinet Council, made up of from fourteen to twenty-eight members, has the duty of administering affairs of state. The cabinet is formed by the Prime Minister and nominally appointed by the throne. It rules only with the confidence of parliament. At the time of presenting his cabinet to parliament, the Prime Minister customarily submits a policy statement as well. In practice his statement has been a brief declaration of good intention in the various areas of government activity which parliament dutifully ratifies as a broad mandate of approval.

The cabinet meets regularly to conduct its affairs under the presidency of the Prime Minister. It has both an administrative and a political secretariat charged with preparing the necessary material for meetings. The cabinet is also served by the various agencies of information and advice in the Office of the Council of Ministers. Burdened with many administrative duties, the cabinet is able to spend little time on the development of policy in a co-ordinated and long-range manner.

The Thai government is organized into twelve ministries besides the Office of the Council of Ministers. In addition there are a number of quasi-autonomous "organizations" which perform certain specialized functions. The ministries are Defense, Finance, Interior, Foreign

[9] Manual of Organization of the Government of Thailand (Institute of Public Administration, Bangkok; in draft form).

Affairs, Justice, Agriculture, Co-operatives, Education, Economic Affairs, Communications, Public Health, and Industry. Each is organized in a similar manner, with a minister's office having authority for policy supervision, an undersecretary's office having powers of administrative supervision, and a number of departments having specialized function. In general the department and its director-general are the units of greatest cohesion. The director-general receives a royal appointment to his position which puts him in a direct relationship with the Prime Minister. At the same time the department is usually the level of organization which has both coherence of activities and unity of budget. Therefore a department can pursue its own policy within its sphere. The director-general is in a position to know his subordinates intimately and, in keeping with Thai traditions of hierarchy and subordination, to call upon their loyalty. To a large extent the director-generals and undersecretaries make up, within the powerful Thai bureaucracy, a kind of administrative elite. Since, however, their lines of loyalty run up and down, there is no more than minimal co-operation as a group. In fact, because the major aim of a director-general is, usually, to expand the activities of his department, he is often in competition with his counterparts for the resources at the disposal of the government as a whole.

Courts of Justice

Thailand has a unified court system with three levels of courts: various jurisdictions of first instance, the appeals courts, and the Supreme (*Dika*) Court. There are also court systems for special groups, such as military courts. Justice is administered in accordance with the codes of law and procedure which define precisely the status of persons, property, and institutions, the nature of crime, the powers of the police, and the procedural safeguards for the rights of litigants and accused persons. The independence of the judiciary which is required by the constitution (Section 103) is established by both the constitution itself (Sections 99–105) and the Judicial Service Act. Judges are protected from interference as far as possible by requiring that all appointments, transfers, and removals of judges be made by the king according to law and with the approval of the Judicial Commission, which consists of certain ex officio members and a majority elected by the kingdom's judges.

Under the constitution (Section 106) there is an extraordinary tribunal consisting of the President of the Supreme Court, the chief judge of the appeals court, the director-general of the Department of Public Prosecution, and three members appointed by the parliament. This tribunal is empowered by the constitution (Sections 113 and 114) to strike down any law which is "inconsistent with or contrary to" the constitution. Such questions are sent to it by any court, and its decisions are deemed final.

Administration

Fundamental to the understanding of politics in Thailand is an appreciation of the position of the administrative organization. In a very real sense it is prior to the problem of power. Government goes on regardless of which leader or group of leaders pulls the levers, and it follows much the same path. Because the ruling class is in general the bureaucracy, because the commercial class is alien and politically intimidated, and because the great and fundamental social class of cultivators is absorbed in the isolated peasant's world of work and religion, free from socially revolutionary pressures, the framework of politics is narrow. The fundamental question is: How shall the rewards of goods, prestige, and power be distributed within the ruling class? Which branch or unit of the bureaucracy will dominate?

Methods of interior administration and local government are at present in a state of flux. (See Chart 1.) Generally speaking, interior administration has been direct and highly centralized. The two basic units of administration are the province (*čhangwat*) and the district (*amphoe*). There are 71 provinces and 411 districts in the kingdom. The senior official in the province is the governor, a professional civil servant of high rank appointed by the Office of the Undersecretary of the Ministry of the Interior. At the provincial level there are also officials of the Police Department and of various ministries such as Education, Agriculture, Finance, and others who work with the governor in conducting the business of the province. The senior official in the district is the district officer, a professional official appointed by the Department of the Interior (in the Ministry of the Interior) who works with officials from other ministries much as the governor does at the provincial level. The district officer and other officials are under the control of the governor and represent the lowest level of professional administration.

Within the district there are two levels of administrative units, the lowest being the villages or hamlets (*muban*) which are in turn grouped into communes (*tambon*). Each village has a headman chosen from among the villagers. The headmen within a commune choose one of their number to be commune chief. Neither of these two offices is part of the official service.

In addition to administrative units rural society may be understood in terms of natural communities. Such communities are not necessarily related to the administrative divisions and in fact are often divided among various administrative units.[10] A natural community is generally oriented to a Buddhist temple and often a school as well which provide social centers.[11] Such communities have no formal corporate or institutional structure although patterns of social organization are evident. In them such personages as venerable monks, headmen, and educated men assume places of leadership. The fact that the government often fails to take account of such communities in its administrative organization is an obstacle to the creation of local responsibility and local centers of strength. This situation, on the other hand, may be agreeable to the central government.

In recent years efforts have been made by the central government aimed toward the development of local self-government. In fact, as long ago as 1933 an act for the establishment of self-governing municipalities was passed, but the experiment was not very successful. Since 1952 a series of legislative enactments have established new institutional arrangements aimed at self-government. These are the elected provincial and commune councils, the sanitary district, and the reorganized municipalities.[12] It is still too early to draw conclusions on these efforts.

National Politics

National political leaders in Thailand are not chosen by the public. They thrust themselves on the country. The organizers and leaders of the three great coups of 1932, 1947, and 1957 have served as national political leaders. In the past twenty-five years three men who were not members of the inner circle of a coup group have held the

[10] A striking example of this is to be found in the central plains community of Bang Chan which has been intensively studied by scholars from Cornell University. This natural community includes at least seven hamlets which are divided between two communes and two districts. See Lauriston Sharp *et al.*, *Siamese Rice Village* (Bangkok: Cornell Research Center, 1953), p. 17.

[11] *Ibid.*, pp. 16–18.

[12] Sai Hutačharoen, *Progress in the Department of the Interior* (Bangkok, n.d.; mimeographed), pp. 13–20. *Administration*, Special Volume no. 1 (Bangkok: Dept. of the Interior, 1956), contains relevant documents. (Both works are in Thai.)

office of Prime Minister. Their combined tenure was less than two years, and they all held office more or less on the sufferance of a power behind the throne.[13] Participation in the three coups has been the pathway to positions of power for all other top leaders, notably Phraya Phahon Phonpayuhasena, Field Marshal Phibunsongkhram, Nai Pridi Phanomyong, Nai Khuang Aphaiwong, General Phao Sriyanon, Field Marshal Sarit Thanarat, and General Thanọm Kitthikačhọn. Because these three events were promoted from within the government, all political leaders of note have had official careers. Since each coup was a military operation, military officers have predominated. A central aspect of successful political leadership has been the ability to command the loyalty of the military, particularly the army units in the capital. The only period of civilian predominance in the political arena was between 1944 and 1947 when the army was rather hangdog after the Japanese war fiasco.

The three big coups produced three corresponding organizations which served to perpetuate the exclusiveness of the group of promoters, to maintain the group in power, and to set policy. These three shadowy groups, the People's Party of 1932, the *Coup d'Etat* Group of 1947, and the Military Group of 1957, have been informal, unpublicized, and rather cryptic in their operations. Their irregularly held meetings have been secret, and the internal power struggles have been known only by leaks or by inference. Both the People's Party and the *Coup d'Etat* Group eventually split into irreconcilable factions which resulted in the collapse of control by the group as such.

Within the framework of quasi-formal organizations and the institutions of government, the personal clique is the basic unit. Cliques are, of course, not a uniform kind of institution but only a system of loyalties of uncertain stability. The clique takes a variety of forms and is built on a variety of direct personal relationships. Larger political organizations are pyramided from these cliques. No doubt the primary clique is based on family ties—father-children, husband-wife, brother-sister, and so on. Centuries of quasi-feudal social relations in Thailand have, however, competed with family ties. At present such loyalties as teacher-student, classmates, unit loyalties in the military, and various kinds of friendship loyalties are important in Thai society. Cliques may also be extended beyond the purely personal tie through the capacity to reward followers with power, privilege, and wealth.

[13] These three were Phraya Mano (1932–1933), M. R. Seni Pramoj (1945), and Nai Pote Sarasin (1957).

Power depends, therefore, upon the ability to inspire and manipulate loyal followers who serve to promote, protect, and maintain the leaders' position.

The manner in which the various elements of political power relate to each other is unstable in Thailand. The constitutional system has not functioned as expected, and there has been no final decision on the problem of regularizing and channeling the struggle for power. The method of popular elections provided in the constitutions for the choice of national leaders has yet to be effective. Considerable confusion and no small degree of dissatisfaction surround the twenty-five-year history of elections. In that time there have been eight general parliamentary elections held under six different electoral laws. These elections have had their uses, however. Perhaps the most tangible is the draining off of excess political energy, particularly in the provincial areas. Election has served as a pathway to positions of secondary leadership. The groups which emerge from the coups must develop control of parliament, and men of influence among members of parliament may therefore be invited to share in the peripheral benefits of power.

The electoral process is also necessary to the leaders of the coup groups for another reason, however. Although leadership is determined by other means and policies and government action are decided in other quarters, elections serve to legalize the ruling group. The Thai nation and particularly the bureaucratic elite not entirely inaccurately conceive of their world as a jungle in which the natural man is a wild beast with an insatiable appetite for power. In such a world a strong desire for law and legitimacy is not surprising. In the old days the king was made legitimate by the splendid trappings and ceremonial of his court. Under the constitution the ceremonial of election is required for the group in power. The public, in fact, seems not so concerned about the political outcome of elections as that they be held in a seemly, clean, and orderly manner.[14]

Coups and rebellions are an ever-present threat to positions of power. In the past twenty-five years there have been no less than eleven attempts, not all successful, to overthrow the government by force. In the same period there have been twenty-seven cabinets, each of which has been the result of major or minor shifts of political power. Political instability is in large part a matter of perpetual struggle for political status. Such a struggle is a necessary hypothesis in an

[14] David A. Wilson and Herbert P. Phillips, "Elections and Parties in Thailand," *Far Eastern Survey* (Aug. 1958), pp. 113–119.

explanation of Thailand's political system. Political status is a composite of three elements—power, money, and fame—which can be manipulated to maintain a kind of equilibrium. Control of certain key positions in the governmental machinery is a necessary precondition of such stability. The instrument of this control is the personal clique, and loyal followers are appointed to key posts. Among the keys to maintaining power are the Prime Minister's office, the ministerial offices, the positions of director-general of police and director-general of the Interior, and military commands, particularly in Bangkok.

After having taken control of such crucial administrative offices, the group which has gained power must, so long as parliamentary government is in effect, control a majority in parliament. The resources of the government are a decided advantage in this endeavor. Patronage is one method of keeping parliamentary members in line because they find cabinet and parliamentary secretary posts attractive. It has become the custom in recent times to reserve a number of these for the elected members of parliament. Friends and supporters of parliamentary members can also be given official positions. Secondly, the government has control over the pork barrel so that in some cases money for promotion of local improvements is given to the loyal member of parliament to use in his province as he sees fit. Thirdly, the government is able to grant privileges to parliamentary members for their own benefit in the letting of government contracts and the disposition of such items as export permits and access to railroad cars. Finally, the government, having the use of considerable official and unofficial funds, is able to pay stipends to its parliamentary supporters over and above their normal salary. All these methods have been used from time to time by the government to ensure its control in parliament.[15]

In the past decade there has been an extraordinary infiltration of political power into the business world along with the development in Thailand of a number of practices which may be lumped together in the term bureaucratic capitalism. This process seems to have begun with the appointment of powerful politicians to the boards of existing corporations (preponderantly Chinese originally) for the purpose of protecting them against state persecution or irregular political extortion.[16] Following their initiation into the business arena, politicians

[15] Prachuab Thọngurai, *The End of Darkness* (Bangkok, 1957), pp. 45–46 (in Thai).

[16] G. William Skinner, "Chinese Assimilation and Thai Politics," *Journal of Asian Studies*, XVI (Feb. 1957), 247–248.

established a number of corporations which enjoyed special advantages in dealing with the state. Control over unbudgeted funds of various government departments has in many cases provided capital for such enterprises. Another development has been the public corporation which is granted a special privileged or monopoly position in certain types of business and is thereby in a strong position to bargain with nonprivileged companies. Thai politicians—like human beings everywhere—have an understandable desire to be rich. In part, however, the motivation for promoting such activities may be found in special problems appearing in the political system during the postwar era. The necessity to go beyond the range of personal appeal and obligation to secure the support of important individuals often calls for provision of financial reward. In recent years the maintenance of political power has become an expensive proposition. The coincidence of this necessity with a political situation in which long-standing anti-Chinese sentiment and policies have made it easier for politicians to exert leverage upon the Chinese business community has made possible the growth of this important kind of political-economic alliance.

· IV ·

Major Problems

THAILAND is relatively free of the pressing and dramatic problems that plague other Southeast Asian or Asian countries. During the great revolutionary period of the nineteenth and twentieth centuries the nation has maintained and strengthened social integration. Plenty of land and reasonable administration have prevented the growth of the more spectacular aspects of rent exploitation and usury. The moderate degree of commercialization has not disrupted the fundamental placidity and uniformity of subsistence-type peasant agriculture. At the same time more than a century of internal peace has permitted the maintenance of effective internal security.

Political Problems

The most immediate problem that Thailand faces is the stability of its political system. Constitutional democracy has hardly achieved very substantial success over the past twenty-five years. The combination of strong and effective bureaucratic government and weak and disorganized extragovernmental organizations has made public control of the government ineffective. At the same time the traditional moral controls of monarchical ideology and the sense of *noblesse oblige* of the ruling class have suffered in the face of Western liberal thought. Government itself has become a much broader, stronger, and more active affair as the techniques of communication, suppression,

59

and regulation have developed. In a moral sense the ancient traditions of government have been corrupted, and since the Second World War in a very practical sense the bureaucracy and political leaders have been corrupted. As almost all persons in power stand potentially or actually to gain by the methods of corruption, there is for the moment little real will to end it.

Twenty-five years ago the bureaucracy, much strengthened by the reorganization and development of the previous forty years and by the new techniques of communication and control imported from the West, was cut free of the restraints of absolutism. This operation was not carried out by a strongly institutionalized parliament as in Britain, by a smarting middle class as in France and the United States, or even by a band of revolutionaries disciplined, for better or worse, as in Russia, but by the bureaucracy itself. As much as the leadership of the Thai revolution might have wished things to be otherwise, it was not able to muster any popular interest outside the bureaucracy upon which to base itself. As a result, politics has become a matter of competition between bureaucratic cliques for the benefits of government. In this competition the army—the best organized, most concentrated, and most powerful of the branches of the bureaucracy—has come out on top.

When the monarchy faltered and royal authority was overthrown, the ideological framework from which moral purpose and direction were drawn was thrown over as well. The rather alien idea of popular control of the state was substituted for the ancient and admittedly limited and outworn monarchialism. If parliamentary democracy is conceived as a process wherein diverse aroused social interests are expressed through organizations outside the government and are synthesized by representative institutions into a statement of the public will which gives moral direction and meaning to public power, then it has not proved suitable for Thai society. In centuries of bureaucratic monopoly of power the interest groups, the public corporations, and the free institutions had not developed. The bureaucracy, being already in control of the substance of society, could not be controlled by society. Behind the flimsy veil of parliamentary government the bureaucracy has been left to struggle within itself for power.

The failure to produce a moral focus of power has left the state in a sort of bureaucratized anarchy. The various departments and branches of the government seek to expand their activities and compete for the resources of the state. But the allocation of these resources is determined by the relative power of the units and inevitably ends in compromise and a spreading thin of effort. Direction and purpose are lost.

This loss of direction and purpose leads to corruption. By current standards ancient government, since it used its power primarily to maintain itself, was a kind of corruption. Its two great functions, war and ceremonial, were to a large extent private matters without particular effect upon the people. But the extent of this "corruption" was limited by the static nature of society and the difficulties of making power effective over distance. Ideology was, of course, also a limitation. In the more dynamic society of commerce the opportunities for state activity and regulation are vast. With the breakdown of discipline and the pressure of inflation the bureaucracy of Thailand seized these opportunities for personal enrichment. In the past ten years the use of public power for personal benefit has become both widespread and institutionalized.

But the breakdown of morale has not been complete. There is widespread revulsion against corruption even as it is going on. The wish for stability and the will to do good are strong. These sentiments have braked corruption to a large extent. The Thai ruling class is also restrained by an appreciation of the futility of killing the goose that lays the golden egg. The inner competition of the bureaucracy also limits to some extent the degree of corruption.

The problem still remains a matter of bringing the state machinery under some disciplining power to give it again a firm and purposeful direction. The Thai political system has fallen between absolutism and democracy. There is no clear road back or forward. Unfortunately political analysts in Thailand do not appear to have a clear understanding of the problem which actually faces them. They seemingly conceive of it as a matter of time, good will, and good men. They look for a solution in the fulfillment of the so-called transitional provisions of the constitution which would mean a fully elected parliament and a withdrawal from the scene of powerful politicians based in the bureaucracy. There is no clear conception of constructing bases of countervailing power and arousing expressions of popular will outside of the government. It is difficult to see a way out of the cliquism and corruption until some such extragovernmental power appears.

Economic Development

Economically the country has more than adequate resources to maintain its present living standards even in the face of considerable population growth. Food is the great surplus product, and the demands of housing and clothing in the tropics are minor. But the economy is at present bound to its agricultural base and single-crop emphasis. In order to develop the basis for a higher living standard, the nation faces the substantial problem of shifting some effort away from the single crop of rice as well as into industrial rather than purely agricultural pursuits. The government is undertaking a number of activities in the line of economic development, but in the words of a Thai government Economic Survey Group report:

A peculiar difficulty in the case of Thailand is that not only is there no systematic plan for economic development but there is no very intense demand or desire for economic development. Thailand is a relatively well-to-do country. If much of its wealth consists in the opportunities provided by nature for the enjoyment of leisure and a good life, it is not out of harmony with the temperament of the people.[1]

The survey refers to conclusions by John A. Loftus, an American acting as economic adviser to the Thai government, who pointed out a situation characteristic of bureaucratic political systems which is an obstacle to orderly efforts toward economic development.

He noted the absence of organized political strength behind alternative schemes for economic development—that is to say, the absence of articulate democratic opinion in support of one line of development rather than another. This, he said, led to a state of affairs in which the competing claims of alternative development schemes became competing claims of different segments of the governmental bureaucracy. There was no inherent machinery for resolving conflicts between Ministries for funds; there tended therefore to be a process of settlement of the conflicts by compromise; with the result that no Ministry got enough money to carry out the projects most urgently needed in the sector of the economy for which it was responsible.[2]

At present the government has undertaken a broad policy of developing basic public utilities largely with the financing of foreign grants and loans. Substantial World Bank loans have been made or sanctioned for improvement of railways and the port of Bangkok and for the construction of dams for power and irrigation purposes. Investment is also directed toward highway development and health and sanitation schemes. For the moment there is little likelihood that the predominantly agricultural nature of the nation's economy will be changed substantially.

[1] Thailand, Economic Survey Group, *Report on Economic Development Plans* (Bangkok, 1957; mimeographed), p. 11.
[2] *Ibid.*, p. 1.

Education

Education is a continuing but not an acute problem in Thailand. Because the country has been independent, the development of general administrative skills has generally kept up with the demands of the nation without the emergence of any sizable unemployed educated group. In the more specialized technical skills, particularly engineering, there is still great shortage. In education of the general public the government has built upon an ancient system of religious education. The number of primary schools has increased greatly in the past three decades, and compulsory primary education is almost universally in effect. The government has continuously poured substantial portions of the national budget into the educational system. Education is, rather, a qualitative problem in Thailand. The steady and rapid expansion of the school system has necessarily meant a general neglect of standards in favor of quantity.[3]

Minorities

One wholesome effect of the sacrifices of territory made under imperialist pressure has been the general homogeneity of the indigenous population. With the exception of the few Malay Muslims isolated in four provinces on the southern border and an even smaller number of primitive hill peoples, the native population of the land is Thai speaking and culturally unified. The country does, however, have a large number of immigrant peoples mostly of Chinese origin,[4] who because of strong national feeling on both sides and because of the economic

[3] The following table indicates the increase in enrollment at various levels of schools in the decade 1944–1954 (see Thailand, Ministry of Education, *Report of Education, B.E. 2485–2497* [A.D. 1942–1955], *and Educational Statistics for Twelve Years* [Bangkok, 1956; in Thai with statistics in Thai and English]):

	Primary	Secondary	
		Junior	Senior
1944	1,828,240	76,650	45,374
1954	2,937,534	176,222	75,712

Combined enrollment in four universities (Chulalongkǫn, Medical, Agricultural, and Fine Arts) increased from 3,266 in 1948 to 5,286 in 1953. The Thammasat figures have been excluded because they include a large number of inactive students who sit only for examination.

[4] There are about 70,000 Vietnamese in Thailand, the great bulk of which are refugees from the Indochina war. There are also small groups of other nationalities. See Lauriston Sharp, ed., *Thailand* (New Haven: Human Relations Area Files, Inc., 1956), pp. 115–119.

position of the immigrants present a substantial and continuing problem.

The seriousness of the problem of the Chinese minority is a matter of the size and distinctness of the group within the whole society. As was pointed out before, the size of the ethnic Chinese community has been estimated at 2,315,000 people in 1955. Of this total number, about 700,000 are China-born, and the remainder were born in Thailand.[5] Ethnic Chinese born in Thailand are generally able to speak Thai as well as Chinese and are usually physically indistinct from the Thai. Although the Chinese community has a number of strong organizations and is highly conscious of its identity, it is not rigidly separated from the Thai community within which it lives. In regard to Bangkok, the home of the largest concentration of Chinese, Skinner has said:

Bangkok society is not a caste system along ethnic lines; class boundaries are by no means coterminous with ethnic-group dimensions, and Chinese and Thai groupings show only a limited tendency to stratify. In this respect, too, models of social structure and functioning which have proved useful in the social analysis of other Southeast Asia countries . . . seem to be only most imperfectly approached by Bangkok (and Thailand) society.[6]

Because the Chinese of Thailand are well integrated in economic groups and work closely with the Thai in a variety of occupational pursuits, the problem is largely a social and political one. Will the Chinese remain culturally distinct or will they assimilate? Will they act as an integrated political group, which would mean with an eye to the political interests of China, or will they be politically motivated by their domestic interests? The government has followed the contradictory policies of containment and assimilation at different times. To quote Skinner again:

In general Thai policies were pro-assimilationist in the pre-modern era and through [Čhulalongkǫn's] reign. A change in Thai policies early in this century reinforced the decline of the assimilation rate brought about by such factors as the rise of Chinese nationalism and education, and the increased immigration of Chinese women. Increasingly in the twenties and thirties, however, Thai policy attempted to arrest the downward course of Chinese assimilation, with only limited success. From 1938 to 1947, the results of a repressive containment policy initially, and of a laissez-faire policy subsequently, were to reinforce the anti-assimilation effect of sociological and

    [5] G. William Skinner, *Chinese Society in Thailand* (Ithaca, N.Y.: Cornell University Press, 1957), p. 183.
    [6] *Ibid.*, p. 310.

international changes, so that the Chinese assimilation rate reached its lowest point by 1947. Thereafter a fluctuating policy has stabilized in a consistent pro-assimiliation course, while at the same time forcing a search by Chinese for a secure relationship with the Thai elite. In the absence of a considerable increase in the impact of Chinese Communist power in Thailand and of another reversal of Thai policy, the rate of Chinese assimilation may be expected to remain moderately high in the foreseeable future.[7]

There is nothing to indicate that the problem of the Chinese minority is in any way critical. The much-discussed economic power of the Chinese has never been exercised cohesively for any purpose and certainly not for political ends. Only on one occasion (1945) has there been public violence which had an interethnic character. The government has been fully able to impose its regulations upon alien Chinese in the face of no more than passive resistance. The problem, therefore, would appear to be the long-range one of whether or not this substantial community of aliens can continue to be regulated and ultimately assimilated into Thai society. This apparently depends, in the main, on three factors: the policy and action of the Thai government, the policy and action of the Chinese government, and the rate of new immigration to refresh the alien community.

The fact that there is no recognized intermediate status between being Thai and being Chinese simplifies the matter of assimilation. A Chinese who speaks Thai, has a Thai name, and assumes various Thai characteristics of behavior is a Thai. Almost all second-generation Chinese immigrants are able to do this. From time to time the Thai government has varied its legal requirements in accordance with the contrasting ends of trying to drive Chinese out or of encouraging them to assimilate. Recently it has tended to adhere to the assimilation course. There has also been a consistent policy to restrict immigration to an absolute minimum in recent years. The Thai government has done its best to forestall either official or unofficial influence from China. Only with reluctance were diplomatic relations established with Nationalist China in 1946, and there is no eagerness at present to recognize Communist China. Although both Chinese governments unquestionably are trying to increase their influence among the Chinese in Thailand, as elsewhere, it is difficult to assess these necessarily clandestine activities. Without doubt the competition between the two governments has made the Thai government's task easier.

[7] G. William Skinner, "Chinese Assimilation and Thai Politics," *Journal of Asian Studies,* XVI (Feb. 1957), 235–236.

Foreign Relations

Thailand has been fated in the modern world of international affairs
to be caught in the middle. In the years of European imperialism before the First World War it was squeezed between France on the
east and Britain on the west and south. In the years leading to the
Second World War in the Pacific it was caught between the rising
Japanese empire and Britain. Following the Second World War and
particularly since 1950 Thailand has been on the border of the Communist world.

There is a consistency in the foreign policies of the kingdom over
the past three decades. By adhering to the side of whatever nation
was most determinedly opposed to China, Thailand has resisted as best
it could the growth of Chinese power in East Asia. In accordance
with this policy Thailand has been closely allied with the United
States since the rise of the People's Republic of China. Thai concern
about China results from both the proximity of the two countries and
the presence of the large Chinese minority in Thailand.

Thailand and China had no diplomatic relations until January 1946.
In view of the delicate situation after the defeat of Japan and the
increased international prestige of China as one of the five great
powers designated in the UN Charter at that time, Thailand found it
expedient to sign a treaty of amity with the Nanking government.
China gained thereby direct official contact with Chinese nationals in
Thailand for the first time. The protection of these nationals was
assured by Thailand in the treaty.

After the Chinese revolution and the flight of the Nationalist government to Formosa, Thailand continued diplomatic relations with
the Nationalists, but on a much less cordial basis. At the same time
various privileges earlier accorded to resident Chinese nationals were
revoked.[8] In its attitude toward the People's Republic of China, Thailand has followed the lead of the United States. The Peking government
has not been recognized, and the seating of the delegation of that
government at the UN has been opposed. Within a few days after the
opening of fighting in Korea in 1950, Thailand announced its intention to contribute troops to the UN command and has maintained a
small force there to the present time. In 1954, deeply concerned about
the expansion of the Vietnam war to its borders with the implication
of spreading Chinese influence, the Thai government became a strong

[8] Skinner, *Chinese Society,* pp. 372–377.

supporter of the idea of a regional defense pact. It was an enthusiastic participant in the drafting of the Manila (SEATO) pact, calling in fact for stronger terms than were finally incorporated therein. Bangkok welcomed the headquarters of the Southeast Asia Treaty Organization, and Thailand has regularly participated in maneuvers of SEATO forces.

The Thai government's attitude toward neighboring countries since the war has been somewhat confused. It was, of course, not clear in the immediate postwar years how sharply the empires of France and Britain had in fact declined. At the same time it was of the first order of importance that Thailand regularize relationships with the world at large, particularly with Britain and France which were rather hostile as a result of Thai co-operation with Japan. The issues involved were settled by negotiations in 1945 and 1946, and a world tour by Pridi Panomyong promoted a revival of Thailand's good name in international affairs. Apparently Pridi also conceived of Thailand as the natural leader in a regional grouping of newly emerging Southeast Asian states. An organization aimed at a loose league of these states was set up in Bangkok in 1947, but Pridi's efforts were aborted by domestic developments, especially the return of Phibun to power.[9] Thailand took its most active role in the affairs of its neighbors in the Indochina war. France was the traditional antagonist of Thailand, and though officially the government remained aloof in the struggle for independence by the Vietnamese, Lao, and Cambodians, there was a strong sentiment of sympathy with the rebellious factions and apparently considerable unofficial support of the rebels from 1946 to 1950.

The victory of the Chinese Communists changed this attitude, however, as it became clear that Vietminh and Peking were closely allied. The year 1950 marked a revival of Thailand's policy of co-operation with the United States. In September and October of that year the two countries signed agreements for technical, economic, and military assistance. Since then Thailand has received over $100 million of American aid as well as several loans from the World Bank. In 1950 Thailand recognized the Associated States of Indochina—Vietnam, Cambodia, and Laos—and clamped down on support for the Vietminh.[10]

[9] John Coast, *Some Aspects of Siamese Politics* (New York: Institute of Pacific Relations, 1953), p. 38.

[10] Russell H. Fifield, *The Diplomacy of Southeast Asia, 1945–1958* (New York: Harper, 1958), p. 250.

A changing international atmosphere in South Asia has confronted Thailand with the problem of reconciling a policy which is closely linked to the militant antagonism of the United States toward China with the fact that Chinese influence in the area has become greater and at the same time less truculent. It would appear that Thailand's future course is to a large extent dependent upon the success with which the United States is able to maintain this type of policy. In spite of the growth of some sentiment in the country for a *rapprochement* with China, the government has up to the present taken no steps away from its close association with the United States and the West. If Thailand should break away from the anti-Communist camp, it is unlikely, barring an actual Communist coup (an improbable event), that the Thai nation would move beyond the fundamentally pro-Western neutralism of Burma and India.

SUGGESTED READING

GENERAL WORKS

Blanchard, Wendell, ed. *Thailand.* New Haven: Human Relations Area Files Press, 1957. A revision of Lauriston Sharp's handbook with a certain amount of political and economic data added. Often inaccurate.

Graham, Walter A. *Siam.* 2 vols. London: Alexander Moring, 1924. The second edition of an excellent handbook of information about Thailand, much of which is still relevant today.

Sharp, Lauriston, ed. *Thailand.* Subcontractor's Monograph. New Haven: Human Relations Area Files, Inc., 1956. A handbook primarily of sociological information.

Thompson, Virginia. *Thailand: The New Siam.* New York: Macmillan, 1941. Another handbook of information of all kinds about Thailand as it was immediately before the Second World War.

NEWSPAPERS AND PERIODICALS

Bangkok Post. One of the two important English-language dailies in Bangkok.

Bangkok World. One of the two important English-language dailies in Bangkok.

Journal of the Siam Society (between 1940 and 1944 known as the *Journal of the Thailand Research Society*). Published since 1904, this journal is an important source for any student of Thailand. Its main emphasis is on art, archaeology, ethnography, and history. A number of good short articles were republished in *Selected Articles from the Siam Society Journal.* (Siam Society Fiftieth Anniversary Commemorative Publication.) 2 vols. Bangkok: Siam Society, 1954.

Siam Rath Weekly Review. An English paper giving translations from the

Thai press and other interesting material. It is associated with a leading Thai-language newspaper.

I: The Historical Background

Dhani Nivat, Prince. "The Old Siamese Conception of the Monarchy," *Journal of the Siam Society*, XXXVI (1947), 91–106. A discussion of the conceptions of law, justice, and duty which were a part of the traditional Thai kingship.

Heine-Geldern, Robert G. *Conceptions of State and Kingship in Southeast Asia*. (Southeast Asia Program, Cornell University, Data Paper no. 18.) Ithaca, N.Y., 1956. (Also published in *Far Eastern Quarterly*, II [1942], 15–30.) Discussion of the magical and cosmological conceptions which informed kingship and the state in ancient Southeast Asia.

Landon, Kenneth P. *Siam in Transition*. Chicago: University of Chicago Press, 1939. A review of changes in Thailand from the revolution in 1932 up to 1939.

Vella, Walter. *The Impact of the West on Government in Thailand*. (University of California Publications in Political Science, vol. IV, no. 3.) Berkeley and Los Angeles: University of California Press, 1955. A careful essay on the political changes in Thailand brought about by the penetration of the West during the last hundred years.

——. *Siam under Rama III*. Locust Valley, N.Y.: J. J. Augustin, Inc., 1957. Detailed history of the reign of the last wholly traditional king of Thailand which sets the stage for the period of Western penetration.

Wales, Horace G. Quaritch. *Ancient Siamese Government and Administration*. London: Bernard Quaritch, 1934. Standard source on traditional Thai political and administrative institutions.

——. *Siamese State Ceremonies*. London: Bernard Quaritch, 1931. Detailed description of royal ceremonies of Thai kingship.

Wood, W. A. R. *A History of Siam from the Earliest Times to the Year A.D. 1781, with a Supplement Dealing with More Recent Events*. Rev. ed. Bangkok: Siam Barnakich Press, 1933. An account of the rise and fall of kings and dynasties.

II: The Contemporary Setting

Andrews, James M. *Siam: 2nd Rural Economic Survey, 1934–1935*. Bangkok: Bangkok Times Press, 1935. Important as a source of information on rural Thailand before the Second World War.

Benedict, Ruth F. *Thai Culture and Behavior*. (Southeast Asia Program, Cornell University, Data Paper no. 4.) Ithaca, N.Y., 1952. A perceptive study, actually written during the Second World War, on some elements of Thai national character and basic institutions of society.

Coughlin, Richard J. "The Chinese in Bangkok," *American Sociological Re-*

view, XX (1955), 311–316. A discussion of the strength of the Chinese community and its resistance to assimilation.

———. "Some Social Features of Siamese Buddhism," *Asia: Asian Quarterly of Culture and Synthesis* (Saigon), II (1952), 403–408. Valuable, though perhaps somewhat overstated, analysis of some of the relationships between religion, society, and personality in Thailand.

———. "The Status of the Chinese Minority in Thailand," *Pacific Affairs,* XXV (1952), 378–389. Examination of government policies toward the Chinese.

de Young, John. *Village Life in Modern Thailand.* Berkeley: University of California Press, 1955. A summary of what is known of the social aspects of life in rural Thailand.

Embree, John F. "Thailand—A Loosely Structured Social System," *American Anthropologist,* LII (1950), 181–193. Provocative article on lack of rigidity in Thai social structure compared with Vietnam, Japan, and even the United States.

Fogg, Ernest L. "Labor Organization in Thailand," *Industrial and Labor Relations Review,* VI (1953), 368–377. An account of the development of the labor situation and the organization of labor.

Ingram, James C. *Economic Change in Thailand since 1850.* Stanford: Stanford University Press, 1955. A detailed economic history of Thailand.

Janlekha, Kamol Odd. *A Study of the Economy of a Rice Growing Village in Central Thailand.* Bangkok: Ministry of Agriculture, 1957. Intensive study of Thailand's rural economy.

Kassebaum, John C. *Thailand: Economic Farm Survey, 1953.* Bangkok: Ministry of Agriculture, 1955. Statistical data on Thailand's rural economy.

Landon, Kenneth Perry. *The Chinese in Thailand.* London and New York: Oxford University Press, 1941. An early study of the most important minority group in Thailand.

———. "The Monks of New Thailand," *Asia* (Concord, N.H.), XL (1940), 129–132. Account of the role of the monk in Thai society and how it has changed.

Lewis, Norman. *A Single Pilgrim.* New York: Rinehart, 1954. Amusing and instructive novel about life mainly in North Thailand.

Pendleton, Robert L. "The Agriculture of Siam," *Foreign Agriculture,* X (1946), 154–167. Description of the state of Thailand's agriculture at the end of the Second World War.

Sharp, Lauriston, *et al. Siamese Rice Village: A Preliminary Study of Bang Chan, 1948–49.* Bangkok: Cornell Research Center, 1953. A wealth of information and an analysis of a village in central Thailand.

Skinner, G. William. "Chinese Assimilation and Thai Politics," *Journal of Asian Studies,* XVI (Feb. 1957), 237–250. Discussion of policy of the

Thai government toward Chinese immigrants and how it has affected assimilation.

——. *Chinese Society in Thailand: An Analytical History.* Ithaca, N.Y.: Cornell University Press, 1957. Detailed history of the Chinese community and the development of its social position.

——. *Leadership and Power in the Chinese Community of Thailand.* Ithaca, N.Y.: Cornell University Press, 1958. A rigorous investigation of the character of leaders and leadership in this alien minority.

Zimmerman, Carle C. *Siam: Rural Economic Survey, 1930–31.* Bangkok: Bangkok Times Press, 1931. The first of several such surveys which provide much information on rural Thailand.

III: The Political Process

Berrigan, Darrell. "Thailand: New Cast, Same Play," *Reporter,* XVII (Nov. 28, 1957), 12–14. Report of the coup of 1957.

——. "Thailand: Pibul Tries Prachathipatai," *Reporter,* XIV (June 14, 1956), 30–34. Account of Phibun's attempts to establish democracy by fiat.

Coast, John. *Some Aspects of Siamese Politics.* New York: Institute of Pacific Relations, 1953). Narrative of political events from 1932 to 1952.

King, John Kerry. "Thailand's Bureaucracy and the Threat of Communist Subversion," *Far Eastern Survey,* XXIII (1954), 169–173. A speculation on the possible disaffection of elements of the Thai administration because of political isolation.

MacDonald, Alexander. *Bangkok Editor.* New York: Macmillan, 1949. The experiences in the immediate years after the Second World War of the founder of a leading English-language newspaper.

Mosel, James. "Thai Administrative Behavior," in William J. Siffin, *Toward the Comparative Study of Public Administration.* Bloomington, Ind.: Indiana University, Department of Government, 1957. Perceptive essay on some of the social and psychological factors which enter the environment of the Thai civil servant.

Peterson, Alec. "Britain and Siam: The Latest Phase," *Pacific Affairs,* XIX (Dec. 1946), 364–372. Account of the negotiations between Britain and Thailand after the Second World War.

Phillips, Herbert P. "The Election Ritual in a Thai Village," *Journal of Social Issues,* vol. XIV, no. 4 (1958). An analysis of the election process as a social ritual rather than a matter of political issues.

Pickerell, Albert, and Daniel E. Moore. "Elections in Thailand," *Far Eastern Survey,* XXVI (June and July 1957), 92–96, 103–111. Account of events surrounding the election of February 1957.

Reeve, W. D. *Public Administration in Siam.* London and New York: Royal

Institute of International Affairs, 1951. Brief description of Thai government and administration.

Sharp, Lauriston. "Peasants and Politics in Thailand," *Far Eastern Survey,* XIX (1950), 157–161. Examination of the political attitude of some Thai peasants toward the central government.

Stanton, Edwin F. "Spotlight on Thailand," *Foreign Affairs,* XXIII (Oct. 1954), 72–85. Discussion of the international forces bearing on Thailand.

Thompson, Virginia. "Government Instability in Siam," *Far Eastern Survey,* XVII (1948), 185–189. Account of the *coup d'état* of 1947 which returned Phibun to power.

———. "Siam and the Great Powers," *Foreign Policy Reports,* XXI (March 1, 1946), 322–331.

———, and Richard Adloff. "The State's Role in Thai Economy," *Far Eastern Survey,* XXI (1952), 123–127. Discussion of postwar economic policies of the Thai government and their political significance.

Udyanin, Kasem, and Rufus D. Smith. *The Public Service in Thailand.* Brussels: International Institute of Administrative Sciences, 1954. A brief introduction to the present state of Thailand's civil service.

Wilson, David A., and Herbert P. Phillips. "Elections and Parties in Thailand," *Far Eastern Survey,* XXVII (1958), 113–119. An effort to put the election process in its larger political and social context.

PART TWO : BURMA

By Josef Silverstein

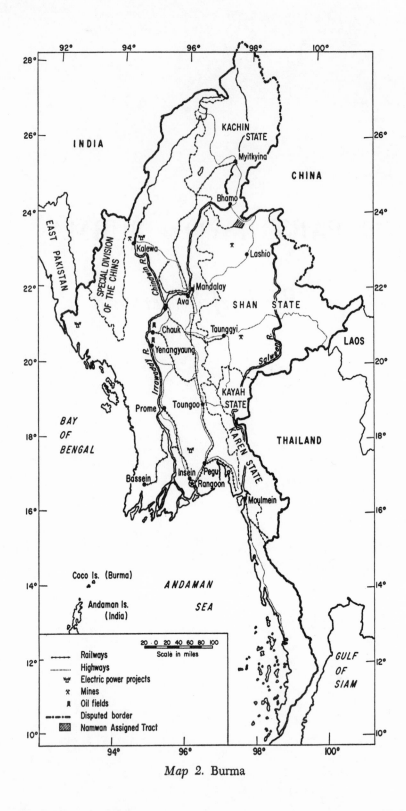

Map 2. Burma

· V ·

The Historical Background

THE geography and the long political history of Burma together provide the background to contemporary developments. At least three physical factors bear particular attention. First, Burma has a predominance of north-south valleys, mountains, and rivers. The major lines of communication follow the contours of the land, and Burma's cities and important towns are located along a north-south axis in the interior rather than near the borders or the seacoast. Second, the country divides naturally into two distinct areas—the plains and delta and the mountains. The political and cultural heartland of historic Burma was centered in the valley which is watered by the Irrawaddy and Chindwin rivers and protected on three sides by a semicircle of mountains. South of this area, the delta plain, which is interlaced with rivers and streams, is the political and economic center of modern Burma. The two regions join to form the present political subdivision referred to as Burma proper. The mountain area is less populated, and its inhabitants are in a more primitive state of political development than those living on the plains; travel is difficult, large towns are few, and there is little to attract the plains people. These mountain districts are today subdivided into five semiautonomous states. Third, Burma has been and continues to be partially isolated from its neighbors. The mountains provide a land shield as a major obstacle to merchants and would-be conquerors. Ancient Indian traders came to Burma by way of the sea. This contact was not sustained, however, and by the time European traders began to penetrate Southeast Asia, the normal trade routes bypassed Burma. Burma's relative isolation affected the attitude of its people toward the world and contributed to their lack of preparedness to meet the rapid penetration of European soldiers and traders in the eighteenth and nineteenth centuries.

The Pattern of History to 1885

The political history of Burma before the British conquest can be summarized as a never-ending struggle between at least four different indigenous groups and between the peoples of Burma and their neighbors. The predominant groups in the internal struggle were the Burmans,[1] whose home was in the Irrawaddy Valley, the Mons or Talaings, who lived in the south, the Shans from the north, central, and eastern parts of Burma, and the Arakanese, whose home was the semiisolated area in the west which bears their name. The other indigenous groups played no important part in the struggles.

In Burma's long history there were three relatively short periods of political unification prior to the British conquest. The first took place in the eleventh century when the Burman kings successfully conquered their immediate neighbors and established an empire which lasted for two hundred years. This period of the Pagan dynasty was Burma's golden age and was characterized by the flowering of an Indian-influenced Burman culture,[2] evidence of which can still be seen in the ruins of the city of Pagan. The period ended in A.D. 1287 when the armies of Kublai Khan drove the Burman king from his throne and destroyed the empire.

The second unification of Burma came in the sixteenth century when a new line of Burman kings—whose home was in Toungoo—subdued their neighbors and re-established Burman rule in roughly the area which is incorporated into modern Burma. The Toungoo kings were successful in forcing the Shans to accept permanent Burman suzerainty.

[1] The terms Burman and Burmese have no precise and accepted meanings. Such leading scholars as J. S. Furnivall and G. E. Harvey use "Burman" as a political term, identifying the citizens of Burma, and the term "Burmese" as an ethnic term, identifying a particular indigenous group. While in Burma, the writer found that the two terms were used in an opposite manner. Throughout this essay, following contemporary usages, Burman will be used in the ethnic sense and Burmese in the political, covering all the inhabitants of the country—Burmans, Karens, Shans, Kachins, Chins, Mons, and so on.

[2] John F. Cady, *A History of Modern Burma* (Ithaca, N.Y.: Cornell University Press, 1958), pp. 4–9.

In Burma's wars with Siam during this period neither country gained a permanent victory; a major result of this warfare was the depopulation of the area of lower Burma. By the beginning of the seventeenth century the vigor of the new dynasty was spent, and Burma again became the center of quarreling groups.

The last unification under indigenous rule came in the eighteenth century, when a third line of Burman kings rose in the north and forged a new empire. One of its initial conquests was the kingdom of Arakan which ceased to exist as a separate state when its king and 20,000 subjects were deported to upper Burma. The new dynasty engaged in numerous adventures against Assam, Manipur, and Siam and successfully defended Burma from four invasions by the armies of China. Burma's imperialism brought the country into contact with British power in India. Friction between the two over Assam and Manipur and rebellious activity in Arakan finally precipitated a war which lasted two years. Superior British military technology and equipment helped the invaders score easy military victories; disease and poor communications gave the victors their major setbacks. The war ended in 1826 with the signing of the Treaty of Yandabo,[3] by which Burma ceded Arakan and Tenasserim, renounced all claims to Assam and the right to interfere in Manipur affairs, and promised to pay an indemnity.

After the war Burma neither improved its military technology nor established friendly and realistic relations with the British. A trivial incident provided the Westerners with a new pretext to renew the fighting in 1852. All of lower Burma was annexed after the well-prepared British met only token resistance.

During the next two decades the Burman king tried to reform his government and establish friendly relations with the British. The arrival of the French as a major power in Southeast Asia in the 1870s and 1880s however, alarmed the British and caused them to use an incident between a British commercial firm and the Burman king in 1885 as a pretext to start the third Anglo-Burmese War. British military operations began in November, and by the end of the month the Burman king surrendered. Following their victory the British, on January 1, 1886, proclaimed the annexation of the remainder of Burma.

Although the political history of this pre-British period suggests a record of warfare and instability, its social history provides a different

[3] W. F. B. Laurie, *Our Burmese Wars and Relations with Burma* (2d ed.; London: W. H. Allen and Co., 1885), pp. 1–76.

picture. Society at the local level proved to be relatively stable. Organized under the leadership of hereditary chieftains called *myothugyis*,
the people performed the services for which they were obligated
and paid their taxes. Each village had a headman who, under certain
conditions was inferior to the chieftain. Because authority was personal rather than territorial, the people continued to owe allegiance
to their chieftains regardless of where they lived. When disputes
arose among the people, both the chieftain and the headman served
as arbitrators and based their recommendations on the moral teachings
of the Buddha and local custom. Even though a Burmese version of
the Code of Manu called the *dhammathat* existed, it played a relatively
unimportant role in the everyday lives of the people. No formal system
of courts and no class of legalists developed to serve society.

Most of the people were cultivators; they farmed either royal or
state lands which were operated under limited leases or their own
land which they or their ancestors reclaimed from the jungle or
swamps. These reclaimed lands were the property of the cultivator as a
member of a village. Although the owner had the right to sell or dispose of his property, his family had first right to buy it back. Since
most of the people practiced subsistence agriculture with a small
surplus for taxes and barter, there was economic stability based on
widespread small landholding. Because the chieftain acted for the
people in dealing with provincial and royal government, village life
remained relatively insulated from the struggles for power around the
throne and among contending ethnic groups.

Social stability in precolonial Burma drew its main strength from
the fact that nearly all Burmans and the peoples under their direct
rule shared a common religious faith—Buddhism. The monkhood or
sangha served the community by providing teachers and schools.
Learning was available to all, and even the meanest peasant learned
to read and memorize the moral teachings of the faith. All male adherents entered the religious order during some period of their lives
and became monks for a limited time. Education, participation in
the religious hierarchy, and feeding the monks to earn merit for the
next rebirth all served to foster close relationship between the people
and their religion and bind the community together.[4] The teachings
of the Buddha, as expressed by the peoples of Burma, place full responsibility upon the individual to live a meritorious life in order

[4] John S. Furnivall, *Colonial Policy and Practice* (New York: New York University Press, 1956), pp. 12–13.

to have a better rebirth in the next existence. This emphasis upon self-reliance proved valuable for social stability in a country plagued with continuous warfare.

Colonial Rule, 1826–1948

An appraisal of colonialism in Burma suggests several major developments which radically altered the society, changed the political and economic institutions, and thrust Burma from a backwater into the main stream of world events. The introduction of law and order throughout Burma contributed to the breakdown of traditional institutions and to the stability previously found only at the local level. In converting Burma into a commercial granary and the world's largest rice exporter, colonialism contributed to the growth in tenancy, moneylending, and the alienation of the land. The introduction of Western concepts of government and politics and the attempt to prepare the people for self-rule by gradually introducing new techniques created a new indigenous political elite which was divided over the question of gradualism versus immediate self-government. The encouragement and protection of minorities at the expense of the dominant Burmans, plus the introduction of large-scale immigration of Indians as laborers and financiers, gave rise to a new social problem which exploded into violent communal riots during the 1930s. These several changes, together with the Second World War, stimulated the peoples of Burma to demand independence.

Prior to the third Anglo-Burmese War, the primary interest of the British was to establish law and order. The territories under their control were governed by a centralized and bureaucratic administration which sought to accomplish its purposes as inexpensively as possible. Local government, being relatively stable, remained unchanged and met with little interference by the Europeans.[5] After the third war, the British were faced with a series of rebellions and organized banditry which cost them enormous sums of money, men, and material, but did not seriously threaten their rule. The support and sympathy given by the local chieftains to the insurgents were major reasons for Chief Commissioner Crosthwaite's decision to replace the traditional system of local government with a new one modeled on the Indian pattern. The changes included making authority territorial instead of personal, eliminating the local chieftains, elevating

[5] John S. Furnivall, "Fashioning of Leviathan," *Journal of Burma Research Society*, XXXIX (1939), 11–137; Furnivall, *Colonial Policy and Practice*, pp. 35–39.

the village headmen to positions as salaried officials responsible to the central government rather than to the local community.[6] These changes had an important impact on the local society because they removed authority from the one official—the chieftain—who was able to exercise real power over the people. In addition they elevated a class of functionaries who had no prestige and who therefore lacked the means for persuading the people to obey the new laws.

The elimination of the monarchy also marked the end of the royal religious council which, in the past, had authority to discipline the monks. With no new council or governing body to censor the hierarchy, discipline in the order deteriorated. Concommitant with this development was the rise in English and Anglo-vernacular schools which concentrated on training for government and commercial employment rather than on righteous behavior. The slackening in public demand for traditional education deprived the Buddhist monks of their chief social function, and the bonds between them and society weakened. The removal of the local chieftains and the deterioration of the Buddhist order were two of the main causes for the breakdown of traditional society in Burma. During the twentieth century crimes of violence and social unrest increased continually in spite of the expansion of the colonial police force, the courts, and the administrative system.

The shift from subsistence to commercial agriculture began between the second and third Anglo-Burmese wars. Stimulated by the increase in demand for rice in India and Europe and helped by the opening of the Suez Canal and the improvement in sea transportation, the British encouraged the peoples in upper Burma to move south and cultivate the rich delta soils. In addition the colonial authorities opened Burma to immigration of Indian laborers, merchants, and moneylenders. Both Burmese and aliens moved into the delta and established new communities which were unlike those from which they came. Few social bonds united them. Coming as individuals or isolated families they owed no allegiance to a traditional chieftain, nor were they subject to social pressures and the observance of lifelong friends. Furthermore, they came to depend upon Indian moneylenders for the annual capital to meet their needs. Since land ownership was a legal right, land could be sold, traded, or repossessed without considering the rights either of the village or of the owner's family, as had been customary under the Burman kings.

[6] Furnivall, *Colonial Policy and Practice,* p. 74.

Tenancy, rack-renting, and land alienation became commonplace, and people drifted from area to area, with no ties to bind them. The system produced rice; it also allowed the land to fall into alien hands and created a landlord class which dealt in land speculation rather than in cultivation. This also contributed to social dislocation and unrest.

Before the twentieth century the British made no effort to introduce institutions of self-government in Burma. The first political reforms which provided nonofficials in the administrative councils came in 1897 when the Chief Commissioner was raised to Lieutenant Governor and given a council of nine (English, Indians, or Burmese) with limited legislative authority. The Morley-Minto Reforms of 1909 provided for expansion of the council to fifteen, with two members elected by a restricted electorate representing the European business community. In 1917 the Secretary of State for India announced that Britain promised eventual self-government for India. The Burmese interpreted the announcement as applicable to their country because it was then a province of India. British wavering, however, and a delayed decision not to apply the reforms to Burma precipitated a storm of protest from the peoples of Burma and signaled the awakening of Burmese political consciousness. Local agitation forced the British to reconsider, and in 1923 the system of dyarchy (whereby certain subjects were transferred to ministers responsible to the Legislative Council and the others were reserved to the Governor) granted to India was also introduced in Burma.

The agitation which developed in 1917–1918 marked the first widespread political protest. Prior to that time organized protests were limited to calling for the end of the deterioration of discipline in the Buddhist hierarchy and of the desecration of sacred shrines by non-Buddhists. The protesters were organized in a nonpolitical Young Men's Buddhist Association (YMBA). The events connected with the announcement of the Secretary of State for India transformed this nonpolitical movement into a political one under the title General Council of Burmese Associations (GCBA). It was broadly based, nonreligious in membership, and political in its objectives. A second development took place in 1920 when the university students called a national strike to protest against the education plans connected with a new university. The strike marked the entry of students into national politics.

From 1923 to 1941 there was a steady growth in self-government and politics. The Act of 1921—implemented two years later—gave Burma its first elected assembly. Of the 103 seats, 79 were filled by popular election. Under the system of dyarchy, the subjects of forestry and education were transferred to ministers nominated by the Governor and responsible to the legislature. Since all other subjects were under the Governor's control and had first call upon revenues, the transferred subjects gave the Burmese ministers prestige, but little power. In this period, the GCBA split into shifting factions mainly over the question of participating in politics or remaining aloof and fighting for a new political system. Beginning in 1928 the investigations of the Simon Commission followed by the Round Table discussions led to Burma's separation from India and the establishment of a new constitution.

The constitution of 1935 provided for the separation of Burma from India and more self-government. Cabinet government, a bicameral legislature in which the lower house of 132 members was fully elected, and the transfer of nearly all internal subjects to ministers responsible to the parliament were the key features of the new law. The Governor still reserved the most important subjects such as finance, defense, and foreign affairs, administered the Frontier Areas without being required to consult parliament or his ministers, and held extreme emergency powers in reserve. During the four years in which the constitution was operative (1937–1941) four Burmese Prime Ministers held office and made a creditable start at tackling some of Burma's worst problems—land alienation, immigration, and credit. Such leaders as Dr. Ba Maw and U Saw made a real effort to work within the framework of the constitution. The Second World War interrupted constitutional and political progress in Burma; but although the experiment was brief, the people could look back upon almost two decades of experience with elections, parliamentary government, and political responsibility and parties. If they did not operate the institutions exactly as they were intended, at least they had time enough to learn how they were supposed to work and to begin adjusting them to local needs.

Along with these developments was one which created tension and violence rather than peace and unity. The British attempted to protect the minorities from the dominant Burmans. Those indigenous minorities who lived on the frontier such as the Shans, Kachins, Chins, and others were administered separately from the rest of Burma under the direct authority of the Governor, and those minorities living among the Burmans, such as the Karens, were given reserved seats in the legislature in order to protect their interests. The Indians, too, were accorded special treatment. Even in the earliest legislative councils at the turn of the century Indians were appointed to them. Later, they too were granted special seats in the elected assemblies. Under the pretext that Karens, Kachins, and Chins made better soldiers than Burmans, members of the indigenous minority groups were recruited in the British-Burma army, and Burmans were not. Ethnic groups generally divided along occupational lines so that the indigenous peoples were identified with agriculture and the Indians and Chinese were identified with urban occupations. This division was destroyed during the 1930s when farmers lost their lands and were forced to move to the cities in order to find work. Direct competition for urban occupations led to violent communal riots during this period. Developments and policies such as these made the people conscious of their ethnic and cultural differences and kept the society divided.

The Second World War and the Japanese invasion of Burma brought British rule to an abrupt end. Fear of the invaders caused all of the British and thousands of Indians to evacuate Burma; many of the Burmese civil servants and political leaders went with the government into exile at Simla in India. The majority of the indigenous population did not leave the country and underwent new experiences which helped to shape their ideas and demands once the war was over.

Four years of war and Japanese occupation paved the way for important political change. The Japanese were never able to assert complete control over Burma because they were harassed by the Allies and were forced to promise freedom to the people in order to win their support. The war provided conditions which gave the Burmese an opportunity to make important social and political gains. They were able to create an army under Japanese sponsorship which was commanded by Burmese. Led by Aung San—who secretly trained in Japanese-occupied Hainan island with twenty-nine other "heroes" [7] —the Burma Independence Army followed the invading Japanese from Thailand to Burma adding recruits as it progressed. Although the name of the Burmese army changed from "Independence Army"

[7] The "Thirty Heroes" were a group of young Burmese who were smuggled out of Burma prior to the war and trained under the Japanese in anticipation of an opportunity to help expel the British from their land.

to "Defense Army" in late 1942 and to "National Army" in 1943, after the Japanese granted nominal independence to Burma, the army remained an indigenous product and on March 27, 1945, revolted against the Japanese and joined forces with the Allies.

During the Japanese occupation the Burmese received a vast increase in administrative experience by filling many important positions in the government. When Japan allowed them to proclaim independence on August 1, 1943, a government headed by Dr. Ba Maw was permitted to take charge of much of the administrative apparatus under the watchful eyes of the Japanese.[8] Although this government had no real effect outside the urban areas, its operation provided invaluable experience to the people and gave them confidence in their ability to govern themselves. In this period of nominal independence a resistance movement arose under the direction of the Anti-Fascist People's Freedom League (AFPFL), the leadership of which incorporated a number of Burmese who had been co-operating with the Japanese. The AFPFL opened its ranks to all the peoples of Burma, regardless of ethnic group, religion, or political beliefs, and after the war emerged as the most important voice in Burmese politics.

The war caused a radical change in the economy and society. Destruction of the internal system of communications caused whole areas to become isolated and deficient in basic foods and clothing.[9] Destruction of other key military targets such as harbors and military installations caused the people to leave the urban areas and return to rural communities where many remained after the war.

In the spring of 1945 the Allies drove the Japanese out of Burma. Thus, when the Second World War ended in August 1945, government in Burma was under the control of the British Military Administration. Its chief concern was to re-establish law and order and restore the normal conditions of living. To distribute needed supplies and collect and export rice, the British organized the economy with the assistance of former British commercial firms as their managers, a move which the Burmese interpreted as calculated to re-establish the prewar economic order.

In October the Burma government in exile returned and took charge of the administration. Governor Dorman-Smith brought with him a

[8] Thakin Nu, *Burma under the Japanese* (London: St. Martin's Press, 1954), pp. 39 ff.
[9] James R. Andrus, "Burmese Economy during the Japanese Occupation," in *Burma under the Japanese* (Simla: Government Printing and Stationery, 1944), II, 173–181.

parliamentary approved policy which stated that Britain's ultimate aim was to grant self-government to Burma. It also stated that internal economic and political conditions made it necessary to continue suspension of the 1935 constitution and leave all power in the hands of the Governor and his council; as soon as possible a small nominated legislature was to be created, and at least three years might elapse before representative government was re-established.[10] The policy failed because the AFPFL refused to co-operate on the grounds that it was regressive and its goals too distant and uncertain. The AFPFL —its hand strengthened by the solidarity of its popular support, by its military forces, and by its determined leadership—called for an immediate election, a constitutional convention, and self-government.[11] The Governor's failure to win the AFPFL's backing and his inability to find local leaders who would oppose it and capture popular support led to a breakdown in his efforts to implement official policy. Dorman-Smith returned to England in June 1946 and in August was replaced as Governor by Hubert Rance, the former director of civil affairs under the military administration.

Rance's arrival was greeted by a police strike which quickly grew into a general strike. To avoid strife, he consulted with London and was permitted to negotiate with Aung San and the AFPFL. On September 26 Rance announced the formation of a new Executive Council which included six members representing the AFPFL and three independents, with Aung San the AFPFL leader, serving as chief councilor. The change led to a quick settlement of the strike and marked the beginning of a new phase in Burmese-British relations, a period of co-operation.

Although the AFPFL co-operated with Rance, the Burmese were not convinced of British sincerity until after Prime Minister Attlee announced in Parliament on December 20, 1946, that the British government was going to invite the Burmese to come to England to discuss the transfer of power and give the peoples of Burma a chance to decide whether or not to remain in the Commonwealth. The meeting in London in January 1947 resulted in an agreement which promised that elections would be held in April and a Constituent Assembly convened in May, that the Governor's Executive Council

[10] *Burma: Statement of Policy by His Majesty's Government, May, 1945* (London: H.M. Stationery Office, 1945).

[11] *From Fascist Bondage to New Democracy: The New Burma in the New World* (Rangoon: Nay Win Kyi Press [1945?]), an official pamphlet of the AFPFL.

would until the transfer of power act as the interim government of Burma in charge of all subjects, that the Frontier Areas would decide whether or not to join with ministerial Burma, and that a High Commissioner for Burma would be appointed immediately.

Between the London meeting and the April elections, the frontier peoples met at Panglong in the Shan States to decide whether or not to join with Burma. The Shans, Kachins, and Chins agreed, but the others in attendance remained uncommitted. The agreement was in no way to prejudice the future right of the peoples to remain autonomous, politically, financially, or socially. To measure the sentiments of the frontier peoples, the British Parliament created an Enquiry Committee under David Rees-Williams to take testimony and make recommendations on the unification of the Frontier Areas and ministerial Burma. In its report the committee recommended that the Frontier Areas be represented in the Constituent Assembly, that because of their backward nature and the absence of electoral lists their delegates be chosen indirectly, that they have full and equal rights with other representatives, and that they have a veto over all decisions relating to their areas and upon all questions of the future federal union.[12]

As agreed, elections took place in April. The AFPFL won an overwhelming victory by capturing 172 of the 182 noncommunal seats. Their affiliate, the Karen Youth Organization, took all 24 Karen-reserved seats because the older Karen organization—the Karen National Union—refused to participate in the election. The parties of the right also boycotted the election. The Communists, having been expelled from the AFPFL, at first refused to contest seats; they later entered on an individual basis and won seven out of twenty-six contests.

In the historic Constituent Assembly, Aung San set the theme by presenting a seven-point resolution based upon an earlier statement agreed to by the AFPFL. Among his points were the following: that Burma should be an independent sovereign republic called the Union of Burma; that all power emanate from the people; that the constitution should guarantee justice—social, economic, and political—to all; and that the minorities must be granted safeguards.[13] On the next day the Assembly elected a Constitutional Committee of seventy-five

[12] *Frontier Areas Committee of Enquiry*, pt. 1 (Rangoon: Government Printing and Stationery Office, 1948), pp. 22–32.

[13] Ministry of Information, *Burma's Fight for Freedom* (Rangoon, 1948), pp. 92–93.

and a series of subcommittees to undertake the work of writing the constitution. The parent body then recessed, and while the Assembly committees were at work, Aung San convoked a Rehabilitation Conference to examine the problems of reconstruction and suggest future economic goals for the nation. The conference embodied its ideas in a two-year plan for economic development.

In the midst of mapping the political and economic future of the country, Aung San and six members of the Executive Council were assassinated; Governor Rance and the local police saved the situation by speedily reorganizing the government and by rounding up the assassins. Thakin Nu [14] accepted Rance's invitation to head the Executive Council and pledged to follow the road marked out by Aung San. The loss of Aung San at this critical juncture was immeasurable; as a prewar and wartime resistance leader and as the symbol of the drive for political independence he held the confidence of the peoples of Burma and was clearly acknowledged as the postwar architect of national unity and independence. His successor was a long-time friend and co-worker who had retired from politics after the war and had returned only after Aung San persuaded him in 1947 to accept the office of vice-president of the AFPFL.

The constitution was completed, and a final settlement was negotiated with Great Britain and signed by Nu and Attlee on October 17, 1947. It provided that Burma was to be a fully sovereign and independent state outside the Commonwealth, that Britain was to cancel a debt of £15 million, and that if British property was nationalized equitable payment would be paid.[15] A supplementary defense agreement also was negotiated; the British Parliament ratified the treaty in December, and Burma became independent on January 4, 1948.

A Decade of Independence, 1948–1958

Independence did not bring utopia to Burma. All activity during the first decade was overshadowed by a lingering insurrection which kept the country in a state of semiwar. There were three significant

---

[14] U Nu was the Prime Minister of Burma until October 28, 1958. The prefix Thakin or master was adopted by Nu and other nationalists in the 1930s as a symbol of their defiance of British rule. At the present time, Nu and others have dropped this prefix because the Burmese are masters in their own house. Nu has returned to the traditional prefix Maung. On the other hand, the people use U or uncle, the traditional term of respect for an elder, a leader, or an esteemed person, when they address him.

[15] *Burma's Fight for Freedom,* pp. 101–110.

groups which resorted to arms in an effort to gain their political objectives. Beginning in March 1948 the Communists initiated the revolt. Shortly thereafter the People's Volunteer Organization (PVO)—created by Aung San as the military arm of the AFPFL—split in its loyalty to the government, and a dissident group joined the Communists in revolt. By the time that the government was in a position to put down these two forces, a third and larger group, the Karen National Defense Organization (KNDO), rebelled and encouraged a large number of Karen soldiers in the Union Army to desert. Only an absence of unity among the various rebel forces, the leadership of Nu, and the government's ability to build a new army saved the nascent Union. By 1952, when the new army was about to take the offensive and end the revolt, a new complication developed; remnants of Chiang Kai-shek's Nationalist Chinese Army who had escaped from China and taken refuge in Burma joined forces with the indigenous rebels in the Shan State and posed a new threat to the Union. On March 25, 1953, the Burmese asked the United Nations to help remove the foreign soldiers from their territory. The United Nations passed a mild resolution taking note of the existence of "foreign forces" on Burmese soil and left the problem to be settled through a private arrangement between the United States, Thailand, Burma, and the Formosa government. Unfortunately the effort failed to evacuate more than 5,500 Chinese, leaving many more to plague the local population.

In dealing with the indigenous rebels the government used peaceful as well as warlike methods. Amnesties were offered on numerous occasions, and although they did not move the die-hard rebels, they did obtain significant results. By 1958 the rebels appeared to have become demoralized, and many responded to the government's offer to leave the jungle, lay down their weapons, and rejoin society. Some were welcomed back as heroes by high officials of the government, and evidence indicated that the rebellions were ending.

Against this background Burma has made important gains, both political and constitutional. At the outset the provisional parliament, which lasted until 1952, was without a real opposition to the dominant AFPFL. In 1950 a small pro-Soviet group in the AFPFL was expelled over criticism of Burma's foreign policy in connection with the war in Korea and its efforts to capture the party for its own purposes. It re-formed as the Burma Workers and Peasants Party (BWPP). The first national election, held in 1951–1952 under trying conditions, resulted in a continuation of the overwhelming dominance of the AFPFL in parliament. The BWPP captured the largest number of seats won by parties opposing the AFPFL and became the official opposition. The second national election, held in 1956 under much-improved conditions, again resulted in an AFPFL victory; the margin was smaller, however, and a formidable opposition emerged under the name National Unity Front (NUF) (wherein the BWPP was the largest constituent group). After the second election Prime Minister Nu stepped out of office for nine months, while U Ba Swe, Socialist and AFPFL leader, took the reins of government. Nu's announced purpose was to purge the party of corrupt elements, but his attempted purge was unsuccessful. An inner party struggle in the AFPFL developed during this period and lingered until May 1958, when it erupted into an open split. To test the strength of his faction Prime Minister Nu called a special session of parliament in June and in a vote of confidence was sustained by a slender majority. Because the results were inconclusive, the Prime Minister announced that new national elections would be held in the fall. Political rivalry between the two AFPFL factions, however, and the return to legal political life of many former rebels who were either outright Communists or Communist sympathizers caused political unrest and uncertainty throughout the country; as a result the Prime Minister, on September 26, announced to the public in a special radio broadcast that he planned to resign from office on October 28 and that he had asked the head of the Union Army, General Ne Win, to replace him as head of the government and ensure that free and fair elections would be held throughout the country. As agreed, Nu stepped down, and the Chamber of Deputies in the Union parliament elected the general as his successor. Aided by ministers who are political independents, the new Prime Minister has been able to restore some of the national confidence in the government, and plans are being made to hold new national elections sometime before April 1959.

The past decade produced an interesting sequence of events which altered the thinking of the government on economic matters. As a party with a socialist philosophy the AFPFL sought to establish a socialist state immediately after independence was granted. After nationalizing a few industries, passing a land nationalization act, and drawing elaborate reconstruction and development plans, the government was forced to retreat on all fronts because of lack of trained technicians, administrators and money. The projects could be financed as long as the state earned surplus revenues from its sale of rice on the world market; after the Korean War, however, the demand decreased, and Burma was left with unsold surplus stocks. Therefore it was forced to shelve its plans and seek new revenues to pay for projects already under way. The change in the economic situation forced Burma to re-examine its methods, prospects, and goals; in June 1957 U Nu proclaimed a new economic policy which promised less socialism and more free enterprise. He and the AFPFL leaders assured the people that socialism was still the ultimate goal, but they realistically announced that a phase of state and private capitalism would precede it.

Although a decade has passed since independence, the peoples of Burma are aware that they have neither created the state which they envisioned in 1948 nor completely rebuilt their war-devastated economy. They are aware also that the country still possesses rich resources, a growing population, and a group of leaders who have learned a great deal through experience and who are willing to try bold solutions as long as there is a chance that they might work. These, balanced against the legacy of war, insurrection, and inexperience, suggest some of the strengths and weaknesses which condition the economic and political development of Burma.

· VI ·

The Contemporary Setting

BURMA today includes an area of about 261,610 square miles which lie, for the most part, in the latitudes of the tropics. The territory is richly endowed with fertile land, plentiful rainfall, and a variety of natural resources; it also possesses areas which are blighted by wind erosion and denuded of top covering because of poor agricultural practices as well as districts which are barely inhabited because of extreme malarial conditions. Under British stimulation the alluvial soils of the delta were cultivated commercially, and in addition to becoming the world's largest rice exporter Burma produced most of the food needs required by the people of the country.[1]

Among its natural resources Burma has had an abundant supply of teak and other woods. Beneath the land's surface there are a variety of minerals such as petroleum, lead, zinc, tin, tungsten, and precious stones. All, with the exception of petroleum, are located away from population centers in isolated regions and are difficult and costly to extract.

Burma is endowed with a river system which provides the country with a natural north-south transport network. The Burmese first, and the British afterward, added a highway system which includes everything from jungle paths to modern paved roads. The road network

[1] James R. Andrus, *Burmese Economic Life* (Stanford: Stanford University Press, 1948), p. 98.

provides the major lateral transport system in the country. The British also developed a good rail system which, prior to the Second World War, included 2,060 miles of track, good equipment, and trained crews. The main rail lines lie parallel with the rivers and highways, and relatively few east-west spur lines were constructed.[2]

The war took a heavy toll in Burma's economic resources. Even today, as the country struggles to match its prewar exports, it is handicapped by limited livestock, outmoded farming equipment, domestic insecurity, bad transportation, and poor storage facilities. Burma's oil production prior to 1958 was below internal needs and until 1957 was without the refining facilities of the main Syriam plant. Export of teak and minerals is low because of inability to exploit the resources, again the result of lack of internal security and insufficient equipment and trained personnel. Human resources have been only partially developed, primarily because of a shortage of modern schools and trained teachers.

The People and the Organization of Society

Although no complete census has been taken and reported since 1931, samples and population projections based on the earlier figures indicate that there were about 19.2 million people in Burma in 1954.[3] Compared with the other countries of Southeast Asia, Burma is the least crowded. It has been estimated that it has sufficient good farm land to provide every man, woman, and child with 1.23 acres.[4]

Probably the most useful system of classification of the peoples of Burma is according to their origin, that is, as either indigenous or alien. Within the indigenous group, the major subgroups if classified along ethnic lines are the Burmans, Karens, Shans, Mons, Kachins, and Chins. The present constitution of Burma provides a separate state for each except the Mons who, for the most part, have been assimilated by the Burmans. Anthropologists find it meaningful to identify the indigenous peoples according to whether their culture can be classified as a hill or a plains type. By hill culture they usually mean a culture in which the people live on the slopes or tops of hills

[2] *Ibid.*, pp. 226–234; Knappen, Tippetts, Abbett, McCarthy, *Comprehensive Report: Economic and Engineering Development of Burma*, I (Rangoon, 1953), 256–280.

[3] United Nations, *Demographic Yearbook* (New York: United Nations, 1955), p. 106, Table 1.

[4] Robert Huke, "Geography and Population," in Frank N. Trager and others, *Burma* (New Haven: Human Relations Area Files, Inc., 1956), I, 69, Table 2.

in small units with relatively autonomous and uncomplicated political organizations and are usually animistic in their religion, practice a shifting, slash and burn type of agriculture called *taungya*, use crude tools, and hunt and raise nearly everything they eat.[5] The Kachins, Chins, and hill Karens fit roughly into this pattern. Plains culture is defined to mean people who live in the valleys or on the plains, whose social and political organization extends beyond the village or family group and is more complex, whose religion, language, arts, and crafts are influenced by Indian culture, whose centers of population are permanent, and whose main agricultural occupation is wet rice farming.[6] The Burmans, Mons, Shans, Arkanese, and delta Karens fit generally into this category.

The dominant religion throughout Burma is Buddhism. It is of the same variety that is practiced in Ceylon, Thailand, Cambodia, and Laos. Buddhists in Burma have resisted almost all efforts of the missionaries to convert them to Christianity. Among the plains people only the non-Buddhist delta Karens have accepted conversion to Christianity on a large scale. The hill-culture peoples, on the other hand, have been very receptive to the missionaries of both Christianity and Buddhism. Today Buddhism enjoys special recognition in the constitution as the faith professed by the majority of citizens of the Union and is gaining adherents at the expense of the other religions.

Among the alien minorities in Burma the Indians, Chinese, and Europeans are the major groups. The Indians and Chinese trace their existence in Burma to the earliest times, both having entered the country via land and sea. No census figures exist, but it is usually estimated that there are just under a million Indians in Burma and approximately 300,000 Chinese. Both make their homes generally in the urban areas and play an important part in the commercial and financial life of the country. Although the Burmese once feared that the British immigration policy would permit a flood of Indian immigrants, the war and the present restriction on immigration have made that impossible. The major problem today in regard to foreign immigrants is the illegal entry of Chinese across Burma's northern frontier. Only a few thousand Europeans now live in Burma. Since independence in 1948 their numbers have decreased steadily. Na-

[5] John K. Musgrave, "An Introduction to the Anthropology of Burma," in Trager, *Burma*, II, 598–620; Edmund R. Leach, *Political Systems of Highland Burma* (London: G. Bell and Sons, 1954).

[6] Musgrave, *op. cit.*, pp. 600–620.

tionalism and socialism have reduced their economic opportunities, and today few, if any, come to take permanent residence or seek citizenship in Burma.

Principal Political Forces

After thirty years of political experience under British and Japanese rule the peoples of Burma have developed the organizations, techniques, and institutions which make it possible for the politically conscious to organize, capture, and hold power or influence those in power. In their attempt to establish parties and institutions modeled on those found in the West, the political leaders have been successful in duplicating the broad forms; within the forms, however, they have created their own patterns which blend Western-type institutions with traditional concepts of leadership and government. The politically aware see a need to work constantly among the unaroused and uncommitted population in order to increase political participation and draw them into the political process.

The political forces at work in Burma today can be divided into three groups, those who seek to capture and hold power, those who seek to influence the holders of power, and neutral groups who are uncommitted but who represent both potential seekers and influencers of power.

Chief among those who seek to capture and hold power are the members of political parties. The contemporary parties established during and after the Second World War bear little relationship to the prewar parties. Prior to its split in 1958 the AFPFL was countrywide, with a national appeal. Through its affiliate mass organizations —the Trade Union Congress, Burma; the All Burma Peasants Organization; the Federation of Trade Organizations; and the Women's Freedom League—it provided leadership, organization, and information for the inarticulate masses. In the 1956 general election it received 1.84 million votes or 47.7 per cent of the total.[7] If the vote of its associate parties in the states, other than Burma proper, are added to this figure, it received 2.16 million or 55.9 per cent. As the dominant party of the postwar period its ideology permeates the constitution and the legislation of the past decade.

Other parties such as the National Unity Front (NUF) seek to win

[7] At the time of the 1956 election 8.57 million people registered to vote, and almost half that number cast their ballots (Josef Silverstein, "Politics, Parties, and the National Election in Burma," *Far Eastern Survey*, XXV [1956] 177–184).

power and adherents from the AFPFL. A blend of several opposition parties which joined in 1955 to contest the last national election, it was without widespread organization, prestige, and patronage and did not have the mystic appeal associated with the AFPFL as the party of Aung San which won Burma's independence. The NUF seeks to represent and influence the same elements in society as the AFPFL and to provide an alternative to it; but a majority of its members are strong supporters of the Communists and would like to see some radical changes in the present form of the government. In the 1956 election it was able to win 1.17 million votes or 30.4 per cent of the total vote. It has worked hard during the postelection period to provide responsible parliamentary opposition. The Arakan National United Organization (ANUO) differs from the other two in that it is local in appeal and represents a landowning class concentrated in one region of the country. Its representation in parliament is out of proportion to its strength. In the 1956 election it polled 38,900 votes or 1 per cent of the total vote and won five seats. Its chief aim is to win statehood for Arakan. Another party of note is the Burma Democratic Party (BDP); it seeks to be a national party, represents the interests of free enterprise, and calls for Burma to enter into an alliance with the United States. The party is the personal vehicle of its leader, U Ba Sein, and is one of the few contemporary versions of a prewar party. In the last election it received 113,091 votes or 2.9 per cent of the total, but it failed to win a seat in parliament because the vote was scattered throughout the country. Collectively these parties have accepted the limitations established by the constitution and have sought to work within its framework.

Among the forces which do not necessarily seek power but nevertheless desire to influence it are the students. Their participation in politics has been an important phenomenon since the birth of the nationalist movement in 1920. Because the universities and the majority of the technical and high schools are in the large cities and towns, the movement is mainly urban. Since independence, education has been free. Students gather in the urban areas from all parts of the country; those who return home carry their new ideas and techniques to a rising generation of younger brothers and sisters as well as to a respectful generation of elders. Partly in this way and partly through direct recruiting and proselytizing among the youth in the rural areas near the cities and towns, student influence has been significant. Traditionally the students have been nationalistic, against authority

and government, and sympathetic to the forces in revolt. They seek
political experience and hope to win recognition as future leaders of
Burma. They have always catered to the politicians and in turn have
been courted by them.

The press, like the students, seeks to influence and not to capture
power. No statistics exist to indicate how many people read or are
influenced by the papers, but there is no doubt that their influence
is important. The government is extremely sensitive to their opinions
and their reporting of the news. As inquirer, critic, and reporter, the
press in its frequent interviews with the Prime Minister acted as the
unofficial opposition during the period of 1951–1956 when there was
no significant opposition in parliament. The press is relatively free
and publishes in all the major languages of Burma.[8] From time to time
the government has attempted to silence a critical newspaper; its
general policy, however, is to encourage free and responsible reporting and not to restrict it. With the joint support of the Burma
Journalist Association and the government, classes in journalism were
started in 1956 and are open to all without tuition charges. The
Journalist Association is strong and independent and has defended
against all challenges its right of free expression. Although most of
the newspapers are concentrated in Rangoon, they circulate in all
the larger cities and towns. The ideas which are propagated are as
varied as the number of papers that print them. The newspapers take
their stand in elections, call attention to corruption and needed improvements, open their columns to letters from their readers, and
sponsor essay and other contests which call attention to the point of
view they are supporting.

The parties seek to capture and the students and the press seek
to influence the workers and peasants. Unlike urban labor, the peasantry is not a cohesive, politically conscious, well-organized force
with a common set of values and goals. As the largest identifiable
group in Burmese society, it is conservative in nature and local in
outlook. Although a peasants' organization has been operative since
before the Second World War, most peasants still look to the traditional local leadership provided by the village headmen, the elders,
and the Buddhist monks.

Urban workers were largely unorganized before the Second World
War; those who were organized were mainly Indians. The world

[8] In 1955 there were seven Indian, eleven Burmese, five Chinese, and six
English newspapers.

depression, however, forced the Burmese to leave agriculture and seek employment in the cities and in the growing oil industry. Congregated in the cities or in accessible areas, such as the oil fields, they were readily available for organization by student and Thakin leaders. The parties of the left have been most active among them, but today both factions of the AFPFL through their trade union mass organization affiliates provide labor with its most active leadership and in turn can count upon the unions to provide workers for mass demonstrations and for election support. For years to come both labor and the peasantry will be major targets for the attention of competing political parties.

Until September 1958 the military remained outside the political struggle. Its main job was to re-establish law and order throughout the country and defend the nation against invasion. The army represents no special ethnic or political group; its members are drawn at large from the nation and are integrated into national units. As such they owe a common allegiance and fight, in the words of their leaders, "for the preservation of the Union." Before the current crisis most observers agreed that the military was nonpolitical and that its leadership was dedicated to the principle of civilian supremacy. Although it was accused by some of being a partisan force with ties to the AFPFL, its activities from 1951 to 1958 support the view that it was above politics. It commands the respect of the people, has a good reputation in the areas where it has fought or has been stationed, and because of its size, its leadership, and its experience [9] represents a potentially strong political force.

The present military leaders in the top echelons served during the period of the Japanese occupation and are close comrades in arms with the present ruling elite; they chose to disassociate themselves from politics when General Ne Win left the cabinet in 1950—after holding office temporarily during the worst period of the insurrection—and refused to take political power again until the 1958 crisis. He accepted political responsibility then because he was one of the few people in public life who commanded the respect and confidence of the leaders of both factions of the AFPFL, the army, and the people throughout the nation. He demonstrated his respect for the con-

[9] Under a presidential proclamation in 1952 the army took charge of an area in the Shan State and held it under military government for two years as a result of the insurrection in that state. See Josef Silverstein, "Politics in the Shan State: The Question of Secession from the Union of Burma," *Journal of Asian Studies,* XVIII (Nov. 1958), 51–53.

stitution by accepting power only after the Chamber of Deputies elected him Prime Minister, by acknowledging that he intended to remain in political power for a limited time—six months—and by choosing a cabinet composed of distinguished civilians drawn from the administration and the judiciary. At the next level leaders are recruited from the ranks, and their social and economic origin is peasant or petty civil servant. The officers have close ties with their men and have not created any identifiable military caste. This may not hold for the future, because a military academy for new officers has been established in the Shan State which may produce a class of officers with an elitist attitude. If the political parties can settle their present differences and restrain themselves from attempting to draw the army into their personal quarrels, it will probably remain outside of politics; if the parties cannot, the army might assume a political role such as is seen in Thailand or Indonesia.

The situation with paramilitary and home-guard units is somewhat different. The Union Military Police (UMP), recruited originally during the early stages of the insurrection by the Socialists and the AFPFL, is under the direction of the Home Minister. Technically it is a police force; it is trained, however, along military lines and is expected to give support to the army. Having been recruited and trained by the Home Ministry, it has a political complexion. In order to neutralize it during the current AFPFL party split the Prime Minister relieved the Home Minister of his duties and in April 1958 took charge of the office and the UMP.[10] The home guard or Pyusawthi was recruited and armed by the government to protect isolated communities from the insurgents in 1955–1956. It quickly became the pocket army of local political leaders and was used in some instances to terrorize the population. Early in 1958 the Prime Minister ordered it to disband as soon as possible and AFPFL members to resign immediately from its leadership and ranks.

Buddhism has great political importance in Burma because it transcends class, occupation, and other social divisions and has been one of the most important catalysts in uniting Burmese society. Prior to the Second World War political leaders sought the support of the monks and used them to further their political ambitions. During the past decade a religious revival has taken place in Burma under the leadership of U Nu and other political and judicial figures. The government has supported pagoda building and examinations and

[10] *Nation*, April 28, 1958, p. 1.

prizes for monks who show exceptional ability in learning and reciting the scriptures. Laws have been passed which strengthen the religious leaders in disciplining the Buddhist hierarchy; money has been made available for all sorts of works of religious merit. The Buddhist revival and celebration which took place between 1954 and 1956 gave the majority of Burmese Buddhists a renewed sense of identity and pride; it emboldened both religious and lay leaders to demand formal recognition of Buddhism as a state religion and instruction in the faith in public schools. Thus far the government has resisted both demands. Although Buddhism is primarily a religious and moral force, its political potential is great, and no leader or party can safely ignore it or act in any way detrimental to it. Buddhism historically has served a special function in the lives of most of the people of Burma, and its revival by the national leaders has won support and sympathy from the peasants and workers such as no political action has done.

Finally, mention must be made of the insurrectionists who today play a declining and changing role in the political lives of the people. There has always been a tradition of revolt in Burmese society. In numerous ways it has expressed itself in royal pretenders, dacoity, and outright rebellion against constituted authority. The insurgents of the past decade included a variety of individuals and groups who differed in origin, aims, and tactics; their common denominator was their use of force and violence to solve their grievances. With the growing strength and efficiency of the army, plus the willingness of the government to grant amnesty to the rebels who return to society, most appear to be laying down their arms and drifting back to their villages without surrendering formally while others have accepted the amnesty terms publicly and have been welcomed as heroes by the government and allowed to participate in the legal political struggle. A recent decision by the Nu government to allow formerly outlawed parties to be reconstituted [11] permitted one of the AFPFL's chief rivals, the underground People's Volunteer Organization, now called the People's Comrade Party (PCP), to become a legal organization. The order made it possible even for the Communist parties to reform legally if they accepted the terms of the amnesty offer. Since a large portion of the insurgents have been Communists or Communist sympathizers, their return to society suggests that a dedicated group, which never accepted the political decisions of

[11] *New York Times*, Aug. 1, 1958, p. 13.

1947–1948 and chose, rather, to try to overthrow the government
after independence was granted, will have a new opportunity to win
adherents by peaceful, persuasive means instead of by the violence
of the past ten years. They always have had a nucleus of supporters
in parliament and society at large; now they will be able to unite
these people and make a real effort to capture power and alter the
system by legal means. Their success or failure will depend in part
on whether or not the present leaders of Burma can solve their own
internal differences and continue to hold the confidence of the peoples of Burma.

Political Leadership

The leaders of Burma since 1945 came to political maturity during
the Second World War. At that time they built the organizations,
developed the plans and techniques, and established contact with
the people. Most of them, either in the government or in the opposition, worked together at one time or another in the AFPFL or one
of its affiliate organizations. The governing elite in Burma proper is
composed of men—all of them about 40 years of age—from middle
or lower income groups whose fathers were petty civil servants, schoolteachers, or farmers. Most of them were students together at the
University of Rangoon or at Mandalay College, shared a common
experience in the student strikes of their day, and participated in the
Thakin Movement and in labor organizational work. All are strong
nationalists and subscribe to an ideology based upon a selection of
ideas from classical liberalism, socialism, and Buddhism. Their approach has been pragmatic and not dogmatic. Their hold on the people
stems from their having shared the experience of war by remaining in
the country and in having worked with Aung San in the formative
days of the independence struggle.

There is also an older generation of leaders, who are outside of the
AFPFL. Such men as U Kyaw Min, Dr. E Maung, Dr. Ba Maw, and
others were educated in England and earned their reputation as members of the bar, in the British controlled civil service, or in prewar
politics. They have tended to look upon the present ruling elite as
half-educated upstarts who were not able to prove their ability in
competitive examinations for the few overseas scholarships available
in Burma under British rule. These older men still participate in politics
and command personal followings that give them prestige and importance in the territory from which they come. They frequently

try to form alliances with a new generation of rising leaders in education, government, and the military who have been educated abroad —largely at government expense—and who, since returning, feel superior in training to those in power. As more foreign-educated Burmese rise in position, the competition between them and those with a purely local education will undoubtedly increase.

Leadership among the peoples in the states other than Burma proper is more traditional, arising in the main from the chieftain classes which still exert considerable authority over their people. This is gradually changing; in the Shan and the Kachin states a rising class of new popular leaders is coming forward and beginning to assume an important role both in state and in national politics. The stimulus for this change stems from post-Second World War conditions and from the support and guidance offered by the AFPFL in the states.

Burma, unlike India, had an administrative bureaucracy composed mainly of alien personnel. When the war came, most of the Indians and all British personnel evacuated the country. The Burmese in the lower ranks moved up rapidly to fill the vacated higher posts. After the grant of independence, the AFPFL discouraged some of the best-trained administrators from continuing in office for fear that they were too closely allied to colonial thinking and therefore hostile to the new government. As a result the few trained older personnel who stayed on absorbed the bulk of the work, and the lower ranks were filled with partially trained and inexperienced men and women. For these reasons the bureaucracy did not provide a stable administrative organization around which the new state could develop. Administrative inefficiency in the government, stemming from the breakdown caused by the Japanese invasion in 1942 and continuing after the war, still persists. Burma's present leaders have been unable to enjoy the support of a well-trained and efficient administration; instead, they have felt obliged to create a new administration staffed with workers who are politically loyal but are in the main unskilled.

At the village level the headmen, the elders, and the Buddhist monks still provide the immediate leadership of the peasant population. They exercise a strong conservative influence and act as an insulation between the people and the political figures representing the government or the mass organizations. Although the government is beginning to make a real effort to break their hold by implementing its bill on democratization of local administration, the problem of public security and the isolation of the rural communities continue to impede rapid change at this level. To overcome this type of resistance, the AFPFL and the government have sought to undermine the traditional leaders by making the people dependent upon mass organizations and co-operatives for special services. Members of the All Burma Peasants Organization have held statutory jobs on land nationalization and *Pyidawtha* [12] committees. The government has also used its control of certain commodities—such as yarn—to get peasants engaged in home weaving to form co-operatives under national leaders in order to get needed raw materials. In spite of the government's efforts, the traditional local leaders are not likely to be eliminated until there is a basic change in the general character of the rural society.

[12] *Pyidawtha* literally means "pleasant royal country," but it is freely translated and used to mean welfare state. See Cady, *op. cit.*, p. 647. The *Pyidawtha* Conference held in 1952 was called in order to examine the conditions of economic development and plan for the future. See *The Pyidawtha Conference: Speeches and Resolutions* (Rangoon: Government Printing and Stationery Office, 1952).

· VII ·

The Political Process

WHEN the members of the Constituent Assembly met to draw up the constitution, they produced a draft which blended liberal-democratic ideas and practices—inherited from the British—with the socialist ideas and values expressed in the draft resolution of the AFPFL.[1] The constitution satisfactorily answered the major question which perplexed the Burmese, namely, how to construct a union in which people who formerly were separated could join together in such a manner as to benefit from unity and still continue to have a nominal degree of independence. When the drafters finished their work, the elected Assembly accepted the document with unanimous approval.

The Constitution of 1947 and the Formal Structure of Government

In answering the paradoxical question posed above, the drafters constructed a constitution embodying features which combine to produce the desired effect: the individual is emphasized over the state; the state is provided with a guide for future action toward social wel-

[1] Maung Maung, in *Burma in the Family of Nations* (Amsterdam: Djambatan, Ltd., 1956), p. 114, states that the Yugoslav constitution was consulted more frequently than other sources; he also points out, however, that the Irish and the United States constitutions were given attention. See Alan Gledhill, "The Burmese Constitution," *The Indian Yearbook of International Affairs, 1953* (Madras, 1954), pp. 214–224, for the fullest discussion of the AFPFL draft constitution.

fare goals which are embodied in the directive principles; a cabinet system of government is created in which the states have direct representation; a unique doctrine of federalism blends the Union and the states and appears to give the states more freedom than is the actual case; provision is made for an independent judiciary; local government is reserved for the states to work out according to their own interests.

The conflict between liberal and socialist principles is clearly seen in the constitution's discussion of the rights of the individual. In the tradition of liberal democracy, the constitution begins with a declaration that all power emanates from the people (Article 4). Following this the authors discuss at length the individual, his identity, rights, and privileges. Under the constitution all men are national citizens (Article 10). Citizenship is automatic to all members of indigenous groups and to the children of naturalized citizens. Although the constitution's main concern is with the citizen, it recognizes the noncitizen and discusses him under the broad heading of "persons"— which presumably include both citizens and noncitizens (Article 20).

Citizenship confers rights. Chief among them are the rights of equality before the law and of economic opportunity and the rights of freedom—to hold property, to maintain the inviolability of the home, of speech, and of assemblage, to form associations, to have freedom of mobility, to enter any trade or profession, and under certain circumstances to operate a public utility. Under normal conditions, citizens are entitled to due process of the law (Article 27). Women are entitled to equal pay with men for equal work. All "persons" are guaranteed religious freedom; and no minority can be denied an education at state schools or forced to accept religious instruction.

The citizen must accept certain limitations. Following socialist ideas, private property may be expropriated or limited in quantity "if the public interest so requires, but only in accordance with law" (Article 23.4). Monopolistic practices are forbidden (Article 23.3). The state is declared to be the ultimate owner of all lands. It may regulate, alter, or abolish land tenure and "resume possession of any land and distribute [it] . . . for collective or cooperative farming" (Article 30). The state declares itself to be the protector of the worker in his right to organize, to obtain safe working conditions and holidays, and to promote "schemes for housing and social insurance" (Article 31). Although the constitution includes class terms, the central focus is neither a particular class nor even the state; throughout, the individual is the main object of discussion.

The directive principles of state policy are "intended for the general guidance of the State," and unless there is specific legislation by parliament, they are not enforceable in law. They include such ideas as the right of all to work, to maintenance in old age, to rest and leisure, and to education. The concept of directive principles probably was borrowed primarily from the Indian constitution.

Modeled after the prewar institutions described in the constitution of 1935, the present constitution provides that there shall be a parliamentary-cabinet system of government at the national level. The titular head of state is the President, who is elected by a joint session of parliament for a five-year term and is eligible for one re-election. The President summons, prorogues, and dissolves parliament on the advice of the Prime Minister. In most situations he has little or no real power. Although all executive action is taken in his name and he must promulgate all legislation, he has no veto power and is little more than a figurehead except in a particular type of emergency. If the Prime Minister loses the confidence of the Chamber of Deputies, the President can refuse the Prime Minister's request to dissolve the parliament and instead can request the Chamber to nominate a new leader. If the Chamber fails to comply within fifteen days, the President must dissolve the parliament and call for new elections (Article 57). In the event that conditions arise while parliament is not in session which call for the immediate promulgation of special ordinances, the President is empowered to take such action and the ordinances will have the force of law until withdrawn or rejected at the next session of parliament (Article 110). The President's one exclusive power is the right to grant pardons. He may be removed by impeachment for high treason, violation of the constitution, or gross misconduct (Article 54).

The parliament of the Union, like its 1935 predecessor, is bicameral. The dominant body is the Chamber of Deputies, which is popularly elected and allotted twice the number of seats given to the second house, the Chamber of Nationalities.[2] All citizens over 21 who are not disqualified by reasons established in the constitution may stand for election in either house (Article 74–76); all citizens over 18 are eligible to vote (Article 76.2). The life of each parliament is a maximum of four years; it can be less if the Chamber of Deputies is dis-

[2] The membership of the Chamber of Deputies is now fixed at 250 members.

solved before that time, and it can be more if a grave emergency has been proclaimed in accordance with the constitution. When the Chamber of Deputies is dissolved, the Chamber of Nationalities automatically is dissolved too; new elections must be held within sixty days to fill both bodies.

The pre-eminence of the Chamber of Deputies over the second house is apparent from an examination of its special rights and functions. It alone nominates the Prime Minister, and he in turn is responsible exclusively to it. It alone has the right to initiate money bills. The second chamber has the right to take twenty-one days to examine each money bill, but it cannot prevent the bill's passage, nor can it insist that its proposed amendments be accepted by the Chamber of Deputies (Article 105).[3]

The Chamber of Nationalities represents the states. Its total membership is fixed at 125, and the seats are distributed between the six states according to a fixed ratio established in the constitution.[4] Although the Chamber is an elected body, the Constitution provides that in specific states only certain classes, ethnic groups, or individuals may represent their state in this house.[5] In theory the Chamber of Nationalities, being represented by special ethnic and social groups, can perform a useful service by considering legislation from a point of view different from that of the Chamber of Deputies. This has not developed, however, because party discipline has imposed substantial uniformity in both chambers.

With the exception of money bills, both houses share the power to initiate legislation. If they do not agree on the exact wording of a measure, the President of the Union must convoke a joint session, and a majority vote of the combined membership decides on the disposition of the measure. Also in joint session, the parliament approves all appointments of Justices to the High and Supreme Courts; all constitutional amendments must be approved by a two-thirds vote of parlia-

[3] Even if the Chamber of Nationalities makes amendments, the Chamber of Deputies "may accept or reject all or any of the recommendations."

[4] Maung, *op. cit.*, p. 119: Shan, 25; Karen, 15; Kachin, 12; Chin, 8; Kayah, 3; Burma proper, 62. Originally the Karens were allotted 24 seats because there was no separate Karen State. After the establishment of their state the Union parliament altered the number of Karen representatives and gave the additional seats to Burma proper.

[5] In the Shan State only the chiefs may elect and be elected to the Chamber of Nationalities. In the Kachin State half the representatives in this Chamber must be Kachins and the remainder non-Kachins. In the Kayah State the representatives in this house are named in the Union constitution by their hereditary title.

ment, sitting in joint session—if the measure relates to a state, the vote must include a majority from that state's representatives—after the measure has received previous approval in each house separately (Articles 207–210). Parliament has the power to declare war and make peace.[6] All treaties must be laid before parliament, and if any require domestic legislation to implement them, parliament must approve of their ratification (Article 213).

The actual head of the government is the Prime Minister; together with his cabinet he forms the Union government (Article 114). All cabinet members are responsible collectively to the Chamber of Deputies; all must be members of parliament. The ministers are appointed by the President after being nominated by the Prime Minister; they in turn serve at the Prime Minister's pleasure and must resign if he asks them to do so, if the cabinet falls in a vote of confidence, or if the Prime Minister resigns from his office. The constitution makes provision for nonelected members of parliament to hold the office of Prime Minister or to accept the responsibility for one of the ministries. This is intended as a temporary expedient; the nonelected officials must resign after six consecutive months in office (Article 116).

The executive authority of the Union extends to all matters in "which the Parliament has power to make laws and in accordance with the provisions of any treaty or agreement" (Article 122). The Prime Minister is required to keep the President informed on all domestic and international matters of policy. He and his government are responsible for the presentation of an annual budget (Article 125). Parliament has the power to inquire, amend, postaudit, and reject, but the government has the initiative in formulating policy and the responsibility for all executive actions. Attached to the Union government, but not a member of parliament or the cabinet, is the Auditor-General. He is responsible for auditing all accounts, must submit reports to the Chamber of Deputies, and is barred from holding any further government office after his term of appointment ends.

Probably the most distinctive and interesting feature of the constitution is the concept of the federal union (see Chart 2). Although the drafters did not attempt to define their ideas about federalism, these

---

[6] In connection with this power the Union constitution contains two imperatives against war. In Chapter XII the Union of Burma "renounces war as an instrument of national policy" (Article 211), and in Chapter VII it declares that "war shall not be declared and the Union shall not participate in any war except with the assent of Parliament" (Article 123). Both these restrictions are stated to be inoperative if actual or imminent invasion exists.

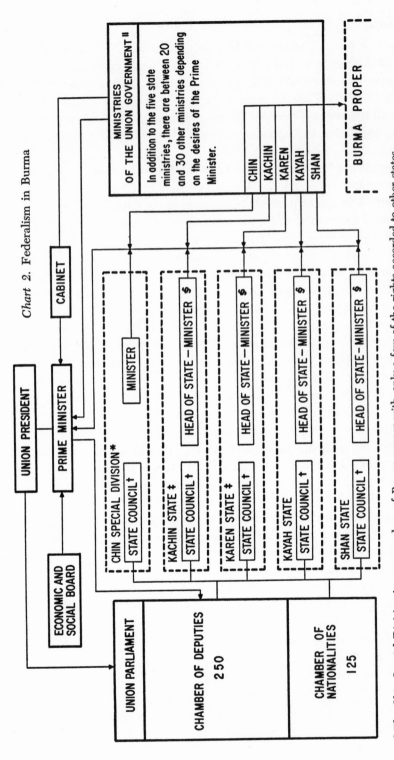

Chart 2. Federalism in Burma

* The Chin Special Division is an appendage of Burma proper with only a few of the rights accorded to other states.
† Members of the Union parliament from the states other than Burma proper automatically hold all seats in the state councils.
‡ Although the constitution recognizes the right of secession, it denies this right to the Kachin and Karen states.
§ A member of parliament appointed as minister for his state becomes thereby the head of his state.
‖ The Union government is also the government of Burma proper.

are implicit in the relationships which exist between the Union government and the states. In conformity with the federal idea the constitution provides for a separate system of government in each of the several states. In all except Burma proper the executive authority is granted to an indirectly chosen head of state. Legislative power is vested in the several state councils; each state has the right to decide on the form and structure of local government in its territory.

With Burma proper disregarded for the moment, note must be taken of the fact that the constitution gives each unit—the Union and the several states—separate and distinctive legislative powers (Article 90, 90.2). Schedule III of the constitution provides a Union and a state legislative list which enumerates the competency of each legislative body. The state list grants the state councils power to legislate on such matters as the state constitution, public service and administration, police power, simple justice and local prisons, education and culture, and state economic affairs—including agriculture, fisheries, and land policy, public works, and markets and prices. The Union legislative list contains all these powers in addition to such national powers as foreign affairs, finance, and war and peace. The reason for the overlap is that Burma proper is administered directly by the Union government, and, therefore, the Union government must have both national and state powers in dealing with the problems which it confronts. All legislation must be promulgated by the President; although he has no veto on Union legislation, he has a thirty-day suspensive veto in connection with state legislation. During that thirty-day period he may call upon the Supreme Court for its advice on questions of the constitutionality of any piece of legislation, and he may return the bill unsigned to the state council if the Court advises that the act does not conform to the constitution (Articles 169–170).

The rigid line of division between the Union and the states is badly blurred in many other places. According to the constitution the Union government enjoys greater authority and special powers. The states may, if they elect to, surrender their rights and powers to the Union (Article 92.3); the Union government, however, may not surrender its powers. In a proclaimed state of emergency, the Union parliament is empowered to legislate for any state on any subject regardless of the legislative lists (Article 94.1). Laws enacted under a proclamation of emergency may remain in effect for six months after the proclamation ceases to be operative (Article 94.4). At all times state laws are inferior to Union legislation regardless of whether or not the laws were enacted before the national laws.

The line of separation becomes less pronounced when a close examination is made of the state governments and the relations between the states and the Union. As noted above, Burma proper does not have a state council, nor, for that matter, does it have any separate state institutions. The Union government and the Union parliament is the government of Burma proper. To all intents and purposes Burma is a unitary state if Burma proper is considered alone (i.e., separate from the other five states). But because both the Union parliament and the government include a large minority of representatives from the other states, the people of Burma proper do not have full and exclusive authority in their own area.

In the other five states as well, the people do not have exclusive power over the institutions and the decisions concerning their territory. The constitution provides that all state offices are to be filled indirectly. That is, members of the state council are also members of the bicameral Union parliament. A state legislator sits in two houses; part of the time he legislates in the national interest and part of the time in the interest of his own state. Because election to the Union parliament is the source of his mandate, it takes precedence over his state seat. When the Union parliament is dissolved, the legislator automatically loses his state as well as his Union seat.

The Union government enters state politics in still another way. The head of state, in each state except one,[7] is filled automatically by the person whom the Prime Minister chooses as his minister for that particular state. The combined minister–head of state owes his position solely to the Union Prime Minister and not to any legislative or elective body. The state council has no authority to remove him, nor can it participate in his selection beyond offering advice to the Prime Minister. As a result of this unique arrangement the office of head of state is secondary to the holder's responsibility as Minister in the Union government.

In terms of privileges, the states do not enjoy equal rights. The constitution provides that every existing state has the right of secession

[7] The exception is the Chin Special Division which is an appendage of Burma proper with special privileges. There is a Chin Affairs Council wherein the parliamentary members sit. There is no head of state, however. The minister for Chin affairs is in charge of Chin general administration, education, and culture; the Council has no legislative power.

unless otherwise expressly provided in the constitution (Article 201); thus far the Kachin and Karen states have been expressly denied this right (Article 178 and the Karen State Amendment Act of 1951). The states which have the right of secession were not able to exercise it before January 4, 1958 (Article 202).

Finally, all the states enjoy equal rights to raise revenue among the people in their own territory. Since the economic base of each state differs, and none can raise enough to be self-supporting, all must look to the Union treasury to augment their revenues in order to finance their expenditures. The state budgets are scrutinized by the Union President to see that they meet the conditions "imposed by the Union, in respect of any contributions from the Union," and all state budgets are included in the Union budget (Articles 164.2, 177.2).

If the federal structure is more nominal than real, it must be recognized that it meets the exigencies of the situation in that it gives the important minorities a territory of their own with their leaders in charge of what autonomy has been granted and with the right to protect and preserve their culture. In devising a system where real power remains with the central government and only incidental powers pass to the states the Burmese have constructed a novel arrangement which satisfies the pride of the various minorities without sacrificing the paramountcy and effectiveness of the Union.

The constitution declares that the judiciary shall be independent. It provides for a Supreme and a High Court and for a system of inferior courts to be established throughout the nation by acts of parliament. The High Court has both original and appellate jurisdiction. It is given "exclusive original" jurisdiction in all matters arising out of a treaty and in disputes between the Union and the states or between the states in any other matter "as may be defined by law" (Article 135). The Supreme Court is the court of final appeal. It may review all decisions of the High Court and any other court established by law. It also may give advisory opinions upon the request of the President.

All Justices of both the Supreme and the High Courts are nominated by the President and approved by the parliament. Their number, salary, and other conditions are determined in law and cannot be changed during a Justice's tenure without his consent.

Venerating a legacy of the British—the rule of law—during the past decade the Justices of the Supreme and High Courts have established an enviable record for independence of action and for estab-

Burma

lishing a calm and peaceful atmosphere in their courts. The place of
the Supreme Court in the present judicial system is comparable to that
of the Privy Council under British rule. This became evident almost
from the birth of the Union when U Saw, the convicted plotter of
Aung San's death, attempted to appeal to the Privy Council after the
grant of independence; he was refused by the Council and forced to
seek a final consideration by the newly established Supreme Court.

In the face of internal political difficulties wherein the Union and
the constitution have been in constant danger of being overthrown,
the Supreme Court has worked unremittingly to establish a tradition
of due process of law in Burma.[8] In spite of the grave conditions which
have prevailed, the Court has worked to protect the individual against
the arbitrary action of the government. A clear case in point arises
out of the question of preventive arrest. According to the state legislative list, a state may enact laws permitting "preventive detention for
reasons connected with the maintenance of public order" (List II,
no. 3.3). The constitution also recognizes the laws which were in
effect at the time of the transfer of power (Article 226); one such law
was the Public Order Preservation Act (POPA) of 1947, which included provisions which made it possible to detain a suspect up to two
months or, under certain conditions, indefinitely. Section 9.1 of the
act provided that "no order made in exercise of any power conferred
by or under this Act shall be called into question in any Court." [9]
Using the powers granted by the act, the Union government made
several hundred arrests of suspects and held them in jail for years without preferring charges, bringing them to trial, or releasing them on
bail. Numerous persons challenged the validity of the act even while
the Union was in mortal danger of being overthrown. The Court
acted firmly and independently by striking out Section 9.1 on the
ground that "no legislative provisions in the Union can validly exclude this Court from enquiring into the legality or the sufficiency of
any decisions of the judicial or quasi-judicial body." [10] In reviewing

[8] For a discussion of the Court's principles as expressed by the first Chief Justice,
see U Ba U, *My Burma* (New York: Taplinger Publishing Co., 1958), p. 203.

[9] As quoted in Winslow Christian, "Burma's New Constitution and Supreme
Court," *Tulane Law Review*, XXVI (December 1951), 50–51.

[10] *Burma Law Reports*, 1948, S.C. 767. For an excellent discussion of this act
and other problems of constitutional law see N. A. Subramanian, "Some Aspects
of Burmese Constitutional Law," *Indian Yearbook of International Affairs, 1956*
(Madras, 1957), pp. 123–155.

the government's use of POPA the Court has released persons arrested for distributing literature which called for the murder of the Prime Minister and other acts calculated to incite the public. The Court has not seen fit to overthrow the act, but in numerous cases it has established precedents which indicate clearly that "preventive detention must satisfy a two-way test, the one substantial and the other procedural. The grounds must be sufficient to support a detention order and there must be a scrupulous observance of the prescribed procedure." [11] Other instances exist to uphold the claim that the Court refuses to be intimidated by outside influences and is determined to establish a model of independent and responsible action.

Unfortunately a dearth of trained legal minds prevents the whole court system from maintaining the high standards of the Supreme and High Courts. As a result incompletely trained and, in many cases, politically motivated magistrates and judicial officers have filled the lower courts; their handiwork must be corrected by an overcrowded, overworked review tribunal system.

Finally, it must be noted that no specific declarations are made in regard to local government institutions or practices. Article 91 declares that on the basis of regional autonomy parliament can make laws and delegate specific administrative, cultural, and economic matters. In conformity with this mandate a Democratization of Local Administration Act of 1949 was passed and then superseded in 1950 by a new act under a similar title. Since local government is a state-reserved subject, the above-mentioned act applies only to Burma proper, and its extension, in part or in full, is a matter for each state to decide.

The constitution provides the institutional framework within which the people of Burma have governed themselves for the past decade. During that period some of the institutions have been ignored or altered, whereas others have been respected and made to work as intended. In order to understand the way in which the political process works, it is necessary to turn now to the informal level of politics and examine the electoral, decision-making, and decision implementation processes.

[11] Subramanian, *op. cit.*, p. 140.

Political Parties

The Burmese constitution, like that of the United States, is silent on the question of political parties. If a legal mandate is sought, it probably lies in the right of individuals to assemble peacefully, to express their opinions and convictions, and to form associations.[12]

Burma's party system is currently in flux as a result of a split in the AFPFL which has divided the ruling elite for the first time since independence. If the present struggle is put aside for the moment, an examination of the AFPFL's structure and activity during the past decade will provide a useful background to contemporary events and also suggest some of the ways in which the present leaders might realign themselves.

Prior to 1958 it was reasonable to say that although Burma had a multiparty system the AFPFL dominated the political scene; and it was not until the 1956 election that an important second party emerged. In many ways the AFPFL was the only modern party in Burma. It had a national organization, a meaningful program, and an ideology to provide a guide for its future action. Its chief opposition since 1956—the National Unity Front (NUF)—was different in that it had no nation-wide organization in the same sense as the AFPFL; rather its structure was built out of a confederation of all participating groups.[13] Therefore, it had no single ideology or much of a program beyond working to unseat the party in power and replacing it as the government of Burma. The NUF's strength lay in its leadership, its unity of purpose, and the fact that it offered itself as an alternative to a people who had become a little weary and disenchanted with the governing party.

As a coalition party the AFPFL was a combination of ethnic groups, mass organizations, independent members, and at least one political party—the Socialist Party. During the past decade the Socialists have been the most influential group in the coalition and have provided it with leadership and ideas. In the preindependence, post-Second

---

[12] Burmese Constitution, Chapter II, Fundamental Rights, Article 17, i, ii, iii.

[13] The Front came into existence when a number of opposition parties formed an alliance to contest the 1956 election. They agreed to pool their efforts and not compete with each other for seats. Originally twelve parties formed the All Opposition Alliance. It included all political ideas from right to left and such diverse personalities as U Kyaw Min, ANUO; Thakin Lwin, BWPP; Ba Sein, BDP; Dr. E. Maung, Justice Party. The coalition split into two parts, the NUF, lead by the BWPP and the Justice Party, and the Burma National Bloc (BNB) lead by Dr. Ba Maw. A few, such as Kyaw Min and Ba Sein, withdrew altogether.

World War period the Socialists contested with the Communist Party led by Than Tun for control of the AFPFL and its constituent mass organizations—the Trade Union Congress, the Peasants Organization, and the Women's Freedom League. After the Communist Party was expelled from the AFPFL in 1946, the only real challenge to Socialist Party leadership came from independents such as U Nu, the president of the AFPFL. The Socialists' power came from two sources, the position of their party in the coalition and their control of the mass organizations. In 1949 during a critical phase of the insurrection against the nascent independent government of Burma, the Socialist Party disagreed with Prime Minister Nu and other non-Socialist leaders in the party and withdrew as a constituent group in the AFPFL. Individual Socialists remained in the AFPFL, however, by retaining their control of the mass organizations. Since the question of dual loyalties never was raised, no problem arose over this curious arrangement. As a result the Socialists have remained an important force in the party, despite the fact that their organization was outside the formal framework of the AFPFL. Although some observers consider the Socialists to be the real leaders of the AFPFL, it must be recognized that much leadership is provided by independents and ethnic-group leaders representing the minorities in Burma. These leaders—though sympathetic toward socialist objectives—were not and never have been Socialist Party members. Because of the strength and influence of the independents and minority-group leaders, conflicts over policies and programs have existed between the Socialists and non-Socialists in the AFPFL. In addition the Socialists have never presented a completely united front, and after the 1958 split in the AFPFL they were to be found on both sides.

The NUF is a coalition, but with a difference; it is a coalition of near equals. The groups included range from the liberal-democratic Justice Party of Dr. E Maung to the Marxist Burma Workers and Peasants Party of U Ba Nyein, U Chit Maung, and Thakin Lwin and the People's Unity Party of Thein Pe Myint. In parliament (1956–1958) the NUF co-operated with the Arkanese National United Organization (ANUO), a conservative, right-wing party. As a party of co-equals the constituent groups retain their previous identity and their hold over their own organizations. Their parliamentary unity was unbroken until the AFPFL split and forced them to decide which faction they would support. Their claim to the title of the official opposition vanished when the AFPFL split occurred and the dissident

AFPFL group took command of the opposition seats in the special session of the parliament in June 1958 on the basis that they outnumbered the NUF.

The structure of the AFPFL emerged during the last years of the Second World War and was institutionalized at the first All Burma AFPFL Congress in 1946. At that time direction of the party rested with the thirty-six-member Supreme Council responsible to the National Congress.[14] Between meetings the Executive Committee of the Supreme Council directed the party's operations. According to the AFPFL's constitution, members of the Supreme Council were to be elected by the subordinate units of the party and the mass organizations. In addition the elected leaders were authorized to co-opt or appoint additional members to the party's highest council without referring their appointments back to the general membership.

There are two types of members in the AFPFL—direct and indirect. Direct or independent members joined a branch of the AFPFL; indirect members entered the AFPFL through membership in an affiliate organization. Because leaders depend upon personal followings to elevate them into the ruling circle, the heads of affiliate organizations hold tight control over their own organizations. It has been possible for independent or direct members to rise to the top through the AFPFL organization. U Nu is a case in point. Without any personal organization, U Nu continued from 1947 into 1958 as head of the AFPFL.

In January 1958 the AFPFL held its third All Burma AFPFL Congress. At the time it was stated that the party had a total membership of 1,368,014, of which 488,014 were direct members. The balance was made up of affiliate groups as follows: the All Burma Peasants Organization (ABPO), 550,050; the Federation of Trade Organizations (FTO), 100,243; the Trade Union Congress, Burma (TUCB) 140,584; the Women's Freedom League (WFL), 57,454; and the Karen Youth League (KYL), 31,669. The membership was represented at the Congress by 2,180 delegates; 1,153 represented the direct membership and 967 the affiliate groups, while the AFPFL state parties were allotted 30 in the Shan State, 20 in the Kachin State, and 10 in the Kayah State.[15] The new Supreme Council was enlarged to 261 mem-

---

[14] *The Constitution of the AFPFL* (Rangoon [1949?]; in Burmese). The constitution provides that an annual national conference shall be held. Because of the internal political situation, however, none were called between December 1947 and January 1958.

[15] *Nation,* Jan. 12, 1958, p. 1.

bers, of which 156 were elected through township and district AFPFL organizations and the remainder by the affiliate organizations. In addition, fifteen persons were co-opted by the elected council. U Nu was re-elected president; he chose an Executive Committee of fifteen and accepted five additional co-opted members.[16] A struggle arose behind the scenes over the naming of the secretary-general. The Socialist faction, led by Kyaw Nyein and Ba Swe, wanted Thakin Tha Khin, whereas U Nu demanded and got Thakin Kyaw Tun (ABPO) for the office. A compromise was effected by appointing Tha Khin as assistant secretary-general. The Congress was memorable because U Nu declared that as of that date the party was no longer a coalition, but a unitary party, and that all affiliates must accept the party ideology and a subordinate status in the AFPFL. In addition he rejected Marxism "as a guiding political philosophy or as the ideology of the AFPFL." [17] He stated that Burma's goal must be a socialist state which "can fully guarantee fundamental rights, economic security, a high standard of living, firm morality, opportunity to practice religion in a positive way . . . maintenance and preservation of our traditions, culture and heritage." [18]

After the election in 1956 the 48 elected NUF candidates banded together in parliament as the NUF and took the seats reserved for the official opposition.[19] Offices of the NUF were opened throughout the country in order to build an organization. No new structure was created, however; rather the former opposition parties merely subordinated their names to the winning NUF title and continued in their previous ways. Thus, for example, the Burma Workers and Peasants Party in Mongwa took charge of the NUF there because the BWPP's candidates were elected from that area, whereas the Justice Party in Prome established the NUF organization because the Justice Party candidate was successful in the election. The hub of NUF activity is the parliamentary group in Rangoon; it sets the party line and takes command of NUF activity. The Rangoon headquarters talks about their party being organized according to Lenin's doctrine of democratic centralism; in fact it is leader-dominated with no voice from below.

Neither in the AFPFL nor in the NUF is there a clear line by which

[16] *Ibid.,* Jan. 31, 1958, p. 1.
[17] Ministry of Information, *Burma Weekly Bulletin,* n.s., VI (Feb. 6, 1958), 376.
[18] *Ibid.*
[19] By mid-1957 the NUF lost five seats through re-elections which were held after the Ministry of Judicial Affairs ruled that the original elections were faulty.

new leaders can rise automatically to the top. Most of the present leaders in both parties are the men who originally organized the movements which they lead. In theory the AFPFL, with its widespread organization and affiliates, was the best equipped to select, train, and elevate leaders from the ranks. The NUF does not have similar mass organizations, but it does have strong support from the university student leaders; their parties and organizations provide the NUF with a ready-made recruiting ground and willing adherents.

A few words must be said about the 1958 split in the AFPFL. Although it had been rumored openly in Burma for years that factions in the leadership were antagonistic, apparently it was not until 1958, when internal security was being re-established and the country was beginning to run smoothly, that the leaders dared to split their organization and allow their differences to be aired publicly. Prime Minister Nu took a major step on April 23, 1958, when he decided that he no longer could keep peace between antagonists—Thakin Tin and Kyaw Tun, the leaders of the All Burma Peasants Organization, and Kyaw Nyein, Socialist leader—and openly broke with Kyaw Nyein by joining the other side and removing a Kyaw Nyein follower, Thakin Tha Khin, from his post as Home Minister. The split forced U Ba Swe, leader of the TUCB and former Prime Minister, to take sides, and he chose to support Kyaw Nyein. In the public debate it became clear that the split between Nu and Kyaw Nyein dated back to 1956, when Nu resigned as Prime Minister to purge the AFPFL of corruption and dishonest leaders. His attack at that time upon Kyaw Nyein's followers led to a party rift which brought Kyaw Tun to the support of Nu against Kyaw Nyein; although the split was repaired temporarily, an undercurrent of ill feeling between the protagonists lingered. The fight was resumed at the 1958 All Burma AFPFL Congress over the office of secretary-general and questions of party ideology. In order to avoid a split at that time it was agreed that Kyaw Tun would take the office of secretary-general and—it is claimed by Kyaw Nyein's followers—resign in forty-five days in favor of Thakin Tha Khin. When Kyaw Tun refused to resign at the expiration of the time limit Nu's present opponents charged Kyaw Tun with bad faith. At the Congress, Nu agreed to allow Kyaw Nyein to build an organization of Burma youth and accept it in the AFPFL. When Kyaw Nyein decided to raid the ranks of the ABPO in the area of Insein for membership during March and April, it became clear to Nu that the two factions were irreconcilable. At this point Nu decided to choose sides; he joined with Kyaw Tun against Kyaw Nyein and after private negotiations in the party headquarters and public press interviews, both sides agreed to allow the Union parliament to decide which faction would continue to govern Burma. Although Ba Swe was not an instigator of the split, he felt that Nu's action of taking sides forced him to act also; apparently to counteract Nu's action Ba Swe joined with Kyaw Nyein. An undercurrent of difference between Nu and Ba Swe has existed since the Congress over Nu's long statement on ideological problems. Nu's declaration of January 30, 1958, that Buddhism and Marxism were not compatible was directly contrary to Ba Swe's earlier pronouncement made in 1951 claiming that the two were "not merely similar. In fact they are the same in concept." [20] Thus the break between the two in May 1958 was to be expected.

In spite of the public claims of Kyaw Nyein and Ba Swe of mass support, Nu was able to hold a large bloc of AFPFL representatives. In addition he gained the support of the NUF and many representatives of the other states. On June 4 he re-organized his cabinet, including three Arakanese—with Kyaw Min becoming the Finance Minister—and two members from the Karen and Kachin states in addition to retaining the ministers who had remained loyal to him from the outset of the break.[21] On June 9 parliament supported Nu by a vote of 127 to 119 on a question of no confidence raised by Ba Swe. After the balloting the opponents embraced and shook hands and promised to wage a clean campaign in the new election scheduled for 1959.[22]

Following the special session of parliament, the Kyaw Nyein–Ba Swe group on June 23, 1958, attempted to engineer the expulsion of Nu and eight others from the AFPFL by a special vote in the party's Executive Council. The maneuver was not wholly successful; U Nu and his supporters decided to fight for the control of the old organization and its name. The two groups compromised by sharing the name—the Nu faction adopted the name "Clean" AFPFL and the Kyaw Nyein forces called themselves "Stable" AFPFL; the two groups divided the mass organizations—the Clean AFPFL keeping control of the All Burma Peasants Organization and the Stable AFPFL keeping control of all the rest. Nu's faction later successfully split off important segments of the membership in the Trade Union Congress and the Women's Freedom League and used them as the nuclei of two

---

[20] Ba Swe, *The Burmese Revolution* (Rangoon: Ministry of Information, 1952), p. 7.

[21] *New York Times*, June 5, 1958, p. 13.   [22] *Ibid.*, June 11, 1958, p. 17.

new organizations subsumed under the Clean AFPFL—the Union of Burma Labor Organization and the Union Women's League. Added to these, Nu's group created a new mass organization, the Union Youth League, to compete with Kyaw Nyein's youth group formed in the spring of 1958. Throughout the summer and early fall the two factions campaigned to strengthen their support among the people; the Stable AFPFL worked through its party and mass organizations while the Clean AFPFL sponsored frequent trips by U Nu, Daw Khin Kyi—the wife of Burma's martyred hero, Aung San—and others in order to make their appeal for support directly to the people. As the campaign went on, both factions sought to undermine the confidence of the people in their opponent.

Because the two factions were of nearly equal strength, they nullified each other; this resulted in giving the NUF a particular advantage in making political demands as a price for its parliamentary support. The NUF, however, was not a united organization on this issue. One of its affiliates, the Justice Party, moved into the camp of U Nu's party when Dr. E Maung, the head of the Justice Party, accepted a government portfolio as the Minister of Judicial Affairs. The two pro-Communist affiliates of the NUF, the Burma Workers and Peasants Party and the People's Unity Party, sought to gain political objectives in exchange for their support. U Nu refused to bargain with them but was willing to continue to accept their support in parliament if they gave it with no strings attached. The Kyaw Nyein forces took a strong anti-Communist line and were adamant in their refusal of all NUF support. Because of this situation U Nu was uncertain that he could survive a no-confidence vote in the scheduled August budget session of parliament, and therefore he asked the Union President to cancel the meeting. This action, in addition to the growing bitterness of the electioneering and the uncertainty connected with the question of how committed U Nu was to the pro-Communist groups in parliament, caused fear, doubt, and confusion in the public's mind.

The army's concern with the deteriorating political situation was communicated to the public as early as June 23, 1958, when General Ne Win, in an address to the Seventh Annual Commanding Officers' Conference, cautioned those fellow officers who were in close association with political leaders in both factions of the divided AFPFL that it was their first duty to be loyal to the constitution; if an officer could not keep this loyalty primary, there was no room for him in the defense services. Second and more important, Ne Win called upon the political leaders to settle their differences within the framework of the constitution and not to involve army personnel in political quarrels.[23] As the two political factions of the AFPFL became more extreme in their attacks upon each other, rumors began to circulate that an army coup was imminent; U Nu attempted to put this rumor to rest by denying it in a speech delivered to the All Burma Conference of the Clean AFPFL. On September 4, 1958, in a radio address to the nation Nu attempted to assure the people that the army was loyal to the constitution and that it was his "duty to defend, in the interests of truth and justice, the Burma Army which is a part of the administrative machinery which is under my charge." [24] All doubt ended on September 26 when U Nu again addressed a radio audience and announced that conditions in the country made it impossible to hold free and fair elections in November as scheduled; therefore, in order to have such an election before April 1959 he had asked General Ne Win to succeed him as Prime Minister and to re-establish order throughout the country and provide the necessary conditions for holding an election. In an exchange of letters between U Nu and Ne Win which were made public, Ne Win agreed to accept the office provided that the Chamber of Deputies elected him and that his cabinet include no members from the active political parties. He promised to suppress crime and corruption and create conditions which would make it possible to hold elections before his six-month term is over.[25] Using the radio the next night, the Prime Minister-designate informed the army that his assumption of power did not mean that it was empowered to interfere in the political life of the country. Its duty was to re-establish and maintain order and to create a peaceful atmosphere for the holding of an election; it was not the army's role to work for the advantage of any political party.[26]

Whether it was U Nu's idea or the army's that Ne Win succeed U Nu in office has not been established conclusively; both principals in the case insist that it was Nu's idea; at any rate, Nu remained in office as he predicted and resigned on October 28, 1958. A Burmese editorial added a new dimension to the question by stating that "if the initiative for turning over the government did really come from U Nu, he must be rated a statesman; if not he would still rate as a diplomatist for succeeding in keeping the word 'coup d'état' out of

[23] Ministry of Information, *Burma Weekly Bulletin*, n.s., VII (July 3, 1958), 83.
[24] *Ibid.*, n.s., VII (Sept. 18, 1958), 173.
[25] *Ibid.*, n.s., VII (Oct. 2, 1958), 193.   [26] *Ibid.*, p. 194.

the references to the situation in Burma." [27] Ne Win, as agreed, accepted the office of Prime Minister after the Chamber of Deputies elected him to succeed Nu. As an old personal friend of the leaders in both factions of the AFPFL his assumption of office has been favorably received by the politicians as well as the public. In keeping his word to select nonpolitical and nonmilitary figures as his ministers, Ne Win remains a neutral in the current political struggle between the Clean and the Stable factions of the AFPFL. It will take more time before the citizens and the political observers will know which of the two factions will emerge as the dominant party in Burma, whether Ne Win will be successful in playing the "honest broker" and avoid having to call the army into active participation in Burma's political struggles, and whether a two-party system will really emerge in Burma.

Elections

Thus far there have been two national elections since independence. According to the constitution the first should have been held within eighteen months after the establishment of the Union. The insurrection prevented it from taking place at the assigned time, and it was not until 1951 that conditions existed whereby it was possible to hold one. At that time it was necessary to hold the election in stages—one part of the country after another—so that available troops could be moved successively into each area to provide security for the candidates and the voters. The chief contestants for seats were the AFPFL, the Burma Workers and Peasants Party, the Independent Arakanese Parliamentary Group (IAPG), and some minor parties which eventually gravitated to the BWPP. The victory clearly was in favor of the AFPFL. Out of the 239 seats contested, the AFPFL won 147 in its own name (about 200 if affiliates were included); the opposition won only 30 seats, and the remainder went to independent candidates.[28] The size of the opposition might have been somewhat larger except that the BWPP withdrew candidates to emphasize its charge that the election was unfair.[29]

The election revealed two interesting aspects of Burmese politics. The use of the single-member constituency ensures that there is no splitting of the vote; the winner takes all, even with a plurality of one.

[27] *Nation*, Sept. 28, 1958, p. 4.   [28] *Asian Annual* (London, 1954), p. 15.
[29] Foreign observers reported that the election was as fair as possible under existing conditions. See the *Economist*, Feb. 9, 1952, pp. 349–351, for an example of such a report.

And the Burmese electoral system, like its British model, does not demand that a candidate be a resident of his constituency. The parties are able to select the candidates and give them financial backing. Thus the candidate is obliged to the party and not to his constituents, and party solidarity in parliament is assured. These two factors, combined with the use of the forementioned three-stage election, gave an unusual result. Candidates who were unsuccessful in one constituency stood a second time in another. The AFPFL alienated many voters by forcing second-rate candidates on some of the constituencies; in such cases the people frequently responded by giving an enthusiastic vote to the opposition candidate. A case in point was the overwhelming victory of U Kyaw Min (IAPG) in his constituency in Arakan, where corrupt AFPFL petty politicians had enraged the voters.

The second national election, held in 1956, duplicated the earlier overwhelming victory of the AFPFL. It also produced a new factor in Burmese postwar politics—the emergence of an opposition large enough to make its voice heard in parliament. Although the AFPFL won 148 seats in its own name, the NUF won 48, the ANUO (formerly the IAPG) 6, affiliates of the NUF 2, and independents 9; the remainder went to affiliates of the AFPFL.[30] The NUF fought the election on the issues of ending the insurrection by peaceful means and stopping corruption in government and faulty administration of state enterprises. The AFPFL countered with a campaign based on recounting its past achievements and promising more in the future. At the time of the election the country was undergoing a mild inflation, while a restriction on imported goods and internal insecurity continued to plague the people. The army was able to provide sufficient security for elections to be held on the same day in all but nine districts. The government made great efforts to correct the conditions which had provoked charges of corruption and coercion in the first election. In view of existing conditions, most observers agreed that it, too, was fair.[31]

Again the use of the single-member district provided some interesting results. For instance, the party which polled the third largest vote in Burma proper, the Burma Democratic Party, failed to win a single

[30] The voting in the nine constituencies postponed in 1956 was not completed until May 1958. For a breakdown of the vote by parties and localities, see Josef Silverstein, "Politics, Parties, and the National Election in Burma," *Far Eastern Survey,* XXV (1956), 177–184, and Geoffrey Fairbairn, "Some Minority Problems in Burmese Politics," *Pacific Affairs,* XXX (1957), 287–313.

[31] *Nation,* May 15, 1956, p. 1.

seat. The Burma Nationalistic Bloc, on the other hand, polled approximately 40,000 less votes than the Democratic Party and managed to win one seat. The vote against the AFPFL affiliates in states other than Burma proper and the continuing discontent in Arakan with the AFPFL's leadership helped to reduce its majority. Although neither factor was important enough to jeopardize the dominant strength and victory of the AFPFL, they suggest that the party had much work to do if it intended to win back its original adherents.

The Opposition

One of the significant developments of the first decade of independence has been the gradual growth of a formal opposition with power enough to force the government to explain its actions and fight for its programs. From the time of the Constituent Assembly in 1947–1950, no formal opposition existed in the provisional parliament of Burma. In 1950 a group of extreme left-wing Socialists attempted to capture the AFPFL for their own interests; when forced to resign, they reorganized as the Burma Workers and Peasants Party and emerged as the opposition. Up to that point all discussions and legislation was passed without any real questions raised. It should be noted also, however, that the years 1948–1950 included the worst period of the insurrection; the members of parliament who remained loyal to the Union were only too glad to see the government give leadership and accept responsibility. It was also during this period that some of the most socialistic legislation was passed; a law nationalizing the Irrawaddy Flotilla Company and a Land Nationalization Bill were passed, timber collection and sales were made a state monopoly under the State Timber Board, and the collection and sale of rice were established as a state monopoly under the State Agricultural Marketing Board (SAMB).

Between 1950 and 1956 the real opposition was the press. The members of parliament who were opposed to the party in power were too few to do more than raise questions, debate, and criticize. They were excluded from all standing committees; they were insufficient to initiate a vote of no confidence. The government proceeded with its business as if there were no parliamentary opposition. The press, on the other hand, played an important role as critic of the government. U Nu, who was anxious to develop a parliamentary tradition, initiated the idea of the frequent press conference in which newsmen could engage him in a free exchange. Here the Prime Minister was subjected to the searching inquiry one normally associates with parliamentary debate. These meetings were reported fully, and follow-up stories and editorials were written; as a result the public was informed about corruption, bad management, and incompetency as well as the successes of the government. Early in the independence period some elements in the AFPFL sought to silence press criticism of the government through violent methods. U Nu responded to this lawlessness by his fellow members with vigorous denunciation of such tactics and worked continuously for the development of a free and responsible press.

In 1954 the government introduced a measure which would have made criticism of public servants, ministers, and officials a criminal offense. The AFPFL easily pushed the measure through the Chamber of Deputies with no opposition because the BWPP and the IAPG members walked out in protest against the measure. Only the organized protests of the Burma Journalist Association and the press were able to muster public opposition; as a result the government withdrew the measure and never revived it. Today the press is relatively free and growing, and it continues to be a strong adjunct to the opposition in parliament.

The parliament of 1956 is beginning to measure up to the expectations of those who looked forward to the day when Burma would have a legislature with a responsible opposition. The formal opposition up to June 1958 was composed of the NUF, the ANUO, a few independents, and members of splinter parties. It has been well led, with its spokesmen articulate and well trained, and it has had sufficient strength to enter a motion of no confidence. In addition its size has made it mandatory that some of its members be included on all standing committees. Although it did not have sufficient power to bring the government down, it forced explanation of governmental actions and plans. In an effort to meet this new challenge, the AFPFL in the 1957 budget session not only presented the customary budget and the Finance Minister's analysis of the nation's economy, but in addition U Nu read a 132-page statement on policies and conditions in the country. After 1956 the government could no longer ignore the opposition. The trend following a decade of independence indicates that the roots of parliamentary government have struck deep, and the chances seem good that representative government will endure.

Governmental Decision Making

According to the constitution, the cabinet is the formal body that makes the decisions which shape the policies of the government. Composed only of ministers, the cabinet meets weekly and works on the basis of a formal agenda which is prepared in advance by the cabinet secretary. The Prime Minister presides, and minutes are taken and kept secret. Decisions are arrived at by common agreement, and discussion of issues continues until there is a consensus. The pre-eminence of the Prime Minister was clearly demonstrated when the government delayed its presentation of the budget in 1955 because the Prime Minister was abroad and no one else could take responsibility for the final draft.

The most important economic and financial decisions are taken in the first instance not in the cabinet but in a special board under the chairmanship of the Prime Minister. This Economic and Social Board was originally created in 1952 as a planning branch under the Ministry of National Planning and Religious Affairs. The next year it was moved to the office of the Prime Minister and reconstituted; since then it has become a sort of supercabinet. As late as 1956 its composition consisted of the following eight members: the Prime Minister; the Ministers for National Planning and Religious Affairs, Mines and Defense, Industry, and Finance and Revenue; the chairman of the Economic and Social Advisory Council; a representative of the Union Bank of Burma; and the executive secretary of the Economic and Social Board. This board seeks the consensus of its members, but in fact no decisions are taken until the Prime Minister decides, and apparently no decision is taken against his will. Although the decisions of this board must be confirmed by the cabinet, this in effect is almost automatic, since the key cabinet officers have already cast their vote and committed themselves by their decisions on the board.

More important than this formal structure of decision making is the informal, extraconstitutional process. It is at this informal level that the party—the AFPFL—brings its weight to bear. Before any decisions are taken in the cabinet or even by the Economic and Social Board, the major questions are discussed and decided in the party's Executive Committee. This committee of fifteen, which includes the Prime Minister and many cabinet officials, also contains members who hold no political posts and have no responsibility except to the party. In a published exchange of letters between Kyaw Nyein and U Nu the Prime Minister stated that he worked constantly to abide by the policy decisions of the party on internal and foreign matters. When Kyaw Nyein accused him of placing so many fetters upon the ministers that they were nothing more than head clerks, Nu replied, "Was it I who placed the controls upon the Ministers? It was the Executive Committee which ordered these checks." [32] The same letter reveals that when Nu returned from his trip to Russia in 1955 he made his first report to a joint meeting of the Executive Committee and the cabinet. The Executive Committee of the AFPFL is the shadow government which makes the basic policy decisions, and, unlike the formal cabinet, it is responsible to no one except a handful of party leaders.

The past decade, however, includes instances when U Nu made personal and in some ways impetuous decisions which add a third dimension to governmental decision making in Burma. Although he has been called the "serene statesman" by some, his temper and anger were demonstrated in a singular decision which he made in the heat of the moment. At the time of the 1956 school examinations, just prior to the elections, there was a student riot in which one of the students was shot and killed. U Nu, in order to mollify the enraged students and their families, decided without consulting others to pass all the pupils taking the examinations. His action had the long-term effect of overburdening an insufficiently staffed school system with a large percentage of students who were unqualified.[33] A different example of Nu's personal decision making is his occasional apparent reliance upon the revelations of a favorite astrologer. In this practice he is acting in consonance with Burmese tradition as well as in keeping with his own beliefs. The exact instant of Burma's independence in 1948 was calculated in this manner; Nu also determined the most auspicious hour to move out of the Prime Minister's residence after he resigned in 1956. In effect, governmental decision making in Burma can be characterized as follows. Basic policy decisions are made in the Executive Committee of the AFPFL. These decisions are confirmed in the cabinet or, if they involve economic

[32] "Kyaw Nyein–U Nu Exchange of Letters, July 3–6, 1956," *Nation*, May 10, 1958, pp. 5–6.
[33] *Nation*, March 23, 1956, p. 1; Silverstein, "Politics, Parties, and the National Election in Burma," p. 181.

questions, in the Economic and Social Board and then the cabinet. At any time, however, the Prime Minister may make a personal decision and impose it upon the hierarchy, both formal and informal.

Implementation of Decisions

Burma's problem has been not in arriving at decisions, but in carrying them out. An examination of the Land Nationalization Act will reveal the difficulties which have beset implementation of this key measure—one which had the support of the party, the government, the parliament, and a large percentage of the people. One of the rallying cries of the prewar nationalists was the call for aid to the agriculturists; land alienation and exploitation were regarded as two of the worst abuses that the farmer faced. As if to honor a pledge, one of the first pieces of legislation passed, without opposition, in the parliament of 1948 was the Land Nationalization Act. Based on Chapter III of the constitution, the act's purposes were to take over all land held by nonagriculturists and to distribute it among tenant farmers, to confirm the land rights of owner-cultivators, to survey and record landholdings, and to bring waste lands into production by distributing it to landless peasants. The ultimate goal, as seen by the Minister of Agriculture and Forests, Thakin Tin (also president of the All Burma Peasants Organization), was to establish "collective farming and mechanization." [34] In reality the act was hastily drawn and contained numerous defects; for instance, there were no provisions for nonfarming landowners who might take up cultivation rather than have their land confiscated, nor were the provisions for eventual compensation to owners clearly stated. The government's haste was due to pressure it felt because of the activity of the rebelling Communist Party among the peasants. Although passed with fanfare, the act was not implemented at once for a number of reasons —the absence of land records and maps destroyed during the war, the insurrection's limitation of the government's effectiveness throughout the country, and the absence of trained personnel to administer the act.

In 1950 a pilot project established in Syriam for testing the act's provisions and the possibilities of carrying them out failed because of such reasons as poor administration, the political activity of the All Burma Peasants Organization and its attempts to dominate the

[34] *The Land Nationalization Act, 1948* (Rangoon: Ministry of Information, 1948), p. 8.

various land committees charged with deciding the basic questions of which lands were to be taken by the government and which were to be exempt, and the sheer unworkability of some of the act's provisions. A new act was passed in 1953 carrying the same title but changed so that it corrected many of the earlier defects, and a new ministry was created prior to the act's passage for the explicit purpose of implementing its provisions.

In 1953, with an improvement in internal security, the government again experimented with the act in eight townships in eight different districts (involving 142,737 acres of land).[35] This time a corps of trained administrators worked directly with village and township committees composed in the main of local agriculturists. Slowly, as the areas came under government control and as administrators became available, the government expanded its scope. In 1955–1956 it was reported that 752,563 acres of land in 49 townships in 28 districts were added;[36] by the end of 1957, out of a total of 20 million cultivated areas, 2,656,248 acres had been covered by the act.[37] Of this total, 1,156,442 acres were distributed to 141,132 peasant families, and 1,263,449 acres were exempted because they were the property of agricultural families. Compensation thus far has been paid only for land taken by the government in the years 1953–1954 and 1954–1955. Each former owner has received 2,500 kyats[38] in cash and the remainder in unnegotiable "Government of the Union of Burma Bonds" which bear 3 per cent interest and mature fifteen years after date of issue. "After a period of five years, ten per cent of the value of such bonds will be redeemed every year."[39] Actual cash payment since 1956–1957 amounted to 4,400,000 kyats.

Some writers have decried the government's action in this field as being inadequate and not really revolutionary, as the Socialists had promised—they say that actually the act legalizes what in effect existed (agriculturists and squatters could not and would not be put off the land).[40] This appraisal does not take note of all the facts

[35] *Burma: The Seventh Anniversary* (Rangoon: Ministry of Information, 1955), p. 18.

[36] *Burma: The Ninth Anniversary* (Rangoon: Ministry of Information, 1957), p. 46.

[37] *Burma: The Tenth Anniversary* (Rangoon: Ministry of Information, 1958), p. 68.

[38] One kyat is equal to 21 cents in American currency.

[39] *Burma: The Tenth Anniversary*, p. 68.

[40] See Hugh Tinker, *Union of Burma* (London: Oxford University Press, 1957), pp. 238–245, for a good discussion of this point.

because it ignores the intent of the act as stated in the law. That
the government is moving slowly and that the scope of its actions is
limited only attest to the persisting difficult conditions which have
hampered the act's implementation. Clearly, the history of the act
demonstrates the great difficulties which face the government in
carrying out legislation even when there is widespread support.

Local Government

Finally, note must be taken of the practices of local government.
At the time of independence local government was bureaucratic, with
control centered at Rangoon; the key official was the deputy commissioner or district officer, who had the widest powers in dealing
with the villages and townships below him. The various democratically
elected councils created in the 1920s were actually nonfunctioning;
village government rested in the hands of the British-appointed
headman, who was advised by the elders and the Buddhist monks in
the village. Since the nationalist leaders were wedded to the idea of
creating a new society at all levels, they proceeded—as one of their
first acts after the establishment of the independence of Burma—to
organize an inquiry committee on local government which was to make
recommendations for future government reorganization at the local
level. The committee, under the chairmanship of U Lum Baw, public
service commissioner, tendered an interim report and a model bill
in August 1948.[41] The aim of its proposals was to "create in each
village a little republic which, within the law and rules laid down
by duly-elected higher authorities, shall have full power to order
its own officers." [42] Using the model act as a basis, the government
rushed its own bill through parliament. In the haste to pass and
implement legislation—in order to meet the challenge of the insurrectionists—the bill was drafted imperfectly. After its passage the
government chose not to implement it because of the insurrection
and inability to provide continuous security anywhere outside of
Rangoon.

In 1952 a general discussion of welfare and democratic reforms
was revived at the *Pyidawtha* Conference. Here U Ba Swe, then
Defense Minister, moved that a new bill be drafted and imple-

[41] Ministry of Home Affairs, *The First Interim Report of the Administration Reorganization Committee* (Rangoon: Government Printing and Stationery Office,
1948).
[42] *Ibid.*, p. 4.

mented as conditions improved and as public receptivity increased. The renewed effort of the party and the government after the conference resulted in the drafting and passage of a new law which in 1955 the government began to put into effect. This called for an end of bureaucratic control and the establishment of a hierarchy of councils from the village to the district; the village councilors were to be elected by a compulsory vote of the inhabitants, and the township and district councils were to be elected indirectly. Powers were scheduled to be transferred gradually to the newly elected bodies which, in the end, would make them independent of the control of the central government and each council partially responsible to the one above it. In June 1956 the government released a statement pointing out the reasons why the act was taking so long to get into operation. It said that no attempt was being made in areas where law and order were not fully restored. It held, further, that there was a need to educate the people so that they would show greater interest in the act and, finally, that the existing provisions of the act must be improved through experimentation.[43] Thus, although the national leaders moved ahead slowly to create an atmosphere of receptivity among the people for a change, government below the national level remains largely the same as it was at the outset of independence a decade ago.

In the states other than Burma proper, local government is a state subject. So far none of the states has passed any local legislation, and there, too, the system of local government remains as it was before independence. Because the people in these states are politically more backward, there is little demand from them to alter the existing system. Presumably if reforms in local government can be carried out successfully in Burma proper, there will be movements to imitate them in the other states.

[43] *Burma: The Ninth Anniversary,* p. 54.

· VIII ·

Major Problems

IN many ways Burma is more fortunate than its neighbors. It has
no problem of population pressure; food is easily grown, and considerable unused arable land is still available. Burma's development
is not impeded by any rigid class or caste system, nor is there great
disparity between the wealthy and the poor. Although Burma's transportation system is neither modern nor adequate, the country does
have a river system which can be adapted to the future transportation needs of the nation.

In its attempt to create a semisocialist state, the government of
Burma has assumed responsibility for economic and social planning.
The state controls the revenues which are realized from government-
marketed exports; as the licensing body for foreign trade and the
controller of foreign exchange it determines who shall buy what from
whom. As the bearer of the national ideology it decides the education policy and makes all major decisions in the field of health and
welfare. The governing elite, not the masses, is the chief advocate
of economic development; therefore, so long as the limited wants of
the people are satisfied and they are allowed to live, more or less,
in their accustomed manner, no strong pressure from below is placed
upon the government to get on with its often unfulfilled promises.

Internal Security

Up to 1957 internal security was Burma's most serious internal problem. In the Prime Minister's speech on June 8, 1957, outlining Burma's new Four Year Plan he said that in 1951 Burma committed its first major blunder in turning its full attention and efforts away from the war against the insurgents to concern for "the national economy and social services." Even today, after mass surrenders by the insurgents, an air of fear and insecurity pervades large areas outside of the cities and garrisoned towns. The occasional derailment of a train, ambush of a motorcade, or raid upon an isolated village keeps alive the war of nerves which affects all—the farmer in the field, the worker in the rice mill, and the traveler on the road. Even though only a relatively few insurgents remain active in the field, the nature of the terrain and poor rural communications give them an advantage over the government, which must maintain large field forces in continual tracking operations. This demands a large military establishment and the diversion of resources to the military and away from civilian needs.

The government has made a sincere effort to go as far in accommodating the demands of the insurgents as is consistent with maintaining national unity. The Karens have their state, and their people are well represented in the military, governmental, educational, and other aspects of Burmese life. The members of the People's Volunteer Organization (PVO) and the various Communist organizations who revolted have largely returned to their peasant occupations or, under the Rehabilitation Program, have learned new trades and have found employment in urban or semirural areas. The government's adamant refusal to negotiate with a hard core of rebels who continue to hold their arms and demand the right to negotiate as a foreign power as well as its willingness to accept the insurgents back without loss of their civil rights is winning wide popular support.

The main problem today involves the deepness of the split in the governing party—the AFPFL—and whether or not the faction which loses power will attempt to capture it by force of arms. If both sides in the AFPFL dispute do as they say they will—accept the democratic decision of the parliament and the national election in the spring of 1959—it is possible that the problem of insurgency will not be revived on a national scale. A decade of insecurity has left the population weary of the fighting and hostile to a renewal of it; nearly twenty years of war and insurrection, however, have established a tradition of revolt and insurgency which may not disappear with pledges of peace and recourse to the electoral processes for the settlement of political disputes.

Economic Problems

U Nu's speech—mentioned above—provides still another revealing insight into the contemporary problems of Burma. He summed up his government's second blunder as "launching . . . our plans without first preparing the ground systematically." As a result he noted four negative consequences: buildings and machinery were ordered and built before plans were made for the production and supply of the raw materials; machinery was delivered before the buildings to house it were completed; in many cases this resulted in waste and inefficiency; absence of a modern accounting system and of trained accountants made it impossible to compute costs and measure the efficiency of state enterprises.

In 1958, after a decade of experimenting with socialist solutions (as understood by the Burmese), U Nu and many of his followers were ready to move toward the right in economic terms and invite capitalists to invest in the economy as long as they can be controlled and provide know-how and managerial skills. This is believed to be a temporary measure in order to build the economic base from which it will be possible to construct a socialist state in the future. It has become apparent to the governing elite that the wrong system of priorities has been followed. At the expense of agriculture, which is the mainstay of the economy, revenues in the past decade were channeled into industrial development rather than reinvested in order to improve crops and methods of production and distribution and forward diversification of agricultural production. U Nu made just this point and went on to emphasize that the change in the nature of the economy must be gradual and not at the expense of the major revenue producer—agriculture.

This re-evaluation of the economic policy has grown slowly in the minds of some Burmese leaders. Prior to 1953 Burma enjoyed a seller's market, and the government was encouraged to believe that the inflated price of rice would continue for many years to come. When the world price dropped, the Burmese did not react immediately and as a result were left with large unsold stocks. In late 1954, however, faced with more discriminating buyers and a more competitive market, they had to re-examine their whole system of purchasing and marketing arrangements. It became evident that the government-operated State Agricultural Marketing Board (SAMB) was inefficient and staffed with unqualified personnel at all levels. Without a proper accounting system its managers did not know exactly how much rice was on hand, where it was located, or what was its condition. Storage facilities were inadequate to house the crops, and much damage was caused by rodents and exposure to the weather. In addition poor milling facilities caused excessive damage to the grain, and this, too, caused Burma's export rice product to be rejected or classified as a lower grade. The SAMB is being reorganized; with the aid of cash incentives farmers are prodded into using improved seed.[1] Foreign technical aid is being used in agricultural extension work and in experimentation with new methods and seed. Belatedly, Burma is giving serious attention to what is undoubtedly its most pressing—if not its major—economic problem.

In the attempt to find new markets, Burma has had a sobering experience in trading with the Soviet Union and its satellites. Beginning in late 1954 with China and in 1955 with Russia and the other eastern European countries, Burma negotiated clearing accounts agreements by which it exchanged rice for manufactured goods. All negotiations are between states and in terms of currency; through a bookkeeping arrangement, the account is to be cleared in cash at the end of the treaty period. Thus far Burma has had its greatest success with China and Czechoslovakia and the least with Russia. The goods which were imported under these arrangements have not been up to the quality which Burma was accustomed to receiving from England, the traditional supplier. As a means of unloading rice stocks this arrangement has been satisfactory; as a means of obtaining useful and needed manufactured items it has not been uniformly successful.

Transportation was one of the hardest hit sectors of the entire economy during the war. Both the British and the Burmese spent considerable time, money, and man power in the repair, rebuilding, and replacement of old equipment and in experimenting with new methods and materials. Unfortunately the insurgents hampered the government's efforts by sabotaging the equipment and rail lines.

[1] The farmer receives 285 kyats ($59.85) per 100 baskets (4,600 pounds) regardless of the quality of his product. If he uses improved seed, he is given 5 kyats ($1.05) extra for the same quantity.

The state is continuing in its efforts, having received equipment from the Japanese under the Burma-Japan Reparation Agreement and the Joint Japan-Burma Fund for Economic Co-operation. In 1956 it obtained a loan from the International Bank of Reconstruction and Development for the reconstruction of rail facilities and harbor installations. More than this is needed, however, for Burma's motor roads are probably worse than those of any other Asian country. Little or no repair has been carried out since the start of the war in 1941. The monsoonal rains, the narrow steel-rim wheels of the ancient oxcarts, and the fighting between the government forces and the insurgents have further deteriorated what remains of a road network already badly damaged during the war.

U Nu stated in his speech of June 8, 1957, that Burma's programs for industrialization must be changed. "To step-up production in the economic field, the operation of all industrial and mining enterprises, except certain key projects, should not be entrusted solely to those who are interested in getting salaries; they should be entrusted also to those who have profit motives." He urged that the success of the joint ventures warranted extensive use of this method. In carrying out this basic change small investors should be encouraged to support these enterprises. It was his belief that such measures would help build Union solidarity because the people would have an economic stake in the community. He suggested also that Japanese reparation funds be used to purchase light machinery and supplies and that indigenous businessmen be encouraged to use this equipment for the development of cottage and light manufacturing industries. In effect Nu launched a full-scale attack upon the past economic activity of the government and called for relaxation of its rigid hold on the economy. Although Nu urged that Burma adopt a more liberal type of economic policy for the present, neither he nor his associates were ready to abandon the AFPFL's ultimate economic goals. Control will remain in the hands of the state whether through regulation or the right to buy out the private investors. Although Nu indicated that the time was not ripe to build a socialist state, he and his party look forward to that day after a proper economic base is established and the trained managerial skill is available.

Education

Education is the key building block in the creation of a new and united Burmese society. In order to prepare the public to take its place in the modern world, J. S. Furnivall—a special adviser to the Union government—in a confidential report on education prepared in 1951 said that the educational system must fulfill two objectives: it must satisfy the economic need of providing the skills and technology necessary to produce sufficient leaders and technicians to meet future needs, and it must also fill the social need of providing the training and instilling the values which will lead to the integration of the society.[2] His ideas were embodied in the educational program adopted at the *Pyidawtha* Conference in 1952. The "Education Plan for the Welfare State" which resulted from the conference [3] called for a regional expansion in school facilities and the utilization of all human and physical resources available. By the end of 1957 it was possible to see progress toward the realization of some of these goals. In Table 1 is given the government's report on the expansion in student attendance. The government reported in January 1957 that

Table 1. Public and private school enrollment in the Union of Burma

Grade of school	Pupils enrolled				
	State schools				Private schools
	1954	1955	1956	1957	1956
Primary school	737,400	1,003,400	1,155,800	1,522,187	17,975
Middle school	80,400	105,200	144,200	164,759	31,412
High school	23,200	29,800	31,700	68,001	66,759
Technical institutes	200	400	600	590	
Artisan training	125	150	250	404	
Teacher training	5,900	2,600	3,600	4,325 *	

* Includes attendance at in-service training and refresher courses.
Source: *Burma Weekly Bulletin*, n.s., VI (Nov. 28, 1957); from a chart originally published as Table 53 in *Economic Survey of Burma, 1957*, p. 278.

up to that date there had been an increase of 6,891 primary, 343 middle, and 112 high schools since the *Pyidawtha* Conference.[4]

The government clearly aspires to be the sole educator of the people. It therefore takes a negative attitude toward private education.

[2] John S. Furnivall, *Planning for National Education* (Rangoon, 1951; mimeographed).
[3] The *Pyidawtha Conference: Speeches and Resolutions* (Rangoon: Government Printing and Stationery Office, (1952), p. 98.
[4] Schools in existence in 1956 were as follows:

Grade of school	State schools	Private schools
Primary	10,226	200
Middle	415	204
High	220	210

In the postwar period the Baptists, who for decades served as teachers
for the Karens and other peoples of Burma, were denied permission
to open a new intermediate college after Judson College—formerly
their institution—had been integrated with the University of Rangoon.
The English-language high schools are under pressure to give more
training in Burmese, and all private schools must register with the
government. Although parents recognize the superior training offered
by some of the private schools, enrollment in them is decreasing as
pressures increase to send all children to public schools.

Because the state has attempted to make rapid strides, serious problems have arisen as a result of inadequate planning and failure to
prepare the people for the numerous changes. Because schooling is
free to all and the best job opportunities are open to those with a
degree or certificate, there has been a tremendous expansion in the
student bodies of the schools. To meet this demand the government
established an emergency teacher program which has proved to be
grossly insufficient. Most of the teachers are inadequately trained and
poorly paid and look upon the job as an interim occupation leading
to a better position. An absence of books and other teaching materials has handicapped those who would like to do a competent
job. In addition the archaic nature of the vernacular language makes
it necessary to use English to explain concepts and ideas which as
yet are impossible to describe in Burmese. Since English is not
taught until the fifth grade and then only as a second language,
most of the students are unqualified to pursue higher studies which
require competency in English. Thus, although a new engineering
college has been erected and technical and vocational schools have
been built and opened, many students hesitate to enter because they
are unable to follow instruction which, in the main, is in English.[5]
The problem of student discipline caps all others as it is a gauge
which measures the unrest and instability of the society. The students
are restive and assertive because their future is unclear. Agitated on

[5] In 1957 an educational inquiry commission was formed by the government to
make recommendations for the improvement of the educational system. Among
the decisions announced on April 4, 1958, were the following: the English examination in the matriculation exams would be adjusted to the comprehension possible for students who started to learn the language in the fifth grade; Burmese
should be the language of instruction for the first two years of university work
beginning in 1960; English will remain the language of instruction for Honors
work and Master's candidates. The newspapers announced that the decision of
the government had the prior approval of the AFPFL Executive Committee. See
the *Nation*, April 4, 1958, p. 1.

all sides by politicians and insurgents and their plight publicized in the press, the students are uncertain of their responsibilities, status, and freedom. No one will quarrel with Nu regarding his suggestion of June 1957 that education must become nonpolitical; no one, however, has found a way to divorce politics from education.

National Unity

The decade of independence and insurrection has had a dual impact upon the nation. Having forged the Union out of divergent and, in many cases, conflicting ethnic and religious groups, the government has been charged with arrogance and disregard for the minorities; at the same time it has been accused of catering to the minorities at the expense of the dominant Burmans. An element of truth lies in both extremes. It is a fact that the Union is intact and relatively stable; but discontent exists in many areas and underlines the fact that a uniformly strong common national feeling has not emerged throughout Burma. According to the constitution the Shan and Karenni states can secede from the Union if an overwhelming desire is manifested in a popular vote by the leaders and the people of those states. This has not developed as yet, and probably never will. In spite of the publicity which a few of the chiefs in Shan State have received in their talk of withdrawing, the majority of the Shan chiefs and people are loyal to the Union and recognize that their fortunes are directly linked with it. The majority of the chiefs are willing to go along with the Union's demand for more democratization in their state, and they agreed on August 18, 1951, to transfer their remaining powers to the people of their state. By mid-1958 the chiefs still had not transferred their powers because of their still unmet demand for compensation. Since the Union government is now willing to pay some compensation and has earmarked funds to pay the Shan chiefs, no real secession movement seems likely to develop. In Karenni—now officially designated the Kayah State—no such movement is afloat, nor is there talk of any.

It is among those who lack the legal right to secede from the Union that real discontent is harbored. The largest minority, the Karens, made their military bid in 1949 to withdraw and establish an autonomous state, and they failed. Today they have a state with their own elected leaders in the Union of Burma. The President of the Union is a Karen, and he stands as a symbol of political unity between the Burmans and the Karens. Further, the Karens have not been discriminated against in high offices in education and in government. Even the army includes a large number of Karens as officers and soldiers. Although there is a political cleavage among the Karens over who shall lead them, the leadership has gone by default to the younger men who supported the AFPFL and stood for compromise when the insurrection erupted. The Karens, as a community, still are dissatisfied with the small size of their state, its location, and the fact that it is not viable economically and that it does not include some of the rich delta area where Burmans, Mons, and Karens are intermingled. Some resent the fact that, although education is a state subject, they do not enjoy complete freedom of action because they must teach and use Burmese in the schools in order to enable their young people to enter the universities. There is a genuine feeling of resistance to this indirect process of Burmanization in which the dominant language, religion, dress, and customs are becoming more widespread. Some Karens have a feeling of helplessness in the face of this tide. What will probably continue to keep the two communities apart for years to come is the recent history of bloody civil strife; the majority of Karens want peace, but the continued existence of guerrilla Karen forces (KNDO) gives hope to the dissident Karen elements who have not become reconciled to contemporary realities.

The Arakanese and Mons present a different kind of problem. They are agitating for separate states or autonomous regions. The territory included in Arakan is inhabited by a mixture of Arakanese, Indians, and Pakistanis. Only in certain areas are the Arakanese a majority. They are bitter toward the AFPFL for having sent "carpet-bagger" politicians as administrators and men of authority. In addition they feel that the Union government discriminates against them in administration, education, and appointments to office. The chief Arakanese complaint is that they have not received treatment equal to other minorities. They have grown rigid in their demands for statehood and more vocal in their efforts to win popular support. Until June 24, 1958, the government's policy toward them was different from its policy toward the Karens; it was adamant in its refusal to give special consideration to Arakanese complaints, although Arakanese claims were investigated by the 1948 Regional Autonomy Inquiry Commission. Because of the mixed nature of the population in the Arakan region, the problem would not be disposed of by creating a new state. The problem of the Mons, too, is not easily disposed of for many of the same reasons noted in the case of the Arakanese. The government and the Arakanese could not find common ground and a new basis for discussion before the present AFPFL split caused U Nu to invite three Arakanese, formerly opposed to his government, into his cabinet. Although he still is opposed to separate states for ethnic minorities, the Prime Minister announced publicly in June that "as the Shans, the Kachins, the Kayahs, and the Karens have their own States, I will not stand in the way any longer, if the Mons and the Arakanese want separate States. If there is a distinct and clear evidence that . . . [they] desire separate States, I promise we will try our utmost to make it possible for the creation of Mon and Arakanese States." [6] A month after this statement over one thousand Mon rebels took advantage of the government's offer of amnesty, surrendered, and were welcomed back into the society. A few weeks later, on August 22, 1958, the government declared their political organization, the Mon People's Front (MPF), a legal organization because it "demonstrated the change that had taken place in its policy, from that of pursuing an armed insurrection to that of confining its activities within democracy." [7] Both moves toward favorable consideration of minority claims will help remove some of the long-existent tensions in Burmese society.

Two alien minorities should be mentioned in connection with the problem of national unity—the Indians and the Chinese. The Indians, who wish to become citizens of the Union, have not found it easy. Some 40,000 have made application, but only about 6,000 so far have received citizenship.[8] Those who have citizenship demand the rights of citizens—especially property rights, which in Burma mean the right to own and operate businesses and have a share of the nation's import and export licenses. Many Burmese refuse to think of the nationalized Indian as a Burmese. They resent his differences in dress, occupation, religion, and way of life. Burmanization has had only a minor effect upon the Indians, and even so only upon small groups or upon individuals. An example of Burmese attitudes is found in the case of U Raschid, who has been the Minister of Trade and Mining and held other major offices. Although Nu has the utmost faith in him and has entrusted him with numerous important missions and responsibilities, the leaders of the Burma Chamber of

[6] Ministry of Information, *Burma Weekly Bulletin*, n.s., VII (July 3, 1958), 88.
[7] *Ibid.*, n.s., VII (Aug. 28, 1958), 151.
[8] *Hindu Weekly Review*, Nov. 4, 1957.

Commerce protested his appointment as Minister of Trade. The man in the street still sees U Raschid as an Indian; he does not accept him even though he was active in the Nationalist movement beginning in the mid-thirties as a coleader with Aung San and U Nu in student politics at the University of Rangoon.

The problem of the Chinese minority is different. Despite the fact that the Chinese way of life, their dress, and their language are unlike those of the Burmese, the Chinese are looked upon with greater favor than the Indians. More intermarriage takes place and less racial tension exists than between the Indians and the Burmese. To the "average" Burmese the Chinese are like distant cousins regardless of the fact that they may act and look different. Even though the Chinese compete in business, they too are faced with the domination of Indians in a number of commercial fields. Only recently, in the face of large-scale illegal Chinese immigration, is the Burmese attitude beginning to become less receptive than in the past.

So far the Union has not blended the indigenous people into any real national unity; nor have the aliens who live among them been accepted. For a decade the government has been pursuing a dual policy toward this problem. On the one hand, it seeks to Burmanize the nation and is trying to blend the diverse groups into one by using a common language, reviving and missionizing Buddhism, and encouraging the adoption of Burmese dress and culture. On the other hand, it is consciously pursuing a policy of diversity in unity. That is, the principal minority peoples have been given their own states, with their leaders in charge, they have control over education up to the university level, and they have been permitted to preserve much of their culture. All faiths—Eastern and Western—have their places of worship and have the use of public facilities when they are needed. Religious minorities, such as the Catholics, have received Union aid for religious activity. Political minorities are not discouraged so long as their activities are legal. On every front the government can point to actions which bear out this conscious policy of allowing diversity among the people with respect to relatively minor issues in the hope of developing unity among them on the larger issues of loyalty and national identity. This formula is not fully effective, however, because the minorities, aware of an ever-increasing Burmanization, are not convinced that the government will continue to acquiesce to cultural diversity in those matters not of central importance to national unity.

Foreign Relations

Three problems absorb the thinking and energies of the Burmese leaders in their relations with the outside world. Two immediate considerations are their relations with China and the marketing of Burmese products in order to pay for outside materials and technical assistance. The third problem—the prevention of a third world war and the maintenance of peace in Asia—is the overriding concern and provides the element that gives unity to Burmese foreign policies.

There are several key assumptions implicit in Burma's foreign policy. It is believed that war will not solve world problems, but will complicate them, perhaps even destroy civilization. The alignment or neutrality of individual small nations will not count for much in the total picture; moreover, each such alignment with power blocs contributes to the increase of world tensions. A corollary to this is the belief that alignment will compromise the independence of Burma and therefore must be avoided. Burma's leaders recognize that in order to obtain the internal objectives of building a new and better society their country must have outside technical and material aid; they will accept such aid provided they are regarded as equals of the donor and provided that acceptance does not imply commitment to any military or power bloc. Finally, they believe that their moral force can provide a small, but important contribution to the maintenance of world peace. These assumptions are predicated on the following conditions: Burma's small size and population; its location between two giants, China and India; its economic needs; memory of the last war and the devastation that it wrought.

Without question the main problem is Burma's relations with China —most immediately, the border dispute and the illegal immigration of Chinese. The border issue is a legacy of the colonial period when the British and the Chinese were unable to agree on its complete demarcation. The dispute was precipitated in 1948 when the Nationalist Chinese government refused Burmese payment of rent for a border area "perpetually" leased from China under a treaty agreement between Britain and China in 1897.[9] The border territory received world-wide attention in 1956 when a leading Burmese English-language newspaper made public that Chinese Communist troops had occupied the disputed area. The government, through diplomatic channels, moved to find a solution and even sent the temporarily

[9] The territory is the Namwan Assigned Tract. See the map of Burma.

retired Prime Minister, Nu, to Peking to negotiate with the Chinese. Nu returned with a tentative settlement plan which called for Burma to surrender the leased territory and three Kachin border villages in exchange for China's recognition of the Burmese version of the rest of the border between the two nations. This settlement has not received ratification and negotiations continue, but there has been a lessening of tension, and both nations have pulled back their troops.

Although the border dispute is highly important, an equally serious and less noticeable issue is developing as a result of the illegal immigration of Chinese across the border and the smuggling of goods in and out of Burma. A steady stream of Chinese continues to move from South China into Burma where they become absorbed in the resident Chinese community. The Burmese authorities are constantly making arrests and deportations, but the influx greatly exceeds those expelled, and as a result the feeling of anxiety and fear created by this problem is augmented by the suspicion that the Chinese government does nothing to discourage its continuance. Akin to this problem is the increase of smuggling, ranging from opium to manufactured goods. Since Burma needs to hold down imports in order not to drain its dwindling reserves of revenues, the influx of luxury items has adversely affected the economy.

In the face of these "Chinese problems" it is important to note the nature of formal relations between the two countries. Burma has been completely correct in its behavior toward China. It was the first nation to recognize the new government of the Communists and has consistently advocated the seating of the present regime in the United Nations. The Communist Chinese too have been proper neighbors in a formal sense. When the Kuomintang Nationalists escaped from China into Burma and launched attacks against China from their sanctuary, the Chinese Communists did not try to follow these enemies into Burma or request permission from Rangoon to do so. Instead Peking left the matter up to the Burmese, who are still wrestling with the problem—one that continues as a potential source of friction between Peking and Rangoon. On the purely diplomatic side there have been repeated exchanges of missions—diplomatic, cultural, sports, and so on—which have taken place between the visit of Chou En-lai in 1954 and the visit of the Deputy Prime Ministers of Burma, U Kyaw Nyein and U Ba Swe, to Peking in December 1957. Both countries are pledged to uphold the "Five Principles"—mutual respect for each other's territory and sovereignty, nonaggression, noninterference in each other's internal affairs, equal and mutual benefit, and peaceful coexistence. They have signed trade agreements and established a regular air-line service between the two countries. In spite of this apparent Chinese good will the Burmese are anxious to find a definite solution to their China problem so that the tensions will relax and the threat of war will recede.

Outside the range of immediate problems but important to Burma are its relations with India. India, as Burma's other large immediate neighbor, is the counterpoise to China. Although there are unsettled problems between the two, the personal good will which exists between Nu and Prime Minister Nehru creates an atmosphere of friendship and respect which has helped the two nations solve some of their problems. India helped Burma in its hour of need by selling weapons to the Burmese government when the insurrection began in 1948, by informing Burma of a plot between two English adventurers and the Karens prior to the Karen revolt, and by offering Burma a substantial loan during its financial crisis of 1955. In addition India still remains, as it was before the Second World War, Burma's best rice customer. In spite of the good will on the leadership level the Indians are unhappy about Burma's treatment of their countrymen and Burmese failure to settle Indian property claims. Moreover, some Burmese are critical of their preseparation debt with India and of the settlement which was made in 1954. The political reality of Burma's need of India as a counterweight to China has helped it to move closer to India—at least on the diplomatic and political levels.

In securing aid, both technical and material, to augment its own economic resources, Burma would prefer to pay from funds realized from the sale of its own products. Its earnings are not, however, sufficient. Burma has received significant economic aid from international organizations and through bilateral agreements. One of the first nations to provide aid under a bilateral arrangement was the United States through its Economic Co-operation Administration. In 1956 it agreed to sell $21 million worth of surplus agricultural products for Burmese currency. This provided Burma with much-needed cotton and foodstuffs without draining foreign exchange reserves. In addition the United States agreed to buy from Burma with American currency 10,000 tons of rice to be distributed in Pakistan, and the Burmese promised to use the money to pay for American technical assistance. In 1957 the United States agreed to lend Burma $25 million in U.S. currency and $17 million in Burmese currency on a long-term basis for use in economic expansion and development. Russia has not overlooked the opportunity of building friendship with Burma through gifts and aid. When Khrushchev and Bulganin visited Burma in 1955, they promised to build a sports stadium and a technical institute for training Burmese in scientific agriculture and to establish tractor stations. At the same time the Burmese insisted upon giving the Russians a gift in return—rice. In January 1958 Russia gave Burma a loan of from 20 to 30 million kyats (approximately $4.2 to $6.3 million) for two irrigation dams and 15 million kyats (approximately $3.1 million) for the establishment of a farm-implement factory. China at the same time gave Burma a loan of 20 million kyats for a textile factory. Under the Colombo Plan the Burmese have received both material and technical benefits. Burma has tried to hold to its principles in that it has accepted aid and loans from all quarters and at the same time has tried to preserve its independence of action.

In his travels around the world U Nu has spoken favorably of the United States to the Chinese and Russian leaders and of those two countries when he visited America. As a participant in an informal Asian arrangement whereby the Prime Ministers of Burma, Ceylon, India, Indonesia, and Pakistan met irregularly and informally to discuss mutual problems, Burma was a cosponsor of the much-publicized Bandung Conference in 1955 in which Communist China participated with other Asian nations in the general discussions. Via religion Burma expanded its relations with its Asian neighbors; for two years (1954–1956) a Buddhist synod was in progress in Rangoon, and all Theravada Buddhist nations were invited to participate and take over a portion of the leadership responsibilities. Cambodia, Laos, and Thailand sent large delegations of ecclesiastics and political figures to Burma; better understanding between these nations appears to have resulted. The Burmese Socialists have been active as sponsors of the Asian Socialist Conference wherein leaders from all countries can exchange ideas and become better acquainted with one another's culture and aspirations; the conference also has provided the Burmese with an unofficial forum to try out their policy ideas.

In Burma's effort to promote world peace and the easing of world tensions, it has worked both within and without the United Nations. In the United Nations, Burma stood with the West and condemned Russian brutality in Hungary in 1956 and voted to accept the United Nations report on the Hungarian uprising in September 1957. It exercised its independence by voting to condemn the actions of England, France, and Israel in Egypt in 1956 and has voted to seat Red China in the United Nations at every session in which the question has been raised. Burma's attitude has been based squarely upon personal knowledge of what war can do to the people and the economy of a country. Consequently Burma has sided with small nations which were victims of aggression, because it tends to project itself into the position of the invaded nation.

Because Burma stands between India and China and because it must trade with East and West to earn the income needed to pay for the welfare state which the leaders have promised the people, foreign relations will rank as the most important problem to face Burma for many years to come.

SUGGESTED READING

OFFICIAL PUBLICATIONS OF THE UNION OF BURMA

Central Statistical and Economics Department. *Quarterly Bulletin of Statistics.*

Economic and Social Board. *Pyidawtha: The New Burma.* Rangoon, 1954. A report on Burma's economic plans.

Ministry of Home Affairs. *Interim and Final Reports of the Administration Reorganization Committee.* 2 vols. Rangoon, 1948–1951.

Ministry of Information. *Burma.* A quarterly; every January issue is called the Anniversary Number and contains a survey of events during the year past.

——. *Burma Weekly Bulletin.*

——. *Kuomintang Aggression against Burma.* Rangoon, 1953.

Ministry of Natural Planning. *Economic Survey of Burma.* Issued annually at the time that the budget is being considered by parliament.

Union Bank of Burma. *Monthly Review.*

——. *Quarterly Bulletin.*

NEWSPAPERS AND PERIODICALS

Atlantic, Special Supplement, CCI, no. 2 (Feb. 1958), 99–170. An excellent cross section of contemporary political and social leaders who discuss current problems and trends in Burma.

Burman.

Guardian. Both daily and monthly. The monthly is developing into the most important monthly in Burma and draws articles from Western writers as well as Burmese.

Nation.

New Times of Burma.

V: The Historical Background

Baxter, James. *Report of Indian Immigration.* Rangoon: Government Printing and Stationery, 1941. An official report on Indian immigration made just prior to the Second World War.

Cady, John F. *A History of Modern Burma.* Ithaca, N.Y.: Cornell University Press, 1958. Especially good development of the period of colonial rule in Burma.

Christian, John L. *Burma and the Japanese Invader.* Bombay: Thacker and Co., Ltd., 1945. A rewritten version of the author's earlier study, *Modern Burma*, with new material about Burma and the Second World War. Excellent bibliography.

Collis, Maurice S. *Last and First in Burma.* London: Faber and Faber, 1956. Drawn from official papers supplied by former Governor Dorman-Smith, it attempts to explain the Governor's actions during the 1945–1946 period.

———. *Trials in Burma.* London: Faber and Faber, 1938. A good firsthand account of British rule during the 1930s by a former civil servant.

Donnison, F. S. V. *Public Administration in Burma.* London: Royal Institute of International Affairs, 1953. A brief but useful summary of the growth of the British administrative system in Burma; very pro-British. Written by a former British civil servant.

Furnivall, John S. *Colonial Policy and Practice.* New York: New York University Press, 1956. A comparative study of colonialism in Burma and Indonesia. The Burma section expands the thesis propounded in the author's *Political Economy* with much new material added.

———. "The Fashioning of Leviathan: The Beginning of British Rule in Burma," *Journal of the Burma Research Society,* XXIX (1939), 1–137. An excellent account of the efforts of the British colonial administrators to establish their authority in Tenasserim in 1826.

———. *An Introduction to the Political Economy of Burma.* Rangoon: Burma Book Club, 1931. The first effort to apply an economic analysis to Burma; a strong criticism of British rule. Recently reprinted in Burma.

Hall, D. G. E. *Burma.* London: Hutchinson's University Library, 1950. A good short history.

———. *Europe and Burma.* London: Oxford University Press, 1945. A short diplomatic history of Burma's relations with the West.

Harvey, Geoffrey E. *History of Burma from the Earliest Times to 10 March 1824.* London: Longmans Green, 1925. A very good history of precolonial Burma with detailed and well-documented notes at the end of the text.

Maung Maung. *Burma in the Family of Nations.* Amsterdam: Djambatan, Ltd., 1956. A short history of Burmese diplomacy. The appendicies contain many documents which are extremely difficult to obtain.

Mountbatten, Louis. *Report to the Combined Chiefs of Staff by the Supreme*

Commander, South-east Asia 1943–5. London: H.M. Stationery Office, 1951. Official report of the recapture of Burma by the Allies in the Second World War.

Nu, Thakin. *Burma under the Japanese.* Ed. and trans. by J. S. Furnivall. New York: St. Martin's Press, 1954. A firsthand account of Burmese politics and society during the Second World War.

Pe Maung Tin and Gordon E. Luce. *The Glass Palace Chronicles of the Kings of Burma.* London: Oxford University Press, 1923. A translation of the Burmese royal chronicles describing the period of the Pagan dynasty; excellent example of precolonial indigenous historical writing.

Sens, Nirmal C. *A Peep into Burma Politics, 1917–1932.* Allahabad: Kitabistan, 1945. A good short study of Burmese politics during the period of political awakening among the peoples of Burma.

Silverstein, Josef. "Transportation in Burma during the Japanese Occupation," *Journal of the Burma Research Society,* XXXIX (1956), 1–17.

Sutton, Walter D., Jr. "U Aung San of Burma," *South Atlantic Quarterly,* XLVII (1948), 1–16. A short biography of Aung San with emphasis upon the last five years of his life.

VI: The Contemporary Setting

Andrus, James R. *Burmese Economic Life.* Stanford: Stanford University Press, 1948. Excellent survey for the period prior to independence.

Brant, Charles. *Tadagale: A Burmese Village in 1950.* (Southeast Asia Program, Cornell University, Data Paper no. 13.) Ithaca, N.Y., 1954.

Dobby, E. H. G. *Southeast Asia.* 2d ed. New York: John Wiley Co., 1951. Chapters ix, x, and xi are devoted to Burma; best geographical study of Burma available.

Hanks, Lucian M. "The Quest for Individual Autonomy in Burmese Personality," *Psychiatry,* XII (1949), 285–300. Work of a social psychologist based on wartime experience in the Arakan area.

Knappen, Tippetts, Abbett, McCarthy. *Comprehensive Report: Economic and Engineering Development of Burma.* 2 vols. Rangoon, 1953. A survey undertaken by American engineers and economists for the purpose of developing and recommending an economic plan.

Leach, Edmund R. *Political Systems of Highland Burma.* London: G. Bell and Sons, 1954. Based upon a field study; provides a detailed and interesting study of Kachin social and political life.

Marshall, Harry. *The Karen Peoples of Burma: A Study in Anthropology and Ethnology.* Columbus: Ohio State University Press, 1922. The best study of the Karens available.

Mi Mi Khaing. *Burmese Family.* Calcutta: Longmans Green and Co., 1946. A very readable account of Burmese life and customs written by a well-to-do Burmese.

Shwey Yoe (pseud. of J. G. Scott). *The Burman: His Life and Notions.* London: Macmillan, 1910. A standard work on Burman customs, dress, and society.

Tinker, Hugh. *The Union of Burma.* London: Oxford University Press, 1956. A general survey of politics, economics, and society in Burma from 1948 to 1956.

Trager, Frank N., and others. *Burma.* 3 vols. New Haven: Human Relations Area Files, Inc., 1956. A general survey of Burma with contributions by authors who have visited Burma and have a continuing interest in the country. This study is very uneven in quality.

VII: The Political Process

Brohm, John. "Burmese Religion and the Burmese Buddhist Revival." 2 vols. Doctoral dissertation, Cornell University, 1957; to be published soon by the Monograph Board of the Association for Asian Studies. Vol. II includes the best study available of the contemporary relationship between religion and Burmese politics.

Christian, Winslow. "Burma's New Constitution and Supreme Court," *Tulane Law Review,* XXVI (1951), 47–59.

Constituent Assembly of Burma, *The Constitution of the Union of Burma.* Rangoon: Government Printing and Stationery Office, 1948; also reprinted in A. J. Peaselee, *Constitutions of Nations,* 2d ed. 3 vols., The Hague: M. Nijhoff, 1956. Neither copy of the constitution includes any of the amendments to the law.

Gledhill, Alan. "The Burmese Constitution," *Indian Yearbook of International Affairs, 1953* (Madras), II (1954), 214–224. A good summary of the main provisions in the constitution with special emphasis on the sources of the document.

Maung Maung, "Portrait of the Burmese Parliament," *Parliamentary Affairs,* X (1957), 204–209.

Nu, U. *Burma Looks Ahead.* Rangoon: Ministry of Information, 1953.

——. *Forward with the People.* Rangoon: Ministry of Information, 1955.

——. *From Peace to Stability.* Rangoon: Ministry of Information, 1951.

——. *Toward Peace and Democracy.* Rangoon: Ministry of Information, 1949. This and the three foregoing works form a collection of Nu's speeches which indicate his political philosophy and trace the first seven years of Burma's independence.

Silverstein, Josef. "Politics in the Shan State: The Question of Secession from the Union of Burma," *Journal of Asian Studies,* XVIII (Nov. 1958), 43–58.

——. "Politics, Parties, and the National Election in Burma," *Far Eastern Survey,* XXV (Dec. 1956), 177–184.

Subramanian, N. A. "Some Aspects of Burmese Constitutional Law," *Indian*

Yearbook of International Affairs, 1956 (Madras), VI (1957), 123–155.

Thomson, John S. "AFPFL—Continuity in Burmese Politics," *Antioch Review*, XVII (1957), 297–313.

Tinker, Hugh. "Nu, the Serene Statesman," *Pacific Affairs*, XXX (1957), 120–137.

Trager, Frank N. "The Political Split in Burma," *Far Eastern Survey*, XXVII (Oct. 1958), 145–155.

VIII: Major Problems

ECONOMIC PROBLEMS

Allen, Robert L. "Burma's Clearing Accounts Agreements," *Pacific Affairs*, XXXI (1958), 147–164. A comprehensive analysis of Burma's experience in trading with Russia, China, and the satellites.

Hagen, Everett E. *The Economic Development of Burma.* Washington: National Planning Association, 1956.

Lloyd, J. "Planning a Welfare State in Burma," *International Labor Review*, no. 69 (Aug. 1954), pp. 117–147.

Lockwood, Agnese N. "Burma's Road to Pyidawtha," *International Conciliation*, no. 518 (May 1958), pp. 385–450.

Thet Tun. "Outline of a Socialist Economy for Burma," *Journal of the Burma Research Society*, XXXVII (1954), 59–76.

Trager, Frank N. *Building a Welfare State in Burma.* New York: Institute of Pacific Affairs, 1958.

CULTURAL PROBLEMS

Fairbairn, Geoffrey. "Some Minority Problems in Burmese Politics," *Pacific Affairs*, XXX (1957), 287–313. A brief examination of minorities in Burma, especially the Shans and the Arakanese.

Kyaw Thet. "Burma: The Political Integration of Linguistic and Religious Minorities," in P. Thayer, *Nationalism and Progress in Free Asia.* Baltimore: Johns Hopkins Press, 1956.

——. "Cultural Minorities in Burma," in H. Passim, ed., *Cultural Freedom in Burma.* Rutland: C. E. Tuttle Co., 1956.

Thompson, Virginia, and Richard Adloff. *Minority Problems in Southeast Asia.* Stanford: Stanford University Press, 1955. Problem of minorities discussed by groups rather than by country, therefore presenting some interesting and revealing comparisons.

FOREIGN RELATIONS

Fifield, Russell H. *The Diplomacy of Southeast Asia; 1945–58.* New York: Harpers and Co., 1958. Pages 167–229.

Hinton, Harold C. *China's Relations with Burma and Vietnam.* New York:

Institute of Pacific Affairs, 1958. A well-documented short historical account of diplomatic relations which attempts to trace a line of continuity between the past and the present.

Kozicki, Richard J. "The Sino-Burmese Frontier Problem," *Far Eastern Survey,* XXVI (1957), 33–38.

Thant, U. "Burmese View of World Tensions," *Annals of the American Academy of Political and Social Sciences,* no. 318 (1958), 34–42.

Thomson, John S. "Burma: A Neutral in China's Shadow," *Review of Politics,* XIX (1957), 330–350.

——. "Burmese Neutralism," *Political Science Quarterly,* LXXII (1957), 261–283.

Tinker, Hugh. "Burma's Northeast Borderland Problems," *Pacific Affairs,* XXIX (1956), 324–346.

Trager, Frank N. "Burma's Foreign Policy, 1948–56: Neutralism, Third Force, and Rice," *Journal of Asian Studies,* XVI (Nov. 1956), 89–102.

——, P. Wohlgemuth, and Lu-yu Kiang. *Burma's Role in the United Nations, 1948–55.* New York: Institute of Pacific Relations, 1956.

PART THREE : INDONESIA

By Herbert Feith

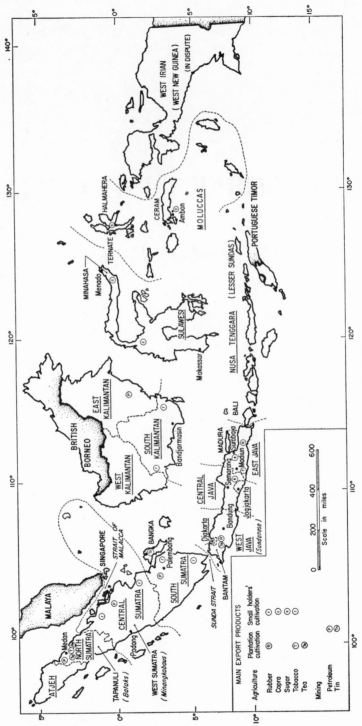

Map 3. Indonesia

· IX ·

The Historical Background

THE patterns of history are everywhere the creatures of geography; Indonesia is no exception. Its location, its archipelago nature, the calmness of its seas, the ruggedness of its mountains, and the volcanic fertility of its soils—all these have had profound effects on the civilizations of which today's Indonesia is heir. They are of great importance, too, in relation to the political context in which these civilizations have evolved.

Indonesia is situated on the trade route between China on the one hand and India, Western Asia, and Europe on the other. Thus for millennia it has been the center of trading empires and the recipient of a diversity of cultural influences from outside. But because it straddles the world's largest and most scattered archipelago, Indonesia as a unit must do battle with geography to maintain itself. With its seas international waterways, it has traditionally been exposed to every kind of penetration from outside—except at those times when its shores have been controlled by a power with considerable naval strength. The calmness of its seas, more easily traversible than many a rugged stretch of its land, has ensured a continuity of cultural contact and interchange between the peoples of the different islands. But the seas have nevertheless been an important obstacle in the way of achieving and maintaining a political unity covering the whole archipelago.

Finally, Indonesia is a tropical country par excellence. Heavy rain-

fall characterizes almost the whole of its area. Much of it outside
Java is covered by tropical forest. But where young and active vol-
canoes have created and continue to create great soil fertility, as in
Java, intensive agriculture has been able to develop. Indonesian history, acted on this geographical stage, may be regarded as a series of
interactions between the naval power required for an all-Indonesian
empire and the military and bureaucratic power which could be
established on the basis of the intensive agriculture of Java.

Early History

If the theories most widely accepted today are correct, the ancestors
of the great majority of Indonesians came to the archipelago in suc-
cessive waves of immigration from mainland Southeast Asia and
South China in the two thousand years before the Christian era. At
the beginning of the Christian era Indonesian society was in the New
Stone Age and the Bronze Age, and some iron was used. Wet rice
agriculture was practiced in a number of areas, and the ox and
buffalo had been domesticated. The Indonesians possessed considerable navigational skills and were probably already playing an active
role in inter-Asian trade. Small monarchical states held power in the
port towns and over the villages of the wet rice valleys. In the mountains and much of the plain country dry rice agriculture by shifting
cultivation provided the basis of economic organization, and the clan
was the central political unit. It is probable that such characteristically
Indonesian means of cultural expression as the wayang puppet theater,
the gamelan orchestra, and the batiking of cloth date back to this
period.[1] Spirit worship was the main religious form.

In the first three centuries A.D., Hinduism came to the archipelago,
and with it Buddhism. How its impact was made is still a subject of
considerable controversy among historians. It is clear that there was
no mass migration from India to Indonesia or any political conquest
of the archipelago. Some of the Hindu religious and cultural impact
came through Indian traders who settled in Indonesian ports. Much
of it is believed to have come through small groups of Indian
Brahmans who were invited to positions of influence at Indonesian
courts.[2] But certainly the impact was major—in the field of religious

[1] D. G. E. Hall, *A History of South East Asia* (London: Macmillan, 1955), p. 8.
[2] J. C. van Leur, *Indonesian Trade and Society* (The Hague: van Hoeve, 1955),
pp. 249 ff.

practice, in literature and architecture, and also in the techniques of organization of the state and of religious legitimation of kingly authority.

The first clear picture of Indonesian political organization is in the seventh, eighth, and ninth centuries. It is a picture of sometimes two, sometimes four or five, major kingdoms, centered on the islands of Java and Sumatra and claiming suzerainty and in some cases tribute from a much larger number of smaller principalities throughout the Indonesian archipelago and on the Malay Peninsula.

Shrivijaya, centered on the east coast of South Sumatra, was probably the most powerful of these kingdoms. In the late seventh century it held territory on the Malay Peninsula and in West Java as well as in Sumatra. By naval power it was able to control much of the trade flowing between China on the one hand and India and the Arab world on the other through the two important straits of Malacca and Sunda. Within the archipelago its commerce held a dominant position, and its ships traveled to both India and China. Shrivijaya was a Buddhist kingdom and an important center of Buddhist learning.

The other main center of political power in this period was the Central Java kingdom of Kalinga. It was this kingdom which bequeathed to the world the most magnificent of Indonesia's architecture including the Borobudur, an eighth-century Buddhist monument, and the ninth-century Hindu temple at Prambanan. These monuments attest not only to the artistic greatness of its civilization but also to the complexity of its governmental organization and the size of the labor force available to its rulers: Borobudur has three miles of galleries and four hundred statues of the Buddha.

The pattern of the states of Indonesia throughout the period of Hindu and Buddhist royal authority and later under Islam—in fact until Dutch military and naval power was able to play a decisive role in the archipelago's politics—may be seen in terms of two main types, of which Kalinga and Shrivijaya serve as examples.[3] The kingdoms of the Kalinga type were inland states centered on Java. Their wealth and power were based on wet rice agriculture on the volcanic plains of the east and central parts of the island, on the exchange of labor services and crop tithes for irrigation, and on a quasi-hereditary bureaucracy with military as well as administrative functions.

[3] *Ibid.*, pp. 104 ff.

The kingdoms of this type played no major role in inter-Asian trade, but the later ones did participate in the interinsular trade of the archipelago.

The states of the Shrivijaya type, on the other hand, were coastal states whose power was not military and bureaucratic but naval and commercial. These states did not exercise authority over large land areas, nor did they build large waterworks. But they sponsored extensive royal and patrician trade, exploiting Indonesia's strategic position astride the principal routes of inter-Asian commerce.

Throughout this long period, however, a large number of Indonesians lived beyond reach of the main states. The sway of the major Javanese kingdoms rarely involved the exercise of governmental power over a majority of the population of that island. In much of Java, as in almost all parts of the other islands of the archipelago, the dominant economic pattern was not wet rice but dry rice agriculture, based on systems of shifting cultivation. In these areas clan organization played a central role, and few large political units existed.

Furthermore most kingdom and empires attained little stability of governmental power. An empire would arise as one of a large number of petty local rulers established wider powers, exacting tribute and a certain degree of obedience from other local rulers by dint of repeated punitive expeditions against them. It would fail as he failed, either militarily or in terms of retaining the local rulers' loyalties. Political power over more distant territories was, in Wertheim's words, "confined . . . . to periodical embassies carrying gifts from the vassal to the suzerain. . . . The transition from internal to external relations between princely rulers was a gradual one." [4]

The greatest of the old Indonesian empires, which lives in the minds of Indonesian nationalists today, was the fourteenth-century empire of Majapahit. Based on East Java, this was predominantly an inland state. Yet it developed considerable naval as well as military strength. At the height of its power it ruled Java, Bali, and Madura and probably parts of Sumatra, Kalimantan (Borneo), Sulawesi (Celebes), and the Moluccas. But Majapahit's power too was relatively short-lived. It disintegrated as geography gradually asserted its dominance over technology and administration, and a plurality of major states reappeared.

The final fall of Majapahit in the early sixteenth century was

[4] W. F. Wertheim, *Indonesian Society in Transition* (The Hague: van Hoeve, 1956), p. 52.

closely related to the appearance of a new factor in the archipelago's politics, Islam. Communities of Moslems from the Arab countries and India had traded and lived in Indonesia for several centuries. Their religion was adopted by Indonesian merchant nobles and princes at a time of world-wide expansion of Islam's political power, when its influence was growing rapidly in India at the expense of Hinduism.

Successful first in several North Sumatran trade ports and in Malacca on the Malay Peninsula, Islam quickly expanded eastward in the late fifteenth and the sixteenth centuries. By the end of the 1530s some rulers as far east as the Moluccas had become Muslims, and Hindu Majapahit in East Java had fallen before a coalition of Muslim commercial states on Java's north coast.

Like Hinduism, Islam spread because of its value in legitimizing political power and aspirations. But unlike Hinduism it brought few major technical innovations. It did, however, result in the introduction of a written code of law. And its gradual penetration into Indonesian religious, cultural, and social life in the course of the next four centuries has wrought profound effects. These effects were in a sense all the greater because Hindu and animist beliefs and practices were clung to by many, both nobles and peasants, who nominally came to be Muslims. For this created the basis of a social and religious dualism which was to become of major importance in the present century.[5]

The Coming of the West

The early sixteenth century saw also the beginnings of European expansion in Indonesia. The first Europeans, the Portuguese, were concerned with entering and monopolizing the much-coveted trade in the spices of the Moluccas, the "Spice Islands." At the same time they sought to spread Catholicism and to wage the world-wide battle against Islam. From the time of their capture of the important Islamic center of Malacca in 1511 they engaged in intensive military exploits in the archipelago for seventy years. They did not succeed in monopolizing the spice trade completely, but gained enormous profits from it nevertheless. Their missionary successes, on the other hand, were modest in the extreme. Rather than winning them converts, their penetration induced a rapidly increasing number of

[5] B. J. O. Schrieke, *Indonesian Sociological Studies*, II (The Hague: van Hoeve, 1957), 232 ff.

Indonesian princes to accept Islam as a political counter to their power.[6]

Following the Portuguese came the Dutch. Arriving at the very end of the sixteenth century, the Dutch came to the Indies with a single intention, to trade. To do this they had to wrest the spice trade from the Portuguese and to hold it against the competition of British, Indonesian, and other Asian traders. But the Dutch East India Company, engaged in the military and navel ventures which this made necessary, was essentially a commercial concern. To build and keep a monopoly it had to establish forts and maintain garrisons in various parts of the archipelago; it also had to control certain small Moluccan islands territorially if it was to restrict spice output in order to maintain high prices. More than this it did not want to do. It had no lust for territorial expansion.

But in Indonesia as in India, the powerful commercial and maritime position which the Western joint-stock company gained was a standing challenge to the interests and prestige of the states of the area. These states—particularly the inland kingdom of Mataram in Central and East Java and the port-centered commercial and maritime powers of Bantam in West Java, Atjeh in North Sumatra, and Ternate in the Moluccas—were by no means weak in relation to the Westerners. Thus the seventeenth century saw the Dutch company forced more and more into military and political activity—against the wishes of its directors in Amsterdam. By the end of the century not only did it hold several Moluccan islands and forts at a number of points on the Moluccan trade route, but also its control of the straits of Malacca and Sunda had had the effect of weakening many of the Indonesian states. And from its center of Batavia it had succeeded in dominating the ports on the north coast of Java.

The eighteenth century saw a further consolidation of the company's power in Java. For most of this century it was receiving tribute from the petty rulers of the island, as Mataram had in the sixteenth and seventeenth centuries. But although dominating Java, it administered only a small part of it directly. In fact its governmental impact was in many ways similar to that of the Javanese empires. This period did see the introduction of coffee and sugar cultivation, however, on a system of forced deliveries. It saw also the rapid growth of the hitherto small Chinese community, a community now

---

[6] Van Leur, *op. cit.*, p. 113; see also Harry J. Benda, *The Crescent and the Rising Sun* (The Hague: van Hoeve, 1958), pp. 14 ff.

used by the company as intermediaries in tax collection and middle-man trade. And it saw the concomitant decline in the trade of the indigenous Javanese.

Outside Java the company's power did not grow. In Sumatra a number of coastal principalities became its vassals, but in general it exercised little influence on this island.[7] In the second half of the century its hold on interinsular commerce grew weaker, its officials became more and more corrupt, and there were sharp rises in its debt. By 1799 this debt stood at 134 million guilders, and its charter was about to expire. The charter was not renewed; instead the Netherlands government took over its holdings and its debts.

There had been few premonitions in these first two centuries of Dutch penetration of the radical transformation that it was later to bring about. Only with severe qualifications can one speak, in the language common to both parties in the Indonesian-Dutch debate of this century, of "three hundred and fifty years of colonial rule."

The Nineteenth Century—Deepening Colonial Penetration

A deepening of the Western governmental and economic impact developed in Java in the early part of the nineteenth century. This began as an indirect result of the Napoleonic wars—first between 1808 and 1811, when the Dutch Bonapartist Marshal Daendels governed the Netherlands' Indonesian possessions on France's behalf and later between 1811 and 1816 under Lieutenant-Governor-General Raffles in the period of the British interregnum. In this period many new roads were built, and rural administration was systematized and made more intensive. Raffles' monetary land taxes brought with them the first direct contact between the government and the village heads of the island.

But the crucial acceleration of the pace of change came after the colony reverted to Holland in 1816, and particularly after 1830, with the introduction of extensive forced cultivation under what is known as the "Culture System." Now unchallenged in its political dominance in Java, Holland could organize the systematic and intensive exploitation of the island's land and labor. Thus the Javanese peasant was obliged to grow commercial crops for the government—legally on one-fifth of his land, in practice generally on two-fifths or more.[8]

[7] Van Leur, *op. cit.*, pp. 110–116.

[8] See John S. Furnivall, *Netherlands India* (New York: Macmillan, 1944), pp. 115 ff.

As a revenue-raising technique this was a magnificent success. Between 1834 and 1877 Netherlands India made a net contribution of
837,400,000 guilders to the Dutch treasury. In Java the system
brought enormous economic change. The island now came to produce
a great variety of crops—coffee, sugar, tea, tobacco, indigo, cinnamon,
and cotton. A number of these could be grown only on large estates.
But several others, notably sugar, were grown on village wet rice
fields, sugar crops alternating with rice crops. This system of rotation was highly profitable to the government and so gave it an interest
in furthering the process whereby the system of wet rice cultivation
was spreading to almost every part of the island. Thus an interest
in irrigation arose. Here one sees an important connection between
the Culture System and the phenomenal rise in Java's population in
the nineteenth century. Irrigation works and the extension of wet rice
agriculture, combining with civil security, pest control, and the communications improvements which made more effective famine relief
possible, were the principal factors explaining how the island's
population, an estimated 4.5 million in 1815, had risen to 28.4 million
by 1900.

The Culture System also had important political consequences. It
forced the government to have large-scale influence in the affairs of
the village. A considerably expanded European civil service supervised the growing and delivery of the crops. At the same time the
system made it important for the government to maintain and
strengthen the authoritarianism of local rule. The Indonesian regents,
quasi-feudal petty rulers who had been in large part incorporated
into the Dutch civil administration, were accorded a substantial stake
in the system. They were readmitted to acknowledged hereditary
status and given both grants of land and a share of the crops produced
by the villagers. For the next hundred years and more the regents,
with the Indonesian section of the Indies civil service which centered
round them, formed a major instrument of colonial power and authority. Inside the village, the village head's position was strengthened. Javanese trade declined further, now becoming definitely subordinate to Chinese trade.

From the 1850s there was strong criticism of the Culture System
in the Netherlands, on both economic and humanitarian grounds.
By the 1870s Dutch colonial policy was made by the representatives
of a newly vigorous industrial capitalism which sought easier investment and a larger market in the Indies. The result was the gradual

abolition of forced cultivation for the government, the passing of control over cultivation from government officials to private contractors, and an increase of investment in private plantations. But the vestigial Javanese commercial class was too weak to avail itself of the opportunities provided by the new laissez-faire situation. On the contrary, the new economic order further increased the numbers and power of its already dominant competitors, the resident Chinese merchants and moneylenders.

No fundamental changes were made in the governmental structure developed under the Culture System. The central task of the civil administration, both European and Indonesian, remained the same— to create and maintain conditions under which both land and labor were supplied cheaply for the cultivation of commercial crops. More and more money penetrated the Javanese village, undermining the subsistence character of its economy. But many of the corroding effects of this on the existing social order were countered by government pressure in favor of traditional social and political relationships.

The "outer islands" experienced colonial government very much later than Java. It was, in fact, only in the last thirty years of the nineteenth century that large areas of these islands were brought under effective Dutch control. By the 1870s the Dutch government had come to fear that other European powers would establish themselves in the archipelago if it did not extend and intensify its influence. In addition it had come under pressure from Dutch industry searching for raw materials. So in the following decade it pressed the rulers of the remaining principalities in Sumatra, Kalimantan (Borneo), Sulawesi (Celebes), the Lesser Sunda Islands, and West New Guinea to sign treaties virtually placing themselves under Dutch control. Most rulers acceded to such pressure. Where one did not, the government resorted to military action. The result was a number of minor wars and one major, long, and costly war against Atjeh in North Sumatra.

By 1909 Dutch authority was established over almost all of what was to be known as Netherlands India. In most of the newly acquired areas existing rulers were allowed to retain their positions and some of their internal governmental functions. But at the same time the European civil service was given wide powers, not only of supervision and intervention, but of direct administration in a number of fields such as road and dam building, forestry, and the control of village budgets.

The Twentieth Century—The "Ethical Policy"

As the nineteenth century drew to a close in a series of economic depressions it was clear that the further development of Dutch enterprise in the Indies, and particularly outside Java, required that the government provide business with a variety of new ancillary services. At the same time a wave of humanitarian indignation in the Netherlands at the officially admitted trend of declining welfare in the Indonesian population led to pressure for a new colonial policy. Thus in 1901 there was born the "Ethical Policy" whereby the government would play a direct and active role in providing a variety of economic and social welfare services.

As a result of the Ethical Policy exploration and surveying were intensified, railways and roads were built, and interinsular shipping was expanded. Schemes were initiated for forest conservation, soil development, veterinary improvement, and the expansion of agricultural and fisheries production. Irrigation was further extended and public health work expanded.

In terms of social development probably the most important of all these efforts to modernize the country was in the field of education. In 1900 no more than 1,615 Indonesian children were attending Dutch-language primary schools, the only type which provided significant access to Western ideas. The total number in village primary schools, many of them Christian missionary schools recently established in the outer islands, was then only 150,000—in a total population of approximately 35 million.[9] To meet the rapidly rising demand of the civil service and private agencies for Indonesian personnel with elementary clerical and technical skills, the government began to establish large numbers of village schools. More important still, it relaxed somewhat its restrictions on admission to Dutch schools. The door was opened to the rise of a small but crucially important new class of Indonesians with Western education.

Government welfare services provided under the Ethical Policy and the increasing world demand for tropical products which arose in the first decades of this century combined to attract a large flow of new investment. British and American as well as Dutch investors channeled capital into the colony—into such Java-grown crops as sugar, coffee, and tea and, more particularly, into the products characteristic of the outer islands, tobacco, rubber, tin, and oil. Outside

[9] *Ibid.*, pp. 367–368.

Java, and especially in areas such as East and South Sumatra, estate agriculture and mining developed rapidly, creating whole new communities.

The same period saw a dramatic development of export agriculture carried on by Indonesian small holders in many parts of the land-rich outer islands. In Sumatra and Kalimantan shifting cultivators began to grow rubber for overseas markets, and in Sulawesi and the Moluccas they planted coconut palms in order to export copra. Here was one way in which colonial rule had dynamic economic effects. In many parts of the outer islands, mostly areas where trading groups had continued to play a relatively important role, the early twentieth century saw a significant expansion of Indonesian entrepreneurship.

The history of Indonesia in the years between 1901 and 1942 is the history of contradictions in the Ethical Policy. The Ethical Policy modernized Indonesia. It provided a variety of welfare services to the Indonesian population. The comprehensiveness of the paternalistic Dutch administration, the thorough training of its personnel, and the high technical standards of its specialized services were probably successful in preventing further falls in levels of living. The policy produced increasing prosperity in parts of the outer islands. In general it enabled agricultural production to keep pace with the continuing rapid growth of population—at least until the last years before the Second World War. By virtue of its respect for authoritarian social and political institutions it did not allow a large-scale disorganization of village society such as developed, for instance, in parts of Burma. Nor did it allow the development of a large landowning class, as in the Philippines. But its conservatism resulted, in Java at least, in a stifling of dynamic economic growth. By bolstering traditional social patterns, the Ethical Policy prevented the village capitalistic development which the money economy was tending to produce.[10]

The policy created two dynamic new social groups, however, the Indonesians of Western education and the smaller group of capitalistic small holders of Sumatra and to a lesser extent Sulawesi and Kalimantan. In this way it put an end to the period of merely passive Indonesian reactions to the colonial impact. But this meant that it had created its own heirs; and by this time the legacy had become all

---

[10] See Clifford Geertz, *The Social Context of Economic Change: An Indonesian Case Study* (Cambridge: Massachusetts Institute of Technology, Center for International Studies, 1956); John S. Furnivall, *Colonial Policy and Practice* (New York: New York University Press, 1956).

too precious. Economically, the Netherlands was more dependent on its colony than any other Western colonial power in Asia. Its nationals had investments there worth approximately 2,634 Dutch guilders ($1,300 million).[11] In addition the community of Netherlanders resident in Indonesia was relatively very large—208,269 in 1930 if Eurasians are included—and all of the community, Eurasians as well as "full-bloods," had a strong interest in the colonial relationship.

A sharp conflict of interests thus developed. The new Indonesian social groups, particularly those with Western secondary and higher education, grew strongly resentful of the caste structure of colonial society which rated them as the permanent inferiors of the Europeans and frequently denied them the positions for which they were trained. At the same time they were increasingly aware of their ability to rally support from the mass of the population. The European population of the Indies became more and more concerned to protect its privileges.[12]

The Rise of the Nationalist Movement

Conflict between a rising Indonesian nationalism and a colonialism determined to defend its central interests was the major theme of political history in the crucial decades before the Second World War. The theme unfolded with the rise of a variety of nationalist parties and organizations. The first of these, Boedi Oetomo (Noble Endeavor), a body advocating educational, cultural, and economic uplift, was established in 1908. It attracted some thousands of members, mainly from aristocratic groups in Java—civil servants and secondary school students—but drew relatively little mass interest.

Four years later the first directly political organization was established, the Islamic Association (Sarekat Islam). Its impact on the hitherto apparently tranquil society of the colony was much more dramatic. A militantly nationalistic organization, anti-Dutch, anti-Chinese, opposed to the Indonesian aristocracy and demanding complete independence, Sarekat Islam was led by merchants and lowly born members of the new group of the Western-educated. With branches in many parts of Sumatra and Sulawesi as well as in Java, it claimed a membership of almost two and a half million (in 1919).

[11] This was the 1940 figure; from Sumitro Djojohadikusumo, *Persoalan Ekonomi di Indonesia* [Economic Problems in Indonesia] (Djakarta: Indira, 1953), p. 8.

[12] Wertheim, *op. cit.*, pp. 148 ff. For a discussion of social and psychological aspects of this conflict see Soetan Sjahrir, *Out of Exile* (New York: John Day, 1949).

Its village appeal was in fact principally reactionary, representing peasant antagonism to increasingly rapid economic and social change and expressed through traditional village religious leaders.[13] But at the same time it afforded a massive demonstration of the ability of the urban nationalist leadership to canalize agrarian discontent.[14]

As early as 1917 there existed inside the Sarekat Islam a Marxist group with Dutch as well as Indonesian leadership, and in 1920 a part of this group transformed itself into a Communist Party. Tension soon developed between the Communist and non-Communist branches of Sarekat Islam, and in 1921 members of the Communist Party were prohibited simultaneous membership in the Islamic Association. The subsequent struggles between the two now separate organizations, together with increasingly effective government efforts to bar the access of political leaders to the mass of the people, resulted in a great weakening of the organized hold of nationalism on the peasantry. In late 1926 and early 1927 a section of the Communist leadership launched a minor revolt in West Java and Central Sumatra, and this gave the government an opportunity for severe repressive measures. Large-scale Communist activity was thus brought to an end. The Sarekat Islam became much less active at the same time.

Specifically Muslim political energies were henceforth more frequently channeled through organizations with a more strongly religious character. The most important of these were the urban-centered Islamic reform organization Muhammadijah and its more strongly rural traditionalist rival, the Nahdatul Ulama. Though primarily concerned with religious and social welfare activities, these two large organizations, and particularly the modernist and Western-education-minded Muhammadijah, were important agents of the growth of national self-consciousness.

But at the same time the center of anticolonialist politics was shifting to a third major current which was neither Communist nor specifically Islamic. In mid-1927 a group of students and recent graduates in Bandung, led by the young engineer Soekarno, established the Indonesian Nationalist Party (PNI). Many of the group had studied in Holland and had there become involved in the nationalist "Indonesian Association"; others had been active in small nationalist study clubs in Indonesia. The new organization demanded complete

[13] Benda, *op. cit.*, pp. 42–45.
[14] George McT. Kahin, *Nationalism and Revolution in Indonesia* (Ithaca, N.Y.: Cornell University Press, 1952), p. 66.

Indonesian independence. To achieve this it urged self-reliance and nonco-operation with the Dutch authorities. Thanks in part to Soekarno's oratorical ability, its influence expanded rapidly. The government reacted in 1929 by arresting its leaders and ordering the dissolution of the organization.

A number of smaller nationalist organizations continued to function. Some of their leaders persisted in attempts to follow the Soekarno policy of organizing a mass following. Others like Hatta and Sjahrir, recently returned leaders of the Indonesian Association in Holland, concentrated on the training of small nationalist cadres. But under a governor-general who believed that "we have ruled here for 300 years with the whip and the club and we shall still be doing it in another 300 years," [15] these organizations were severely hampered in their activities. All of them were seriously affected by a new wave of arrests and exilings in 1933 and 1934. This resulted in the banishment of Soekarno, Hatta, Sjahrir, and many others to remote parts of the archipelago, a banishment from which they were to be released only with the coming of the Japanese.

Nationalist political activity continued. But by the middle 1930s its main focus had shifted from politics to such fields as journalism, social welfare work, co-operatives, and particularly education. The government, its budget reduced by the depression and its fear of Indonesian intellectuals steadily mounting, curbed educational expansion.[16] For Indonesian nationalists this became a central political issue. In order to help provide wider educational opportunities and at the same time propagate their own ideas, many of the nationalist leaders became teachers in private schools. Many taught in the schools of the modernist Muslim Muhammadijah, many others in those of the secular nationalist educational body Taman Siswa.

The government had made a beginning with representative government in 1918. It had agreed then to the existence of a People's Council, an advisory body whose membership would be partly nominated and partly elected, but indirectly and on the basis of a small and racially delineated franchise. In 1931 it agreed that Asians—Indonesians and

[15] Governor-General de Jonge in 1936, quoted in Sjahrir, *op. cit.*, p. 112.

[16] In 1939–1940, there were 2,178,732 Indonesians receiving vernacular primary education and 88,223 primary education in Dutch; 42,941 were receiving secondary education (lower secondary in the large majority of cases), and 637 university education (*Statistical Pocketbook of Indonesia, 1941* [Batavia: Kolff, 1947], p. 22). In the same year the number of Indonesians graduating from tertiary institutions in the country was 37 (Kahin, *op. cit.*, p. 32).

"Foreign Orientals" together—should have a majority on the Council. But beyond this point there was no progress. The Council remained an advisory body. Its wishes could always be overridden by the Governor-General. The nonco-operating section of the nationalist movement boycotted it.

In 1936 the People's Council called for a conference to discuss plans for the development of Indonesia over a ten-year period toward self-government within the limits of the existing Dutch constitution. But the request was rejected by the Netherlands government. Even after the Nazi invasion of Holland in 1940, Indonesian nationalists were offered no more cause for hope than a vague statement that there would be a reorganization of the Indies' relations with the Netherlands after the war.

What little legislative experience Indonesians obtained under Dutch rule was in the politics of virtually permanent opposition. At the regional level, as at the level of the country as a whole, there were few opportunities for Indonesians to participate actively and share responsibility. Regional legislative assemblies existed, but they were popularly elected bodies only in one or two areas specially favored by the Dutch, such as Minahasa in North Sulawesi and Ambon in the Moluccas—areas with a large Christian population and high literacy which had become recruiting places for the colonial civil service and particularly the army. And in fact the importance of regional councils was small, for the government functioned with a high degree of centralized control from Batavia.

Even in village government there was little effective democratic participation. In formal terms village heads were popularly elected, at least in Java. In reality hereditary or quasi-hereditary succession remained the normal pattern throughout the archipelago. Moreover, the scope of effective autonomy had declined sharply as a result of the administrative changes of the Ethical Policy.

Similarly in the government service Indonesians played a relatively small role. There were no Indonesian governors and but one Indonesian department head. In 1940 only 221 of the 3,039 civil service positions classified as "higher rank" were held by Indonesians.[17] The armed forces were virtually closed to Indonesians till shortly before the Japanese attack, unless they came from the specially privileged areas such as Minahasa and Ambon. No Indonesian was allowed to be even a middle-ranking officer. Unlike its neighbor colonial powers, Great

[17] Kahin, *op. cit.*, p. 34.

Britain and the United States, Holland did not accept the necessity of a future cession of self-government to its colony.

The Japanese Occupation, 1942–1945

When the Japanese inflicted their quick defeat on the Dutch in early 1942 and moved in to occupy the archipelago, they inaugurated a period of momentous change. The three and a half years of military and naval occupation shook the foundations not only of the governmental structure which the Dutch had laboriously built, but of society itself. Its catalytic effects were even greater.

Soon after the Japanese arrived, they arrested the great majority of the European residents of the colony. After humiliating them publicly, they placed them in camps for the rest of the occupation. Their places were at first taken by Japanese officers. As the numbers of these did not suffice, however, Indonesians had to be found. They were fairly soon brought into government posts higher than they had occupied under the Dutch.

To rally Indonesian support for their war effort, the Japanese attempted to use the popular leaders of the nationalist movement and of Muslim organizations in their propaganda work. Many of these leaders, most prominently Soekarno and Hatta and a number of important leaders of the old Sarekat Islam, the modernist Muhammadijah, and the traditionalist Nahdatul Ulama, co-operated. They did so even after they had become disillusioned with Japanese rule, partly because of necessity and partly also because they saw that they could in turn obtain concessions from the Japanese, both for their own interest groups and for the general development toward Indonesian independence.

Through the secular nationalist leaders and the Muslim leaders the Japanese established mass organizations with branches throughout village Indonesia. But significantly they maintained a separation and a competition between the organizations under each of these two sets of leaders. Thus they welded Indonesian Muslims into a greater unity, bringing the Muhammadijah and the Nahdatul Ulama into a single Muslim mass organization, Masjumi. At the same time they sharpened the long-standing divisions between the actively Muslim community on the one hand and on the other the less positively Muslim social groups who found political leadership in aristocratic and secular nationalist elements.[18]

[18] Benda, *op. cit.*, pp. 103 ff.; see also Willard H. Elsbree, *Japan's Role in South-*

The organizational burgeoning under the Japanese was particularly marked at the level of youth. Quasi-military youth organizations, established both on an Islamic and a secular basis, imbued a large group of the youth of Indonesia with a radical and anti-Western nationalism. At the same time they were provided with a knowledge of, and respect for, the techniques of totalitarian government.

In September 1943 the Japanese authorities in Java and Sumatra established an Indonesian-officered auxiliary army. By 1945 this numbered about 120,000 men.[19] Thus far more Indonesians acquired military experience than at any time in the Dutch period, and Indonesian nationalism acquired a source of great potential power. Japanese encouragement of the Indonesian language, the modernized Malay sponsored by the prewar nationalist movement as a future national language, added further to the potential strength of nationalism.

Japanese rule was both ruthless and inefficient. By their frequent confiscations of food, their secret-police methods, and their arbitrary beatings, by the fact that they took perhaps as many as 300,000 Indonesians out of the country to do forced labor on the Asian mainland (from which many were never to return), and by their inability to check a runaway inflation or relieve severe conditions of famine —in all these ways the Japanese caused tremendous social dislocation and earned the intense hatred of the great mass of Indonesians, peasants in particular. This hatred flared up in a number of local insurrections. It also provided considerable opportunities for the left-wing nationalist-led underground contact organizations, which gained strength particularly toward the end of the occupation.[20]

But it was through the leaders who co-operated with the Japanese that Indonesian nationalism was given its strongest stimulus. The Japanese authorities made possible an unprecedented degree of organizational contact between the urban nationalist leaders who worked with them and the mass of the village population. This was so particularly beginning in late 1944 when the Japanese were being forced to retreat from much of the South Pacific. Then they promised Indonesian independence "in the very near future" and relaxed many of their earlier restrictions on the propagation of Indonesian nationalism. At the same time they began to open high administrative posts to

---

east Asian Nationalist Movements (Cambridge, Mass.: Harvard University Press, 1953), pp. 76 ff.

[19] Kahin, *op. cit.*, p. 109.   [20] Sjahrir, *op. cit.*, pp. 244 ff.

Indonesians, both to persons from the old aristocratic civil service and to some of the younger group of nationalist intellectuals. In March 1945 they allowed the establishment of an Investigating Committee for the Preparation of Independence, and in early August an Indonesian Independence Preparatory Committee, both bodies headed by Soekarno and Hatta.

Thus the Japanese occupation, a shattering experience in many ways, did help to produce a situation from which it was possible to go on to the achievement of independence. At the same time it contributed to the necessity that this should be achieved by revolutionary means.

The Revolution, 1945–1949

On August 17, 1945, two days after the Japanese surrender, Soekarno and Hatta proclaimed the Republic of Indonesia. Within three weeks the new Republic, of which Soekarno became President and Hatta Vice-President, had a temporary constitution, an advisory Central National Committee of 135 men, a cabinet responsible to the President, and the support of virtually every group in Indonesian society, including all of the anti-Japanese underground organizations. Before the end of September it had succeeded in wresting arms from a large number of Japanese soldiers and in establishing a functioning administration in most parts of the country, an administration in which young intellectuals and university and secondary school students played a major role.[21]

But Holland was in no way prepared to accept an independent Indonesia. Regarding the Republic as a Japanese creation, the Dutch government expected to be able to overthrow it quickly and hurried troops to the area.

The first Allied troops, the British, landed in Java in late September. Already the Republic was showing its preparedness for revolutionary action by the determination with which it was fighting for whatever arms and local power the Japanese still held. But the revolutionary potentialities of the situation became actual when Dutch troops landed under British cover a short time later. By the end of the year there was widespread Dutch-Indonesian fighting throughout the archipelago. Indonesian resistance was particularly effective in Java and Sumatra, where the Japanese had given Indonesians substantial military training.

The last three months of 1945 saw also a series of major govern-

[21] Kahin, *op. cit.*, pp. 134 ff.

mental and political developments inside the Republic. The Central National Committee was given legislative powers. The presidential cabinet headed by Soekarno was replaced by a new cabinet responsible to the Central National Committee and led by the former underground leader, Sjahrir. In response to an official call for a multiparty system, a number of parties and party-associated organizations were established or re-established.

Thus there came into existence the Masjumi (Consultative Council of Indonesian Muslims) led by many of the leaders of the wartime Masjumi and also by a number of "religious socialists" who had not been prominent in the older body. At the same time the second Indonesian Nationalist Party arose, led by many of the leaders of the 1927 PNI of Soekarno, a number of them men who had held prominent positions in the Japanese period. The Socialist Party, led by Sjahrir and a fellow underground worker, Amir Sjarifuddin, emerged as a powerful party with a strong youth organization. The Indonesian Communist Party was re-established. At the same time several organizations of national-Communist political orientation sprang up and quickly attained prominence as leaders of the demand for a radically nationalist policy of nonnegotiation with the Dutch.

The new Sjahrir cabinet was prepared to negotiate with the Dutch, as were all of its successors. But there was strong domestic pressure against this, much of it from military units—both of the army proper and of guerrilla organizations—which the government could not fully control. In this situation, with two governments functioning alongside one another, each claiming sovereignty over the country as a whole, clashes were unavoidable. Thus the years 1946–1949 were a time of intermittent negotiation and fighting.

In the course of 1946 the Netherlands established control over a number of cities and surrounding areas in Java and Sumatra, but the great majority of the people of these two islands continued to be governed by the Republic. Outside them the Dutch were more successful, being able to suppress nationalist military resistance and to exercise governmental functions. From the middle of 1946 onward they began a process of establishing in the areas under their control states which would ultimately, the Dutch said, be members of a federal state of Indonesia.[22]

Repeated negotiations produced only limited agreement. At the

[22] A. Arthur Schiller, *The Formation of Federal Indonesia* (The Hague: van Hoeve, 1955). See also Kahin, *op. cit.,* pp. 351 ff.; Hubertus J. van Mook, *The Stakes of Democracy in Southeast Asia* (New York: Norton, 1950), pp. 219 ff.

end of November 1946 British pressure on the two parties resulted in the signing of the Linggadjati Agreement, by which Holland agreed to recognize the Republic as the *de facto* authority in Java and Sumatra and consented to co-operate with it toward the achievement of a sovereign federal Indonesia. But this agreement, which was strongly criticized by many on both sides, was little more than an agreement to agree. It provided few answers to immediate problems and frictions.

By July 1947 the Dutch had 150,000 soldiers in Indonesia. Then, charging the Republic with failure to comply with the Linggadjadi Agreement, they lodged a full-scale attack on parts of its territory. India and Australia launched protests against this action with the United Nations Security Council. But the Council merely called for a cessation of hostilities and established a three-man Good Offices Committee to help toward a resolution of the conflict. The Dutch were permitted to retain the areas which they had been successful in wresting from the Republic, which included most of the important estate and mining areas in Java and Sumatra. When in January 1948 the pressure of the United States chairman of the Good Offices Committee resulted in the signing of a second negotiated agreement, the Renville Agreement, the terms merely reflected the weaker military position of the Republic. Like the earlier Linggadjati Agreement it failed to put an end to the fighting.

Meanwhile Sjahrir had left the prime ministership. Under his successor, Amir Sjarifuddin, the leader of the pro-Communist wing of the Socialist Party (whose non-Communist wing was led by Sjahrir), there was a considerable rise in the strength of the Indonesian Communist Party and groups of similar outlook. This resulted in part from economic deterioration produced by the Dutch blockade of Republican territory and the influx of large numbers of refugees from the Dutch-held areas.

After the signing of the Renville Agreement in January 1948 Sjarifuddin's cabinet fell and was replaced by one led by Hatta, a cabinet composed mainly of ministers of the Muslim Masjumi and the nationalist PNI. Soon afterward strong tensions developed between this cabinet and a left-wing coalition of parties led by Sjarifuddin, which opposed the cabinet's policy of continued negotiation with the Dutch. The tensions grew when in August 1948 Musso, a leader of the Indonesian Communist Party in the 1920s, returned dramatically from a long exile in the USSR and quickly succeeded in merging the left-wing coalition into an expanded Communist Party of which he assumed leadership.

The situation came to a head in September; at that time a group of second-echelon Communist leaders at Madiun in East Java proclaimed a revolt against the Soekarno-Hatta government. The uprising lasted little more than a month, but bloody battles were fought before the Republican government suppressed it. Musso was killed in action. Amir Sjarifuddin and a number of other important leaders were subsequently executed. Indonesian communism suffered an important setback.[23]

In December 1948 the Dutch launched a second major attack on the Republic. With blitz tactics, heavy arms, and air support they quickly captured the Republic's capital, Jogjakarta, in Central Java, and seized most of its top leaders, including Soekarno and Hatta, to exile them on the island of Bangka, off Sumatra. Further, they succeeded in establishing control over all the cities and larger towns in Java and most of those in Sumatra, though certainly not of the surrounding village areas or the road system.

This time, however, the response of the Security Council was much more strongly anti-Dutch. World opinion had been aroused, and the U.S. Congress was exerting pressure for America to take a stand against the Netherlands. With the Communists scoring victory upon victory in China, U.S. State Department thinking was beginning to place more emphasis on the importance of Asia. Moreover, there was a change in the department's attitude toward the Indonesian Republic after the Republic had shown itself ready and able to suppress a Communist revolt.

The following year saw a gradual but decisive turn of events. Republican guerrilla resistance was so vigorous that it was virtually impossible for the Dutch to administer the territory they had newly acquired. Republican scorched-earth policies were increasingly dangerous to Dutch business interests in the country. These factors, combined with growing U.S. pressure on The Hague and the threat of a suspension of Marshall Aid, finally persuaded the Netherlands to change its policies basically. Thus in the course of 1949 the Dutch government came to accept the necessity of transferring full sovereignty to Indonesia and of transferring it to an Indonesia which, though federal in constitutional form, would probably be dominated politically by the Republic.

The terms of this transfer were eventually worked out in a Round

[23] Kahin, *op. cit.*, pp. 256–303. See also Ruth T. McVey, *The Soviet View of the Indonesian Revolution* (Cornell Modern Indonesia Project, Interim Reports Series; Ithaca, N.Y., 1957), pp. 58–83.

Table Conference between the Netherlands, the Dutch-sponsored federal states, and the Republic, held at The Hague between August and November 1949. Arrangements were made at that conference for the coming into existence of the federal Republic of the United States of Indonesia (RUSI), to consist of the fifteen Dutch-created states and the Republic, but with the latter in a clearly dominant position. To this state Holland would transfer sovereignty over the Netherlands Indies "completely, unconditionally and irrevocably."

But the Round Table Conference agreement was yet a compromise settlement. It had proved impossible to arrive at any agreement with regard to the future of West New Guinea (West Irian); therefore the Indonesian delegations conceded that the *status quo* should prevail there, with the stipulation that the area's political status would be determined through negotiations between Holland and Indonesia in the course of the next year. The Indonesian delegations agreed also to the creation of a Netherlands-Indonesian Union—which was, however, an organization without substantive powers. They agreed that the new state should extend a number of guarantees to Dutch investors in Indonesia and to personnel of the Dutch and Netherlands Indies administrative services, that it should continue to maintain consultative relations with Holland in the case of major financial decisions, and, most important, that it should take over the large Netherlands Indies debt of 4,300 million guilders (nearly $1,130 million). These were major concessions which continued to be criticized strongly in Indonesia for a long time. But the prestige of Soekarno and Hatta and the support of the two major parties, Masjumi and PNI, ensured their acceptance.

Political Developments since Independence

On this basis the federal Republic of the United States of Indonesia was established on December 27, 1949. Soekarno was sworn in as its President and Hatta emerged soon afterward as its Prime Minister. He headed a cabinet selected largely without heed to party, including Masjumi and PNI men, a number of nonparty ministers, and five ministers, chosen from the federal states.

Very soon, however, it became clear that the federal structure of Dutch-established states, many of them geographically and politically unreal units, was crumbling with the victory of the revolutionary Republic and the departure of the Dutch. Most of the leaders of the federal states were quickly persuaded to accede to the strong popular demand for a unitary Indonesia. Within a little over seven months the RUSI structure had been negotiated out of existence and replaced by the unitary Republic of Indonesia. Where the transition was marred by violence, as in parts of West Java, South Sulawesi, and the Moluccas, this was the result more of rear-guard actions of units of the Netherlands Indies army than of popular opposition to the unitary state. Conflicts of regional interest existed, but the Dutch attempt to harness them failed. Nationalism was by far the stronger force.

From 1950 political power has been in the hands of the leaders of the 1945 Republic. This group, however, has become increasingly divided in the course of exercising power in socially diverse Indonesia. In the early postrevolutionary period political power was shared mainly between the Masjumi and the nationalist PNI. These were the two largest parties in the temporary parliament, the Masjumi having 47 seats and the PNI 35—in an assembly of 234 members. The Masjumi headed the first two cabinets of the unitary state, and the PNI the next two. The Socialist Party of Sjahrir, much smaller, with 15 representatives in parliament, was able to exercise considerable indirect influence particularly through sections of the Masjumi and PNI in sympathy with its ideas. The Communist Party, with 14 members and some support from a number of other parties, was still weak in mass support, following its defeat at Madiun in 1948 and the brief arrest of several thousands of its members and supporters by the Masjumi-led government of Dr. Sukiman in August 1951. But its strength grew rapidly from 1952 onward. That was also the year of the establishment of the Nahdatul Ulama as a political party. This conservative Islamic religious and social organization, which had been a constituent of the Masjumi of the Japanese period and of the post-1945 Masjumi, then announced its existence as a separate party and withdrew its eight parliamentary representatives from the Masjumi group in the House. It was not then regarded as a major force, but with its great success in the 1955 elections it emerged as the country's third-largest party.

In addition a large number of smaller parties have continued to play an important role. For a cabinet to have a working majority it has usually been necessary to include the representatives of many parties. Sharp conflicts have arisen between the parties of the coalitions and frequently inside these parties. In a number of cases cabinets have had to capitulate in the face of conflict with such extraparliamentary centers of political power as the President, the army and the leadership of particular regions. No less than seven cabinets have held office since December 1949, none for longer than two years. In general cabinets have been weak and unable to take resolute action on contentious issues except at the risk of being overthrown.

For some time it was hoped that the country's first general elections would produce political crystallization, a greater measure of stability, and thus a government in a stronger position to act firmly in tackling the country's pressing problems. When elections were held in 1955 —both for parliament and for a Constituent Assembly—they did produce a certain crystallization. The new House of Representatives with 260 members is dominated by four parties, the PNI and the Masjumi with 57 seats each, the Nahdatul Ulama with 45 seats, and the Communist Party with 39. The numerous small parties which had exercised considerable influence before the elections gained little representation. But the elections did not produce political or governmental stability. The resulting disappointment undermined faith in constitutionalism.

In the two years before the elections the unity of the nationalist leadership was further weakened by a process of party polarization. Electioneering greatly widened the gap between the Masjumi and the PNI, with the Communists and the Nahdatul Ulama aligned with the PNI and the small Socialist Party aligned with the Masjumi. The same period saw an increasing rift between President Soekarno and Vice-President Hatta, the former more and more a partisan of the PNI, the latter becoming more closely linked with the Masjumi.

In early 1956, just after the elections, the attempt was made to close the gap. A cabinet of all the major non-Communist parties took office under Prime Minister Ali Sastroamidjojo of the PNI. But deep-seated divisions continued to exist. The new cabinet proved itself as incapable as its predecessors to deal resolutely with the host of problems facing it. Before long it began to reap the fruits of a rapidly growing disillusionment with the whole parliamentary system.

Since December 1956 Indonesia has been in the grip of protracted crisis. Dissatisfaction with the course of the country's politics erupted in that month in a series of bloodless coups which put the reins of government of Central, North, and South Sumatra in the hands of army-led regional councils. Charging the Ali Sastroamidjojo cabinet with corruption, "red tape," overcentralized government, and financial neglect of their areas, the leaders of these councils announced that they no longer recognized it. At the same time they themselves began to channel a part of the exports of their areas, denying Djakarta the foreign exchange. Djakarta was able to overthrow the North Sumatra council from within. But the Central and South Sumatra regimes continued in power, and defiance of the capital spread elsewhere. In March 1957 bloodless coups of a similar type placed power in the hands of army-led councils in East Indonesia and Kalimantan. These events forced the Ali Sastroamidjojo cabinet to resign.

The leaders of the regional councils now demanded a new cabinet in which the Sumatran-born Hatta, who had resigned from the vice-presidency in early December 1956, would play a dominant role. But this did not come about. With the formation of the present cabinet of the nonparty leader Djuanda—a cabinet centering on the PNI and Nahdatul Ulama and containing several Communist sympathizers —President Soekarno's influence in the national government remained paramount.

The year 1957 saw a gradual widening of the breach between Djakarta and the regional councils. A new proclamation of martial law provided a framework for negotiation with the military commanders in the rebel areas. Furthermore, Djakarta made certain concessions to the demands for regional autonomy and increased its budget allocations to the areas outside Java. Numerous conferences were held. But certain basic disagreements about the economic organization and political character of the national government persisted. President Soekarno remained a dominant power in Djakarta; Hatta remained a private citizen.

The solution which Soekarno offered to the crisis in the country's politics was "guided democracy" or "democracy with leadership," which would be initiated by the establishment of a new high advisory "National Council" under his chairmanship and a cabinet of all parties including the Communists. This clearly afforded little basis for agreement with the regionalists whose political orientation was predominantly anti-Communist. The regionalist leaders voiced alarm when the mid-1957 provincial and regency elections in Java showed a rise in Communist strength there—from 5.5 million votes in 1955 to approximately 6.9 million (25.6 per cent of the total Java vote). Tensions mounted as the year wore on, with Djakarta and the regions maneuvering against one another by all means short of violence.

The hopes of negotiated settlement faded quickly after an attempt made in November 1957, apparently by the followers of a strongly anti-Communist army officer Colonel Zulkifli Lubis, to assassinate President Soekarno. This coincided with a defeat for Indonesia in the UN General Assembly, on the question of the Indonesian claim to West Irian. Shortly thereafter worker groups attempted a series of take-overs of Dutch property. A few days later the army took over the management of all Dutch enterprises.

The economic consequences of this were immediately serious, particularly in areas dependent on interinsular shipping for their rice. When the government attempted to force the regions to stop their illegal external trading, the issues came to a climax. The regional leaders demanded the resignation of the Djuanda cabinet and its replacement by a cabinet led by Hatta. But Djakarta did not respond. Finally, on February 15, 1958, a "Revolutionary Government of the Republic of Indonesia" was established at Padang in Central Sumatra with a Masjumi leader and leading economist, Sjafruddin Prawiranegara, as Prime Minister. Djakarta reacted by resorting to military action. A civil war had broken out.

The events of the next few months suggest that the regionalist leaders, or that majority of them who became associated with the rebel government, greatly overrated their chances of success. In all probability they did not expect that the central government would use military force against them. When it did, with great speed, they found their positive support to exist only in Central Sumatra and parts of North Sumatra and North Sulawesi. Even in these areas many rebel troops showed little inclination to fight. All the major towns of the rebel-held area were in government hands by the end of June. Sizable guerrilla resistance was continuing, however.

The widespread fear that the civil war would lead the major world powers to intervene in Indonesia's domestic struggles was not realized. The rebel forces received assistance from the Nationalist Chinese government on Formosa and the services of several individual American flyers. The central government, having been refused American arms, bought planes and ships from Czechoslovakia, Poland, and the USSR. But neither power bloc intervened on a major scale. There were indications of an improvement in relations between the Indonesian and U.S. governments after April 1958 when the United States indicated willingness to assist Indonesia by selling it small arms and surplus rice.

The aftermath situation in the second half of 1958 found the country with its territorial political unity substantially restored. But the consequences of the rebellion were still evident particularly in the form of serious inflation. Moreover, many of the basic political conflicts remained unresolved.

· X ·

The Contemporary Setting

NO single adjective better characterizes present-day Indonesia than "postrevolutionary." Indonesian society today is vastly different from Indonesian society twenty years ago, because of independence and of the way in which it was achieved and because of the tumultuous political and social changes of the Japanese occupation and particularly of the revolution.

The racial caste structure of colonial society crumbled with the defeat of the Dutch and the subsequent surrender of the Japanese. New social groups quickly attained positions of leadership and prestige. With the revolution the aristocratic regents were suddenly less powerful than the young nationalist intellectuals. The hierarchical general administrative service of which the regents had been the main support lost much of its importance to the new army units, the teachers, and the information officers. In Java and Sumatra, Indonesians from all parts of the archipelago fought alongside one another, using the nationalist-sponsored Indonesian language and thus overcoming much of the separateness between cultural groups which the colonial establishment had tended to perpetuate. New mass organizations arose, undermining local loyalties and replacing them with loyalties to the nation and to political ideologies. Hundreds of thousands of young men had been uprooted from their villages to do forced labor for the Japanese in Burma and Thailand, and even larger numbers left their villages to fight in the army or in guerrilla bands against the returning Dutch. Large-scale physical destruction and forced migration added to the disruption of the social order.[1] The pace of change was tremendous. Its impact was the greater because of the contrast with the conservation of traditional relationships which had characterized the Dutch regime.

To a considerable extent social instability has continued throughout the postrevolutionary period. For many of the half-million or so revolutionary fighters and many of the others uprooted by the eight years of turbulence, no suitable work could be found. They have gained new horizons, which make it impossible for them to accept the restrictive social conditions of their villages. But they lack the formal training which would enable them to find satisfactory urban employment. They therefore constitute a restive element, challenging established social authority in town and village alike. A small number of such persons form the core of the bandit-rebel Darul Islam movement, which has continued to operate in stretches of mountain country in West Java, South Sulawesi, and several other areas throughout the postrevolutionary period. Many more have found a place in civilian society, but, dissatisfied with it, are quickly responsive to every kind of radical politics.

Social Institutions—The School and the Political Party

The period since 1950 has, however, seen the emergence of new channels of social integration. In this period power has been in the hands of the nationalist leaders of the revolution, the majority of whom are persons of Western secondary or higher education. Under these leaders education has had a role of central importance. Ability and achievement have assumed increased importance, relative to race and birth, in the determination of a person's social status. Education has become one of the chief ladders of personal advancement.

Every postrevolutionary government has placed great emphasis on educational expansion. The result has been a dramatic fall in illiteracy —from 89 per cent of the adult population in 1940 to 57 per cent in 1955[2]—a threefold increase in primary school enrollments, and still larger increases in enrollments in secondary schools and universities.

[1] Willem F. Wertheim, *Indonesian Society in Transition* (The Hague: van Hoeve, 1956), pp. 152 ff.

[2] Djawatan Pendidikan Masjarakat (Mass Education Department), *Statistik* (Djakarta, 1955). These figures refer to literacy in Latin script only.

The school has become a central social institution in urban and particularly in rural life.[3] The rapidly increasing number of Indonesians with training of every sort has helped to fill the important gaps left in the economic machine of the country by the departure of large numbers of Dutch administrative and technical personnel. On the other hand education has proved a socially disintegrating force where lack of economic expansion has made it impossible for schooled young people to find the positions which they have been led to expect as their due.

For much of the postrevolutionary period the system of political parties and their associated organizations have been as influential in society as the school. During the revolution the political parties were important agencies through which the nationalist elite could organize popular support. Subsequently they expanded their activity in preparation for the country's first elections in 1955, encouraged by the government's conviction that the mass of the people should become politically conscious.

At the village level party branches are frequently no more than groups of followers of such traditional and still extremely influential leaders as the village head and the local religious teacher. But the important new fact is that social conflict can henceforth be given legitimate expression, in communities hitherto substantially "closed" and forbidding any open expression of conflict. Almost all of the many new voluntary associations which sprang up during and after the revolution—women's and youth organizations, co-operatives, religious organizations, private schools, labor and peasant unions, and so on—are associated with one of these parties. In large and small towns and even in villages in the more "detraditionalized" areas, political power has come to be exercised by coalitions of local political party leaders. District officers and even village heads have lost a part of their authority.[4]

[3] Clifford Geertz, *The Social Context of Economic Change: An Indonesian Case Study* (Cambridge: Massachusetts Institute of Technology, Center for International Studies, 1956), pp. 35 ff. See also Andrea Wilcox, *The Determinants of Political Action in a Sundanese Village* (Cornell Modern Indonesia Project, Ithaca, N.Y.), forthcoming.

[4] Willem F. Wertheim, "Changes in Indonesia's Social Stratification," *Pacific Affairs*, XXVIII (March 1955), 41–52. See also Geertz, *op cit.*, pp. 141 ff.; Herbert Feith, *The Indonesian Elections of 1955* (Cornell Modern Indonesia Project, Interim Reports Series; Ithaca, N.Y., 1957), pp. 12 ff.; Ann R. Willner, "Social Change in Javanese Town-Village Life," *Economic Development and Cultural Change* (University of Chicago), VI (April 1958), 229–241.

Today the political party, like the school, is a channel of personal advancement. It is also a central focus of conflict between groups struggling for power at the national level. Within the intelligentsia-led nationalist elite which obtained power in the revolution, conflict has developed as various sections have associated themselves with different interests in society; the parties have provided an important arena for this conflict.

Most political parties have continued to be dominated by leaders from the old revolutionary elite. But in almost every party the position of this group is being challenged more and more by other groups. It is challenged first by a younger generation of men of higher Western education, second by persons who act as spokesmen of propertied interests. Finally and most powerfully, it is challenged by the leaders of mass organizations—veterans' leagues, trade unions, religious organizations, and so on—with which the parties are linked. In some cases these changes have lessened the importance of the party itself. A tendency has appeared, growing particularly since the 1955 elections, for the mass organizations and military, regional, and other power groupings to act independently on the political stage, bypassing the political parties.

Social Forces—Bureaucracy, Army, Business Communities, Labor

Perhaps the most important center of social power in postrevolutionary Indonesia is the bureaucracy, greatly enlarged as compared with the prewar period and continuing to grow at the present time.[5] In considerable measure the bureaucracy of today is the product of the revolution. Not only have many revolutionary fighters been rewarded by civil service posts, but the leading positions in the service have been filled by prominent nationalists—often lawyers, doctors, journalists, or former teachers in nationalist schools who had not worked in the prewar colonial civil service. Thus the government service continues to be regarded as the spearhead of the nationalist effort toward social rebuilding. The functions of government are even wider today than under the paternalistic Dutch administration, and

[5] At the end of 1953 the total number of civil servants with permanent status (including police personnel and employees of autonomous regions) was 599,721, compared with 144,974 in the Netherlands government service in 1930 (*Statistik, 1956* [Djakarta: Central Bureau of Statistics, 1957], p. 200; *Indisch Verslag,* 1933 [Netherlands Indies Report, 1933], pp. 347, 363).

the bureaucracy has extensive power to determine the ways in which government policy is to be implemented. In fact its influence extends to virtually every aspect of Indonesian life. This arouses little or no opposition, however, for Indonesian society sees only a blurred line between governmental and nongovernmental areas of activity and grants priority to the former. At the same time the bureaucracy is loose and fragmented in its internal power structure, anything but monolithic, and thus is itself a major scene of struggle for political power.

The 200,000-man army, even more important as a center of power today, is a product of the revolution in even greater measure. A small group of its officers and men were members of the Netherlands Indies army before the war. A much greater number obtained their first military experience in the Indonesian auxiliary army established by the Japanese. Another similarly large group first became involved in military organization in the course of the revolution, joining either the army or one of the irregular local bands which were later incorporated in it.

Highly heterogeneous in composition and divided by its susceptibility to a variety of local and political party pressures, the army has nevertheless a certain cohesion of both interests and outlook and on one or two occasions in the present period has shown that it can achieve a high degree of unity on political issues. In such instances its actions in the political field have been of decisive importance. Having played a central role in the revolution, politically and administratively as well as militarily, the army has never completely abjured politics since. In the crisis period since December 1956 it has again been openly involved in politics, as both participant and arbiter. Its governmental role has grown with great rapidity in the same period.

One major consequence of independence has been to increase opportunities for Indonesian entrepreneurship. Indonesian business activity has expanded, both in Java, where it had grown extremely weak in the colonial period, and in the outer islands, where its decline had never been so complete and was in considerable measure offset by the development of small holders' rubber and copra in the early part of this century. The rapid growth of co-operatives is one manifestation of this new activity. In addition a small but politically important group of Indonesian businessmen has arisen as a result of the government's attempt to place Indonesians in all key positions in the economy. Revolutionary political leaders and government functionaries are now large-scale importers and bankers, thus creating the beginnings of a form of bureaucratic capitalism. One may say that a small "new" capitalist class has taken its place alongside the small group of "old" Indonesian capitalists.

The role of the Chinese community, now approximately two and a half million strong, has undergone considerable change. Both the Japanese occupation authorities and the Indonesian revolutionary administration preferred Indonesian trading groups to Chinese. Moreover, during the revolution there occurred outbreaks of anti-Chinese feeling which resulted in the widespread repudiation of debts to Chinese moneylenders and in the permanent expulsion of Chinese residents from villages and small towns in the areas of fighting. In the postrevolutionary period the Chinese have recovered much of their earlier position in the larger towns, despite the continuation of government policies strongly preferring native Indonesian business. Some Chinese capital, forced out of external trade, has gone into small and medium-sized industry. In the internal distributing trade Chinese enterprise continues to play the major role.

Politically, however, the Chinese as a community are in a weak and exposed position. There is little social contact between Chinese and Indonesians, and popular anti-Chinese feeling runs high. Even that majority section of the Chinese population who have adopted Indonesian citizenship are not accepted as Indonesians and consequently suffer discrimination in a number of areas.[6] Nevertheless the position of the minority is partially safeguarded by the fact that many members of the Indonesian nationalist elite have common interests with Chinese in business enterprises.

At least until late in 1957, when the take-over actions against Dutch enterprises were launched, Western-owned and Western-run enterprises were a major component of the Indonesian economy—particularly in estate agriculture, mining, shipping, banking, and exporting. But even before 1957 the political power of the European owners of capital had shrunk beyond recognition. No longer did there exist a government strongly under their influence. No longer could their interests dominate labor policy. Their very foreignness was a source of political weakness.

Since December 1957 the position of Dutch capital has been even weaker. Many Dutch enterprises, though still formally in their original

[6] See Donald E. Willmott, *The National Status of the Chinese in Indonesia* (Cornell Modern Indonesia Project, Interim Reports Series; Ithaca, N.Y., 1957).

owners' possession, are operated by Indonesian managers subject to military control boards. British and American assets continue to be under the authority of their owners, and some of these, United States oil companies in particular, have markedly increased the size of their investments in recent years. But non-Dutch capital also is in a position of relative political weakness.

One aspect of this political weakness is the strength of the large and militant new labor unions. These unions, virtually a new phenomenon, so different are they in size and power from their small prewar forerunners, are a political factor of the first order in Indonesia, whether facing foreign employers, Indonesian employers, or the government. The total number of labor unionists is variously estimated at between one and a half and two and a half million. A slight majority of these are members of the unions affiliated with the All-Indonesian Trade Union Organization (SOBSI), which is linked with the Indonesian Communist Party, and approximately a quarter belong to union federations associated with one of the other political parties.[7]

Elements of Continuity—Economic Structure and Traditional Social Divisions

Certain important features of Indonesian society, and particularly of the country's economy, were relatively little affected by the turbulent events of the Japanese occupation and the revolution. There were patterns which, far from being changed, were accentuated.

Indonesia's economy is still highly dependent on the prices which its export products, mostly industrial raw materials, can fetch on a fluctuating world market. This one-sidedness had proved extremely costly in the Great Depression. In the later 1930s the Dutch government took steps to alleviate it by encouraging small-scale industry, but the results were modest when the war intervened. In the postrevolutionary period industrialization has had high priority in Indonesia's economic planning, and a number of successes have been achieved. But the pace has been slow. The economy remains, like that of other Southeast Asian countries, predominantly agricultural and extractive. To satisfy an expanded demand for foreign-produced commodities and also for government revenues, Indonesia is heavily dependent on the export of rubber, oil, tin, and copra.

Another aspect of this one-sidedness is the fact that the exports on

[7] See Stephen W. Reed and others, eds., *Indonesia*, Subcontractor's Monograph, Human Relations Area File 57 (New Haven, 1956), pp. 939–941.

which Indonesia depends are produced by a very small number of areas of the country. As is shown on Map 3, estate and mine production is nearly all concentrated in a few areas of North Sumatra, South Sumatra, and West Java. Small holders' rubber and copra are grown in wider areas, but almost entirely outside Java. Java, which serves as the main supplier of foodstuffs and local manufactures for the domestic market, produces less than a quarter of the country's annual exports. The pressure of the exporting areas for budget and foreign exchange allocations in proportion to their earnings has been a political factor of primary importance in regional relationships, particularly since about 1953 with rising domestic inflation and a fixed exchange rate reducing the value of the exporters' income. In the period since 1956 regionalist groups have had their independent centers of political power principally in those parts of the country, such as Sumatra and North Sulawesi, which have a "strong" position vis-à-vis the national government because they produce a large proportion of the country's exports.

Paralleling and frequently aggravating economic tensions of this type are the traditional and deeply rooted divisions between the many ethnic, cultural, and linguistic groups—the Javanese of East and Central Java, the Sundanese of West Java, the Minangkabaus of West Sumatra, the Bataks of Tapanuli in North Sumatra, the Dajaks of Kalimantan or Borneo, and so on. These divisions do not always give rise to social conflict, but they contribute heavily to its aggravation in a number of areas. Where one ethnic group holds a position of political or economic superiority over others—as in the case of the Javanese in West Java and the Bataks in North Sumatra—ethnic feeling is a political factor of considerable independent importance.

Some religious divisions are also of great social and political significance. This is not the case with cleavages between the Muslim majority and the 2 per cent Hindu minority in Bali or the scattered 4 per cent of Protestants and 1 per cent of Catholics. But it is the case with the divisions inside Islam.

The Islamic community is divided along two main lines. First there is a major social cleavage, particularly in East and Central Java, between communities of *santri,* devotedly Islamic persons often associated with town or village trade, and communities of *prijaji* or *abangan*—aristocrats or peasants in the Javanese context—who are nominally Islamic but at the same time critical of Islam (and whose real religious beliefs and practices are frequently influenced more strongly by Hinduism and animism than by Islam). A second main type of cleavage, also social as well as religious, is that inside the community of devotedly Muslim *santri*.[8] This is the division between modernism and religious reform on the one hand and religious conservatism on the other. Modernism, which has close links with urban small trade, finds its main organizational expression in the Muhammadijah and its main political expression in the Masjumi. Conservatism, which is more particularly linked to small landlordism, finds religious and political outlets in the Nahdatul Ulama.

The village has been greatly affected by the upheavals of the revolution—and yet in some ways it has been little affected. Socially a great deal has changed in the lives of that 75–80 per cent of the Indonesian people who live in villages. They have become much more aware of the world beyond their own village and district. Their position has improved in that the great increase of social fluidity makes it possible for some children of peasant origin, through schooling and activity in political parties and mass organizations, to rise in the social scale. There have been no basic changes in the condition of the village's economy, however.

Under colonialism money made major inroads on the earlier self-sufficiency of the village. But the traditional structure of village society which colonial government policy sought to maintain counteracted the tendencies which the impact of money set up toward a general dynamization of the economy. The process can be seen most clearly in Java. There the Western impact produced no rise in productivity or levels of living, but merely what has been called "static expansion," [9] the extension of wet rice agriculture to more and more areas, accompanied by an enormous growth of population.

Dutch colonialism did not produce a problem of large landlordism as Spanish colonialism did in the Philippines. It did bring about large-scale peasant indebtedness, in particular to Chinese moneylenders and their agents. In Java it gave rise to an agricultural and economic problem more acute and more difficult of solution than exists in any other of the Southeast Asian countries. It resulted in a situation in which tremendous population pressure exists alongside

[8] Clifford Geertz, "Religious Belief and Economic Behavior in a Central Javanese Town," *Economic Development and Cultural Change*, IV (Jan. 1956), 134–158; see also Robert R. Jay, "Santri and Abangan: Religious Schism in Rural Central Java" (unpublished dissertation, Harvard University, 1956).

[9] J. H. Boeke, *Economics and Economic Policy of Dual Economies as exemplified by Indonesia* (Haarlem: Tjeenk Willink, 1953), p. 174.

economic stagnation, with peasants owning, share-owning, or working, as laborers, tiny and uneconomic plots of an average size of about two acres and often less than half an acre. These, moreover, were constantly subject to further subdivision with the further growth of the agricultural population.

This pattern of "shared poverty," [10] with the large-scale disguised unemployment which accompanies it, has not been changed substantially by the revolution. Some factors have operated to alleviate it, for instance, the expansion of rural small industry and the program of resettling persons from Java in the outer islands, particularly Sumatra.[11] The greater receptivity on the part of villagers to new agricultural methods has produced a slight rise in production per acre. The number of villages in which forms of communal land ownership continue to prevail has dwindled to a small minority, and in many parts of Java there has developed an increased economic differentiation within the village, with the village elite growing considerably richer. The developmental effects of these changes, however, have been largely offset by deterioration in transport facilities and by the greater shortage of village credit as a result of withdrawal of the Chinese from this field in many areas. Overshadowing all other developments, the continuing rapid rise of the population has aggravated the acuteness of the whole problem. From a little over 70 million in 1940 Indonesia's population rose to an estimated 85 million in 1956. Java's population rose in the same period from 48.4 million to 55.1 million.[12] In Java, at least, village levels of consumption have fallen—from an already very low prewar level.[13]

The problem is less immediately serious in the islands outside Java because of their relative abundance of land and somewhat higher levels of living, because of cultural forms more favorable to capitalist enterprise, and because indigenous trading groups were never completely eliminated in their (relatively short) colonial period. Here too, however, village agriculture has remained largely static. Only in

[10] Geertz, "Religious Belief and Economic Behavior."

[11] In 1953, a good year for resettlement, 48,354 persons were involved in the program (*Statistik, 1956*, p. 16). But the annual increase in Java's population is estimated to be 900,000.

[12] Biro Pusat Statistik (Central Bureau of Statistics), *Statistical Pocket Book of Indonesia, 1957* (Djakarta, 1957), p. 11.

[13] See Benjamin Higgins, *Indonesia's Economic Stabilization and Development* (New York: Institute of Pacific Relations, 1957), p. 177.

rare cases has productivity risen more rapidly than population. More-over, the economies of these areas have suffered from the deteriora-tion which has taken place in road and sea communications.

Cities and towns have grown to be two, three, or four times their prewar size, partly as a result of population increases not absorbed by expanding opportunities within the village economy. This swelling of the urban labor market has tended to depress wages for urban work. Thus, although the growth of trade unionism along with the sympathetic attitude of governments has bettered the position of workers in industries where unionization has been possible, it is doubt-ful whether there has been any general improvement in the position of the wageworker.

The mass of the Indonesian people, in rural and urban areas alike, have experienced great social ferment. But as yet no way has been found to channel the new energies in order to produce the economic rewards which the revolution promised. This situation has obvious implications for social and political stability.

Political Orientations

Indonesian political thinking of the present period is most strongly influenced by the outlook of the nationalist elite which led the revolu-tion. In very large measure this elite is a product of Western educa-tion. A small section of its membership, the section most closely linked with Indonesian business in the prewar period, was educated in tradi-tional Islamic schools. But by far the greatest part gained a Dutch university or secondary education. And the role which the men of this group play today is more a result of their Western education than of their parents' social position.[14]

All nationalist leaders have been deeply affected by the impact of the West upon their country and themselves. Their nationalism may be seen partly in terms of their adherence to the democratic ideals which their colonial rulers preached but did not practice in Indonesia and partly in terms of their concern that their country should become the equal of the countries of the West in prosperity and power. As an outgroup in colonial society, having relatively few links with aristo-cratic or commercial interests, the nationalist leadership was charac-

[14] See Soelaeman Soemardi, "Some Aspects of the Social Origins of the In-donesian Political Decision-Makers," *Transactions of the Third World Congress of Sociology* (London: International Sociological Association, 1956).

terized by a high degree of social radicalism, and much of it was under strong Marxist influence. The Japanese occupation produced a radicalization of its nationalism, at the same time strengthening its authoritarian aspects. Through the revolution the group became committed to what it saw as a complete reshaping of society, and it was confident of achieving this, principally through political action. Its mood is conveyed by such words as "dynamic," "liberation," "struggle," "upbuilding," and "enlightenment."

Democratic values play an important role in the thinking of the Indonesian elite. They are prominent in the country's Five Principles of State, first formulated by Soekarno in 1945: Faith in God, Nationality, Humanity, People's Sovereignty (or Democracy), and Social Justice.[15] But a number of Indonesian leaders, Soekarno prominent among them, have advocated a distinctively Indonesian form of democracy, a form which gives expression to *musjawarah,* the traditional Indonesian method of coming to agreement not through majority decisions but by a search for something like the Quaker "sense of the meeting." In one way this attitude expresses the syncretism which is a feature of the Indonesian and particularly the Javanese intellectual and religious tradition, the cast of thinking which emphasizes an ultimate mystical and aesthetic unity of things underlying what appear as material conflicts and logical incompatibilities. In addition, however, it should be seen in relation to the strong emphasis, in the political thinking of many of the leaders and particularly of those more closely linked with the aristocratic tradition of Java, on the need for authoritarian leadership.

The division of greatest importance in the elite's thinking is closely related to the contrast between leaders linked with the vestigial Javanese aristocracy and others having different ties, often with trading groups strong in the islands outside Java. In another sense it represents the contrast between two different types of reaction to the West. It is the division, in religious and cultural as well as social thinking, between the Islam and moderate socialism of the leaders of the modernist Muslim party, Masjumi—men like the party's Sumatra-born chairman and former Prime Minister, Mohammad Natsir—and the mystical Hindu-influenced "Javanese religion" and radical cultural nationalism of the Javanese leaders of the Nationalist Party (PNI),

[15] Soekarno, *The Birth of the Pantja Sila* (Djakarta: Ministry of Information, 1953).

men like the party's late deputy chairman, Sarmidi Mangunsarkoro.[16] It parallels the socioreligious division described above between the devotedly Muslim *santri* and the nominally Muslim *prijaji* and *abangan*. And at the level of policy orientation it parallels the division between those whose primary concern is with economic development and those who would give priority to noneconomic objectives, involving principally the nation's prestige and its cultural identity.

Intellectuals of both these two main currents describe themselves as democrats and socialists, and almost all of them are Muslims of one sort or another. Their ideas have much in common, and their precepts for government policies perhaps more. But the postrevolutionary period has seen a series of political developments whereby divisions between them have been brought to the fore.

At the same time the period has seen a decline in the attraction of the intellectuals' democratic ideology at the level of the newspaper-reading public. At this level democracy has always been understood in a way different from that of the intellectuals; numerous older attitudes toward political authority have been woven into the meaning of the new symbol. In the present period there are many ideological currents with influence among the Indonesian newspaper readers. But constitutionalism is relatively weak among them. If any one current can be said to dominate, it is radical nationalism.[17]

[16] See, for instance, Mohammed Natsir, *Some Observations concerning the Role of Islam in National and International Affairs* (Southeast Asia Program, Cornell University, Data Paper no. 16; Ithaca, N.Y., 1954); Sarmidi Mangunsarkoro, *The Philosophical and Cultural Foundations of Our Education System* (Djakarta, 1945).

[17] For an analysis of political values held at the level of the newspaper-reading public see Guy J. Pauker, *Indonesian Images of Their National Self* (Santa Monica, Calif.: Rand Corporation, 1958).

· XI ·

The Political Process

POLITICS in Indonesia today substantially bypasses the country's constitution. Particularly since the development of the regional crisis in December 1956, constitutionalism has been undermined by deeds and even by words. Nevertheless a large group of Indonesia's leaders remain devoted to constitutional principles. Furthermore, the constitution guided and contained the country's political process fairly adequately for the greater part of the postrevolutionary period. This process cannot be understood without some knowledge of it.

The Constitution

The Indonesian constitution, like so much else in the country, is the product of its revolution. Indonesian lawyers had for decades been trained to be conversant with Dutch constitutional practice. But next to no basis for a democratic constitutional system existed in Indonesia, either in the country's prewar experience—of government by a governor-general with a weak representative council—or in the forms of its political organization under Japanese military rule. Thus, when Indonesian independence was proclaimed in August 1945, a constitution was adopted which had hurriedly been prepared in the previous few months, out of the void as it were.

Promulgated in this way, the constitution was not regarded as sacrosanct. Several of its central features were changed later in 1945, although the document itself was not amended. An entirely new constitution was written at the time of the establishment of the federal Republic of the United States of Indonesia in December 1949; and this was replaced by a third constitution with the return to the unitary form of government in August 1950. The 1950 constitution is operative today; but it too is only a temporary constitution.[1] A 520-man Constitutional Convention elected in 1955 is currently working on the permanent basic law which is to replace it. The tentativeness of Indonesia's constitutions and the frequency with which they have been changed stand in contrast with the relative continuity of constitutional arrangements in countries such as the Philippines and India, which enjoyed greater democratic opportunities under prewar colonial governments and experienced no revolutionary upheaval, or relatively little, in the period after the war.

All of Indonesia's constitutions demonstrate the attachment its leaders have felt to democratic values. The 1950 constitution has a preamble and a long series of directive principles or ideological clauses which reflect the central ideas of European democracy (responsible government, religious freedom, and equality before the law) and of socialism (the right to work and to strike, equality of opportunity, and co-operative economic organization). It establishes a European-type parliamentary system of government. It makes the President largely a figurehead, as also the Vice-President. A Prime Minister heads a cabinet which is responsible to parliament and can be overthrown by it. Parliament consists of one house only and is elected for a four-year term by universal suffrage.

Governmental Institutions

In actual practice the various Western institutions have been shaped by the circumstances of Indonesia's politics and its social and cultural context. This is very clear in the case of the presidency, which has consistently been much stronger than the 1950 constitution provided.[2] Under this constitution the President is required to act on the advice of the cabinet in every situation, virtually the only exception being his prerogative to select "formateurs" to form a new

---

[1] See "The 1945 and 1950 Constitutions of the Republik Indonesia," *Indonesian Review* (Djakarta), I (Feb.–March 1951), 137–157; Amos J. Peaslee, ed., *Constitutions of Nations* (The Hague: Nijhoff, 1956), II, 368–392.

[2] See A. K. Pringgodigdo, *The Office of President in Indonesia as Defined in the Three Constitutions in Theory and Practice* (Cornell Modern Indonesia Project, Translation Series; Ithaca, N.Y., 1957).

cabinet. In addition he may under certain circumstances dissolve parliament, a power which he could conceivably exercise independently of cabinet advice, but which in fact has never been used.

In actual practice President Soekarno has wielded very much greater powers. He has on occasion vetoed the appointment of a minister or refused to sign an emergency law. He has appointed himself to form a cabinet. He has frequently used his oratory in ways not endorsed by the cabinet of the day or even running counter to its policies. In 1957 he initiated the formation of the "National Council," introducing a new factor in the country's political institutions. Informally the weight of his approval or disapproval of a policy has been a political factor of utmost importance throughout the postrevolutionary period.

At the same time he is responsible to no parliament and no electorate. Indeed the office of President is in principle elective, and it may be that President Soekarno, who was originally elected in 1945 by a small committee of prominent nationalist leaders, will one day stand as a candidate in a large presidential election. But so far no procedures exist for presidential elections. None will be held until such time as they are called for under the new constitution currently being prepared by the Constitutional Convention.

The power exercised by the President in excess of constitutional prescription is to be traced principally to the personality of Soekarno and his role as the foremost leader of the struggle for independence. Soekarno is a charismatic leader, a man of great personal dynamism whose leadership is believed by many to have supernatural sanctions. He is the leader of an egalitarian movement, but at the same time he is the "father of his people."

Soekarno has been a principal nationalist leader for more than thirty years. It was he who proclaimed independence. His oratory, which is highly sensitive to the feelings of particular regional and social groups, provides him with mass support unequaled by that of any other Indonesian leader. Thus he is, in a sense, too big for his formal constitutional position. He himself has insisted that his role as President must not be seen as negating his role as a revolutionary leader. His prerogatives have frequently been the subject of party controversy, with one section of the political elite agreeing with his view and another affirming a literal interpretation of the constitution. In practice his power has circumscribed the capacity of several cabinets for action.

The vice-presidency, held by Dr. Mohammad Hatta until his resignation in December 1956, has also acquired an importance greater than the constitution provides. Under the constitution the Vice-President is to assist the President and to replace him in the event of his death or inability to exercise the duties of his office. But Hatta is an old-time nationalist leader, whose prestige is exceeded only by that of Soekarno himself. He had been part of the Dwitunggal, the "duumvirate" of Soekarno and Hatta which had existed since the beginning of the Japanese occupation. Further, the two leaders, both nonparty men, have been widely regarded as complementing one another, both in terms of training, personality, and outlook (Hatta's skills as economist and administrator and his practical realism moderating the fiery enthusiasm of the architect, orator, and aesthete Soekarno) and in terms of their regional origins (Hatta being Sumatran and Soekarno Javanese). Soekarno-Hatta unity has long been a symbol of the unity of Indonesia and continues to be even since Hatta's resignation from the vice-presidency.

Thus there existed the tradition of something like a copresidency. Hatta had considerable indirect political influence, until he became estranged from Soekarno in the years between 1952 and his resignation in 1956. Even before his decline in influence, however, Hatta never acted in excess of his constitutional prerogatives. In response to repeated calls for a presidential cabinet headed by him—a request which was in conflict with the 1950 constitution, although there had been three such cabinets under the earlier constitutions—Hatta stated that he would head such a cabinet only in response to a request from parliament. Since his resignation no Vice-President has been appointed.

The functioning of parliament has in good part been in accordance with the conceptions embodied in the 1950 constitution. Both the temporary parliament of 1950 and the parliament elected in the 1955 elections have been forums for free criticism of government policy and practice. They have made wide use of the right of inquiry into government action and some use of legislative initiative. The requirement that all treaties should have parliamentary ratification before becoming valid has been an important foreign policy factor. Parliaments have also used their right to initiate motions of no confidence in a cabinet. And whereas no cabinet has fallen as a direct result of a no-confidence motion from parliament, several have resigned because of an anticipated inability to maintain their parliamentary majorities.

Parliamentary procedure, which follows European models, is adhered to faithfully—with consequent long delays and a large, more or less permanent backlog of government bills. This bridle on executive action is partly counterbalanced by a provision whereby cabinets may proclaim emergency acts which are valid without parliamentary approval, provided only that they are presented to the next session of parliament for ratification. A further factor giving the executive ascendancy over parliament has been the budget. Here parliament has in fact been deprived of one of its crucial constitutional powers in that cabinets have failed, in all but one case, to submit their annual budgets to it for ratification prior to the year of their operation.[3]

In those instances in which the institution of parliament has failed most strikingly, it has been as a result of failures in the functioning of the party system and of cabinet government. Parliament itself has functioned with a considerable degree of consonance with the provisions of the constitution; at least it did so until the end of 1956.

The country's legal and judicial system has a relatively long continuous existence. It was a peculiar feature of Dutch colonial government that the attempt was made to develop a multiple legal system, with native courts of customary law and religious courts existing alongside courts administering Western statutory law. Independence has eliminated the racial distinction and produced a considerable extension of the scope of statutory law. But justice in religious and related matters continues to be administered independently, and the customary law of particular ethnic communities is still operative in many fields.[4]

The various judicial organs have generally maintained high standards in their day-to-day work, laboring as they have under all the difficulties consequent upon rapid social change, understaffing, and the uncertainty and confusion which characterizes the country's multiple legal system. But where politics have become involved, legal guarantees have frequently proved to be weak. In a number of cases long periods of time have been allowed to elapse before arrested persons have been brought to trial. This has happened particularly when the army has arrested persons suspected of connections with the extremist Muslim Darul Islam. Several cabinets have taken actions in-

[3] Miriam S. Budiardjo, "The Provisional Parliament of Indonesia," *Far Eastern Survey*, XXV (Feb. 1956), 17–23.

[4] See Johannes Leyser, "Legal Developments in Indonesia," *American Journal of Comparative Law*, III (July 1954), 399–411.

jurious to freedom of the press. Newspaper offices have been raided by politically irate bands of city youths, and the offenders were not punished. In a number of important cases political pressures have distorted the processes of law, with lawyers reluctant to take over a defense case against the government.

Since the proclamation of martial law in March 1957 the effectiveness of the citizen's legal guarantees has been reduced as a result of the arbitrary manner in which some military commanders have used their new powers. In this same crisis period the press has lost much of the high degree of freedom it previously had to criticize cabinets, the President, and the army. Furthermore, there has been a rise in the importance of political violence, particularly in Djakarta where gangs have operated with "protection" from one or other government agency.

Constitutionalism faced one of its severest tests in the giant experiment of the 1955 elections. These elections were held at a time of acute tensions; their political outcome was almost entirely unpredictable, as were their social consequences. Virtually none of the electors had ever cast a vote except in village elections. Indeed the elections were frequently postponed. But eventually they were held, and it is widely agreed that they were successful. Undoubtedly they were organizationally and in terms of the maintenance of security and also in terms of the level of participation. In both the elections, the parliamentary election and the subsequent election for the Constitutional Convention, no less than 87 per cent of eligible voters—and every citizen over 18 years of age or married was eligible—cast a valid vote.

More important, they were genuine elections. Notwithstanding the fact of pressure from several government agencies in favor of particular parties, ordinary voters were able to register their social and political preferences with a wide degree of freedom and consciousness of choice. The parties which emerged successful—the "big four," PNI, Masjumi, Nahdatul Ulama, and Communist Party—were those which were able to identify themselves with major social forces.[5]

But the elections did not achieve what was widely expected of them. They did not regenerate the functioning of Indonesian democracy; they afforded no way out of the situation of unstable, weak, and ineffective government which had prevailed since 1950. Indeed they

[5] See Herbert Feith, *The Indonesian Elections of 1955* (Cornell Modern Indonesia Project, Interim Reports Series; Ithaca, N.Y., 1957).

probably aggravated the seriousness of political divisions. These shortcomings have been attributed by some to faulty electoral mechanics, in particular to the type of proportional representation system used in Indonesia which makes the member of parliament responsible to his party and not to his constituents. But for a more basic explanation one must look at the problems of political instability and governmental weakness in broader context.

Problems of Governmental Weakness

These problems come into focus as the functioning of the institution of cabinet is examined. No less than seven Indonesian cabinets have held office since August 1950. A total of more than twenty-three weeks has been spent in cabinet crises after one cabinet has resigned and before another was formed. Even more important, cabinets have been severely limited in the range of policies they were able to pursue; some indeed were virtually hamstrung. This is partly because of the multiplicity of parties and the fluidity of relations between and inside them; no cabinet until the present one has been a coalition of less than eight parties, and the major parties have been deeply divided internally for much of the period. In addition the weakness of cabinets has resulted from the constant threat of veto and intervention by such powerful extraparliamentary forces as the army leadership, the President, and, more recently, regional political groups.

The difficulties facing the governments of the period become clear as one looks at the way in which they have fallen. The Masjumi-led cabinet of Mohammad Natsir (October 1950–March 1951) was forced to resign over an issue of representation on regional legislative councils: its leadership had earned the antagonism of President Soekarno, as well as of the PNI-led opposition, by its refusal to abrogate the Round Table Conference agreements unilaterally when Holland was adamant in resisting Indonesia's claim to West New Guinea. Its successor, the Masjumi-PNI–led cabinet of Dr. Sukiman (April 1951–February 1952), had the positive backing of the President. But it too fell before it had achieved many of its program goals, largely as a result of intraparty disagreements in the main government parties, which came to a head over a secretly negotiated agreement for U.S. economic and military aid. The next was the cabinet of the PNI leader Wilopo, also a cabinet including the two main parties, but with the ministers drawn from the less strongly pro-Soekarno fractions of these parties. When this cabinet fell after fourteen months (April 1952–

June 1953), the immediate issue was its handling of the problems of illegal peasant squatting on foreign-leased estate land. Behind this there was pressure from the majority section of the PNI and from the President, who opposed the cabinet's personnel policies in the army.

In the period of these three cabinets, of Natsir, Sukiman, and Wilopo, the most important political division was not one between parties but inside them. It was certainly not a division between right and left. It was a cleavage at once between two types of outlook and two loose federations of cliques. At the level of ideas it was between economic development-oriented persons influenced by the Socialist Party leader Sjahrir and anti-Socialist Party nationalists whose principal concern was not economic, but cultural and political. At the more important level of factions and interest groups one can speak of it as a division between a younger anti-Soekarno wing, with associations with the central army leadership of the time, and an older pro-Soekarno wing. There were great similarities in the policies pursued by each of the "wings" when in office; their antagonisms were in large part merely those between "ins" and "outs." Nevertheless the lines were being drawn at this time for the political polarization which was to develop later.

All of these three cabinets found it difficult to implement their policies. They have a number of important achievements to their credit, particularly with regard to economic and social rehabilitation. But they failed in some of their central tasks. Whenever a seriously divisive issue arose—the party composition of the regional councils, the terms of U.S. aid, army reorganization, concessions to foreign investors, and a number of others—cabinets had either to postpone action or, if they embarked on the policy they believed necessary, to run the great risk of being forced to resign. This resulted partly from the fact that parties shifted their allegiances rapidly. In particular the PNI and Masjumi, both then deeply divided internally, swung quickly as between the army-backed politics of the younger generation of men like Natsir and Wilopo and the pro-Soekarno politics of men prominent in prewar nationalist politics like Sukiman and Ali Sastroamidjojo. At a more basic level no cabinet possessed the governmental resources to act decisively in the face of strong sectional opposition.[6]

Wilopo's successor was Ali Sastroamidjojo of the PNI whose cabinet

[6] Herbert Feith, *The Wilopo Cabinet, 1952–1953: A Turning Point in Post-Revolutionary Indonesia* (Cornell Modern Indonesia Project, Monograph Series; Ithaca, N.Y., 1958).

was able to maintain itself for almost two years (July 1953–July 1955). In this cabinet the Masjumi was not represented, but the conservative Muslim Nahdatul Ulama, which had split away from the Masjumi in 1952, acted as an important junior partner of the PNI. The cabinet, which had President Soekarno's strong support, was eventually obliged to resign by the leadership of the army; the immediate issue was the personnel policy of the Minister of Defense. It was followed by the Burhanuddin Harahap cabinet, led by the Masjumi, with the Nahdatul Ulama holding prominent portfolios in the four months before it withdrew its ministers. This cabinet was in office for seven months (August 1955–March 1956), in which time the country's first elections were held; it resigned when the newly elected parliament had assembled.

Intraparty divisions were much less important in the two and a half years of these two cabinets. The approaching elections for which most parties campaigned heavily over a period of years effected a closing of ranks, particularly in the two major parties. They also produced a general polarization. The PNI forged a working alliance with the Communists and co-operated closely for most of this time with the Nahdatul Ulama. The counterpart of these links was an association of the Masjumi with the Socialists and the small Christian parties. President Soekarno, increasingly involved in day-to-day politics, identified himself with the PNI-led group of parties. An important and generally preponderant section of the leadership of the army supported the group led by the Masjumi. Vice-President Hatta, whose differences with the President were now major, was more and more closely linked with the Masjumi-Socialist bloc.

The cleavage between the country's two main power groupings grew in the course of this period; the Communists, who had previously stood outside the main body of nationalist leadership, now became involved in its divisions. At the same time the issues and alignments of interest-group politics came to correspond more to the issues and alignments of the Cold War. The Pro-Soekarno wing, with which the PNI was now clearly identified, stressed anti-Western themes both in foreign policy and in relation to Western capital invested in Indonesia; the anti-Soekarno wing, led by the Masjumi, took an increasingly pro-Western stand. The divisions between the two wings were henceforth much more than merely divisions between "ins" and "outs."

Nor were these divisions any longer merely divisions inside a single intellectual-led revolutionary elite. The influence of intellectuals in the parties declined in this period, as the parties developed closer relations with the centers of social power. The elections considerably hastened this development in that they obliged the parties to seek out their potential support, not only at the village level, but also among those who could organize the village vote and those who could pay for this organization. The Masjumi became more closely linked with the older Indonesian capitalism of the towns and rural areas— small holders' rubber and copra, the batik industry, and small-scale distributive trade—and the PNI with the growing bureaucratic capitalism of the cities, particularly banking, large-scale importing, and shipping. At the same time mass organizations and their leaders, the organizers and mediators of ideas, grew increasingly powerful inside every party, also challenging the intellectuals' influence. As the parties developed responsiveness to sectional vested interests and mass organizations, the divisions between them tended to grow.

Furthermore, the results of the elections showed the parties with great clarity where their regional support lay. The PNI, NU, and Communist Party each obtained more than 85 per cent of their total vote in Java and more than 65 per cent of it in East and Central Java, the area of the ethnic Javanese. On the other hand only 25.4 per cent of the total Masjumi vote came from East and Central Java, another 25.9 per cent from West Java and Djakarta, and 48.7 per cent from the less densely populated outer islands. Thus the PNI, like the NU and the Indonesian Communist Party, emerged from the elections as a Java-centered party, a party of the ethnic Javanese, and the Masjumi emerged as the party of the non-Javanese.

The period of the Ali and Burhanuddin cabinets produced no improvement in the ability of governments to govern and, in fact, some deterioration. The actions of these two cabinets, one the counterpiece of the other, were severely circumscribed by considerations of party political interest. In a number of fields they pursued their interests to the extent of disregarding the rules of constitutional behavior. Government actions favored the elections interests of the government parties, and there was a major increase in the power of political parties, particularly of the PNI, within the bureaucracy.

When to deal with difficult long-term problems, particularly economic ones, would have meant taking risks in relation to their own survival, these cabinets did not deal with them. Their approach was essentially an *ad hoc* one. Thus they promoted little progress in the formulation of policy with regard to such basic and politically difficult problems as regional autonomy, the role of foreign capital, and civil service and army reorganization. All this was left till "after the elections."

But the two postelections cabinets have operated under even more restrictive political circumstances. Internally divided and challenged by the increasing disrespect of various extraparliamentary groups for their constitutional authority, they have been in an even weaker position than their predecessors to effect policies for long-term development.

The first of them, the second cabinet of Ali Sastroamidjojo (March 1956–March 1957), was a coalition of all the main non-Communist parties emerging from the elections. Led by the PNI, it also included Masjumi and NU members in prominent positions. It was nevertheless internally divided and showed itself incapable of decisive action even in its first months of office—a fact which led to many public expressions of dissatisfaction with the whole constitutional system.

But, despite its divisions, the cabinet was predominantly a pro-Soekarno coalition. Thus it aroused the opposition and open intervention of anti-Soekarno sections of the army. These were now no longer the dominant force within the central leadership of the army. But they did remain powerful in the military areas outside Java, which, as the 1955 elections had shown, were the domain predominantly of the Masjumi and the smaller Christian parties. So it was that the extraparliamentary challenges to the Ali cabinet came from the army-led regional councils in Sumatra and East Indonesia. The bloodless coups executed by these councils in their areas eventually achieved their aim of forcing the cabinet's resignation.

Politics in the Current Crisis

Of the period of the present cabinet, of the nonparty leader Djuanda, it is difficult to make any assessment. It is operating in a situation at once critical and confused. Formed by President Soekarno himself in April 1957, the Djuanda cabinet is an "emergency business cabinet." Some of its ministers are members of parties or political organizations—mainly from PNI and NU and also from Communist-sympathizing organizations—but they do not sit as representatives of these bodies.

Brought into existence to deal with an emergency situation, the Djuanda cabinet has nevertheless been in a weak position to govern.

This is partly because the rebellious regional movements in the islands outside Java were able until February 1958 to maintain and consolidate their power and, by channeling an increasing share of their export revenues into their own areas, to make the economic position of the central government precarious. In addition it results from the proclamation of martial law in March 1957, which involved a large-scale transfer of legal and political authority from civil to military agencies. This proclamation was tantamount to a recognition of the power which the military leaders of the defiant regional movements in Sumatra and East Indonesia had arrogated to themselves. More important, it placed greatly increased powers in the hands of the chief of staff of the army, Major General A. H. Nasution, and of regional military commanders in Java and Kalimantan. This power grew further with the outbreak of the rebellion or civil war in February 1958 and soon came to extend to virtually the whole of the country. In 1957 and 1958 a number of the most important policy decisions were taken by the army and issued in the form of military decrees. At regional and local levels army officers have come to play an exceedingly important role both as policy makers and as co-ordinators, leaders, and channelers of organizational political activity.

A final factor weakening the position of the cabinet has been the increasingly open political role of President Soekarno. It was he who formed the cabinet, and an important section of its membership feels itself responsible to him rather than to the Prime Minister. Moreover, he exerts strong influence in major policy matters through his chairmanship of the "National Council." This Council was created in May 1957 as part of the implementation of the President's conception of Guided Democracy, or Democracy with Leadership, which would supersede liberal parliamentary democracy. The new institution is a top-level body of persons appointed by the Djuanda cabinet largely at the President's suggestion to represent the "dynamic groups in society"—workers, peasants, veterans, youth, women, national entrepreneurs, journalists, artists, intellectuals, religious groups, particular regions, and the armed forces.[7] The precise status of the 45-member body is not clear. The Djuanda cabinet does not regard it as more than an advisory body. But considerable prestige has been conferred on it, and the President has been able to use it to apply strong pres-

[7] Roeslan Abdulgani, "Indonesia's National Council: The First Year," *Far Eastern Survey*, XXVII (July 1958), 97–104.

sure on the cabinet to follow policies favored by him. Its political composition is such that it is unlikely ever to oppose President Soekarno.

Thus the Djuanda government has frequently appeared as something less than a government. Some of its most important actions, its decisions relating to the regional crisis and its December 1957 decisions in the matter of the taking over of Dutch enterprises and the expulsion of large numbers of Dutch residents, appear to have been taken not by the cabinet itself, but by forces outside it, in particular the President and the central army command. So on contentious issues the cabinet has appeared as a mere broker of political forces. In 1957 and till February or March 1958 large areas of the country accepted its instructions only in part. Now as then it must constantly vie with the President and the chief of staff of the army for the last word in important decisions.

As the power and prestige of cabinet has declined in the crisis conditions of the Djuanda cabinet, so too parliament and the party system have grown less important. Parliament has continued to function, as has the Constitutional Convention. But the deliberations of both bodies have attracted little attention, for the focus of political contention has been seen to lie elsewhere and the most important matters of policy have been debated in conferences of military commanders, in *ad hoc* joint consultations of military and political leaders, and in the National Council rather than in parliament. The same period has witnessed considerable discussion, some of it by high public officials, of the possibility of radical changes in the whole constitutional structure.

Similarly the political parties, which played so central a role in the period before and immediately after the 1955 elections, have lost a good deal of their importance—despite the fact that provincial and regional elections were held in different parts of the country in 1957 and 1958. A number of the major parties have become relatively inactive, their leaders divided from one another along lines of regional origin, in terms of differing attitudes to particular military leaders, or according to their point of view on the issues involved in the civil war. In one sense the current situation is similar to that which prevailed before the beginning of campaigning for the 1955 elections. Politics again operates mainly as between organized groups in cities and towns. Village support is again of only limited importance.

The Communist Party, however, continues to be united and active, not only in urban areas but in many peasant communities as well. It is free from the ideological uncertainties which have sapped the vigor and *élan* of most other parties as disappointment has grown with the parliamentary and party system. And it has achieved an unmatched degree of organizational effectiveness. Confident that its voting appeal has grown, it protested vigorously throughout 1958 against suggestions that the second parliamentary elections be postponed. (Scheduled originally for November 1959, these are now to be held sometime in 1960. But this too continues to be in dispute.)

It would seem that a process has been started whereby cabinet and parliament are to become less powerful than other political institutions and perhaps even displaced by them. The Western-type constitutional forms which have been unable to provide Indonesia with effective government appear to be disintegrating. But it is as yet too early to discern the nature of the new institutions which are emerging or to assess the likelihood of their being able to succeed where their predecessors have failed.

Basic Causes of Political Instability

It has been argued here that continuing political instability and the closely related inability of governments to tackle the basic problems of the country have produced a progressive undermining of constitutionalism. But to explain this instability and the lack of achievements of governments it is necessary to examine the social and political situation of the country in a wider context.

Indonesia is a country whose island nature and long history of divisions makes political consensus difficult to maintain. It is a country with a multiplicity of diverse and conflicting social interests and a wide diffusion of political power. Thus its leaders' strong will to unity must contend with centrifugal tendencies derived from both history and economic structure. Desiring determined government, they are restricted because of the existence of a great number of small power centers, each in a position to veto some types of government action. These facts lie behind the splintered and fractionalized system of political parties which has contributed so much to political instability.

Moreover, as has been noted, colonial rule left Indonesia with a variety of acute problems. When independence was achieved, it came to a country whose agricultural capacity was increasingly unable to keep up with its rapid rate of population growth. It came to a country whose economic structure was one-sidedly export-oriented and whose governmental machine was heavily dependent on raw materials exports and the prices these fetched on a sharply fluctuating world market. It came to a country whose people had not been trained to take over its government, but who, on the contrary, had been barred from both political and administrative participation except at low levels.

The problems which this heritage presents for the governments of independent Indonesia are all the more formidable as a result of the eight years of Japanese occupation and the revolution. In those eight years great physical destruction was wrought. But, more important, the severest blows were dealt to Indonesia's social structure. And the way was cleared for yet further rapid social change in the postrevolutionary period.

In particular, the Japanese occupation and the revolution created a new group of persons taken out of their traditional roles in villages and towns to become soldiers and mass organizers. These people were promised a stake in the new society of independence. But the new society has had to operate on the basis of the old economy. Economically the country's problems remain substantially as before. So, for large groups of those who fought in the revolution, there have simply not been enough rewards or opportunities for new social integration. Nor has the economy expanded rapidly in the postwar period; such new employment opportunities as have been created have been more than offset by the rapid development of education.

Thus there exists a sizable group of children of the nationalist revolution who have remained dissatisfied with its fruits. These people, an important minority of what we have called the newspaper-reading public, are the chief source of political ferment. It is they who provide the dynamic energy of movements giving vent to "oppositionist" feeling—whether they are directed against the Dutch, the Chinese, or "Djakarta."

The role of the group is the more important because its members can find support in a much wider group of people affected by ongoing social change. Their leadership is easily accepted by wageworkers, by the urban unemployed and semiemployed, by peasant groups in a number of areas, and by many of the large group of the newly educated who cannot find the type of employment which they have been led to expect as their due. At the same time the social forces with a major interest in social stability are weak in Indonesia, partly because the group of Indonesians with ties to established property continues to be relatively small.

Finally, one must consider the weakness of governments in terms of the sparsity of the resources which they command. Operating against a background of highly stimulated economic and social aspirations in a large section of the population, Indonesian governments are severely limited in the instruments of control which they have at their disposal.

Constitutionally they are weak—meaning here cabinets, which have been the center of government power at least until the present crisis— because of the power of the President and of parliament. Unlike cabinets in most parliamentary countries, they have had to share with the President the important power to order a dissolution.

Politically they have strength because of the great prestige of government as such and because of their opportunities of channeling nationalist ideology through such agencies as the Ministries of Information, Education, and Religion. But here, too, the potentiality of rivalry between cabinet and President is an important limiting factor. Patronage is one of the most important weapons of governments. They can buy off opposition by virtue of their ability to dispose of government posts, overseas trips, import licenses, and so on. But this is effective only for members of the political elite, not at the level of the larger and ultimately decisive group of the newspaper-reading public.

Furthermore, the agencies through which they can enforce their will are beset with numerous weaknesses. The power and authority of the members of the general administrative service—the regents and district officers—have been radically curtailed by the upsurge of nationalist and democratic feeling and by the development of political parties and mass organizations at the local level. The police remains obedient and relatively cohesive. The small navy and air force proved their effectiveness in the military actions of 1958, though they had failed earlier in putting an end to large-scale smuggling activity. The army, however, is a heterogeneous body, revolutionary in its origin, political in its traditions, and subject to various local pressures. Its successful actions against the 1958 rebellion have served to strengthen the power of its central command, but important divisions continue to exist. The army has never been prepared to accept government decisions uncritically and is not prepared to do this now. And a number of areas exist where it is unable to exert power because of the influence of the rebels of 1958 or of the Darul Islam and other earlier rebel-bandit groups.

Finally, as will be shown in the following section, the government's controlling capacity is seriously impaired by weaknesses in its system of administration.

Political Behavior

In the foregoing discussion reference has been made to the concept of three levels at which Indonesian politics operates, the level of the political elite, the level of the newspaper-reading public, and the mass level. In terms of these arbitrarily delineated categories the mass level is relatively unimportant in the national political process. It is of great importance in what may be called "detraditionalized areas"—cities and towns, estate and mine areas, and some areas of small holders' export production. And it became more generally important with the onset of heavy village campaigning for the 1955 elections. But this situation ended shortly after the elections. Although many millions of villagers and town workers have retained membership of the parties in which they were enrolled in the period of campaigning, this fact has been of little significance since then, at least at the level of national politics.

On the other hand the newspaper-reading public is a constantly important political factor. Indonesia has a total daily press circulation of something over 800,000; [8] one may estimate the number of persons actually reading newspapers regularly or semiregularly at approximately two million. This group of the population—persons with at least primary education, city people, town people, and some prominent village people—is in effect "public opinion" as far as the day-to-day and month-to-month politics of the capital is concerned. The members of this group are in a position to press, through political parties, trade unions, religious organizations, and so on, for particular sectional interests. Their feelings on political issues are important in keeping government action within the limits of common nationalist consensus. They become decisive when a government acts in violation of this consensus—as in 1952 when the Sukiman cabinet's Foreign Minister secretly signed an agreement to accept U.S. aid on terms which, it was feared, would lead to military obligations.

Above this group is the political elite, the top leadership of the nationalist revolution and those who have become linked with it by

[8] The figure given by the Ministry of Information for September 1, 1955, is 821,560. See *Almanak Pers Indonesia, 1954–1955* [Indonesian Press Almanac, 1954–1955] (Djakarta: Indonesian Press and Public Opinion Institute, 1955).

virtue of economic power, power over mass organizations, or family ties. This is the group to which Robert Bone referred when he wrote that "Indonesian political life is a kind of poker game played by a few thousand people all of whom have known each other much too long and too well." [9] But the size of the group is probably no more than five hundred persons. Most political decisions are taken on the basis of consensus in this very small group, which includes higher civil servants, army officers, politicians, youth and student leaders, newspaper editors, importers, bankers, and professors, most of them in the capital. After a political crisis, the minimum agreement necessary for decisions is re-established through the balance within this group. At the same time many of its members act as spokesmen for the much larger group of the newspaper-reading public, both on issues of broad nationalist consensus and on matters affecting sectional interests.

It is this elite group which has become increasingly divided in the postrevolutionary period, with sections of it involved with centers of economic and social power—propertied groups and collective bodies such as trade unions, veterans' organizations, and military units. Nevertheless a great deal of unity continues to characterize the elite. The conditions of capital-city social life have worked to integrate the powerful mass leaders of low educational attainment into the pattern established by the intellectuals. Intermarriage has had a similar effect, at the same time forging links between elite members of mutually antagonistic parties and interest groups. Despite the aggravation of the conflicts inside the elite, its members continue to have common interests. These factors go far to explain the remarkable compromise solutions which it has been possible to effect in the case of a number of Indonesia's political crises.

The smallness of Indonesia's political elite gives personal factors a role of very great importance. Thus family, clan, and regional relationships, disciple relationships, the role of persons with "fatherlike" personal influence over others, and simply personal likes and dislikes—all these factors can be decisive in the making of political decisions.

Moreover, elite politics in Indonesia has its own style rooted in traditional Indonesian thinking and cultural attitudes as well as in a variety of reactions to the impact of the West. Thus the country's

[9] Robert C. Bone, "The Future of Indonesian Political Parties," *Far Eastern Survey*, XXIII (Feb. 1954), 17–24; see also James H. Mysbergh, "The Indonesian Political Elite," *ibid.*, XVI (March 1957), 38–42.

tradition of consultation, compromise, and synthesis is undoubtedly a factor of major importance at the level of elite politics.[10]

The Indonesian political process is thus immensely complicated. Its basic elements are revolutionary change, social diversity, and a wide diffusion of power. The levels at which the process functions are many, and the interaction between them follows a variety of channels. Finally, it operates in a cultural context of its own, a context which itself determines the role of institutions adopted from other countries. It cannot be understood except on its own terms.

[10] Soedjatmoko, "The Role of Political Parties in Indonesia," in Philip W. Thayer, ed., *Nationalism and Progress in Free Asia* (Baltimore: Johns Hopkins Press, 1956), pp. 128–140.

· XII ·

Major Problems

INDONESIA faces most of the problems common to the Southeast Asian countries, many of them in more acute forms than those of its neighbors. As an archipelago nation historically divided and its several islands uneven in economic development, it has major difficulties to surmount in maintaining national unity. Economic tasks are extremely formidable, some of them unmatched in any other Southeast Asian country, principally because of the serious agricultural situation in Java with its increasingly adverse ratio of population to resources. At the same time much is expected of Indonesian governments because a revolution has aroused critical political awareness in the mass of the people (at least in Java) to an extent greater than in any of the neighboring countries.

On the other hand Indonesia has certain advantages over its neighbors. The new social ferment which the revolution brought to town and village alike has made possible great achievements in the field of education; it has made possible a significant measure of democratization of local government and affairs; it has removed some important barriers to economic expansion. Indonesia's social class structure is such that relatively few strong barriers stand in the way of egalitarian social reform. In addition the geographical situation shields the nation from some of the immediate external dangers which the countries of mainland Southeast Asia must face.

The Indonesian revolution was fought for independence. Yet independence was and is seen merely as a bridge to the attainment of social justice and higher levels of prosperity. The Indonesian leadership of the present time is therefore charged with bringing about economic development.

Set in its political context, this means both more and less than economic development in the sense in which economists use the term. The Indonesian leaders' goal is not only raising per capita income in the population at large, but also—and this is perhaps of more immediate importance—achieving a "national economy" with Indonesians in positions of leadership and management. From the point of view of political stability the development which Indonesian governments are required to furnish is not simply a matter of long-term planning for a general rise in prosperity. It is equally important that this development should involve the economic and social integration of the groups of Indonesians to whom governments are most immediately accountable, first the persons of the elite and secondly those of what we have called the newspaper-reading public. In particular it must involve the half million or so former revolutionaries who constitute the most dynamic section of the newspaper-reading public. Political instability and the disintegrative tendencies manifesting themselves particularly since 1956 may be seen as the result of the regime's failure to implement policies which are developmental in a long-term sense and at the same time are adequate to the task of integrating these old revolutionaries.

The Economy

Indonesia's economic problems go back ultimately to the peasant cultivating his tiny plot of land. Of the 80 per cent or so of the Indonesian labor force engaged in agriculture, the greatest part consists of small cultivators operating on a labor-intensive basis with little or no capital. A small but increasing minority produce for the world market: they are the small holders who furnish rubber and copra and to a lesser extent sugar, tobacco, coffee, and tea. The great majority grow basic foodstuffs, rice, maize, cassava, sweet potato, soya beans, and green vegetables on what is still substantially a subsistence basis.

Indonesian peasants are poor, and the structure of their economy is such that they are in danger of growing poorer. In Java this is directly related to the smallness of plots and the pressure of the population on land. There are few opportunities on the island for increasing the acreage under crops, for its percentage of forest land is already so low that erosion is a serious problem. Thus peasant plots are tending to become even smaller as the population grows. At the same time much of the rural labor force is underemployed, even in areas where cottage industry exists. Here is a problem whose dimensions call for comparisons with the poorest and most densely populated areas of India and China.

Outside Java the problems are similar to those of the relatively plentiful areas of Southeast Asia. Land is generally not very scarce, and population pressure is still a phenomenon of little more than local significance, despite the fact that population is growing even faster than in Java. At the same time these areas too are faced with most aspects of the vicious circle of technical and economic "underdevelopment"—the interaction of lack of capital, underemployment of labor, lack of saving habits, and lack of purchasing power. Although great differences of economic pattern exist—between such areas of relatively developed capitalism as West Sumatra and such tradition-bound regions as the eastern Lesser Sunda Islands—it is clear that the Indonesian islands outside Java are in general in urgent need of the dynamic impulses generated by economic development.[1]

What, then, is the government's answer to the situation in peasant agriculture—extreme in Java but serious also elsewhere? In part it is one of technical improvement. The government's agricultural extension workers have had success in promoting the use of fertilizers and of superior seed strains. Because of this work, whose effectiveness can be traced partly to changes in peasant attitudes produced by the revolution, production of staple foods has risen. The policy goal of making Indonesia again self-sufficient in rice production, as in the last year of the prewar period, has yet to be attained. But the increase in rice production from 5,805,000 tons in 1951 to 7,300,000 in 1956 is cause for considerable satisfaction.[2] The same may be said for the improvements in livestock and in land and sea fisheries.

An important focus of government effort is credit creation and the fostering of small-scale industrial activity in or near the village. Village Indonesia in the postrevolutionary period has been especially thirsty for credit. Governments have attempted to meet this need

[1] Justus M. van der Kroef, "Indonesia: Centrifugal Economies," in James W. Wiggins and Helmut Schoeck, eds., *Foreign Aid Re-examined: A Critical Appraisal* (Washington, D.C.: Public Affairs Press, 1958), pp. 197–220.

[2] Bank Indonesia, *Report for the Year 1951–52* (Djakarta, 1952), p. 136, and *Report for the Year 1956–57* (Djakarta, 1957), p. 131.

partly by expanding credit through old and new banking institutions and partly by encouraging co-operatives. The growth of co-operatives has been a notable feature of economic development in Indonesia, particularly in that it has been the result mainly of autonomous self-help in the village. By the end of 1955 there were in existence 11,400 co-operative societies of different types with a total membership of approximately 2 million and accumulated capital amounting to more than 300 million rupiah (approximately $26 million).[3] It is doubtful, however, whether even this constitutes a quantitatively satisfactory tackling of the twin problem of village savings and capital accumulation.

The governments have been concerned to maximize the production and export yields of estates and mines. But their efforts have run up against a number of political difficulties. In part this stems from the fact that the great majority of the enterprises concerned are owned by foreigners, or were until the take-overs of Dutch enterprises in December 1957.

One difficult problem for these enterprises has been that of labor costs. Miserably low as estate workers' wages are by any Western comparison, they are high compared with wages paid for estate work in a number of other tropical countries and also high compared with wages paid in Indonesia in colonial times. This is the result both of the strength of the labor unions and of the generosity of the country's new labor legislation which incorporates such progressive (but for Indonesia expensive) features as the seven-hour day and a number of bonuses and social service provisions. In addition government conciliators and arbitration tribunals have frequently favored labor before foreign management, partly because of nationalist and labor sympathies and partly because of the greater political pressure which labor unions are able to exert.

A somewhat parallel problem is the one of illegal squatting on estate land. This dates back to the prewar period. It was aggravated during the Japanese occupation and the revolution when governments called on villagers to occupy unused plantation land, particularly for rice growing. Postrevolutionary governments have attempted to return some of this land to the estates, but retransfers of land have proved to be political dynamite, partly because of the power of the peasant unions, to which the squatters are naturally strongly attracted.

[3] See Mohammad Hatta, *The Co-operative Movement in Indonesia* (Ithaca, N.Y.: Cornell University Press, 1957), pp. 93, 94.

In 1953 an attempt at forcing a retransfer in East Sumatra produced a shooting incident and five deaths and was in part a cause of the fall of the Wilopo cabinet. After that governments acted with great circumspection, and there were few evictions. The number of squatters on estate lands has grown steadily throughout the postrevolutionary period, especially in East Sumatra.[4]

Sensing insecurity, most estates have done little replanting in the whole of the present period. Many have followed a policy of maximizing immediate profits, with a view to reducing gradually their assets in the country, and some have actually closed down operations. With the December 1957 take-overs of Dutch assets many Dutch estates came under the supervision of military boards, and most Dutch members of their technical and administrative staffs left the country. This produced a further production decline and heightened the sense of insecurity in the whole estate sector of the economy. In the oil sector, on the other hand, where well over half of the capital is American, there have been no take-overs and several sizable new investments.

Since 1951 there has been a tendency for the volume of exports, as measured by government statistics, to decline. In part this was because of the smuggling of export commodities to Singapore, the Philippines, and British Borneo. Stimulated by the currency discrepancies which resulted from domestic inflation and the pegging of the rate of exchange, the smuggling trade made important inroads into the volume of government-controlled foreign reserves, particularly in the period between 1954 and the first half of 1958.

With rubber and oil accounting for approximately 60 per cent of the foreign exchange earnings in any one year, Indonesia was strongly affected by the Korea war boom in raw materials prices and again by the post-Korea slump. The boom was damaging in that it created pressures for heavy overseas spending and so made the subsequent return to normal import levels politically and psychologically difficult. The slump forced the country to import at much lower than normal levels. This was as important in generating political pressures against the government of the day as it was in creating difficulties for development planning. Moreover, it had drastic consequences for government finances, as Indonesia's budgetary structure is built pre-

[4] See Karl J. Pelzer, "The Agrarian Conflict in East Sumatra," *Pacific Affairs*, XXX (June 1957); Clark E. Cunningham, *The Post-War Migration of the Toba Bataks to East Sumatra* (Cultural Reports Series, Southeast Asia Studies, Yale University; New Haven, 1958).

dominantly on export and import duties. In 1952 these constituted
59 per cent of government receipts.[5] Thus a further result was a government deficit producing severe inflationary pressures.

Reacting strongly against the disadvantages at which their country
has been placed by the almost exclusively raw material-producing
nature of its economy, Indonesian leaders are anxious for a rapid
development of industry. In the first three years of the postrevolutionary period government industrial policy concentrated primarily on
small-scale and cottage industry, with the establishment of industrial
processing and advisory "centers" in rural areas and encouragement
of ex-guerrillas to enter such fields as brick- and tilemaking and saw-
milling. The subsequent period saw an increased emphasis on larger
operations. Some success has been achieved in both fields. Textile
production more than doubled between 1951 and 1955. The number
of printing plants was greatly augmented, as was the number of rubber remilling units, and Indonesia acquired a caustic soda factory, a
desiccated coconut factory, and, in 1957, a large new cement plant.

Since January 1956 a Five Year Plan has been officially in operation.
This plan has a fairly strong industrial emphasis, calling for the establishment of two hydroelectric *cum* irrigation schemes and an iron and
steel industry. The first two years of its operation, however, provide
little cause for optimism, at least with regard to these major projects.
This is due principally to the political crisis which has engulfed Indonesia in the 1956–1958 period. But it reflects also certain political
factors which have slowed down industrial development—in fact
development generally—in the whole of the postrevolutionary period.

Indonesian governments of this period have lacked the effective
power needed to pursue long-range goals of prosperity and development and at the same time satisfy immediate political demands. On
the whole they have tended to do the latter at the expense of the
former. There have been strong moves in the dirction of "Indonesiani-
zation," the extension of Indonesian ownership and control machinery
into such previously foreign-dominated sectors as importing, banking,
shipping, plantation agriculture, rice milling, and exporting. This has
done something to satisfy political demands, but its economic effects
have generally been negative.

One important political brake on planned development has been
the weakness of governments vis-à-vis parliament. A number of im-

[5] Stephen W. Reed and others, eds., *Indonesia*, Subcontractor's Monograph,
Human Relations Area File 57 (New Haven, 1956), p. 1057.

portant government bills in the economic field have been held up by parliaments for as long as three or four years.

Large and frequent budget deficits, the result in part of a political inability to resist patronage pressures and reduce expensive liabilities, in part also of the need for heavy military spending, have produced a continuing inflation. Rising sharply after 1953, this had become a problem of major proportions by 1958, with the cumulative effects of the regionalist rebellion coming on top of an already unsound financial situation.

Finally in this connection one must consider the effect of two other factors which have functioned as a brake on economic development— the country's low level of bureaucratic efficiency and the continued existence of civil insecurity.

Administrative Problems

Independent Indonesia has had an extreme shortage of trained administrators, as well as of government technical personnel, throughout its period of existence. This fact has its roots in the colonial policies of Holland which resulted in few Indonesians obtaining thorough training and fewer administrative responsibility. In part, too, it is due to the fact that government work offers little financial attraction for persons with university or completed secondary training. The revolution produced a radical equalizing of the government's payroll, a leveling off of the ratio of highest to lowest salaries. In consequence there is now a large discrepancy between the salaries which skilled persons may receive in government compared with private employment. Many such persons have therefore left the service. Furthermore, many of those who remain feel that their presence is a favor they confer upon the government, and this creates important obstacles to discipline and consistent personnel policies.

On the other hand the bureaucracy is heavily overstaffed at the lower levels. This is partly because two separate administrative services had to be fused after the withdrawal of the Dutch and the collapse of their puppet federal states. More important, it is a result of the political necessity to reward large numbers of ex-fighters with government posts. In addition it has been impossible to prevent the civil service from continuing to expand. And this expansion, owing in large part to local political pressures for the acceptance of young persons finishing school, has been chiefly at levels where overstaffing already exists. Civil service and army salaries together have eaten away roughly 50 per cent of the government budgets in the last four years. Whenever a government leader has called for a reduction in civil service personnel or, more daring still, army personnel, there have been immediate and vociferous reactions, both from civil service unions and from political parties.

In recent years there has been relatively little left of the moral *élan* and sense of purpose which characterized much of the revolutionary civil service. The relative importance of national loyalties in relation to sectional and family ties has declined. This, combined with the fact of low salaries for higher civil service personnel, has given rise to corruption. In the years immediately preceding the general elections of 1955, governmental corruption developed on a particularly serious scale; it then acquired a degree of public acceptance, at least inasmuch as it was seen as corruption for party campaigning funds. Civil servant corruption has been reduced since the launching of army-led anticorruption drives under the martial law regulations invoked in March 1957.

On the other hand political nepotism, which was also greatly stimulated in the period immediately before the elections, continues to characterize the government service. It is frequently remarked that particular ministries or sections of ministries are the domain of one or another party or faction. When there is competition or conflict between sections of the government service or, as is more usually the case, a signal absence of co-operation, long unbreakable deadlocks frequently ensue.

Inertia is perhaps the biggest single problem of the administrative system. Administrators tend to avoid decisions, delegating these upward or, at the higher levels, deferring them. Where radical reorganization is required, it is frequently thought to be impossible of accomplishment. Instead, therefore, a variety of new regulations are superimposed on an already-overcomplicated system of rules; cumbersomeness and inefficiency are the result.

There is very great variety within the Indonesian administrative system, and to make any general assessment of its level of performance would be extremely difficult. It is certainly adequate to the requirements of its role in much of Indonesian society, particularly rural society. On the other hand it is undeniably failing in many aspects of its "modern" and "developmental" role.

Moreover, dissatisfaction with it has long been high among certain groups, helping to build up anti-Djakarta feeling. "Red tape" and administrative bungling have been resented especially in the more distant islands whose representatives cannot easily come to Djakarta to press their claims personally. One important aspect of the regionalist movements of 1956 and 1957 is that they were directed against Djakarta's inefficiency in dealing with regional problems.

Civil Security

In the first two years of the postrevolutionary period the government registered major successes in the restoration of security. It persuaded large numbers of members of irregular guerrilla bands to return to normal civilian life, and it defeated three distinct challenges from groups of soldiers of the old Netherlands Indies army.

By 1952, however, it had become clear that in certain areas there was a problem of former Republican guerrillas which was unlikely to be solved rapidly. The problem was most serious in parts of West Java and South Sulawesi, and in both of these areas the core of it was the extremist Muslim Darul Islam, a movement working for, and actually claiming to be, an Islamic state.[6] In 1953 the area of insecurity became more extensive with the outbreak of an armed rebellion in Atjeh in North Sumatra and the association of this with the Darul Islam movement. Although never developing the proportions which civil insecurity has had in Burma, this situation had serious effects on production and general political stability. In 1953 there were 655 village officials and guards who were killed in West Java alone, and army casualties averaged one man per day. Material losses for that year were estimated at 115,000 rupiah (approximately $10,000) per day.[7]

Continuing pressure by the best-trained units of the Republic's army produced definite improvements in the situation between 1953 and 1956. This was above all the case in West Java, where rebel-bandit strength came to be confined to relatively small areas of rugged mountain terrain. In some other regions, such at Atjeh, the proportions of the problem were reduced by negotiation. But the crisis situation in 1957–1958 appears to have increased the scope and effectiveness of Darul Islam activity in several parts of the country.

In any event a hard core of Darul Islam rebels continues to exist

[6] See C.A.O. van Nieuwenhuijze, "The Darul Islam Movement in West Java," *Pacific Affairs*, XXIII (1950), 169–183; "The Problem of Security," *Indonesian Affairs* (Ministry of Information, Djakarta), II (June–July 1952), 8–13.

[7] A. H. Nasution, *Tjatatan Sekitar Politik Militer Indonesia* [Notes on Indonesian Military Policy] (Djakarta: Pembimbing, 1955), pp. 91 ff.

in West Java and several other areas, particularly South Sulawesi. Economically and socially, it throws its shadow over a much larger area than it actually controls. This is a situation which is unlikely to be changed rapidly. As the Malayan "emergency" has shown, overwhelming military superiority can fail of success against small and tightly knit rebel groups enjoying some popular support and operating by terrorism. Darul Islam's strength results partly from the fear which its cruelty inspires. But in addition its ideological attraction as a radically Muslim movement, a radically anti-Dutch movement, and a movement of regional resistance to Djakarta further explains its strength.

Government effectiveness against the rebel and bandit organizations has been limited by frequent cabinet changes and changes in top military personnel. It has also suffered because of vacillation between a military and a negotiated solution to the problem. Again, the fighting strength of the army is adversely affected by political factors which have made impossible the radical reorganization of it which most of its leaders regard as necessary. Thus the revolutionary army has been allowed to grow old; the average age of its soldiers was 34 in 1954.[8] Finally, budgetary stringency has limited the army's effectiveness. Especially since 1953 it has been short of supplies, and poor soldier welfare conditions have been a constant grievance.

The year 1958 has seen the development of civil insecurity of a new type. The "Revolutionary Government of the Republic of Indonesia," divested of its control over major towns, is continuing to operate as a guerrilla movement. Its followers have inflicted considerable damage on government enterprises and production facilities in parts of Sumatra and Sulawesi.

Education

Education is a field in which independent Indonesia has shown some of its greatest advances—just as limitation of educational opportunities was one of the severest shortcomings of the colonial administration. Whereas 2,021,990 children attended primary schools in 1939–1940, the figure had risen to 5,882,348 by 1954–1955. There are good grounds for believing that all children between the ages of 8 and 14 years will be attending school by the target year of 1961 or soon thereafter.[9] The expansion has been even more dramatic in the

[8] *Ibid.*, pp. 203 ff. and *passim.*
[9] See *Statistik Pendidikan dan Pengadjaran, tahun 1953–54* [Educational Statis-

secondary field. Whereas 21,875 pupils attended junior secondary schools of all types in 1939–1940 and 4,660 senior secondary schools (including technical and vocational schools), the figures for 1953–1954 were 338,667 and 66,314.[10] And they have risen considerably since that year. University enrollments have expanded tenfold.

Standards have indeed fallen compared with before the war, particularly at the secondary level. An equally serious shortcoming is that the system fails to attract good students to technical and business schools. The ambition of the better students is a professional career or, failing that, a clerical one.

Most important of all, there are signs in several areas that the large growth in the number of persons with primary and lower secondary schooling is increasing social instability.[11] The present regime will have to pay politically unless it can end the discrepancy which now exists between its educational expansion and the pace of economic development.

Nevertheless the educational picture may well be cause for pride. There can be no doubt that the school has continued the process of democratization begun by the revolution, particularly in rural society. Liberal scholarship allowances have made it possible for children of even some of the poorest groups of villagers to study at secondary schools.

At the same time education has been important in the welding of national unity. Interregional understanding has been furthered by the system of posting secondary schoolteachers to areas outside their place of origin. Schools and mass education work have contributed to the assimilation into something like an all-Indonesian culture of the many small and remote ethnic groups hitherto in scant contact with other cultures.

Education has played a major role in spreading the use of the Indonesian national language. Because Indonesian is the language of instruction in primary schools in all parts of the country, at least from

tics, 1953–1954] (Djakarta: Education Ministry, 1954); *Pengadjaran Sekolah Rendah dan Sekolah Landjutan, 1954–55* [Primary and Secondary Education, 1954–1955] (Djakarta: Central Bureau of Statistics, 1957). In early 1953 an additional 1,784,050 children were attending Muslim schools under the Ministry of Religion. See *Statistik Pendidikan dan Pengadjaran, tahun 1953–54*, p. 10.

[10] *Statistik Pendidikan dan Pengadjaran, tahun 1953–54*, pp. 4–12.

[11] F. L. Barloga and others, "Report of Technical Education Survey Team," *Ekonomi dan Keuangan Indonesia* [Economics and Finance in Indonesia] (Djakarta), VIII (Oct. 1955), 637–683; A. van den Ende, "Onderwijs en Maatschappelijke Behoefte" [Education and Social Need], *ibid.*, X (Feb. 1957), 116 ff.

the fourth class upward, it is now known by an important group of villagers everywhere, including many areas where no person understood it in 1950. In Indonesia, unlike the Philippines, Burma, and India, the introduction of an indigenous national language has called forth little or no opposition from any linguistic or cultural group. This is partly because a form of the language has been a lingua franca of trade in the archipelago for hundreds of years and partly because it is not the language of a dominant cultural group.

National Unity

The period since December 1956 has made it clear that none of Indonesia's many problems is more important than that of national unity. Anti-Djakarta feeling has been rising gradually in most parts of the country throughout the postrevolutionary period. In 1956 it emerged as active defiance of the central government in a number of very important areas outside Java. And in 1958 it gave rise to a major rebellion.

Some observers have explained these developments in terms of the ethnic and cultural diversity of Indonesia, stressing the existence of long-standing feelings against Java and against the ethnic Javanese in that one-third of the country's population who live outside the central island. These are significant factors. But regionalism has been directed more against Djakarta than against Java or the ethnic Javanese. The men who led the regionalist movements of 1956–1958 are as much Republicans and old revolutionaries as the leaders of the central government. Their grievances were more the product of their concern for the economic welfare of their region than of their feelings as members of an ethnic, cultural, or linguistic group of Minangkabaus, Bataks, or Minahasans. At the same time they reflect the dominant economic orientation of particular regions outside Java, an orientation as sympathetic to capitalistic entrepreneurial activity as that of the main Javanese leadership to bureaucratic economic organization.

The leadership of the regionalist movement came principally from areas which contribute heavily to Indonesia's foreign exchange earnings. In one sense an objective conflict of interests exists between these areas and Java, and indirectly Djakarta. Whereas the exporting areas are concerned to import both capital and consumer goods on a scale approximating the value of their exports, the Djakarta leadership must concern itself also with Java, which has relatively little export production. This, moreover, is not only because Java can exert immediate political and patronage pressure. It is also because Java is poor and in great need of developmental stimulation.

Conflicts of economic interest came to the fore also on the issue of regional autonomy. The development of the crisis may be traced in good part to the slowness of the central government in granting the regions significant local autonomy or the taxing powers which would enable them to promote development on the basis of their own resources. It may be traced also to the inefficiency of the administrative system, overcentralized and cumbersome as it is. A further contributing factor was the apprehension felt in the islands outside Java— which the elections of 1955 had shown to be strongholds of the Masjumi (and to a lesser extent the Socialist and Christian parties)— at the increasing strength of communism in Java and the permissive attitude of the central government and President Soekarno toward it.

The political and military defeat of the regionalist leaders who launched the Padang rebellion has afforded an important temporary check against centrifugal tendencies. Furthermore, it has shown that a strong will to effective unity continues to exist throughout the country. The regionalists honored fully the symbols of nationalism and national unity throughout 1957. They modified their attitude somewhat in February 1958, when they resorted to an open disavowal of the central government and President Soekarno. Soon thereafter they found much of their support falling away. In a sense, therefore, the failure of the rebellion can be seen as evidence of the great support still enjoyed by the all-Indonesian nationalism associated with the name of the President.

Nationalism apart, there are a number of powerful factors making for continued unity in the country. Java is an important market for several products of the outer islands, as the outer islands are for numerous Javanese products. There are large numbers of Sumatrans in Java, and large numbers of Javanese in Sumatra. And many personal links exist between the regions through individuals at or near the level of the political elite, links of common schooling, common nationalist and revolutionary experience, and intermarriage.

But regionalism is by no means dead; the grievances which produced the centrifugal pressures of 1956–1958 have yet to be alleviated. In the present period the central government is faced with the necessity for determined action if the new militarily established unity is to be maintained. It has the difficult task of setting its house in order economically. It must come to a general and quickly implemented

settlement on the long-standing problems of financial relations between the center and the regions and the allocation of development
funds among different parts of the country. And it must tackle the
whole question of regional autonomy. This involves decisions not only
on such matters as the status of particular areas and the ethnic groups
in them, but also on fundamental questions such as that of the future
position of the hierarchical general administration and its role in relation to other government agencies and to the elected regional assemblies and their executive arms.[12]

It has been argued by a number of overseas observers, and more
recently by some Indonesians, that federalism would provide the most
effective framework for the solution of these problems. In view of the
unhappy memories which most Indonesian nationalists have of the
federalism which the Dutch sponsored in opposition to the revolutionary Republic, it is more than likely that another formula will be
preferred. But it would seem that to be politically and economically
practicable it will have to be one which gives the regions outside
Java more money and more power over its spending than they had
before 1956.

A less immediate but nevertheless important problem of national
unity is that of Indonesia's Chinese minority. The country has three
major and constitutionally recognized minorities, the roughly 2,500,000
persons of Chinese ancestry, the 85,000-strong Arab minority, and the
perhaps 50,000-strong Eurasians; but only the first of these three is a
major political factor. Historically a tool of the colonial power, the
Chinese minority has long been socially separate in most parts of the
country from the community of native Indonesians. Its economic power
has often made it the target for vigorous Indonesian hostility.

The rise of China as a great power and the growth of Indonesian
communism have provided a new context for the old antagonisms.
Although traditionally nonpolitical and concerned primarily to enjoy
secure conditions under which trade may go on, the Indonesian
Chinese are in large part attracted by the newly powerful China. A
small minority of them, mainly newcomers born outside Indonesia,
are active propagandists for communism. But almost all look to Peking
to give them protection in the exposed position which they occupy
vis-à-vis Indonesian nationalism.

[12] See John D. Legge, *Problems of Regional Autonomy in Contemporary Indonesia* (Cornell Modern Indonesia Project, Interim Reports Series; Ithaca, N.Y.,
1957); Gerald S. Maryanov, *Decentralization in Indonesia as a Political Problem*
(Cornell Modern Indonesia Project, Interim Reports Series; Ithaca, N.Y., 1958).

Since 1956 there has been a marked rise in the volume of public expression of anti-Chinese feeling. The same period has seen the introduction of a number of military decrees aimed specifically at members of the Chinese community, in particular discriminatory taxes and the closing down of Chinese schools. The year 1958 saw the beginnings of a new emphasis in the officially channeled anti-Chinese campaigning, that is, the singling out of Chinese residents who are citizens or supporters of the Republic of China on Taiwan (which was unofficially helping the Sumatran and Sulawesi rebels). Military decrees ordering the taking over of Chinese business enterprises and schools were pointed directly at supporters of the diplomatically unrepresented Kuomintang regime. In this way it was possible for the demands of Indonesian nationalism to be met—at a time when economic adversity had created heavy pressures toward scapegoatism—without arousing resentment in Peking.

Foreign Relations

Indonesia, like Burma, India, and Ceylon, pursues a policy of nonalignment in the Cold War. Indonesian leaders speak of it as an active independent policy aimed at safeguarding world peace. This policy rests in part on a jealous and sensitive concern for the preservation of Indonesia's new and hard-won independence and for its maximum freedom of international action. It represents also an attitude critical of both the Western and the Soviet-group countries, their social values, and their past policies toward Indonesia. In addition it is rooted in the carefully reasoned belief of a number of Indonesian leaders that their country can best contribute to world peace from the vantage point of nonalignment and a lack of prior commitment to either world bloc.

The policy is also explained in terms of Indonesia's domestic position. Of greatest importance for the maintenance of Indonesia's independence, its leaders argue, is domestic political stability. For this to be achieved it is imperative that the Cold War be kept from Indonesia's shores. So it has been an aim of foreign policy to avoid any international involvement which could widen internal divisions.[13]

Indonesia's military planning is based essentially on these con-

[13] See Mohammad Hatta, "Indonesia's Foreign Policy," *Foreign Affairs*, XXXI (April 1953), 441–452, and "Indonesia between the Power Blocs," *ibid.*, XXXVI (April 1958), 480–490; "The Historical and Philosophical Background of Our Independent Foreign Policy," *Indonesian Affairs* (Ministry of Information, Djakarta), I (July 1951), 8–13.

siderations. Thus it has refused to join the Southeast Asia Treaty Organization. Its leaders are aware that SEATO offers a degree of protection, whether Indonesia belongs to it or not. But their attitude is that, being militarily weak and having only a tiny navy, Indonesia cannot protect itself against attack by a major power. The most that could be presented to the would-be attacker is the threat that the people's guerrilla resistance would make occupation of Indonesian territory a costly and thankless task.

The nation's efforts must therefore be bent, its leaders believe, toward strengthening internal political unity and relieving international tensions, particularly in Asia. Its sponsorship of the Colombo Powers consultations (between the Prime Ministers of India, Pakistan, Ceylon, Burma, and Indonesia) and of the Asian-African conference held in Bandung in April 1955 and its active role in the United Nations, particularly on colonial issues, are motivated in part by concern for the lessening of world tensions. Concern to gain prestige for Indonesia as one of the leaders of Asia is another important aspect of this type of foreign policy activity.

The independent foreign policy has the support of all parties in Indonesia, including, officially, the Communist Party. Important differences of emphasis exist however, as between groups advocating greater or lesser degree of co-operation with the U.S.-led and Soviet-led blocs of states. These came into prominence with the development of the regional crisis, and particularly with the outbreak of civil warfare in early 1958. But, significantly, both parties in the conflict have continued throughout to take their stand on the basis of the independent foreign policy. At the level of the newspaper-reading public, at least, the feeling continues to be dominant that Indonesia must avoid every Cold War entanglement.

Indonesia has not been a major recipient of foreign aid, partly because governmental weakness and administrative delays have made a rapid rate of capital absorption impossible. Most of the aid has been received in the postrevolutionary period has come from the United States—in the form of an Export-Import Bank loan of $100 million, technical assistance, and surplus commodities aid.[14] There have been smaller amounts in technical assistance from the United Nations and through the Colombo Plan. Since 1955 Indonesia has made use of

[14] Total U.S. aid in the period 1950–1958 has had a value of $300 million. See statement of J. C. Baird, Director of U.S. Operations Mission, Djakarta, in *P.I.A. News Bulletin* (Djakarta), May 8, 1958.

East German and Czechoslovak credits and technical personnel, and late in 1957 parliament approved acceptance of a Soviet loan of $100 million.[15] Indonesian foreign policy aims to draw maximum advantage from the fact that the country is uncommitted in the Cold War. This is important particularly in relation to the periodic need for new arms supplies and also at those times when a foreign loan becomes urgently necessary in order to meet the situation created by a critical depletion of foreign exchange reserves.

The most problematical aspect of Indonesia's foreign policy concerns relations with its former colonial master. The fact that Indonesia had to fight against Holland for over four years before its independence was recognized has left a deep mark on the thinking of almost all groups of Indonesians. In this respect no comparison is possible with any other Southeast Asian country, except possibly Vietnam.

Since 1950 relations between Holland and Indonesia have been disturbed by two principal issues, first by the strong economic position which the Dutch have continued to enjoy in Indonesia for almost all of this period—particularly in estate agriculture, banking, large-scale trading, and interinsular shipping—and secondly by the problem of sovereignty over West Irian or West New Guinea.

The West Irian issue, an important prestige question for both countries, has been particularly important in making good relations difficult. Since 1952 Holland has refused to enter further negotiations on this issue, thereby intensifying Indonesian feeling and obliging all political groups in the country to advocate and pursue strongly anti-Dutch policies. The last conference between the two countries, a meeting to discuss economic relations between them, broke down in early 1956. Thereupon the Masjumi-led government of Burhanuddin Harahap announced unilateral abrogation of the Round Table Conference agreement of 1949. Several months later the second Ali Sastroamidjojo cabinet decided on repudiation of 3,000 million guilders (approximately $780 million) of the old Netherlands Indies state debt which Indonesia had assumed under the 1949 agreement, that is, of that strongly resented part of the debt which represented the costs of Holland's postwar military operations against the Republic.

In November 1957 an Asian-African nations' motion in the UN General Assembly, asking that the President of the Assembly should initiate

[15] For a stimulating discussion of the implications of this new development see Charles Wolf, Jr., "Soviet Economic Aid in Southeast Asia: Threat or Windfall," *World Politics*, X (Oct. 1957), 91–101.

further Indonesian-Dutch negotiations on the Irian issue, failed to obtain the necessary two-thirds majority in the Assembly. There had previously been official statements, including some made by President Soekarno, to the effect that Indonesia would resort to independent action if this happened. When it did, Djakarta labor groups in Dutch enterprises began under PNI and Communist leadership to take over control of their firms. The cabinet, divided internally, took no action against them. Finally, several days later, the military stepped in and decreed what were described as temporary take-overs of Dutch business, temporary until Holland should agree to discuss the issue of sovereignty in West Irian. At the same time the cabinet ordered the expulsion of unemployed Dutch residents, and some government spokesmen called for more widespread expulsions. Large numbers of Dutch residents immediately began to leave.

It would be wrong to assume that this means that the Dutch no longer have an economic role to play in Indonesia. Some thousands of Dutch persons continue to work in Indonesia, many of them in high technical and business posts. But the decline in the Dutch role has been spectacular. No other nation of the area, with the exception of North Vietnam (and possibly South Vietnam), has rid itself so completely of its former colonial master. Dutch-Indonesian relations continue to be characterized by bitterness.

Indonesian leaders are right in more senses than one when they say that their revolution has not been completed. Its momentum continues.

SUGGESTED READING

IX: The Historical Background

Allen, George C., and Audrey G. Donnithorne. *Western Enterprise in Indonesia and Malaya.* London and New York: Macmillan, 1957.

Benda, Harry J. *The Crescent and the Rising Sun.* The Hague and Bandung: van Hoeve, 1958. A major and fully documented study of Indonesian Islam. Although concerned primarily with the period of the Japanese occupation, the author devotes two substantial chapters to Islam in the previous decades.

Boeke, J. H. *Economics and Economic Policy of Dual Economies as Exemplified by Indonesia.* Haarlem: Tjeenk Willink, 1953. A presentation of the dual economy theory, which continues to arouse considerable argument among economists and other social scientists.

Brand, Willem, Hubertus J. van Mook, and others. *The Indonesian Town: Studies in Urban Sociology.* The Hague and Bandung: van Hoeve, 1958.

Three major research reports made by Dutch investigators of the prewar period. It was edited, with a long introduction, by the editors of Selected Studies of Indonesia by Dutch Scholars.

Burger, D. H. *Structural Changes in Javanese Society: The Village Sphere and the Supra-Village Sphere.* (Cornell Modern Indonesia Project, Translation Series.) Ithaca, N.Y., 1957. A sociological interpretation of aspects of the Western impact, particularly in the nineteenth century; includes a highly interesting discussion of the aristocratic culture of Central and East Java.

Coast, John. *Recruit to Revolution.* London: Christophers, 1952. The very readable story of an Englishman's involvement with the cause of the revolutionary Republic, with personality sketches of a number of Indonesian leaders.

Coolie Budget Commission. *Living Conditions of Plantation Workers and Peasants on Java in 1939–1940.* (Cornell Modern Indonesia Project, Translation Series.) Ithaca, N.Y., 1956. A comprehensive report of the Netherlands Indies government, classified and unpublished until recently.

Djajadiningrat, Idrus Nasir. *The Beginnings of the Indonesian—Dutch Negotiations and the Hoge Veluwe Talks.* (Cornell Modern Indonesia Project, Monograph Series.) Ithaca, N.Y., 1957. A scholarly investigation of relations with Holland in the early period of the revolution.

Furnivall, John S. *Netherlands India: A Study of Plural Economy.* New York: Macmillan; Cambridge, Eng.: Cambridge University Press, 1944. An excellent general history of Indonesia in the colonial period. At the same time it is a presentation of the Furnivall theory of plural economy which has relevance for all of Southeast Asia.

Geertz, Clifford. *The Development of the Javanese Economy: A Socio-Cultural Approach.* Cambridge: Massachusetts Institute of Technology, Center for International Studies, 1956. An anthropologist's essay which throws new light on several of the central problems of Javanese history.

Haar, Barend ter. *Adat Law in Indonesia.* Ed. and with an introduction by E. Adamson Hoebel and A. Arthur Schiller. New York: Institute of Pacific Relations, 1948. A comprehensive survey of adat or customary law. The author was one of the leaders of the school of adat law specialists.

Kahin, George McT. *Nationalism and Revolution in Indonesia.* Ithaca, N.Y.: Cornell University Press, 1952. This sensitively written history of the Indonesian revolution is essential reading for anyone wishing to understand the country's political situation in the present period. It also contains important chapters on prewar colonial society and the early history of nationalism.

Kat Angelino, A. D. A. de. *Colonial Policy,* vol. II. The Hague: M. Nijhoff, 1931. A major work describing the structure and problems of colonial government in the Netherlands Indies.

McVey, Ruth T. *Comintern Colonial Policy, 1920–1927, and Its Effects on the Development of Indonesian Communism.* (Cornell Modern Indonesia Project, Monograph Series.) Ithaca, N.Y., 1959. A comprehensive study based on detailed research.

——. *The Soviet View of the Indonesian Revolution.* (Cornell Modern Indonesia Project, Interim Reports Series.) Ithaca, N.Y., 1957. Based on a full examination of Soviet materials, this paper goes far toward explaining Soviet and Communist actions in the 1945–1949 period.

Raffles, Sir Thomas Stamford. *History of Java.* London: Black, Parbury, and Allen, 1817.

Schiller, A. Arthur. *The Formation of Federal Indonesia.* The Hague and Bandung: van Hoeve, 1955. A legally oriented account of the governmental structure established in the Dutch-held areas of Indonesia in the period 1946–1949.

Schrieke, B. J. O. *Indonesian Sociological Studies.* Pt. I, The Hague and Bandung: van Hoeve, 1955; pt. II, The Hague and Bandung: van Hoeve, 1957. Selections from the work of an outstanding Dutch sociologist and historian. Included are studies of the social structure of precolonial Indonesia, of the role of Hinduism and Islam, and of the early Western impact, as well as the report of an investigation into the social roots of Communist influence in West Sumatra in the 1920s.

Sjahrir, Soetan. *Out of Exile.* New York: John Day, 1949. A collection of letters written by Sjahrir in the 1930s, from his various places of political exile in East Indonesia. Sensitively written and highly readable, the book is to be recommended not only for the understanding it provides of the thinking of the man who was to become Indonesia's first Prime Minister, but also as an introduction to the problems facing the Indonesian intellectual today.

Soemardjan, Selo. "Bureaucratic Organization in a Time of Revolution," *Administrative Science Quarterly,* II (Sept. 1957), 182–199.

Vandenbosch, Amry. *The Dutch East Indies: Its Government, Problems, and Politics.* Berkeley and Los Angeles: University of California Press, 1944. A comprehensive account of the system of government as it was on the eve of the Japanese occupation.

van Leur, J. C. *Indonesian Trade and Society.* The Hague and Bandung: van Hoeve, 1955. A recently translated collection of the main works of a Dutch historian who did path-breaking work in challenging the Europe-centered view of Asian history.

van Mook, Hubertus J. *The Stakes of Democracy in Southeast Asia.* New York: Norton, 1950. The parting words of the last Dutch Governor-General.

Vlekke, Bernard H. M. *Nusantara: A History of the East Indian Archipelago.* Cambridge, Mass.: Harvard University Press, 1945.

Wolf, Charles, Jr. *The Indonesian Story.* New York: John Day, 1948. A full account of the Indonesian—Dutch negotiations of 1945–1947 which culminated in the Linggadjati Agreement.

Woodman, Dorothy. *The Republic of Indonesia.* New York: Philosophical Library, 1955. An introductory book by a British journalist.

X: The Contemporary Setting

Alisjahbana, Takdir. "The Indonesian Language—By-Product of Nationalism," *Pacific Affairs,* XXII (Dec. 1949), 388–392.

Geertz, Clifford. "Religious Belief and Economic Behavior in a Central Javanese Town: Some Preliminary Considerations," *Economic Development and Cultural Change,* IV (Jan. 1956), 134–158. A brilliant exposition of social and economic aspects of religious cleavage in Central and East Java.

——. *The Social Context of Economic Change: An Indonesian Case Study.* Cambridge: Massachusetts Institute of Technology, Center for International Studies, 1956. Mimeograph. An analysis of developmental and anti-developmental consequences of the colonial system of sugar cultivation. It includes many valuable insights into the political process in contemporary rural society.

Higgins, Benjamin. "The 'Dualistic Theory' of Underdeveloped Areas," *Economic Development and Cultural Change,* IV (Jan. 1956), 99–115. An answer to the Boeke theory in terms of modern development theory.

Jay, Robert R. "Local Government in Rural Central Java," *Far Eastern Quarterly,* IV (Feb. 1956), 215–227. A valuable article which throws light on social as well as institutional aspects of local government.

Kennedy, Raymond. *Field Notes on Indonesia: South Celebes, 1949–1950.* Ed. by Harold C. Conklin. New Haven: Human Relations Area Files, 1953. Interesting jottings on a great variety of aspects of rural life in this area.

Palmier, Leslie H. "Changing Outposts: The Western Communities in Southeast Asia," *Yale Review,* XLVII (Spring 1958), 405–415. Stimulating reading and of considerable relevance to Westerners proposing to live in Southeast Asia.

Reed, Stephen W., and others, eds. *Indonesia.* Subcontractor's Monograph, Human Relations Area File 57. New Haven, 1956. A three-volume handbook on Indonesia. It contains useful material on a great variety of subjects, but is not uniformly reliable.

Soelaeman Soemardi. "Some Aspects of the Social Origins of the Indonesian Political Decision-Makers," in *Transactions of the Third World Congress of Sociology.* London: International Sociological Association, 1956. Important conclusions from research on the biographies of cabinet ministers, parliamentarians, and senior civil servants of the present period.

Supomo. "The Future of *Adat* Law in the Reconstruction of Indonesia," in

Philip W. Thayer, ed., *Southeast Asia in the Coming World.* Baltimore: Johns Hopkins University Press, 1953. Pages 217–236. An address by a man who was regarded as his country's foremost adat law scholar and also occupied high political and diplomatic posts.

van der Kroef, Justus M. "Economic Development in Indonesia: Some Social and Cultural Impediments," *Economic Development and Cultural Change,* IV (Jan. 1956), 116–133. A stimulating discussion of social aspects of the role of labor, entrepreneurship, and bureaucracy.

———. *Indonesia in the Modern World.* Vol. I, Bandung: Masa Baru, 1954; vol. II, Bandung: Masa Baru, 1956. A sociologist's essays on a great variety of historical, economic, social, and political problems. The author has a full acquaintance with the Dutch literature on Indonesia and contributes a number of stimulating interpretations of his own. But, partly as a result of the wide range of subjects covered, a number of these essays are marred by inaccuracies.

van der Veur, Paul. "The Eurasians of Indonesia: Castaways of Colonialism," *Pacific Affairs,* XXVII (June 1954), 124–137.

van Nieuwenhuijze, C. A. O. *Aspects of Islam in Post-Revolutionary Indonesia.* The Hague and Bandung: van Hoeve, 1958. A series of essays written by a former Islamic affairs specialist of the Netherlands Indies government.

Wertheim, W. F. "Changes in Indonesia's Social Stratification," *Pacific Affairs,* XXVIII (March 1955), 41–52. A discussion of the rise of collectivist social forces and values in the present period.

———. *Indonesian Society in Transition.* The Hague and Bandung: van Hoeve, 1956. A major work of social analysis, both historical and contemporary. The author, a neo-Marxist, is a leading Dutch authority on modern Indonesia.

Widjojo Nitisastro, and J. E. Ismael. *The Government, Economy, and Taxes of a Central Javanese Village.* (Cornell Modern Indonesia Project, Translation Series.) Ithaca, N.Y., 1959.

Willmott, Donald E. *The National Status of the Chinese in Indonesia.* (Cornell Modern Indonesia Project, Interim Reports Series.) Ithaca, N.Y., 1956. A short but comprehensive study based on sociological field research.

Willner, Ann R. "Social Change in Javanese Town-Village Life," *Economic Development and Cultural Change,* VI (April 1958), 229–242.

XI: The Political Process

Bone, Robert C. "The Future of Indonesian Political Parties," *Far Eastern Survey,* XXIII (Feb. 1954), 17–24. Includes some vivid description of the atmosphere of elite-level politics.

Budiardjo, Miriam S. "The Provisional Parliament of Indonesia," *Far East-*

ern Survey, XXV (Feb. 1956), 17–23. The best account of the role of parliament in the postrevolutionary period.

Feith, Herbert. *The Indonesian Elections of 1955*. (Cornell Modern Indonesia Project, Interim Reports Series.) Ithaca, N.Y., 1957.

——. *The Wilopo Cabinet, 1952–1953: A Turning Point in Post-Revolutionary Indonesia*. (Cornell Modern Indonesia Project, Monograph Series.) Ithaca, N.Y., 1958. Includes material on the main parties of the present period and on the role of the army.

Kahin, George McT. "Indonesia," in George McT. Kahin, ed., *Major Governments of Asia*. Ithaca, N.Y.: Cornell University Press, 1958. Pages 471–592. A comprehensive and up-to-date survey of the structure and functioning of Indonesian government and politics.

——. "Indonesian Politics and Nationalism," in W. L. Holland, ed., *Asian Nationalism and the West*. New York: Macmillan, 1953. Pages 65–196. Valuable material on the parties and on governmental and political developments in the 1950–1951 period.

McVey, Ruth T. *The Development of the Indonesian Communist Party and Its Relations with the Soviet Union and the Chinese People's Republic*. Cambridge: Massachusetts Institute of Technology, Center for International Studies, 1954.

Natsir, Mohammad. *Some Observations concerning the Role of Islam in National and International Affairs*. (Southeast Asia Program, Cornell University, Data Paper no. 16.) Ithaca, N.Y., 1954. A good introduction to the thinking of the chairman of the Masjumi, who is a theologian and political theorist as well as a party leader.

Pauker, Guy J. *Indonesian Images of Their National Self*. Santa Monica, Calif.: Rand Corporation, 1958. Also in *Public Opinion Quarterly*, XXII (Fall 1958), 305–325. An illuminating study of political values at the level of the "newspaper-reading public," based on an analysis of entries submitted in a press-conducted essay competition.

——. "The Role of Political Organizations in Indonesia," *Far Eastern Survey*, XXVII (Sept. 1958), 129–142. Contains a number of valuable insights into the functioning of mass organizations, the political role of the army, and the prospects of communism in Indonesia.

Peaslee, Amos J., ed. *Constitutions of Nations*. The Hague: M. Nijhoff, 1956. Vol. II, pp. 368–392. Gives full text of present (interim) constitution of 1950.

Pringgodigdo, A. K. *The Office of President in Indonesia as Defined in the Three Constitutions in Theory and Practice*. (Cornell Modern Indonesia Project, Translation Series.) Ithaca, N.Y., 1957. The author is a leading constitutional authority who has been the director of the cabinet of the President.

Roeslan Abdulgani. "Indonesia's National Council: The First Year," *Far Eastern Survey*, XXVII (July 1958), 97–104. An excellent exposition of the ideas of "guided democracy" or "democracy with leadership." The author, a leading PNI intellectual, is deputy chairman of the National Council.

Soedjatmoko. "The Role of Political Parties in Indonesia," in Philip W. Thayer, ed., *Nationalism and Progress in Free Asia*. Baltimore: Johns Hopkins Press, 1956. Pages 128–140. A highly stimulating paper on the operation of parties in the context of elite and village society, particularly in the period before and during the 1955 elections.

Soekarno. *The Birth of the Pantja Sila*. Djakarta: Ministry of Information, 1952. The original formulation, in a speech of 1945, of what were to become the Five Principles of State of the Republic; a basic text for all students of Indonesian political thought.

XII: Major Problems

Bank Indonesia. The annual reports of this body, the central bank of Indonesia, are excellent compilations of economic data. Prior to the financial year 1953–1954 the name was "Java Bank."

Biro Pusat Statistik (Central Bureau of Statistics). *Statistical Pocket Book of Indonesia, 1957*. Djakarta: Biro Pusat Statistik, 1957. By far the most useful compendium of statistics (demographic, economic, educational, etc.) available in English.

Bone, Robert C. *The Dynamics of the Western New Guinea (Irian Barat) Problem*. (Cornell Modern Indonesia Project, Interim Reports Series.) Ithaca, N.Y., 1958. A major piece of research which provides the fullest available coverage of the problem.

de Meel, Hans. "Demographic Dilemma in Indonesia," *Pacific Affairs*, XXIV (Sept. 1951), 266–283. A pessimistic view of Indonesia's population problem.

Ekonomi dan Keuangan Indonesia [Economics and Finance in Indonesia]. A monthly journal edited by a group of leading Indonesian economists, this publication contains many articles of high standard on economic and related subjects. A number of the contributions are in English.

Finkelstein, Lawrence S. "The Indonesian Federal Problem," *Pacific Affairs*, XXIV (Sept. 1951), 284–295. An early article on the problems of central authority and regional autonomy in the postrevolutionary period.

Fryer, Donald W. "Economic Aspects of Indonesian Disunity," *Pacific Affairs*, XXX (Sept. 1957), 195–208. A geographer's view of the recent regional crisis.

Hatta, Mohammad. "Indonesia between the Power Blocs," *Foreign Affairs*, XXXVI (April 1958), 480–490.

——. "Indonesia's Foreign Policy," *Foreign Affairs*, XXXI (April 1953), 441–452.

Hawkins, Everett H. D. "Prospects for Economic Development in Indonesia," *World Politics*, VIII (Oct. 1955), 91–111. A useful introductory survey.

Higgins, Benjamin. *Indonesia's Economic Stabilization and Development.* New York: Institute of Pacific Relations, 1957. Although short, this is the best and most comprehensive general work on the country's economic problems.

Hutasoit, M. *Compulsory Education in Indonesia.* UNESCO, 1954. The aims of Indonesia's educational system as seen by the secretary-general of its Ministry of Education.

Indonesia, Republic of, Ministry of Information. *Basic Information on Indonesia.* Djakarta: The Ministry, 1953. A useful reprint collection of articles from Indonesian government and other publications; articles on education, health, and economic affairs, as well as on the press and political parties.

Legge, John D. *Problems of Regional Autonomy in Contemporary Indonesia.* (Cornell Modern Indonesia Project, Interim Reports Series.) Ithaca, N.Y., 1957. A historian's investigation of the problems of centralization and decentralization, based on field experience in the crucial 1956–1957 period. Included is a valuable discussion of factors contributing to the development of the regional crisis.

Maryanov, Gerald S. *Decentralization in Indonesia as a Political Problem.* (Cornell Modern Indonesia Project, Interim Reports Series.) Ithaca, N.Y., 1958. A short but rigorously executed examination of the political attitudes involved in the regional conflict. It incorporates insights gained in field work carried out in Indonesia in 1958.

——. *Decentralization in Indonesia: Legislative Aspects.* (Cornell Modern Indonesia Project, Interim Reports Series.) Ithaca, N.Y., 1957. A careful study of basic institutional problems underlying the political ones.

Paauw, Douglas S. "Financing Economic Development in Indonesia," *Economic Development and Cultural Change*, IV (Jan. 1956), 171–185. An examination of Indonesian taxation, with reference to the problems of central and decentralized control.

Pelzer, Karl J. "The Agrarian Conflict in East Sumatra," *Pacific Affairs*, XXX (June 1957), 151–159. A valuable introduction to the problems of estate land tenure, peasant squatting, and ethnic antagonism which have undermined government authority in this important area.

Soedjatmoko. *Economic Development as a Cultural Problem.* (Cornell Modern Indonesia Project, Translation Series.) Ithaca, N.Y., 1958. A stimulating essay, first published in the Indonesian literary review *Konfrontasi*.

van der Kroef, Justus M. "Indonesia: Centrifugal Economies," in James W.

Wiggins and Helmut Schoeck, eds., *Foreign Aid Re-examined: A Critical Appraisal.* Washington, D.C., Public Affairs Press, 1958. Pages 197–220. A very valuable discussion of the social and historical context of economic enterprise in Java as compared with the outer islands of Indonesia.

——. *The West New Guinea Dispute.* New York: Institute of Pacific Relations, 1958. A short but useful treatment of the problem.

PART FOUR : MALAYA AND SINGAPORE

By J. Norman Parmer

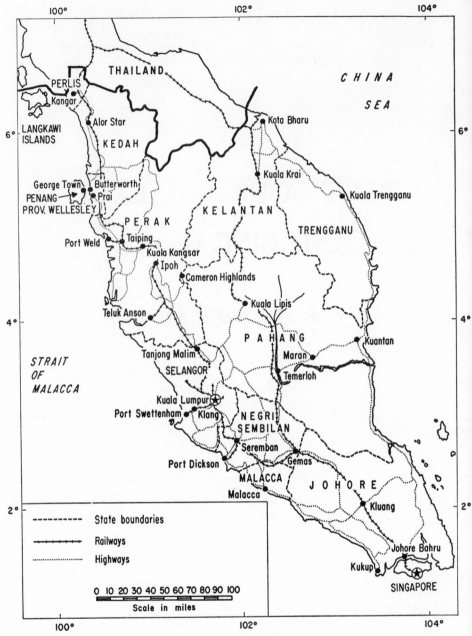

Map 4. Malaya and Singapore

· XIII ·

The Historical Background

JUTTING sharply and narrowly southward to form the southernmost extension of the Asian continent is the Malay Peninsula. At the strategic center of Southeast Asia, it has for centuries been both a bridge and a barrier for Asian peoples. Whoever dominated the peninsula usually controlled the Strait of Malacca—the major water transit between Southern and Eastern Asia. Firm and judicious exercise of control meant wealth and influence to those in command; the alternative was war and piracy. Today the Federation of Malaya occupies some 51,000 square miles of the southern part of the peninsula; off its tip, which is just above the equator, is the State of Singapore, an island of about 220 square miles.[1]

Pre-European History

The pre-European history of Malaya [2] is mainly linked with ancient India and Indonesia. Culturally, its early history is a part of the story of Indian religious-cultural influences on the older indigenous cultures of Southeast Asia. Malay rulers are today enthroned by officials in

[1] A geographical description of Malaya can be found in E. H. G. Dobby, *Southeast Asia* (3d ed.; London: University of London Press, Ltd., 1953), ch. vi.

[2] Before the Federation of Malaya obtained independence in 1957, "Malaya" was often used to refer to both the Federation of Malaya and Singapore. Since independence, "Malaya" is used to refer chiefly to the Federation. In these chapters the use of "Malaya" generally follows this time sequence.

Brahmanic postures surrounded by Hindu and tantric Buddhist symbols, and the colors of the Federation's official ensign are probably derived ultimately from the colors of the four sides of Mount Meru in Indian mythology. Politically, Malaya's early history is largely bound up with the rise and fall of empires in the islands of the nearby Indonesian archipelago. Two contemporary Malay rulers claim descent from the rulers of Shrivijaya, the Sumatra-based, Mahayana Buddhist empire which held sway over much of the peninsula between the eighth and thirteenth centuries. In the latter century the peninsula was threatened by the emerging Thai kingdom in the north, and thereafter, until the present day, occasional Thai incursions have been a characteristic of Malaya's political history. In the fourteenth century, however, Malaya was probably under the rule of the Java-based, Hindu empire of Majapahit. The fifteenth century saw an independent state grow up around the city of Malacca. At first Hindu, the rulers of this prosperous and worldly city soon accepted Islam. Malacca's Malay rulers sent tribute to the Ming emperor of China and through their trading connections spread Islam eastward.[3] It was at Malacca in 1509 that the Europeans first made contact with Eastern Asia.

The European Period to 1942

The Portuguese, motivated by a desire to obtain wealth and to destroy Moors, captured Malacca after a bloody struggle in 1511. To Albuquerque, the Portuguese Governor-General at Goa in India, it was a key fortress for control of the Indian Ocean. It was, further, a commercial entrepôt and a jumping-off point for Portuguese excursions to the Spice Islands and to China and Japan. For 130 years the Portuguese clung to Malacca, giving it a Roman Catholic and mixed-blood population still evident today. Under the Dutch, who displaced the Portuguese in 1641, Malacca's fortunes declined, and Batavia, the newly established Dutch base on Java, took its place as the area's principal port and commercial entrepôt.

Both the Dutch and Portuguese guarded against attacks from nearby Malay and Indonesian rulers and strove to enforce a monopoly of trade. A challenge to the Dutch monopoly came from British country ships.[4] The enterprising captain of one of these, Francis Light, acquired

[3] R. J. Wilkinson, "The Malacca Sultanate," *Journal of the Malayan Branch of the Royal Asiatic Society*, XIII, pt. II (Oct. 1935), 22–67.

[4] Country ships were ships built in Bombay, Calcutta, or Pegu, owned by British or Indian firms or individuals and permitted by the British East India Company to engage in trade between Asian ports, notably between Bombay and Canton.

Penang island off Malaya's west coast from the sultan of Kedah and occupied it for the British East India Company in 1786. Napoleon's occupation of the Netherlands prompted the British to seize Malacca, less than a decade later, although British rule there was not finally secured until the Anglo-Dutch treaty of 1824. The most important British position in the Straits was established on Singapore island in 1819 by Thomas Stamford Raffles. To this East India Company official, famed for his enterprise, advocacy of free trade, and scholarly interests, must go the principal credit for founding the British empire in Southeast Asia.

Penang, Malacca, and Singapore were administered initially by the East India Company and later by the British India Office. In 1867, partly because of demands by local British merchants, they were transferred to the Colonial Office and constituted as a crown colony. The government of the Straits Settlements was similar to that of other British crown colonies and changed little prior to 1942 when the Settlements fell to the Japanese. The Governor was all-powerful and responsible only to the Crown, although he seldom acted without attempting to obtain the support of his executive and legislative councils and ascertaining the views of private organizations. Executive and legislative councils had official and unofficial members, and among the latter were a minority of Chinese and members of other Asian communities. The councils were kept small and tidy, and all members were either appointed by the Governor or were members ex-officio. The economic life of the Settlements was commercial and maritime. Raffles' policy of free trade was a great fillip to Singapore during the nineteenth century when Dutch policy in Indonesia was one of monopoly and restriction. Singapore quickly became the greatest entrepôt port in all Southeast Asia.

When the East India Company acquired the Straits Settlements, it showed little interest in the Malay States on the peninsula. To be sure, the company did not want to see any important power entrenched there, but neither did it wish to undertake unprofitable administrative and probable military commitments. The States were partly the fragmentary remains of the old Malay empire of Malacca which because of their rulers' factionalism and because of European and Siamese incursion had failed to unite and evolve an effective political system. Their governments consisted of rulers or sultans and vassal chiefs or rajas; pretenders to the thrones were numerous, and warfare between the states was frequent. The indigenous people spoke the Malay language; their religion was Islam underpinned with Hindu and animistic beliefs. Political confusion and physical insecurity increased from the 1850s when large numbers of immigrant Chinese laborers entered the States to work tin mines being developed by entrepreneurs in the Settlements. Malay unwillingness or inability to cope with bloody, multifactional struggles between Chinese miners, organized into secret societies, finally occasioned British intervention in the States. In 1874, largely at the behest of British and Chinese Straits merchant entrepreneurs, the Governor with Colonial Office approval signed a treaty with the dispossessed heir to the throne of Perak.

Treaties written in the 1870s and 1880s with the rulers of Perak, Selangor, Pahang, and Negri Sembilan exchanged British protection for British Residents whose advice was to be accepted in all matters save those concerning Malay custom and the Islamic religion. The Residents quickly became the *de facto* wielders of power. In 1895 the four states were joined in a nominal federation known as the Federated Malay States (FMS), and subsequently a centralized administration was established. The inauguration of a Federal Council in 1909, primarily upon the request of British plantation owners and managers, completed the edifice which remained with few alterations until 1942.

The structure of the FMS government was similar to that of a crown colony although the individual states remained juridically sovereign British-protected countries. At the top was a High Commissioner who was the Governor of the Straits Settlements. The British Residents meeting several times each year were a kind of weak executive council. Much of their work was actually undertaken by the High Commissioner's deputy who remained in Kuala Lumpur, the Federation's capital. The Federal Council with official and unofficial members was in practice a colonial legislative council. Beneath the Federal government were state governments—each composed of a sultan, a Resident, and a British-created State Council whose role was advisory. Of great importance in day-to-day administration were districts within each state, directly ruled primarily by British administrative officers responsible to the Residents. Within the districts were smaller units called *mukims* ruled by Malay *penghulus* or headmen. These men were answerable to district officers as well as to their own traditional chiefs and were usually chosen with some deference to local Malay opinion.

During its short history the FMS was troubled with two related constitutional questions. The one concerned rivalry between the High Commissioner, who as Governor remained most of the year in Singapore, and his deputy in the FMS. Power became heavily concentrated in the office of the deputy, and the High Commissioner took steps to reduce that power. The deputy's position was defended by businessmen who desired a strong on-the-spot Federal executive. The other issue was a conflict of interests between alien capitalism and the Malay people. Rapid economic development had occurred allegedly without Malay participation. The FMS government was British-conceived and British-operated and was primarily a political framework for Western enterprise. The state governments, where Malay authority and prestige were thought to lie, had been eclipsed almost entirely by the Federal government. British officials were divided on the wisdom and propriety of this development. But the weight of opinion was with those who were perhaps influenced by Lugard's Dual Mandate—the Malays should enjoy some of the substance as well as the forms of power. First in the 1920s and then more seriously in the 1930s, steps were taken to decentralize the powers of the FMS government to the state governments. Attempts to reduce the power of the High Commissioner's deputy in Kuala Lumpur were linked with these efforts at decentralization.

Decentralization along with other discriminatory policies brought the permanently domiciled Chinese and Indians to charge the British with being pro-Malay and practicing "divide and rule." The policies which these groups particularly protested were discrimination against non-Malays in ownership of land,[5] classification of China-born persons of long residence as aliens, provision of free education only to Malays, and the refusal to admit non-Malays to higher government administrative positions. But only a handful of Malayans [6] debated these issues. The majority of non-Malays retained their transient character, particularly as the government made no attempts to assimilate them. Their interest in Malaya was economic, and their politics, if any, were reflections of politics in their homelands. Beginning in the 1930s a handful of Malays, mostly aristocratic intelligentsia, experienced some feelings of modern nationalism out of fear for the extinction of their culture by the powerful alien and materialistic influences accompanying British rule. With these exceptions, prewar Malaya was free of

[5] A policy of reserving ricelands exclusively for Malays was partially reversed, after the Second World War began, by the leasing of small areas to Chinese. The policy was protested by Malays but was explained as necessary because of Malaya's dependence on imported rice.

[6] That is, any Malay, Chinese, Indian, or other person who makes his permanent home in Malaya.

popular politics. This remarkable situation was encouraged by the efficiency and benevolence as well as the judicious use of the police and intelligence machinery of the British government.

The ultimate goal of decentralization was to join the four federated states with five other Malay states which had come under British protection. These five were Johore, whose rulers had long had close relations with the British, and Perlis, Kedah, Kelantan, and Trengganu, which in 1909 exchanged Thai for British suzerainty. These states differed significantly from each other in degree of political and economic development, and their position vis-à-vis Britain differed from that of the four federated states. The British officers assigned to each sultan were styled advisers rather than Residents, and Malay participation in government was generally more substantial. In short, indirect rule was more of a reality in these five unfederated states. This helps to explain why many outstanding post-Occupation Malay leaders have come from former unfederated states. By 1941, decentralization had made some progress, but the basic powers of the FMS government remained unimpaired.[7]

The Malay States and the Strait Settlements were served by a predominantly British-staffed Malayan Civil Service. The few non-British members were Malays drawn from a Malay Administrative Service established in 1910 primarily for sons of aristocratic families. Non-Malays were numerous in subordinate clerical and technical posts, and British refusal to admit them to higher positions was regarded as one aspect of the pro-Malay policy. In the Settlements, a Straits Settlements Civil Service was open to all British subjects, but it was used chiefly to staff minor positions.

British rule, whichever form it took, brought stability, security, and prosperity. Among Malayans, those who benefited primarily were immigrant Chinese. The Malays, as farmers and fishermen, left wage labor to the moneygrubbing, pork-eating nonbelievers. Chinese labor, capital, and entrepreneurial skill felled the jungle, cultivated the early plantations, mined the tin, and worked the docks. From the mid-nineteenth century, Singapore became a great labor mart for indentured Chinese coolies. They were employed under hard conditions upcoun-

---

[7] Good accounts of pre-Second World War British policies in the Malay States are found in Rupert Emerson, *Malayasia: A Study of Direct and Indirect Rule* (New York: Macmillan, 1937), and Lennox A. Mills, *British Rule in Eastern Asia* (London: Oxford University Press, 1942). On constitutional development see Roland St. J. Braddell, *The Legal Status of the Malay States* (Singapore: Malay Publishing House, Ltd., 1931).

try; poorly paid, often badly treated, and working in unhealthy places, early death was commonplace. Conditions gradually improved, however, and Chinese continued to come to Malaya in vast numbers until 1941.[8]

The age of untrammeled *laissez faire* was passing when British rule was extended to the mainland. Hence such measures to attract capital as road and railway building, provision of hospitals, establishment of experimental plantations, and schemes to import labor—all were undertaken by the government. But British and European capital was slow to enter the States. Few British capitalists could compete with Chinese tin-mine operators. The latter invested little capital, resorted to profit-sharing schemes in hard times, and sometimes made as much profit from selling food and opium to their laborers as from ore output. Only in the 1920s with the introduction of costly tin dredges to work the mainly alluvial deposits did European capital come virtually to dominate the industry.

Tin played an indispensable role in the economic development of Malaya, but rubber has been the pre-eminent industry of the twentieth century. Seeds of the *Hevea brasiliensis* tree were brought to Malaya in the 1870s from Brazil by way of London. Booming rubber prices by 1910 saw proprietary plantations transformed into share companies in which British merchant houses of the Settlements took an important hand. After the First World War some 2.1 million acres were in rubber. Further planting brought total acreage to 3.1 million in 1931 and 3.5 million in 1940. Rubber exports rose dramatically from some 6,000 long tons in 1910 to nearly 200,000 tons after the First World War and to nearly 500,000 tons in some years of the 1930s. Malaya accounted for a high of about 57 per cent of world exports in 1932; thereafter exports declined to about one-third of the world total.[9]

British planters were handicapped in the early years by a shortage of labor. Chinese were regarded as difficult to manage and too demanding of high wages. Planters resorted to South Indians who had been coming to the Straits in small numbers first as penal and subsequently as

[8] See William L. Blythe, "Historical Sketch of Chinese Labour in Malaya," *Journal of the Malayan Branch of the Royal Asiatic Society*, XX, pt. 1 (June 1947), 64–114. Prior to 1933, immigrants were mostly men. Thereafter until 1938 the government restricted male immigrants but freely admitted women. The result was a large influx of female immigrants resulting in a greater degree of permanence to the Chinese community.

[9] Sir Andrew Mcfadyean, *The History of Rubber Regulation, 1934–1943* (London: George Allen & Unwin, Ltd., 1944), pp. 226–229.

indentured laborers since shortly after the Settlements were founded. From the 1870s the government encouraged private importation of Indians in the belief that it was politic to have more than one kind of labor upon which to draw. In 1907 Indian immigration was organized on a quasi-official basis, and tens of thousands of Indians annually entered Malaya through the 1930s.[10]

Although capital was invested in a number of other export crops and minerals, rubber and tin production dominated the economic life of the country. Large output and good prices for rubber and tin were unattended by an effective and sustained demand for high wages and social services. Hence Malaya was a source of great profits for British and Malayan Chinese capitalists and of foreign exchange for Great Britain. But when rubber and tin prices in London and New York were poor, as in the early 1920s and again in the 1930s, calamity struck Malaya. The most serious complications were averted by permitting or assisting unemployed Chinese and Indians to return to their home-lands. Capitalists were not, however, happy at losing their labor and were anxious to avoid wide swings in market prices, characteristic of both tin and rubber. They resorted to international control schemes. The imperfect Stephenson scheme (1922–1928) was replaced by the International Rubber Regulation Agreement (1934–1944). Three inter-national tin-control schemes operated between 1931 and 1941.

Singapore remained a great entrepôt port in spite of the neomercan-tilistic policies which accompanied late-nineteenth-century European imperialism. Business lost to traders shipping directly to and from other Asian ports was compensated for by financing, processing, and shipping the products of the Malay States. Merchants attributed the colony's great prosperity to the free-port policy, and they rather suc-cessfully defended it against the imperial preferences and quotas adopted throughout the British empire from 1932.

In summary, capital investment in Malaya in the late nineteenth and twentieth centuries was dramatic and spectacular but decidedly spe-cialized. Unaccompanied by a significant expansion of food and con-sumer-goods production, the inflow of immigrants from China and India served to make Malaya heavily dependent on imports, including some 50 per cent of its food requirements. The most significant legacy

[10] J. Norman Parmer, "Colonial Labor Policy and Administration: A History of Labor in the Rubber Plantation Industry in Malaya, 1910–1941" (Ph.D. disser-tation, Cornell University, 1957; to be published by the Association for Asian Studies), pp. 56 ff.

of this rapid economic growth, however, was the creation of a plural society of perhaps unique proportions. In 1940 the total population of the Malay States and the Straits Settlements was estimated to be 5.5 million persons, consisting of 2.3 million Malays, 2.4 million Chinese, and 0.75 million Indians.

The Japanese Occupation and Its Aftermath

When the Japanese attacked Malaya in December 1941, the British were required to fulfill the protective provisions in their treaties with the Malay rulers. The attack came with such boldness that the defenders were for practical purposes unprepared. The giant Singapore naval base, begun in the 1920s and opened in 1938,[11] proved no obstacle. Nor did the airdromes and military bases to which Australian and Indian as well as British troops were dispatched late in 1941. Malaya fell in a little over two months. The defeat was so humiliating that it evoked bitter and exaggerated charges of complacency and decadence against British officials and businessmen.[12]

The Japanese joined Sumatra to Malaya and ruled both as a colonial territory with no pretense of eventually granting independence. The Chinese were treated badly, but the Malays were favored with government appointments. The Indian population was encouraged in its Indian nationalist sympathies; the Azad Hind, or Free India government, was enthusiastically organized in Singapore in 1943. The Japanese were unable to use the large productive capacity of the country's plantations and mines. But Indian laborers were sent to work on the infamous Burma-Thailand "death railway." Malaya's dependence on imports caused considerable hardship in spite of Japanese efforts to increase local food production and invent substitutes for a variety of goods.[13]

[11] For a brief but good history of the base see C. Northcote Parkinson, *Britain in the Far East: The Singapore Naval Base* (Background to Malaya Series no. 7; Singapore: Donald Moore, 1955).

[12] Numerous books have been written about the Japanese invasion of Malaya. Authoritative accounts are A. E. Percival, *The War in Malaya* (London: Eyre & Spottiswoode, 1949); Russell Grenfell, *Main Fleet to Singapore* (London: Faber & Faber, 1952); Sir George Maxwell, comp., *The Civil Defence of Malaya* (London: Hutchinson, 1944). Interesting critical accounts are Ian Morrison, *Malayan Postscript* (London: Faber & Faber, 1942), and E. M. Glover, *In 70 Days* (London: Frederick Muller, 1946).

[13] Concerning the Japanese occupation of Malaya see United States, Office of Strategic Services, Research and Analysis Branch, *Japanese Administration in Malaya*, R. & A. no. 2072 (Washington, 1944; mimeographed); Chin Kee Onn, *Malaya Upside Down* (Singapore: Jitts & Co., 1946).

Armed resistance to the Japanese was maintained primarily by Chinese who were aided, mostly in the last months of the war, by British officers and supplies sent from India.[14] Many of the underground fighters were Communists who had been active among Chinese laborers in Singapore factories and on upcountry plantations and mines in the late 1930s. They apparently spent as much time in preparation for postwar activities as in harassing the Japanese. When the Japanese surrendered, more than two weeks passed before British forces arrived in strength in September 1945. The Communist-led guerrilla forces set up kangaroo courts to take vengeance upon collaborators. During this period also clashes occurred between Malays and Chinese. For a time communal warfare seemed imminent.

The net effects of the Japanese invasion and occupation of Malaya were a disillusionment with British power, a general stirring of Malay political consciousness, the articulation of communal antipathy, the improvement of the Communist Party organization, and a general expectation of social and economic change for the better when the Occupation was over.

The first months after the Occupation were eventful and tumultous. A popular expectancy of important change prevailed, and numerous organizations were formed to give expression to ill-defined hopes. The British Military Administration took a fairly tolerant attitude and did not enforce prewar controls restricting political activity. The Malayan Communist Party (MCP) was permitted to operate. Early in 1946 newly organized, generally Communist-controlled trade unions called general strikes which the government regarded as challenges to its authority. These were met with police action, and thereafter unions concentrated their activities on economic grievances which in view of food shortages and inflation were many and genuine.

The Malay States

The Colonial Office made plans during the war for the constitutional reorganization of Malaya. A rationalization of government and an attempt to define the status of domiciled non-Malays were considered desirable. To achieve these objectives new treaties would have to be

[14] A special Allied organization, Force 136, aimed to promote underground operations in Japanese-occupied Southeast Asia. For an exciting account of one officer's experiences in Force 136's operations in Malaya, see F. Spencer Chapman, *The Jungle Is Neutral* (London: Chatto & Windus, 1953).

written with each of the Malay rulers.[15] A situation was envisaged in which British troops would have reconquered Malaya, and the Malay rulers, appearing in an equivocal position, would not oppose the planned changes. This set of circumstances failed to come about. Nevertheless the Colonial Office proceeded about as planned.

The opportunity was taken to obtain the prewar object of a union of all the Malay States. The new government, to be known as the Malayan Union, was to embrace the nine states as well as the two British Settlements of Penang and Malacca. The new treaties, signed in late 1945, did not revive the prewar protectorate status but provided for a transfer of sovereignty from the rulers to the British Crown. The government was to be headed by a British Governor assisted by appointed executive and legislative councils. Resident commissioners would preside over State and Settlement councils with limited powers. The rulers were to have little else to do than advise on Malay custom and religion. A still more radical change was the intention to grant citizenship to all persons, Malay and non-Malays, on an equal basis. Singapore was to be constituted as a separate crown colony.[16]

The Malayan Union constitution became effective on April 1, 1946. It immediately evoked two kinds of protest. The most effective protest came from numerous organizations formed among the Malay community and presenting a common front in the United Malays National Organization (UMNO).[17] They criticized the Union as a scheme imposed arbitrarily to deprive the Malays of the privileged status which they had enjoyed before the Occupation. The country would be turned over to aliens. The Malay protest was encouraged by "pro-Malay" British who felt that the Malayan Union was a usurpation of Malay sovereignty and a betrayal of Malay trust. Another protest was led by domiciled, Western-educated non-Malays, who in Singapore expressed their views through the Malayan Democratic Union (MDU). To these people the Malayan Union was autocratic and illiberal and seemed

[15] Great Britain, Colonial Office, *Report on a Mission to Malaya,* by Sir Harold MacMichael, Colonial no. 194 (London: H. M. Stationery Office, 1946).

[16] Great Britain, *Malayan Union and Singapore: Statement of Policy on Future Constitution,* Cmd. 6724 (London: H. M. Stationery Office, 1946); Great Britain, *Malayan Union and Singapore: Summary of Proposed Constitutional Arrangements,* Cmd. 6749 (London: H. M. Stationery Office, 1946).

[17] For an analysis of the UMNO and other political parties active in the years 1945–1948 see T. H. Silcock and Ungku Abdul Aziz, "Nationalism in Malaya," in William L. Holland, ed., *Asian Nationalism and the West* (New York: Macmillan, 1953), pp. 298 ff.

likely to perpetuate British rule indefinitely. It gave no recognition to aspirations for democratic government.[18]

Those who did not denounce the Union merely displayed apathy. In July 1946 the Governor began consultations with representatives of the rulers and the UMNO on constitutional revision. Proposals were tentatively agreed upon which would replace the Union with a federal government.[19] A consultative committee of "influential representatives of the non-Malay communities" was then appointed to collect non-Malay opinions on the matter. This committee's recommendations, made early in 1947,[20] did not fundamentally alter the proposals for a federal government.

Non-Malay opponents of the Union apparently failed to see clearly enough that the issue was between the Union and something less favorable to them. In any event they now opposed the federation as well. In order to obtain wider support the MDU took the lead in forming the All-Malaya Council of Joint Action (AMCJA) in December 1946. This was a loose coalition of quite diverse organizations. It charged that the consultative committee of non-Malays was unrepresentative and vainly sought to present its arguments to the Colonial Office in London. The Malays in the AMCJA, anxious to maintain their Malay identity, subsequently formed their own coalition chiefly around the anti-imperialist and pro-Indonesian Malay Nationalist Party (MNP). This Malay coalition, the Pusat Tenaga Ra'ayat or PUTERA, allied with the AMCJA early in 1947. AMCJA-PUTERA leaders rather belatedly began work on a model constitution which was published toward the end of the year. It called for a strong federal government including Singapore and a popularly elected legislature with a responsible executive. Temporary protection was provided for the Malays. The sultans were to remain as constitutional rulers, and Malay majorities were to be guaranteed in the Federal and state legislatures for nine years. A Malayan citizenship was accorded to all born in

[18] On behalf of those who framed the Union constitution it may be argued that the Union was a cleanly structured government basically unfettered by anachronistic elements. It was a government which would, in large measure, square with the social and economic, if not the political, realities of Malaya. It provided what the British regarded as a sound basis on which constitutional reform could be ultimately introduced.

[19] Malayan Union, *Constitutional Proposals for Malaya: Report of the Working Committee* (Kuala Lumpur: Malayan Union Government Press, 1947).

[20] Malayan Union, *Constitutional Proposals for Malaya: Report of the Consultative Committee* (Kuala Lumpur: Malayan Union Government Press, 1947).

Malaya, and aliens could obtain citizenship fairly simply. The proposals met with no success.

The Federation of Malaya was inaugurated on February 1, 1948. The principal constitutional instrument of the new government was the Federation Agreement, 1948. It recognized the sovereignty of each ruler in his state and revived the prewar protectorate relationships with Britain. The principle of a strong central authority was, however, maintained by assigning most powers to the Federal government. The Federal government was headed by a High Commissioner, appointed by the Crown, and consisted of executive and legislative councils appointed by the High Commissioner. The Legislative Council had seventy-five members with an unofficial majority appointed in order to represent racial and economic interests. The High Commissioner was charged with the responsibility of safeguarding "the special position of the Malays" and "the legitimate interests of other communities." Qualifications for Federal citizenship favored the Malays. It should be noted that Federal citizenship did not actually or potentially confer nationality. The Federation was little more than a powerful administrative apparatus linking together ten sovereignties; a person might be a national of any one of the nine Malay states or a British national.[21] Finally, a Conference of Rulers was formed which was to consult with the High Commissioner on questions of policy, particularly immigration policy, and give assent to bills passed by the Legislative Council. The British Settlements of Penang and Malacca were included in the Federation;[22] Singapore remained a separate crown colony.

The Federation was a more logical step in the constitutional development of Malaya than was the Malayan Union. But the MDU and its allies bitterly denounced the Federation as a step backward—a return to the prewar pro-Malay policy and a revival of the partnership between British imperialism and Malay feudalism. Such popular support as they had appeared to dwindle. Much of it had come from trade unions with Communist leaders.[23] Early in 1948 the government took

[21] See F. G. Carnell, "Malayan Citizenship Legislation," *International and Comparative Law Quarterly*, Oct. 1952, 504–518.
[22] Federation of Malaya, *The Federation Agreement, 1948* (Kuala Lumpur: Federation of Malaya Government Press, 1952). When Kuala Lumpur is the place of publication, the publisher is the Federation of Malaya Government Press unless otherwise noted.
[23] S. S. Awberry and F. W. Dalley, *Labour and Trade Union Organisation in the Federation of Malaya and Singapore* (Kuala Lumpur, 1948).

steps to separate the Malayan Communist Party from its trade union adjuncts. At about the same time MCP policy appears to have changed from peaceful political activity to armed revolt.[24] The Communist rebellion, styled the Emergency, began officially in June 1948. Most political parties and trade unions then disbanded or became moribund.

The Emergency was similar to the guerrilla warfare waged against the Japanese. Small tough bands of men, mostly Chinese and including many who had fought against the Japanese, totaled perhaps five thousand and were supported by some members of the Chinese community. They attacked plantations, mines, civilians, and police and military forces. Their objective was to disrupt the economy and ultimately to gain political control. Although they failed, the Emergency cost thousands of lives and hundreds of millions of dollars needed for social services and economic development. Moreover, since Emergency Regulations reduced freedom of speech and assembly and generally created an atmosphere discouraging political activity, the Emergency delayed constitutional reform.

The terrorists, as they were called, attained their greatest success late in 1951 when they ambushed and killed the British High Commissioner, Sir Henry Gurney. General Sir Gerald Templer, who was subsequently dispatched to Malaya, employed against the terrorists swift and massive counterattack, greater use of informers, collective punishment of whole villages, and stringent control of food supplies. The resettlement of more than a half million persons—mostly Chinese farmers and part-time laborers—from their isolated houses on the jungle fringe into guarded villages was completed. The object was to cut off the support which these "squatters" gave to the Communists out of sympathy or fear. General Templer was unable to bring an end to the Emergency, but the terrorists became manageable, and the morale of at least part of the public was raised. Critics, however, expressed the belief that police state conditions did not hold the solution. The Emergency Regulations, which permitted extreme penalties and indefinite detention of thousands of suspected persons, were criticized. To defeat the Communists positive measures were needed to win popular

[24] Writers have often expressed the view that the Communist shift to armed revolt in Malaya and elsewhere in Southeast Asia in 1948 was directed from outside the area and communicated to Southeast Asian Communist leaders at the "Calcutta Conference" of Southeast Asian youth in February 1948. A good treatment of the subject in which the author expresses doubt of this view is found in Ruth McVey, *The Calcutta Conference and the Southeast Asian Uprisings* (Cornell Modern Indonesia Project, Interim Reports Series), Ithaca, N.Y., 1958.

support for the government; it was necessary that the government show its good intentions by making progress toward self-government.

The Federation Agreement clearly stated the intention of eventually granting self-rule. But preconditions of self-rule were the emergence of a Malayan national unity and, because of the Emergency, the restoration of law and order. Nevertheless some limited political reforms were attempted. In 1951 six Malayan members of the Federal Executive Council were assigned portfolios. Municipal elections were held in 1951 and 1952 among minuscule electorates, and a Federal ordinance in 1952 made possible the setting up of popularly elected town and village councils. Once popular government at the lowest level had given experience in self-rule, elections were to be extended to state governments and ultimately to the Federal government. In 1952 also citizenship requirements were liberalized, making it possible for more non-Malays to become Federal citizens. This "parish pump" approach to constitutional reform and the failure to create a Federal nationality when extending citizenship were criticized as insufficient proof of British intentions to grant self-rule.[25]

Criticism notwithstanding, local elections brought a revival of party politics. The parties were conservative in respect to the economic and social backgrounds of their chief spokesmen, and each stood for independence. They differed with regard to their leaders' personalities, on the rate of speed toward independence, and on the nature of Malayan unity which British authorities had declared prerequisite to freedom. Did Malayan unity mean merely political co-operation between communities, or did it mean some kind of synthesis of the Malay, Chinese, and Indian cultures?

One point of view was represented by the Independence of Malaya Party (IMP). Its leaders advocated measured steps toward self-government over a ten-year period and talked of a Malayan unity which seemed to imply a cultural amalgamation. Open to all "Malayans," it appeared to be an enlightened attempt to keep communalism out of politics. The party was, however, generally defeated at the polls. One reason was that the favors shown it by the government caused it to be stigmatized as having British backing.

Political success went to parties making a communal appeal. The United Malays National Organization revived under new leadership, and the Malayan Chinese Association (MCA) was formed as a kind

[25] See Victor Purcell, *Malaya: Communist or Free?* (London: Institute of Pacific Relations, Victor Gollancz, Ltd., 1954), pp. 217–229.

of spokesman for the Chinese to government and to the Malay community. The two parties joined forces in 1952 to contest the Kuala Lumpur municipal elections. Their success caused them to continue as an Alliance in other elections in subsequent years. Unfavored by the British, Alliance leaders were outspokenly critical, advocated a rapid introduction of self-rule, and declared that the only practical Malayan unity was co-operation between communities. Independence could not wait on a Malayan nationality based on cultural fusion.

A party which emphasized social and economic questions was the Pan-Malayan Labour Party (PMLP). It mixed a class appeal with a Malayan, noncommunal approach and an aggressive anti-British, nationalist stand. The party was badly handicapped by lack of funds, dissension, opportunism, and the Emergency. Trade union organization was reviving, partly in response to British encouragement, but unions did not support the party because of legal barriers and official urgings to avoid politics. The PMLP had few election successes.[26]

Besides encouraging a noncommunal political party, British authorities endeavored to use the powers of government to attenuate the plural-society problem. The fundamental thesis was that prospects for national unity would be improved if the Chinese would yield some of their economic power to the Malays and if the Malays in turn would give the Chinese some of their political power. The Rural Industrial Development Authority (RIDA) was established in 1950 to try to strengthen the economic position of Malay peasant farmers.[27] Co-operative rice mills, a processing plant for rubber small holders, and a boatbuilding and repair yard for fishermen were RIDA projects. Committees were appointed to investigate ways of getting Malays into business—to make Malay capitalists, said critics—and to determine why Malays failed in business. The first yielding of Malay political power to the Chinese was the liberalization of citizenship qualifications in 1952. In 1953 Chinese and Indians were permitted to enter the Malayan Civil Service in the ratio of one non-Malay to four Malays. This was a nominal concession as long as the British occupied some 80 per cent of the administrative positions.

The relative political and economic positions of the Malay and Chinese communities changed little prior to independence in 1957. A

[26] J. Norman Parmer, "Trade Unions and Politics in Malaya," *Far Eastern Survey*, XXIV (March 1955), 33–39.

[27] Federation of Malaya, *Report on Rural and Industrial Development Authority, 1950–1955*, by D. E. M. Fiennes (Kuala Lumpur, 1957).

major reason was that Chinese economic power was strongly entrenched and backed by decades of hard work, business experience, and accumulated capital. Another reason was that prior to independence it was questionable how much the Malays really had to exchange. Most real political power was in British hands; much of what was termed Malay power was really political privilege. Finally, efforts to strengthen the Malays economically were never concerted, sustained, or adequately financed—probably because of uncertainty over ultimate goals. Little encouragement was given to suggestions that legislation might be employed to transfer economic power from one community to another.

Potentially of greater significance in developing national unity were efforts from 1950 to create a system of national schools. Education in Malaya has been largely a private responsibility, and many children have received little or no schooling. The government has paid the whole cost only in respect to Malay children. The result has been that education is still conducted in a variety of schools in a miscellany of tongues with different curricula by teachers who are sometimes poorly qualified. Christian mission schools, teaching in English, occupy a prominent role. But claiming a much larger number of students are Chinese and Indian vernacular schools. Many of these have inculcated loyalty to China and India.[28] A unified system of education is needed, and ultimately it could be the most effective means of developing a Malayan nationality. But in the short run, public debate on education policy has seemed likely to intensify communal feelings. The Chinese particularly have opposed national schools and have argued that cultural autonomy and political loyalty are not incompatible. The Malay view is generally otherwise. A national education law was finally enacted in the Federation early in 1957. It was fairly represented as "the maximum degree of agreement that can at present be achieved on this controversial and contentious field of education."[29]

While Malayan unity was being discussed in terms of economics and education, political activity continued to revive. Popularly elected local government was steadily extended, and in 1954 the first state elections were held. Earlier a large committee of British and Malayans met to

[28] Stanley Spector, "Students and Politics in Singapore," *Far Eastern Survey,* XXV (May 1956), 65–73.

[29] Federation of Malaya, *Legislative Council Debates Official Report . . . 6th and 7th March 1957* (Kuala Lumpur, 1957), col. 2542. The law was based on Federation of Malaya, *Report of the Education Committee, 1956* (Kuala Lumpur, 1956). See pp. 297–298 below for a brief description.

consider elections to the Federal Legislative Council.[30] The Alliance, unsuccessful in its demand for a three-fifths elected majority and elections by November 1954, staged popular demonstrations and an effective country-wide boycott of government. The first national elections were held in July 1955 for 52 seats in an expanded 98-member Federal Legislative Council. Candidates stood in single-member territorial constituencies and were directly elected by simple majority votes. The High Commissioner, in selecting members of the Executive Council after the elections, appointed Legislative Council members who had popular support there.[31] Federal citizenship was the chief qualification to vote, and an estimated 1.6 million persons were eligible for voluntary registration. Approximately 1.25 million persons, mostly Malays, registered, and the voter turnout was over one million.

The UMNO-MCA Alliance, now joined by the Malayan Indian Congress (MIC), published a comprehensive platform promising economic development, expansion of social services, Malayanization of the public services, an attempt to end the Emergency by meeting with Communist leaders, revision of the Emergency Regulations, a national education policy acceptable to all communities, and a drive against official corruption.[32] Alliance candidates emphasized their record of opposition to Britain and presented the Alliance as the most satisfactory combination of political forces for obtaining *merdeka* (freedom). They promised to seek a constitutional commission from abroad as a step toward attaining independence within four years. The Alliance was the only organization with a full slate of 52 candidates, entering 35 Malays, 15 Chinese, 1 Indian, and 1 Ceylonese. It won an overwhelming victory, polling more than 800,000 votes and capturing 51 of the 52 seats. The election of some Chinese in predominantly Malay constituencies was hailed as evidence of the communal harmony achieved by the Alliance.[33]

[30] Federation of Malaya, *Report of the Committee Appointed to Examine the Question of Elections to the Federal Legislative Council* (Kuala Lumpur, 1954).

[31] The Federation of Malaya experienced a departure from the usual course of constitutional reforms in British dependencies in that the Federal Legislative Council moved directly from an all-appointive body to one in which a majority of members were popularly elected. Usually there is an intermediate step in which a minority is elected. The majority was, however, a small one (Federation of Malaya, *Introduction of Elections to the Federal Legislative Council* [Kuala Lumpur, 1954]).

[32] The Alliance, *The Road to Independence* (reprinted in the *Malayan Mirror*, [Kuala Lumpur, irregular], June 16, July 1, 1955).

[33] For discussions of the Federal elections of 1955 see Francis Carnell, "The

Victorious Alliance leaders together with representatives of the Malay rulers proceeded to London in January 1956. Earlier the High Commissioner had declared that the Emergency should no longer be regarded as an obstacle to advances toward self-government.[34] The London talks resulted in important Executive Council posts being turned over to Malayans and creation of the office of Chief Minister. Agreement was reached on the terms of reference of a commission to make recommendations on a new constitution. Independence was to be proclaimed by the end of August 1957, if possible.[35]

The constitutional commission's five members were drawn from Commonwealth countries and placed under the chairmanship of Lord Reid of the United Kingdom.[36] Its terms of reference determined the basic outlines of governmental structure, namely, a federal form of constitution with a strong central government employing parliamentary democracy and presided over by a constitutional head of state. The commission had, however, to deal with several vital and controversial questions on which the communities differed sharply. These were the issues of citizenship qualifications, national language, and Malay privileges. The commission was admonished to safeguard "the special position of the Malays and the legitimate interests of other communities."

Public and private hearings were held in the Federation between June and October 1956. Broadly stated, in regard to citizenship the Malays wanted a stiff residential requirement as well as other qualifications. The Chinese favored citizenship by birth and a simple residential

Malayan Elections," *Pacific Affairs*, Dec. 1955, pp. 315–330. Additional commentary can be found in Irene Tinker, "Malayan Elections: Electoral Pattern for Plural Societies," *Western Political Quarterly*, June 1956, pp. 258–282. The official report is Federation of Malaya, Supervisor of Elections, *Report on the First Election of Members to the Legislative Council of the Federation of Malaya* (Kuala Lumpur, 1955).

[34] Federation of Malaya, *Legislative Council Debates Official Report . . . 30th November to 9th December 1955* (Kuala Lumpur, 1956), cols. 156–157.

[35] Other important decisions included: the High Commissioner would consult with the Chief Minister on future Executive Council appointments, the Federation would remain in the sterling area after independence, and the Federation and Britain would become allies in a defense and mutual assistance treaty. See Federation of Malaya, *Report of the Federation of Malaya Constitutional Conference held in London in January and February 1956* (Kuala Lumpur, 1956).

[36] In addition to Lord Reid the members of the commission were Sir Ivor Jennings from Britain, Sir William McKell from Australia, B. Malik from India, and Justice Abdul Hamid from Pakistan. A Canadian appointee withdrew for reasons of health and was not replaced.

qualification for foreign-born. The Malays wanted the Malay language to be the sole official language whereas the Chinese wanted kuo-yü, the Chinese national language, to have equal status. The Malays insisted that special privileges which they possessed (namely, reservation of civil service positions, scholarships, business licenses, land) be written into the constitution. The Chinese argued that these were unfair and could not be continued indefinitely. Alliance leaders submitted one memorandum rather than permit representations from each member party. Considerable strain was thereby placed on the partnership; a split was avoided by the plea that disunity would delay independence.

The Reid Commission's recommendations were closely drawn. Favoring the Malay community, they endeavored to gain a substantial amount of crucial non-Malay support. The main points were the granting of citizenship to those born in the Federation on or after independence day and the acquisition of citizenship rather simply and easily for those born in the Federation before independence day. Foreign-born persons resident in the Federation on independence day and showing proof of eight years' residence were to be entitled to citizenship. A comprehensive loyalty oath and a knowledge of Malay were further required. Malay was recommended as the national language; but the English, Chinese, and Indian languages might be used for ten years in the Federal legislature. Malay privileges were to be examined by the Federal legislature after fifteen years with a view to their reduction or abolition.[37]

These recommendations were revised by representatives of Britain, the Malay rulers, and the Alliance in the spring of 1957.[38] As a result the constitution became more conservative and favorable to the Malays. Foreign-born persons resident in Malaya on independence day and showing proof of eight years' residence were to be eligible for but not entitled to citizenship;[39] English but not the Chinese and Indian languages was to be retained in the legislature; Malay privileges were to be the responsibility of the Malay monarch, and no provision was made for their review. Islam was to be the religion of the Federation.

[37] Great Britain, Colonial Office, *Report of the Federation of Malaya Constitutional Commission, 1957*, Colonial no. 330 (London: H.M. Stationery Office, 1957). A description and commentary of the Reid Commission's recommendations are found in J. Norman Parmer, "Constitutional Change in Malaya's Plural Society," *Far Eastern Survey*, Oct. 1957, pp. 145–152.

[38] Federation of Malaya, *Constitutional Proposals* (Kuala Lumpur, 1957).

[39] For a full statement on citizenship qualifications, see note 5 of Chapter XV.

Chinese protests over the revisions placed the Malayan Chinese Association and its alliance with UMNO under further stress. Chinese objections within and without the MCA were not countenanced, however, and the Alliance-controlled Federal Legislative Council unanimously approved the final draft constitution in July. Other arrangements were completed, and the formal transfer of power was effected on August 31, 1957. The first Yang di-Pertuan Agong or Supreme Head of State was crowned on September 1. The new constitution was not, however, to be fully implemented until 1959, when Federal elections were to be held.

What may be said by way of conclusion about postwar constitutional and political developments in the States? From the constitutional talks between the British and Malays in 1946, the British based their policies on the assumption that the Malays were the most articulate and important political force in Malaya. The Federation constitution of 1948 was concrete expression of this belief, and with it the British returned to their traditional policy of basing their position in the States on a Malay alliance. An important difference was that before the war the alliance was with the Malay rulers and the aristocracy. From 1946 the new Anglo-Malay alliance was somewhat more broadly based and may be more aptly termed co-operation with popular and conservative Malay leaders.

The Malay community might be the most vigorous and broadly based political force in Malaya, but the British realized the vital need of securing a share of power for those Chinese and Indians who regarded Malaya as their home. In fact a cardinal aspect of British policy was to obtain a place for the "Straits-born Chinese," persons of long residence, of wealth and influence, of the professions, and of English education. Malay nationalism had to be kept from becoming too narrow. The British offered counsel to the Malays who were told not to regard the Federation as a permanent arrangement but as a breathing space in which to try to improve their position vis-à-vis the other communities. At the same time, the British undertook to draw a line, in the form of constitutional citizenship provisions, between the desirable, indeed indispensable, non-Malays and others whose loyalty lay outside Malaya. And they sought to induce the Straits-born Chinese and persons of similar outlook to engage in political activity. Most of this element had eschewed politics, and some, especially the older generation, were inclined to regard themselves primarily as British subjects and above the rank and file of Malayans.

The British viewpoint with regard to those people who were politically the most important and desirable in the country did not *ipso facto* establish them in power. Britain's task was somehow to have these people create effective political forces that would serve as a basis of power to which authority could be transferred. The political forces needed to be friendly to Great Britain and British economic interests and have good prospects of retaining power for some years—to provide stable and positive, effective government. A vital aspect was timing. Britain was not anxious to give up its position in Malaya. The Emergency was for a time legitimate reason for the British to postpone their departure. The plural society also presented opportunities to delay political progress. But to tamper with communal feelings was exceedingly dangerous and might easily destroy what possibilities there were for the ultimate emergence of a satisfactory basis of power. The British did encourage Malayan politicians, notably through the Independence of Malaya Party, to adopt a conservative nationalism. Was this a praiseworthy endeavor or a political delaying action? Much suggests that it was altruistic. Moreover, to assert that it was a mere maneuver probably credits British authorities with more capacity for Machiavellian calculation than is warranted. Nevertheless Chinese and particularly Malay leaders regarded British backing of the IMP as an attempt to delay independence. They were consequently spurred to form a political alliance. They sought to prove to the British that they could cooperate. In their success they formed a basis of political power.

The Alliance met British criteria. Its leaders were conservatives, men of affluence and of British education. Through the UMNO the Alliance was able to count upon the support of most of the Malays, and through the MCA, upon those Chinese whom both the British and the Malays could trust. There were flaws, but a better basis of power was not likely. A further delay would only bring forth political forces less congenial and probably less durable. From the time the Alliance demonstrated its strength in the Federal elections of 1955, British authorities worked to ensure friendly British relations with its leaders and to promote its continued success. The constitution of 1957 —the constitution of the independent Federation—represents an effort on the part of Alliance leaders and British authorities to fix in juridical form, at least for some years ahead, the combination of forces which constitutes the basis of Alliance power. The Anglo-Malayan defense treaty of 1957 supplements and caps the constitutional arrangements.[40]

[40] See p. 305.

Singapore

Singapore was established as a separate crown colony on April 1, 1946—when the Malayan Union was inaugurated. The step was protested at the time by members of the Malayan Democratic Union and others. It was explained as desirable in view of Singapore's "special economic and other interests." [41] Britain's interest was clearly to keep Singapore apart from the peninsula. Singapore was the bastion of British and Commonwealth military, naval, and air forces in the East. Its trade was lucrative, its government amply supplied with revenue. Moreover, exclusion of Singapore, with its large Chinese population, was in the political interest of the Malays.

Compared to that of the Malay States, the post-1946 constitutional history of Singapore is a fairly simple story. Unlike the mainland, Singapore has not had to accommodate its constitution to Malay monarchies; nor, with a population 80 per cent Chinese, has it had to grapple with plural-society problems of the same magnitude. Rather the major obstacle to a generally orderly progress toward self-rule has been the incitement of Chinese national feeling among much of the population as a result of government policies and of Communist activity, particularly among students in Chinese schools.

Extremely small electorates chose a minority of seats in the colony's Legislative Council in 1948 and again in 1951. Reports of a local committee in 1953 and of a constitutional commission in 1954 led to major reforms.[42] Twenty-five members of a thirty-two-member Legislative Assembly were to be popularly elected by an expanded, automatically registered electorate. A nine-member Council of Ministers was to be established, made up of three ex officio members and six persons appointed by the Governor from the majority party or parties in the Assembly on the advice of a Chief Minister. The Governor retained powers to override the ministers and the Assembly and to suspend the constitution. The constitution was an improved form of dyarchy aimed at encouraging the development of parliamentary government and a party system.

Prior to these reforms the Progressive Party dominated Singapore's narrow politics. The Progressives were relatively cautious and, like

[41] Great Britain, Colonial Office, *Report on a Mission to Malaya,* Colonial no. 194 (London: H.M. Stationery Office, 1946), p. 3.

[42] Singapore, *Constitutional Commission, Singapore* (Singapore: Government Printing Office, 1954).

the Independence of Malaya Party in the Federation, its leaders were stigmatized by opponents as colonial "stooges." The reforms stimulated the formation of new parties. In the first elections under the new constitution in April 1955 about half the electorate of 300,000 or approximately 12.5 per cent of Singapore's population voted. None of the parties secured a majority, but one of the new parties, the Labour Front, obtained a plurality of ten seats. By joining with the successful candidates of a minor party and utilizing the help of appointed Assembly members and the ex officio ministers, the Labour Front was able to form a government.[43] It was still in power in mid-1958.

In its campaign the Labour Front espoused a moderate socialism and called for a fully elected and multilingual legislature and repeal of the Emergency Regulations. As a government it did not have an easy time. The party was handicapped by lack of a majority, by disunity, and, during the first year of its rule, by its well-intentioned but inexperienced and mercurial leadership. The most vociferous and sustained opposition in the Assembly came from the People's Action Party (PAP) which had won three of the four seats it contested. Also socialist, it sought supporters among Chinese-educated workers and students and endeavored to embarrass the Labour Front government by encouraging strikes and political demonstrations resulting in violence and bloodshed.

In addition to coping with civil disturbances the Labour Front had the task of negotiating further constitutional reforms. The Labour Front Chief Minister led an all-party delegation to London in April 1956 seeking sovereign independence within one year. The Secretary of State for the Colonies proposed instead that Singapore have internal self-rule, with Britain retaining control of external affairs, defense and internal security. Retention of control over internal security was explained as necessary because of its relationship to external defense. On this point negotiations collapsed.[44] The Labour Front's Chief Minister resigned in protest in June 1956, but his colleagues did not join him and one of them became Chief Minister.

With constitutional talks deadlocked, the government turned its attention to the question of subversion. To many, the colony's political

[43] See F. G. Carnell, "Political Ferment in Singapore," *Far Eastern Survey*, XXIV (July 1955), 97–102.

[44] Great Britain, *Singapore Constitutional Conference*, Cmd. 9777 (London: H.M. Stationery Office, 1956).

security had become precarious. In October 1956 a campaign to eliminate criminal and subversive elements was begun. Full use was made
of public security legislation [45] to arrest, detain, and banish suspected
persons. By the end of 1957 a large number of Chinese students, newspapermen, trade unionists, and PAP leaders, one of whom was a
member of the Legislative Assembly and member of the 1956 delegation to London, had been arrested and detained. An official "white
paper" alleged Communist control of the PAP.[46]

In the meantime a new all-party delegation had gone to London
in March 1957 for fresh talks on the constitution. Points agreed on
the year before were accepted, with slight modifications, by both
sides. Singapore was to be known as the State of Singapore; a parliamentary government popularly elected by a special Singapore citizenship [47] would have control over internal affairs while Britain retained
control over external affairs and defense. The previously difficult question of internal security was resolved by assigning this responsibility
to an Internal Security Council of seven members. Over the protests
of the Singapore delegation, the Secretary of State insisted that known
subversives be barred from participation in the first government under
the new constitution.[48] The Singapore Legislative Assembly approved
these proposals on May 1, 1957.

The PAP was unhurt by the arrest and detention of some of its
leaders. In December 1957 it won a plurality of seats in city council
elections and in July 1958 won a city council by-election. City government under a PAP mayor proved to be fairly competent although
tumultuous and, in the eyes of some, disastrously chaotic. If city election results portended a PAP victory in Singapore State elections—
probably to be held before April 1959—Singapore's future political
stability seemed in doubt. PAP spokesmen added to the disquiet by
suggesting that they would free their imprisoned colleagues should
they form a government. Britain appeared determined, however, to

[45] From 1955, succeeding the Emergency Regulations.

[46] Singapore, *The Communist Threat in Singapore*, Sessional Paper no. Cmd. 33
of 1957 (Singapore: Government Printing Office, 1957).

[47] More than 330,000 persons had registered as citizens of Singapore by the
end of January 1958, approximately doubling the electorate (*Straits Budget*
[Singapore, weekly], Feb. 5, 1958, p. 4). For citizenship qualifications, see note
9 of Chapter XV.

[48] Great Britain, Colonial Office, *Report of the Singapore Constitutional Conference Held in London in March and April 1957*, Cmnd. 147 (London: H.M.
Stationery Office, 1957)

go ahead with the new constitution,[49] and another all-party delegation, returning from London in May 1958, where it had gone to work out last-minute "snags," reaffirmed the all-around intention to proceed.

Constitutional progress in postwar Singapore was more orderly than in the Federation. But although Singapore earlier achieved a measure of self-rule, a reasonably stable basis of political power failed to develop. Singapore's population is racially fairly homogeneous; but economically, and especially culturally, it is sorely divided. Persons who appeared to have common political interests but with varied cultural backgrounds failed to unite and even avoided political activity. The failure to evolve an effective basis of power delayed further constitutional reforms. Nevertheless British authorities were determined to proceed lest politicians avoid putting their own houses in order and continue to wave the anti-imperialist banner and drive themselves into extreme positions. But even the new constitution would not give complete independence—that did not seem practical even to most Singapore politicians. Singapore was destined to be part of a larger political entity. What should that be? Some Singaporeans undoubtedly preferred to remain with Britain. Many talked of independence through joining the Federation. But the Federation government was not prepared to add a million or more factious Chinese to its already large Chinese population. Any other choice was not likely to be acceptable to either Britain or the Federation. The solution probably lay in some kind of confederation of the two territories. In any event, constitutional progress beyond that already agreed upon depended on the development of a basis of political power satisfactory to Great Britain. Before that occurred, Singapore seemed certain to experience some stormy politics.

[49] Statement by the British Prime Minister, Harold Macmillan, in Singapore, Feb. 13, 1958 (*Straits Budget,* Feb. 19, 1958, p. 10).

· XIV ·

The Contemporary Setting

A HAPPY legacy of British rule in Malaya is one of the best-developed communication systems in Southeast Asia. About one thousand miles of efficient government railways are supplemented by more than six thousand miles of paved roads on which Chinese-owned bus companies provide good transportation at moderate cost. Frequent air service is available to major towns. Government-owned telephone and telegraph services and electric power facilities, already sizable, are steadily being expanded. It is the west coast that has experienced major economic development. Three-fourths of the country is still covered by tropical rain forest or jungle.

The Economy

Heretofore the Malayan economy in the twentieth century has rested chiefly on export agriculture, mining, and commerce.[1] Among export crops rubber is today the most important. In 1956 the Federation and Singapore had over 3.5 million acres planted in rubber—more than half of all land under cultivation. Estates (100 acres or more) accounted for 2.0 million acres; small holdings (less than 25

---

[1] T. H. Silcock's *The Economy of Malaya* (Background to Malaya Series no. 2; Singapore: Donald Moore, 1954) is a useful introduction to the subject. He observes that the Malayan economy really consists of the subsistence economy, the plantation and mining economy, and the mercantile economy.

acres) and medium holdings (25–99 acres) exceeded 1.5 million acres. Two-thirds of the estate acreage was European, mainly British, owned. Small holdings, numbering nearly 400,000 in 1953,[2] were mostly owned or cultivated by resident Malay farmers; medium holdings, totaling about 7,000, were worked by Chinese and others for mostly absentee owners of all communities. The output of the total acreage in 1956 was about 626,000 long tons—below the postwar peak of nearly 700,000 tons in 1948 but above a low of about 574,000 tons in 1953. The decline and subsequent rise in production appeared to be the result of decreased yield from aging rubber trees followed by increased yield from younger trees coming into production. Estates and small and medium holdings accounted for 56 and 44 per cent respectively of total production. Malaya's 1956 output was approximately one-third of the world's natural rubber production and one-fifth of total (natural and synthetic) world production.

Some 300,000 estate workers—their wages scaled to market prices —rely on rubber production for their livelihood. Another perhaps 300,000 small holders and their families are dependent on rubber for a substantial part of their living. Thousands of other persons depend indirectly on rubber for their incomes. The Federation government, too, is affected; export duty on rubber—scaled to prices—is a primary source of revenue. Income tax payments and the level of consumption of du.ied imports vary according to the level of prosperity in the rubber industry. Further, rubber is the chief earner of foreign exchange. Natural rubber prices have fluctuated widely but have generally been good since the end of the Japanese Occupation. Proposals to stabilize rubber prices through international agreement have been considered (but not acted upon) by representatives of rubber producing and consuming nations through the International Rubber Study Group. The profits to be obtained from rubber have forced other crops into the background. Nevertheless the Federation presently has important estate or small-holder acreages in coconuts, oil

[2] Some individuals operated several small holdings or "lots." Acreage of small and medium holdings is an estimate. The figures for the numbers of small and medium holdings are taken from Federation of Malaya, *Report of the Mission of Enquiry into the Rubber Industry of Malaya* (Kuala Lumpur: Federation of Malaya Government Press, 1954), p. 4. Other statistics in this paragraph are based on data in Federation of Malaya, Department of Statistics, *Rubber Statistics Handbook, 1956* (Kuala Lumpur: Federation of Malaya Government Press, 1957). In this chapter when Kuala Lumpur is the place of publication, the publisher is the Federation of Malaya Government Press.

palms, and pineapples. Other crops have been successfully produced for export in the past.

Tin is second only to rubber in value of exports and as a base of government revenue. In the nineteenth century, government revenues from tin and ancillary enterprises did much to make subsequent economic development possible. Today the Federation is the world's largest tin producer, accounting for approximately 40 per cent of world production. In 1957 nearly 60,000 tons of concentrated tin were produced—approximately two-thirds by European-owned mines. Tin producing and consuming nations have joined in an International Tin Agreement to try to stabilize widely swinging tin prices; [3] controls were first applied late in 1957. The success of the scheme was jeopardized by large and unexpected Russian tin exports. The total effect in Malaya was sharply reduced output accompanied by significant unemployment. As with rubber in agriculture, tin has diverted attention from searching for and developing other mineral products.[4]

The commercial sector of the Malayan economy is mainly the entrepôt trade of Singapore and of Penang to a lesser extent. It involves the entry and reshipment of the output of Southeast Asian plantations, mines, and other enterprises as well as of the manufactured goods of the United States, Europe, Japan, and elsewhere. Ancillary to this trade are rubber mills, tin smelters, shipbuilding and repair services, suppliers of ships' fuel and stores, packing and warehousing facilities, assembly plants and parts depots, great banking houses, huge oil storage and distribution facilities, insurance underwriters, and ship brokers. European firms control 50 per cent or more of import-export operations. They are especially strong in shipping, banking, insurance, and the import and sales of heavy machinery. Chinese and some Indians predominate in the importing and processing of raw materials and in the distribution of imported consumer goods. The trend, long evident, is toward the Chinese obtaining a larger share of the total trade. In 1956 Singapore handled nearly 17.5 million tons of cargo valued at about US$2.5 billion.[5]

[3] For an analysis of the agreement as well as some interesting commentary on the Malayan tin industry see Siew Nim Chee, "The International Tin Agreement, 1953," *Malayan Economic Review*, II (April 1957), 35–53.

[4] High-grade iron ore is mined on an important scale and appears capable of expansion. Most of the annual production, which in 1957 approached 2.5 million tons, is shipped to Japan. Bauxite and ilmenite could become important.

[5] F. C. Benham, *Economic Survey, Singapore, 1957* (Singapore: Government Printing Office, 1958), p. 25. The value of the Malayan dollar is fixed in sterling

A large measure of Singapore's trade (about 20 per cent by value in 1956) is with the Federation. Conversely, about 40 per cent of the Federation's foreign trade by value is with or through Singapore. The value of Federation exports depends chiefly on rubber and tin prices; of imports, on the cost of food and consumer goods. The Federation's over-all trade balance [6] since 1946 has been favorable. In 1956, of Singapore's and the Federation's total foreign trade valued at US$2.8 billion, about 36 per cent was with the United Kingdom and sterling-area countries; 12 per cent, with the United States and dollar countries; and 14.5 per cent, with Western European countries. The remaining trade was chiefly with Japan and Southeast Asian countries. Singapore and the Federation had a very favorable balance of trade with the United States and Western Europe and an unfavorable balance with the sterling area and neighboring Southeast Asian nations. [7] The decade ending in 1956 witnessed the significant trend wherein the United States took an annually smaller percentage of Malayan rubber exports (about 15.8 per cent in 1956), and Britain, Western European countries, and Japan took a generally larger share of rubber exports. [8] Chiefly because of the Federation's favorable trade balance, the over-all balance of Singapore and the Federation tends to be favorable.

Today the three traditional sectors of Malayan economy are bolstered by a fourth. Manufacturing has become increasingly important and currently contributes significantly to personal incomes, government revenues, and savings of foreign exchange. A World Bank mission observed in 1954 that Malayan industrial activity is probably exceeded in Asia only by Japan, India, and Hong Kong. Industrial development has not come about primarily as a result of cheap and abundant raw materials and labor. It has proceeded largely from the capital produced from the rubber and tin industries, from the need to process the output of the estates and mines and to supply services to com-

---

at 2s. 4d.; amounts in U.S. dollars are herein transposed from Malayan dollar amounts at three Malayan to one U.S. dollar.

[6] This is not to be construed as balance of payment since nontrade transactions have not been taken into consideration. Nontrade figures often represent a large outflow of capital. The balance of payments picture therefore is less bright than is suggested by trade figures only. Information on nontrade transactions is not readily available.

[7] Federation of Malaya, *Annual Report, 1956* (Kuala Lumpur, 1957), p. 121.

[8] Federation of Malaya, Department of Statistics, *Rubber Statistics Handbook, 1956*, p. 39.

merce, and from the fact that Malaya is a ready market for consumption goods.[9]

With respect to government revenue and expenditure, the power to tax in the Federation is concentrated in the Federal government, and most revenues are obtained from import and export duties and income taxes. The vagaries of rubber and tin prices have made accurate budget planning impossible. Federal revenue rose from approximately US$147.8 million in 1950 to US$245.2 million in 1951, declined to US$206.7 million in 1953, and was US$267.3 million in 1957. Federal expenditure has been high because of the cost of the Emergency, the rising cost of administration, and the increased demand for social services. Deficits occurred in 1949, 1953, 1954, and 1957.[10] The Federation's liabilities (public debt, interest-free long-term liabilities, and short-term financing less accumulated sinking funds) were approximately US$268 million at the close of 1956. On the same date revenue surpluses amounted to about US$146.1 million.[11] Much of the debt was held internally, and debt servicing, including sinking-fund appropriations, represented about 5 per cent of 1956 revenue.[12] The debt situation was probably satisfactory, but additional deficits seemed likely for some years in view of plans for economic development and expansion of social services.

Singapore, clinging to its reputation as a free port, has a simple revenue structure dependent mainly on an income tax and duties on liquor, petroleum, and tobacco. The colony has usually had an annual surplus which in recent years has substantially helped to pay for expanding social services. The public debt has been small and has been covered by investments of surplus revenue. Indicative of the future, however, were Singapore's expenditures for 1957, estimated at US$107 million against revenue estimated at US$78 million, the difference being due chiefly to capital development costs.[13]

Negotiations leading to Federation independence involved eco-

[9] International Bank for Reconstruction and Development, *The Economic Development of Malaya* (Baltimore: Johns Hopkins Press, 1955), pp. 119 ff.

[10] Revenue figures and deficit information are taken from various annual reports of the Federation of Malaya. The revenue figure for 1957 is not strictly comparable to previous years; it is taken from Federation of Malaya, *Treasury Memorandum*, Federal Legislative Council Paper no. 76 of 1957 (Kuala Lumpur, 1957).

[11] Federation of Malaya, *Annual Report, 1956*, pp. 89–93.

[12] Federation of Malaya, *Financial Statements for the Year 1956*, by C. E. Gascoigne (Kuala Lumpur, 1958), pp. 84–85.

[13] Benham, *op. cit.*, pp. 23–24. Revised estimates suggested that the budget would approximately balance.

nomic and financial arrangements of importance. The Federation chose to remain in the sterling area and to continue curtailment of dollar imports. Federation and Singapore contributions of hard currencies to the sterling pool have been very substantial; between 1948 and 1957, their U.S. dollar contributions totaled about 1.9 billion.[14] Malaya has aided the postwar economic recovery of Britain and has provided dollars which other sterling-area members have used for economic development. Malaya is further linked to the sterling area by investments of revenue surpluses and other government funds in empire and Commonwealth government securities. Membership in the sterling area was important to the Federation in the first years of independence to avoid disrupting the long-standing financial orientation of the country and to maintain confidence and stability in the Malayan dollar which is fully backed and freely convertible into sterling.

The Society

The rapid economic development of Malaya would not have been possible without the hundreds of thousands of immigrants who came to Malaya during the course of British rule. Many of these became domiciled after 1930 because of depression, war, and immigration policies. The resulting heterogeneity of contemporary Malayan society cannot escape the visitor. He can see Malay rice farmers, policemen, taxi drivers, and politicians; Chinese shopkeepers, building laborers, factory owners, and university professors; Indian doctors, lawyers, estate laborers, and night watchman; Singhalese and Eurasian clerks; British plantation managers; Australian mine operators, and American engineers.

A preliminary report on the 1957 census placed the Federation's population at 6.3 million.[15] A rough estimate of the communal composition of this total would give the Malays 3.1 million, the Chinese 2.3 million, and the Indians .7 million. The report indicated a population for Singapore of 1.5 million. This was somewhat higher than

[14] Information on this subject is not readily available. This figure is, however, fairly accurate. It is based upon the difference between Pan-Malayan (i.e., Federation, Singapore, and British Borneo territories) imports and exports to dollar countries as given in Federation of Malaya, *Annual Report, 1956*, p. 121, plus figures for 1957 stated by the Federation Finance Minister in the Federal Legislative Council on March 17–18, 1958. In October the minister was reported to have said that Malaya's net U.S. dollar earnings for the past decade had averaged about US$300 million per year (*Straits Budget*, Oct. 22, 1958, p. 18).

[15] *Malay Mail* (Kuala Lumpur, daily except Sunday), May 11, 1957, p. 5.

previously estimated and was laid to an inflow of Chinese from the Federation. Singapore's population was roughly 80 per cent Chinese, 10 per cent Malay and Indonesian, and 6 per cent Indian. The three major domiciled communities contrast sharply in their physical appearances, languages, religions, and mores. Few can speak, and still fewer are literate in, each other's languages; [16] market Malay is a lingua franca for many whereas English serves the same purpose for some. Intermarriage is unusual, and groups within communities tend to follow traditional economic pursuits.

Since the Japanese Occupation the main determinates of population increase have been birth and death rates. All three communities have high and similar birth rates (about 45 births per 1,000 population per year) but differ significantly in respect to infant mortality. The Malays have the largest number of infant deaths, the Chinese the smallest number. The difference is due to the poorer health facilities and greater poverty of the rural Malays. Infant mortality rates are generally declining; the over-all death rate is about 10 per thousand, indicating a very high net rate of increase of about 3.5 per cent.[17] Half or more of the population is under the age of 21.

Census enumerators use "Malaysian" to describe both the indigenous Malay and the Indonesian immigrant who, being of the same ethnic stock and cultural orientation, has readily been assimilated. Indonesians have come to the peninsula for centuries, and a large number have come from Java and Sumatra within the past fifty years.[18]

The main centers of Malay population are Kedah, Perlis, Kelantan, and Trengganu where the kampong or Malay village is the most common feature of the countryside. In Singapore, Johore, Selangor, and Perak the Malays are a minority. All Malays are Muslims,[19] and the village mosque is a focal point of Malay society. The Malays are overwhelmingly small agriculturists. Perhaps 50 per cent are engaged in rice cultivation, usually producing one crop per year. Another substantial proportion grow rubber as well as part of their food require-

---

[16] The 1947 census indicated an over-all literacy rate of nearly 500 per thousand for males and less than 200 per thousand for females. The Malays had the lowest literacy rates; the Indians, the highest. A good exposition of communication in Malaya's plural society is found in Norton Ginsberg and Chester F. Roberts, Jr., *Malaya* (Seattle: University of Washington Press, 1958), ch. vi.

[17] Federation of Malaya, *Annual Report, 1956*, pp. 8–10; Singapore, *Annual Report, 1956* (Singapore: Government Printing Office, 1958), pp. 17–22.

[18] T. E. Smith, *Population Growth in Malaya* (London: Oxford University Press, 1952), pp. 16 ff.

[19] They belong to the Shafiite sect of the Sunna or orthodox tradition.

ments. Malay holdings are quite small, approximately two to six acres, with ownership sometimes shared between several families. The effects on the Malay farmer of the rapid development of an export and money economy during the last half century have barely been investigated. The worst experiences of other agricultural societies may not have occurred in Malaya, however. Legislation has aimed at making Malay farmers secure in their land. Nevertheless they have fallen victim to Indian moneylenders, to Chinese shopkeepers, and, in some instances, to aristocratic Malay landlords. Rural indebtedness, tenancy, land fragmentation, rack-renting, and absentee landlordism are, for example, decades old in the Kedah "rice bowl." [20] The Malay community also predominates in fishing.

Malays have also shown interest in government clerical employment, the teaching profession, and the police and military forces. A traditional disinterest in wage employment has been changing since the Japanese Occupation. The Malay farmer, or more likely his son, has tended to leave his rice field for the estate or the town. In 1956 nearly 20 per cent of rubber estate workers were Malays.[21] This drift from the rice fields was sufficiently disturbing to cause the government to investigate in 1952. Only in the northeast, in Kelantan, do the Malays occupy an important position in commerce and light manufacturing. Generally, Malays are poor; those few who are middle class usually have an aristocratic background and have acquired wealth through control of land or through a government connection.

Given the class structure of the Malay community and the entrenched position of non-Malays in the economy, opportunities for upward movement are not very numerous. The peasant's son may currently aspire to service in the army, the police, the teaching profession, or the civil service and perhaps to a political career. Before the Occupation, government positions were largely held by the sons of rulers, rajas, or chiefs. Today scholarships are available to the intelligent Malay schoolboy, and places are reserved for him in the higher institutions of learning. Rajas' sons still abound in government service, but numerous men of more humble background can also be met.

[20] On Malay rice farming see Federation of Malaya, *Report of the Rice Production Committee,* vol. I (Kuala Lumpur, 1953). See also the work of another committee, Federation of Malaya, *Final Report of the Rice Committee* (Kuala Lumpur, 1956).

[21] Federation of Malaya, Department of Statistics, *Rubber Statistics Handbook, 1956,* p. 37.

The term "Chinese" covers a great diversity. Most Chinese immigrants came from the coastal regions of South China, within which are important district and linguistic differences. These differences have persisted in Malaya although they have weakened with the spread of the national language and the birth of generations of Malayan-born. More than 60 per cent of Malayan Chinese have been born in Singapore or the Federation.[22] The Chinese have settled chiefly on the western side of the peninsula and in Singapore, and probably well over 50 per cent of the Federation's Chinese live in towns. The religion of most Malayan Chinese consists of a variety of popular beliefs and practices—many local to Malaya—which are loosely classified as Buddhism and Taoism.[23] A growing number of young people appear to be without strong religious beliefs.

The Chinese have an important position or an ethnic monopoly in virtually every phase of the economy and in the technical branches of government. The community is prosperous and well to do. But this generalization covers extremes running from poor laborers, market gardeners, and domestic servants through a middle class of shopkeepers, technicians, and landlords to wealthy owners of mines, estates, and factories. The opportunities for easy class advancement seem to have lessened in recent years as the rate of growth in Malaya's basic industries has slowed or halted. Upward movement is still possible, however. The obstacles are not solely economic. Linguistic differences, kind and degree of education, and extent of Malayan assimilation are important factors.

The term "Indian" embraces those who came from, or the descendants of persons who came from, widely separated parts of India and with various religious backgrounds. But the Tamil-speaking Hindu from South India accounts for the large majority. He is found working chiefly on government public works and on European plantations, particularly in Selangor, Perak, and Negri Sembilan. Here the Indian population is largest. A few Indians are found in nearly every economic endeavor. Almost as many are in the professions as are Chinese and Malays combined. Indians in commerce, finance, or the profes-

[22] M. V. Del Tufo, *A Report on the 1947 Census of Population* (Kuala Lumpur, 1949), p. 84.

[23] See Alan J. A. Elliott, *Chinese Spirit Medium Cults in Singapore* (London School of Economics and Political Science, Department of Anthropology, Monographs on Social Anthropology, n.s., no. 14; Norwich: Jarrold & Sons, Ltd., 1955), pp. 24 ff., and various articles by Marjorie Topley in *Journal of the Malayan Branch of the Royal Asiatic Society.*

sions are affluent, but the large majority of laborers are poor indeed. Nearly 50 per cent of the Indian community in 1947 was born in Malaya.[24]

Class mobility among the Indian community appears to be slight. Economic differences are powerfully backed by differences in language, caste, and education as well as the paucity of opportunity. This situation has resulted in restiveness among young men who are increasingly reluctant to follow their fathers as wage laborers. Possibly the only thing in common among all Malayan Indians is their love and pride for India. Indian lawyers have appreciated this and have since the 1930s believed that their political fortunes in Malaya rest upon obtaining the support of Indian laborers.

Political Forces

In such a heterogeneous society, potential political forces and their possible alignments would appear to be numerous. Up to mid-1958 many groups and associations which might ordinarily be thought of as having political interests had not often entered politics, although politicians had claimed or had begun to bid for the support of certain of them. Among the reasons for their relative lack of political activity were the absence of political experience, legal barriers and official pressures against political activity, the lack of strong belief by some in the wisdom of advancing their interest through political action, and the conviction of others that their particular interests should be subordinate to broader interests.

To cite some examples, most Federation trade unions have avoided politics because their leaders have not been convinced of the futility of economic action to secure their goals. They also have the example of unions being used as weapons of political parties in the period 1945–1948. In addition political action as a union was illegal in the Federation prior to 1955.[25] The civil service and also the predominantly Malay police and military forces have been strictly enjoined from engaging in politics. The subordination of particular to broader interests was seen in the winning of independence. Another broad interest of special importance to the Malays has been communal solidarity. Malay youth, women, and religious leaders have engaged in politics

[24] Del Tufo, *op. cit.*, p. 85.

[25] See J. Norman Parmer, "Trade Unions and Politics in Malaya," *Far Eastern Survey*, XXIV (March 1955), 33–39, and "Trade Unions in Malaya," *Annals*, CCCX (March 1957), 142–150.

but usually in combination for the purpose of winning independence and because of their desire to maintain Malay unity. Another broad interest important to numerous Malay and Chinese community leaders has been the desire for intercommunal harmony.

Some of the considerations which have deterred groups and associations from politics are still valid. Freedom from Britain has not, for example, removed the broader interests of communal solidarity or mutual understanding. A result of independence, however, has been participation in politics by more groups and associations. The balance of political forces that will ultimately emerge is difficult to foresee although there have been many developments upon which to speculate. The truth is that politics is still in a formative stage; neither the Federation nor Singapore has yet experienced enough political freedom. More elections will help clarify the picture; thus political leaders and observers look forward to the elections in both territories in 1959 under new constitutions.

POLITICAL PARTIES IN THE FEDERATION

Of the dozen or more parties in the Federation, few can yet claim to have formed effective national organizations. The oldest and largest of the legal parties is the United Malays National Organization (UMNO).[26] Formed in 1946 to give unity and direction to Malay protests against the Malayan Union, it has been led by Malays of aristocratic and middle-class backgrounds, especially from Kedah and Johore. The leader of the new party from 1946 was Dato Onn bin Ja'afar, former *mentri besar* or prime minister of Johore and member of the sultan's household. Dato Onn, who was hailed on the eve of independence in 1957 by the retiring British High Commissioner as "the father of political thought and development" in Malaya,[27] left the UMNO in 1951 to found the all-communities Independence of Malaya Party (IMP).

The forerunner of the IMP was the Communities Liaison Committee formed in December 1948. Its purpose was to bring community leaders together to discuss communal problems and explore means of attaining national unity. Malcolm MacDonald, the forward-looking British Commissioner-General in Southeast Asia, helped to inspire the

[26] All parties are required to register with the government and file details of their organization and activities. If registration is refused or rescinded, the party becomes an illegal organization.

[27] Federation of Malaya, *Legislative Council Debates Official Report . . . 14th and 15th August 1957* (Kuala Lumpur, 1957), col. 3071.

committee's formation. In forming IMP, Dato Onn was unable to carry an important number of Malays with him. Nor did he receive the non-Malay support which he had expected. IMP amounted to little more than a handful of English-educated urban Chinese and Indians. Seeking to recoup his political fortunes, Dato Onn founded Party Negara early in 1954. Negara claimed to be noncommunal but espoused in vain a narrow Malay nationalism in an attempt to win the Malays from their continuing support of UMNO. Defeated in the Federal elections in 1955 and in a by-election in 1957, many Malayans were inclined to believe that the political career of Dato Onn, in his sixties, was at an end.

When Dato Onn left the UMNO, leadership went to Tengku Abdul Rahman, an uncle of the sultan of Kedah. Rahman, a Cambridge-educated lawyer, has shown considerable ability in leading the Malays in a moderate nationalism. At the time of independence his prestige was very high; he is virtually the first and only Malayan national leader of stature to emerge. Now in his fifties, Rahman as Prime Minister has surrounded himself with British advisers to whom he listens but follows only as he sees fit. Other top leaders of UMNO include Dr. Ismail bin Dato Abdul Rahman, an Australian-trained medical doctor from Johore, and Dato Abdul Razak bin Dato Hussain, a lawyer from the Pahang aristocracy.[28]

The Malayan Chinese Association (MCA) has been almost the only spokesman of the Chinese community. Formed in 1949, its activities were initially more welfare than political in nature, and it did much to alleviate the hardships of squatter resettlement. In assuming a more definite political role since 1952, MCA leaders have been motivated by a belief that Malayan Chinese must take a constructive self-interest in politics. The MCA, however, has never been supported by the Chinese community in the same way as the Malays have supported UMNO. This has been due to divisions in the community as well as a traditional Chinese reluctance to enter politics.

Fierce struggles have occurred for MCA party positions. The principal founder and first president of the party was a Straits-born Chinese, Dato Tan Cheng-lock, a pioneer rubber planter and lead-

[28] Dr. Ismail has held ministerial posts for Agriculture and Commerce and Industry and subsequently became the Federation's first ambassador to the United States. Dato Abdul Razak has held the difficult job of Minister for Education and subsequently became Deputy Prime Minister and Defense Minister.

ing prewar Chinese spokesman. He was succeeded as MCA president in March 1958 by Dr. Lim Chong Eu, a British-educated physician from a well-known Penang family. His election was followed by a large turnover of MCA officers. Also prominent and regarded by some as the Federation's most influential Chinese figure is Colonel Henry Hau Shik Lee. Lee, who was the principal founder of the UMNO-MCA Alliance, was ousted from MCA leadership late in 1956 but returned to a position of power in March 1958.

Opposition within and without the MCA to its acceptance of the revisions of the Reid recommendations crystallized in the Federation of Chinese Guilds and Associations (FCGA), which claimed to represent more than a thousand Chinese organizations. Lau Pak Khuan, spokesman for an older generation of Perak Chinese and former MCA supporter, led a protest delegation to London in the name of the FCGA. It produced no tangible results, and thereafter little was heard from the organization; but this did not mean that the views it represented were no longer lively ones.

The Malayan Indian Congress (MIC) was organized after the Japanese Occupation, but it had prewar roots in an older generation of Indian professional men who were inspired by India's struggle for independence. Party leadership was much criticized in 1954 for its advocating the election of some Federal Legislative Council seats on a communal basis. Joining the UMNO-MCA Alliance in 1955, the MIC has sought to be the spokesman for Indians loyal to Malaya. It has apparently not been able to command the strong support of the Indian community. This is attributable to divisions in the community and also to the struggle for party offices. Since 1955 V. T. Sambanthan, a Tamil-speaking rubber planter and businessman, has been MIC president. Numerous Indians outside the MIC are of actual or potential political importance.

The background of UMNO-MCA-MIC Alliance leaders is obviously conservative. A comprehensive statement of their social and economic policies was issued prior to the Federal Legislative Council election in July 1955 and has subsequently been elaborated. The Alliance stands for extension of education, health, housing, and welfare services; recognition of trade unions and fair treatment of labor; economic development through government encouragement and assistance to local and foreign private enterprise; fair taxes; and, insofar as possible, a balanced budget. In June 1958 Tengku Abdul Rahman described the Alliance as a "rightist" party, one most suited to the needs of the people for the present.[29]

Opposition to the Alliance has fundamentally followed three tacts, namely, member parties have betrayed the communities which they represent by compromising between themselves; unity based on communal organizations serves to perpetuate communal differences and delay achievement of real Malayan unity; and the Alliance is an association of reactionary capitalists and aristocrats. Only subsequent to independence have the opposition parties had some success against the Alliance—in a Federal by-election and local elections. Alliance leaders regard their opponents seriously and have renewed earlier efforts to achieve better organization. In 1958, member parties were asked to approve a constitution for the Pakatan Perikatan or Alliance Organization. The UMNO, MCA, and MIC apparently would have retained their separate organizations but would have been subject to the policies of the new party's executive. UMNO members raised considerable objection but finally gave their approval. Alliance leaders subsequently decided to postpone the project. The most serious opponents of the Alliance early in 1958 appeared to be Malay communal parties and left-wing groups organized around the Labour Party of Malaya.[30] The Chinese community was without effective opposition parties, generally managing to keep opposition groups within the MCA itself.

The Malay communal parties included Dato Onn's Party Negara, which continued to espouse a narrow Malay nationalism. Another was the Pan-Malayan Islamic Party (PMIP), which held one of the two non-Alliance elected seats in the Federal Legislative Council. Its president was Dr. Burhanuddin Al-helmy, who is popularly known as an Islamic scholar and is a long-time champion of Malay nationalism and ties with Indonesia. Inspired by talks with the Indonesian leaders Soekarno and Hatta, he was a principal founder of the Malay Nationalist Party in 1945.[31] A third Malay party was the Party Ra'ayat (People's Party), whose leader was the English-educated, sometime journalist Inche Ahmad Boestamam. Boestamam was detained in 1948 under the Emergency Regulations and was released in 1955. He sought to offer the Malays a left-wing party and avoided links with Negara

[29] *Straits Budget,* June 11, 1958, p. 16.

[30] The Pan-Malayan Labour Party became the Labour Party of Malaya in 1954.

[31] Burhanuddin attended the Bandung Conference in 1955 where he reportedly presented himself as Malaya's representative. For this he was strongly criticized by Tengku Abdul Rahman.

and the PMIP. Up to mid-1958 the Malay parties had had few election successes.

The victories had been won by the People's Progressive Party (PPP) and the Labour Party of Malaya. The PPP secretary-general, D. R. Seenivasagam, won a Federal Legislative Council by-election in November 1957. A Ceylonese lawyer, Seenivasagam successfully ran against an important MCA official in a predominantly Chinese constituency. In December the Labour Party defeated Alliance candidates in town council elections in the Federation. In Penang the Labour Party won control of the council, and the party's chairman, D. S. Ramanathan, who is a teacher in a Methodist mission school, became mayor. Alliance defeats were put down to the Malay minorities in the constituencies contested, the conclusion being that Chinese and Indian support for the MCA and MIC was lacking.[32]

The Labour Party and Party Ra'ayat formed a National Socialist Front in 1957. The Front would clearly make a class appeal, and its platform in the 1959 Federal elections would probably call for public ownership of major industries, social reform legislation, help to local industries, opposition to communism, and repeal of the Emergency Regulations. At the same time the Party Negara and the PMIP talked of a Malay National Front.

While the legal parties made plans, significant developments had occurred in respect to the Malayan Communist Party (MCP). The MCP is the oldest political party in Malaya although it probably cannot claim an unbroken history.[33] Formed in 1927 out of the revolutionary committee of the Malayan Kuomintang Party, it was early set back by police action but revived in the late 1930s to organize Chinese workers in Singapore and the Malay States. Then followed the Occupation, the years of legal existence in 1945–1948, and the Emergency from June 1948. By 1955, when the Federal elections were held, the Communists were on the defensive though by no means beaten. After the Alliance victory, Tengku Abdul Rahman met with Chin Peng— the Malayan-born, English- and Chinese-educated general secretary of the MCP—to discuss an amnesty. The talks failed because of dis-

---

[32] *Straits Budget*, Dec. 18, 1957, p. 3.

[33] See Gene Z. Hanrahan, *The Communist Struggle in Malaya* (New York: Institute of Pacific Relations, International Secretariat, 1954); René Onraet, *Singapore—A Police Background* (London: Dorothy Crisp & Co., 1947); Harry Miller, *The Communist Menace in Malaya* (New York: Praeger, 1954); Lucian W. Pye, *Guerrilla Communism in Malaya: Its Social and Political Meaning* (Princeton: Princeton University Press, 1956).

agreement on several points but in particular over the party's demand for legal recognition.[34] An MCP conditional peace bid early in 1957 was rejected. But in September, just after independence, the Alliance government made a final amnesty offer which was extended through July 1958. This led to the highest surrender rate ever attained but failed to bring the Emergency to an end. Earlier, in October 1957, the MCP declared that it was willing to end the struggle and pledge its loyalty to Malaya. It also called for recognition of various political parties, diplomatic relations with all countries, a neutralist foreign policy and alignment with the Asian-African group of nations, a merger with Singapore, and the release of all political "offenders."[35] The MCP is still predominantly Chinese in spite of strenuous efforts before and since the Emergency began to recruit Indians and Malays, which may indicate that the communal appeal is still much stronger than the class appeal.

POLITICAL PARTIES IN SINGAPORE

Singapore's half-dozen important political parties date mainly from 1954–1955 when constitutional reform greatly broadened the scope for political activity. The size of the parties is difficult to estimate. The prominent parties roughly represent cultural and economic divisions among the Chinese. The Liberal-Socialist Party is the result of a merger of two right-wing parties of well-to-do persons previously separated because of differences in education: the one Chinese and the other British. The Labour Front—first under David Marshall, a criminal lawyer, and then under Lim Yew Hock, a white-collar trade unionist—formed a coalition government after the elections of April 1955. It is supported by members of the Singapore Trades Union Congress (STUC) as well as by some professional persons and stands for a moderate, pragmatic variety of socialism without radical changes in Singapore's commercial economy.[36] Marshall, who claims to stand for "entrepôt socialism," left the Labour Front to form the Workers' Party late in 1957, taking with him some Labour Front supporters.[37]

[34] See Federation of Malaya, *Report by the Chief Minister of the Federation of Malaya on the Baling Talks* (Kuala Lumpur, 1956).

[35] *New York Times*, Oct. 6, 1957, p. 25.

[36] See remarks by Francis Thomas, Labour Front Minister for Communications and Works, in Singapore, *Singapore Legislative Assembly Debates Official Report* (Singapore: Government Printing Office, 1957), II, no. 25, April 29, 1957, cols. 1842–1847.

[37] For a discussion of the Labour Front and other left-wing parties, particularly

Further to the left is the People's Action Party (PAP). Its leadership is divided roughly between young English-educated, professional persons and Chinese-educated leaders of students and militant unionists outside the STUC. In August 1957 party control passed to the latter group. Shortly thereafter the government alleged that the PAP had become a Communist front and arrested a number of party officials. Subsequently the English-educated, "moderate" leaders resumed control of the party. They include the principal founders of the PAP—Lee Kuan Yew, a Cambridge-trained lawyer, and Dr. Toh Chin Chye, a University of Malaya physiology lecturer. The Australian-educated mayor of Singapore, Ong Eng Guan, is also regarded as a PAP moderate. These men appear to be in the unhappy position of having to rely upon the police action of their political opponent, the Labour Front government, to maintain control of the party.

The Malay minority in Singapore is represented principally by a Singapore United Malays National Organization. It joined with a Singapore Malayan Chinese Association to help the Labour Front form a government in 1955. Inche Abdul Hamid bin Haji Jumat, chief UMNO spokesman, became Minister for Local Government, Lands, and Housing. Singapore UMNO's appeal is communal, but its supporters are divided between right and left. The former are inclined toward the Labour Front; the latter, toward the PAP. The Singapore Indian community has numerous organizations, but none are very active politically. Indians have instead supported other parties.

---

in Singapore, see Charles Gamba, "Labour and Labour Parties in Malaya," *Pacific Affairs*, XXXI (June 1958), 117–130.

· XV ·

The Political Process

FORMAL political processes in the Federation and Singapore were by late 1958 still to be proved by experience. Little could be said about the informal political processes, since the framework in which they would operate was yet to be fully established and political forces were themselves to some extent inchoate. No study had been made of the informal processes insofar as they had developed. Therefore, this chapter is chiefly concerned with a brief description of the formal structures of the governments which were to be created.

The Federation

The constitution [1] of the Federation of Malaya became effective on Independence Day, August 31, 1957. It declared Islam to be the religion of the Federation but guaranteed the right to practice other religions. It established a federal government consisting of a monarch, a conference of rulers, a cabinet, a two-house parliament, a judiciary, and five public service commissions. The constitution also provided for state governments and dealt with a variety of other important matters, such as citizenship, elections, division of powers between the Federal and state governments, special rights and privileges, and fundamental liberties.

[1] Federation of Malaya, *Constitutional Proposals* (Kuala Lumpur: Federation of Malaya Government Press, 1957). In this chapter when Kuala Lumpur is the place of publication, the publisher is the Federation of Malaya Government Press.

The monarch, who is given the title Yang di-Pertuan Agong, or Supreme Head of State, is chosen for a five-year term by the nine Malay rulers, assembled in the Majlis Raja Raja, or Conference of Rulers, from among themselves on the basis of seniority. The first Yang di-Pertuan Agong was the ruler of Negri Sembilan, Tuanku Abdul Rahman ibni Al-marhum Tuanku Muhammad.[2] The Conference of Rulers also chooses a Deputy Supreme Head of State and picked the ruler of Selangor for the first incumbent of this office. Other major functions of the Majlis Raja Raja are to advise the Yang di-Pertuan Agong on certain appointments;[3] to consent or withhold consent to certain laws, mainly those affecting their position and privileges or altering state boundaries; and to deliberate on questions of national policy in company with the Federal Prime Minister and state chief ministers, whose advice must be accepted. The Conference must also be consulted on any change in policy affecting Malay privileges.

The Yang di-Pertuan Agong's responsibilities are to summon and dissolve parliament, to appoint a Prime Minister and cabinet, to assent to bills passed by parliament, to "safeguard the special position of the Malays and the legitimate interests of other communities," and to make numerous important appointments. The Yang di-Pertuan Agong performs these duties after consultation with various authorities and generally must act in accordance with the advice of the cabinet. He may, however, exercise discretion in acting upon a request to dissolve parliament as well as in appointing a Prime Minister, a Chief Justice, a Public Services Commission, and a Police Service Commission. When appointing the Prime Minister, the Yang di-Pertuan Agong must choose a person who is a citizen other than by registration or naturalization and who is a member of the House of Representatives and able to command the confidence of the majority of that house. If the Prime Minister loses the confidence of the House, he may request that parliament be dissolved. If this is denied by the Yang di-Pertuan Agong, he must resign. Other members of the cabinet are chosen from either house on the advice of the Prime Minister, and the cabinet is collectively responsible to parliament.

The first Federal parliament will take office after the elections

[2] He has legal training and experience and comes from a state which has one of the country's economically and politically most sophisticated Malay populations.

[3] Notably appointments to Supreme Court judgeships, the office of Chief Justice, the office of Auditor-General, the Election Commission, and Public Services Commission.

under the new constitution in 1959. The Dewan Negara or Senate will have 38 members, 22 elected by state legislatures and 16 appointed by the Yang di-Pertuan Agong. Appointments are to honor distinction in public service or in public life and to give representation to minorities. Senators hold office for six years, half being elected or appointed every three years. Provision is made for the possible eventual direct election of all Senators. The other house is the Dewan Ra'ayat or House of Representatives. It will have 100 members directly elected in single-member territorial constituencies.[4] Representatives meet at least once every six months and hold office for five years unless parliament is dissolved sooner. Bills are initiated in either house, but money bills may originate only in the House of Representatives. Both houses pass on bills, but Senate approval is not required on money bills or on bills passed by the House a second time after the lapse of one year in which the Senate has not acted. Constitutional amendment requires a two-thirds vote of the total membership of each house. Malay is the official language of parliament, but English may be used for ten years from Independence Day. Members of the House of Representatives as well as of the state legislatures are elected by persons who are 21 years old, have resided for six months in the constituency in which they intend to vote, and are citizens.[5]

[4] The first House of Representatives in 1959 will have 104 members. The Reid Commission was of the opinion that a fair delimitation of 100 new constituencies would not be possible until after most new citizens were registered, a process which was thought likely to be still in progress well into 1959. Rather than delay, the commission recommended that for the first elections the existing 52 constituencies be split into two. See Great Britain, Colonial Office, *Report of the Federation of Malaya Constitutional Commission, 1957,* Colonial no. 330 (London: H.M. Stationery Office, 1957), p. 31.

[5] Citizenship or nationality is acquired primarily in three ways: by law, by registration, and by naturalization. Persons who were citizens before Independence Day or who were born in the Federation on or after Independence Day are citizens by law. Persons born in the Federation before Independence Day are entitled to be registered as citizens if they are 18 years old, have resided in the Federation for five of the preceding seven years and intend to reside permanently in the Federation, are of good character, and have an elementary knowledge of Malay. The last requirement was waived if application was made within one year of Independence Day. Persons not born in the Federation but resident there on Independence Day may apply to be registered as citizens if they have resided in the Federation for eight of the preceding twelve years and meet the above qualifications. The language qualification was also waived for one year where the applicant had attained the age of 45. Decisions of the registration authority cannot

The judiciary is a single system composed of a Chief Justice and a Supreme Court and subordinate courts established by parliament. The Supreme Court has original, appellate, and revisional jurisdiction as provided by Federal law, has jurisdiction in disputes between states or between a state and the Federation, and may, upon application by a party engaged in proceedings in a lower court, interpret the constitution. As is provided by Federal law, an appeal from the Supreme Court to the Yang di-Pertuan Agong can be referred to the Judicial Committee of the Queen's Privy Council for a report or recommendation.[6] Provision is made for the independence of the Supreme Court; once appointed, judges cannot be removed prior to retirement at the age of 65. Minor courts concerned with Malay custom and Islamic law lie outside the system and are provided for by state law.

In respect to the eleven states, the Federal constitution guarantees their constitutions and sets out the structure of their governments. Each is headed by a hereditary ruler (in the nine former Malay states) or a governor (in the two former British Settlements of Malacca and Penang). A governor holds office for four years and is appointed by the Yang di-Pertuan Agong acting in his own discretion after consulting the state's chief minister. Each state has a popularly elected legislative assembly and an executive council appointed by the ruler or governor on the advice of his chief minister, who must be able to command the support of a majority of the legislative assembly. The executive council is collectively responsible to the assembly. The Federal parliament may admit other states to the Federation

---

be appealed except on a point of law; the registration authority is a permanent three-man Election Commission appointed by the Yang di-Pertuan Agong after consultation with the Conference of Rulers. Persons who were not resident in the Federation on Independence Day may apply for naturalization if they are 21 years old, have resided in the Federation for ten of the preceding twelve years and intend to reside permanently in the Federation, are of good character, and have an adequate knowledge of Malay. Persons obtaining citizenship by registration or naturalization must take an oath renouncing loyalty to any other state and swearing allegiance to the Federation.

The constitution further provides that all Federation nationals are Commonwealth citizens. This means that a Federation national when in another Commonwealth country may exercise such privileges as that country extends to Commonwealth citizens. If, however, he exercises rights conferred exclusively on citizens of that country, then he loses his nationality just as if he were exercising rights in a foreign country.

[6] Great Britain, Commonwealth Relations Office, *Federation of Malaya Agreement,* Cmnd. 383 (London: H.M. Stationery Office, 1958).

and alter the boundaries of existing states. In the latter event, however, the consent of the state legislative assembly and the Conference of Rulers is necessary.

The constitution divides legislative and executive powers between the Federal and state governments, the powers being assigned in Federal, state, and concurrent lists. The Federal list includes almost all the major activities of government. Federal predominance is further assured by articles giving precedence to Federal law where state law is inconsistent with it, when uniformity between states is desired, and in several matters concerning land use. The Federal government is also empowered to conduct research, to make investigations, to give advice, and to implement national economic development plans—any state powers to the contrary notwithstanding. State governments may legislate in respect to Islamic law and Malay custom; land, including reservation of land for use by Malays and mining; agriculture; and local government services and public works, including housing. Responsibility is shared (the concurrent list) in such matters as social welfare, public health, town and country planning, and drainage and irrigation. The states are assigned residual legislative powers. Because of the great importance of land to economic development, the Federal constitution provides for a National Land Council of Federal and state representatives to formulate policy on land use and administration of laws.

The power to tax, borrow, lend, and spend lies primarily with the Federal government, and such powers as the states have in this matter are assigned in the Federal constitution. The principal sources of state income are Federal grants based on state population and road mileage, the revenue from fees, licenses, rents, fines, and entertainment taxes and tin production—each state receiving 10 per cent or more of the Federal export duty on the tin it produces. The Federal constitution established a National Finance Council composed primarily of state representatives which is to be consulted by the Federal government on financial matters affecting the states.

A single article in the Federation constitution charges the Yang di-Pertuan Agong with the responsibility of safeguarding the "special position of the Malays and the legitimate interests of other communities." He must, however, act in accordance with the advice of the cabinet. Specifically, the Yang di-Pertuan Agong is empowered to direct any public service commission or other authority to reserve for Malays—in such proportions as he considers reasonable—positions in the Federal public services, Federal scholarships, places in Federal educational facilities, and Federal permits and licenses to engage in business. The Yang di-Pertuan Agong may not cause any person to be deprived of public office, cause any person in public office not to be treated impartially in respect to his terms of service, or cause a person to be deprived of any scholarship or other educational privilege. Neither the Yang di-Pertuan Agong nor any Federal law may cause a person to be deprived of any right, privilege, permit, or license enjoyed by him or cause a refusal to renew such permit or license to him or to his heir or successors. Nor can any Federal law require a permit or license in a business where none was previously required and then refuse same to a person engaged in that trade or business prior to the law's coming into force. Finally, parliament is forbidden to restrict any business solely to Malays. The constitution also undertakes to preserve Malay land reservations while protecting non-Malays. Private property may not be declared a Malay reservation, and a practical limit is placed on the declaration of unused land as new Malay reservation.

Fundamental liberties are guaranteed by the Federal constitution, and protection is assured against banishment, slavery, forced labor, retroactive laws and repeated trials, deprivation of property, and discrimination in public education. These liberties are, however, importantly qualified. Parliament may restrict freedom of speech, assembly, association, and movement in the interest of security, public order, or public health and is the final authority on such restrictions. In addition parliament may enact emergency laws having effect for one year which deny basic liberties if organized violence occurs or is feared likely to occur. Except as specifically stated, opportunities are not given for individuals to obtain redress against unlawful executive acts or to challenge the constitutionality of laws.[7] Finally, a broad exception is made to equality before the law by the privileges accorded to Malays and the efforts to safeguard the economic interests of non-Malays.

[7] The Reid majority proposals allowed "reasonable" restrictions by parliament on fundamental liberties, thus opening the way for the courts to interpret the law. The Reid proposals also provided for redress against executive acts and for challenge of the constitutionality of laws. The final draft deleted these features. The deletions were criticized in the Legislative Council. See Federation of Malaya, *Legislative Council Debates Official Report . . . 14th and 15th August 1957* (Kuala Lumpur, 1957), cols. 3135 ff. See also *Straits Times* (Singapore, daily), Aug. 14, 1957, p. 8; Aug. 16, 1957, p. 8.

Singapore

The main features of a constitution for the new State of Singapore which was scheduled to be established early in 1959 were worked out in a series of conferences in London between 1956 and 1958.[8] As agreed in these meetings, the constitution supplemented by royal instructions and Singapore legislation will provide that the head of the State of Singapore and the Crown's representative be a Malayan-born person with the Malay title Yang di-Pertuan Negara. He will hold office for four years, and Singapore will be consulted prior to his appointment. Except in certain matters noted below, the Yang di-Pertuan Negara will act according to the advice of a Prime Minister and Council of Ministers who will be collectively responsible to a fully elected fifty-one-member Legislative Assembly. The Assembly will experiment with debate in English, Chinese, Tamil, and Malay. The right to elect members to the Assembly will rest upon a Singapore citizenship.[9] Persons under detention at the time the constitution becomes effective are to be barred from participating in the first

[8] Great Britain, *Singapore Constitutional Conference,* Cmd. 9777 (London: H.M. Stationery Office, 1956) and *Report of the Singapore Constitutional Conference Held in London in March and April 1957,* Cmnd. 147 (London: H.M. Stationery Office, 1957).

[9] By legislation enacted in October 1957 Singapore citizenship is obtainable primarily in three ways: by law, by registration, and by naturalization. All persons born in Singapore and all persons born outside of Singapore if their fathers were born in Singapore are citizens by law. Persons who are citizens of the Federation or citizens of the United Kingdom and colonies and who are of age and of good character and have lived in Singapore for two years prior to application are entitled to be registered as citizens. Persons who have resided in the colony for eight years prior to when the law came into operation and are of age and of good character may be registered as citizens if application is made within two years of the date the law came into operation. Refusal to register such applicants need not be explained and cannot be appealed. Persons may become citizens by naturalization who have lived in Singapore eight of the preceding twelve years, have lived there for twelve months prior to application, are of age and of good character, and intend to reside in Singapore permanently. Persons seeking citizenship by registration or naturalization must take an oath of allegiance and loyalty. Persons who might be citizens of another country by that country's laws must divest themselves of that citizenship before becoming permanent citizens of Singapore. Commonwealth citizens may become citizens of Singapore on the same terms as apply to Federation citizens if their countries are so designated by the Singapore government. Anyone who became a citizen within three months of the law's coming into operation could be deprived of his citizenship within the twelve months following without prejudice to a subsequent new application. See Singapore, *Report from the Select Committee on the Singapore Citizenship Bill,* Sessional Paper no. Cmd. 18 of 1957 (Singapore: Government Printing Office, 1957).

Assembly. There will be an independent judiciary and a public services commission. United Kingdom armed services will be permitted
to retain and add to the lands which they possess. The proposed constitution will protect minorities and includes the statement that "it
shall be the deliberate and conscious policy of the Government of
Singapore at all times to recognise the special position of the Malays
who are the indigenous people of the Island and are in most need
of assistance." [10]

This government is to have complete responsibility for the affairs
of Singapore except for internal security, external relations, and defense. External relations and defense will be the responsibility of a
United Kingdom Commissioner in Singapore. In order that the United
Kingdom and Singapore governments may maintain close liaison on
defense and external relations—the trade and cultural aspects of which
will be shared with Singapore—an Intergovernmental Committee is
to be established by administrative action once the new constitution
becomes effective. In respect to internal security, the constitution
will provide for a seven-member Internal Security Council composed
of the Prime Minister and two other Singapore ministers, three representatives of the United Kingdom, and a minister from the Federation
government. The United Kingdom Commissioner is to be one of the
three United Kingdom representatives and chairman of the Council.
The United Kingdom government also intends to retain the right to
suspend the Singapore constitution; and if such action becomes necessary, the Commissioner will take over the government of Singapore.
The proposed constitution can be amended by Singapore in respect
to "matters of purely internal concern." The United Kingdom will
also be able to make amendments but will do so only in agreement
with the Singapore government. It was proposed that the new constitution be reviewed at the end of four years, if not sooner, and,
if no agreement was reached, that it should remain in force.

[10] Great Britain, Colonial Office, *Report of the Singapore Constitutional Conference Held in London in March and April 1957,* Cmnd. 147, p. 5.

· XVI ·

Major Problems

THE Federation of Malaya obtained political freedom in probably the most favorable circumstances possible in Southeast Asia in the middle of the twentieth century. The transfer of power was peaceful. The country had extensive capital investments, substantial undeveloped land, and a small population. A large and growing number of entrepreneurs, administrators, and technicians were available to assume responsible positions. These were important assets in dealing with numerous difficult problems. As for Singapore, the island colony was not dissimilar in respect to the value of its economic resources and the caliber of many of its citizens. But it had special problems; and full independence, if feasible at all, was some time off.

Economic Problems of the Federation

Malaya is undoubtedly overly dependent upon prices received for rubber and tin exports.[1] At the same time, the capital investments and earning powers of those industries are very large in relation to the country's population. The result is great wealth for some, a comparatively good standard of living for many, and substantial public assets in the form of communication facilities, buildings, utilities, schools, and hospitals. This relatively favorable situation is quickly

[1] A brief introduction to the subject of Malayan economic problems is Lim Tay Boh, ed., *Problems of the Malayan Economy* (Background to Malaya Series, no. 10; Singapore: Donald Moore, 1956).

changing. First, the population is increasing rapidly. From 6.3 million in 1957, the Federation's population is likely to reach 8.5 million by 1967. The labor force will increase from 1.6 million to an estimated 2 million by 1967.[2] Secondly, rubber and tin are now mature industries, and although manufacturing is capable of expansion, few important new industries are in sight. The fundamental economic problem, therefore, is how to provide jobs for the rising labor force as well as government revenue for expanding social services. If economic expansion cannot be achieved, the people of the Federation not only will fail to attain the higher standard of living to which they aspire but will see the disappearance of the comparatively high standard which many of them presently enjoy. The government seeks a solution by encouraging existing industries to achieve efficiency and by endeavoring to attract local and external capital into new enterprises.[3] Its efforts are being conducted within a framework of national economic planning.

The first attempt at economic planning was a draft development plan for the period 1950–1955.[4] Implementation was handicapped by the Emergency, a distortion of costs during the 1951–1952 Korean War years, the insufficiency of the original plan, and inadequate institutional tools.[5] In 1954 a World Bank mission surveyed the Malayan economy and recommended an expenditure in the Federation of US$258.9 million (in Singapore, US$203 million) over the period 1955–1959. A central bank was also proposed to free Malayan currency from its full monetary backing and to establish and manage credit facilities. This and other institutional recommendations would assist economic development and help to create a national in place of a colonial economy.[6]

A new five-year plan was approved in October 1956.[7] To run from

[2] Federation of Malaya, *Legislative Council Debates Official Report . . . 4th to 13th December 1957* (Kuala Lumpur: Federation of Malaya Government Press, 1958), cols, 4243–4247. In this chapter when Kuala Lumpur is the place of publication, the publisher is the Federation of Malaya Government Press.

[3] An informative report on the prospects for industrial development is Federation of Malaya, *Report of the Industrial Development Working Party* (Kuala Lumpur, 1957).

[4] Federation of Malaya, *Draft Development Plan of the Federation of Malaya* (Kuala Lumpur, 1950).

[5] See Federation of Malaya, *Progress Report on the Development Plan of the Federation of Malaya, 1950–1952* (Kuala Lumpur, 1953), pp. 5 ff.

[6] International Bank for Reconstruction and Development, *The Economic Development of Malaya* (Baltimore: Johns Hopkins Press, 1955).

[7] Federation of Malaya, *Report on Economic Planning in the Federation of Malaya in 1956* (Kuala Lumpur, 1957), p. 3.

1956 through 1960, it became the economic program of the Alliance government. The plan envisages an expenditure of US$452.7 million with 25.4 per cent allocated to agriculture, mining, and industry; 25.2 per cent to transportation and communications; 7.9 per cent to power; 9.5 per cent to education; 5.2 per cent to medical facilities and rural health schemes; and 7.4 per cent to municipal public works and low rental housing programs. Most of the money is being obtained by drawing on financial reserves, by internal loans, and by assistance from and loans raised in the United Kingdom. Some US$77 million will have to be raised elsewhere. Additional borrowing will be required for costly long-range projects not in the plan. These include a hydroelectric development, an irrigation scheme, and a new east-west railway.

A large part of the funds is earmarked for the rubber industry. Natural rubber producers believe that they can successfully compete with synthetic rubber if their production costs can be reduced.[8] The chief means of lowering costs is to replace aging rubber trees with new high-yielding strains. Replanting is costly, but some companies began long ago. Less farsighted or less financially able producers were prompted by the government beginning in 1951. Replanting surcharges on rubber exports were collected and subsequently paid out. In 1954 an inquiry mission found that the replanting rate was unsatisfactory and recommended in effect that producers be compelled to replant.[9] The World Bank also made recommendations on the question. In 1955 the government introduced a new program. It has sought to encourage estates and small holdings to invest their profits in replanting by offering them substantial assistance out of general revenue. The results of this program added to previous efforts have produced significant progress. At the end of 1958 estates probably had half or more of their 2 million acres in high-yielding trees. Small holders lagged behind, but during 1958 the government initiated a major campaign to have small holders replant. By the end of that year about 20 per cent of the more than 1.5 million acres in small and medium holdings would probably be replanted.[10] Independ-

[8] A discussion of natural rubber production costs and the general position of natural rubber vis-à-vis synthetic is found in Lennox A. Mills, *Malaya: A Political and Economic Appraisal* (Minneapolis: University of Minnesota Press, 1958), pp. 155 ff.

[9] Federation of Malaya, *Report of the Mission of Enquiry into the Rubber Industry of Malaya, 1954* (Kuala Lumpur, 1954).

[10] *Natural Rubber News* (Washington, D.C., monthly), Aug. 4, 1958, p. 1.

ence saw some estates change hands.[11] Nevertheless the prospects for the industry seem favorable. Rubber production is rising and seems likely to continue to rise at an increasing rate. Within a few years Malayan output may surpass Indonesian production. Malaya will then be the world's leading producer of natural rubber.

That Malayan authorities have an optimistic view of the industry's future was suggested by their stand at the fourteenth meeting of the International Rubber Study Group in June 1958. Price stabilization internationally for certain products would appear to be a natural corollary of national economic planning for countries with lopsided export economies. The Federation departed from its own past position and that of its neighbors by opposing price stabilization.[12] The feasibility of stabilization might have been questioned generally in 1958, but stabilization for the Federation would probably have meant restricted output, reduced revenues, and curtailment of replanting. Without controls Malaya's annual production seems certain to increase while the cost of production for many of its producers will decrease. In such circumstances lower rubber prices will not necessarily hurt Malayan producers. The purpose of replanting is, in fact, to make natural rubber profitable at a lower price—one competitive with synthetic rubber. Lower prices will, however, almost certainly hurt other Asian producers who are still heavily dependent on low-yielding trees. Conceivably, if Malayan production increases fast enough, a period of declining prices may permit Malayan producers to gain a larger share of the natural rubber market at the expense of their high-cost neighbors. Eventually, the Federation will probably again favor international rubber price stabilization but not before its industry has become more competitive with synthetic rubber by greatly reducing the cost of production.

In respect to attracting capital for new enterprises, the Alliance government in 1958 sought to encourage new foreign capital investment by enacting legislation guaranteeing "pioneer industries" five-year tax holidays on certain conditions. An agency was planned which would grant medium- and long-term loans. Local enterprises were to be assisted through selective tariff revision. Institutional arrangements included the creation of an Industrial Development Division

[11] One authority estimates that about one-tenth of European-owned estates have been acquired by Asians (a statement by Sir Eric Macfadyen reproduced in *Natural Rubber News,* July 1958, p. S-3).

[12] The official government position was to welcome any "realistic proposal" for price stabilization (*Straits Budget,* July 2, 1958, pp. 3–4).

in the Ministry of Commerce and Industry. Toward its major development projects the government was successful in raising some capital.
Its first postindependence local loan for US$16.6 million was over-
subscribed. A proposed British loan had to be postponed, but the
United States granted a US$10 million loan for development of Port
Swettenham and the World Bank agreed to lend funds for the first
stage of a hydroelectric project in the Cameron Highlands. Against
these encouraging developments were continued unemployment and
sharply reduced revenues attending lower rubber and tin prices. The
Federation's deficit for 1958 threatened to be about US$45 million
on a record budget in excess of US$300 million.[13] The government
decided to revise and stretch out the five-year development plan.

In conclusion, the Federation's economy seems unlikely to alter
radically in the short term. Most development capital will probably
have to be found within the country. Actually economic problems,
though formidable, do not appear insoluble providing the government—the political framework—is stable and enlightened. Over the
long run the wealth, industry, skills, and sophistication of the Malayan
people may give them a distinctly superior economic position in Southeast Asia.

Economic Problems of Singapore

Estimates that Singapore's population will reach 2 million by 1965 [14]
are probably low. The problem here too is to expand the economy
in order to create jobs and revenue to pay for social services. In this
task Singapore is on the defensive against neighboring countries seeking to export raw materials and import manufactured goods directly.
The neomercantilism of the imperial powers has given way to the
economic nationalism of newly independent states—which now include the Federation. Singapore's merchants, bankers, and entrepreneurs have too much experience and capital at their command,
however, to be easily displaced. Moreover, strategically located in a
generally disturbed area, the island is hardly less in the twentieth
century than in Raffles' day a haven, a secure place to do business.
But will Singapore itself remain politically stable and secure? And
will the entrepôt trade, even if efficient services are maintained, earn

[13] Federation of Malaya, *Second Supplementary Estimates of Expenditure, 1958*
(Kuala Lumpur, 1958), p. 1.
[14] F. C. Benham, *Economic Survey: Singapore, 1957* (Singapore: Government
Printing Office, 1958), p. 11.

enough to meet the needs of the rising population? It is questionable that commerce has in the past provided for the people's needs to the extent presently regarded as a minimum standard of living.[15] If trade is not enough, should the island industrialize? Much has already been accomplished, but any further industrialization would probably require government assistance and a compromise of the sacrosanct free-trade policy. In the meantime, development of Singapore's social services is progressing.

The Federation's Plural Society

Most problems in the Federation are ultimately concerned in some way with its plural society. The two major approaches to a substantive solution to this problem have been (1) measures to raise the living standards of the rural Malays and generally to strengthen and widen Malay participation in the economic life of the country and (2) to establish a national school system with a Malayan-oriented curriculum.

The economic approach seeks to help Malays become prosperous farmers and small businessmen. The chief measures have been the extension of credit, establishment of vocational and commercial training facilities, provision of technical advisory services, development of marketing facilities, encouragement of co-operative societies, and improvement of rural health and education. Continuance of these reformist measures seems assured for some time in that the constitution discourages attempts to displace present businessmen by executive or legislative action. Hope is also placed on the development of the interior and the East Coast in the belief that the Malays will obtain a share of new large-scale economic development. This would reduce popular pressure on non-Malays to yield some of their economic strength. Such a hope may not, however, be easily realized since without careful regulation those already possessing capital and experience would benefit most from new development.

The other approach to resolving the plural society problem, that is, through a system of national schools, reached an important landmark in 1957 when a national education program was given legislative sanction. The principal feature is a six-year primary education taught in the Malay, Chinese, or Tamil languages with a common curriculum

[15] See Singapore, *Report of the Committee on Minimum Standards of Livelihood*, Sessional Paper no. Cmd. 5 of 1957 (Singapore: Government Printing Office, 1957).

and English as a compulsory subject.[16] Initially, the program does not aim at compulsory education but seeks to provide primary education for all those who desire it.[17] Time will be necessary to obtain money, facilities, and qualified teachers as well as to make adjustments in respect to existing facilities and teachers. To the credit of the Alliance government, the program was ahead of schedule at the end of 1957. Primary enrollment was then approaching one million students.[18] The program also plans several types of secondary education from two to six years' duration. The medium of instruction here may be Chinese or Tamil, but Malay and English are to be compulsory in all schools. Over-all the program has met some of the non-Malay objections to national schools, but controversy on educational policy continues as not all aspects of the program are fully accepted.

The best progress to date in meeting the plural-society problem lies in the moderation and responsibility shown by many leaders of the Malay, Chinese, and Indian communities. Ultimately, the crucial test will probably be whether life in their plural society has given Malayans the restraint, the ability for second thoughts, and an appreciation of the other fellow's feelings that is sometimes lacking in societies where the population is more homogeneous or where one ethnic group dominates. The knack of compromise so vital to a democratic system ought to be especially well understood in Malaya where everyone belongs to a minority.

Political Problems of the Federation

The fundamental political problem in the Federation is to maintain political stability as a means to social and economic progress. Inseparable from this is the need to make parliamentary government work because stability ultimately will probably depend not only on the satisfaction of material aspirations but also on the association of the people with governmental decisions. At the time independence was attained, the Alliance provided a relatively stable government. The question was whether it would continue to dominate the political scene and if not whether there were other political forces actually or potentially strong enough to form an effective government.

[16] A system of local control is to be established. But the Federal government will set policy and provide teachers and inspectors. See Federation of Malaya, *Report of the Education Committee, 1956* (Kuala Lumpur, 1956), pp. 5–19.

[17] *Ibid.*, pp. 20–21.

[18] Federation of Malaya, Department of Statistics, *Monthly Statistical Bulletin of the Federation of Malaya* (Kuala Lumpur, monthly), Feb.–March 1958, p. 163.

Alliance strength in the Federal elections in 1955 was derived almost entirely from overwhelming Malay support for UMNO. The Malays have had the preponderance of voting power and have used it effectively by remaining united. Their unity has stemmed from a desire to be rid of British rule and also from the anxiety of possibly being submerged by non-Malays. Since the Malays will probably retain their voting superiority for some years, they should be able to dominate elections if they remain united.[19] Independence has not removed the desire for unity for the sake of self-preservation and, in fact, probably has increased it. On the other hand conflicting interests do exist within the community, and these appear to be more pronounced with independence achieved. The question arises whether the desire for communal solidarity outweighs the ambitions of separate groups.

In the circumstances, interest attaches to the Malay opposition parties. Their principal line of attack is that UMNO is not concerning itself enough with Malay interests. The revisions of the Reid constitutional commission's recommendations were aimed at blunting their criticism.[20] Subsequently, however, they have found issues. Citizenship qualifications are criticized as too liberal to non-Malays. "Malay" rather than "Malayan" is demanded as the nationality of the people. The government is accused of not promoting the use of the Malay language and of not expanding Malay educational facilities. Allegedly too little is being done to raise Malay living standards. Because British persons have been retained in high positions, independence is said to be a sham. Part of the criticism takes a religious bent; the government is criticized for not giving more financial assistance to the Federation's Islamic college.

[19] No adequate citizenship figures were yet available in mid-1958. An estimate would be that out of a total population of 6.3 million persons about 3.0 million would be eligible to vote by age and citizenship. Not all persons eligible for citizenship under the new constitution would necessarily seek citizenship, however, and this would likely be true especially of the non-Malays. In the 1955 Federal elections persons qualified to vote by citizenship and age were thought to total about 1.6 million, the large majority of whom were Malays. During the first year of independence, when special dispensations were in effect, hundreds of thousands of new citizens, apparently mostly non-Malays, took up citizenship. The potential electorate in the 1959 Federal elections may be estimated at about 2.5 million persons, with the Malays in the majority. The commissioner of elections was reported in July 1958 to have said that the Malays would dominate the electoral rolls for at least the next ten years (*Malay Mail*, July 1, 1958, p. 5). As in 1955, voter registration for the 1959 elections is expected to be voluntary.

[20] See p. 260 for a statement of these revisions.

Malay opposition leaders deny that they seek to split the community, but their success will depend on capturing all or part of the UMNO organization or winning the Malays away from UMNO. Either way, they will have to exploit the growing political articulation of separate groups in the Malay community. These include rice farmers, ex-servicemen, teachers, the educated youth, and the small but growing number of wageworkers. Not least important are the men of standing in local Malay communities—an indigenous leadership upon which British rule did not much intrude. In 1955 many of the latter supported UMNO. Among the opposition parties the Pan-Malayan Islamic Party appears to have good prospects for attracting Malay support from UMNO. PMIP leaders with their nationalist, Islamic, and Indonesian sympathies probably represent an alternative to the Western-educated Malays who have thus far led the community in a moderate nationalism. UMNO members' criticism of the proposed Pakatan Perikatan suggested that perhaps a Malay reaction to moderation had set in. Nevertheless, in mid-1958, Tengku Abdul Rahman and his colleagues appeared to continue to enjoy the support of the large majority of the Malay people.

When the Alliance was formed, critics predicted its early demise since the Malayan Chinese Association and the UMNO appeared to have so little in common and so much in conflict. It has thus far confounded the critics largely because its Chinese partners have considered it vitally important to have connections with the politically powerful Malays. The Chinese have been motivated by a concern for the future security of their business and property interests and usually quite as much by a genuine Malayan loyalty.

Virtually from the beginning of the Alliance the officers of the Malayan Chinese Association have had the unenviable job of arriving at policies on such issues as citizenship, language, and education acceptable both to their Malay partners and to the Chinese community for whom the MCA claims to speak. This most difficult task when coupled with a conflict of personalities within the organization caused MCA internal affairs to be in a state of almost perpetual crisis. The persons who appeared to enjoy ascendancy in the party in 1957— the year of constitution making—were English-educated Chinese with long Malayan roots (the Straits-born or their equivalent) and with almost no psychological ties to China.[21] They were able to agree to

[21] Maurice Freedman has observed that the Straits-born in Singapore have become increasingly identified with the Chinese community there through a process

the revisions of the Reid recommendations as well as to the national education policy. Their accommodation to Malay views caused much resentment, however, among other Chinese whose principal strength lay in the urban artisan and commercial guilds, chambers of commerce, and clan and district associations. These people are Malayans, but they have strong psychological ties to China.[22]

The struggle within the MCA has been between Chinese who are economically and socially conservatives. Probably none of the contending groups has ever been able to command the support of the several hundred thousand strongly China-oriented working class and rural Chinese. These often harassed people have not had, nor are they likely to have, any political spokesmen if secret societies and the Malayan Communist Party are excepted. The intercession of a well-to-do and paternal-minded community "leader" to seek the benevolence of the all-powerful government official is no longer acceptable to them. No purpose is served by saying that they have shunned politics and contacts with government, except to emphasize how difficult they are to reach. Actually they will probably not give support to any truly Malayan political party until Malayan education and advances in their standard of living have worked to assimilate them. Until that occurs, these Chinese are certain to cause political as well as social problems.

In 1958 the MCA remained divided. Nevertheless the change in party leadership early in the year suggested an attempt to obtain more party unity as well as a renewed effort to rally Chinese community support behind the MCA. The outcome of these efforts would probably not be known until the Federal elections in 1959. The Chinese seem likely, however, to shed some of their traditional reluctance to engage in politics now that British rule has ended. If Chinese voters support the MCA (and the Indians, the MIC), the

which he calls "retro-assimilation" brought about by "the pressure of the forceful majority, and no doubt urged on by the fall from their earlier economic power" (Maurice Freedman, *Chinese Family and Marriage in Singapore* [Colonial Office, Colonial Research Studies no. 20; London: H.M. Stationery Office, 1957], p. 230). Something like this is happening in the Federation, but closer identification of the Straits-born Chinese with the China-born Chinese community need not necessarily mean alienization or Sinicization of the Straits-born. Singapore's being predominantly Chinese presents a different social milieu for politics than does the Federation with its Malay population.

[22] Some of them in the past have been associated with the Kuomintang Party in Malaya or in China, and hence they are sometimes—rather exaggeratedly—labeled as "Kuomintang."

MCA (and the MIC) may become more important to the Alliance, particularly if the Malay opposition parties succeed in reducing Malay support for UMNO. The new MCA officers appeared determined to keep the Alliance intact.

If the Alliance remains in control of government beyond the 1959 Federal elections—as in mid-1958 it seemed likely to do—continued political stability is probable. The Alliance will need a responsible and forward-looking opposition in the Federal parliament, however, to help it make good on its plans for social and economic progress. Such an opposition probably can be provided only by the Federation's democratic socialists.

Malayan politics is sometimes said to have two possible courses: the one communal, the other class. Some argue that the class appeal is the only one which can effectively vanquish communalism, and they hope that a democratic socialist party will emerge which would help resolve communal differences and otherwise offset the preponderance of conservative elements in Malayan society. Such a party would also draw support away from the Communists. Actually the most effective political organization reflecting class interests to emerge to date has been on the right, namely, the Alliance, rather than on the left.

It is difficult to speculate sanguinely about the early emergence of a strong democratic socialist opposition in the Federal parliament. The socialists do have a role to play. And their major political opportunities have waited on the attainment of independence. But they have been handicapped by "socialist opportunism," the strength of communal feeling, and the Emergency. Their greatest support appears to lie in urban centers where middle- and working-class Chinese and Indian voters are found. They do not, however, have such constituencies to themselves; and if the Alliance produces tangible benefits, some of their appeal will be lost. The socialists are also an object of Communist subversion, and to avoid official interference in their affairs they have to police their ranks carefully. This may be an impossible task. The government will have to exercise great responsibility in cleaning out subversives in the ranks of those who are likely to be its most vigorous critics. Such a situation is not conducive to the successful working of parliamentary government. To win an important number of seats in the Federal parliament the socialists require better and more comprehensive organization, more trustworthy candidates, better financing, and a greater following among those who have the votes—the Malays.

The chances for the development of a responsible and enlightened opposition in the Federal parliament in the near future seem poor. Neither separately nor in combination are the Malay parties or the socialist parties likely to form an effective opposition. At their best, they might be able to win enough seats between them to ensure that no majority emerges. Were that to happen early in the Federation's experience with self-rule, political stability would probably disappear and the whole parliamentary experiment be placed in jeopardy.

If the prospects for continued governmental stability are fair and those for the early emergence of an effective opposition are poor, what are the chances for the successful working of parliamentary government? Among the political factors the newness of the machinery, the lack of experience in operating it, and the weakness of the party system militate against the success of parliamentary government. In addition political responsibility is little developed, and a tradition exists from before and during British rule for concentrating power in the hands of a few. Another liability is the presence of the Malayan Communist Party bent on subverting the constitution. On the other hand most Malayan political leaders know best and tend to admire British parliamentary government. The conservative constitution is probably an asset; its federal structure may prove an advantage if some issues can be debated in the States before reaching the Federal level or if the state legislatures give both opportunity and experience to embryo statesmen. The attainment of independence peacefully and the retention of ties with the Commonwealth are positive factors. Commonwealth membership is a happy alternative to potentially explosive ties with either China or Indonesia. No doubt if Malaya can become a truly united nation, its people will ultimately work out their own philosophy and system of government, modifying the machinery which British and pioneer Malayan statesmen have bequeathed to them.

Political Problems of Singapore

The fundamental political problem in Singapore is not whether political stability will be maintained or parliamentary government be workable. Rather the problem is how to arrive at an effective combination of political forces which can assume authority and provide stability. A satisfactory basis of power has to emerge before there can be any further constitutional advance or discussion of merger with the Federation. Singapore has enough social groups with a broad identity of interests to provide a basis of political power. Heretofore these groups have disastrously wasted their strength by supporting several parties whose chief *raison d'être* has been the conflicting personalities and ambitions of their founders. Another election may help to unite those with similar interests.

Should stability be achieved, the problem will still exist of how to cope with tens of thousands of Chinese students and workers who are strongly motivated by Chinese nationalism *cum* communism and whose leaders are prone to violence. The solution, if there is any, seems to require continued judicious use of the police coupled with the firm implementation of such social, economic, and educational measures which over a period of many years may weaken the sources of discontent.

The Malayan Communist Party

At the end of July 1958 the Alliance government's amnesty offer to the Malayan Communist Party lapsed, and military and police action was stepped up to end the Emergency. The amnesty had induced many surrenders, and Communist strength was placed at about one thousand, lower than at any other time since the Emergency began.

Quite apart from the fact that Communist parties elsewhere in Southeast Asia are adopting policies of co-operation with constituted authorities, the Malayan Communist Party has good reasons for wanting peace, at least for the present. With an independent Malayan government functioning and fuller scope for legal political activities, more can be gained by attempting to achieve power through a peaceful and constructive pose than by rebellion. Communist leaders insist, however, on legal recognition of the party. Since both they and the Alliance government are adamant on this point, the Emergency will probably drag on, perhaps ultimately to an indefinite conclusion.

Recognition or not, the MCP is attempting to penetrate legal political parties, trade unions, student associations, and other organizations. It has two courses open to it. One is to espouse democratic socialism, decry communalism, and have its members join trade unions and socialist organizations. The other is to further communalism by playing on Chinese nationalism and cultural pride and exploiting the actual or alleged grievances of the Chinese community. In order, therefore, that leadership of much of the Chinese community should not go to the Communists, it is important that the present leaders of the Chinese community actually lead. Their ability to do so will depend in part on the degree of political effectiveness which they can attain in an electorate and government dominated by the Malays.

Federation Foreign Policy

With attainment of independence the Alliance government was confronted with numerous foreign policy problems. Its initial reaction was to approach foreign affairs cautiously. But although it wanted friendship with all nations, several factors would clearly influence the determination of foreign policy. These are membership in the Commonwealth,[23] the Emergency, the plural society, the country's dependence on trade, and its strategic position in Southeast Asia. The nature and direction of foreign policy would, of course, importantly affect the Federation's economic and political development.

The first major foreign policy step was a defense and mutual assistance treaty with Great Britain. It provides British assistance against external attack, in coping with the Emergency, and in the training and development of Federation armed forces. The Federation in return promises to co-operate and to take such action as it considers necessary in the event of attack on any Far Eastern British territory or dependency. Moreover, both countries agree to consult on measures to be taken in the event of a threat to peace in the Far East. Britain is permitted to maintain forces in the Federation including a Commonwealth Strategic Reserve. These forces may not be used to fulfill Southeast Asia Treaty Organization commitments since the Federation is not a member of SEATO. They may, however, be freely redeployed from the Federation to SEATO bases.[24] The Anglo-Malayan treaty has no time limit; and it effectively carries on, now on the basis of equality, the long-standing British relationship with the peninsula. It should provide sufficient security for the new nation to make the politically contentious question of Federation membership in SEATO unnecessary. Singapore, whose foreign relations remain a British responsibility, is a major SEATO base.

Diplomatic recognition has been extended to all nations except East Germany, North Korea, North Vietnam, Outer Mongolia, the People's Republic of China, and the Republic of China (Formosa). Embassies have been established in Britain, Australia, India, Japan, Indonesia, Thailand, and the United States. Diplomatic relations

[23] The Federation is the tenth member and the first monarchy.
[24] Great Britain, *Proposed Agreement on External Defence and Mutual Assistance,* Cmnd. 263 (London: H.M. Stationery Office, 1957).

have not been established with any Communist nation. The possibility of recognizing Peking is held out once the Emergency has come to an end.

In the 1957 United Nations General Assembly [25] the Federation voted against India's move to discuss the question of United Nations representation for the People's Republic of China. At the same time it voted with the majority for the admission of South Korea and South Vietnam. The Malayan representative spoke in support of the Indonesian claim to West Irian and voted in favor of Indonesia and the Netherlands holding further negotiations. The Federation has joined with the Afro-Asian group of nations in favoring freedom for Algeria, in supporting Arab nationalism and noninterference in Arab affairs, in calling for revision of South African racist policies, and in attempting to find a solution to the problem of Formosa. The Federation also criticized Soviet intervention in Hungary. Disarmament is favored if linked to effective international control and cessation of production of atomic materials. A summit conference was supported if preceded by foreign ministers' meetings.

Tengku Abdul Rahman, who is Minister for External Affairs as well as Prime Minister, has made good-will visits to Ceylon, Thailand, South Vietnam, and Japan since independence. He has observed that Southeast Asian nations would do well not to concern themselves unduly with world power politics when they have so many problems at home. He has stressed the idea of mutual help among Asian nations and has informally suggested a "united front" against Communist infiltration in Southeast Asia. The Prime Minister has also proposed that Asian nations draw up a charter guaranteeing fair treatment to investors of external capital.[26]

The Federation has some special problems in respect to Indonesia. Many Malays have intimate ties with Sumatra and Java, and on broad issues they are inclined to identify Malay with Indonesian interests. Not a few Malay leaders have in the past talked vaguely of eventual "unity" with Indonesia. Therefore some concern has been expressed over minor flaws which have developed in the two countries' relations. The Federation's apparent initial hesitation to give more concrete support to Indonesia in the United Nations on the West Irian

[25] The Federation was admitted as the eighty-second member of the United Nations on September 17, 1957.

[26] The proposal was made at the 1957 meeting of the United Nations Economic Commission for Asia and the Far East held in Kuala Lumpur (*Malay Mail*, March 5, 1958, pp. 1–2).

issue was criticized in the Djakarta press. Indonesians have accused the Federation and Singapore of harboring smugglers engaged in dealings with Indonesian rebels, although both governments have declared strict neutrality. Singapore has almost unavoidably been host to a number of Indonesian rebel leaders. The two countries may also divide on the question of rubber price stabilization. Nevertheless UMNO leaders profess warm friendship for Indonesia, and the Alliance government has sought a cultural pact with this neighbor.

The trend of foreign policy has understandably been toward closer friendship with the Commonwealth and non-Communist nations. This fact has not been lost on Alliance opponents. They, as well as some members of UMNO, have been critical of the Anglo-Malayan treaty. Rahman has stoutly defended the treaty and otherwise maintained that the Alliance has an independent foreign policy. In general the Prime Minister and Alliance leaders have been reluctant to discuss foreign affairs at length, taking the view that any extended debate on foreign policy would rather fruitlessly draw attention from more urgent domestic problems.

SUGGESTED READING

PERIODICALS

Journal of the Malayan Branch of the Royal Asiatic Society, Singapore. Successor to the *Journal of the Straits Branch of the Royal Asiatic Society,* Singapore, vols. I–LXXXVI, 1878–1922. Vol. I began in 1923; issues vary. The journal contains original contributions to the history and social sciences of the Malay Peninsula.

Malaya, London, monthly. Formerly *British Malaya.* Monthly journal of the Association of British Malaya, an organization of retired British civil servants and businessmen with Malayan interests, it has economic and political commentary, company reports, news of old Malayans, and miscellany.

Malayan Economic Review, Singapore, biennially. Vol. I began in 1956. The journal of the University of Malaya Economics Society, it contains useful articles by the faculty, graduate students, and others.

Malayan Historical Journal, Kuala Lumpur. Vol. I began in 1954; issues vary. It is the journal of the Malayan Historical Society.

Useful articles are also occasionally found in *Eastern World* (London), *Far Eastern Survey* (New York), *Far Eastern Economic Review* (Hong Kong), *Malayan Journal of Tropical Geography* (Singapore), and the *Geographical Review* (New York).

XIII: The Historical Background

Allen, G. C., and Audrey G. Donnithorne. *Western Enterprise in Indonesia and Malaya.* New York: Macmillan, 1957. A well-written and sympathetic account of European enterprise in Malaya and Indonesia over the past seventy-five years with emphasis on the years since 1945.

Bauer, P. T. *The Rubber Industry: A Study in Competition and Monopoly.* Cambridge: Harvard University Press, 1948. An examination of the Malayan and Indonesian rubber industries during and subsequent to the Great Depression, 1929–1933. It is sympathetic to the small holder and critical of rubber regulation schemes as established. It contains much useful information on Malayan rubber production, estate labor, and small holders.

Clodd, H. P. *Malaya's First British Pioneer.* London: Luzac & Co., 1948. A biography of Francis Light, who founded the Settlement on Prince of Wales Island or Penang in 1786.

Coupland, Sir Reginald. *Raffles of Singapore.* 3d ed. London: William Collins Sons & Co., Ltd., 1946. A competent study.

Emerson, Rupert. *Malaysia: A Study in Direct and Indirect Rule.* New York: Macmillan, 1937. Best analytical study of British rule in Malaya to 1937; provocative and critical.

Fermor, Sir Lewis Leigh. *Report upon the Mining Industry of Malaya.* Kuala Lumpur: Federated Malay States Government Press, 1940. A detailed study of the mining industry including information on its history, geological background, methods of production, legislative aspects, and relationships with agriculture. It was undertaken on government invitation.

Hill, A. H., trans. "The Hikayat Abdullah—An Annotated Translation," *Journal of the Malayan Branch of the Royal Asiatic Society,* XXVIII, pt. III (June 1955), 1–354. The autobiography of Munshi Abdullah, a Malay of Arab and South Indian ancestry, who was employed as a scribe and teacher by Raffles and others; valuable for description and commentary on early-nineteenth-century Malacca and Singapore.

International Rubber Regulation Committee. *The History of Rubber Regulation, 1934–1943.* Ed. by Sir Andrew Mcfadyean. London: Allen & Unwin Ltd., 1944. A favorable history of international rubber regulation; some useful tables on rubber acreages, exports, and prices.

Jones, S. W. *Public Administration in Malaya.* London: Royal Institute of International Affairs, Oxford University Press, 1953. A good account of the constitutional, legal, and administrative history of British Malaya told by a former Malayan civil service officer.

Knorr, K. E. *Tin under Control.* Stanford: Food Research Institute, Stanford University Press, 1945. A comprehensive study of tin and particularly of international tin control schemes of the 1930s. The author is critical and regards the schemes as generally unsuccessful.

Maxwell, Sir George, and Sir Eric Macfadyen. *Problems of Administration in British Malaya.* New York: Institute of Pacific Relations, International Secretariat, 1944. Reproduction of articles in the journal *British Malaya* in 1943. A historical survey with many interesting insights by Maxwell, former Federated Malay States Chief Secretary.

Mills, Lennox A. "British Malaya, 1824–1867," *Journal of the Malayan Branch of the Royal Asiatic Society,* III, pt. II (Nov. 1925), 1–338. The only comprehensive history of the States Settlements in the nineteenth century. Chapters include the Anglo-Dutch treaty of 1824, Anglo-Siamese relations in 1824–1867, East Indian Company policy, and Chinese relations with the Malay States.

——. *British Rule in Eastern Asia.* London: Oxford University Press, 1942. Pages 1–372 concern Malaya. Best pre-Second World War survey of British policy and administration in respect to commerce, primary industries, labor, and social services. The emphasis is on the 1930s, and there is much statistical data.

Onraet, René Henry de Solminihac. *Singapore: A Police Background.* London: Dorothy Crisp & Co., 1947. The memoirs of a police officer concerning crime, communism and subversion, Chinese secret societies, opium, and similar topics prior to the Japanese Occupation.

Parkinson, C. Northcote. *A Short History of Malaya.* Singapore: Donald Moore, 1954. A brief, interesting, and occasionally provocative essay on the British connection with the peninsula.

Purcell, Victor. *The Chinese in Malaya.* London: Oxford University Press, 1948. A comprehensive survey, largely historical, of the Chinese community in Malaya. The author observes that economic rivalries are the basis of communalism and suggests that Marxian class appeal is not sufficient to bridge communal differences.

Stahl, Kathleen. *The Metropolitan Organization of British Colonial Trade.* London: Faber & Faber, Ltd., 1951. Pages 63–121 concern Malaya. This is a useful account of British commercial organization in Malaya with brief histories of the four largest British firms and a good description of the agency house system.

Swettenham, Sir Frank A. *British Malaya: An Account of the Origin and Progress of British Influence in Malaya.* First published 1906, revised 1948. London: George Allen & Unwin, Ltd. The early history of the Malay States under British rule mixed with the personal recollections of the States' best-known British administrator.

Thompson, Virginia. *Postmortem on Malaya.* New York: Macmillan, 1943. A critical general survey of Malaya on the eve of the Japanese invasion.

——, and Richard Adloff. *The Leftwing in Southeast Asia.* New York: William Sloane Associates, 1950. Ch. v concerns Malaya; a description of parties and politics, 1945–1948.

Wilkinson, R. J. *A History of the Peninsular Malays with Chapters on Perak and Selangor.* 2d rev. ed. (Papers on Malay Subjects.) Singapore: Kelly & Walsh, 1920. An ably done history of the Malays to c. 1874. It includes chapters on the Malacca sultanate and the Dutch and Portuguese periods.

Winstedt, Sir Richard O. *Malaya and Its History.* 2d rev. ed. London: Hutchinson's University Library, 1951. A well-written historical survey, partly a condensation of the author's numerous earlier works on the history of the Malay States.

——. *The Malays: A Cultural History.* Rev. ed. London: Routledge & Kegan Paul, Ltd., 1950. A survey of Malay religious beliefs, of social, political, and economic systems, of literature, and of arts and crafts as they used to be and, in part, still are.

Wurtzburg, Charles Edward. *Raffles of the Eastern Isles.* London: Hodder & Stoughton, 1954. The most complete biography of Raffles.

XIV: The Contemporary Setting

Carnell, Francis G. "Communalism and Communism in Malaya," *Pacific Affairs,* XVI (June 1953), 99–117. A good discussion of the dangers of communalism and communism.

Dobby, E. H. G. *Southeast Asia.* 3d ed. London: University of London Press, Ltd., 1953. Chs. vi–viii inclusive deal specifically with Malaya. This is a scholarly and comprehensive geographical study.

Elliott, Alan J. A. *Chinese Spirit Medium Cults in Singapore.* (London School of Economics and Political Science, Department of Anthropology, Monographs on Social Anthropology, n.s., no. 14.) Norwich: Jarrold & Sons, Ltd., 1955. A study of what the author regards as the most typical manifestation of overseas Chinese religious orientation.

Firth, Raymond. *Malay Fishermen: Their Peasant Economy.* London: Kegan Paul, Trench, Trubner & Co., Ltd., 1946. A scholarly study of the economics of the Malay fishing community of Perupok, Bachok district, Kelantan, based on research done before the Japanese invasion. The author observes the need to increase output but notes that the success of technical improvements will be dependent on social changes.

Freedman, Maurice. *Chinese Family and Marriage in Singapore.* (Colonial Office, Colonial Research Studies no. 20.) London: Her Majesty's Stationery Office, 1957. An interesting and scholarly study, the first of its kind, of the Chinese family in Singapore. The purpose of the work was to see how traditional Chinese kinship characteristics have been altered by migration, Western influence, nationalism, and colonialism. The broadest conclusion is that Chinese society in Singapore is more than an ex-

tension of Chinese society in China and that kinship relationships have
weakened or significantly altered because of the above influences.

Gamba, Charles. *Labour Law in Malaya.* Singapore: Donald Moore, 1955.
A discursive survey of labor and trade union legislation.

Ginsburg, Norton, and Chester F. Roberts, Jr. *Malaya.* Seattle: University
of Washington Press, 1958. Produced originally as a Human Relations
Area Files project, this co-operative study is one of the most comprehensive works on Malaya ever published. Based chiefly on secondary
works, it contains a vast amount of factual information on contemporary
Malaya.

Hanrahan, Gene Z. *The Communist Struggle in Malaya.* New York: Institute of Pacific Relations, International Secretariat, 1954. An account of
the Malayan Communist Party in its international and Malayan historical
setting with a description of its policies, strategy, and tactics. Documents
in appendices include the party's constitution.

Josey, Alex. *Trade Unionism in Malaya.* Singapore: Donald Moore, 1954. A
critical discussion of trade unions and official trade union policy and a
statement of the case for democratic socialism in Malaya.

Mason, Frederic. *The Schools of Malaya.* Singapore: Donald Moore, 1954.
A brief essay on Malaya's schools with a short commentary on educational
policy.

Miller, Harry. *The Communist Menace in Malaya.* New York: Praeger,
1954. A popular account of the "Emergency" through 1953 by a British
journalist.

Parkinson, C. Northcote. *Templer in Malaya.* Singapore: Donald Moore, Ltd.,
1954. A favorable treatment of General Sir Gerald Templer's administration in Malaya.

Parmer, J. Norman. "Constitutional Change in Malaya's Plural Society,"
Far Eastern Survey, XXVI (Oct. 1957), 145–152. A commentary on the
1957 constitution and on some of the political aspects of its drafting.

Purcell, Victor. *Malaya: Communist or Free?* London: Institute of Pacific
Relations, Victor Gollancz, Ltd., 1954. A rather hurried and uneven survey
of post-Occupation political developments. It is provocative and critical
of British policies and particularly of General Sir Gerald Templer.

Pye, Lucian W. *Guerrilla Communism in Malaya: Its Social and Political
Meaning.* Princeton: Princeton University Press, 1956. A political and
sociological analysis of Malayan communism with references to the history
of the Malayan Communist Party based on interviews with surrendered
Communist terrorists.

Siew Nim Chee. *Labour and Tin Mining in Malaya.* (Southeast Asia Program, Cornell University, Data Paper no. 7.) Ithaca, N.Y., 1953. A comprehensive and useful study of labor in the tin-mining industry.

Silcock, T. H. *The Economy of Malaya: An Essay in Colonial Political Econ-*

omy. Singapore: Donald Moore, 1954. A good introduction to Malaya's several economies with a commentary on its strengths and weaknesses.

——. "Forces for Unity in Malaya," *International Affairs*, XXV (Oct. 1949), 453–465. The author considers various possible British policies and advocates a policy of attempting to foster national unity. He suggests how this might be done and enumerates favorable factors. It is one of the most thoughtful articles written on post-Occupation Malaya.

——, and Ungku Abdul Aziz. "Nationalism in Malaya," in William L. Holland, ed., *Asian Nationalism and the West.* Part III, pp. 267–345. New York: Macmillan, 1953. A good analytical study of post-Occupation political developments with numerous historical references.

XVI: Major Problems

International Bank for Reconstruction and Development. *The Economic Development of Malaya.* Baltimore: Johns Hopkins Press, 1955. A good survey of the Malayan economy with recommendations for utilization of resources for the period 1955–1959.

Lim Tay Boh. *Problems of the Malayan Economy.* Singapore: Donald Moore, 1956. Thirteen short talks on population, rural poverty, credit, banking, wages, and other topics.

Mills, Lennox A. *Malaya: A Political and Economic Appraisal.* Minneapolis: University of Minnesota Press, 1958. A series of essays dealing chiefly with the Emergency, communalism, politics, and the rubber industry.

Parmer, J. Norman. "Malaya's First Year of Independence," *Far Eastern Survey*, XXVII (Nov. 1958), 161–168. A brief statement of political and economic problems.

Smith, T. E. *Population Growth in Malaya: An Analysis of Recent Trends.* London: Royal Institute of International Affairs, Oxford University Press, 1952. An interesting and useful study based on data obtained in the 1947 census. It will become outdated when results of the 1957 census are reported.

PART FIVE : VIETNAM

By *Wells C. Klein*
and *Marjorie Weiner*

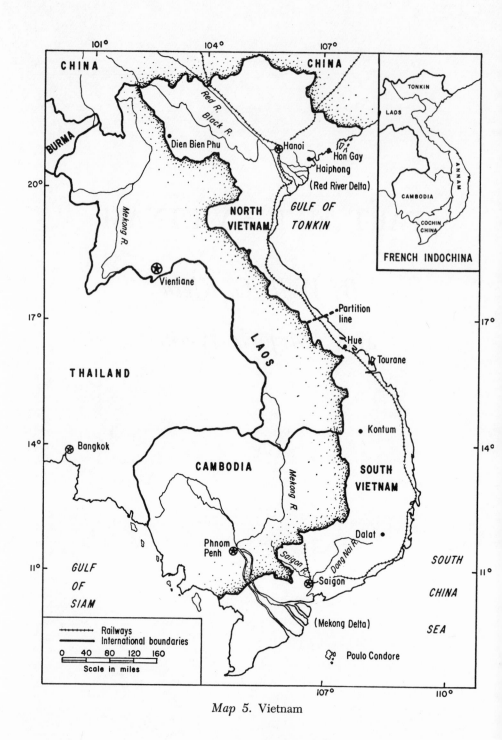

CHINA

CHINA

BURMA

Red R.

Black R.

• Dien Bien Phu

⊕ Hanoi

Hon Gay

Haiphong

(Red River Delta)

20°

Mekong R.

NORTH
VIETNAM

GULF OF
TONKIN

⊗ Vientiane

17°

Partition
line

Hue

LAOS

Tourane

17°

THAILAND

• Kontum

14°

⊗ Bangkok

CAMBODIA

Mekong R.

SOUTH
VIETNAM

14°

Dalat •

Phnom
Penh

Saigon R.

Dong Nai R.

SOUTH

11°

GULF

OF

SIAM

⊗ Saigon

(Mekong Delta)

CHINA

11°

SEA

Poulo Condore

Railways
International boundaries

0   40   80   120   160
Scale in miles

TONKIN

LAOS

ANNAM

CAMBODIA

COCHIN
CHINA

FRENCH INDOCHINA

107°

110°

Map 5. Vietnam

· XVII ·

The Historical Background

THROUGHOUT history the countries of Southeast Asia have been subject to influences stemming from two great civilizations, those of China to the north and of India to the west. Most of these countries have been influenced to a far greater degree by India than by China, either as a steppingstone for Islam or through Hinduism and Hinayana Buddhism. Since Vietnam was for a thousand years part of China, it stands unique in Southeast Asia, and traditional Vietnamese culture has long evidenced striking similarities to that of tenth-century China.

Vietnamese history is that of a people rather than of a geographic area, for present-day Vietnam is far more extensive than it was under Chinese rule or throughout most of its subsequent independent existence. During their early history the Vietnamese were confined to Tonkin, the area today adjacent to south China. Only after achieving independence in the tenth century did the Vietnamese begin expanding southward until in the eighteenth century they controlled what today is known as Vietnam.

Contemporary Vietnam is said to resemble two baskets, one at each end of a long pole. In the north is Tonkin, centered about the intensively cultivated and highly productive Red River delta. From Tonkin, Vietnam extends southward along the east coast of the Indochinese peninsula. This portion of the country, Annam, is characterized on the coast by small fertile deltas interspersed by rocky prominences jutting out to the sea. Inland are the mountains of the Annamite chain and the high plateau country inhabited by aboriginal mountain tribes and until recently devoid of Vietnamese settlers. Farther south the thin coastal strip widens and eventually merges into the flatlands of Cochin China and the rich alluvial soil of the Mekong delta, the farthest limit of Vietnamese expansion.

The first verified date of importance in Vietnamese history is the founding of the kingdom of Nam-Viet, in 208 B.C. Composed of parts of present-day southern China together with Tonkin and northern Annam, Nam-Viet was incorporated into China in 111 B.C.,[1] and for over a thousand years was to be the Chinese province of Chiao Chi.

The first millennium A.D. were the "formative years" of traditional Vietnamese culture. If, at the end of this period, Vietnam was not the "little China" it has often been called, it was at least so influenced by Chinese culture that at the level of the aristocracy it had lost all but vestigal evidences of its former self and at the village level had taken on numerous Chinese characteristics. Perhaps the most important aspects of Chinese culture adopted by the Vietnamese were the political and social organization represented by the mandarinate and the moral precepts embodied in Confucianism. Ostensibly all authority emanated from the emperor who held "the mandate of heaven." In practice, however, it was the hierarchical mandarin bureaucracy which ruled Vietnam. Membership in the mandarinate, with its promise of prestige and financial reward, represented the most desirable status in Vietnamese society.[2] To become a mandarin the candidate spent many years in preparation for the examinations which would determine his degree of knowledge and resultant official rank. To absorb the wisdom of the past was considered the primary requisite for the moral perfection thought to be the basis of good administration, and study was concentrated on rhetoric, ancient Vietnamese and Chinese history, poetry, ethics, and "the science of government."[3]

[1] D. G. E. Hall, *A History of Southeast Asia* (New York: St. Martin's Press, 1955), p. 170.

[2] In general Vietnamese social structure permitted little social mobility except that resulting from appointment to the mandarinate or that, at the village level, resulting from the acquisition of land which constituted the basis of wealth and prestige in the village.

[3] Joseph Buttinger, *The Smaller Dragon* (New York: Praeger, 1958), pp. 283–305 and footnotes. See also Pierre Huard and Maurice Durand, *Connaissance du Viet-Nam* (Paris: Imprimerie Nationale, 1954), pp. 83–86.

In its ideal form the mandarinate system meant that the country's ruling class was identical with its educated minority. The ideal of advancement according to ability was not, however, always realized. The mandarinate had both honest and corrupt elements; which group gained ascendancy depended on the personality of the emperor—the degree of authority he was able to exert—and whether or not the country was in a state of civil war or disorganized in its aftermath.

The Chinese Confucian ideal on which the mandarinate was based represents a single hierarchy of values that the mandarins had a vested interest in maintaining. What Hsiao-Tung Fei says of traditional China is also applicable to traditional Vietnam. The mandarins "monopolized authority based on wisdom of the past. . . . Their main task was the perpetuation of established norms in order to set up a guide for conventional behavior." [4] The values inherent in Confucianism and manifest in the mandarin system gave rise to few impulses for social change, and those which did develop were easily suppressed by the self-perpetuating aristocracy.

The commune was the basic administrative and social unit in Vietnam. In some instances it was a single village community and in others a small group of contiguous villages. In either case the commune was a clearly defined administrative and social unit governed by a council of notables co-opted from among the rich landowners who formed the village aristocracy and to whom might occasionally be added a few men of eminence such as the village teacher. [5] A Vietnamese proverb says, "The king's law bows before village custom," and as long as the commune paid its taxes, provided military recruits, and maintained internal order, it was subject to little interference from the mandarinate.

When in 939 Vietnam gained its independence from China, there was no decisive break with the past; Vietnamese rulers maintained essentially the same form of social and political organization to which the country was accustomed under Chinese domination. The only significant change was an almost immediate redirection of Vietnam's military efforts toward the new goal of territorial expansion to the south.

The major obstacles to Vietnamese expansion were two states with

[4] Hsiao-Tung Fei, *China's Gentry* (Chicago: University of Chicago Press, 1953), p. 74.
[5] Paul Mus, "The Role of the Village in Vietnamese Politics," *Pacific Affairs*, XXII (Sept. 1949), 266.

cultures bearing considerable Indian influence—Champa in Annam
and, to the west beyond Champa, the powerful Khmer empire, under
which the famed Angkor Wat was built. Vietnamese expansion was
neither constant nor peaceful, but whereas Cham and Khmer objectives appear to have been confined to military victories and plunder,
the Vietnamese followed up their successful forays with colonization,
thus slowly expanding their territory.

The issue with Champa was finally settled in 1471 when the
Vietnamese won a decisive battle destroying forever the unity and
military strength of that kingdom. Today, little that is discernible remains of Champa except for a few Indic ruins strangely out of place
in Sinicized Vietnam and a small fast-disappearing minority of Cham
interspersed among the numerous Vietnamese in southern Annam.[6]

Having vanquished the Cham, the Vietnamese were free to continue
their territorial expansion, this time at the expense of Cambodia—as
the remaining territory of the once extensive Khmer empire is now
known. The Vietnamese met with little formal resistance and easily
moved into the rich Mekong delta. By the middle of the eighteenth
century they reached their farthest limits of expansion, for the Mekong
delta presented vast reaches of relatively unpopulated land ideally
suited for rice cultivation.[7]

The last phase of Vietnamese territorial expansion coincided with
the beginning of permanent European contact. From the sixteenth to
the nineteenth century four European nations—England, France, the
Netherlands, and Portugal—jockeyed for commercial and religious
position in Vietnam. Although by the beginning of the eighteenth
century European trade with Vietnam had declined, Western missionary activity, particularly by the French, continued despite the
opposition of the mandarinate which viewed Christianity as a threat

[6] The relationship of Champa and Vietnam presents an interesting historical
problem. The two peoples and contrasting cultures lived side by side for the
better part of seven centuries, often in a state of military equality; yet the culture
of Indianized Champa seems to have made little impression on that of the Vietnamese. Why the Chinese-acquired institutions of Vietnam maintained such remarkable stability in the face of these cultural influences historians find difficult
to explain.

[7] The Vietnamese established their suzerainty over Cambodia in 1658, but in
order to retain its control Vietnam had to fight several wars with Siam, the last of
which ended in compromise. From 1847 until the French took over, Vietnam and
Siam "exercised a kind of common protectorate over Cambodia" (Buttinger, *op.
cit.*, pp. 305–306; see also Walter Vella, *Siam under Rama III* [Locust Valley, N.Y.:
J. J. Augustin, Inc., 1957], pp. 94–114).

to the ordered social structure that maintained the ruling class in its dominant position. Soon, however, the mandarinate came to consider that the missionaries were an entering wedge for European military penetration and territorial acquisition as well, and as a result anti-Catholicism had become so intense by 1750 that all but a handful of missionaries were forced to leave the country or go into hiding.[8]

French pre-eminence among European powers in Vietnam began in 1802 when a prince of the feudal Nguyen family, Phuc-Anh, unified strife-torn Vietnam and from his capital at Hue declared himself the Emperor Gia-Long. For his ultimate success Gia-Long was considerably indebted to a French missionary, Pigneau de Behaine, with the result that throughout Gia-Long's reign France was the only European country with permanent representatives in Vietnam.

Gia-Long's policy toward the West was one of noninvolvement. He hoped to avoid the dangers which emanated from Europe by being courteous to all and friendly with none. But upon Gia-Long's death his succesor, Minh Mang (1820–1841), took a much stronger position and revived persecution of the missionaries. To Minh Mang and the mandarinate, missionaries were an integral part of Western imperialism. The policy of the Nguyen emperors toward the West, first of noninvolvement and then of enforced isolation at the expense of the missionaries, was an attempt to maintain the old order. The rulers of Vietnam sought to close off the country and thereby avoid contagion from the West. In so doing they antagonized French commercial and military interests and, even more important, the missionaries and their growing support in France. There is little doubt that the Nguyen policy of isolation and persecution contributed to the dismemberment of Vietnam and afforded the pretext needed when France finally decided in 1857 that it too wanted a Far Eastern colony.

The dismemberment of Vietnam began in September 1857 when the French took the port Tourane with a force of fourteen vessels and twenty-five hundred men. Initially the attack was a success, but the French were unable to move inland and instead turned southward to Saigon, thereby delineating the course of colonial conquest. In February 1859 Saigon was captured, and two years later a treaty was signed between the French and Tu Duc, the fourth Nguyen emperor and the last to reign independent of the French. France acquired the three provinces adjacent to Saigon, and Vietnam agreed not to cede any part of its territory to another foreign power without first securing

[8] See Buttinger, *op. cit.*, chs. iv and v, especially the footnotes.

French permission. The final annexation of Cochin China was completed in 1867, when Admiral de la Grandière occupied the entire south on the pretext that anti-French rebels were using districts still under Vietnamese control as a base of operations and refuge.

The second period of conquest commenced in 1883 after a hiatus resulting from the Franco-Prussian War and civil discord in France. A force of six hundred men stormed and took Hanoi and began the long and bitter pacification of Tonkin. At the same time a French fleet bombarded Hue, the imperial capital, and shortly afterward forced the Vietnamese to sign a treaty making Tonkin and Annam French protectorates. Vietnamese independence came to an end on August 25, 1883.

The French Impact

French colonialism had two major effects on the course of Vietnamese history, first, the dislocation of traditional patterns and the emergence of a poorly integrated society combining both French and Vietnamese features and, secondly, the creation of a nationalist response which, as it worked for the overthrow of French rule, brought new political, economic, and social concepts into Vietnam.

Under French rule Vietnam was neither conceived of nor administered as a single entity, but was divided into three separate regions: Cochin China, a French colony, and the two protectorates of Tonkin and Annam. In 1887 these were combined with Cambodia, a French protectorate since 1864, to form the French Indo-Chinese Union [9] administered by a Governor-General responsible directly to the Ministry of Colonies in Paris. French rule was characterized by a succession of vacillating policies accompanied by a rapid turnover of high officials and frequent administrative reorganization. Much of the difficulty was attributable to Paris which lacked firsthand knowledge of Vietnamese affairs, yet was unable to refrain from constant meddling through administrative directives or by appointing new Governors-General who were often selected for political reasons and not on the basis of experience in colonial administration.[10]

As in other colonies the pattern of French colonial administration in French Indochina was hierarchical, "government from the top down

[9] The French protectorate of Laos was added to the Indo-Chinese Union in 1893, and a final addition was made in 1898 with the inclusion of the territory of Kwangchowwan which France leased from China.

[10] Between 1892 and 1930 Indochina had twenty-three Governors-General in addition to an even greater number of colonial ministers.

rather than from the bottom up."[11] Cochin China was divided into provinces, each administered by a French official responsible to the Governor of Cochin China, who in turn reported to the Governor-General. Tonkin and Annam also became, for all practical purposes, French colonies, though they preserved the theoretical status of protectorates. In contrast to Cochin China the French maintained a façade of Vietnamese control in Tonkin and Annam by allowing the mandarinate to carry out most administrative functions, though under the close supervision of French officials who retained effective political control.[12]

By the turn of the century French colonial policy was largely dictated by one dominant consideration—exploitation of the colony for the benefit of France. Vietnam was regarded as a source of raw materials and food for metropolitan France and its dependencies and as a market for the products of French industry. The economy was dominated by a combination of private French investors and the Bank de l'Indochine which served to channel metropolitan capital into the colony and to direct its investment at highly profitable rates. French interests permeated all sectors of the economy but exercised almost exclusive control over mineral extraction, the rubber industry, and manufacturing. The Chinese community controlled the rice trade and was active in retailing, while Vietnamese economic ambitions were generally confined to landowning, where profits were derived from high rents and usurious rates of interest on money advanced to tenant farmers.

The economic impact of French rule did not change the preponderantly agrarian nature of the Vietnamese economy, and by 1940 the peasantry still constituted 85–90 per cent of the total population. The structure of land ownership, however, was considerably altered. In Tonkin and Annam the pattern had been fairly well fixed in advance of the French so that, despite the economic changes that took place, in the 1930s more than 98 per cent of proprietors still cultivated their own land in Tonkin and 89 per cent in Annam.[13] But because of population pressures holdings were fragmented and provided little

[11] Rupert Emerson, *Representative Government in Southeast Asia* (New York: Institute of Pacific Relations, 1955), p. 171.

[12] Cambodia and Laos were protectorates whose status and administration were comparable to that of Tonkin and Annam.

[13] Virginia Thompson, *French Indo-China* (New York: Macmillan, 1937), p. 144. Many proprietors, however, were so heavily in debt that they owned land in name only, moneylenders holding real control.

more than subsistence for the majority of the population.[14] In contrast to Tonkin and Annam land was abundant in Cochin China, and there emerged a pattern of large estates owned by both French and Vietnamese landlords. It is estimated that prior to the Second World War approximately three-quarters of this land was held by absentee owners and cultivated by tenants. The economic organization of Cochin China was further modified by the growth of the rubber industry; this created a labor shortage that was met by transplanting thousands of Tonkinese workers to the south where they lived and worked under conditions approximating peonage.

French remolding of the traditional Vietnamese social order took place at the expense of the basic unit of Vietnamese society, the commune. This highly autonomous economic and political unit could not endure within the centralized administrative system which the French imposed upon Vietnam. French-trained Vietnamese officials were given authority formerly held by the village notables, who thereby lost prestige and with it much of their tradition-based authority over the villagers. With the breakdown in local authority, much village communal land was lost to speculation by notables and mandarins, and following upon the disruption of this traditional form of social insurance came an increase in pauperism and vagrancy. The growth of urban centers and a cash economy also contributed to the destruction of communal life, as did the French emphasis on individual as against collective responsibility. The village persisted as a physical unit under the French, but it lost much of the cohesiveness and recognized autonomy which in former days had made it the arbiter of behavior for the Vietnamese peasant and the single locus of rural life.

Colonialism did not substantially alter the basic social structure of traditional Vietnamese society, but it did much to change its composition and to widen the gap between the upper class and the rest of the population. With the growth of mining, manufacturing, and the rubber industry came the development of an indigenous proletariat, a new phenomenon in Vietnam; and in Cochin China the expansion of rice production gave rise to a new class of absentee landowners. French education also contributed to reshaping class structure by enlarging

[14] In Tonkin 62 per cent of the peasantry eventually owned less than nine-tenths of an acre and 30 per cent less than four-tenths of an acre. Conditions in Annam were only slightly better (Ellen J. Hammer, *The Struggle for Indochina* [Stanford: Stanford University Press, 1954], p. 65).

the upper class and by substituting French for Vietnamese values in the outlook of many Vietnamese.

French colonialism left its deepest imprint in Cochin China which, as a very recent Vietnamese territorial acquisition, had not developed the deep-seated traditions that were evident to the north. The fact that it was also the area of greatest French economic penetration and was administered as a colony also contributed to the greater impact of French institutions. To a lesser but significant degree Tonkin was also subject to French influence, especially in urban centers where industry was concentrated. Annam, however, primarily because of its poverty, was the least affected of the three regions of Vietnam. Here the royal court remained, its traditional ceremonial role maintained, but its political authority usurped by the French.

The Growth of Nationalism

The roots of Vietnamese national unity extend back to the period of Chinese rule, but as a force dedicated to self-determination and enjoying wide popular support nationalism did not emerge on the Vietnamese scene until after the First World War. It required the disintegration of traditional ways and the influence of Western ideas to develop the leadership and the popular base of support which gradually transformed "traditional feelings of cultural unity into an intense nationalism." [15]

Early Vietnamese resistance to colonial rule was concerned with removing the French and restoring the Nguyen dynasty; its leaders were mandarins of the old order who were uninterested in social or political reform. During the decade before the First World War, however, the objectives of Vietnamese resistance began to change as French economic penetration and cultural imperialism progressed. By 1911, when the Chinese revolution overthrew the Manchu dynasty, Vietnamese nationalism, though not yet supported by the masses, had developed a broader social base and had begun to incorporate concepts of social and political reform. The Chinese revolution provided a strong stimulus to its growth, China soon becoming the Mecca for young Vietnamese revolutionaries and the early Kuomintang the model for Vietnamese nationalist organization.

The First World War constituted an important turning point in the

[15] Milton Sachs, "Marxism in Viet Nam," in Frank N. Trager and Associates, *Marxism in Southeast Asia: A Study of Four Countries* (Stanford, Stanford University Press; forthcoming).

Vietnamese struggle for self-determination. In 1915 France, locked in what appeared to be a losing battle with Germany, turned to its colonies for support, and some 100,000 Vietnamese soldiers and workers were sent to Europe.[16] For the first time large numbers of Vietnamese were exposed to ideas of political and social equality. They came into contact with socialists and Frenchmen who espoused anticolonial sentiments; they saw what Western technology could create. When these men returned home after the war, they carried their newfound knowledge and ideas into a stratum of Vietnamese society which until then had felt the yoke of Western civilization but had seen none of its promise.

During the twenties, as nationalist sentiment continued to grow, important elements of the revolutionary movement began to coalesce into the two organizations which were to be predominant in the Vietnamese nationalist movement. In 1925 Ho Chi Minh organized the Association of Vietnamese Revolutionary Youth [17] which became the Indochinese Communist Party (ICP) in 1930. The ICP was a relatively late arrival in the nationalist camp, and its membership in Vietnam did not exceed a few hundred. Thus, though well organized, it could not yet compete with its major rival, the Viet Nam Quoc Dan Dang (VNQDD), or the Vietnamese Nationalist Party.[18]

The VNQDD was organized in 1927; its aim was the revolutionary overthrow of French rule and the establishment of a republican government along the lines of the Chinese Kuomintang, of which the VNQDD was the Vietnamese counterpart. In 1929, after an unsuccessful assassination attempt on the Governor-General which precipitated a series of arrests, the VNQDD leadership decided on an all-out revolutionary effort. On the night of February 9, 1930, the Vietnamese garrison at Yenbay on the Chinese border rose in revolt, killing its French officers. Yenbay was supposed to be one of a number of

[16] Thompson, *op. cit.*, p. 480.

[17] Ho Chi Minh was born Nguyen Van Thanh (or Nguyen Van Cung) in 1890. After attending high school in Hue, Ho left Vietnam in 1911 as cabin boy on a merchant vessel and in 1919 turned up in Paris under the name Nguyen Ai Quoc (Nguyen the Patriot). He became a member of the French Socialist Party, and when this split in 1920, he was with the group which formed the French Communist Party. In 1923 he went to Moscow as the French delegate to the Congress of the Peasant International (Krestintern); he remained there for more than a year to study communism before accompanying Mikhail Borodin, the senior Soviet adviser to the Kuomintang, to Canton, where he ostensibly worked as a translator in the Soviet Embassy (Robert Shaplen, "The Enigma of Ho Chi Minh," *Reporter,* XII [Jan. 27, 1955], 13–14).

[18] Hammer, *op. cit.*, pp. 79–80.

uprisings, but the government had been alerted, and the VNQDD revolution was virtually stillborn. The French response was immediate and effective, and the VNQDD was destroyed as an effective organization until it reappeared under Chinese auspices during the Second World War.

In 1930 the ICP, seeking to take advantage of popular unrest and capitalize on the failure of the VNQDD, staged a series of demonstrations which led to strikes in urban areas and finally, in two provinces, to open peasant-backed rebellion.[19] The Communists actually established "soviets" in two provinces before the French succeeded in reasserting their authority. French retribution for the Communist revolt was swift and brutal. Unlike the VNQDD, whose organization was loose, the ICP was hurt but not destroyed by French countermeasures. By 1933 the party was once again operative.[20]

During the late 1930s ICP adherence to the Popular Front cost the party a sizable portion of its support, especially in the south where Trotskyists [21] took advantage of the Stalinists' difficulties in justifying their sudden turnabout in policy and co-operation with the French. The Popular Front, its rationale deriving from European politics, failed to appeal to the Vietnamese. With the fall of the Popular Front in 1938 the ICP was driven underground, with many of its militants arrested, and on the eve of the Second World War the Trotskyists were the dominant Communist organization in Cochin China.

The Second World War and the Viet Minh

Japan wanted Indochina as a springboard for military adventures to the south and as a source of rice, rubber, and coal supplies for the home islands.[22] After a series of ultimatums, negotiations, and even a

[19] By 1931 ICP membership had grown to about 1,500, augmented by some 100,000 peasants affiliated in peasant organizations (*ibid.*, p. 92).

[20] *Ibid.*, pp. 83–86.

[21] The Trotskyists were first organized in 1932 but from almost the beginning they were ideologically divided. One group, centered in Saigon, joined with the Stalinist ICP in the publication of "La Lutte" (The Struggle) and entered a joint legal political slate in municipal elections. A second group, while supporting La Lutte's candidates, were more bitterly opposed to the Stalinists. The southern coalition eventually broke up when both Trotskyist groups refused to collaborate with the Stalinists in support of the Popular Front which required the cessation of revolutionary agitation for independence and cooperation with the French. Sachs, *op. cit.*

[22] See Andrew Roth, "French Indo-China in Transition," in Levy, Lacam, and Roth, *French Interests and Policies in the Far East* (New York: Institute of Pacific Relations, 1941).

brief but bloody clash between French and Japanese troops, the Vichy administration in Indochina capitulated, and in July 1941 Japan was in complete control of the French colony. The form of the Japanese occupation, however, was quite unique in Southeast Asia; for internal administration and security functions remained in French hands until almost the end of the war, thus enabling the Japanese to use the colony and its resources without assuming the burden of governing. The strange balance between French and Japanese authority was maintained until March 1945, when the Japanese became fearful of the growing pro-Ally sympathies of the French. Only then, after nearly four years of co-operation, did the Japanese fully displace the French.

During this period the Vietnamese nationalists were far from inactive. In May 1941 Ho Chi Minh convened the Central Committee of the ICP in southern China and launched the Vietnam Independence League (Viet Nam Doc Lap Dong Minh Hoi), better known as the Viet Minh. This was a nationalist coalition with Communists in key positions. Among its leading members were such people as Vo Nguyen Giap and Pham Van Dong,[23] later to become, respectively, commander in chief of the Viet Minh army and Vice-Premier of the Democratic Republic of Vietnam (DRV). Ho Chi Minh assumed the title of secretary-general.

The Viet Minh almost immediately ran into difficulties, for the Kuomintang, which had Communist problems of its own, was distrustful of the Viet Minh leadership. In early 1942 Ho Chi Minh was arrested, and later the same year the Chinese were instrumental in organizing another Vietnamese nationalist coalition, the Vietnam Revolutionary League (Cach Menh Dong Minh Hoi), known as the Dong Minh Hoi. The new movement was established as a counter to the Viet Minh—one that would be more amenable to the policies of Kuomintang China, from which it received a regular subsidy. The Viet Minh, though officially a member of the Dong Minh Hoi, understandably gave it no more than superficial support.

The Allies looked to the Dong Minh Hoi to provide an espionage

[23] Vietnamese names are written with the family name first and the given name last, and this is the form followed in these chapters. It is common practice for Vietnamese to address each other by the given name, since most family names are quite common and their use makes identification difficult. There are instances where this practice is not followed. For example, Ho Chi Minh is always referred to as President Ho, and Ngo Dinh Diem is called either President Ngo or President Diem.

network in Indochina, but it was soon obvious that without active Viet Minh participation little intelligence would be forthcoming, since the Viet Minh appeared to be the only movement with an organization in Vietnam capable of keeping track of Japanese military activities. It was for this reason that Ho Chi Minh was released from jail in 1943 and given direction of the Vietnamese nationalist movement operating from China.[24]

During the period between 1943 and the Japanese coup of 1945 the Viet Minh concentrated its energies on perfecting and expanding its organization, especially in northern Vietnam where the Viet Minh directed the Vietnamese independence movement despite Dong Minh Hoi pretensions to power. By 1945 the Viet Minh had some 10,000 men under arms [25] and held *de facto* control over large areas of rural Tonkin despite French efforts to prevent the spread of its authority.[26] In the south, however, several factors combined to limit Viet Minh activities. Cochin China was the stronghold of the Cao Dai and Hoa Hao religious sects,[27] both of which resisted Viet Minh penetration of the areas they controlled. Viet Minh effectiveness was also hampered by the existence of a strong Trotskyist movement and the simple fact of geographical distance from the northern base of operations.

When the Japanese executed their coup in March of 1945, the Vietnamese as well as the French were taken by surprise. Had Japan simply usurped French control, the balance of power between nationalist and occupying forces would not have been significantly altered. The Japanese did not want to assume the burden of direct government, however, and in order to avoid this responsibility and to provide continuity in the administration of Vietnam they made a decision which was to have historic consequences.

It had been the French assumption that the Emperor Bao Dai would "rule" as a puppet king under the colonial system, as had all the Vietnamese emperors since the death of Tu Duc. But the Japanese

[24] Hammer, *op. cit.*, p. 96.   [25] *Ibid.*, p. 97.

[26] Philip Devillers, *Histoire due Viet-Nam de 1940 à 1952* (Paris: Editions du Seuil, 1952), p. 113.

[27] The Cao Dai, a religious sect combining the beliefs of many faiths, was formed in Cochin China in 1926. In 1935 under a new "pope" it became a nationalist as well as religious organization and looked toward Japan for aid in liberating Vietnam. The Hoa Hao was formed among the peasantry of lower Cochin China in 1939. It too was a religious sect, but was based on "reformed" Buddhism. Like the Cao Dai, the Hoa Hao shortly took on nationalist overtones and sought the expulsion of the French from Vietnam (Bernard B. Fall, "The Political-Religious Sects of Vietnam," *Pacific Affairs*, vol. XXVIII [Sept. 1955]).

saw in the young emperor a solution to the problem which French recalcitrance had presented them. Immediately after ending French rule the Japanese turned to Bao Dai, who on March 11 proclaimed Vietnam an independent nation—independent, that is, from the French. The Japanese continued in their position of authority, and the powers of Bao Dai's government were limited by their presence.

.The Viet Minh did not support the new Bao Dai government and was in no way beholden to the Japanese. With the French removed the Viet Minh was thus able to step up its activities. In the far north, where Japanese troops did not replace the French, the Viet Minh quickly consolidated its control over what was called the "liberated zone" [28] and with the end of the war made its bid for power. Bao Dai's government was unable to rule, and the Japanese, though they would have preferred leaving Vietnam in more friendly hands, still considered the Viet Minh preferable to the French and did not prevent it from assuming political and military control. Only in Cochin China did the Viet Minh have difficulty; there the end of Japanese rule left a power vacuum which none of the rival nationalist factions were strong enough to fill alone. The Viet Minh eventually organized a "Committee of the South," but its authority within the committee was only marginal, and the Viet Minh had continual difficulty in maintaining its ascendancy. Because of better advance preparation by the Viet Minh there was less competition among contending nationalist groups in Tonkin and Annam. At the end of the war the Viet Minh moved into Hanoi, set up a provisional government, and called for the abdication of Bao Dai who, as it turned out, was at the same time considering asking Ho Chi Minh to form a new government. Outside of the Viet Minh no effective government existed in Vietnam, and when Bao Dai's advisers also urged that he accede to the Hanoi government, he did, abdicating on August 26. The ex-emperor was immediately made Supreme Political Adviser to Ho Chi Minh's government and provided an important symbol of legitimacy for the new regime. On September 2, 1945, the Democratic Republic of Vietnam came into official existence when, before a crowd assembled in Hanoi, Ho Chi Minh read the Declaration of Independence of Vietnam.

An Uneasy Interlude

Throughout the years of the Second World War, Viet Minh strategy had been directed toward gaining control of the nationalist movement and establishing an independent Vietnamese government under

[28] Devillers, *op. cit.*, p. 132.

its auspices. The Viet Minh hoped to demonstrate Vietnam's ability to govern itself and by so doing enlist great-power support for the cause of independence. It argued that France abdicated its right to rule on failing to defend Vietnam from the Japanese. The Viet Minh objective was almost achieved; only in Cochin China did France gain the opening wedge needed to re-enter Vietnam and then only with the aid of a decision reached halfway around the world. At the Potsdam Conference in 1945 it was agreed that Nationalist China would accept the Japanese surrender and evacuate Allied prisoners of war north of the 16th parallel in Indochina and that British forces would undertake the same operation in the south. Although the decision may have seemed a simple expedient, its implementation set the stage for the subsequent war.

In accord with the Potsdam decision British troops, under the command of General Douglas Gracey, arrived in Saigon on September 12, 1945. They found the city peaceful but tense. The Committee of the South was in control of the administration, and relations between the Vietnamese and the 20,000 French civilians were strained. General Gracey's orders from Vice-Admiral Mountbatten, Supreme Allied Commander in Southeast Asia, were explicit and were confirmed on September 18: "Sole mission: disarm the Japanese. Do not get involved in maintaining order." Yet two days later Gracey issued "proclamation No. 1 from the Allied Control Commission" in which he affirmed his "responsibility for maintaining order." [29] In a series of directives aimed at undermining the authority of the Committee of the South, the British banned the Vietnamese press, forbade all meetings and demonstrations, imposed a strict curfew, and proclaimed martial law. Then on September 22 the British quietly armed over a thousand of the French troops who had been interned by the Japanese, and the next day, augmented by a contingent of paratroopers newly arrived from France, the French executed a *coup d'état*, taking over the government of Cochin China from the Committee of the South. Terror reigned during the days which followed. The French vented their accumulated anger against the Vietnamese in a wave of violence which went unchecked by French and British forces, and the Vietnamese retaliated with even greater violence. A truce was finally arranged on October 1, but it lasted for only ten days; the Vietnamese would not accept a return to colonialism and the French would not tolerate Vietnamese independence.

During the short-lived reign of the Committee of the South the Viet

[29] *Ibid.*, p. 158.

Minh had been busy strengthening its hold over the nationalist movement principally at the expense of the Trotskyists, many of whom were
arrested, assassinated, or, by one means or another, removed from the
scene. Under the direction of the veteran Communist Tran Van Giau,
the consolidation process continued after the French coup, even while
the nationalist forces were being dispersed by General Leclerc's
"mopping up" operation. Nonetheless Viet Minh ambitions for total
control in areas outside of British and French positions were soon
frustrated by the Cao Dai and Hoa Hao. With much of their strength
deriving from religious allegiance and with well-defined and fairly
secure territorial bases, both the Cao Dai and the Hoa Hao were able
to prevent serious Viet Minh penetration of their organizations. In
fact the ultimate effect of Viet Minh pressure was not to bring the
Cao Dai and Hoa Hao into line, but to drive both groups into an un-
easy alliance with the French, thus completely destroying any possibility for a united front against colonial forces in the south.

In Tonkin and Annam, as contrasted with Cochin China, the Viet
Minh had been considerably more successful in rallying support during the early 1940s, and prior to the arrival of the Chinese no other
nationalist groups were in a position to contest seriously its authority.
To further consolidate its position the Viet Minh did not hesitate to
use force, especially against the leadership of rival organizations, weak
as they may have been. In order to extend its base of popular support, especially among the peasantry, the Viet Minh initiated a series
of programs designed to secure the loyalty of the Vietnamese population. A vigorous campaign against illiteracy was launched, prostitution, gambling, and the use of opium were banned, the head tax was
ended, universal suffrage and general elections were announced.[30] To
make the Viet Minh appear as broad a nationalist coalition as possible its leaders dissolved the ICP in November 1945, stating that
"those followers of Communism desirous of continuing their theoretical studies will affiliate to the Indochina Association of Marxist
Studies." [31] In all, the Viet Minh was remarkably successful in its
efforts to secure popular support. Those nationalists who had previously been opposed to Ho Chi Minh's coalition generally remained
so, but the uncommitted majority were impressed and supported the
Viet Minh.

In accordance with the Allied decision Chinese forces commanded

[30] Hammer, *op. cit.*, pp. 141–142.
[31] *Republique* (Hanoi), no. 7, Nov. 18, 1945; quoted in Sachs, *op. cit.*

by General Lu Han arrived in northern Vietnam in mid-September 1945. With them came the Dong Minh Hoi and the VNQDD. Operating under an umbrella of Chinese protection, these organizations soon established themselves in several strategic areas so that despite wartime pre-eminence and subsequent proselytizing the Viet Minh was suddenly faced with serious competition. Furthermore, the Chinese almost immediately pressured Ho Chi Minh to include his pro-Kuomintang adversaries in the DRV government. Chinese interference and the growing strength of the Dong Minh Hoi and the VNQDD compromised but did not destroy the Viet Minh's hold over the north. As promised, the government held elections for a National Assembly in early 1946; opposition members held a variety of important posts in the new government, but it continued to be controlled by the Viet Minh with Ho Chi Minh still President.

The Chinese finally agreed to leave Vietnam in the spring of 1946, but only after exacting numerous concessions from the French, among which were granting Chinese residents in Vietnam a legal status equivalent to that of French nationals and renunciation by the French of extraterritorial rights in the China. When the conditions for Chinese withdrawal were finally agree to, the question of French interests in the north came to sudden prominence. The French were determined to protect these even at the price of war; but there were some 25,000 French civilians in Hanoi who in a sense were Viet Minh hostages. Furthermore, if the French were to attack in March, as they planned if no satisfactory agreement was reached, there was reason to believe that the Chinese might intervene. The Viet Minh was also concerned with the implications of the Chinese withdrawal, for it was in no position to withstand a French attack either politically or militarily. In addition if the Viet Minh delayed agreement until after the Chinese left Vietnam, its bargaining position would be greatly weakened. Thus, with urgency felt by both sides, an agreement was signed on March 6, 1946, between the French Commissioner in Northern Indochina, Jean Sainteny, and two representatives of the DRV, Ho Chi Minh and Vu Hong Khanh, the latter representing the VNQDD. France recognized the Democratic Republic of Vietnam as a "free state, having its own government, parliament, army and treasury, belonging to the Indo-Chinese Federation and to the French Union." [32] The French

[32] Text in Allan B. Cole, ed., *Conflict in Indo-China and International Repercussions: A Documentary History, 1945–1955* (Ithaca, N.Y.: Cornell University Press, 1956), pp. 40–41.

agreed to a referendum to determine whether Tonkin, Annam, and Cochin China should be united and to a gradual withdrawal of French troops from Vietnam. The DRV in turn agreed not to oppose French forces sent to relieve the Chinese. A final provision stated that details of implementation would be negotiated at a later date.

In retrospect it seems clear that the March 6 accord was a diplomatic victory for France. Its recognition of the DRV constituted a realistic appraisal of the existing situation, whereas the peaceful entry of French troops into the north was something which otherwise could have been achieved only at tremendous cost in French lives and property. The referendum and troop-withdrawal provisions presented no immediate problem to the French since they could be placed in operation only when details were worked out; this meant more negotiations after the French were firmly entrenched in Hanoi.

The March 6 agreement had been worked out between Ho Chi Minh and Jean Sainteny, moderates in their respective camps. Immediately after its terms were made known, the agreement was attacked by the more extreme elements on both sides. The fact that both the Dong Minh Hoi and the VNQDD were represented in the DRV government, and therefore party to the agreement, helped spread the "guilt" on the Vietnamese side, but even then it required Ho's great prestige to secure Vietnamese compliance. In the French ranks Sainteny and his colleagues were subject to a bitter verbal barrage. High Commissioner Admiral Georges Thierry d'Argenlieu declared his "amazement" at the agreement, and in the months that followed he became the leader of the French elements which eventually scuttled one of the few accords ever reached between France and the Vietnamese nationalists.

The Vietnamese were anxious to iron out the "details" of the March 6 agreement in order to unify Vietnam and define its independent status. In the latter part of April 1946 a conference was held at Dalat, but it proved a failure when no agreement was reached on the two basic questions of what constituted a "free state" and under what conditions a referendum would be held. Optimists hoped that another meeting, this time in France, would lead to peaceful relations between the two peoples, but the conference held at Fontainebleau in early June failed to reach agreement on the very same issues which had remained unresolved after Dalat. It became increasingly clear that settling the status of Vietnam would require compromise on fundamental issues—but by whom? The French seemed determined that the "mistakes" made by Sainteny should not be realized, and Ho Chi Minh would go no further. In fact he could go no further and still retain control of the nationalist movement.

The Fontainebleau Conference was finally terminated without agreement when Admiral d'Argenlieu torpedoed it from afar by fostering and then officially recognizing a Cochin Chinese separatist movement in violation of the March 6 agreement. Ho Chi Minh finally signed a *modus vivendi* with the French government. It meant agreement on minor issues, but the question of Cochin China and the definition of a "free state" remained unresolved.

Following the failure at Fontainebleau the situation in the north rapidly deteriorated. On November 22 fighting broke out in the port city of Haiphong. Peace was restored but only momentarily, for the French commander was instructed to give the Vietnamese a "serious lesson." The next day the French bombarded the Vietnamese quarter of the city, killing more than 6,000 people according to the conservative French estimate.[33] On December 19, after the French ordered the disarming of Viet Minh militia, the Vietnamese attacked French positions in Hanoi. Fighting soon spread throughout Tonkin and Annam; the war had begun.

French refusal to recognize the national aspirations of the Vietnamese made the outbreak of war almost inevitable. Regardless of what the ultimate aims of the Viet Minh leadership may have been, in 1946 they represented the will of the vast majority of the Vietnamese people. Included in the Viet Minh ranks or lending active support to its policies were members of such diverse groups as Catholics, Communists, socialists, democrats, the bourgeoisie, peasants, mandarins, and members of the imperial court at Hue. Even such groups as the Dong Minh Hoi and the VNQDD, which had reason to fear the Viet Minh, still preferred it to a return to French rule. The number of pro-French Vietnamese in 1946 was indeed small.

Bao Dai versus Ho Chi Minh

The war lasted seven and a half years and on both sides was fought with extreme violence and cruelty. The French controlled the cities and larger towns, but with the exception of the Cao Dai and Hoa Hao areas the Viet Minh in general controlled the countryside. The war had its ups and downs, but neither side was strong enough to force a military decision. French armor was as useless against Viet Minh

[33] Hammer, *op. cit.,* p. 183.

guerrillas operating from forest and swampy ricelands as were Viet
Minh light arms against heavily fortified French positions. Not until
1953, when the Viet Minh used heavy artillery obtained from Communist China, did the military balance change sufficiently to alter the
pattern of control in Vietnam.

The war can be divided into two periods, each of which reflects
different policies in Vietnam and abroad. During the first it was generally a domestic affair between the French and the Viet Minh. With
the second period, commencing in mid-1949, policies began to shift.
On the international scene the Cold War had begun, and both the
United States and Communist China, which by then had defeated the
Nationalist forces on the mainland, now took a more active interest in
the Vietnamese war. Internally, the Communists ceased to hide behind the subterfuge of a nationalist coalition and took more overt
control of the Viet Minh movement, and on their part the French
attempted a political counter to Viet Minh popularity by setting up
what was supposed to be an alternative to the DRV—a Vietnamese
government under ex-Emperor Bao Dai.

In December 1947 the French persuaded Bao Dai, who was then
living in Hong Kong, to re-enter Vietnamese politics; and, following
months of negotiation, he signed the Ha Long Bay agreement with the
French in June 1948. This agreement recognized the independence of
Vietnam but so hedged it with military, political, economic, and administrative restrictions that many anti-Viet Minh nationalists were
unwilling to go along with Bao Dai. French negotiators had expected the Ha Long Bay agreement to cut the ground from under the
Viet Minh's claim to be the representative of Vietnamese nationalism,
but its many restrictions and the reluctance of the French government
to ratify the agreement if anything strengthened the Viet Minh position. Bao Dai whose intelligence has never been deprecated, soon
recognized this fact and refused to be identified with the government
of General Xuan which resulted from the Ha Long Bay agreement,
but instead went to France where he argued for greater independence.[34]

The French believed that without support from Bao Dai the Xuan
government was useless as a political alternative to the Viet Minh.
Using this lever, Bao Dai declined to return home until the French
agreed to the unification of Vietnam and greater Vietnamese freedom
in internal affairs. The French finally acceded to the ex-emperor's de-

[34] *Ibid.*, pp. 214–231.

mands, and in the Elysée Accords of June 1949 gave Vietnam at least some of the outward symbols of independence. Tonkin, Annam, and Cochin China were at last unified, and Vietnam joined the French Union as an associated state. Bao Dai returned home and declared himself chief of state. The new government, now with Bao Dai at its head, was permitted its own army and police force and took over many administrative functions from the French. Yet no real transfer of power took place. French troops still walked the streets of Saigon and Hanoi, and the French military controlled the Vietnamese army. French nationals retained their privileged status, and their economic interests were protected by the agreement. Finally, fiscal policy continued in French hands, with the Vietnamese piastre tied to the French franc.

The "Bao Dai solution" failed in its intent. In the French design Bao Dai was supposed to draw nationalist support away from the Viet Minh, but he was of no use to the French unless he accepted less than did Ho Chi Minh. But to compete with the already-established Viet Minh and to rally nationalist forces to his government, Bao Dai had to offer as much if not more than Ho, and this the French would not allow. Bao Dai was caught between the French and the Viet Minh and could not represent an effective alternative until the French quit Vietnam and left real power in Vietnamese hands. This they refused to do.

During the years 1945–1948 the Viet Minh made no radical changes in the economic and social organization of the areas under its control. Its leadership was known to be Communist, but its policies gave little indication of this. By 1949, however, the nature of the Viet Minh regime visibly began to change. When victorious Chinese Communist armies arrived at the Tonkinese border in December, the Viet Minh began looking to the north for substantial military support. Before long the DRV was drawn into alignment with the Soviet bloc, perhaps as part of the price of Chinese aid. In December 1951 all pretense was abandoned when the old ICP was revived as the Workers Party (Dang Lao Dong).

In the spring of 1950 Communist China began sending military aid to Vo Nguyen Giap's army. Shortly after, the United States, in line with President Truman's Communist-containment policy, declared its willingness to send economic and military aid to the French in Indochina. Where previously the basic issue had been nationalism versus colonialism, now the question of communism came to the fore, clouding the nationalist issue and providing the French with a new argument for their continued presence in Vietnam. The American government soon acquiesced to the revised French view of the Indochina war—that the basic issue was communism—even though some American government officials (and a number of Americans outside of government) questioned whether nationalist aspirations had been met with the formation of the Bao Dai government. By 1953 the United States was paying close to 80 per cent of the cost of the French military effort,[35] but it was only in 1954 when the French position was rapidly deteriorating that the United States exerted real pressure on the French government to recognize the validity of non-Communist nationalist demands.[36]

The military balance between the French and the Viet Minh began to change when Vo Nguyen Giap's army started receiving increased quantities of arms from Communist China, including heavy artillery. The final showdown began in late 1953. The French held a heavily fortified position at Dien Bien Phu in northwestern Tonkin near the Laotian border; here the Viet Minh chose to strike. The battle raged furiously as the world watched. By all accounts the French defense was heroic, but Viet Minh strategy and arms were superior. Dien Bien Phu fell on May 7, 1954, and the Viet Minh prepared to advance on the Red River delta toward Hanoi and Haiphong. There was apparently little that the French could do to stop them.

As the French position in Tonkin worsened, the war became more distinctly an international issue. In March 1954 the French government requested direct United States military intervention, and for a time the American government gave the request active consideration. One reason the United States eventually declined to enter the conflict was that the British refused to support such a venture pending a last attempt to arrive at a peaceful solution through a meeting of the Great Powers at Geneva. By the time the conference was convened, the situation in Vietnam clearly constituted an immediate threat to world peace.

The Viet Minh delegation at Geneva was headed by Pham Van Dong, but the Communist side was generally represented by Chou En-lai of Communist China. The Western nations were unable to

[35] *Ibid.*, p. 313. American aid began in 1950 and averaged $500 million annually.

[36] One possible reason for American reluctance to pressure Paris on Indochina was the fact that the United States was trying to persuade France (the attempt was unsuccessful) to join with its traditional enemy, Germany, in the European Defense Community and thus found the exerting of effective pressure on France in the Far East difficult.

concur on a general policy, and for a while it looked as though the conference might fail to reach any agreement. But when Pierre Mendès-France, upon becoming Premier of France declared that if a satisfactory settlement was not reached by July 20 he would resign, prospects for a solution brightened. France was tired of "la sale guerre" with its drain on the French economy and its cost in French lives. Dien Bien Phu had been a rude awakening, and its military consequences were alarming. On the other hand the Viet Minh was in a difficult position. It had demonstrated military superiority but could no longer proceed independently of China and Russia—the price of Communist-bloc support—and when its mentors decided that the time was not propitious for further military action, the Viet Minh was forced to accede. One reason for Russian and Chinese agreement on Indochina seems to have been the fear of American intervention which might involve China and spark the Third World War.

Agreement was finally reached on the night of July 20–21, 1954. Those portions of the Geneva accords which dealt with Vietnam (Cambodia and Laos were also included) were agreed on between the French and the DRV. Bao Dai's State of Vietnam did not sign the accords and declared itself not bound by them. The provisions of the agreement affecting Vietnam were: (1) partition of Vietnam at the 17th parallel along the Ben Hai River, with the north going to the DRV and the south to France; (2) staged withdrawal of all troops to their respective zones, to be completed within 300 days; (3) military equipment to enter Vietnam on a replacement basis only and troops on a rotation basis only; (4) free movement of civilians between the two zones until the end of the 300-day troop evacuation period; (5) national elections to unify Vietnam to take place within two years; (6) establishment of an International Armistice Control Commission composed of representatives of India, Canada, and Poland with an Indian as chairman.[37]

The results obtained at Geneva are generally considered a diplomatic victory for the West, though, as it turned out, not for France. The Viet Minh, poised for further battle, found the ground cut out from under it, whereas the French were saved from almost certain military defeat in the north. The Viet Minh counted on the elections stipulated in the Geneva agreement to unify Vietnam under its

[37] *Further Documents Relating to the Discussion of Indochina at the Geneva Conference,* Miscellaneous no. 20, 1954 (London: H.M. Stationery Office, June 1945).

control, for without doubt it still enjoyed the sympathy, if not the active support, of a considerable majority of the population. July 1956 passed by without national elections, however, and instead of having to contend with the unpopular French south of the 17th parallel, the Viet Minh was faced with an independent nationalist government unhampered by the presence of French troops and protected by the promise of American military intervention in the case of renewed hostilities.

South Vietnam after the Geneva Conference

In the dark days of early 1954 the French were under heavy American pressure to reconstitute the Vietnamese government along more independent lines with a Premier who unequivocally represented Vietnamese interests. A new set of agreements was reached by April 1954. Although too late to affect the course of the war and lacking the "completeness" which the French had promised, they did provide the basis for independence. The question of who was to be Premier was settled on June 16 when Bao Dai appointed Ngo Dinh Diem to replace the incumbent Prince Buu Loc. Diem was an anti-Communist nationalist whose reputation was uncompromised by co-operation with the French.

When Diem came to office, he did not come to power. In South Vietnam, French wartime policies left the Cao Dai and Hoa Hao in military and political control of large areas which they administered almost as independent states. In Saigon, Bao Dai had sold control of the police to the Binh Xuyen, an army of onetime river pirates who also controlled gambling and prostitution in the capital city. To further complicate matters, Ngo Dinh Diem found that he lacked control of his own army, whose commander in chief, Major General Nguyen Van Hinh, talked openly of taking over the government. Were these problems not enough, the South was shortly inundated with a flood of homeless refugees from North Vietnam whose total number before the May 18 cutoff date is officially reported to have reached 888,127 persons.[38] (Some 75,000 are thought to have arrived after May 18.) To deal with these problems Diem had no organized backing, lacked administrative and political experience, and was unpopular with the French, who still held real power in the South. In the summer of 1954 the question discussed in Saigon was not whether Diem would

[38] *Fourth Interim Report of the International Commission for Supervision and Control in Vietnam* (London: H.M. Stationery Office, Dec. 1955), p. 21.

fall, but when. Yet Diem lasted and is today President of the Republic of Vietnam.

The threat posed by General Hinh was disposed of when the United States chargé d'affaires in Saigon intimated to Bao Dai and the French that any government which did not control its own army was unlikely to be the recipient of American aid. Hinh's replacement with a commander of Diem's choice did not yet secure him control of the army, but it reduced the chances of open rebellion from at least one direction. The next task which faced Diem was that of the "sects"—the Cao Dai, Hoa Hao, and Binh Xuyen. The basic issue between Diem and these sects was state versus private government. During the war years the French had proved a steady source of income and armament for the sects, who in exchange gave military support to the French. Now that the war was over, this comfortable source of income was shortly due to end. It was Diem's intention to incorporate the sect military forces into the national army, thereby depriving the opposition of its military strength. The sects were willing to see this incorporation of most of their troops, whom they could no longer afford to pay, but in exchange they wanted a political settlement which guaranteed their virtual political and territorial autonomy. On the other hand Diem wished to discuss political questions only after integration; and the situation was stalemated. By skillful political maneuvering he managed to stave off any open breach and in fact induced several sect leaders to "rally" to the government with their troops. The bulk of the sect forces, however, remained adamant in their opposition to Diem.[39]

In the early spring of 1955 Diem took the initiative and closed the "Grande Monde," the largest gambling establishment in the Far East, owned by the Binh Xuyen and providing the bulk of their income. In March the major sect leaders came together in a "United Front of All Nationalist Forces" and presented Diem with an ultimatum—that he either comply with their demands or resign. At the same time they requested Bao Dai to dismiss Diem. Ngo Dinh Diem refused to comply, and Bao Dai equivocated. The situation in Saigon was extremely tense. Armed Binh Xuyen patrols roamed the streets, and the President was virtually a prisoner in his palace. Which way the national army would turn in the event of open hostilities represented the unknown factor in the power equation. Fighting first broke out on the night of March 29–30 between troops loyal to Diem and the Binh

[39] Roy Jumper, Winston-Salem, N.C., unpublished manuscript.

Xuyen, but by early morning the French Commissioner, General Paul Ely, arranged a truce, which was precariously maintained for three weeks.

Diem knew that his political future hinged on the outcome of his struggle with the sects. During the truce period his political stock was at its lowest ebb. General Collins [40] returned to Washington on April 20 and is known to have advocated replacing Diem with someone more acceptable to the sects and France. Other Americans, however, including State Department personnel and some of the American military advisory group in Vietnam, argued for Diem's retention, and American policy continued as before. On April 26 Diem decided to force the issue and removed the Binh Xuyen chief of police, substituting a regular army colonel of his own choice. Two days later the issue was joined when Diem refused to heed Bao Dai's summons to France for "consultation." Fighting commenced on April 28, and by April 30 a sizable portion of the area between Saigon and its sister city, Cholon, was destroyed. The French attempted to impose a cease-fire but to no avail.

During the short battle two important events occurred almost simultaneously. First, the United Front coalition of sects fell apart, and the Binh Xuyen were caught fighting alone. Secondly, at the crucial moment the army proved loyal to Diem, thus enabling him to drive the Binh Xuyen from the city and in a few weeks decimate its ranks. April 1955 was the turning point in Diem's bid for real power. Before this time he was Premier, but in name only. After the end of April, with the army now committed, he was able to begin consolidating political power.

In an attempt to regain the political initiative and strengthen their position, the leaders of the Hoa Hao and Cao Dai, operating through a political coalition known as the People's National Revolutionary Committee, convened a congress which called for the immediate removal of Bao Dai. Diem allowed the committee to generate popular sentiment for this, but several months later when he called for a national referendum to choose between himself and Bao Dai, it was Diem and not the Revolutionary Committee which benefited. This marked the end of the Revolutionary Committee as an important political force, and several months later it was forced to dissolve itself. After this most of the Hoa Hao leaders resorted to military action against Diem

[40] General J. Lawton Collins was President Eisenhower's personal representative to Vietnam during this crisis period.

but were eventually defeated by the government's "pacification campaigns." The Cao Dai leaders were more circumspect, and though they yielded to Diem and formally abjured politics, the Cao Dai still exists as an important religious organization.

The referendum was held on October 23, and the French, now resigned to Vietnamese independence, accepted the inevitable result. Diem won with a reported 98 per cent of the vote, and three days later the Republic of Vietnam was declared a sovereign state with Ngo Dinh Diem its first President.

· XVIII ·

South Vietnam:

The Contemporary Setting

DURING the few years which have elapsed since the accords signed at Geneva divided Vietnam into two separate states, far-reaching changes have occurred in the South. The French have withdrawn, and with their departure the once unifying issue of colonialism has receded, revealing a variety of divisions in Vietnamese society which were to a large extent previously obscured by anti-French nationalism. Together with the all-pervasive issue of communism, the nature of these divisions and their physical and economic setting must be appreciated if the political process in South Vietnam is to be understood.

Land and People

Although Vietnam extends a thousand miles from north to south, because of its elongated shape it has a total area of only 126,600 square miles, of which about 65,700 square miles, or slightly more than half, constitute South Vietnam. The South is therefore larger in area, but its population of approximately 12,000,000 persons is less than that of the North, with about 14,600,000 persons. This gives the South an average population density of 183 persons per square mile, compared with 240 persons per square mile in the North. The larger ratio of population to land in North Vietnam is due to the high population density of the Red River delta, one of the greatest densities in the world, which more

342

than offsets the fact that the North has no city comparable to Saigon in size.

In ethnic composition South Vietnam is relatively homogeneous in comparison with other countries of Southeast Asia. The two largest minority groups are the Chinese, numbering approximately 800,000 persons, most of whom live in Saigon's twin city, Cholon, and the hill tribes of the high plateau and mountain regions northeast of Saigon which are thought to number in the neighborhood of 250,000. In addition there are a few as yet unassimilated Cham living near the southeastern seaboard and a sizable number of Khmer dispersed along the Cambodian border. But of the total population of South Vietnam close to 90 per cent are culturally and linguistically Vietnamese.

The Economy

The basic characteristics of South Vietnam's economy evolved during the colonial period but were modified by the subsequent effects of war and partition. Although Saigon and the major towns were spared heavy damage during the war, the nation's communications network was badly disrupted. Roads fell into disrepair, many bridges were destroyed, and approximately one-third of the total railway track was rendered unusable. In addition silting blocked passage in much of the economically vital 2,900-mile network of inland waterways which run through the Mekong delta, and half the boats and junks which once plied these waterways were either destroyed or sunk.[1] Considerable progress has recently been made in rehabilitating the nation's transportation system, but there still remains much to be done before the lack of basic facilities ceases to handicap the economy.

The war also had a pronounced effect on rice production and the distribution of population in South Vietnam. Because of unsettled conditions in the countryside, during the war hundreds of thousands of peasants fled the land seeking safety in Saigon and the larger towns. It is estimated that 20 per cent of the cultivated land in the Mekong delta was abandoned prior to 1955 [2] thereby producing both a sharp reduc-

[1] Economic Commission for Asia and the Far East (ECAFE), *Economic Survey of Asia and the Far East, 1957* (Bangkok: United Nations, 1958), pp. 168–169. The South's coastal fleet was also badly damaged during the war. In 1956 it was composed of seventeen ships with only one-tenth the prewar tonnage (ECAFE, *Economic Survey of Asia and the Far East, 1956* [Bangkok: United Nations, 1957], p. 171). This has created difficulties in transporting goods, especially rice, to the coastal regions in the northern part of South Vietnam.

[2] David Wurfel, "Agrarian Reform in the Republic of Vietnam," *Far Eastern Survey*, XXVI (June 1957), 86.

tion in rice production and a serious unemployment problem.[3] The government has attempted to solve both the unemployment and production problems by enticing the new urban population back to the land through a series of agrarian reform measures. But at least partially because of the opposition of the large landowners, agrarian reform has been modest in scope, and although it has probably been responsible for some of the recent increases in rice production, it has failed to solve the problem of unemployment by inducing a mass return to the land.

Prior to 1954 the northern and southern regions of Vietnam were complementary in resources and production, with products of northern industry exchanged for southern rice.[4] Partition brought an end to this trade and created new problems for both regions. Whereas most of Vietnam's limited industrial capacity and almost all of its coal went to the North, South Vietnam inherited both the rich rice-producing lands of the Mekong delta and the important rubber and dry crop areas to the north and east of Saigon.

The French colonial policy of restricting industrial development left South Vietnam with an economy based almost exclusively on the production of food and commercial crops. Although secondary crops including maize, tea, copra, sugar cane, cotton, coffee, and tobacco are grown, rice and rubber are the backbone of the South's economy and its two principal export commodities. The present level of rubber production exceeds prewar output by about 61 per cent.[5] But because of reduced production resulting from land abandonment and the migration of large numbers of peasants to urban centers, rice production is only now reaching the 1939 level.[6]

[3] Saigon has grown from a prewar population of 500,000 to approximately 1,900,000 persons today without a commensurate increase in employment opportunities or housing (ECAFE, op. cit., 1956, p. 169). The unemployment problem has been further complicated by the large number of North Vietnamese refugees who remained in Saigon, the 75,000 persons left jobless by the withdrawal of the French expeditionary corps, and some 57,000 men demobilized from the Vietnamese army (ibid.).

[4] Under colonial rule Vietnam's limited industrial capacity was concentrated in the north, which supplied one-half of Vietnam's total cloth requirements and all of its coal. In turn approximately one-half of the south's rice surplus went to the agriculturally deficient north (ECAFE, op. cit., 1957, pp. 168–169).

[5] Vietnamese rubber production in 1938 was 43,200 tons (ECAFE, op. cit., 1956, p. 197). Despite wartime damage to some of the trees, annual rubber production was 70,800 tons in 1956 (ECAFE, op. cit., 1957, p. 221).

[6] ECAFE, op. cit., 1957, p. 170. Taken alone, gross production figures are often misleading. Since 1939 the population of what is now South Vietnam has risen on

Because of the effects of partition South Vietnam is particularly deficient in industrial capacity. Since 1954 a few new factories have been established, notably for textiles and for paper, glass, aluminum, and plastic products. These additions have, however, been offset by reduced production in other industries, with the result that the over-all trend of industrial production appears to be slightly downward.[7]

Economic organization in South Vietnam is not greatly different from what it was during the colonial period. French capital has retained a dominant position in manufacturing and the rubber industry, whereas the Vietnamese, though commencing to expand their economic horizons, are still primarily engaged in agriculture and commerce. Until recently the Chinese dominated the rice trade and other strategic areas of the economy, but in 1956 the government ordered that they either become Vietnamese citizens or withdraw from eleven important areas of economic activity.[8] But by employing numerous subterfuges, including the taking of a Vietnamese wife, the Chinese remain in control of large sectors of the economy in spite of the considerable official pressure to which they are subject.

The basic structure of landownership in the South is also much the same as it was before partition and the agrarian reform program. The major changes which have taken place are in areas where North Vietnamese refugees are being resettled on abandoned land. In addition to a number of less ambitious undertakings, the government, with financial aid from the United States, is developing four large resettlement projects. The showpiece is Cai San in the south where 40,000 persons are being resettled on 75,000 acres of riceland. Two other less advanced projects are also on ricelands in the Mekong delta, and another is located in the highland region where large, relatively unpopulated areas in a militarily strategic region present a security problem to the government.

Social Organization

Vietnam has retained its essentially two-class structure, though it is possible to discern the rudimentary beginnings of something like a middle class in the lower army echelons, in the government bureaucracy, and in the numerous small businesses which have sprung

---

the order of 40 per cent. Thus, even though present rice production equals that of 1939, per capita production, and consequently surplus available for export, is still markedly below prewar output.

[7] *Ibid.*, p. 171.   [8] See below, page 381.

up in the wake of independence and with the withdrawal of French and, more recently, Chinese capital. The socioeconomic upper class of South Vietnam is composed of the top echelon of the government bureaucracy, higher-ranking army officers, landowners and wealthy businessmen, professionals such as doctors and lawyers, and many intellectuals. Social mobility is not a characteristic of southern Vietnamese society, and as a prerequisite, membership in the upper class usually requires a combination of at least two of three qualifications: wealth, "family," and education. An exception to this rule may be the group of young army officers for whom ability and personal loyalty provide a basis for advancement. The vast majority of the Vietnamese are still occupied with cultivation of the land or with village artisanry. They and wage laborers, whose numbers (and unemployment) have grown with the development of urban concentrations and wartime conditions, constitute what might be termed the lower class in Vietnamese society.

In addition to what may be conceived of as the horizontal class structure of Vietnamese society, there are groupings based on common aspirations, political alignments, occupation, and other identities of interest. In varying degrees they exert influence on the course of government. Politically the most important element is the army.

In a nation in which government control rests to such a large extent on personal or family loyalties and on "subsidizing" group allegiances, the support of the national army is a requisite for continuance in power. This is one reason why the showdown with the Binh Xuyen in the spring of 1955 was so important. Diem not only routed the Binh Xuyen, but at the same time won over the army. From that time Diem has given the military a great deal of attention in order to ensure its continued loyalty. Soldiers are well paid by Vietnamese standards,[9] well trained and equipped, and evidence an *élan* which is sadly lacking elsewhere in the country. Much of the army's support is based on personal loyalty to the President who, bypassing formal organization, often deals directly with young field commanders and military chiefs of province. Diem has thus far retained for himself the title and function of Secretary of State for Defense.[10]

Once that he was sure of its support, Diem used the military as

[9] Bernard B. Fall, "South Viet-Nam's Internal Problems," *Pacific Affairs*, XXXI (Sept. 1958), 259.

[10] Roy Jumper, "Mandarin Bureaucracy and Politics in South Vietnam," *Pacific Affairs*, XXX (March 1957), 55, footnote 16.

an instrument to consolidate and extend government control. Of twenty-two chiefs of province in the southern region (formerly Cochin China) in April 1957, fourteen were army officers, and of these nine were at the same time commanders of military subzones.[11] In the less secure areas the army, endowed with political as well as military power, actually constitutes a sort of parallel government responsible directly to the President.[12]

The bureaucracy has a vested interest in maintaining the government of the Republic of Vietnam, though not necessarily as Ngo Dinh Diem's government. For this, if for no other reason, government functionaries are generally anti-Communist. The bureaucracy, as it must, lends outward support to the government, but it should not be considered a group which as a whole is unreservedly in support of President Diem.

Upon coming to office in 1954, Ngo Dinh Diem was confronted with an ineffective bureaucracy dominated by French selected and trained personnel generally unsympathetic to the new regime. To remedy the situation the President replaced many old-line bureaucrats with army officers and administrative personnel from central and northern Vietnam [13] and concentrated power in the hands of a few trusted individuals, most important of whom are his brothers Ngo Dinh Can and Ngo Dinh Nhu. Personal loyalty, always a prominant consideration, became the dominant criteria for recruitment into government service.[14] To develop more active support in the bureaucracy the government embarked on a campaign of political education of its members, including regular classes with required attendance.[15] One governmental publication reports that such studies have helped induce the bureaucracy to "strengthen their ideological conceptions and make them understand better the meaning of the People's Communist Denunciation Campaign." [16] To enhance its con-

[11] United States Operations Mission to Vietnam, *Saigon News Roundup*, no. 77, April 12, 1957.

[12] Jumper, "Mandarin Bureaucracy and Politics in South Vietnam," p. 56.

[13] *Ibid.*, p. 55.

[14] Jumper reports an associate of President Diem's as saying, "You cannot be sure of a man unless you know him yourself. When you rely upon the recommendation of a second person, the gates are thrown open to invasion by your opponents" (*ibid.*, p. 51).

[15] Roy Jumper, "The Communist Challenge to South Vietnam," *Far Eastern Survey*, XXV (Nov. 1956), 166.

[16] *Record of Governmental Achievements, July 1955–July 1956* (published by the Vietnamese government, n.d.), p. 28.

trol the government also stimulated the formation of a League of Revolutionary Civil Servants to which all civil servants are "invited" to belong and which functions as a vehicle for the political education program.

The political position of the wealthy elite—absentee landowners and businessmen—is based on their economic power, on the technical and administrative skills they can offer or withhold from the government, and on their membership in other groups (e.g., intellectuals). That the wealthy elite have been able to exert a conservative influence on the government is evident in the moderacy of the agrarian reform program. There exists, however, a basic conflict of interests between the wealthy elite and Diem. The former represent the *status quo* in social and economic terms, whereas the President, if he is to widen his base of support and effect any sort of "revolution," a term he often uses, represents change of a sort inimical to the interests of this group.

Intellectuals and university students have considerable political importance. Although Diem has effectively ousted the French, not all intellectuals are persuaded that his government will last and are willing to be associated with it. The government's resort to political repression has also alienated members of this group. Nevertheless the President has the allegiance of a number of North Vietnamese intellectuals and students whose acquaintance with the Viet Minh is firsthand and who regard communism as the outstanding threat to Vietnam.[17]

Most Vietnamese, though nominally Buddhist, practice varying combinations of Buddhism, Confucianism, Taoism, ancestor worship, and animism. For them religion is an individual and family matter and consequently requires little formal organization. In contrast, Catholicism is a religion with a hierarchical organization which can be mobilized for political purposes. Although the Catholic Church in South Vietnam does not engage in secular activities as actively as in, say, Spain, it does not confine itself to strictly religious matters. In the days of the refugee exodus following the Geneva accords the Church was very active politically.

[17] The schism in the ranks of the intellectuals may be illustrated by reference to the students at the University of Vietnam in Saigon who are politically divided over the issue of whether the University Students Association should actively participate in the government's anti-Communist campaign. The division is regional as well as political, with North Vietnamese students supporting Diem and accusing the southern students of being pro-Communist (Jumper, "The Communist Challenge to South Vietnam," p. 165).

Catholicism was introduced into Vietnam by the French, and it is understandable that many members of the upper class are Catholic converts. For this reason and because of the Church's organization, Catholics in general—quite apart from those Catholics who are refugees from the North—are a group of political importance even though they form only about 4 per cent of the population of South Vietnam. Two divergent political tendencies are apparent among the nonrefugee Catholics. As members of the landholding class many are unsympathetic to the Diem government for personal financial reasons. On the other hand both the Catholic orientation of the government (Diem is a devout Catholic and a number of members of the government are also Catholic) and the fact that the Church supports the government despite occasional differences operate to encourage southern Catholic support.

The North Vietnamese refugees constitute a once extremely important group whose influence seems to be on the wane as the government's need for its support lessens. In the uncertain days following Geneva when the army's loyalty was in doubt, the refugees were the only group completely committed to Diem. The great majority of the refugees are Catholic. In most instances they were led south by the village priest, who assumed the role of political as well as religious leader, and they maintained village units intact in southern refugee camps. During the initial period refugees were extensively used to provide evidence of popular support for the government by means of numerous demonstrations; and, though unarmed, many were for a long time encamped in the immediate environs of Saigon where their numbers could be brought into play on short notice. Both as Catholics and as North Vietnamese fleeing from the Viet Minh, refugee loyalties naturally gravitated toward Diem. More recently both the degree of refugee allegiance to the President and his need for their backing have diminished. The inevitable problems involved in resettlement have tended to reduce unqualified refugee support of the government, though perhaps not of Diem personally. With the army now fully committed and the power of the sects broken, the government finds itself in a considerably less precarious position, one in which refugee support is less vital. Nonetheless most of the refugees, Catholic and non-Catholic alike, are still firmly behind the government.

The Communists in South Vietnam are an element of considerable political importance, whose strength is difficult to assess but who clearly have significant influence in important sectors of Vietnamese society. At the time of the Geneva Conference the Viet Minh in the south was well organized and controlled most of the countryside beyond the outskirts of Saigon. It is unquestionable that it claimed at least the passive support of a large majority of the southern population. It is equally as certain that today Communist influence is considerably less than in 1954. The nationalist and democratic aura which the Viet Minh managed to weave about themselves prior to Geneva still lingers on, and the Communists have endeavored to maintain the illusion. But the issue of colonialism is no longer paramount, and the Diem government is actively competing for southern loyalties. Nonetheless the Communists still have considerable strength especially among the peasants,[18] and their influence is by no means confined to the countryside. It is significant among the urban proletariat and extends into the upper class where many members of the intelligentsia and bureaucracy are thought to be sympathetic to communism.

In the long run, especially in the event of open hostilities between the Republic of Vietnam and the Communists, the political allegiance of the peasantry will be a critical factor. Both sides realize this, and competition for peasant loyalties constitutes the basis of the struggle between Diem and the Communists for control in the countryside. But who is winning, where peasant allegiance may be said to lie, is an open question. The political and military leaders whom the Viet Minh left behind to operate covertly in the South are of the peasantry and are instructed to lead exemplary lives, to behave so as to attract rather than alienate the peasants—conduct which contrasts sharply with the actions of many local government officials. In addition the Communists have benefited from the fact that the government of South Vietnam has refused to recognize titles to land conferred on the peasants by the Viet Minh. In fact the question of landlordism is one of the most important, if not the most important, of the issues in the conflict between Diem and the Communists, an area of competition in which the government's agrarian reform program is making only slow progress.

In more immediate political terms the peasantry as a group is less important than either the bureaucracy or the military. They are largely unorganized, and, except as members of other groups (e.g., refugees or Communists), they do not play a direct political role. Peasant

[18] Jumper, "The Communist Challenge to South Vietnam," p. 161.

interests are advanced primarily in terms of the competition for their loyalties.

In some respects the position of the urban proletariat is analogous to that of the peasantry. Neither group is directly connected with the structure of power or process of government, yet in the ideological battle waged between Diem and the Communists the support of both groups is a primary objective. It is in this indirect sense that they influence the government. There is little doubt that many workers are Communist-oriented, especially among the unemployed. In counteracting Communist influence the government is obliged to recognize the social and economic needs of the workers, and there is some evidence that their interests are receiving greater recognition. Trade unions are a relatively new phenomenon in South Vietnam and are closely controlled by the government. But within limits they are today acting in the worker's behalf in wage, hour, and working conditions disputes.[19]

Overlying the socioeconomic and group differences in Vietnamese society is a third social division based on regional identification. Historically Tonkin and Annam were the seats of Vietnamese culture. The south was the frontier, and the Cochin Chinese were considered much as uncultured frontiersmen by their compatriots in the center and north. The regional identifications and antagonisms which have always characterized Vietnam have been accentuated by the present situation. The seat of the government of the Republic of Vietnam is in Saigon in the south, and resentment is engendered among southerners by the fact that the President and many of his closest advisers are from central and northern Vietnam and by the extensive use that Diem has made of refugees from the north in his administration. The influx of North Vietnamese peasant refugees and what is considered by some to be the preferential treatment accorded them have also stimulated southern hostility. In turn the Vietnamese from the north and center now living in South Vietnam feel themselves isolated, away from home and among countrymen whom they consider uncultured and materialistic. Furthermore, as in the case of the students from the north, they often find it difficult to understand why many southerners are not more adamant in their opposition to communism.

[19] Bernard Fall indicates that "continuous strikes for higher wages" by plantation workers are actually pricing Vietnamese rubber out of the world market (Fall, "South Viet-Nam's Internal Problems," p. 248).

· XIX ·

South Vietnam:

The Political Process

THE system of government as it exists and operates in the Republic of Vietnam today has as its base a written constitution promulgated by President Ngo Dinh Diem on October 26, 1956. In examining the provisions of the constitution it should be kept in mind that they were framed for two main purposes: to give legal sanction to already-operative governing institutions and to broaden the area of popular participation in government. Up to that time the government's primary concern had been directed toward establishing security and stability and filling the vacuum created by the destruction of the political forces holding power when the Geneva accords were made. This formalization of governmental functions is therefore the end result, rather than the initiator, of the political system: it must be studied within the context of the constitution's limited role in providing a framework for the actual distribution of power within the government of Vietnam.

The Formal Organization of Government

The writing of the draft constitution was at first assigned by presidential decree[1] to a Constitutional Commission composed of well-

---

[1] Presidential Decree no. 25, Tong Thong Phu (Presidency), Nov. 28, 1955, in *Vietnam Presse Spéciale*, no. 679, Nov. 30, 1955. *Vietnam Presse* is the official government news agency.

known lawyers, including prominent ministers in the government.[2] Several foreign experts, notably American and Philippine, were consulted. Following the election of the National Constituent Assembly, however, the President incorporated some general principles in an address to the Assembly on April 17, 1956,[3] and turned over to the Assembly the task of elaborating a draft constitution. When a fifteen-man Constitutional Committee was chosen by the Assembly, four members of the original commission were on it, as chairman, vice-chairman, secretary, and reporter, thus ensuring a measure of familiarity and continuity with the previous commission's draft. From April 28 through July 1 the National Assembly debated its committee's draft, with members of the committee playing a prominent role in defending the proposals or accepting modifications. The Assembly's proposed constitution was submitted to the President on July 2. He returned it to the Assembly on October 15 with specific recommendations for changes, most of which were readily adopted by the Assembly in the final draft.[4]

The constitution provides for a presidential system of government patterned in some respects upon the American constitution but with a less clearly defined separation of powers. (See Chart 3.) The President is vested with the executive functions and also with the "leadership of the Nation" (Article 3).[5] He is directly elected by universal suffrage and secret ballot on a ticket which also includes the Vice-President. The term of election is for five years, and both are eligible for re-election for two additional terms. The President is the supreme commander of the armed forces, appoints and dismisses all military and civil servants, names ambassadors, accredits foreign diplomatic representatives, and represents the nation in foreign affairs. With the consent of the Assembly, the President ratifies international treaties,

[2] Nguyen Huu Chau, Presidency; Vu Quoc Thong, Social Action; Vu Van Mau, Foreign Affairs; Bui Van Thinh, Interior; Tran Chanh Thanh, Information; and Nguyen Van Si, Justice.

[3] He proposed that Vietnam should be a republic with sovereignty vested in the people, with separation of powers between executive and legislature, and with an independent judiciary. See *The Constitution of the Republic of Vietnam* (Saigon: Secretariat of State for Information, Oct. 26, 1956), pp. 4–6.

[4] Most of the President's suggestions were minor, since key members of his cabinet were on the Assembly's Constitutional Committee which wrote the draft (J. A. C. Grant, "The Vietnam Constitution of 1956," *American Political Science Review*, LVI [June 1958], 443–444).

[5] According to Bernard Kalb, Vietnamese officials state that the sentence was added to the revision at the suggestion of President Diem (*New York Times*, Oct. 27, 1956).

Chart 3. The structure of government in the Republic of Vietnam

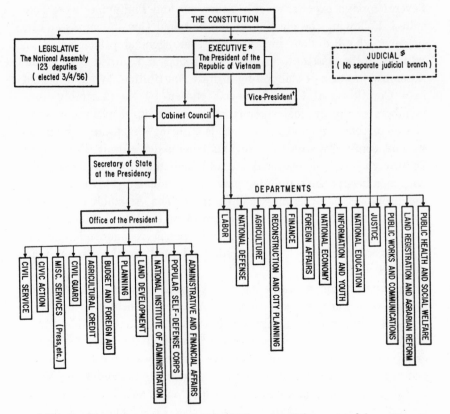

* The President at present retains the Defense portfolio, assisted by a Deputy Secretary of State for Defense.

† The present Vice-President is also the Secretary of State for National Economy.

‡ The Cabinet Council includes all heads of departments, plus the Secretary of State at the Presidency, the Deputy Secretary of State for National Defense, and certain heads of services at the Office of the Presidency.

§ The court system is in the process of reorganization.

declares war, and concludes peace treaties. He may submit bills of law to the National Assembly for consideration and may veto all or part of legislative acts. To override the presidential veto requires a three-quarters vote of the entire membership of the National Assembly. The President is further empowered to enact his suggested budget by decree if one has not been voted by December 31, but he may not expend more than a quarter of the total amount of money he requested from the National Assembly in any fiscal quarter. In case of emergency the Assembly can confer on the President the power to legislate by decree within defined time limits. He may also enact legislation by decree while the Assembly is in recess. In addition the President may sign decrees temporarily suspending laws in regions which he has declared to be in a state of emergency. With the consent of the Assembly the President may organize a referendum the results of which are binding on both legislature and executive.[6]

The powers conferred on the President by the constitution give him broader authority than is enjoyed by the President of the United States: this is most obvious in matters of budgetary control and in the power to veto parts of legislation and to legislate by decree in an emergency. The right to organize referendums could also become a strong weapon in the hands of an ambitious President since referendums can be manipulated in authoritarian regimes by those who run them.

Extraordinary powers are reserved for the first President, designated in Article 96 as the "President of the Republic who was charged by the people in the referendum of October 23, 1955, with establishing a democratic regime." Under Article 98 he can suspend civil liberties completely during the first legislative term, which ends on October 1, 1959:

The President of the Republic may decree a temporary suspension of the rights of freedom of circulation and residence, of speech and the press, of assembly and association, and of formation of labor unions and strikes, to meet the legitimate demands of public security and order and of national defense.[7]

The National Assembly is composed of deputies elected by direct and universal suffrage with secret ballot for a three-year term of office. The constitution grants them immunity for anything said on the Assembly floor and makes the status of deputy incompatible with any other elective or appointive public office. "The National Assembly votes the laws. It approves international treaties and conventions" (Article 55). Deputies share with the President the right to introduce

[6] The proposal for the referendum was made to cover issues that might arise on which the executive and legislative branches were in conflict (Grant, *op. cit.*, p. 449).

[7] The "emergency" provisions bear an ominous likeness to Latin American constitutional measures, and the "suicide clause" of Article 98, providing for the suspension of constitutional guarantees, is similar to Article 48 of the Weimar Constitution which was used to sidetrack parliamentary government in Germany (Grant, *op. cit.*, p. 450; see also Gwendolen M. Carter, John H. Herz, and John C. Ranney, *Major Foreign Powers*, 3d ed. [New York: Harcourt, Brace, 1957], p. 413).

legislation. They may override a presidential veto and serve on the Constitutional Court [8] which pronounces upon the constitutionality of laws.

Probably the most controversial aspect of the legislative section is Article 42, which permits the National Assembly to delegate legislative authority to the President in time of emergency. Since the Assembly is presently dominated by government partisans, no contest of will has yet arisen which might portend the future of executive-legislative relations.

Despite the constitutional guarantee that "the Judiciary shall have a status which guarantees its independent character" (Article 4), the judiciary is in fact neither separate nor equal. "Historically, the Vietnamese judiciary has been a puppet of the executive," [9] and the guarantees necessary for judicial independence—life tenure and inviolability—appear nowhere in the constitution. Although the President has decreed that magistrates shall enjoy "independence and irremovability," [10] to date the judiciary has not been conspicuously courageous in handing down decisions unfavorable to the government. Since magistrates can be transferred by the Department of Justice at will, the threat of exiling a Saigon judge to a remote province can be used as an effective form of pressure by the executive. The actual organization of the court system is left to statutes and is still in the process of revision.

The constitution provides for a National Economic Council, charged with "suggesting ideas and rendering its opinion on economic projects and proposals" (Article 82). The Vice-President of the Republic acts as its chairman, and members are chosen "from among professional associations, from the various branches of economic activity, from various social organizations relating to the economy, and from among economists." There have as yet been no appointments to the Economic Council, and it exists only on paper.

The Vietnamese constitution includes in its main text a "bill of rights" guaranteeing such basic civil rights as freedom of speech, assembly, press, and religion and equality before the law. These rights, however, may be severely restricted by exercise of police powers. Thus even the right to travel abroad is subject to qualifications and

[8] The Court is to consist of four deputies, four judges or lawyers appointed by the President, and a chairman appointed by the President with the National Assembly's consent (Article 86), but it has not yet been appointed.

[9] Grant, *op. cit.*, p. 450.

[10] *Record of Government Achievements, July 1955–July 1956* (published by the Vietnamese government, n.d.), p. 39.

exceptions, as "in cases of restrictions by law for security, national defense, economic, financial reasons, or in the public interest" (Article 13). Economic liberties, like the right to form trade unions, to strike, and to receive equal pay for equal work, are present, but also in restricted form. In short, all rights are subject to "the legitimate requirements of general security, morality, public order, national defense" (Article 28).

The constitution aims at harmonizing the rights of the individual with his duties as a citizen:

The State recognizes and guarantees the fundamental rights of the human person in his individual capacity and in his capacity as a member of the community.

The State shall endeavour to establish for all equal opportunities and the necessary conditions for the enjoyment of their rights and the performance of their duties [Article 5].

This is an expression of the official philosophy of the regime, "personalism," or the importance of the human person and personality. The citizen is viewed as a member of the family, which is recognized by the state as constituting "the foundation of society" (Article 25). The constitution further defines the duties of the citizen in terms of the anti-Communist nature of the Republic and the citizen's task to protect its principles, which include "the republican form of Government, the democratic regime, national freedom, independence, and unity" (Article 28).

It is unfair to evaluate the constitution solely in terms of its workability to date, because the exigencies of the present situation in South Vietnam impede a balanced application of its measures. The distribution of power is unequal and could permit an arbitrary use of authority on the part of the executive. On the other hand nothing in the basic provisions necessarily militates against the future development of truly representative institutions culminating in a vigorous Assembly responsive to public will and expressing it at the highest levels. The Assembly's unimpressive record to date stems in part from being allowed to debate only unimportant issues [11] and from having

---

[11] Bernard Fall, who recently returned from South Vietnam, maintains that the Assembly "has developed a very vocal opposition group over the past two years and its sessions exhibit a refreshing give-and-take." But the Assembly is hamstrung by the fact that, during the first two years of its existence, its authority has been circumvented since most important government business has been carried on by presidential decree. See Bernard B. Fall, "South Viet-Nam's Internal Problems," *Pacific Affairs*, XXXI (Sept. 1958), 253.

government-sponsored measures forced through by the progovernment majority.[12]

The constitution does not provide for the organization of government below the national level. During the Bao Dai regime Vietnam
was divided into three regions, North, South, and Center, with the
plateau region, the Pays Montagnards du Sud (PMS), enjoying a
special status as crown domain.[13] The regional governments, administered through governors appointed by Bao Dai, controlled their own
budgets and possessed a great deal of economic and political autonomy. In order to replace this loose structure with a highly centralized
chain of command controlled by the executive, President Diem deprived the regions of center and south Vietnam of their juridical personalities and independent budgets,[14] transforming them into primarily
administrative units. The duties of the presidential delegates to the
regions, now drastically curtailed, appear to be largely supervisory
—to co-ordinate, study, and advise—but not to initiate policy.[15] This
sweeping reorganization has not yet been completely carried out.

The President has also expanded central executive power over the
local administrative apparatus at the expense of the regional governments by channeling presidential authority primarily through the
thirty-odd province chiefs.[16] These have in the past been drawn
largely from the ranks of the trusted young officers, but recently the
trend has been to return the provinces to civilian control.[17] The province is granted juridical personality and an individual budget, allocated

[12] For example, on May 29, 1958, the Assembly voted a draft "family" bill
sponsored by Madame Ngo Dinh Nhu, the President's sister-in-law. It had aroused
widespread criticism and opposition both within and outside the Assembly, since
it abolished divorce except in special cases, but the deputies did not dare defy
Madame Nhu and reject a measure she vigorously defended.

[13] *Times of Vietnam,* Jan. 28, 1956.

[14] Presidential Decree no. 17, Dec. 14, 1955, in *Saigon Daily News Round-up*
(*NRU;* published by the United States Operations Mission to Vietnam), no. 170,
Aug. 1, 1956 (derived from the Vietnamese newspaper *Thoi Cuoc*). The former
region of north Vietnam and part of center Vietnam were taken over by the
government of North Vietnam following the Geneva accords.

[15] *Ibid.,* no. 238, Oct. 29, 1956 (*Dan Nguyen*).

[16] Roy Jumper, "Problems of Public Administration in South Vietnam," *Far
Eastern Survey,* XXVI (Dec. 1957), 184.

[17] Especially in the south, where the "pacification campaigns" against the sects
combining political, social, and military activities were conducted under over-all
military command, the army has played an important role in areas usually reserved
to civil authorities. For example, Truong Tan Buu pacification operations in
southeast Vietnam were described as "military and administrative." See *NRU,* no.
181, Aug. 14, 1956 (all papers).

by the central government, and the province chief is responsible for the application of laws and the maintenance of security and order. Provinces are further divided into districts, cantons, and villages.

The constitution authorizes the President to appoint secretaries of state [18] responsible to him, each of whom heads a government department. Policy formulation within a department is carried on by a personal "cabinet" on the French model appointed by and responsible to the Secretary of State and usually made up of his trusted political aides whose jobs depend on his.

The Executive Office, called the Office of the Presidency, is also headed by a Secretary of State with cabinet status. Up to the present, it has served as the real locus of executive power. Within the Presidency are such services as the Directorate of the Budget, the Press Service, Civic Action,[19] and the National Institute of Administration. At various times the Presidency has concerned itself with problems rightfully the domain of the regular departments. A strong Secretary of State, however, can often maintain the integrity of his own department's decision-making authority.

The cabinet as a group is not an important organ of power. Decisions involving the departments are usually made through personal contact between the individual Secretary of State and the President. The fluctuating importance of his department can often serve as an indication of the Secretary's standing with the President.[20] Although over-all governmental supervision is probably exercised by the Presidency, the President's brother Ngo Dinh Nhu serves as his "political adviser" and is believed to be Diem's most trusted policy maker. He has a large sphere of authority permitted him both in decision making and implementation at the executive level.

An increasingly important political role has been assumed by members of the bureaucracy occupying positions usually thought to be neutral in Western countries. Successful efforts to transform this group into politically active and effective proponents of government policy

[18] The term Secretary of State refers to the head of a department, formerly called minister, and should not be confused with the American Secretary of State, whose Vietnamese counterpart is the Secretary of State for Foreign Affairs.

[19] An organization concerned with propaganda at village levels.

[20] For example, Nguyen Ngoc Tho, a close friend of the President, enjoys broad powers as Secretary of State for the Economy. By provision of the constitution the President was empowered to choose the Republic's first Vice-President, with Assembly approval, and appointed Tho (Jumper, "Problems of Public Administration in South Vietnam," p. 185).

have been made through intensive political indoctrination carried on within each department. Officials are impressed with the necessity of abandoning their traditional policy of *attentisme*, or fence sitting, and of making a positive contribution by entering the political arena. The National Revolutionary Civil Servants League [21] took an important part in the government's effort to get out the vote for the national elections to the Constituent Assembly. Since the bureaucracy completely depends on the President's largesse for position and tenure, it has been, together with the students and refugees, one of the easily manipulated groups most frequently called upon to participate in demonstrations, organize protest meetings, sponsor petitions, and carry out other activities through which the government seeks to demonstrate that its support is widespread and emanates spontaneously from all segments of the population.

The Dynamics of the Political Process

In most of the new nations of Southeast Asia, nationalist and revolutionary fervor has found focus in a movement in which the leader personally symbolizes the struggle for independence. Vietnam is no exception. In the 1940s the Viet Minh under Ho Chi Minh gained the loyalty of a great percentage of the masses as well as that of most of the intellectuals by carrying on the struggle for liberation against the French and translating the desires of the people into deeds. Bao Dai's ineffective leadership and the taint of French collaboration hindered his government's efforts to capture this nationalist sentiment and gain a sizable following. A major problem facing the government of President Diem was the necessity to dissociate itself from its predecessor and to bring forth a leader capable of attracting widespread support to counteract the magnetic appeal of Ho Chi Minh. One goal was achieved by the virulent personal attacks on Bao Dai in the referendum and by the withdrawal of the French expeditionary force. The other is in process of being effected by the build-up of Ngo Dinh Diem as the savior of the Vietnamese nation.

President Diem is not by nature a volatile personality like President Soekarno of Indonesia, for example, nor is he a spellbinding orator capable of capturing public imagination and affection. Born in 1901 of a traditional mandarin family, Diem grew up at Hue in a

[21] Affiliated with the political party, the National Revolutionary Movement (*Times of Vietnam*, Sept. 1, 1956). It is presently headed by Secretary of State for the Interior Lam Le Trinh.

rigid patterned society, sheltered from public contact by the nature of the social system as well as by the high fences and gardens which enclosed the mandarins' homes. He was by inclination reserved and ascetic, and these qualities were reinforced by a Catholic upbringing. He entered into imperial service at the court of Hue and in 1933 became Minister of the Interior in Bao Dai's cabinet. His career was short-lived, supposedly because of French rejection of his reform program.[22] For more than twenty years Diem lived out of the political limelight, although both Bao Dai and Ho Chi Minh offered him positions in their postwar governments. The years prior to the Geneva Conference he spent in Europe and the United States, seeking recognition for himself and his program.

By remaining aloof from both the French-controlled and the Viet Minh governments when many intellectuals were jockeying for position and power within them, Ngo Dinh Diem gained a reputation as a disinterested moderate nationalist, a reputation reinforced by his personal qualities of moral integrity and uncorruptibility. His unswerving belief in Vietnam's heroic "historical mission"[23] and in his own destiny as leader of his people served him well during the chaotic first year of his rule, providing him the courage to be stubbornly uncompromising with opposition, both Vietnamese and foreign. But these very qualities and actions, which would have been assets in traditional Vietnam where authority was based on respect and fear, are not readily translatable into mass appeal. One can admire a stern judge, but it is difficult to respond emotionally to his leadership. In the past Diem's attempts to reach the villagers at their own level were symptomatic of his inability to appear at ease in peasant surroundings: dressed in the sharkskin suit of the French *colon,* he arrived in a long, black limousine and was flanked by his Westernized officials and scores of foreign advisers invited along for the ride. He was also frequently seen robed in the blue satin tunic and black turban of the imperial mandarin, perhaps in an effort to revivify the respect for authority and obedience traditionally accorded to rulers of Vietnam. Of late, Diem has traveled extensively throughout Vietnam in much more informal dress and manner and has made himself more accessible to the peasantry during these trips. But whether in suit

[22] Ellen J. Hammer, *The Struggle for Indochina* (Stanford: Stanford University Press, 1954), p. 86.

[23] "Message on the Promulgation of the Constitution," *President Ngo Dinh Diem on Democracy* (Saigon: Secretariat of State of the Presidency), p. 19.

or tunic, Diem has as yet failed to compete with Ho Chi Minh on Ho's own terms, as a man of the people.

The political philosophy of Ngo Dinh Diem must be examined if the values of the present regime are to be understood, since they reflect in large measure the President's ideas and principles. Diem's personal training and Roman Catholic beliefs have shaped his attitude that there is no compromise possible between good and evil. He equates opposition to his government with evil and is thus unwilling to recognize opponents as a "loyal" opposition. He has thus refused to deal with them on any terms except surrender. Democracy, to Diem, is a theoretical concept viewed primarily in moral terms and based less on the practices of the democratic process than on the ethical conduct and moral obligations of the citizen and the state.[24] The important unit within the state is the national community, and the citizen flourishes as a member of it, subordinating individual good to common welfare. The free development of human personality— the doctrine of personalism—requires that the state aid the individual to realize not only political liberty, but also social and economic freedom.[25] Diem believes that this can best be done by encouraging the people to organize associations within their community for mutual welfare and self-help, with the government channeling economic aid through the local associations. Personalism, then, is a philosophy of political liberties within the context of collective and communal life. It places greater emphasis on spiritual values than on material improvements, and the similarity of some of these views to older Confucian beliefs has an appeal for many conservative Vietnamese.[26] The President expounded this philosophy in his message to the National Assembly on April 17, 1956, in which he outlined his recommendations for the constitution:

Thus we affirm our faith in the absolute value of the human person, whose dignity antedates society and whose destiny is grander than time.

We affirm that the sole legitimate end and object of the State is to protect the fundamental rights of the human person to existence and to the free development of his intellectual, moral and spiritual life.

[24] "Diem betrays marked irritation when queried about the abridgement of civil liberties in South Viet Nam. His conversation reflects an archaic, mandarin temperament" (William Henderson, "South Viet Nam Finds Itself," *Foreign Affairs,* XXXV [Jan. 1957], 285)

[25] Phuc Thien, "Political Philosophy of Ngo Dinh Diem, Part I," *Times of Vietnam,* Oct. 6, 1956. Two other sections of this informative article appeared in subsequent issues of the weekly, Part II on October 13 and Part III on October 20.

[26] "Confucianism and Personalism," *Times of Vietnam,* Sept. 29, 1956. This

We affirm that democracy is neither material happiness nor the supremacy of numbers. Democracy is essentially a permanent effort to find the right political means for assuring to all citizens the right of free development and of maximum initiative, responsibility, and spiritual life.[27]

With concepts of loyalty and obedience accepted as prime virtues in the President's philosophy, it is not surprising that Diem places greatest confidence in members of his family and close personal friends whose allegiance is unquestioned. The influence of his brothers on Diem's policy making cannot be overestimated, although they, like all political figures in South Vietnam, are ultimately responsible to the President. Diem, a strong-willed personality, is front man for no group or individual, but he tends to hold himself aloof from political maneuvering and leaves the daily workings of politics to a trusted few, especially Ngo Dinh Nhu in Saigon in the south and the young, autocratic Ngo Dinh Can in center Vietnam. The beautiful Madame Ngo Dinh Nhu, the President's sister-in-law and official hostess, acts as champion for women's rights in the National Assembly and reportedly participates in palace intrigues with marked success. Ngo Dinh Luyen, ambassador to the Court of St. James and minister to The Hague and Brussels, exerts little influence on internal affairs and is the least powerful brother. Finally, the President's eldest brother, Monsignor Ngo Dinh Thuc, undertakes to speak for the nation's Catholics and refugees. The prelate acts as a moderating influence on the struggle for power within the personal clique and engages in the promotion of such projects for the general welfare as the recently established University of Hue. He has thus gained a larger measure of public respect than the other members of his family who are often viewed as backstage Machiavellian figures and as such serve as scapegoats for criticism which might otherwise be directed against the President himself.

---

article attempts to liken the ideas of Confucianism with "the new doctrine on which is based the national revolution of Vietnam, personalism."

[27] Ngo Dinh Diem, "Message to the National Assembly," *Vietnam in World Affairs*, I (Saigon: Secretariat of State for Foreign Affairs, June 1956), 103. In his message to the opening session of the National Assembly on October 6, 1958, the President stated: "Our society rests on two solid pillars: the family and the community. It is up to us to complete this traditional socio-political duality by the coordinated addition of a third element, cooperative organizations, economic units functioning to ensure the necessary material conditions for the integrated life of the family and administrative units of the community" (quoted in *News from Viet-Nam*, IV [Washington, D.C.: Embassy of Vietnam, Nov. 10, 1958], 6).

The importance of other political leaders in power positions depends largely on the closeness of their relationship with the Ngo family and is continuously subject to change. In the past the strongest figure among these was Tran Chanh Thanh who, as Secretary of State for Information and president of the National Revolutionary Movement often used these organizations to execute Ngo Dinh Nhu's policies. But Thanh's role has been downgraded as Nhu's own Revolutionary Workers Party has increased its activity. Two other young men related to the Ngo family by marriage have also figured prominently in the government, Tran Trung Dung, Deputy Secretary of State for Defense,[28] and Nguyen Huu Chau, a brilliant lawyer and, until recently, the Secretary of State to the Presidency.[29] Membership in the power clique rarely exceeds a dozen personalities whose fortunes wax and wane with the vicissitudes of intraclique rivalries. The narrow composition of this group reflects the essentially authoritarian nature of the government.

A cabinet post may provide these leaders with access to the apparatus of governing power, but it does not ensure them tenure. In the past, political parties have served as personal followings for political leaders rather than as vehicles for marshaling public support. The old-line nationalist groups have been driven into the opposition by their anti-Diem bias, and new parties have been organized to supplant them and to act as a propaganda arm of the government. Although divergencies can be noted between the major progovernment parties, the main efforts of all have been directed toward consolidating the authority of the President. Led by men occupying high positions in the government, these parties may also be said to serve as private propaganda organs held together through personal ties and hopes of political reward. The leader controls the party rather than the party producing the leader; and political parties have thus far failed to function as a source of leadership recruitment for the government.

The largest political party to date is the National Revolutionary Movement (Phong-Trao Cach-Mang Quoc-Gia), organized in 1941

[28] He and Thanh were former officials in the Viet Minh and are probably responsible, to some extent, for the introduction of Communist-type propaganda indoctrination and tactics in, respectively, the army and bureaucracy (Grant, *op. cit.*, p. 458 n.).

[29] Chau has fallen into disfavor because of personal difficulties with the Ngo family and has left government service. Whether he will remain permanently eclipsed is uncertain.

and legalized by the Department of the Interior in 1954 under the leadership of Tran Chanh Thanh, Ngo Dinh Nhu, and Ngo Dinh Can. It tries to operate both as a political party with regional and local affiliates and as a movement encompassing other parties. It claims a membership of more than one million [30] and a base of support wider than that of any other political party. The National Revolutionary Movement (NRM) is, as yet, the only political organization capable of marshaling and organizing popular forces on a national level. It enjoys unrivaled government backing and confidence because of its close adherence to the government line. It employs Communist-type methods to train militant cadres and to develop a vast propaganda apparatus.[31] In the south it must compete with other progovernment parties, but in the center the NRM is all-powerful; no opposition is tolerated by Ngo Dinh Can. Regional rivalries between the two factions in the NRM are deep-seated, and Can's faction appears to have gained the upper hand with the election of Phan Van Nhu from center Vietnam as president of the NRM, succeeding Tran Chanh Thanh.

Most of the policy-making elements of the NRM derive from one of the parties affiliated with it, the Revolutionary Workers Party (Can-Lao Nhan-Vi Cach-Mang-Dang),[32] whose mentor is Ngo Dinh Nhu. A tightly knit covert group whose members are reputedly handpicked by Nhu, the Revolutionary Workers Party (RWP) is organized along cell lines with each member knowing only a few others.[33] It has been rumored that the party intends to tighten its membership by purging the "unreliable" elements and that it will participate more actively on the local level by sending militants down to the village to aid the community development programs. Ngo Dinh Nhu has been very active in labor affairs, and the RWP, in order to emphasize its left-wing character, chose to sit at the far left in the National Assembly. It espouses personalism as its doctrine and is probably the source of inspiration for the President's ideas on this subject.

[30] Press conference of Tran Chanh Thanh, Jan. 22, 1956, *Vietnam Presse Spéciale*, no. 724, Jan. 23, 1956.

[31] It runs a daily newspaper, *Cach-Mang Quoc-Gia* [National Revolution], which receives a government subsidy and often operates in conjunction with the Department of Information.

[32] A more literal translation is Revolutionary Workers Personalist Party, since *Nhan-Vi* means "personalism"; but the translated form popularized by Americans is here used. Inclusion of *Nhan-Vi* is important as a key to understanding the party's philosophy and program.

[33] *Times of Vietnam*, Feb. 25, 1956.

Operating as a kind of "brain trust" for the more amorphous NRM, the RWP members are placed in strategic positions throughout the government. Its influence stems, not from the fact of its being an elite group, but from the complete devotion of its followers to Nhu, who uses this select group to carry out his policies.

Another political party, the Citizens Rally (Tap Doan Cong Dan), merged with the NRM in July 1958.[34] Led by the first president of the National Assembly, Tran Van Lam, it had been a conservative Catholic party supported primarily by southern business classes and government officials. As a strictly regional party it posed the greatest threat to the supremacy of the NRM in the south, and friction had been reported between members of the two parties. At the third convention of the Citizens Rally (CR) in January 1957, President Diem recommended that the group orient its program toward cultural, social, and economic activities, rather than "pure politics." [35] Whether the wealthy southern Catholics who had hitherto allied with the CR will now support the NRM-CR coalition is problematic.

The progovernment party least firmly entrenched in the Ngo circle is also the smallest, the Movement to Win and Preserve Freedom (Phong-Trao Tranh-Thu Tu-Do). Its members are drawn primarily from professional groups, notably lawyers, and it numbers some well-known political figures in its leadership. The Movement to Win and Preserve Freedom (MWPF) charted a reasonably independent course when led by former Secretary of State for the Interior Bui Van Thinh, but under its present leadership [36] the MWPF has hewed closer to the government line. It is the most conspicuous example of an elitist party, top-heavy with ambitious leaders who enjoy little popular support at the local level. Apart from the particular roles of its individual members, the MWPF exerts little influence on the political scene, either within or outside the government.

The failure of these parties to put forth any original and vigorous platform of ideas and action for the National Assembly elections serves to underline their inadequacies as mechanisms to formulate policy, mold public opinion, or represent special-interest groups. The

[34] The new coalition will continue to use the name National Revolutionary Movement, and its chairman is still Phan Van Nhu. In effect the Citizens Rally has been swallowed up by the NRM.

[35] *Times of Vietnam,* Jan. 26, 1957.

[36] Vu Quoc Thong, former Secretary of State for Social Action, now Vice-Speaker of the National Assembly, presently heads the party.

NRM program of action emphasized "consolidation of national independence." [37] Posing as an educational organization of "intellectuals and workers," [38] the RWP did not present a party slate of candidates, though some of its members ran as individual candidates. It outlined a "program of reform of the Social Structure" aimed at balancing "absolutist concepts of liberty . . . and absolutist concepts of the primacy of group interests . . . so that human personality be respected and, at the same time, the common welfare be assured." [39] The CR spoke for a platform of balanced economic, social, political, and cultural aims. Only the MWPF elaborated the democratic freedoms it considered essential to individual development.[40]

With strong government backing, the NRM won a whopping victory in the national elections. In an effort to give a diversified flavor to the electoral campaign, some NRM and RWP members ran as Independents. Although 50-odd official NRM candidates and 44 Independents were elected,[41] 61 delegates were seated as NRM members when the National Assembly organized itself, and only 11 retained their status as Independents, among them Madame Ngo Dinh Nhu. The CR seated 25 delegates, the RWP 15, the MWPF 8, and the Dai-Viet, an old-line party, 1.[42] It is interesting to note that the "big names" for the most part presented themselves as candidates in the center, where the NRM was strongest,[43] or in refugee districts, where the priests could "deliver" the votes.[44] Only two southerners in the political elite, Tran Van Lam and Nguyen Huu Chau, dared run in the highly contested districts of Saigon. Candidates were not required to be resident in the district they wished to represent, and election was on the basis of a plurality of votes within the single-member district. The presence of foreign observers partially accounts for the fact that freer election campaigns were run in the capital. Although 14 per cent of the electorate as a whole failed to vote, less than 5 per

[37] *Times of Vietnam*, Jan. 28, 1956.   [38] *Ibid.*, Feb. 25, 1956.
[39] *Ibid.*   [40] *Ibid.*, Feb. 4, 1956.
[41] *Ibid.*, March 10, 1956. This statistic is unreliable since some candidates began to switch party affiliation before the election.
[42] *Constitution of the Republic of Vietnam* (Saigon: Secretariat of State for Information, Oct. 26, 1956), p. 13. Of the 123 deputies elected, 2 were refused seats, both Independents.
[43] Tran Trung Dung, Ngo Dinh Nhu, and Tran Chanh Thanh received at least 95 per cent of the votes cast in their respective districts in the center.
[44] For example, Madame Ngo Dinh Nhu and Vu Quoc Thong ran in refugee districts.

cent abstained in center Vietnam, whereas more than 20 per cent of the electorate stayed away from the polls in the south.[45]

Except for the candidates already nationally known, deputies were picked on the whole more for their loyalty to the government than for their ability or for their command over popular imagination. A political party label was not as important as whether or not the candidate had government approval. Within the National Assembly, only the NRM exercises strict party discipline,[46] its delegates usually voting as a bloc.

In a regime in which political power is centralized in the hands of a small clique, policy making is necessarily a personalized process. The general public has little means of discovering the process through which government decisions are reached.[47] Nongovernmental interests may exert influence on a narrow range of specific problems, but in general only in a peripheral area of decision making through a tie-in with government officials and agencies. Foreign advisers, notably Americans, play a part in the gathering of information and translating it into programs of action, but their influence is advisory and generally limited to technical matters.[48] The government attempts to involve the general public in its policy making in a curious way which could be described as the manufacturing of consensus. The Department of Information and other official or extragovernmental agencies sponsor meetings, demonstrations, and petitions requesting a certain action or policy in an effort to foster the semblance that some government decisions are taken in response to popular will.

The failure of newspapers to assume leadership in the formulation and dissemination of ideas and in the shaping of public opinion can be accounted for by the poor quality of newspaper reporting and the government's attitude toward freedom of the press. Long accustomed to prohibitive restrictions on news relating to political issues, Viet-

[45] Although these statistics are not reliable, they point up the significant difference between the voting patterns of center and south Vietnam. This may indicate that government pressure and coercive tactics were used more extensively in the center.

[46] During the period that one of the writers was in South Vietnam, she learned from several reliable sources that candidates endorsed by the NRM had to submit an undated letter of resignation to the party chairman before receiving the official nod.

[47] Jumper, "Problems of Public Administration in South Vietnam," p. 185.

[48] According to Fall, an American adviser's recommendation is "in many cases only heeded when it does not clash with the views of the South Vietnamese Presidency" ("South Viet-Nam's Internal Problems," pp. 258–259).

namese newspapers have developed a brand of yellow journalism, not unlike that in the United States at the turn of the century. With competition intense for a narrow reading public, newspapers resort to flamboyant sensationalism to attract readers, and reporting is quite often unreliable. For this reason the government claims that it is necessary to supervise both the content of the newspapers and their distribution. It resorts to a variety of techniques to make sure that only the news it sees fit to have printed reaches the streets. For example, through the Department of Information the government subsidizes "acceptable" newspapers and journals by making large-scale purchases of their issues for distribution in Vietnam and abroad.[49]

Although the government ostensibly lifted press censorship for Vietnamese newspapers in February 1956, an indirect form of control resulted, since in a new ordinance the government imposed severe penalties for publishing anything favoring Communist activities or endangering state security.[50] The first case arising under this ordinance occurred in April 1956, when the editors of the weekly magazine *Van Nghe Tu Do* [Cultural Freedom] criticized Tran Chanh Thanh for unwittingly abetting Communist propaganda by distributing a film contributing to class hatred. (The film depicted a struggle between landlord and tenant.) The magazine's publication license was withdrawn, and several of its editors were arrested on grounds of "(1) having written misleading commentaries favorable to anti-national activities, and (2) having acted in such a manner as to bring disturbance to security and order."[51] The case aroused interest among foreign newspapermen, and probably to avoid unfavorable international publicity the courts imposed lighter sentences on the editors than many observers expected—several months in jail with the sentence suspended.[52]

In another altercation between the Department of Information and a newspaper, *Tien Thu* [Progress], in July 1956, not only was the paper forced to cease publication but a mob, generally believed or-

[49] When discussing the Information Department budget in the National Assembly in 1957, a deputy complained that the 24 million piastres—more than 10 per cent of the department's total budget—asked for the subsidizing of newspapers was too much. Furthermore, he urged the Information Department to aid all anti-Communist newspapers, not only *Cach-Mang Quoc-Gia* (NRM paper), the *Gazette* (quasi-official French-language newspaper), and the *Times of Vietnam* (a pro-government English-language paper). See *NRU*, Feb. 14, 1957 (all papers).
[50] Ordinance 13, Feb. 20, 1956, *Times of Vietnam*, Feb. 25, 1956.
[51] *Times of Vietnam*, May 26, 1956.   [52] *Ibid.*, July 14, 1956.

ganized by the Department of Information, ransacked the newspaper's office while the police made no effort to intervene. An article on this event in the English-language *Times of Vietnam* was censored [53] and its editorial eliminated, despite supposed removal of government censorship and the progovernment bias of the newspaper. Mob action also occurred against two opposition newspapers in September 1957, and those involved were not punished. [54]

It might be asked whether the government's anticommunism program serves, not only to combat communism, but also as a means of achieving less obvious purposes. Parades organized in Saigon for their demonstration effect could hardly be expected to intimidate the Communists, but they might impress the foreigner. More dangerous are the measures, taken in the name of anticommunism and security, which result in the suppression and silencing of non-Communist groups and individuals. According to the Presidential Decree No. 6, dated January 11, 1956, "persons considered dangerous to National Defense and Public Security may . . . be interned in a detention camp" or placed under house arrest. It is an open secret that this ordinance has been used to jail, not only Communists, but also opposition figures. [55]

A major concern of the government is to "get out to the villages." An auxiliary militia, the Civil Guard, acts as a provincial home guard in areas pacified by the National Army and is responsible to the Presidency. Another organization, Civic Action, is concerned primarily with propaganda and activity at the village level. Also under the

[53] *Ibid.*

[54] Grant, *op. cit.*, p. 461. Of all nonmilitary government agencies the Department of Information appears most prone to use violence, both physical and symbolic, to gain its ends. It is generally held responsible for the sacking of the Majestic Hotel in June 1955 by masses of local students, government officials, and refugees brought into the city by the government to demonstrate against the first anniversary of the Geneva accords. The department probably encouraged, at least passively, the mob destruction of newspaper presses in 1957.

[55] In a case involving the weekly *Thoi Luan* [Chronicle of the Times], an attempt was made to implicate the opposition leader, Dr. Phan Quang Dan in the newspaper's criticism of the government (Fall, "South Viet-Nam's Internal Problems," p. 254). Although the editor drew a suspended prison sentence and a heavy fine and the publishing permit was withdrawn, Dr. Dan was acquitted (*Times of Vietnam*, March 15, 1958). Dr. Dan has recently announced that he hopes to register his opposition group, the Free Democratic Party, as a legal political party and publish a newspaper (*ibid.*, April 19, 1958). As for political prisoners, they can be jailed for an indefinite time, and a riot in Chi Hoa jail in May 1956 highlighted their grievances.

Presidency, it is charged with training cadres who "act as liaison agents between the people and the authorities . . . to contact the population to keep them informed on the general policy of the government." [56] The work of Civic Action is carried out in conjunction with programs of adult education and public welfare. According to the director-general of Civic Action, its program is based on personalism.[57] Difficulties were reported between the young Civic Action militants and the established administrative officials who resent encroachments on their authority, but after a period of readjustment the work of Civic Action has been resumed and expanded.[58] Recently teams from the Revolutionary Workers Party have also been going out to the villages to aid in establishing village co-operatives and community development projects. Whether they will be as successful in winning political support in the villages as their Communist counterparts in the North depends in part on their ability to work in co-operation with existing governmental apparatus. The recent recrudescence of terroristic activities in the countryside points up the dangers involved in accepting positions in areas remote from Saigon. The objectives of the terrorists are the "gradual 'insulation' of the central authorities from direct contact with the grass roots [and] serious interference with accurate reporting about the state of the population to the central authorities." [59]

The organization and running of the elections for the National Constituent Assembly served as a focal point for integrated activities on the part of both governmental and extragovernmental agencies and groups and provides some insight into the nature of Vietnamese politics. The ordinance promulgated January 23, 1956, establishing election procedure allowed candidates an extremely short period of time for their campaigns. The date on which the campaigns officially began was February 20, less than two weeks before the election. A special government committee was set up to screen prospective candidates in order to eliminate "unfit" participants,[60] and some opposition figures found their candidatures rejected. Electoral committees were established in each district to control distribution of government money to meet candidates' expenses, as no private ex-

[56] *Times of Vietnam,* Oct. 13, 1956.   [57] *Ibid.,* June 14, 1958.
[58] *News from Vietnam* (Embassy of Vietnam, Washington, D.C.), Feb. 21, 1958, p. 8.
[59] Fall, "South Viet-Nam's Internal Problems," p. 257.
[60] *Gazette,* Jan. 25, 1956.

penditures were allowed. Since the sum was allotted on the basis of the number of voters in each district and was equally distributed among all the candidates, those running in heavily contested districts, notably Saigon, were penalized. The committees also distributed the posters, pamphlets, and handouts for the candidate, thus permitting prior screening of their contents. Newspaper space was given predominantly to government-favored candidates.

Refusing to run against such stacked odds, five opposition parties, which represented the sects and certain intellectuals, boycotted the elections and deplored the lack of campaign freedom.[61] The Communists were, of course, forbidden to enter the race. In view of the careful pruning of the list of candidates and the narrowly circumscribed area for maneuvering, it is not surprising that the campaign was generally bereft of substantive issues and of substantial interest.

In fact the government campaign to "get out the vote" far overshadowed the efforts of individual candidates. Saigon was covered with posters, banners, handbills, pictures, and slogans all exhorting the population to participate in the voting.[62] Loud-speakers blaring speeches and song rolled down the streets at all hours of the day and even into the night. Government officials and members of various social and popular groups paid door-to-door visits to explain the duties of citizens and distribute tracts, primarily in Saigon but also in the provincial towns.[63] Officials and teachers were granted a holiday the day before the election, and, according to government sources, more than 10,000 members of the League of Revolutionary Civil Servants and about 2,000 students guarded the polling areas on the night before the election.[64]

Despite predictions of widespread sabotage efforts by the Communists, election day was generally calm and balloting orderly, although some instances of violence were reported in various provinces, especially in the south.[65] Police arrests of "Viet Minh sympathizers" a short time prior to election day may account in part for Communist

[61] *Times of Vietnam*, Feb. 4, 1956.

[62] A *Times of Vietnam* editorial, Feb. 25, 1956, complained about "last week's wave of posters which were plastered about in bewildering profusion and with a total disrespect for private property and the beauty of our city."

[63] *Gazette*, Feb. 22, 1956.

[64] *Vietnam Presse Spéciale*, no. 758, March 5, 1956.

[65] Here ballot boxes were stolen, grenades thrown near voting booths, and polling officials assassinated (*Times of Vietnam*, March 10, 1956; see also *NRU*, March 5, 1956 [*Troi Nam, Le Song, Thoi Cuoc*]).

failure to disrupt the election, but it is doubtful that an all-out effort was made. Government irregularities during and after the election also occurred. In some districts the number of ballots cast exceeded the resident populations. Military voting in blocs helped to swing a number of unsure districts. Candidates considered politically un-reliable by the government were forced to withdraw from the cam-paign at the last moment. In certain areas ballots for different candidates were marked in different-colored ink that showed through the thin envelope in which they were placed, thus allowing identifica-tion of the voter's choice.

Despite the absence of completely free elections, the large turnout of voters [66] and the fact that nation-wide elections could be held with so little disruption indicate that the government does enjoy some popular support. Although the results do not serve as a fair appraisal of government strength, a large protest vote could have been registered in certain districts in Saigon, where government personalities were running in reasonably free elections. That this did not occur and that a small number of truly independent candidates were elected give evidence of meaningful elections, at least in a limited sense. There is no reason to believe that the government would have lost in a com-pletely free election. It would not have won such a complete victory, but a smaller victory under such conditions might perhaps have been a greater triumph.

[66] They were subject, however, to some psychological intimidation, since census cards were stamped at polling booths to ensure that an individual voted only once, thus providing a way for checking afterward on who failed to vote.

· XX ·

South Vietnam:

Major Problems

THE Republic of Vietnam is a new state, and its government has been faced with a number of complex and trying problems, not all of them within its powers to solve. Although the government has in many instances employed questionable practices in consolidating its political position, it has nevertheless brought to South Vietnam a measure of stability and security, which most observers would have thought impossible a few years ago. Yet serious problems remain, and in many respects the ultimate fate of South Vietnam—whether it achieves political and economic viability—rests on their resolution.

The Economy

The bustling streets and well-stocked shops of South Vietnam's capital and only major city, Saigon, obscure the seriousness of the nation's economic difficulties, the more immediate of which derive chiefly from noneconomic factors. In South Vietnam, a nation born of civil war and confronted with the ever-present threat of political subversion and the possibility of renewed hostilities, questions of economic policy have, of necessity, been subordinated to political and military considerations. Decisions involving major financial commitments such as refugee resettlement and maintenance of a large military establishment were made without regard to whether the economy could support such undertakings, with the inevitable result that South Vietnam is today living beyond its means. This fact is apparent in the difference between total goods and services produced in South Vietnam and total goods and services consumed. The disparity is equivalent to South Vietnam's excess of imports over exports.[1]

As of 1954 the South has faced three critical demands necessitating heavy government expenditures: the reception and resettlement of refugees from North Vietnam, reconstruction of the nation's communication system, and the maintenance and training of a large army. Despite low production levels it is possible that the government could have met a larger portion of its expenditures from domestic resources were tax collection facilities at all adequate. As a result of poor organization, graft, and the shortage of trained personnel, however, tax revenue comprises only a fraction of total assessments. Even were collection facilities more adequate, for political reasons it is still questionable whether the government could greatly increase tax revenue. Because of the pattern of income distribution—the overwhelming majority of the population have only marginal incomes—most additional revenue would have to come from the wealthy elite, a group upon which the government is politically dependent and one which it is in a poor position to antagonize further.

Given the American commitment to South Vietnam, Ngo Dinh Diem has turned to the United States for extensive economic aid,[2] most of which goes to meet the government's budget deficit.[3] A brief glance

[1] In 1955 the market value of gross domestic production of goods and services was approximately 8.5 per cent less than gross expenditures for goods and services during the same period. The 8.5 per cent difference reflects 6,602 million piastres of imports not covered by exports. (Figures are derived from ECAFE, *Economic Survey of Asia and the Far East, 1957* [Bangkok: United Nations, 1958], Table "O.") In 1956 exports covered 27 per cent of imports. In 1957 the gap widened: only 21 per cent of imports were covered by exports. See Bernard B. Fall, "Will South Vietnam Be Next"? *Nation,* CLXXXI (May 31, 1958), 492.

[2] In 1955 American aid to Vietnam totaled $85.5 million; in 1956, $193.7 million; and in 1957, $261.2 million (ECAFE, *op. cit., 1957,* p. 181). For statistical details of American aid to Vietnam see United States Operations Mission to Vietnam, *Annual Reports,* and International Co-operation Administration, *Operations Reports.*

[3] In order to avoid excessive inflation which would result if aid funds were provided without a commensurate increase in consumer goods, American budget support is made available through an arrangement whereby the Vietnamese government "sells" the foreign exchange it receives from the United States to Vietnamese importers in exchange for local currency. The foreign exchange is then used to import consumer goods, and the government applies its local currency

at Table 2 will indicate the precarious financial position of the Vietnamese government and the reason why foreign aid is necessary.[4]

Table 2. Government revenue and expenditure (estimates); in millions of piastres

Year	Total revenue	Total expenditure	Budgetary deficit
1954	5,470	16,954	11,484
1955	5,122	15,697	10,575
1956	7,251	12,471	5,220
1957	8,461	14,160	5,699
1958	8,701	14,375	5,674

Source: Economic Commission for Asia and the Far East, *Economic Survey of
Asia and the Far East, 1957* (Bangkok: United Nations, 1958).

The way in which the exigencies of the government's political and
military position vis-à-vis North Vietnam and opposition elements in
the South impinge on the nation's economy is reflected in Table 3.
Over the past three years the cost of maintaining the army has alone
exceeded the total income from foreign aid.

Table 3. Government expenditures and receipts (estimates); in billions of piastres

	1955		1956		1957	
	Amount	Per cent	Amount	Per cent	Amount	Per cent
Government expenditures						
Defense	7.1	66.3	6.9	55.2	6.6	46.5
Development	1.0	9.3	1.8	14.4	2.4	16.9
Administration	2.6	24.4	3.8	30.4	5.2	36.6
Total	10.7	100.0	12.5	100.0	14.2	100.0
Government receipts						
Government revenue	7.2	67.3	7.3	58.4	8.5	59.9
Foreign aid	3.8	35.5	5.6	44.8	5.7	40.1
Changes in cash balance	—.3	—2.8	—.4	—3.2	—	—
Total	10.7	100.0	12.5	100.0	14.2	100.0

Source: ECAFE, *Economic Survey of Asia and the Far East, 1957.*

proceeds against the budget deficit. Although considerable criticism has been
leveled at the commercial imports program for its emphasis on relatively unpro-
ductive or luxury commodities in lieu of capital goods which would strengthen the
nation's economy, it nonetheless achieves its major purpose, that of balancing increased purchasing power with additional consumer goods, while making additional funds available to the government.

[4] The legal rate of exchange is 35 piastres to one dollar. On the "free market" a
dollar is worth approximately 75 piastres.

Because American aid is on a year-to-year basis, its quantity depends, in part, on domestic considerations in the United States, and its long-term continuation is uncertain.[5] One of the more pressing tasks facing the Diem government, therefore, is to effect a reduction in its present overwhelming dependence on foreign aid. The high level of government expenditure is dictated by political and military considerations, and it would appear that the resolution of Vietnam's "foreign aid dilemma" is dependent on increasing government revenue rather than decreasing expenditure. Although reorganizing the tax structure and increasing the efficiency of revenue collection would help to some extent, an over-all solution to the problem of government finance depends on increasing national production and thereby broadening the tax base to the point where government expenditures can be financed from internal resources.

Increased production is the key not only to reducing Southern dependence on American aid, but also to the long-range problem of economic development. This is a critical area of competition between the Diem government and the Communists; in which direction Southern loyalties eventually swing will depend in large measure on whether the general population comes to identify its economic well-being with the present government or with the Communist program. The outcome of this struggle ultimately hinges on Diem's ability to elicit support, especially from the peasantry, by increasing production and translating the increases into higher standards of living.

South Vietnam's natural-resource base is capable of supporting relatively large increases in national output. Although, with the exception of modest coal reserves,[6] partition left the South bereft of mineral resources, the country is richly endowed with fertile land suitable to both rice and dry crops. The quality and training of South Vietnam's labor force and managerial class, however, presents a serious obstacle to economic development, especially in the industrial

[5] The uncertainty of American funds inhibits long-range planning even though new appropriations are reasonably certain to be forthcoming.

[6] The South imports approximately 120,000 tons of coal annually from the United States and Australia. Partial relief may come from a small government-owned coal mine located at Nong Son, just south of the 17th parallel, which at present produces about 7,200 tons annually but at such high unit cost that for many years the mine was abandoned. Economic and technical assistance from France and the United States should increase output to about 24,000 tons annually at reduced cost. Expanded production at Nong Son will still only partly compensate for the loss of northern resources.

sector of the economy. The government, aware of the problem, has organized vocational schools and is improving general educational standards, but in the long run most skills will have to develop along with, and through, the industrial sector. One additional training ground may be the military. Under American auspices the Vietnamese army is developing into a well-trained partially mechanized corps, and it is possible that many ex-soldiers may find their army-developed skills in demand on the civilian labor market.

Probably the most serious long-range problem affecting economic development is that of securing adequate quantities of investment capital. Were the government of South Vietnam administratively equipped to undertake centrally planned and executed development programs, problems of domestic capital formation would not be unlike those of increasing government revenue. Investment capital could be mobilized by means of forced saving (taxation) to the extent allowed by administrative facilities, the size and breadth of the tax base, and, of course, political considerations. It seems doubtful, however, that the Vietnamese government will itself enter into large-scale economic development at least in the near future, so that the bulk of Vietnam's expansion will have to come from the private sector.

Domestic capital formation in the private sector is limited by three factors: the absence of adequate banking facilities where savings can be mobilized for investment purposes; the high-profit quick-return psychology of Vietnamese businessmen; [7] and the pattern of income distribution wherein most available capital is concentrated in the hands of a relatively few persons usually more interested in maintaining their relatively luxurious levels of personal consumption than in national economic development. The shortage of domestic capital, intensified by heavy withdrawals of French investments at the end of the colonial era, has forced Vietnam to look abroad for investment in domestic enterprises. Unfortunately there is widespread competition for international developmental capital, and in relative terms the Vietnamese situation offers few incentives as compared with more stable and economically promising countries. It therefore seems unlikely that much new foreign capital will be forthcoming until political conditions within South Vietnam as well as relations with the North stabilize to

[7] Returns on investment in land and commerce have traditionally been so high that only very lucrative industrial investments can equal them. The concept of what constitutes a fair return tends to make the cost of investment capital prohibitively high for undertakings in which immediate returns cannot be expected.

the point where investment will seem relatively secure to the foreign investor.

Another obstacle to economic development is the South's basically two-crop economy, one which leaves the country particularly vulnerable to fluctuations in the international market for rice and rubber. In addition the lack of agricultural diversification and the inadequacy of food-processing industries place South Vietnam in the anomalous position of spending scarce foreign currency to import food products which might easily be produced domestically. Still another problem facing the nation is the low yield of both rice and rubber which, combined with the overvaluation of the piastre, leaves the Vietnamese exporter at a competitive disadvantage in international trade. Finally, there is the problem of landlordism.

Because of its political importance agrarian reform has received considerable attention. The government's approach has been three-fold. A decree was issued in January 1955 fixing minimum rents at between 15 per cent and 25 per cent of the total crop, the exact amount depending on the productivity of the land and on "improvements" such as buildings and livestock. Included was a provision calling for contracts between tenants and landlords to enforce the new regulation. By 1957 over 50 per cent of the tenant farmers had signed contracts embodying the new legal rent scale even though landlords evidenced their opposition by delaying tactics. The former Minister of Agrarian Reform is a case in point; a large landowner himself, he was one of the slowest to comply with the law which it was his responsibility to administer.[8]

A second measure limited absentee landholdings to 100 hectares (247 acres) with an additional 30 hectares allowed if the owner is himself engaged in cultivation. The effect of the ordinance, if and when fully implemented, will be to break up the relatively few large landholdings but leave the basic landlord-tenant relationship intact throughout most of the South.[9]

[8] David Wurfel, "Agrarian Reform in the Republic of Vietnam," *Far Eastern Survey*, XXVI (June 1957), 83.

[9] The government's philosophy with regard to land ownership is generally considered fairly conservative. "Agrarian reform does not mean spoliation. It operates with justice and equality, and with respect for private property. The Department of Agrarian Reform, created in 1955, has bound itself to respect the concept of private property. The concept of private holdings is, further, expressly included in the Constitution of the Republic of Viet-Nam" (*News from Viet-Nam*, IV [July 4, 1958]).

A third measure was the establishment of an agricultural credit program. Its primary purpose is to stimulate agricultural production. This is evident in the priorities for consideration of loan requests: agricultural co-operatives, the returning of fallow land to cultivation, and industrial crops.[10] By mid-1957 agricultural credit agencies had extended loans totaling over 200 million piastres.[11]

As to what course the Vietnamese economy will follow in the future and with what degree of government participation, little information is available. In 1957 the government announced a five-year plan with "two major objectives: *first*, to establish the basic elements for an independent national economy and *second*, to initiate projects directed toward the healthy development and growth of this economy." [12] Priority is given to agricultural development,[13] with only 9.1 per cent of the total planned public expenditure going for manufacturing and mining.[14] Crop diversification to reduce dependence on rice and rubber exports is a central item in the program. The plan as outlined will also be concerned with public works and social welfare.

Minority Problems

Of the various minority groups resident in South Vietnam only the Chinese and the mountain tribes constitute anything of a problem. The Chinese first arrived in the south in the late seventeenth century and have since occupied a strategic position in the Vietnamese economy. Until recently the Chinese controlled most of the country's commercial activity and as a result of a series of increasingly advantageous international agreements [15] have enjoyed special political and economic privileges which in the years after 1946 were substantially the same as those of French nationals. It was therefore to be expected that the new government of South Vietnam would even-

[10] *News from Viet-Nam*, III (June 14, 1957).

[11] ECAFE, *op. cit., 1957*, p. 175. The magnitude of this figure may be somewhat misleading in that much of it has gone for emergency needs in refugee resettlement and for the purchase of livestock. It does, however, indicate the importance which the government places on raising agricultural production.

[12] *News from Viet-Nam*, III (July 12, 1957).

[13] In comparisan with agriculture, the industrial sector of the economy has received scant attention. Aware of the deficiency in power resources—a must for industrial expansion—the government proposes to build two modest hyproelectric plants, but beyond this little long-range planning is taking place.

[14] ECAFE, *op. cit., 1957*, p. 22.

[15] The last and most important agreement was that signed between France and Nationalist China in 1946 which led to the withdrawal of Chinese troops from northern Vietnam.

tually act to alter the status of the Chinese resident in the South. As a government publication put it, "such a large percentage of the population composed of resident aliens constituted a considerable infringement upon Vietnamese sovereignty, especially when that population virtually controlled the Vietnamese economy and showed its power to strangle it through speculatory measures." [16]

In August 1956 the government made Vietnamese citizenship mandatory for all Chinese born in Vietnam, and less than a month later it barred to all but Vietnamese citizens eleven important occupations including the rice trade and the operating of small retail shops. [17] The latter action was neither unexpected nor unprecedented. As the Vietnamese government has taken pains to point out, a number of countries, including Thailand, Indonesia, and the Philippines, have enacted regulations discriminating against the Chinese, some much more stringent. The retroactive requirement of Vietnamese citizenship, however, is unique; in other countries enacting similar legislation the individual Chinese has always been allowed choice of nationality.

In moving against the Chinese community the government acted from two motives: economic, to lessen Chinese control over the nation's economy, and political, to end the quasi-extraterritoriality enjoyed by the Chinese and bring them under government control. The possibility of a large body of resident foreign nationals identifying themselves politically with a Communist nation, especially China, posed a serious problem to South Vietnam. This concern for security was expressed by Ngo Dinh Diem when he stated that "with the Communist's persistent infiltration and incitement of Chinese to sabotage, the nationalization of Chinese is not only a favor [to the Chinese], but a strengthening of internal security." [18]

Chinese reaction to the new measures clearly showed the extent of their economic strength. Rice exports all but came to a halt, and the movement of goods within Vietnam was seriously disrupted. The affair extended beyond national boundaries when Chinese merchants in Hong Kong and Sinapore refused to handle Vietnamese rice ship-

[16] *News from Viet-Nam,* III (June 14, 1957).

[17] Bernard B. Fall, "Vietnam's Chinese Problem," *Far Eastern Survey,* XXVII (May 1958), 67. The eleven barred occupations are: fishmonger and butcher; retailer of products in common use; coal and firewood merchant; dealer in petroleum products; secondhand dealer; textile and silk merchants; scrap-metal dealer; grain dealer; transportation (e.g., taxicabs, buses, trucks, boats); rice milling and processing; commission agent.

[18] *Times of Vietnam,* Oct. 13, 1956, p. 2.

ments out of sympathy for their countrymen. Because of American aid the Vietnamese have been able to weather the economic storm; and, possessed of the administrative means to force at least outward compliance, the government has refused to reconsider the citizenship provision of the new regulations. The Chinese have recently softened their economic boycott if only because they too feel the pinch, and the government in turn has somewhat reduced its pressure on the Chinese community. No mutually acceptable solution to the question of Chinese nationality has yet been reached, however, and tension persists.

The mountain tribes of Vietnam also represent a problem, but here it is the Vietnamese who are economically the stronger. During the latter days of French rule when the Pays Montagnards du Sud (PMS), the highland region of the South, was a crown domain governed by French officials appointed by Bao Dai, the mountain tribes were afforded some measure of protection from exploitation by the Vietnamese. To be sure, under the French they provided cheap plantation labor and were required to work out taxes on private as well as public roads, but with these exceptions the mountain tribes were left pretty much alone. Now that the French have departed and the PMS has been integrated into the political structure of South Vietnam, the mountain tribes have an economic relationship with the Vietnamese analogous to that of the Vietnamese vis-à-vis the French during the early colonial period. A weaker and less well organized group, they are easily taken advantage of, especially in commercial transactions in which their lack of familiarity with contract arrangements and relative values leaves them open to all sorts of manipulation.

Education

Education facilities in Vietnam are extremely limited. Part of the problem is a direct result of the nation's underdeveloped economy, poor communications, and predominantly rural nature. As in most countries these factors tend to limit educational opportunities. A second explanation of present inadequate facilities lies in Vietnam's colonial past. Apart from the needs of the mandarinate, the only system of education which existed in traditional Vietnam was found in the commune,[19] and when French rule disrupted communal life, much of the traditional educational system was also destroyed. Although

[19] Le Quang Hong, "Compulsory Education in Vietnam," in *Compulsory Education in Cambodia, Laos, and Vietnam* (Paris: UNESCO, 1955), pp. 115–116.

the French subsequently developed some excellent facilities for higher education and still operate some *lycées* in South Vietnam, these were on a limited scale, and French support to primary education was wholly inadequate.

Since early 1955 the government of South Vietnam has devoted considerable attention to the problem of education. Because of the political importance of literacy it has placed particular emphasis on adult education, employing both Civic Action cadres and regular school personnel to combat illiteracy.[20] Enrollment in primary schools has jumped from approximately 360,000 in 1954 to about 723,000 to-day, and attendance in secondary schools has risen from 21,000 in 1954 to 41,000 at present.[21] Startling as these increases may seem, the number of children receiving formal instruction constitutes less than one-fifth of the school-age population, and education remains a basic national problem.

Public Administration

On assuming the position of president of the Council of Ministers in June 1954, Ngo Dinh Diem had yet to achieve control over the administrative organs he nominally headed. Both the quality of the bureaucracy and the organization of government administration were deficient, but because political survival depended on effective control over the government apparatus, Diem had to ensure the loyalty of the bureaucracy to his administration before he could act on these problems. The President eventually broke the political power of the bureaucracy and secured its tacit loyalty, but this was achieved to the detriment of developing an efficient administration with proper delegation of authority and smooth functioning in the lower echelons. Because it gave first priority to political considerations the government has only recently been able to devote serious attention to personnel and organizational problems.

Graft is not a new phenomenon in Vietnam, but with the general disorganization which followed upon partition, sudden real independence, and the flood of refugees, it grew to alarming proportions. Viet-

[20] The literacy campaign is a good example of the way in which the Southern regime has employed Communist experience and techniques in shaping its own propaganda program. The South now claims an 80 per cent adult literacy (*News from Viet-Nam*, IV [Aug. 29, 1958], 9). This is undoubtedly an exaggerated figure, but the very exaggeration is indicative of the importance the government places on literacy.

[21] *Ibid.*, pp. 4, 6.

namese daily newspapers are replete with references to scandals in public office, and in the year 1955 alone the Saigon press reported over a hundred cases of embezzlement of refugee funds.[22] The problem of actual graft is accentuated by the widespread belief in its universal practice.[23] The expectation of malfeasance in public office has become normative in South Vietnam with the result that informal sanctions are generally lacking. An official who makes a personal financial success of his office without getting caught is ofttimes looked upon with a degree of awe and approbation.

The government's program to combat malfeasance in public office has been inhibited by general public apathy, and its efforts to make regulatory agencies effective have been hampered by the lack of adequate personnel and conflicting lines of authority. Probably the most effective measures taken to date have been the use of informers, a carry-over from colonial days, and the fear of fines and imprisonment engendered by a number of well-publicized cases of corruption in which the sentences have been extremely harsh.

Primary responsibility for much of Vietnam's poor administrative organization devolves upon the nation's colonial heritage, but the present government must also be held partially to blame. Personalized autocratic rule, nepotism, favoritism, the lack of delegation of authority, and responsibility without authority are still problems under the present regime. With authority concentrated at the Presidency and in the few departments which enjoy Diem's confidence, decisions as to policy and its implementation are made by a few, sometimes poorly informed, persons. Information and recommendations seldom flow upward in the administrative hierarchy or from the local to the national level, so that little advantage is taken of the better understanding and technical competence often possessed by lower-level officials and local administrators. This contributes to low morale in the civil service, as does the not uncommon practice of bypassing regular administrative channels and appealing directly to the President or some highly placed official in order to obtain action.

Internal Security

After the Geneva Conference the Communists, as well as most of the world, expected that it would be only a matter of time, two years

[22] Roy Jumper, "The Communist Challenge in South Vietnam," *Far Eastern Survey*, XXV (Nov. 1956), 167.

[23] Roy Jumper, "Mandarin Bureaucracy and Politics in South Vietnam," *Pacific Affairs*, XXV (March 1957), 57.

at the most, before all of Vietnam would be under Viet Minh control. This expectation has not yet been realized, and, barring a decisive change in the international situation, it is unlikely that Vietnam will be unified under the Communists in the foreseeable future. Yet it should be realized that unification under these conditions remains the major goal of Ho Chi Minh's government and that Communist activities in the South continue to be oriented toward this end.

At present Communist strategy is twofold. On the diplomatic front the DRV is pressing for normalized trade relations between the two sections of Vietnam and reunification by means of national elections. At the same time the Communists are operating clandestinely in the South with the purpose of weakening and embarrassing the Diem government and strengthening their influence among the Southern population. It is this second area of activity which constitutes South Vietnam's internal security problem and to which extensive government countermeasures are directed.

The Communists continue to use force as a political weapon, and in recent months there has been a marked increase in the number of attacks on local leaders and government personnel.[24] The fear of reprisal is also thought to play an important role in the Communist program, especially in discouraging peasant co-operation in government programs—either measures against Communist penetration or the agrarian reform program. But, at least for the moment, the greatest threat to the South's security lies not in violence but in Communist propaganda which derides the Diem government as "puppets of the American imperialists" and endeavors to create dissension by appealing to different social groups—peasants, workers, unemployed, students, intellectuals, the Chinese, and tribal minorities—each in terms of how its particular status would benefit from the unification of Vietnam.

The government's response to Communist activities has concentrated on military and political action, in part bypassing the more basic, if less spectacular, area of economic reform.[25] Its anti-Communist campaign has been co-ordinated under the previously described Civic Action program, whose members have been a particular object of Communist attention.[26]

[24] Bernard B. Fall, "South Viet-Nam's Internal Problems," *Pacific Affairs*, XXXI (Sept. 1958), 257–258.

[25] This perhaps results from the fact that political and military measures directed against the Communists are unlikely to antagonize politically important vested interests as would thoroughgoing economic reform.

[26] The Communists have been assassinating government officials in South Vietnam

Foreign Relations and Defense

Since the inception of South Vietnam its foreign policy has been conditioned by a single dominant consideration—its position vis-à-vis the Democratic Republic of Vietnam and the Communist world, especially China. Government foreign policy statements have been among the most outspoken in their opposition to communism and in their support of the West.

South Vietnam's relationship to the United States is of such an intimate nature as almost to preclude the use of the term foreign relations. The South owes its territorial existence to the powers which convened in Geneva in the spring of 1954, but it was primarily American support for Diem that ensured his continuance as President in late 1954 and early 1955, and it was largely a result of American pressure that the French withdrew when they did. It is the United States and the protective umbrella thrown over South Vietnam by SEATO, of which the United States is militarily the most powerful member, that ensures South Vietnam's sovereignty in the face of Communist pressure. In addition it is American economic aid which today supports the Vietnamese economy. This dependence on the United States, although considered by some Vietnamese to impinge on the nation's sovereignty, is, for at least the present, a necessary condition for the continued existence of the Republic of Vietnam.

Now that the French have accepted the loss of their former colony, South Vietnamese relations with France are surprisingly good in view of the history of French involvement in the area. France continues to provide limited economic and technical assistance to Vietnam and vies with the United States as the South's principal trade partner.

Primarily through the personal efforts of President Diem, South Vietnam has gained wide acceptance as an independent member of the community of nations. Cordial relations have been established not only with such Western-oriented Asian countries as the Philippines and Thailand, but with such "neutral" nations as India and Burma as well. Apart from the Communist bloc, with which contact has been assiduously avoided, South Vietnam's relations with only two countries. Nationalist China and Cambodia, can in any way be considered strained. In the case of Nationalist China the issue is that of the citizenship of ethnic Chinese born in Vietnam. The Nationalist government

---

at a rate of about twenty-eight a month (James Reston, "Summit Talk Outlook," *New York Times,* June 3, 1958).

has supported the Chinese community in its contention that the Vietnamese government's action has been unfair and unjustified by precedent in international law. The United States has attempted to arbitrate the dispute, but since it is closely allied with both countries, the American government has found following a middle course an exacting proposition of little avail.

Relations with Cambodia are more of a problem. For centuries Vietnam and Cambodia were periodic antagonists, but of recent years their traditional hostility has been increased by difficulties over the transit of goods from Saigon or up the Mekong River to Cambodia and by disputes over the exact location of the poorly defined border between the two countries. Political differences have also created problems. The Vietnamese accuse the Cambodians of "harboring wanted criminals," and the Cambodians reply that they are providing "political asylum."

The South Vietnamese army of 150,000 men is probably quite capable of meeting any domestic military contingency, but it is patently inadequate to protect the nation against the reported 350,000-man army north of the 17th parallel. The defense of South Vietnam is, therefore, actually more an international than a domestic problem; any military action between North and South Vietnam would undoubtedly involve major powers on both sides of the Cold War, particularly the United States and Communist China, thus threatening world peace.

· XXI ·

North Vietnam

THE government of the Democratic Republic of Vietnam (DRV), the only Communist regime in Southeast Asia, differs markedly from those of other countries in this area.[1] Communist Party control of the governing process and of social and economic activities in the DRV can most readily be compared to the system of control established by the Communist parties in China and the Soviet Union.

The general population of North Vietnam does not necessarily share the official commitment to Communist values, but it gave strong and sustained nationalist support to the DRV in its opposition to the French. Under the aegis of the DRV, the revolutionary war began in the north, and here it was victorious. Although the issue of anti-colonialism had significance throughout Vietnam and indeed served as a unifying bond for diverse groups in all parts of the country, the actual burdens of war were borne most heavily by the northerners.

---

[1] It should be remembered that existing international tension has prevented most Westerners from obtaining access to this area, and those who do are rigidly circumscribed in activity. The Canadian, Indian, and Polish members of the International Control Commission shuttle between the North and the South, but their efforts are solely directed toward implementing the provisions of the Geneva accord of 1954. Therefore data on the North must primarily be culled from radio and news broadcasts emanating from Hanoi, Peking, and Moscow, and information is thereby fragmentary and apt to be tendentious.

They tended to feel closely involved in the struggle and to identify their national consciousness with loyalty to the northern DRV regime as the only force capable of winning independence from the French. As in the rest of Southeast Asia, nationalism was the ideology which gained support for the revolutionary government, and the residue of wartime patriotism is still important in North Vietnam despite the peace settlement in 1954. An additional basis for cohesion and loyalty exists in the demonstrated ability of the DRV to meet many of the needs of a large proportion of its people and to establish a viable political and economic regime. Dissatisfaction with the repressive measures of its police state has, however, already been manifested. And should the DRV be forced to champion causes demanded by the Communist bloc which run counter to the aspirations of Vietnamese nationalism, then communism, stripped of its anticolonial trappings, may be less effective in maintaining popular acceptance of the DRV.

Land and People

The Vietnamese, who comprise about 85 per cent of North Vietnam's total population, inhabit the lowland areas, primarily in the fertile Red River delta, whereas tribal minorities—the Thai, Meo, Muong, Nung, Tho, and others—are generally confined to the mountain areas. Most of the overseas Chinese in Vietnam originally settled in the South or fled from the North at the time of partition.

Rice is the main crop of North Vietnam. This has traditionally been a deficit food area, but with a good harvest in 1957 the DRV was able to produce enough rice for its own needs and to export 14,000 tons to India and 25,000 tons to Indonesia.[2] The mountainous hinterland is generally unsuitable for rice cultivation, although it is rich in other natural resources. Since 1955 the DRV has commanded an excellent seaport at Haiphong. Hanoi, with its population of about half a million, is now the capital of the DRV.

North Vietnam's most important industrial resource is coal. The anthracite mines of Hon Gay, northeast of Haiphong, constitute the major coal basin of all Southeast Asia. The French dismantled much of the machinery before they left, but production has been resumed with new Soviet equipment, though output as yet falls short of the 1938 level. Other mineral resources found in the North include tin, tungsten, chromium, and phosphates.

[2] ECAFE, *Economic Survey of Asia and the Far East, 1957* (Bangkok: United Nations, 1958), p. 250.

Social Structure

Like other People's Democracies, the DRV has attempted to deal with social and cultural issues in the North in accordance with Marxist-Leninist teachings and to remold the social structure in terms of the theory of class conflict. Theoretically the workers constitute the most important group in society, but because of the low level of industrial development there is not a large, politically aware proletarian class in the North. About 400,000 people are presently working in mines, plants, railroads, construction, and other industrial areas. Since the 1956 agrarian reform revolts, which pointed up the "unreliable" nature of the peasantry, the DRV has emphasized the increasingly important role of the workers and has put forth the motto "Reliance on the workers." A new trade union law, promulgated on November 5, 1957, defines the rights and duties of trade union organizations. It officially recognizes "the leading role of the working class with respect to the people's democratic administration." [3] As the DRV increases the scope of its industrialization program and the workers become numerically more significant and technically more skilled, labor can be expected to be more active in the social and political spheres.

Because of their numerical predominance the peasants necessarily provide the basis of any social reconstruction in Vietnam. The DRV has attempted to impose an arbitrary classification of rural society according to the size of landholdings [4] and has stimulated class consciousness among poorer peasants and peasant laborers in the course of implementing the land redistribution measures. Although measures against landlords were undoubtedly stringent, nothing like the mass liquidations in China and Russia have occurred in North Vietnam. This can be explained in part because there was no sizable class of large landlords and also because many landlords fled south during partition. The poorer villager who received his land from the land distribution program thus gained a vested interest in the continued existence of the DRV regime. The agrarian revolts of 1956 indicate,

[3] *Voice of Vietnam*, Hanoi radio, Dec. 17, 1957.

[4] Bernard B. Fall, *The Viet-Minh Regime* (rev. ed.; New York: Institute of Pacific Relations, 1956), Appendix IV, "Viet Minh Population Decree," pp. 172–178. The classification decree divides rural society into five classes: landlord, rich farmer, middle-class peasant, poor peasant, and agricultural worker (predominantly landless). Detailed explanations are provided for determining social categories, including a section devoted to children and students and another to adoption and marriage relationships.

however, that peasant satisfaction over the positive results of this program was tempered by reaction against the repressive measures employed while carrying it out. With the completion of the land reform program, economic differences among the peasantry have been greatly reduced, and the vestigial hold of the landlords on village politics has been eliminated.[5]

The DRV, following the Chinese Communist example, has recognized that the "capitalist" classes, the petty bourgeoisie and the national bourgeoisie, have a role to play. But the small traders have been so heavily taxed that many were forced out of business, and those remaining must compete with government co-operative stores selling Chinese and Russian goods at comparatively low prices.[6] Indications are that the large-scale "nationalist" bourgeoisie will be tolerated for a limited time, so long as its economic functions are deemed useful, but will eventually disappear as the state-owned enterprises squeeze out private industry.

As far as the intellectuals are concerned, the DRV, following Communist dogma, emphasizes that "one should NOT consider them as a special class. One should take into account the family from which they originate when it comes to classify them."[7] After many intellectuals had shown dissatisfaction with the repressive measures of the regime in the fall of 1956, efforts were made to improve their relations with the government. The Workers Party in the summer of 1957 issued a policy statement recognizing that "the intellectuals are a precious capital of the nation" and promising to do "all in its power to create conditions for them to work and study and develop their abilities to serve the fatherland and the people more and more effectively."[8]

Despite the rigidity of this formalized class structure, possibilities for upward social mobility are probably greater in the North than in the South. The criteria of status under the DRV differ more drastically from prewar Vietnam, where wealth, family background, and education formed the primary assets for achieving political and social power. Although education is undoubtedly still an important factor for attaining certain high-level positions, revolutionary activities and proved

[5] B[rian] C[rozier], "Indochina: The Unfinished Struggle," *World Today*, XII (Jan. 1956), 24.

[6] "Problems of the Viet Minh," *Economist*, CLXXVII (Oct. 29, 1955), 395.

[7] Fall, *The Viet-Minh Regime*, p. 177.

[8] *Vietnam News Agency* (*VNA*), Hanoi radio, Aug. 29, 1957; quoted in the Workers Party newspaper *Nhan Dan* [The People].

loyalty to the regime are probably equally important qualifications, whereas a background of wealth and aristocratic family association is presumably a liability.

The Political Process

In North Vietnam the governing process operates within a complex set of quasi-legal and extralegal government forms linked only peripherally with the political system created by the constitution of 1946. The constitution was written at a time when the DRV entertained hopes for Western, particularly American, aid and support in maintaining its independent status. It was of utmost importance, therefore, that the DRV publicize its adherence to the forms and practices of Western democracy, and this was the role which the constitution was written to fulfill. The DRV cited the demands of the wartime situation under which it functioned for nearly eight years as the excuse for circumventing many of the constitution's requirements.

FORMAL STRUCTURE OF GOVERNMENT

The constitution, adopted by the newly elected National Assembly in November 1946, provides for a unicameral legislature (a "People's Parliament"), a President, and a cabinet form of government. The formal structure of government in North Vietnam today actually consists of three major organs, the presidency, the cabinet (Council of Ministers), and the Permanent Committee of the National Assembly, which operate as three concentric circles of power joined together through an "interlocking directorate" of party leadership. The constitution vested executive authority in a President, a Vice-President, and a cabinet including a Prime Minister responsible for cabinet policy. The first government under the constitution, approved by the National Assembly on November 3, 1946, gave to Ho Chi Minh the positions of both President and Prime Minister, and not until 1955 were the two posts separated, with Pham Van Dong becoming Prime Minister.

According to the constitution the People's Parliament is "the body entrusted with supreme powers" (Article 22). Should the People's Parliament dissolve itself, with the consent of at least two-thirds of its members, a small Permanent Committee elected from their number by the deputies is authorized to assume the parliamentary functions until new elections are held (within two months after dissolution). The crucial grant of powers to the Permanent Committee is found in Article 35 which declares that "if the term of office of the People's

Parliament expires during such a crisis as time of war, the Permanent Committee is allowed to prolong their functions for an indefinite time." The National Assembly decided, in November 1946, not to transform itself into a People's Parliament because of the crisis conditions. Until 1956 it had been convened only occasionally to rubber-stamp government decisions—the first time being in 1953 to vote the agrarian reform legislation. Effective legislative powers were thus lodged with the Assembly's Permanent Committee and with the executive branch.[9] In the past two years the National Assembly has been more active in submitting legislation, and three new civil rights laws were passed by the sixth session of the National Assembly in January 1957. These laws guarantee freedom of assembly and association, corporal inviolability, and inviolability of residence and correspondence.[10] The Assembly also appointed a committee to revise the 1946 constitution. The government has announced that this new draft will be presented to the next session of the National Assembly for approval and then submitted to a referendum. Its provisions purportedly include the strengthening of the powers of the legislative branch, more explicit rights for women, and considerable clarification of the powers of the judiciary.[11]

The constitution authorizes the division of North Vietnam into provinces, districts, and villages. A law passed by the National Assembly at its eighth session in April 1958 regulates the organization of regional administration. It specifies that autonomous zones and cities will depend directly on the central administration; provinces, villages, and towns will have Administrative Committees and People's Councils. Districts will have only Administrative Committees. The People's Councils will be elected at the various levels by direct universal suffrage and are authorized to formulate policy on questions of local interest. These policies are to be executed by the Administrative Committee, upon approval of higher authorities. The Administrative Committee provides the channel for enforcing the laws of the state and for carrying out the instructions of higher-echelon Administrative Committees, as well as managing the local administrative machinery.[12] During the war the People's Councils had often been suspended, and

[9] Unless otherwise indicated, information concerning the constitution, local administration, and the judiciary is derived from Fall, *The Viet-Minh Regime.*

[10] *VNA*, Hanoi radio, Jan. 24, 1957.

[11] Bernard B. Fall, "Die Rechtslage in der Demokratischen Republik Viet-Nam," in *Ost-Europa Recht* (Stuttgart, West Germany), no. 1 (1958), pp. 198–211, *passim.*

[12] *Voice of Vietnam,* Hanoi radio, June 18, 1958.

the Administrative Committees had merged with unofficial "Resistance Committees" staffed by political officials appointed and controlled by the Viet Minh.[13] A presidential decree of September 1957 authorized elections for the new People's Councils at all levels.

The constitution makes no attempt to institute a judiciary independent in character or functions. In practice, as Bernard Fall points out, the Communist-dominated local Resistance Committees were instrumental in the appointment of judges at all levels of administration, and village Resistance Committees actually acted as courts themselves. In 1953 special "People's Land Reform Tribunals" were set up to try landlords under the new agrarian reform laws, and "the shift towards the use of the courts as a tool of executive policy was apparent throughout the whole judicial system." [14] These tribunals were abolished in 1956, and the DRV's judicial structure is now being revised.[15]

DYNAMICS OF GOVERNMENT

Led by experienced and disciplined Communists, the DRV is now both theoretically and practically a fully committed member of the Communist world. Its official ideology is Marxism-Leninism, and the governing process is shaped in part by doctrinal considerations and their practical ramifications. It must be remembered, however, that communism is not a widely shared system of values in North Vietnam, but rather provides a general manual of techniques and policy guides whose theoretical base is understood and interpreted by a few in the ruling elite. Mao Tse-tung's success in exploiting agrarian issues and his strategy and tactics in utilizing the peasant base during the long Chinese Civil War have provided a practical example for his southern neighbor.[16] From the Chinese Communists the DRV leadership learned how to exploit what has been termed the "potent and persuasive slogan" [17] of coalition government, including the formula of the "people's democratic dictatorship" representing an alliance of four classes, under the leadership of (and therefore controlled by) the working class, that is, the Communist Party.

[13] Fall, *The Viet-Minh Regime*, p. 28.   [14] *Ibid.*, p. 34.

[15] At the eighth session of the National Assembly the juridical system and the prosecution system were detached from the Ministry of Justice, and a high court and public prosecution board were set up under the direct leadership of the Council of Ministers (*VNA*, Hanoi radio, April 29, 1958).

[16] Z. H. Zoberi, "Lenin and the Freedom Movement in Vietnam," *Contemporary Review*, no. 188 (Oct. 1955), p. 269.

[17] Conrad Brandt, Benjamin Schwartz, and John K. Fairbank, *A Documentary History of Chinese Communism* (Cambridge, Mass.: Harvard University Press, 1952), p. 286.

Political coalitions. Until 1950 the DRV leadership placed primary emphasis on the coalition nature of its government. This was an attempt to gain the adherence of Vietnamese nationalists to its cause and foster the impression that it commanded a broad political mandate. The ability of the Communists first to dominate, and then overtly to control, this coalition was facilitated by French intransigence. No viable alternative was offered to the Vietnamese nationalists by the French even after the Bao Dai regime had been established in the South. The popular organization of the masses was the Viet Minh, which included under its aegis a variety of nationalist organizations and officially claimed some 8 million members.[18] Its influence extended throughout Vietnam by means of a network of People's Committees which formed a hierarchy of authority, linking the national organization to the smallest canton or village. The committees dominated the local administration, performing such duties as collecting taxes and acting upon instructions from above to determine the nature of the government in the local area.

The political effectiveness of the Viet Minh derived from its tightly disciplined, hard core of party organizers and leaders, mostly Communists, who directed policy in the Tong Bo, or Viet Minh Central Executive Committee. The Tong Bo is reputed to have been the real government of the DRV at that time, formulating both national and international policy and using the organs of government as an administrative channel.

Political changes were made in 1955 in response to the shifting international and domestic position of the DRV. With the establishment of the Diem regime in South Vietnam, the DRV found itself in competition with a nationalist government asserting that it offered real independence to the Vietnamese and demanding their allegiance. In order to appeal for peaceful national reunification and gain support in the South, the DRV was once more anxious to emphasize the divergent sources of its support. In September 1955 a new popular organization was formed—the "Fatherland Front" [19]—claiming to represent all segments of the population, all shades of political opinions, and sectional interests of both North and South Vietnam. The Fatherland Front called for reunification of Vietnam through appoint-

[18] J. R. Clementin, "The Nationalist Dilemma in Vietnam," *Pacific Affairs,* XXIII (Sept. 1950), 303–304.

[19] In 1951 the Viet Minh Front had been supposedly absorbed into a new Front, the Lien Viet, which was organized in 1946. The merger, however, was never completed. A Lien Viet Congress in Hanoi in September 1955 declared itself dissolved in order to become the Fatherland Front.

ment of a provisional central government by the separate legislatures
of North and South Vietnam, leaving these legislatures with some
autonomous power. In advocating a coalition government instead of
centralized reunification as called for by official DRV policy, the
Fatherland Front was mirroring Moscow's renunciation of military
means to achieve Vietnamese unity.[20] This scheme was calculated to
appeal to Southern nationalists fearful of Northern Communist domination.

The Workers Party. The Indochinese Communist Party, which supposedly had been dissolved in 1945, re-emerged in 1951 as the Vietnamese Workers Party (Dang Lao-Dong). It proclaimed its role to be
that of the vanguard in the guidance of Vietnam on the path toward
socialism and in the establishment of a People's Democracy which
would be allied with the Soviet Union, China, and other People's
Democracies. It called for the organization of government power
through a People's Democratic Dictatorship based, as in Mao's China,
on an alliance of four classes, under the leadership of the working class.
The platform of the Workers Party states:

The motive forces of the Viet-Nam revolution at present are the people comprising primarily the workers, peasants, petty bourgeoisie and national bourgeoisie, followed by the patriotic and progressive personages and landlords.
The basic mass of the people consists of the workers, peasants and intellectual workers (intellectual workers belong to various strata of the people,
mostly to the petty bourgeoisie). The leading class in the Viet-Nam revolution is the working class.[21]

It is, of course, not the workers as a whole who exercise political
control, but the Workers Party, actually a dictatorship of a very few
revolutionary leaders. The February 1951 Manifesto of the Workers
Party proclaims it to be a "powerful, clear-sighted, determined, pure
and thoroughly revolutionary political party" composed of "the most
revolutionary workers, peasants and intellectual workers." [22] Marxism-
Leninism is its theoretical foundation, democratic centralism its principle of organization.

The Workers Party structure is highly centralized, extending down
through the zone and region, province and village, to the basic unit of

[20] "Vietnam in the Hazard," *Economist*, CLXXX (July 21, 1956), 202.

[21] Allen B. Cole, ed., *Conflict in Indo-China and International Repercussions:
A Documentary History, 1945–1955* (Ithaca, N.Y.: Cornell University Press, 1956),
p. 99.

[22] *Ibid.*, p. 107.

organization, the cell group. Influence and control over the people are maintained by the party's trained propaganda agents (*can bo*) who live in the villages. Their task is not only to explain particular government policies but also to educate the people to "correct thinking," thus making them more receptive to government propaganda. In addition they keep the government informed as to public opinion and attitudes. The agent enters into the activities of all organized village groups, such as children's sections, women's leagues, and peasants' organizations, and works "to make the people feel the presence and the weight of the Central Government." [23] Foreign newspapermen who witnessed the DRV take-over of Hanoi in 1954 reported that as soon as order was established political indoctrination sessions were held twice daily for all residents, including lectures, self-criticism, and learning of DRV slogans, songs, and dances.[24]

Leadership. The outstanding factor contributing to the Communists' ability to capture control of the Vietnamese revolution has been the continuity and cohesion of their leadership. Some were "old guard" Communist companions of Ho Chi Minh in China and Russia who had spent many years in French prisons and received their training in the revolutionary turmoil of the 1920s and 1930s. These and some younger leaders became overt members of the Indochinese Communist Party when it was made legal under the Popular Front government in France. They helped form the Viet Minh in 1941 and are presently members of the Central Executive Committee of the Workers Party. Through their key positions in the administration they control not only party policy but the apparatus of government, the military, the foreign service, and the front organizations.[25]

The undisputed leader of the DRV, its President and mentor, is Ho Chi Minh, whom Philippe Devillers calls "one of the most remarkable leaders of the liberation movement in Asia." [26] The magic of his name and his almost legendary reputation derive from the belief of many Vietnamese that he personally combines most major virtues. A recognized scholar, his fluent command of several modern languages and his knowledge of both traditional Sino-Vietnamese and contemporary Western ideas appeal to Vietnamese respect for education. His

[23] *New York Times*, Jan. 5, 1955.
[24] *New York Times*, Oct. 21, 1954; article by Tillman Durdin.
[25] Fall, *The Viet-Minh Regime*, p. 44.
[26] Philippe Devillers, *Histoire du Viet-Nam* (rev. ed.; Paris: Editions du Seuil, 1952), pp. 182–183.

personal modesty and asceticism, expressed in simplicity of dress and manner, permit him to mix easily with the peasantry as well as officialdom. Ho Chi Minh's portrait is displayed in all homes and shops of the North, and everyone is taught to emulate Uncle Ho's "four virtues: industriousness, frugality, justice and integrity." [27] Most important for purposes of propaganda, "throughout Vietnam he symbolizes the struggle for independence," [28] a cause to which he devoted his life and which he brought to victory. His hold on the imagination and affection of his people emanates, not from appeal to highly charged emotionalism through oratorical ability, but from his roles as "Uncle Ho and Father Ho and President Ho, all in one" [29]—the traditional and familiar scholar, self-sacrificing patriot, and father of his country.

Other influential figures are as follows: Pham Van Dong, the present Prime Minister and Foreign Minister, comes from a family of high-ranking imperial mandarins and attended Chiang Kai-shek's Whampoa Academy for military and political training in China, returning to Vietnam in 1926 to organize cells for the Indochinese Communist Party.[30]

Truong Chinh (real name, Dang Xuan Khu) is reputed to be the theoretician of the Workers Party, of which he was secretary-general until the agrarian reform fiasco in 1956. He was a member of Ho's old Youth League [31] and secretary-general of the Marxist Study Group formed in 1946. He has recently been appointed a Deputy Prime Minister in the government.

Hoang Quoc Viet (real name, Ha Ba Cang), president and founder of the Vietnamese Confederation of Labor, was a charter member of the ICP in 1930 and secretary-general of the Viet Minh Front. He spent five years at the infamous island prison of Poulo Condore, together with Pham Van Dong and Truong Chinh, and was released, like them, in 1936 at the time of the Popular Front.[32]

Vo Nguyen Giap is commander in chief of the army and presently a Deputy Prime Minister and Minister of National Defense. He holds a French doctorate in political economy and was a former high school

[27] Joseph Starobin, *Eyewitness in Indochina* (New York: Cameron and Kahn, 1954), p. 115. Starobin, an American Communist writer who has since broken with the party, traveled in North Vietnam in 1953.
[28] W. Macmahon Ball, "Nationalism and Communism in Vietnam," *Far Eastern Survey*, XXI (Feb. 13, 1952), 26.
[29] Starobin, *op. cit.*, p. 116.   [30] Devillers, *op. cit.*, p. 70.
[31] Le Thanh Khoi, "The Democratic Republic of Vietnam, I," *Eastern World*, VIII (Dec. 1954), 18.
[32] Fall, *The Viet-Minh Regime*, p. 139.

teacher. He early joined the Vietnam Revolutionary Party and learned guerrilla tactics at the Chinese Communist headquarters in Yenan after his release from French prison.[33]

The army. The People's Army of the DRV, composed largely of peasant recruits, is generally regarded as one of the most loyal and reliable instruments of the government. Under Vo Nguyen Giap's guidance the army was developed into a cohesive, disciplined, thoroughly professional fighting corps. In addition to the regular army, regional forces and village militia, enjoying a large amount of local autonomy, were charged during the war with local defense and security. The army is viewed as a means of spreading propaganda among the peasantry, and basic political education for soldiers often preceded military training. The DRV army apparently learned much from Mao Tse-tung who, in his "Strategy of Revolutionary War in China" (1936), said that "we consider the people's army as an organism of propaganda and an instrument to organize the people's power." [34] Instruction in Marxist ideology is coupled with classes on Vietnamese history and daily self-criticism sessions during which the soldiers confess their fears and weaknesses.[35] The army is thoroughly permeated with political commissars, members of the Workers Party who share with the military commander responsibility for military as well as political decisions.[36] Joseph Starobin quotes an army commander as asserting that "the secret of our strength . . . is in our political training." The officer continues:

The units of the Lao Dong Party in each section, and in each company, are the backbone of the Army. They discuss every phase of the coming battles, and the political commissar is the key officer. Except in actual combat, his position is as important as the military commander's.[37]

The DRV has always taken great pains to emphasize to the soldiers the necessity of behaving well toward the peasants so that "the population like and esteem the fighting men." [38] Peasant support and aid was essential for the type of guerilla warfare the DRV waged so successfully, and many of the soldiers, especially in the local militias, were farmers by day.

Mass organizations and political groups. It is fruitless to discuss

[33] Ellen J. Hammer, *The Struggle for Indochina* (Stanford: Stanford University Press, 1954), p. 97.

[34] Quoted in Le Thanh Khoi, *op. cit.*, p. 19.

[35] *Ibid.*, p. 36.

[36] Fall, *The Viet-Minh Regime*, p. 83.

[37] Starobin, *op. cit.*, p. 82.

[38] Le Thanh Khoi, *op. cit.*, p. 36.

other political parties in the North as if they existed as independent entities, for they are under strict governmental control and emphasize their co-operation with the DRV. Both the Democratic Party, which united moderate elements among the business classes and Roman Catholics, and the Socialist Party, established in 1946 under Viet Minh auspices and claiming to represent left-wing intellectuals, have members in the National Assembly, and their party leaders hold important government posts. Neither represents a true opposition, however, or even a critical voice.

A multiplicity of organizations—representing women, peasants, labor, certain Roman Catholic and Buddhist groups, and youth—flourish in the North; but all facets of political, economic, and social activity are in fact guided and controlled by the DRV through the Workers Party. Workers, for example, are organized in a number of unions capped by the General Confederation of Labor. Instead of acting primarily as a bargaining agency for its members, the Confederation serves to carry out government economic policy. According to the 1957 trade union law, "the tasks of the trade union are to organize, educate and unite all manual and intellectual worker forces to serve as the mainstay of the people's democratic administration . . . and to be zealous and exemplary in carrying out all state laws and policies." [39]

Censorship and the Press

In general, freedom of speech and the press has been severely circumscribed by the DRV's policy of strict censorship of newspapers and control over all media of mass communication and propaganda. During the summer and fall of 1956 the government for a brief time eased this close supervision and permitted criticism to be voiced and published. There seem to have been two main reasons for this apparently sudden shift in policy. In February 1956 Nikita Khrushchev initiated a de-Stalinization program in Russia at the Twentieth Congress of the Soviet Communist Party, and in April 1956 Anastas Mikoyan, the Soviet First Deputy Premier, visited Hanoi, apparently to bring the new "line." Mao Tse-tung had also launched his slogan "Let a hundred flowers bloom; let a hundred schools of thought contend," which was designed to promote the flourishing of culture through the competition of conflicting ideologies, presumably on the assumption that Marxism would triumph in open discussion.[40]

[39] VNA, Nov. 20, 1957; see also Fall, *The Viet-Minh Regime*, p. 143.
[40] Harold C. Hinton, "China," in George McT. Kahin, ed., *Major Governments of Asia* (Ithaca, N.Y.: Cornell University Press, 1958), p. 91. Cf. "Ideological

From September until December 1956 a group of intellectuals in Hanoi published detailed criticisms of government policy in a fortnightly newspaper, *Nhan Van* [Humanism]. The paper brought out five issues before it was suppressed, and these were quickly sold out despite intimidation of those found buying, selling, or reading them.[41] Many articles were signed by prominent Vietnamese journalists and men of letters. Their complaints were aimed against "the complete absence of freedom, the lack of civil rights, of a constitution, and of any code of law, and against the high-handed and dictatorial behavior of senior officials." [42]

At the same time the DRV government moved to correct mistakes committed in implementation of the agrarian reform program. Both the Workers Party and the Fatherland Front called for purging those officials responsible for the errors, but affirmed the fundamentally correct nature of the land redistribution policy. Truong Chinh resigned as secretary-general of the Workers Party and was replaced by Ho Chi Minh; the dreaded Land Reform Tribunals were abolished, and a general shake-up of the bureaucracy was reported.[43] On November 3, 1956, the Council of Ministers, presided over by Ho Chi Minh, announced that those wrongly arrested or punished under this program would be released and compensated for injury. They pledged to broaden democracy and "strengthen the basis of . . . the democratic legal processes" by guaranteeing freedom of movement and speech and giving more power to "the organizations elected by the people" [44]—the People's Councils and Administrative Committees and the National Assembly.

---

struggle is not like other forms of struggle. Crude, coercive methods should not be used in this struggle, but only the method of painstaking reasoning" (speech by Mao Tse-tung, "On the Correct Handling of Contradictions among the People," Feb. 27, 1957, in "World Documents," *Current History,* XXXIII [1957], 362).

[41] P. J. H., "Revolt of the Intellectual in North Vietnam," *World Today,* XIII (June 1957), 252.

[42] *Ibid.,* p. 253. Pham Khoi, a respected scholar, decried inept bureaucratic stifling of freedom in arts and letters, in an article published in September 1956 in *Giai Pham Muoi Thu* [Autumn Masterpieces], one of the four newspapers carrying articles opposing government policy. He berated politicians who try to force writers and artists to comply with nonartistic standards and objected to the power of an editor to "correct or reject an article according to his own whim, without anything in the article deserving correction or rejection" (in Hoang Van Chi, ed., *The New Class in North Vietnam* [Saigon; Cong. Dan, 1956], p. 79). Khoi and several other writers were expelled from the writers' association in the summer of 1958.

[43] *VNA,* Hanoi radio, Oct. 29, 1956.

[44] *Voice of Vietnam,* Hanoi radio, Nov. 8, 1956.

Although there is no accurate way of gauging the extent to which the divergent opinions expressed by the intellectuals reflected public opinion, their denunciations of the DRV program of land reform, coupled with the government's self-criticism, clearly struck a responsive chord among the peasantry. In mid-November groups of peasants in the traditionally revolutionary and stanchly pro-Viet Minh province Nghe An demonstrated against the government, seized arms, and attacked soldiers and political agents sent to pacify them.[45] Disturbances spread to the neighboring provinces. Government reaction to these manifestations of peasant dissatisfaction was swift. It attemped to minimize the extent of these "revolts" and to blame them on a few "saboteurs. . . . [who] incited the people to attack the men of the People's Army. . . . [and] to oppose and manhandle the administrative personnel and People's Army personnel." [46]

While repressing these revolts the government also began to move against the opposition newspapers. At first it tried, by counterattack in the government-controlled press,[47] to restrain the contents of their articles without banning the newspapers themselves. Finally, on December 14, a decree was issued which effectively muzzled the press by specifying that newspapers were tools which must "serve the interests of the country and the people, safeguard the People's Democratic Regime, and support the Government of the Vietnam Democratic Republic." [48] *Nhan Van* has not appeared since, and in the summer of 1958 the executive committee of the writers' association applied disciplinary measures against some of its members belonging to the so-called "*Nhan Van—Giai Pham* saboteur group." [49]

The recent emphasis which the government has placed on rewriting the constitution, passing civil rights legislation, and strengthening the powers of the National Assembly indicates an attempt to revise the authoritarian and repressive methods which provoked the first public display of acknowledged and widespread discontent in the DRV. In addition a "mistakes correction" campaign has been initiated, to cor-

[45] *VNA*, Hanoi radio, Nov. 16, 1956.   [46] *Ibid.*, Nov. 25, 1956.

[47] A November 8 editorial in *Nhan Dan*, the official newspaper of the Workers Party, declared that "any act or word which is harmful to the people's unity, which aims to separate the People from the Party and Government, which hurts the reputation of our Regime and Party must be prohibited" (*Voice of Vietnam*, Hanoi radio, Nov. 8, 1956). An all-out attack on *Nhan Van* was published in *Nhan Dan* on December 10, presaging the censorship decree of December 14 (*VNA*, Hanoi radio, Dec. 14, 1956).

[48] *VNA*, Hanoi radio, Dec. 15, 1956.

[49] *Voice of Vietnam*, Hanoi radio, July 10, 1958.

rect the errors committed during the land reform program and to spur intensive ideological study among Workers Party members in rural areas, many of whom were responsible for the excesses committed in 1956. By the end of 1957 the campaign was reported nearing completion and had resulted in "repression of the reactionary and lawbreaking landlords" and in "the reinforcement of the organizations of the party, adminstrations and mass organizations from the provincial down to the village levels." [50]

Problems

An examination of four basic problems—agrarian reform, minorities, industrialization and foreign relations—can serve as case studies of government policy-making and implementation. The way in which the DRV meets and attempts to solve these problems often contrasts sharply with methods and solutions applied by other countries in Southeast Asia, although the problems themselves are by no means completely dissimilar.

AGRARIAN REFORM

In accordance with Communist techniques the cornerstone of the DRV agrarian reform program has been the redistribution of landholdings. At first the government moved cautiously, aiming at satisfying the peasant's land hunger while not alienating the landlord. In the general agrarian legislation of July 1949 only those lands belonging to "French colonialists and Vietnamese traitors" were expropriated. This law also attacked the major problems of excessive land rents and usury rates by reducing rents a flat 25 per cent, regulating moneylending, and guaranteeing certain rights of tenure to the tenant farmer. Preoccupied by the war, the government was lax in enforcing these measures; and landlords, still powerful in the village councils, evaded many of the regulations. By 1953 the government felt secure enough to begin its land reform program in earnest. The National Assembly was convened in December 1953 to approve a drastic program which was promulgated on December 19. In a speech to the National Assembly, Ho Chi Minh explained its purpose: to gain the support of the peasant by placing political and economic power in his hands and to stimulate the whole economy by increasing rice production.[51]

[50] Report to the seventh session of the National Assembly on September 10, 1957 (*VNA*, Hanoi radio, Sept. 11, 1957).

[51] Information for the above paragraph is derived chiefly from Le Thanh Khoi, "The Democratic Republic of Vietnam, II," *Eastern World*, IX (Jan. 1955), 20.

This program, strikingly similar to a previous Chinese Communist decree promulgated in June 1950, gives the farmer full title to the land taken from the landlord class. Those landlords deemed friendly to the Resistance were promised compensation in state bonds redeemable in ten years, but the extent of this compensation was not indicated. By mid-1956, when the land reform program was considered complete, it was reported that some 2 million acres had been redistributed among 2,200,000 peasant families.[52]

In order to implement its program the government, as in Communist China, classified the rural population into five categories: landlords, rich peasants, middle peasants, poor peasants, and landless peasants. Land passed primarily from the hands of landlords to poor and landless peasants. Political teams went to all villages to explain the program and begin the process whereby landlords were to be publicly denounced by peasant mobs, forced to confess their crimes, and then tried and meted out punishment by "People's Land Reform Tribunals." A Chinese Communist slogan originating with Sun Yat-sen, "Land to the tiller," was used during the campaign. Because of the fragmentation of landholdings, the margin between landowner, rich peasant, and middle peasant was often blurred, rendering the necessary classification both difficult and arbitrary. With inadequately trained political agents maintaining a rigid and overzealous interpretation of the laws, a kind of village terror ensued. Those classified as landlords sometimes received brutal treatment at the hands of the peasants and heavy penalties up to the death sentence from the Land Reform Tribunals. Protests against the handling of the agrarian reform program in the villages and discontent with the exorbitant agricultural tax demands and compulsory political meetings found expression in the fall of 1956 in the peasants' uprisings, described previously. A Workers Party communiqué admitted that "the criteria for distinguishing various classes in the rural areas were not well assimilated. . . . As a result, a number of poor or landless peasants themselves have been hit; many middle peasants were also affected, and rich peasants were regarded almost as landlords."[53] The Council of Ministers affirmed its policy of alliance with the rich peasant and promised to readjust land and yield estimates in order to lessen the tax burden.[54]

---

[52] Premier Pham Van Dong's report to the National Assembly on economic rehabilitation (*VNA*, Hanoi radio, April 17, 1958).

[53] *VNA*, Hanoi radio, Oct. 29, 1956.

[54] *Voice of Vietnam*, Hanoi radio, Nov. 8, 1956.

The DRV also attempted to stimulate rice production by encouraging increased co-operative activities among the peasants [55]—organizing mutual aid teams, co-operative stores, and marketing associations—and by rewarding individual efforts through "patriotic emulation" campaigns, which honor farmers and workers with outstanding achievements in production.[56] If the DRV has achieved self-sufficiency in rice production, as is claimed for 1957, then one of the traditional problems facing the North will have been eliminated. Although the government has been very cautious about the actual collectivization of farms, it can be assumed that, as in Communist China, the first step of land redistribution and organization of mutual aid teams will probably be followed by the establishment of communes. The aim of the DRV's three-year agrarian program, as set forth by the State Planning Board in 1958, emphasized collectivization of agriculture in order to increase food production.[57]

MINORITIES

In recent years the DRV has paid special attention to minorities, both religious and ethnic, in an attempt to bring them within the purview of state control. As in the South, the Roman Catholics are the most important religious minority in North Vietnam. Concentrated primarily in the two bishoprics of Phat Diem and Bui Chu, they had initially been strong supporters of the Resistance. In 1945 four Vietnamese bishops had appealed to Pope Pius XII for support in the struggle for independence. But the DRV policy of organizing all segments of the population into government-controlled organizations met opposition from some Roman Catholic clergy who were then persecuted and sometimes expelled from DRV territory. The semi-autonomous position of the bishoprics was destroyed when the French flew paratroopers into Phat Diem in 1949, utilizing it as a base to repell a Viet Minh advance.[58] With the flight of many Roman Catholics to the South after partition, the government has taken pains to em-

---

[55] Pham Van Dong's report to the National Assembly stated that there are now 169 supply and marketing co-operatives with a membership of over 1,200,000 and also 102,000 mutual aid teams comprising 710,000 peasant households (*VNA*, Hanoi radio, April 17, 1958).

[56] A report to the third congress of model manual and intellectual workers in 1958 by Hoang Quoc Viet, president of the General Confederation of Labor, claimed that 35,490 model workers have emerged in the past three years (*VNA*, Hanoi radio, May 13, 1958).

[57] *New York Times*, April 20, 1958.

[58] Hammer, *The Struggle for Indochina*, p. 276.

phasize a policy of freedom of religion. At Christmas 1954 Ho Chi
Minh sent a message to Vietnamese Roman Catholics insisting that the
"Government is sincere in its desire to respect religious freedom." [59]
During the agrarian reform disturbances, many of which took place in
predominantly Catholic areas, the government allowed the justness of
Catholic complaints, with Ho Chi Minh stating: "As for the Catholic
compatriots, the mistakes committed during the land reform have
also infringed upon their religious freedom. The Party, Government
and the Front clearly realize these mistakes and are determined to
correct them." [60] The government has nevertheless been trying to keep
religion within state-controlled limits by pressuring priests and laity
alike to join government-sponsored associations, such as the "National
Liaison Committee of Vietnamese Patriotic and Peace-loving Catholics." Even the law promulgated June 14, 1955, which formalized the
relationship between Church and state and guaranteed freedom of
conscience, contains the warning:

The Government will punish those who misuse religion to wreck the peace,
unity, independence and democracy of the country . . . to prevent the be-
lievers from exercising their civic rights, to encroach upon the freedom of
belief and the freedom of opinion of other persons or to carry out illegal
activities.[61]

Most of the ethnic minorities in North Vietnam occupy the strategically and economically important mountain areas bordering on
China. Thus the relations of these groups with the government has
been a matter of vital concern to the DRV, especially since the mountain peoples are traditionally anti-Vietnamese. Cadres have been sent
into the mountain regions on intensive propaganda campaigns. The
government, as early as 1945, had proclaimed equality for these
groups, and minorities have been given the right to vote and sit in
the National Assembly. In 1955, at a meeting of the seventh session
of the Workers Party, Ho Chi Minh outlined the policy of granting
autonomy to the Thai-Meo area in northwest Vietnam. The Thai-Meo
Autonomous Area, officially inaugurated in the spring of 1955,[62] covers
an area of approximately 19,500 square miles and is inhabited by
about 330,000 members of some twenty minority tribes.[63] It shares a

[59] *New York Times,* Dec. 31, 1954.   [60] *VNA,* Hanoi radio, Nov. 20, 1956.
[61] Quoted in *Daily News Release,* Hsinhua News Agency no. 1983, July 5, 1955
(Hanoi, July 4, 1955).
[62] *VNA,* Hanoi radio, May 7, 1955.
[63] Unless otherwise indicated, information for this paragraph is derived from
"Minorities under the Viet Minh," *Eastern World,* IX (Nov. 1955), 17–18.

common border with the "Thai Autonomous Region" in Yunnan, created by the Chinese Communist government in 1953. The region is described by the enabling decree as "an echelon of local administration placed under the direct control of the central government." Provincial administration is abolished, and local government consists of a twenty-four member Administrative Committee and a People's Council. The Administrative Committee was "elected" at a minorities congress on May 11, 1955, which also adopted a seven-point program giving as its primary tasks the development of agriculture and industry and the propagation of "belief in President Ho Chi Minh, the Lao Dong Party and the Democratic Republic of Vietnam." Although minorities are supposed to govern their own region, any laws enacted by their administrative organs must be consonant with those of the DRV and are subject to approval by the central government. The zone has charge of its own budget but must contribute to the central budget and maintain "financial unity" with the rest of the country. Thus autonomous regional administration, though ostensibly under local control, will provide the mechanism for channeling DRV propaganda and authority.

The government promised that similar autonomous regions would subsequently be set up for other ethnic minorities and in June 1956 announced the establishment of the Viet-Bac Autonomous Area. This area embraces five provinces covering more than 16,000 square miles, with nearly 800,000 inhabitants belonging to fifteen different ethnic groups, notably the Tho and Nung.[64] Its capital, Thai-Nguyen, was the wartime "resistance capital" of the DRV, and the Viet-Bac Area is situated to the southeast of the Thai-Meo Area. A third area, like the other two bordering on China in the north, was organized more recently. Situated between the two others, it is called Lao-Ha-Yen, for the three provinces it includes—Lao-Kay, Ha Giang, and Yen Bay.

Along with the ostensible grants of political autonomy to the mountain peoples, the DRV has made concessions in the cultural field. The Thai script has been standardized, and the Thai language is used in schools of the Thai Area. On March 19, 1955, a central normal school was organized for ethnic minorities, and the government has promised intensified educational training to enable the minorities to participate in the national community on an equal footing with the Vietnamese.

[64] *VNA*, Hanoi radio, June 17, 1956.

INDUSTRIALIZATION AND FOREIGN AID

There are four types of ownership in North Vietnam's economy—state ownership and co-operative, private, and joint state-private enterprises. The state-owned sector includes most large industrial enterprises.[65] Co-operatives operate primarily to purchase and distribute goods. Most of the North's consumer goods are supplied by small-scale peasant handicraft production.[66] The private economic sector (or capitalist sector) is under strict state supervision and control. Large-scale private industry accounted for only a small percentage of the total industrial output in 1956.[67] The three-year plan enunciated by the State Planning Board in 1958 places emphasis on increasing the scope of state enterprises, expanding industrial plants, and encouraging handicrafts.[68] Premier Pham Van Dong reported to the National Assembly that the DRV's foremost task was "to transform the economy along Socialist lines." [69]

Owing to lack of capital, of technicians, and of an industrial base, development of heavy industry has been slow. Most efforts thus far have been geared to creating light industry projects: these produced badly needed consumer goods and expanded urban employment.[70] The DRV, however, shares the general Communist faith in the value of heavy industry and has launched an ambitious industrialization program. The foreign aid which this program requires has been sought primarily from Russia and China. During the summer of 1955 Ho Chi Minh made an important trip to Peking and Moscow, requesting economic assistance, and took with him Truong Chinh, then secretary-general of the ruling Workers Party. He succeeded in obtaining a Chinese aid and friendship treaty promising about $326 million to build factories and provide technicians and equipment for restoring railroads, airfields, and roads.[71] Of special interest to China was the rehabilitation of the railway route from China to the Vietnamese port at Haiphong, rebuilt in 1956 and linked up to

[65] Theodore Shabad, "Economic Developments in North Vietnam," *Pacific Affairs,* XXXI (March 1958), 40.

[66] Premier Pham Van Dong's report to the National Assembly in 1958 related that privately owned small business and handicrafts supplied 58.8 per cent of North Vietnam's industrial output (*VNA*, Hanoi radio, April 17, 1958).

[67] Shabad, *op. cit.*, p. 41.   [68] *New York Times*, April 20, 1958.

[69] *Ibid.*, April 18, 1958; article by Tillman Durdin.

[70] Shabad, *op. cit.*, p. 39.

[71] "A New Manchuria?" *Fortune*, LVI (Aug. 1957), 80.

Kunming by the Chinese in 1957.[72] On the same trip Ho Chi Minh obtained promises of $100 million in aid from Russia to erect textile mills, develop tin and phosphate deposits, and equip a machine-tool manufacturing plant, which was opened in April 1958.

In order to import consumer goods which it cannot obtain from Russia or China, the DRV must earn foreign exchange. Foreign trade is carried on principally with Communist countries. In first place is China, and in second is Czechoslovakia, both of which supply industrial equipment and consumer goods in return for wood, tea, coffee, spices, and anthracite.[73] After partition, France attempted to maintain its tenuous economic position in the North by sending a mission there headed by Jean Sainteny, former French Commissioner for Tonkin and one of the few French officials who had had extensive dealings with the Viet Minh and had managed to retain their trust.[74] The agreement signed in 1954, however, proved disappointing to French businessmen who were asked to provide all the capital for renovating their factories in return for the dubious pleasure of making profits in "Ho Chi Minh piastres," which have little international value because of severe inflation. Most French economic interests in North Vietnam have since disappeared, leaving the DRV economy firmly tied to the Communist bloc.[75]

FOREIGN RELATIONS

North Vietnam's foreign relations reflect the general pattern of Communist satellite relationships with countries both within and outside the Communist orbit. Russia and China are the countries with the most influence on the DVR's domestic and foreign policy, and the United States plays the role of favorite "whipping boy," as leader of the "imperialist bloc" and prime supporter of Ngo Dinh Diem's regime in the South.

Because of its status as the only Communist regime in Southeast Asia, the DRV receives special attention and aid from Communist China and all other countries of the Soviet bloc. For the Vietnamese, haunted by the specter of a thousand years of Chinese domination,

[72] Shabad, *op. cit.*, p. 49. The Kunming-Haiphong railroad was formally inaugurated on March 1, 1958 (*VNA*, Hanoi radio, March 2, 1958).

[73] Shabad, *op. cit.*, pp. 52–53.

[74] *New York Times*, Oct. 13, 1954; article by Tillman Durdin.

[75] The DRV did sign a trade agreement with France exchanging anthracite, green tea, raw silk, and agricultural and forest products for machinery and textiles (ECAFE, *op. cit., 1957*, p. 260).

the dependence of the DRV on Chinese aid and the presence of Chinese technicians and political advisers must present some problems, even to the ruling elite schooled in China. During the agrarian disturbances in the fall of 1956, the Chinese Foreign Minister Chou En-lai paid a sudden visit to Hanoi, which the Hanoi press reported only two days before his arrival.[76] The trip may also have been motivated by a concern over the dismissal of Truong Chinh as secretary-general of the Workers Party, since he is generally viewed as the Vietnamese leader most favorable to China.[77] Vietnamese official speeches made during Chou's four-day visit reflected a desire to emphasize Vietnam's equality of status with China, and a *Nhan Dan* editorial pointedly remarked: "In their relations, the Democratic Republic of Vietnam and the People's Republic of China entirely respect each other's national independence and sovereignty and territorial integrity, and always treat each other with a spirit of equality." [78]

With the Soviet Union the DRV's relations are much less complex. Some observers interpret North Vietnam's emphasis on its friendly relations with Russia as an attempt to maintain freedom of action by balancing Russia against Red China.[79] The replacement of Truong Chinh by Ho Chi Minh may have indicated the resurgence of a pro-Russian faction in the DRV government which Ho Chi Minh is said to lead,[80] although Truong Chinh was appointed a Deputy Prime Minister in 1958. A visit by Anastas Mikoyan in April 1956 was universally lauded in the DRV press as "an unique occasion to strengthen the friendship which unites our two countries," [81] and no unseemly references to "equality" and "mutual respect" marred the adulatory tone of the welcome. Simultaneously with his visit appeared a communiqué from the Workers Party, announcing its support of the resolutions of the Twentieth Congress of the Soviet Communist Party which condemned the cult of the individual. A speech by Ho Chi Minh followed, deploring the "serious mistakes" of Comrade Stalin.[82] When

[76] *VNA*, Hanoi radio, Nov. 16, 1956.

[77] Harold C. Hinton, *China's Relations with Burma and Vietnam* (New York: Institute of Pacific Relations, International Secretariat, 1958), pp. 21–22.

[78] *VNA*, Hanoi radio, Nov. 18, 1956.

[79] Hinton, *China's Relations*, pp. 16–18.

[80] Bernard B. Fall, "Crisis in North Viet-Nam," *Far Eastern Survey*, XXVI (Jan. 1957), 13.

[81] *Nhan Dan* editorial, in *VNA*, Hanoi radio, April 2, 1956.

[82] *Voice of Vietnam*, Hanoi radio, April 27, 1956.

Russian tanks rolled into Hungary—at the same time that North Vietnamese peasants reacted violently against their own government—the DRV warmly endorsed "the disinterested and wholehearted assistance of the Soviet Army." [83]

The DRV's commitment to the Soviet bloc has already cost it a strategic victory since it was Soviet and Chinese pressure which forced the DRV to accede to the Geneva accords at a time when its armies were poised for further conquest. Since then, China and Russia have both paid lip service to the Vietnamese drive for reunification, but the date set by the Geneva accords for nation-wide elections has long since passed, and Vietnam remains divided. Although the policies of Moscow and Peking may preclude aiding the DRV to achieve forcible reunification at this time, they continue to grant it economic support of considerable magnitude which—like American aid to South Vietnam—is undoubtedly of importance to the regime's viability.

SUGGESTED READING

GENERAL WORKS

Cole, Allan B., ed. *Conflict in Indo-China and International Repercussions: A Documentary History, 1945–1955.* Ithaca, N.Y.: Cornell University Press, 1956. A documentary history which spans a vital ten-year period and includes documents pertaining to both internal and international events affecting the course of Vietnamese history. It is well organized, with commentary introductions preceding each section.

Gourou, Pierre. *The Peasants of the Tonkin Delta.* 2 vols. New Haven: Human Relations Area Files, Inc., 1955. (Originally published in French in 1936.) An exhaustive demographic study of Tonkin; too detailed for any but the specialized reader.

Lewis, Norman. *A Dragon Apparent.* London: Cape, 1951. A good travelogue, especially vivid when dealing with the author's observations on the mountain tribes of southern Vietnam.

Newman, Bernard. *Report on Indochina.* London: Robert Hale, Ltd., 1953. A highly readable, personalized account of the author's travels in Indochina, the places he visited, and the personalities he interviewed, including the Emperor Bao Dai.

BOOKS IN FRENCH

Although this selected reading list has been primarily limited to English-language works, there are several books in French too valuable to exclude.

Devillers, Philippe. *Histoire du Viet-Nam de 1940 à 1952.* Rev. ed. Paris:

[83] *VNA*, Hanoi radio, Nov. 5, 1956.

Editions du Seuil, 1952. The best book written on modern Vietnamese history to date, this comprehensive and scholarly study is especially enlightening for the 1945–1950 period. The author, who came to know personally the major protagonists of the Franco-Vietnamese struggle, describes with clarity and perception the Vietnamese as well as the French point of view.

Huard, Pierre, and Maurice Durand. *Connaissance du Viet-Nam.* Paris: Imprimerie Nationale, 1954. This book is a sociological study of Vietnamese traditional life and customs by two authors who speak fluent Vietnamese and have a profound and intimate knowledge of Vietnamese culture. It is too detailed and specialized for the general reader, but it is a superb reference book.

Le Thanh Khoi. *Le Viet-Nam.* Paris: Les Editions de Minuit, 1955. A thorough and knowledgeable history of Vietnam by a well-known Vietnamese scholar. The consistent excellence of this book is marred only in the last chapter when the author substitutes a pro-Viet Minh bias for his scholarly detachment.

Mus, Paul. *Viet-Nam: Sociologie d'une guerre.* Paris: Editions du Seuil, 1952. An analysis of the sociological and cultural bases for the Franco-Vietnamese conflict. The author was in Vietnam during the crucial 1945–1947 period, and his book, although difficult reading, is important for an understanding of the complex problems underlying the war in Vietnam.

NEWSPAPERS AND PERIODICALS

Economist. British weekly magazine, 1954–1958. This magazine contains numerous brief but informative articles on both North and South Vietnam.

News from Vietnam, Embassy of Vietnam, Washington, D.C. The official Vietnamese Embassy news publication for the American public. It often contains useful policy statements and excerpts from speeches, as well as summaries of political events and news about the economy.

Times of Vietnam, Saigon, Vietnam. A progovernment English-language daily with a weekly supplement. It offers a reasonably complete news coverage and an occasionally controversial article.

Vietnam Presse, Saigon, Vietnam. The official government news agency which puts out several daily editions as well as special supplements; invaluable as a source of government information.

XVII: The Historical Background

Buttinger, Joseph. *The Smaller Dragon.* New York: Praeger, 1958. The only history of Vietnam in English, this important book deals with the period prior to French rule, though a chronology of important events after 1883 is included. Much substantive material is also included in footnotes at the end of each chapter.

Cady, John F. *The Roots of French Imperialism in Eastern Asia*. Ithaca, N.Y.: American Historical Association, Cornell University Press, 1954. An analysis of French imperialist policies and philosophy. The book includes an interesting and valuable chapter on the French conquest of Indochina, within this larger context.

Ennis, Thomas E. *French Policy and Developments in Indochina*. Chicago: University of Chicago Press, 1936. A survey of French rule in Indochina; interesting background material, especially concerning the development of French administration and its political philosophy.

Hammer, Ellen J. *The Struggle for Indochina*. Stanford: Stanford University Press, 1954. The most comprehensive book in English on modern Vietnamese history and politics. It is well written and sensitive and is a basic work for an understanding of present-day Vietnam.

———. *The Struggle for Indochina Continues*. Stanford: Stanford University Press, 1955. In this supplement to her earlier book, the author discusses recent events in Vietnam and criticizes the Diem government for its authoritarian methods.

Levy, Roger, Guy Lacam, and Andrew Roth. *French Interests and Policies in the Far East*. New York: Institute of Pacific Relations, 1941. An examination of French economic and trade policies in the Far East; includes material on the early period of the Japanese occupation in Indochina.

Mus, Paul. "The Role of the Village in Vietnamese Politics," *Pacific Affairs*, XX (Sept. 22, 1949), 265–272. An illuminating study of the effect of the course of events in Vietnam on the outlook and thinking of Vietnamese peasants and on traditional village institutions.

Robequain, Charles. *The Economic Development of French Indo-China*. London: Oxford University Press, 1944. A basic analysis of the French colonial economy. Some of the material is too detailed to be of general interest, but much of it is important for an understanding of the French impact as well as of the contemporary economic structure of Vietnam.

Thompson, Virginia. *French Indo-China*. New York: Macmillan, 1937. An important and scholarly work discussing many aspects of Vietnamese life prior to the Second World War.

United States, Department of State, Office of Intelligence Research. *Political Alignments of Vietnamese Nationalists*, by Milton Sacks. Department of State no. 3708. Washington, D.C., 1949. A highly detailed study of Vietnamese nationalists and the nationalist movement, valuable as a reference work and containing important material unavailable elsewhere.

XVIII: South Vietnam: The Contemporary Setting

Alsop, Joseph. "A Reporter at Large," *New Yorker*, XXXI (June 25, 1955), 35–58. A personal account of this well-known correspondent's trip through South Vietnam to see at firsthand Communist-controlled villages in the

Mekong delta. It contains interesting discussions of politics with Communist militants and of the author's contact with Communist official mentality.

C[rozier], B[rian]. "Indo-China: The Unfinished Struggle," *World Today*, XII (Jan. 1956), 17–26. An account of the struggle for survival of the Diem regime in the first years after the Geneva accord, as well as a short sketch of North Vietnam's history during this period.

Fall, Bernard B. "South Viet-Nam's Internal Problems," *Pacific Affairs*, XXXI (Sept. 1958), 241–260. A survey of the most pressing problems facing the government of South Vietnam and a critical account of how they are being faced. The author finds both the economic and security situations deteriorating.

———. "The Political-Religious Sects of Vietnam, *Pacific Affairs*, XXVIII (Sept. 1955), 235–253. A good, clear account of a complex subject: the background, leadership, and political importance of the three "sects" of South Vietnam, the Cao Dai, Hoa Hao, and Binh Xuyen.

———. "Will South Vietnam Be Next?" *Nation*, CLXXXVI (May 31, 1958), 489–493. A recent evaluation of South Vietnam's progress with particular reference to economic problems. The author blames the type of American aid operating in the south for many of the government's economic woes.

Gittinger, Price. "Rent Reduction and Tenure Security in Free Vietnam," *Journal of Farm Economics*, XXXIX (May 1957), 429–440. This article and the one following represent the most recent, detailed descriptions of the implementation of the land reform program in South Vietnam.

———. "Vietnamese Land Transfer Program," *Land Economics*, XXXIII (May 1957), 173–177.

Grant, J. A. C. "The Viet Nam Constitution of 1956," *American Political Science Review*, LVI (June 1958), 437–463. An excellent analysis of the Vietnamese constitution and the political forces which produced it.

Hammer, Ellen J. "Progress Report on Southern Viet Nam," *Pacific Affairs*, XXX (Sept. 1957), 221–235. A thoughtful and balanced evaluation of the political situation in the south and the progress which the government of South Vietnam has made in recent years.

Henderson, William. "South Vietnam Finds Itself," *Foreign Affairs*, XXXV (Jan. 1957), 283–294. An excellent account of the political history of President Diem's government, with an analysis of the problems it has solved, is solving, and must solve to maintain its existence.

Hotham, David. "U.S. Aid to Vietnam—A Balance Sheet," *Reporter*, XVII (Sept. 19, 1957), 30–33. An account of the efforts made by the U.S. Aid Mission in South Vietnam and its primary deficiency—an emphasis on budget support for the Vietnamese army rather than the building up of industry.

Jumper, Roy. "The Communist Challenge to South Vietnam," *Far Eastern Survey*, XXV (Nov. 1956), 161–168. A provocative analysis of the activities of the Communists in South Vietnam, their appeal for the peasants, and the difficulties encountered by the present regime in countering this appeal and rooting out Communist influence.

——. "Mandarin Bureaucracy and Politics in South Viet Nam," *Pacific Affairs*, XXX (March 1957), 47–58. A thoughtful interpretation of the role of the mandarins in the administration under French rule and their usefulness and drawbacks in the present government bureaucracy.

——. "Problems of Public Administration in South Vietnam," *Far Eastern Survey*, XXVI (Dec. 1957), 183–190. An excellent description of the complex administrative machinery inherited by the present government and the problems involved in reforming the colonial bureaucratic structure; especially informative on the process of government and the attempts to modernize the civil service.

Mansfield, Mike. *Report on Vietnam, Cambodia, and Laos to the Senate Committee on Foreign Relations, October 3, 1955.* (U.S. Congress, Senate, Committee on Foreign Relations.) Washington, D.C.: U.S. Government Printing Office, 1955. Senator Mansfield visited South Vietnam during the late summer of 1954 when the nation's future was most uncertain. The Senator was one of the most influential Americans in the shaping of U.S. policy toward Vietnam, and his report is very important.

Sharp, Walter R. "Some Observations on Public Administration in Indo-China," *Public Administration Review*, XIV (Winter 1954), 40–51. A useful description of public administration practices and problems during the later days of French rule in Vietnam. It is of particular interest because it indicates both the formal and informal administrative structure which the present government inherited.

Thai Van Kiem. *Vietnam, Past and Present.* Published under the auspices of the Vietnamese Department of National Education and the National Commission for UNESCO. Paris: Commercial Transworld Editions [1956?]. A rather superficial survey of Vietnamese history and present-day life, with some interesting accounts of Vietnamese legends and some insight into Vietnamese traditions.

Vietnam, National Constituent Assembly. *The Constitution of the Republic of Vietnam.* Saigon: Secretariat of State for Information, 1956. The English translation of South Vietnam's constitution, with a short exposition of its background and major features.

Wurfel, David. "Agrarian Reform in the Republic of Vietnam," *Far Eastern Survey*, XXVI (June 1957), 81–92. A good detailed analysis of South Vietnam's agrarian reform program with attention given to its political setting.

XXI: North Vietnam

Crozier, Brian. "The International Situation in Indochina," *Pacific Affairs,* XXIX (Dec. 1956), 309–324. An examination of the international position of the three states of Indochina as a result of the Geneva accord. It is especially valuable on North Vietnam's relations with the Communist bloc and the issue of reunification of Vietnam.

Fall, Bernard B. "Crisis in North Vietnam," *Far Eastern Survey,* XXVI (Jan. 1957), 12–15. A revealing analysis of the dissatisfaction which found voice in North Vietnam in the fall of 1956 and its political ramifications.

——. *The Viet-Minh Regime.* Rev. ed. New York: Institute of Pacific Relations, 1956. The most complete study of government and politics in North Vietnam to date, based on firsthand information and original documents. The appendix includes some useful Viet Minh documents not available elsewhere.

Foreign Broadcast Information Service. *Daily Reports.* Washington, D.C.; mimeographed. Includes translation of monitored radio broadcasts from Hanoi which provide an invaluable source of information about the DRV's activities and policies.

H., P. J. "Revolt of the Intellectuals in North Vietnam," *World Today,* XIII (June 1957), 250–260. A thoughtful and sensitive analysis of the causes, events, and results of the "revolt of the intellectuals" during the fall of 1956.

Hinton, Harold C. "Sino-Vietnamese Relations," in *China's Relations with Burma and Vietnam.* New York: Institute of Pacific Relations, 1958. Pages 1–25. Mimeographed. An evaluation of present-day relations between Red China and the DRV in the light of historical background.

Hoang Van Chi, ed. *The New Class in North Vietnam.* Saigon: Cong Dan, 1958. A translation of some articles, stories, and poems published in newspapers and magazines in the DRV, chosen for their anti-Communist and antigovernment bias. Especially interesting are those writings which appeared in the fall of 1956.

Le Thanh Khoi. "The Democratic Republic of Vietnam." Pt. I, *Eastern World,* VIII (Dec. 1954), 18–19, 36; pt. II, *ibid.,* IX (Jan. 1955), 20–21. An examination of the political process in North Vietnam by a well-known Vietnamese author sympathetic to the DRV. Useful sections deal with agrarian legislation, political organization and indoctrination of the army, and governmental administrative apparatus.

"Minorities under the Viet Minh," *Eastern World,* IX (Nov. 1955), 17–18. A useful account of North Vietnam's policy toward minorities, with special reference to the establishment of the Thai-Meo Autonomous Area.

Shabad, Theodore. "Economic Developments in North Vietnam," *Pacific Affairs,* XXXI (March 1958), 36–53. A thorough analysis of North Vietnam's economy, based largely on data obtained from Russian sources, with useful interpretations of the economic structure of society.

Shaplen, Robert. "The Enigma of Ho Chi Minh," *Reporter,* XII (Jan. 27, 1955), 11–19. A brief biography of the DRV President Ho Chi Minh, which describes his character in terms of his personal background and that of the Vietnamese revolutionary movement.

Starobin, Joseph. *Eyewitness in Indochina.* New York: Cameron and Kahn, 1954. The author is an American Communist writer who broke with the party in 1956 over the repressions in Hungary. This book records his impressions of his travels in North Vietnam. Although his account is biased, it is nonetheless interesting as one of the few personal accounts available of life under Communist rule in the DRV.

Taussig, H. C. "North Viet Nam's Headaches," *Eastern World,* XI (March 1957), 12–14. A critical account of the implementation of land reform measures in the north and the "headaches" which resulted for the government because of the mistakes committed, by a writer generally sympathetic to the DRV.

Ton That Thien. "Economic Planning in Independent Vietnam," *India Quarterly,* XII (July–Sept. 1956), 298–308. A description of the economic programs of both North and South Vietnam, especially useful with reference to the north.

PART SIX : THE PHILIPPINES

By David Wurfel

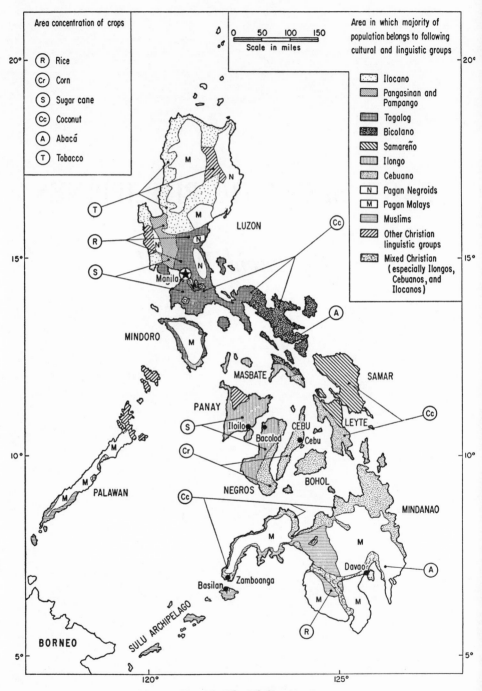

Map 6. The Philippines

· XXII ·

The Historical Background

THE Philippines can boast of no great architectural reminders of the ancient past, no Angkor Wat, as in Cambodia, no Borobudur, as in Indonesia. It is the only nation in Southeast Asia which became subject to Western colonialism before it had developed a centralized governmental structure ruling over a large territory or an advanced elite culture which customarily grew up around a royal court. The consequences of this are far-reaching, distinguishing the Philippines from other parts of the area.

An intense Western impact dating from an earlier stage in cultural development resulted in a greater degree of conversion to Western ways than in any other Southeast Asian country—though Filipinos retain more traits common to the Malay world than is often recognized. Filipinos, earliest to get thorough European educations, were the first nationalists in Southeast Asia. But the subsequent peaceful transition to self-government and independence has dulled the cutting edge of contemporary nationalism. It has also caused less social disruption than accompanied the winning of independence in French, Dutch, or even British colonies. This was conducive to the development of constitutionalism, but at the same time transferred political power to the hands of an economically powerful elite, an elite often unaware of the long-term danger in trying to maintain that power intact.

The Spaniards, on their arrival in the Philippines, found the islands inhabited mostly by brown-skinned Malays, forefathers of today's Filipinos. Some were hunters, others were shifting cultivators on the highlands, and those in the lowlands practiced wet rice cultivation. It was this last group with whom the Spaniards had most contact.[1] The largest stable political unit in the islands was the barangay, a kinship group roughly equivalent in size to a village. The *datu*, or ruler of the barangay, occasionally would join with other rulers in confederations, which seldom endured, however. Rice fields, unlike hills and forests, were never owned in common as in Java or Vietnam. The *datu*, and sometimes the freeholder, had slaves to work his own land and serve in his house. Between these extremes were serfs who were attached to the land, paid half their crops to their masters, whether *datu* or freeholder, and rendered them personal service at feast time or harvest. The customary law of these communities stressed arbitration of disputes and compensation for the aggrieved party, not punishment of the guilty.[2]

Chinese traders had been resident since about A.D. 1000, and some cultural influences from South Asia were carried to the islands by the Indonesian empires of Shrivijaya and Majapahit,[3] yet in comparison with other parts of Southeast Asia the cultural impact of both China and India on the Philippines was of little importance. The peoples of the Philippines were unique in the area in having never adopted either Hinduism or Buddhism. This is sometimes posed as the explanation for the failure of a strong monarchical state to take form. Their religion was animism.

By the early fifteenth century this pattern was being changed, however, with the introduction of Islam via Malacca. Islam was first implanted in Sulu and Mindanao; by the mid-sixteenth century two sultanates had been established there, and the chieftain of Manila had also become a Muslim. It was in the midst of this wave of Islamic proselytizing that the Spaniards arrived. Had they come a hundred

[1] Fred Eggan and others, *Area Handbook on the Philippines* (New Haven: Human Relations Area Files, Inc., 1956), I, 250–260.

[2] See Plasencia, "Las Costumbres de los Tagalos," translated in Emma Blair and James Robertson, *The Philippine Islands* (Cleveland: Arthur Clark Co., 1904), vol. VII; Colin, "Labor Evangelica," in *ibid.*, vol. XL.

[3] Elizabeth Hassell, "The Sri-Vijayan and Madjapahit Empires and the Theory of Their Political Association with the Philippines," *Philippine Social Science and Humanities Review*, XVIII (1953), 3–86. It is doubtful whether any Philippine *datu* was ever tributary to those empires, as is sometimes claimed.

years later or had their motives been strictly commercial, as was at first the case of the Dutch, Filipinos even today might be a Muslim people.

But Spanish colonialist motives were not strictly commercial. A state in which there was a union of spiritual and temporal government deemed ecclesiastical empire as important a goal as profit. Magellan sailed west to find the Spice Islands, but on arrival in the Philippines in 1521 he tried to Catholicize the natives of spiceless Cebu and met death as the result of his involvement. After three further expeditions had ended in disaster, Philip II, "the most Catholic of Kings," for whom the islands were named, decided to send "an expedition to the heathens." It succeeded in establishing the first permanent Spanish settlement, Cebu, in 1565. In 1571 the Spanish city of Manila was founded, in which is today the oldest permanent Western community in any Far Eastern capital.

By the end of the sixteenth century most of the coastal and lowland areas north of Mindanao had been brought under Spanish control with comparatively little bloodshed. Friars marched with soldiers and soon accomplished the peaceful conversion to Catholicism of almost all the natives under Spanish administration. Animists quickly gave way in the face of aggressive Christian evangelism, though animistic beliefs and practices were retained by many of the new converts. The Muslims of Mindanao and Sulu, termed "Moros" because previous Spanish contact with Muslims had been mainly with the Moors, were never completely subdued by the Spaniards, however. That task was not finished until after more than a decade of American rule.

Spanish rule for the first hundred years was, in most areas, exercised by the Governor-General through a peculiar kind of tax-farming system known as the encomienda.[4] By the end of the seventeenth century, however, it was largely inoperative. The Governor-General

---

[4] An encomendero was a Spaniard, and usually a friend of the Governor-General, who was given the right to collect tribute from a certain number of natives, ranging as high as 6,000 families. It was not a land grant, and encomiendas, as such, do not appear to be the origin of large landholdings today. In return for the right to collect tributes the encomendero was to pacify the people, pay for their religious instruction, and put 20 per cent of the amount collected into the royal treasury. Encomenderos, most of whom exercised great cruelty in collecting tributes, seldom fulfilled all of these responsibilities, and frequently none of them. As a result, the system came under attack by the friars. See vols. VI, VIII, XXV, XXXIV, and XLVII of Blair and Robertson, *op. cit.*, for contemporary descriptions and criticisms of the encomienda system.

began to appoint his own representatives, civil governors in pacified provinces and military officers in unpacified ones, to collect taxes directly.

Several provinces remained under military rule to the end of the Spanish regime; in those areas there was almost no native participation in government. But in pacified areas below the provincial level the Spaniards built on indigenous institutions, while changing their content drastically over the years. The barangay was transformed into a territorial unit and made a subdivision of the town, which itself was a subdivision of the province. The *datu*, who had been recognized by the encomendero and required by him to collect tribute, with the regularization of the administration became subordinate to the mayor. The *datu's* once hereditary position was in time made appointive, still with primarily tax-collecting duties.[5] The barangay lost almost all governmental significance in face of the rising importance of the towns. There the wealthier residents, including heads of the barangay, had a small voice in choosing the chief municipal officer and in making certain minor decisions, but centralization was extreme. Because of the power of the Church generally and because of the fact that the parish priest was usually the only Spaniard in town, he was a member of almost all the numerous administrative boards and commissions and had the last say in most municipal decision making.[6]

Within the Spanish central government in Manila, Filipinos held no responsible positions. The Governor-General, appointed by the king, was the colony's most powerful figure, sometimes likened to an independent monarch. He dominated the high court, and as captain general of the armed forces he exercised exclusive personal control over military governors and their provinces. His privilege of engaging in commerce for private profit was legally recognized and delimited; he paid little heed to the limitations. In fact Spanish colonialists generally had no conception of government office as anything more than an opportunity for private gain. Madrid attempted to supervise the Governor-General's activities, but the great distance between mother country and colony made this almost impossible. Even frequent removal—the average term of office was three and a half years, and in the nineteenth century less than two years—and a devastatingly

[5] John Romani and Ladd Thomas, *A Survey of Local Government in the Philippines* (Manila: University of the Philippines, 1954), pp. 2–4, 15–16.

[6] W. Cameron Forbes, *The Philippine Islands* (Cambridge: Harvard University Press, 1945), p. 296.

thorough investigation of the outgoing Governor's administration were ineffective instruments of control.[7]

The Governor-General was also civil head of the Church in the islands. But the archbishop vied with him for political supremacy and, especially in the late seventeenth and eighteenth centuries, frequently won. During the first half of the eighteenth century, in case of death, absence, or incapacity of the Governor-General, the archbishop was legally entitled to act in his stead. In 1781 a traveler reported that the clergy "are more absolute in the Philippines than the King himself."[8] Besides political power the ecclesiastical organization acquired great wealth, mostly in land. Royal grants and devises formed the core of its holdings, but many arbitrary extensions were made beyond the boundaries of the original grants. These extensions and other tenuous interests in land were transformed into ownership toward the end of the nineteenth century when a modern land-title system was adopted.

Though evidence is not clear, there seem to have been three other ways in which large landholdings developed in the nineteenth-century Philippines. The new laws made it possible for some wealthy Filipinos, descendants of *datus,* to formalize traditional land rights—and grab untraditional ones, by making false claims and then manipulating the law against farmers ignorant of its capabilities. Other large tracts were acquired by corporations and individuals, mostly Spaniards, interested in planting sugar and other cash crops. The decline of economic autonomy in the village and the increase in the use of money, accelerated by the formal opening of Manila to foreign trade at the end of the eighteenth century and the completion of the Suez Canal in 1869, also increased the chances for the owner-cultivator to go into debt. Frequently debt proved only a prelude to his loss of ownership, often to a Chinese moneylender. Since interest was usurious and rents oppressive, this increasing concentration of landownership at the expense of the cultivator, who was sensitive to the injustice in the methods of acquisition, contributed substantially to the unrest which exploded in the Philippine Revolution.[9]

[7] See Alejandro Fernandez, "The Spanish Governor- and Captain-General in the Philippines" (unpublished M.A. thesis, Cornell University, 1955).

[8] Guillaume Le Gentil, "Ecclesiastical Survey of the Philippines," in Blair and Robertson, *op. cit.,* XXVIII, 210.

[9] For the most detailed description of nineteenth-century economic developments see Benito F. Legarda, "Foreign Trade, Economic Change, and Entrepreneurship in the Nineteenth Century Philippines" (unpublished Ph.D. thesis, Harvard University, 1955).

A revolution requires educated leadership, however, and tenant cultivators had no access to education. Education in the Philippines until the late nineteenth century was offered only by Catholic institutions. Primary education in such schools was little more than the memorization of the catechism, given in the local dialect. Only those who could afford Manila schools or who received special tutoring from a priest learned Spanish. But with the opening of the Suez Canal, less expensive travel made possible an education in Europe for a rapidly increasing number of young men whose families had profited from the expanded commerce. They were thus confronted with the new ideas sweeping the continent, liberalism and nationalism.

A large percentage of these young men were mestizos, that is, of mixed blood. For generations there had been no Spanish women in the Philippines; as late as 1870, in a pure-blooded Spanish community of nearly 4,000, the male-female ratio was 6 to 1. Miscegenation was inevitable. Mestizos had higher social status in the Philippines than in most other Southeast Asian countries. Nevertheless the mestizo himself was the object of discrimination by Spaniards, many of whom tended to associate mixed blood with illegitimacy. Liberalism taught mestizos doctrines of equality.

A wave of Spanish liberalism brought to the Philippines the education decree of 1863 which sought to establish government-supervised free compulsory education for children aged 7 to 12, with instruction in Spanish. Like other Spanish reform decrees, this one was very incompletely implemented; nevertheless by 1898 there were nearly 200,000 children in school, or 3 per cent of the population.[10] Many reforms proclaimed were never enforced; others were instituted, then revoked. This pattern was a more important stimulus to revolutionary activity than endemic repression and was caused by frequent and violent fluctuations in the Madrid government between liberal and reactionary control. For instance, during the liberal regimes of 1810–1813, 1820–1823, and 1834–1835 the Philippines was represented in the Spanish parliament and thus made conscious of the injustice of its later exclusion.

The Philippine Revolution

The intellectual forerunners of the Philippine Revolution, the "Propagandists," were from the European-educated elite. They did not

[10] Eggan, *op. cit.*, II, 752.

advocate revolution or independence, however, but only asked for the Philippines' assimilation as a regular province of Spain, for civil liberties, and for vaguely phrased reforms. Some Propagandists were Masons and demanded the expulsion of Spanish friars. They found ardent allies among Filipino priests who were resentful of their lack of equality with Spanish clergy. Jose Rizal, physician, sculptor, novelist, and poet, who is now the Philippines' revered national hero, was outstanding among the Propagandists. Spanish authorities falsely charged him with conspiring to lead an armed uprising and had him shot in December 1896. Others of like mind and social status were imprisoned and had their property confiscated. Petitioning Spain for reform became an obviously useless endeavor. More daring moves were in order.

Revolts broke out in several provinces around Manila in late 1896. After months of fighting, severe Spanish retaliation forced the revolutionary armies to retreat to the hills. In August 1897 a truce was negotiated. But after the U.S. naval victory in Manila Bay on May 1, 1898—less than a month after the outbreak of the Spanish-American War—the rebels reorganized, resumed the military campaign, and declared independence in June.

The leadership of the revolt from 1896 to 1898 benefited from the writings of the Propagandists, but did not come from their number. Andres Bonifacio, the founder of the secret society which instigated the 1896 uprising, was a largely self-educated warehouseman in a Spanish commercial firm in Manila and was under strong Masonic influence. Emilio Aguinaldo, military commander of the revolutionary forces and in addition "dictator" of the revolutionary government and finally President of the short-lived Republic proclaimed in January 1899, was the son of a municipal mayor in the province of Cavite and had had some secondary education in Manila. Mass support for these leaders came mostly from tenants of estates owned by the Church. The revolutionary government decreed the nationalization of those lands in 1898 and ordered the Spanish friars—comprising the great majority of the clergy—expelled. It is clear that the revolutionary movement had both social and national goals, but both were frustrated.

The first goal was frustrated by the intrusion of the wealthy landed elite into positions of leadership in the revolutionary Republic, the second by American policy. Though Aguinaldo had gained the impression from Admiral Dewey and other Americans in the Far East that the United States would support Filipino independence, dreams of "manifest destiny" in Washington helped bring about the U.S. annexation of the Philippines. Fighting between Filipino and American troops started early in February 1899, and by May, General Aguinaldo and his men had been driven out of the area around Manila. He was finally captured in 1901. Shortly afterwards the general took an oath of allegiance to the United States and within a year resistance had collapsed.[11]

It is nevertheless significant for the understanding of later developments that the proclamation of a republic marked the Filipinos as the first Asian people to try to throw off established European colonialism. In addition to nationalist fervor they had certain governmental skills as well, derived from experiences in local administration and from the study of law. They had drawn up a constitution, which evidenced familiarity with the constitutions of Europe and America, established a government in accordance with constitutional provisions, and set up administrations in several provinces.[12]

United States Rule

While fighting continued between Filipinos and American troops, the United States annexed the Philippines by the Treaty of Paris signed in December 1899. American opinion was sharply divided on the question of annexation, and the treaty was ratified in the Senate by only one vote more than the necessary two-thirds.

The islands were governed by the military until 1901. In 1899, however, Cornell University's President Schurman had been sent out as the head of a five-man fact-finding commission and had reported to President McKinley that all Filipinos wanted ultimate independence.

McKinley's instructions to the Second Philippine Commission headed by William Howard Taft were actually written by Elihu Root. Aided by the Schurman Commission report they exhibited a high order of statesmanship and became a guide not only to the Taft Commission in establishing civil government, but to future constitutional and administrative development under American direction. The instructions directed, in part, that

[11] See James H. Blount, *The American Occupation of the Philippines, 1898–1912* (New York: Putnam and Sons, 1912), and Teodoro Agoncillo, *The Revolt of the Masses* (Quezon City: University of the Philippines, 1956).

[12] Eduardo Austin, "A Study of the Rise and Fall of the First Democratic Republic in the Far East: The Philippines, 1899" (unpublished Ph.D. thesis, Georgetown University, 1957).

in all the forms of government and administrative provisions which they are authorized to prescribe, the commission should bear in mind that the government which they are establishing is designed not for our satisfaction, or for the expression of our theoretical views, but for the happiness, peace and prosperity of the people of the Philippine Islands, and the measures adopted should be made to conform to their customs, their habits and even their prejudices, to the fullest extent consistent with the accomplishment of the indispensable requisites of just and effective government.

At the same time the commission should bear in mind, and the people of the islands should be made plainly to understand, that there are certain great principles of government which have been made the basis of our maintenance of individual freedom, and of which they have, unfortunately, been denied the experience possessed by us; that there are also certain practical rules of government which we have found to be essential to the preservation of these great principles of liberty and law, and that these principles and these rules of government must be established and maintained in their islands for the sake of their liberty and happiness, however much they may conflict with the customs of law and procedure with which they are familiar.[13]

This colonial attitude of tutelage tempered with tolerance helps to explain varying degrees of conservation and innovation in the American establishment of political institutions in the Philippines. Thus, on the one hand, the Spanish civil law tradition was conserved, and there was no attempt to introduce the jury system. But civil marriage and the writ of habeas corpus were among the important additions. An American-style Supreme Court was superimposed on top of the existing judicial structure. In line with McKinley's instructions to give preference in appointment to qualified natives, the first Chief Justice of the Supreme Court, named in 1899, was a Filipino (with considerable Spanish blood); he was, in fact, the highest-ranking Filipino official in the islands for several years. By 1912 half of the judges of first instance were Filipinos; in 1926 only two out of fifty-five judges were American.[14]

The creation of a Philippine legislature was a clear example of innovation, necessary because there was nothing on which to build in the Philippines' Spanish past, when legislation had been entirely by executive decree. In fulfillment of the provisions of the Philippine Organic Act, passed by Congress in 1902, the American-dominated eight-man Commission, which had been both legislature and Gov-

[13] The instructions may be found in Appendix III of Dean Worcester, *The Philippines, Past and Present* (New York: Macmillan, 1930).

[14] See Forbes, *op. cit.*, ch. vi.

ernor-General's cabinet, became in 1907 the upper house of a bicameral legislature. Several of its members still remained as heads
of executive departments, however. The Assembly, or lower house,
was composed of eighty members directly elected from single-member districts. Even though the size of the electorate was severely
restricted by requirements of property and knowledge of Spanish
or English, this was the first popularly elected legislative body in
Southeast Asia. Except for legislation affecting the "non-Christian
tribes," which was the exclusive prerogative of the Commission, a
bill to be enacted into law had to be approved by both houses.[15]
Until the appointment of a Filipino majority to the Commission by
Governor-General Harrison in 1913, American officials within the
legislature thus had a veto power on all Filipino legislative proposals.

Before 1933 Francis B. Harrison was the only Governor-General
to represent a Democratic administration in Manila. He had been
named by President Wilson and sent out with specific instructions
to prepare the Philippines for "ultimate independence." Meanwhile,
in Washington a Democratic Congress hastened to fulfill long-standing campaign promises to the same end. The Jones Act, passed in
1916, would have fixed a definite date for the granting of Philippine
independence if the Senate had had its way, but the House prevented
such a move.[16] In its final form the act merely stated that it was
the "purpose of the people of the United States" to recognize Philippine
independence "as soon as a stable government can be established
therein." Its greater importance was as a milestone in the development of Philippine autonomy. Under its provisions the Commission
was abolished and replaced by a twenty-four-man Senate. Twenty-
two members were elected from eleven districts, and two were appointed by the Governor-General to represent non-Christian areas.
The electorate was expanded to include all literate males.

There were still substantial restrictions on autonomy, however. The
Governor-General could veto acts of the legislature, which, if overridden, became law only when signed by the President of the United
States. All laws regarding public land, timber, mining, currency, coinage, immigration, and tariff required the President's signature, and
the U.S. Congress reserved the right to annul any Philippine law on

[15] See Worcester, *op. cit.*, ch. xxvi.

[16] Garel Grunder and William Livezey, *The Philippines and the United States*
(Norman: University of Oklahoma Press, 1951), pp. 146–156.

any subject, though it never did so. The legislature's power of the purse was restricted by a provision continuing the previous year's appropriation when no appropriation bill had been passed by the beginning of the fiscal year. During the administrations of Governor-General Harrison in Manila, 1913–1920, and of President Wilson in Washington, Americans did not find occasion to exercise the powers over Philippine legislation which they possessed. After the Republican victory of 1920, however, President Harding's appointee, Governor-General Leonard Wood, vetoed several enactments of the legislature. President Coolidge withheld his signature from one.[17]

The Philippine legislature under American tutelage fulfilled a more important political than lawmaking role. It was, in effect, the instrument of the Nacionalista Party, founded in 1907, which always commanded an overwhelming elected majority. From 1907 till 1921 Sergio Osmeña, Speaker of the lower house, was the unchallenged political leader of that party and of the Filipino people. In 1922 Manuel Quezon, then Senate President, became Nacionalista leader. He controlled the party and both houses of the legislature from that position until the establishment of the Commonwealth in 1935.

From the beginning the most meaningful plank in the Nacionalista platform was independence. In fact the Nacionalistas practically monopolized the political symbol of independence and thus could not be dislodged until the goal was achieved. Parties under colonial rule seek primarily to transfer the locus of sovereignty and transform the constitutional structure rather than to undertake the responsibilities of government under the existing constitution. Though Filipino political leaders were allowed to shoulder those responsibilities to a greater extent than their counterparts in other Southeast Asian colonies, nevertheless they paid inadequate attention to the business of legislation. Americans in the executive office, aided by Filipino cabinet secretaries, usually took responsibility for drafting and pushing important bills and killing undesirable ones. Thus the stage was set for executive dominance of the legislative process under the Commonwealth.[18]

In a way that legislation alone could not accomplish, control of the appointive power greatly strengthened the position of the Nacionalista Party and its leaders at least for a time. To this end Speaker Osmeña and Senate President Quezon, during the incumbency of

[17] See J. Ralston Hayden, *The Philippines* (New York: Macmillan, 1947), ch. viii, and Worcester, *op. cit.*, pp. 733–738, 762.

[18] Hayden, *op. cit.*, pp. 172–174, 197, 315–316.

Harrison and with his assistance, transformed the constitutional structure substantially, without congressional enactment. Through their domination of the Harrison-created Council of State they effectively controlled top appointments. With this and other innovations a quasi-parliamentary system was established. It was abolished, however, by Harrison's successor, Governor-General Wood, who reasserted executive independence of the legislature.

With the exception of the hiatus under Harrison, it was through the executive that American direction of Philippine domestic affairs was maintained until 1935, though a predominantly Filipino judiciary and legislature limited the scope and qualified the effectiveness of that direction. There was actually little more than one decade of thoroughly American administration in the islands, which was too short a time in which to transmit to all Filipino administrators the best traditions of American public service. Whereas Americans formed 51 per cent of the civil service in 1903, they were only 29 per cent in 1913 and 6 per cent in 1923. The sharpest drop came as a result of the drive for "Filipinization" during the Harrison administration. In 1913 there had been only one Filipino bureau chief. By 1925 only one member of the Governor-General's cabinet, the Secretary of Public Instruction who was concurrently Lieutenant Governor-General, and four out of twenty-five bureau directors were Americans. By 1936, the first year of the Commonwealth, 160 Americans, almost all educational administrators or highly skilled technicians, made up less than 1 per cent of the Philippine Civil Service.[19]

A civil service law was early enacted which in its incorporation of the merit principle equaled the best of those in force in the United States at the time. There was strict adherence to this principle in the appointment of Americans. The same generalization can be made about appointments of Filipinos, at least until 1913. But under Harrison the legislature began to play an important role in appointments, though there were no dismissals in violation of tenure.[20] If Filipinization had been more gradual, it would probably have been more difficult for the legislature to encroach on the merit system.

American impact on Philippine local government was even weaker than in Manila. But so Elihu Root had planned it. McKinley's instructions read: "The natives of the islands . . . shall be afforded the opportunity to manage their local affairs to the fullest extent of which

[19] Worcester, *op. cit.*, pp. 299, 768; Eggan, *op. cit.*, II, 967.
[20] See Hayden, *op. cit.*, ch. iv.

they are capable." Here was an excellent example of conservation of existing institutions with modification only in the direction of greater self-government. The only important change in the municipal structure, besides the removal of the parish priest from his paramount position, was the direct election—only by the propertied class at first —of town officials. Provincial governors were also made elective, indirectly in 1910, directly in 1917. Almost all Americans had been removed from provincial government by 1916; none but teachers had ever served at the municipal level.

McKinley's instructions recommending administrative decentralization were, unlike those for local self-government, honored mostly in the breach. Not only would such an innovation have prevented American officials in Manila from giving the fledgling municipal governments the kind of supervision they felt necessary in the first decade to maintain administrative standards, but it also flew in the face of the Spanish tradition of centralism. As long as central supervision meant American supervision, Filipino politicians were against it. In fact, had American supervision continued longer, the resulting antagonisms might have generated a stronger spirit of independence in local government than now exists. But when the Executive Bureau, which supervised local government, ceased to be headed by an American in 1916, local independence suffered.[21]

American Social and Economic Policy

United States preparation of the Philippines for democratic self-government properly contained two parts: one, gradually giving governmental responsibility to those capable of undertaking it; the other, building the socioeconomic base for political democracy. Such a two-pronged policy, however, suffered internal contradictions. Self-government meant, of necessity, assumption of power by those Filipinos who were educationally qualified. But these men came for the most part from the landed gentry,[22] and preservation of their political and economic position was incompatible with democratization of society. Though not always intending, or even aware of, some of the long-range consequences, American administrators did launch programs with a potential for basic social change. In U.S. educational

---

[21] See Romani and Thomas, *op. cit.*, ch. v, and Hayden, *op. cit.*, ch. xi.

[22] For example, 85 out of 93 members of the House of Representatives in 1923 were classified as "landowners" or "lawyers" (Robert Stephens, "The Prospect for Social Progress in the Philippines," *Pacific Affairs,* XXIII [June 1950], 149).

policy the incompatability with continued elite dominance was not
so immediately apparent to those affected. Agrarian reform, on the
other hand, posed a more direct threat and was understood as such;
as a result the policy was frustrated.

Filipino patriots had made clear during the revolution that they
wanted a greatly expanded educational system that was free, compulsory, and secular. The American administration, with missionary
zeal, set out at once to try to satisfy the Filipino's nearly insatiable
hunger for education. By 1922 public school enrollment was already
past the million mark; the school population had expanded 500 per
cent in a generation. Expenditures for education had risen to nearly
one-half of governmental expenditures at all levels. Teachers were
trained so rapidly that by 1927 most of the first wave of American
teachers—765 came before 1902—had gone home and Americans accounted for only little more than 1 per cent of the 26,200 public
school teachers.[23]

There were two statistically measurable results from this tremendous
emphasis on education. Literacy was more than doubled,[24] from 20
per cent of the population over 10 years of age in 1903 to 49 per cent
in 1939, and educated Filipinos were given a common language and
a linguistic key to Western civilization. As a consequence of the decision to make English the language of instruction, even in the primary
grades, by 1939 nearly 27 per cent of the population could speak English, a larger percentage than for any one of the native tongues. But
the more important result was the new avenue of upward social mobility which education offered.[25] Secondary schools were open to the
most determined students, even from the village. Financial sacrifices
by poor families to allow promising offspring to go away to school
were, and are, phenomenal. Nor were the financial barriers to higher
education unsurmountable for the average high school graduate, especially after the introduction of the American institution of the working student.[26] Though it took a generation for its effects to be felt

[23] Worcester, *op. cit.*, p. 402, and Eggan, *op. cit.*, II, 754–757, 928. See also
Hayden, *op. cit.*, chs. xviii, xix, and xx.
[24] It is not known whether all reported literacy is truly functional.
[25] In 1939 there were 76,000 students in public high schools, a level of enrollment
which had been reached a decade earlier, and approximately 60,000 in private high
schools. This was thirty-five times the number of high school students in Indonesia
in 1940 (George McT. Kahin, *Nationalism and Revolution in Indonesia* [Ithaca,
N.Y.: Cornell University Press, 1952], p. 31).
[26] By 1940 there were more than 12,000 students in state-supported colleges and
more than three times that number in private college-level institutions, where
many studied part time (Eggan, *op. cit.*, II, 802–803).

on the national scene, this great expansion of educational opportunity was helping to build a middle class. In educational policy was found the only successful American effort to stimulate Philippine social change.

American attempts to create greater equality of economic opportunity met with less success. In a predominantly agricultural country the pattern of landownership is the most important index of economic democracy. The concentration of ownership in the hands of a few which had accompanied the introduction of new Spanish land laws in the late nineteenth century was the continuing trend in the American period. The new public land law limited corporate acquisition to 2,530 acres and individuals to 355. But legal restrictions had little effect on those politically well-connected Filipinos who were intent on amassing fortunes in speculation or in agricultural exploitation of the vast arable public domain. Furthermore, the homesteading procedure, patterned after provisions in the U.S. public land law, was too complicated for the average peasant to handle, especially when the Bureau of Lands officials, entirely Filipino after 1913, often gave him delay and corrupt connivance with land-grabbers instead of assistance. Throughout the American period less than 35,000 homestead applicants received patents to their land, whereas the number of farmers increased by over 700,000.[27] An antiusury law was equally ineffective in preventing comparatively small loans from causing owner-cultivators' loss of their land. Co-operative credit schemes were tried, but they failed largely because of inadequate government supervision.

The most direct American attempt to transform tenants into owners was the friar-lands purchase of 1904, in which the insular government acquired over 400,000 acres of agricultural land owned by the Catholic orders. But the redistribution of the estates failed to achieve its purpose. Instead of transfering Church ownership to the cultivators, a sizable number of medium and small landlords were created. Poor drafting by Americans of the legal provisions and Filipino administration highly susceptible to landlord pressures were responsible for this failure.

The percentage of farmers who were tenants doubled from 1900 to 1935. The economic frustration of the tenants, unable to find meaningful political expression, erupted in three small rebellions in Central Luzon during the 1920s and 1930s.

[27] Karl Pelzer, *Pioneer Settlement in the Asiatic Tropics* (New York: Institute of Pacific Relations, 1945), p. 111.

Industrialization was conscious policy in the American-ruled Philippines only under Governor Harrison's leadership. Between 1916 and 1919 several laws were passed by the legislature, on Harrison's recommendation, creating investment guaranty funds to encourage private industry and setting up five government corporations with a total capital authorization of $25 million for the development of the coal, iron, petroleum, cement, and other industries. The coal, iron, and cement companies actually undertook operations. Despite the determined efforts of General Wood, Harrison's successor, to "get the government out of business," most of the enterprises mentioned continued under government control, albeit without additional capital or government loans.[28]

U.S. trade policy toward the Philippines contributed very little to the preparation for independence. In 1909 Congress, in the Payne-Aldrich Tariff Act, allowed free entry of Philippine products into the American market and at the same time adopted a tariff law for the Philippines which allowed free entry of all American products.[29] Free trade with the United States undoubtedly stimulated the production of the Philippines' two main export crops, sugar and coconuts, since their U.S. prices were higher than the world price. But agricultural development is not synonymous with balanced economic development and, at least in the Philippines, merely reinforced the socioeconomic and political position of the landed gentry.

Granting Independence

In the midst of the Great Depression the United States finally decided to relinquish sovereignty over the Philippines. The culmination of a series of "independence missions" to the United States and of agitation by American liberals for the fulfillment of the vague pledge in the Jones Act was the passage by a Democratic Congress of the Hare-Hawes-Cutting Bill, even over President Hoover's "lame duck" veto, in January 1933. It provided for independence after a transitional period of ten years of nearly complete self-government. It also made provision for the retention of U.S. military and naval bases in the islands after independence. Senate president and Nacionalista Party head Manuel Quezon especially disliked this last provision. Nor was

[28] See Jose Apostol, *The Economic Policy of the Philippine Government: Ownership and Operation of Business* (Manila: University of the Philippines, 1927).

[29] Grunder and Livezey, *op. cit.*, pp. 104–116. See also Pedro Abelarde, *American Tariff Policy toward the Philippines* (New York: King's Crown Press, 1947).

he pleased with the fact that the independence mission which claimed credit for the act was headed by his political rival, Speaker Osmeña. He therefore persuaded the Philippine legislature to reject the Hare-Hawes-Cutting Act and himself headed another mission to Washington asking for several revisions. This mission, because of its willingness to compromise and Roosevelt's assistance, was able to go home in March 1934 with the Tydings-McDuffie Act, identical to the earlier act except that no specific provision was made for U.S. retention of military, as distinguished from naval, bases.[30]

Philippine independence missions and American liberals, even under the leadership of Roosevelt, could not, however, have obtained such an act without the assistance of some incongruous allies—certain special-interest groups. The depression had caused American farm interests to look desperately for relief, and those who suffered real or imaginary hurt from the competition of Philippine products sought relief in the exclusion of those products. They had failed in a direct attempt to amend the tariff on Philippine exports, but found that the respectable cloak of the advocacy of independence increased the effectiveness of their efforts. Tied to independence was the end of free entry into American markets of Philippine sugar, coconut oil, rope, and other less important items. There was to be, according to the Tydings-McDuffie Act, a gradual application of export taxes in lieu of American tariff over a five-year period, beginning in 1941, before full U.S. tariff duties would be applied to Philippine products. That these economic interests were able to accomplish what they did is partly explainable by the fact that the ratio of American investments in the Philippines and exports to the Philippines to the size of American gross domestic investment and gross domestic product was smaller than such a ratio for other colonial powers.[31]

Under the terms of the Tydings-McDuffie Act the conduct of foreign relations and national defense during the ten-year Commonwealth period remained under American control, and the U.S. President was

[30] For the text see Hayden, *op. cit.*, Appendix I. For the historical account see Grunder and Livezey, *op. cit.*, ch. xii, and David Bernstein, *The Philippine Story* (New York: Farrar, Straus and Co., 1947), pp. 125–132, 136–137.

[31] For example, the Philippine market absorbed less than .2 per cent of the U.S. gross national product. Whereas the U.S. investment in the Philippines in 1940 was $127 million, at the same time Dutch investment in Indonesia amounted to $1,300 million. See *The Philippines: A Report on Business and Trade* (New York: First National City Bank of New York, 1952), p. 7, and Sumitro Djojohadikusumo, *Persualan Ekonomi di Indonesia* [Economic Problems in Indonesia] (Djakarta: Indira, 1953), p. 8.

given the power to approve or disapprove any constitutional amendment or any acts affecting currency, coinage, imports, or exports. In
extremities the United States reserved the right, by presidential proclamation, to intervene in the Philippines for the maintenance of
constitutional government. Despite these rather broad restrictions,
however, Philippine internal autonomy was really complete since,
until the Japanese invasion, the United States neither exercised nor
threatened to exercise any of its restrictive powers.

After acceptance by the Philippine legislature, the first steps in the
implementation of the Tydings-McDuffie Act were accomplished
promptly. A constitutional convention was elected, and a constitution
was framed which bears a strong resemblance to its American model.
After the approval of the constitution by plebescite and by President
Roosevelt, the Commonwealth of the Philippines was inaugurated
on November 15, 1935. The last Governor-General, Frank Murphy,
became the first High Commissioner and as such the representative
of the President of the United States in the islands. As everyone had
expected, Manuel Quezon was elected President by an overwhelming
majority. After the serious split in the Nacionalista Party, caused by
Quezon's rejection of the Hare-Hawes-Cutting Act, was patched up,
Speaker Osmeña had been nominated for the vice-presidency; he
received more votes than Quezon.

Government under the Commonwealth was thus essentially one-
party government; the Nacionalistas' only opposition came from a
number of small, unstable, and unco-ordinated parties, which held no
national offices. Under Quezon's leadership some progress was made
in agrarian reform, in expansion of the educational system, and in the
construction of public buildings and roads. But the prospect of smooth
and relatively painless transition to independence was shattered by
Japanese attack in December 1941.

Japanese Occupation

The Filipinos' reaction to Japanese invasion was unique in Southeast
Asia. The great majority voluntarily determined to resist, though for
most, of necessity, resistance was passive. For those who enjoyed self-
government and were on the threshold of independence from the
United States, Japanese promises had no appeal, especially when given
at the point of a gun. The heroism of Bataan, both American and
Filipino, is well known; it was repeated after Bataan's fall by guerrilla units throughout the Philippines. Because of this spirit of resistance, manifested by more acts of sabotage and open defiance than

anywhere else in Southeast Asia, the Japanese reserved some of their cruelest atrocities for the Filipinos. Nevertheless it can also be said that there was less disruption of the social structure and of the composition of the political elite as a result of Japanese occupation than in any other country of the region except Thailand.

There was a substantial proportion of the elite which collaborated with the Japanese. As many Filipinos are quick to point out, when commenting on "the Japanese time," "not everyone could go to the hills." In the large towns and cities the material advantages of collaborating were many. Moreover, in the urban centers were found some men with long-standing sympathies for Japan and Japanese authoritarian ideology. Most prominent of these was Associate Justice of the Supreme Court Jose P. Laurel, the only Filipino ever to receive an honorary degree from Tokyo Imperial University. All who collaborated say that they were doing so to protect the Filipino people from the full fury of Japanese brutality; some were. But in the face of sharply conflicting factual accounts of the Japanese regime, it is very difficult for anyone without firsthand experience to judge individual motivation.

At any rate a large percentage of the officials of the Commonwealth government served also under the Japanese.[32] From October 1943 an "independent Republic," established under Japanese auspices, operated behind the façade of a constitution. But President Jose Laurel was in fact chosen by the Japanese. He had absolute veto power over the acts of the appointed National Assembly and could, without legislative approval, enter into all kinds of "agreements" with "foreign powers," that is, Japan. In almost every matter the leaders of this "Republic" were forced to do Japanese bidding.

Though most Filipinos did not after the war view collaboration in the same black-and-white terms as did most Americans, nevertheless the Philippines was the only Southeast Asian country in which collaboration became a major postwar political issue. President Quezon, who had headed the Commonwealth government in exile in the United States, died in August 1944, and Vice-President Osmeña assumed the presidency. After the American landing in the Philippines in October, civil government was returned to the Commonwealth, though for several months Osmeña's powers were mostly on paper. The problem of what to do with collaborators was his major headache.[33]

[32] Fifty-three out of 122 members of Congress, including a majority of the Senate (Bernstein, *op. cit.*, p. 209).
[33] See *ibid.*, chs. viii and x.

In November 1944 General Douglas MacArthur, Supreme Commander of United States Armed Forces in the Far East, had declared that he would "run to earth every disloyal Filipino." But his actions, contrary to U.S. policy established in Washington, sabotaged what attempts were made to prosecute collaborators. Most dramatic was his "liberation" in April 1945 of his prewar friend Manuel Roxas, who had been minister without portfolio in Laurel's cabinet and director of the wartime rice procurement agency which supplied the Japanese army, while four other cabinet members were "captured" and imprisoned. This and other assistance from MacArthur launched Roxas' postwar political career and helped to confuse the collaboration issue. Though a People's Court was set up to try those indicted for treason, no important person was convicted. In January 1948 all those either indicted or convicted were given amnesty by President Roxas, except any who may have committed murder, theft, or rape as well. In spite of a feeble attempt to raise the issue again in the 1949 election campaign, it was dead. In the fluidity of Philippine politics "guerrillas" and "collaborators" were by that time to be found on both sides of all political fences.

An Independent Republic—The Roxas Administration

When the Commonwealth Congress was reconvened, Senate President Roxas became its political leader. In January 1946 Roxas declared his candidacy for the presidency and was shortly nominated by a convention of the "Liberal Wing of the Nacionalista Party," thus inaugurating what may develop into a stable two-party system. His platform promised "to prosecute mercilessly those guilty of collaboration," [34] but ten of the sixteen senatorial candidates on his ticket had held high office under the Japanese. President Osmeña, who was nominated by the Nacionalista loyalists, obtained the support also of the Democratic Alliance, which was made up largely of peasant groups in Central Luzon and urban middle-class elements and included some Communists. Most, but not all, ex-guerrillas were found in Osmeña's camp. Roxas campaigned vigorously throughout the country, spending substantial sums, whereas Osmeña, a much older man who really wanted to retire, tended to his official duties, not leaving Manila. In April a slim majority elected both a Liberal President and Congress. In May, Roxas was inaugurated to head the Commonwealth and on July 4, 1946, became the first President of the Republic of the Philippines.[35]

[34] *Ibid.*, p. 241.   [35] *Ibid.*, ch. xii.

One of President Roxas' most pressing tasks was to gain official Philippine acceptance of the Bell Trade Act, passed by the U.S. Congress in April, the terms of which were embodied in an international agreement. Free trade with the United States was thereby extended for eight years after independence, and equal rights, or parity, were given Americans and Filipinos in exploitation of natural resources until 1974. The sugar interests in the Liberal Party were determined to push its approval, since rehabilitation of the sugar industry through preservation of a guaranteed tariff-free market in the United States was one of their main purposes. The agreement was finally approved by the Philippine Congress only because many groups which openly opposed all of the act's main provisions had nevertheless argued "necessity" and recommended approval. The Philippine Rehabilitation Act, in which the U.S. Congress authorized funds to make payments for war damages, had provided that until Philippine ratification of the trade agreement no war-damage claim over $500 should be paid. The final hurdle in ratification was adoption of an amendment to the constitution, since the parity provision was in conflict with Article XIII, which reserved the utilization of natural resources to Filipino citizens. The amendment received a three-fourths majority in a Liberal Congress only after that body had refused to seat ten Nacionalista and Democratic Alliance Congressmen on the grounds that they had been elected with the aid of fraud and violence.[36] The necessary plebiscite was held in March 1947, with Roxas campaigning for "yes." Nearly 60 per cent of the registered voters stayed away from the polls, a high rate of abstention in the Philippines, but those who did vote gave the amendment an overwhelming majority.

Having assured the flow of U.S. rehabilitation funds, the Roxas administration was forced to devote most of its attention to the Hukbalahap (an abbreviation for the Tagalog words meaning "People's Army against the Japanese"). This group was formed in a Central Luzon village in March 1942,[37] including in its leadership several well-known Communists. Though the Huks fought the Japanese, they also occasionally fought other guerrillas whom they termed "reactionary."

After the war, at the same time that most guerrilla groups were given recognition for services rendered to the American cause, Huk

[36] See Shirley Jenkins, *American Economic Policy toward the Philippines* (Stanford: Stanford University Press, 1954), ch. vii.

[37] Russell Fifield, "The Hukbalahap Today," *Far Eastern Survey*, XX (Jan. 24, 1951), 13–18.

leaders Luis Taruc and Casto Alejandrino were imprisoned by the
U.S. army. U.S. military police assisted the Philippine constabulary
and the private landlords' armies, called "civilian guards" or "temporary police," in restricting left-wing political activity, thus encouraging
armed resistance.[38] The size of Huk forces by that time may already
have equaled the Philippine constabulary in Central Luzon. Arms
were easily obtainable; clashes multiplied steadily. In the summer of
1946 Huk Supreme Commander Taruc, out of jail since September
1945, attempted to negotiate a cease-fire with President Roxas, while
insisting that his followers be allowed to retain their arms. But negotiations failed, and Taruc left Manila "for the field."

Roxas then adopted a "mailed fist" policy, which was difficult to
make effective, since in many places the peasants would not co-
operate with the often abusive constabulary. As fighting spread, a
number of political leaders proposed amnesty for the Huks. Roxas,
however, declared the Hukbalahap and the affiliated National Peasants
Union illegal in March 1948. But he did not have time to enforce this
measure, for he died of a heart attack in April.

The Quirino Administration

Vice-President Quirino, a former senator from Ilocos Sur, was thrust
into a leadership position for which he was unprepared. Nevertheless he
moved boldly during his first months in the presidential office, exceed-
ing popular expectations. In June, as the fruit of negotiations with Luis
Taruc, President Quirino declared amnesty for all Huks who "presented themselves with all their arms and ammunition to the duly
constituted authorities." [39] But in spite of an apparent desire by both
Quirino and Taruc to make amnesty work, disagreement developed
when the government insisted that arms, once "presented," be surrendered and the Huks refused to do so. Just before the August 30
deadline for arms surrender, Taruc returned to "the field" and announced by open letter that he was a member of the Communist
Party. The party was, in fact, by that time in firm control of Huk
leadership. Soon thereafter the lines hardened. Quirino announced an
"all out" drive against the Huks.

It was in the midst of dissidence and of a growing number of re-

---

[38] See Hernando Abaya, *Betrayal in the Philippines* (New York: A. A. Wyn,
1946), ch. vii.

[39] *Manila Times*, June 22, 1948; see also July 12 and August 1, 1948, for Taruc's
attitude toward amnesty.

ports of corruption that the 1949 elections were held. President Quirino, running for re-election, was opposed by Jose Laurel, former president of the Japanese-sponsored "Republic" and nominee of the Nacionalista Party, which had attacked Roxas for collaboration in 1946. His other opponent was Senator Jose Avelino, an independent Liberal renowned for his apologias for corruption. The election outcome was decided by the political machine of the majority party which, with armed men, money, and few scruples, delivered a vote of nearly 52 per cent for Quirino. Competent observers estimate that about one-fifth of Quirino's total resulted from fraudulent registration, fraudulent tallying, and voter intimidation.[40]

The way in which the Liberal regime achieved power substantially affected the way it exercised power, that is, corruption bred more corruption. The year 1950 was a low point in Philippine public morality, not rivaled till 1958. The consequences of this kind of administration and of purely economic contingencies, for example, a fall in world copra prices, were declining foreign exchange balances, acute shortages of cash in the treasury, so that salaries of government employees were months in arrears and public works projects had to be halted, and a general lack of faith in the government, which fed the fires of rebellion.

In February 1950 the Hukbalahap changed its name to Hukbong Mapagpalaya ng Bayan ("People's Liberation Army") and openly called for the overthrow of the government. From March to August the Huks held an increasingly daring series of raids, culminating in the temporary capture of two provincial capitals in Central Luzon. They regularly controlled large areas of Luzon's "rice bowl." Huk successes shocked the Quirino administration into a more realistic appraisal of its weaknesses. Several new measures were taken, including the appointment of a new Secretary of National Defense, Congressman Ramon Magsaysay, and the dismissal of incompetent and corrupt army officers. The army's capture of several top-ranking members of the Communist Party in Manila in October frustrated Huk plans for "a much bigger operation" in November.

In 1950 Philippine awareness of basic problems and a determination to solve them received a decisive stimulus from American policy which evidenced increasing concern about the Philippine crisis. Soon after the beginning of the Korean War, in July, President Truman on Presi-

---

[40] James Dalton, "Ins and Outs in the Philippines," *Far Eastern Survey,* XXI (July 30, 1952), 121, citing the report of the Senate Electoral Tribunal.

dent Quirino's invitation sent an Economic Survey Mission to the
Philippines which made an intensive study of Philippine problems and
released its report in October. Besides suggesting changes in fiscal,
monetary, trade, agricultural, industrial, and labor policy, it also recommended the provision of $250 million in U.S. aid to help carry out
the new policies. This aid was to be "strictly conditioned" on steps
being taken by the Philippine government to carry out the suggested
reforms. Implementation of the report was begun with the signing of
an agreement in November in which the Philippines promised to enact
new tax laws and a minimum wage law. In April, after this legislation
had been passed, the first U.S. funds were released.[41]

These moves against the Huks and these positive economic programs were designed to bolster the Quirino administration. But in
the last three years of his incumbency Quirino alienated one of the
most powerful component groups in his party, the sugar planters.[42]
In fact the Liberal Party which entered the 1951 campaign was split
at least three ways. President Quirino was confronted not only by
planters, led by Vice-President Fernando Lopez, but by the millers,
under the leadership of his chief economic adviser, Jose Yulo, and
closely associated with party president Eugenio Perez. All were vying
with the President's personal followers and with each other for party
hegemony. In the midst of this disunity a bill was pushed through
Congress abolishing "block voting,"[43] thus removing an institutional
reinforcement for party regularity. In part because of the uncertain
loyalties of local politicians who directed irregular armed groups that
were attempting to influence voting, the President supported the decision of his Secretary of National Defense, Magsaysay, to guard the

[41] See below, p. 500.

[42] A number of sugar mills, or centrals, which were established after the First
World War had signed contracts with the planters (i.e., landowners or large lessees,
not farm workers) which extended for thirty years. In most cases the planters
agreed to deliver 40–50 per cent of the milled product to the central as payment
for milling. When these contracts expired in the period 1948–1951, planters, much
better organized than they had been thirty years earlier, demanded a larger share
of the crop; but most centrals balked. Therefore the planters, well represented in
Congress, succeeded in getting a bill passed in 1950 which would have given them
70 per cent of the milled sugar. After Quirino had vetoed it, a modified version of
the bill—giving planters from 60 to 70 per cent of the sugar, with smaller centrals
receiving more than larger ones—was introduced in 1951 and finally enacted, becoming law in June 1952 without the President's signature. In the intervening
political struggle, Quirino lost the support of the planters. See the Sugar Act of
1952, Republic Act 809.

[43] See below, pp. 481–482.

freedom of the polls with 24,000 troops. In addition the growth of a nation-wide group of public-spirited citizens to guard the sanctity of the ballot, the National Movement for Free Elections (NAMFREL), encouraged President Quirino to support also the hard-working Commission on Elections which was supervising poll officials. These factors combined to make possible an election considerably more peaceful and more honestly administered than that of 1949. The Liberals lost to the Nacionalistas all nine Senate seats at stake and twenty-three of fifty-two provincial governorships.

Secretary Magsaysay was the focus, sharpened by this election, of whatever popular support remained for the Quirino administration. His reputation was built, in part, on the reconstruction of a disciplined armed force, with good morale and training, both willing and able to pursue the enemy. By 1953 the Huks' armed strength was broken. Magsaysay not only fought them, but he also perceived the underlying needs of the peasants who had become Huks and therefore established land settlement projects for surrendered dissidents.

The Election of 1953

By late 1952 Quirino could see that Magsaysay had become presidential timber and that the consistent support that he, as President, had given the Secretary's policies was not contributing to his own prestige. His support, understandably, diminished. Furthermore, Magsaysay's ferocious honesty was irritating to some of Quirino's less upright associates. A break was inevitable. A quiet offer of Nacionalista backing for the presidency finally caused Magsaysay to hand in his letter of resignation on February 28, 1953; said he, "It would be useless for me to continue as Secretary of National Defense with the specific duty of killing Huks as the administration continues to foster and tolerate conditions which offer fertile soil to Communism." [44] Ten days later Magsaysay was inducted into the Nacionalista Party at Senator Jose Laurel's home. Laurel urged Magsaysay's nomination for the presidency and withdrew his own name from the preconvention jockeying. In the April convention Magsaysay won overwhelmingly; he received the full weight of "old guard" support. They knew that he was the only candidate popular enough to win against the machinery of the majority party, and they thought that he was politically naïve enough to make it possible for them to control him.

The majority of Liberal Party leadership was behind President

[44] *Philippine Herald,* March 1, 1953.

Quirino's bid for nomination and re-election. But the sugar planters and their allies, after losing a floor fight at the party convention, walked out and formed their own Democratic Party, nominating Ambassador Carlos Romulo for President and endorsing Vice-President Lopez' re-election. (The Liberals nominated Jose Yulo to be Quirino's running mate.) The planters' reliance on crop loans from the government-controlled Philippine National Bank [45] created very strong pressure to back the winning side. Thus as the campaign progressed and it became evident that, though the Democrats held the balance of power, they could not win alone, negotiations for coalition with the Nacionalista Party were begun. The coalition was consummated on August 21, with Romulo's withdrawal and Lopez' acceptance of a berth in the coalition Senate slate.

Magsaysay's campaign was unprecedentedly vigorous. He spoke in more towns and villages and shook more hands than any Philippine presidential candidate before him. The campaign was well financed, in part by American private citizens and organizations, and well organized. Besides the support of twenty-three governors and eleven senators, the Magsaysay bandwagon received a unique impetus from the Magsaysay-for-President Movement (MPM). This was a group of young lawyers, businessmen, and ex-guerrillas, most of them with little political experience, who set up a national organization distinct from the Nacionalista Party. MPM leaders were closer to Magsaysay personally than most party bosses. In contrast with Magsaysay's campaign vigor, Quirino spent July and August in the United States undergoing serious abdominal surgery. In fact for a time it was thought that he would not live. Vice-presidential candidate Yulo bore the brunt of the campaigning.

Widespread fears of fraud and intimidation proved unwarranted, because preventive measures had been taken. In a comparatively free and nonviolent election with a higher percentage of registered voters voting (78 per cent) than ever before, Magsaysay received about two-thirds of the votes.

The Magsaysay Administration

President Magsaysay's administration was launched in a wave of enthusiasm. On inauguration day, like President Andrew Jackson, he

---

[45] In the fiscal year 1954, for example, the Philippine National Bank lent nearly 150 million pesos, or about 65 per cent of all crop loans, to the sugar industry. The government's Rehabilitation Finance Corporation was also an important credit source for sugar men.

opened Malacañang to the people, and thousands flocked through the chandeliered halls for the first time. He continued to keep his doors open to all callers. The accomplishments of the Magsaysay administration were important in several fields. For instance, a favorable atmosphere was created for the growth of a free, responsible labor movement. The Bureau of Customs was given a house cleaning, and dishonesty in foreign exchange allocation was substantially reduced. But so much had been expected of Magsaysay—he himself vowed in his inaugural address to achieve the "impossible"—that there was sharp dissatisfaction in some quarters when inevitable failings were revealed. Enthusiasm lagged in the second half of his administration, and there seemed to be indications that he was having greater and greater difficulty in finding men to appoint who were imbued with his ideals. Magsaysay's administrative achievements were probably not as important as his impact on the Philippine political process.

Midway in the Magsaysay administration the popularity of the Nacionalista Party was still high. In the 1955 senatorial election, which marked another step forward in honest poll administration, not one Liberal was elected.[46] The Liberal Party was so pessimistic about its future, and so unsuccessful in its search within its ranks for a strong presidential candidate for 1957, that in July 1956 several Liberal Congressmen proposed that the Liberal Party nominate Magsaysay.

The March 1957 airplane crash on a Cebu mountainside which killed Ramon Magsaysay was a terrible tragedy for the Philippine nation. Most Filipinos felt it as a personal tragedy as well. Several hundred thousand people lined the route of his funeral procession. The loss of this dominating figure not only was cause for mourning, but in addition completely altered the political scene.

The Election of 1957

The headless Nacionalista Party was the scene of greatest disorder. But Carlos Garcia, who as Vice-President had succeeded to the presidency on Magsaysay's death, gained control of the party's machinery by the fullest utilization of the President's powers and won nomination at the convention on the first ballot. The Nacionalista Party

[46] Senator Claro Recto, the President's sharpest critic, had consented, after his nomination on the Nacionalista Party ticket was blocked by Magsaysay, to become a "guest candidate" on the Liberal ticket, without discarding his Nacionalista affiliation, and was elected. A perceptive interpretation of this election is found in John Smail, "Magsaysay and the Philippine Election of 1955" (unpublished manuscript, Ithaca, N.Y., 1957). See also Carlos Quirino, *Magsaysay of the Philippines* (Quezon City: Phoenix Press, Inc., 1958), pp. 213–220.

which nominated Garcia was essentially the pre-Magsaysay party, however. Most of the Magsaysay-for-President Movement, together with other younger elements of the Magsaysay administration, broke with Garcia in May and formed the Progressive Party. Its presidential nominee was former newspaper publisher Manuel Manahan, who had been customs collector under Magsaysay. Its organization was weak.

Jose Yulo, previously "in retirement," announced his willingness to accept the Liberal presidential nomination in April and was for all practical purposes nominated before the convention opened. Representative Diosdado Macapagal, the best Liberal vote getter in 1955, became his running mate. Senator Claro Recto, convinced that he could not get the Nacionalista nomination, joined with Senator Lorenzo Tañada to form the Nationalist Citizens Party, with a strongly nationalistic platform.

In this unique four-cornered race Carlos Garcia became the first Philippine President to win office by a minority vote (41 per cent). In a free, but costly, election his skillful distribution of "pork barrel," patronage, and privately contributed funds snatched victory. Garcia established another first by failing to carry with him his vice-presidential candidate, House Speaker Jose Laurel, Jr. Laurel lost to Macapagal primarily because of the outspoken opposition of the Roman Catholic clergy. The Speaker had led the fight in the House in 1956 for a bill requiring the reading of Rizal's anticlerical novels in all high schools.

Manahan, who campaigned as the "new Magsaysay," handshook his way through more villages than had the late President; he was more nearly the recipient of the martyred hero's mantle of mass popularity than any other candidate. He emphasized the need for more rapid land reform and placed first in most provinces of Central Luzon. Manahan received only 21 per cent of the total vote, however. Recto, like Laurel anathema to the Church, talked mostly of nationalism, on a fairly high intellectual level. His campaign had little appeal for the masses, and he placed a poor fourth with a vote of less than 9 per cent.[47]

The majority of voters are therefore represented by a small minority of elective officials. With the election of a Vice-President and two senators the Liberal Party was saved from the ignominious defeat that it had feared in 1957, but it made a poorer showing in the House,

[47] David Wurfel, "The Philippine Elections: New Trends," *Foreign Policy Bulletin,* Jan. 1, 1958, pp. 60–64.

nineteen of its candidates being elected, than it had in 1953. The Progressives, the third largest party, were left with no national officials whatsoever. At this point it seemed doubtful whether they could maintain their independent existence in such a circumstance.

Garcia's new term began in an atmosphere different from Magsaysay's. Though the President evidenced a certain degree of economic realism by calling for "austerity," for example, a drastic cut in nonessential imports in order to prevent the complete evaporation of foreign exchange reserves, he has not always set the example for other political leaders which would be necessary to make austerity effective. During the first year of the Garcia administration the incidence of official corruption rose sharply. Some critics compared it unfavorably with the Quirino administration.

· XXIII ·

The Contemporary Setting

THE Republic of the Philippines covers 115,600 square miles, making it little more than half the size of Thailand, or of Texas, but double that of Malaya. This area is divided among more than 7,000 islands and is inhabited in 1958 by approximately 23 million people speaking about seventy distinct languages.

The People

These figures paint a picture of greater diversity than actually exists, however. The interisland shipping network makes of the sea more a highway than a barrier; 6,620 islands are smaller than one square mile, whereas the eleven islands of more than 1,000 square miles comprise 95 per cent of the land area and have 90 per cent of the population. Furthermore, 89 per cent of the inhabitants are native speakers of one of the eight major languages.[1] About 4 per cent are Muslims of Mindanao and Sulu, speaking nine different dialects. They are for the most part fishermen and shifting cultivators, midway in cultural development between Christian and pagan Filipinos—except for the younger Muslim leadership which, through educational achievement, is already well integrated into upper-class Filipino culture. Almost all the rest of the languages are spoken by isolated pagan

[1] Fred Eggan and others, *Area Handbook on the Philippines* (New Haven: Human Relations Area Files, Inc., 1956), I, 265–307.

peoples, which together account for only 3.5 per cent of the population.

The eight major linguistic groups are roughly equivalent to the nominal membership in Christian churches, which encompasses over 92 per cent of all Filipinos.[2] Predominant, of course, is the Roman Catholic Church, with about 80 per cent of the population in its fold. The Aglipayans, or members of the Philippine Independent Church, which was an offshoot of the Catholic Church during the revolution and was founded by Father Aglipay and other nationalistic Filipino priests, are next with nearly 6 per cent. The Protestants, with almost 5 per cent of the population, are the third largest Christian group.[3]

The Chinese are the largest alien group in the Philippines and now number over a quarter of a million.[4] They stand on the edge of Philippine politics,[5] but in the midst of the national economic life. In 1953, for example, they were reported to control 42 per cent of the investments in commercial enterprises.[6] Philippine Chinese have become racially and culturally assimilated to a greater extent than is true of Chinese communities elsewhere in Southeast Asia, except perhaps in Thailand. Frequent intermarriage with Catholic Filipinos has usually resulted in offspring who were reared as Catholics and accepted as Filipinos. There is Chinese blood in a large percentage of middle- and upper-class Filipinos today. In recent years, however, the rate of assimilation has been slowing, caused by an increasing percentage of Chinese women, consequently decreasing intermarriage, and by an intensification of Chinese nationalism. Despite the degree

[2] Native speakers of the eight major linguistic groups as a percentage of the total population are as follows (*Statistical Handbook of the Philippines, 1903–53* [Manila: Bureau of Printing, 1954], p. 6, from the 1948 census): Cebuano (Sugbuhanon), 24.7; Tagalog, 19.4; Ilongo (Hiligaynon), 12.3; Ilocano, 12.2; Bicolano, 7.6; Samareño (Waraywaray), 6.3; Pampango, 3.3; Pangasinan, 2.7.

[3] Iglesia ni Kristo, the fastest growing church, led by a Filipino ex-Protestant who calls himself "Bishop," has about 1.5 per cent (Eggan, *op. cit.,* II, 472, 514, 720, 740). Percentages are estimates for 1958 based on the 1948 census and the trend of growth within the various churches, with such corrections of the percentages for pagans, Protestants, and Iglesia ni Kristo as seemed necessary.

[4] Official figures are much lower, but do not account for the large number of illegal entrants. The prewar Japanese community of about 50,000 either retreated with the Japanese army in 1944 or was evacuated in 1945. Americans and Spaniards and other Europeans together account for about 30,000.

[5] One full-blooded Chinese, now a Filipino citizen, is a member of the House of Representatives, however.

[6] Compiled by the Department of Commerce and Industry, quoted in *American Chamber of Commerce Journal,* XXX (1954), 417. The actual figure was probably somewhat higher. See also George Weightman, "The Chinese Community in the Philippines" (unpublished M.A. thesis, University of the Philippines, 1952).

of assimilation already achieved, the Chinese are still the object of Filipino resentment, mainly because of their superior economic status.

Agricultural Economy and Rural Society

The Philippine economy is predominantly agricultural, though somewhat less so than that of the rest of the area. Agriculture provides 39 per cent of the national income, work for 61 per cent of the gainfully employed, and 76 per cent of Philippine exports.[7] Over three-fourths of the value of these agricultural exports is derived from three crops, coconuts, sugar cane, and abacá (the bananalike tree from which Manila hemp is extracted).

In this agricultural economy opportunities for the average farmer are limited, and power is narrowly concentrated. Although the 1948 census showed that 37 per cent of farm operators were landless tenants—an average of 70 per cent in six Central Luzon provinces— the figure may now be as much as 46 per cent or more.[8] Alongside this great landless class are 600 individuals and corporations, constituting .036 per cent of farm operators, who own more than 1,272,000 acres, or about 13 per cent of the nation's farm land. About half of the farmsteads, whether owner- or tenant-operated, are less than five acres.[9] Among the little more than half of all farmers who are full owners of their land, thousands lose their land each year through indebtedness.[10]

The political implications of this ownership pattern and the social organization that accompanies it are unfortunate for a nation aspiring to be democratic. Landlords have dominated rural community leader-

[7] United Nations, *Economic Survey of Asia and the Far East, 1957* (Bangkok, 1958), p. 215, and Office of Statistical Co-ordination and Standards, National Economic Council, *Philippine Statistical Survey of Households Bulletin*, ser. 1, I (May 1956), 11. The accuracy of statistics in the Philippines, though improving and probably now greater than in other Southeast Asian countries, cannot be taken for granted. Even figures such as the above which attempt to describe the economy or society in general terms must be considered approximations.

[8] Generoso Rivera and Robert McMillan, *The Rural Philippines* (Manila: Mutual Security Agency, 1952), p. 42.

[9] Arturo Sorongon, *A Special Study of Landed Estates* (Manila: International Co-operation Administration, 1955), Tables 2 and 4; Bureau of Census and Statistics, *Summary Report on the 1948 Census of Agriculture* (Manila: Bureau of Printing, 1954), Table 7.

[10] See Generoso Rivera and Robert McMillan, *An Economic and Social Survey of Rural Households in Central Luzon* (Manila: Foreign Operations Administration, 1954). This survey showed that 83 per cent of farm owners were in debt, paying interest at rates up to 100 per cent for a period of a few months.

ship in most areas. Their political power was originally derived from the feudalistic, noneconomic obligations that have traditionally been owed by tenants to landlords and from the latter's ability to retaliate against tenants who ignored tradition. Thus, in the face of ejection from their plots for failure to do so, tenants voted in accordance with their landlord's "recommendation." Many also followed their landlord's advice willingly.

These traditions were beginning to be challenged by tenants in Central Luzon under Communist and other radical leadership in the late 1930s. During the Japanese occupation and for a short time thereafter the Huks administered large areas in which landlord political influence was nil. Even with the defeat of the Huks in 1953 Central Luzon landlords did not dare demand the old type of political loyalty and would not have received it even if they had. Portions of Iloilo province have gone through the same transformation. But in parts of the Philippines farther from the leavening influences of metropolitan areas, the traditional pattern is still strong and is only just now being shaken.

In a generally hierarchical rural society landlords also command respect and exercise influence outside their own landholdings, in large part because of their superior educational attainment and of their willingness to assume the culturally imposed obligations, including financial, of paternalistic leadership. Many, as well, are still able to manipulate police and courts for their benefit.

New types of leadership, independent of the old hierarchy, are, however, also developing in the rural Philippines. Until recently there was no official selected from within the village. But the provision, since 1956, for the election of the barrio, or village, lieutenant will reinforce his position as local political leader and may relieve him of some of his former dependence on his superiors, the town mayor and councilors.[11] He has always been the most important channel of information from the outside. The new-style leadership is also being exercised in the parent-teacher associations, perhaps the most active voluntary associations in rural areas since the war, which have not only built more than one-half of all village schools, but have exercised influence outside the realm of educational affairs. Farmers' cooperative marketing associations and tenant unions, for example, the Federation of Free Farmers, are also vehicles for the new type of leadership. In some areas they are quite strong. Nevertheless there

[11] See p. 479.

is still considerable correlation between rural leadership and wealth, educational attainment, and family connections.

Any generalizations about rural society or the agricultural economy in the Philippines must be qualified by geographical differentiation. Area specialization in certain crops creates interest groups with geographical boundaries, which can therefore find effective representation in the legislature. Rice is planted on 45 per cent of Philippine farm land, but domestic production is not enough to meet consumption requirements for this diet staple, and some importation is usually necessary. Only in the Central Luzon plain is there grown a great surplus over local needs; political leaders from this area constitute the "rice bloc," though the term is not frequently used. More common is the use of "tobacco bloc," referring to Congressmen from northern Luzon, where tobacco is the most important crop by value. Almost all production is consumed in the Philippines. Thus the policy goals of the tobacco and rice blocs are substantially the same—price support and restriction of imports.

Opposed to these blocs on one great issue of national economic policy are the producers—both growers and processors—of the three important export crops, coconuts, sugar cane, and abacá. All three of these groups favor giving exporters a free hand in the use of the dollars they earn abroad. The "sugar bloc," consisting of Congressmen from Negros, Panay, and a few districts in Central Luzon, is most vocal and is most powerful, since sugar is the most important industry in the Philippines from the standpoint of capital invested, taxes paid, dollars earned by exports, and government credit received. Coconut producers are scattered throughout the Philippines south of Manila and are not so tightly organized. Abacá production is limited to southeastern Mindanao.

The large producers in each of these interest groups have their own associations. The National Federation of Sugarcane Planters and the National Rice Producers Association are the oldest and most influential. Together, the leaders of these organizations form an important segment of the economic elite.

Industrial Economy and Urban Society

Though agriculture remains predominant, the Philippine economy is developing an industrial sector. The percentage of gainfully employed in agriculture is dropping; manufacturing now provides jobs for over 12 per cent. Almost 15 per cent of the net domestic product, a higher percentage than in any other Southeast Asian country, is derived from manufacturing.

The mode of development is a modification of the Japanese pattern, primarily with private capital. In fact government participation in gross fixed capital formation was estimated in 1956 as only 25 per cent, compared to 29 per cent in Japan and about 50 per cent in Burma.[12] Though foreign private capital, primarily American, has predominated in the past, over half of capital stock in the islands is now Filipino-owned,[13] and more than 80 per cent of commercial bank credit is given by Filipino-owned banks. Government investment is limited in most cases to fields in which private capital will not or could not easily enter, such as hydroelectric power, irrigation, or highways.

Industrialization, even though in its first stages, is creating two new interest groups, which will give better balance to the complex of social forces in the Philippines. On the one hand, an industrial entrepreneurial class—still miniscule—finds, for example, that its desire for more foreign exchange allotments to machinery imports and industrial raw materials puts it in opposition to those who want to import the more immediately profitable luxury items. These young industrialists have come out of the older commercial class or from large landholding families, and they have divided loyalties. But the group as a whole has found it desirable to organize into the Philippine Chamber of Industries to help protect their interests as industrialists.

Urban laborers, on the other hand, are numerous, but too weak economically to wield much power as yet. Labor organizations in the Philippines have grown phenominally since the passage in 1953 of the Industrial Peace Act, patterned after the U.S. Wagner Act. The number of registered unions jumped from 838 to over 2,100 in July 1956. Union members probably account for about one-fourth of nonagricultural wage and salary workers. Top union leadership, most of which comes from the middle class, has now largely adopted the philosophy of the American labor movement. Unions are not formally affiliated with political parties. Union leaders, however, not only publicly announce support for candidates, but occasionally run for office them-

[12] United Nations, *Economic Survey of Asia and the Far East, 1957*, pp. 214–216. Under the recently published Five Year Plan, however, 40 per cent of net investment is to be provided by the government.

[13] See Benjamin Higgins, "Development Problems in the Philippines: A Comparison with Indonesia," *Far Eastern Survey*, XXVI (1957), 161–169. Capital accumulated in the Philippines by permanent resident Chinese should not be termed "foreign capital," nor, on the other hand, is it "Filipino-owned."

selves, although the well-fed myth that union leaders "control" the "labor vote" seems to have even less basis in fact than it has in the United States.

There is an important aspect of Philippine social development which is only partly the result of infant industrialization. Urbanization, as elsewhere in Southeast Asia, seems to be running ahead of industrial development. Already 25 per cent of the population lives in towns and cities, with the great metropolitan area of Manila accounting for nearly 10 per cent. Outside the Manila area are six cities with populations over 100,000. It is likely that noneconomic values of urban life brought to rural areas by mass communications have accelerated migration to the cities even without economic motivation.

Class Structure

Though "peasant"—a term Filipinos do not often use—is a social status not difficult to distinguish, drawing other class lines in the Philippines poses real problems, since for Southeast Asia these lines are comparatively fluid. Kinship and other personal ties across class boundaries help to keep class antagonisms at a minimum in most areas, despite evident extremes of wealth.

The growth of a middle class, a positive contribution to democratic development, is more advanced in the Philippines than in any other Southeast Asian country. Educational opportunities have made entrance into the middle class from below possible for many, especially since the war. The more than 160,000 students enrolled in colleges and universities in 1954 were equal to almost 2 per cent of the labor force. Another important area of middle-class recruitment lies in the very large families among the landed gentry, families with usually twice the national average of three or four children. Income from land alone is not sufficient to support the offspring of most such families in the style to which they become accustomed. Professional or managerial income is necessary as a supplement; often the "supplement" becomes the major source of income.

In the Philippines "middle class" is not synonymous with "bureaucracy," in contrast with some countries in the area, since the government service cannot possibly absorb even the majority of the products of the educational system. In May 1956 about 8.5 per cent of the labor force were professional and technical men, managers and administrators, or clerical and office workers. Only about one-third of these were government employees.

The upper class is composed of large landholders and of large industrial and commercial entrepreneurs—and their lawyers. The political power of landlords, including some with medium holdings who retain the political position of wealthier owners, is relatively greater than their economic power. There are still a number of very wealthy, but politically neutral, alien businessmen. Nevertheless, to a larger extent than in any other Southeast Asian country except bureaucratic-capitalist Thailand and Communist North Vietnam, the Philippine economic and political elites are coterminous. But, unlike Thailand, it is more common for economic power to beget political power than vice versa, though there are a number of professional politicians who did not join the upper class, or the more restricted economic elite, until after achieving high public office. In the past decade an increasingly important number of the middle class has moved into the political elite, retaining their middle-class economic status. The political elite today includes top national government officials, both elected and appointed, the President's advisers, unofficial as well as official, some of the provincial governors, and private persons either formally or informally related to the political parties. It probably does not number much over two hundred.

Interest Groups

Politics has frequently been called the Philippine national pastime; there is certainly a strong tendency toward the politicalization of leadership in all occupations and interest groups. Three occupational groups which, besides serving as avenues of entrance into the political elite, have potential or actual political influence are the army, the press, and public school teachers.

Because the Philippines won its independence peacefully, the army was never glorified as the leader of a nationalist revolution. The recipient of training for many years in the American nonpolitical military tradition, it is today one of the least politically oriented armies in Southeast Asia. There were individual officers during the Quirino administration who were deeply involved in politics, both locally and nationally. But this politics was of a personal, extramilitary nature. During Magsaysay's incumbency in the National Defense Department a military *élan* was developed and given nonmilitary goals, for example, land settlement or mediation of tenancy disputes. President Magsaysay appointed many young officers to civil posts in his search for honest and efficient administrators, thus providing entrance for some into the political elite. But this meant no easy interchangeability of military and political "hats," since most of them were required to resign their active commissions. After Magsaysay died, many were even forced out of their civilian jobs because of the antagonism of "old guard" politicians.

During the Magsaysay administration top military leaders felt little need to engage in concerted political action, since, on the whole their goals were already being served by the civilian government. As evidence, although the constabulary continued to fulfill the responsibilities of election supervision thrust on it by the Commission on Elections, there was never any substantiated charge of political favoritism against it as an organization. Only once, by threatening to resign, did the military leadership attempt as a group to influence Congress openly, and this failed. The attempt merely increased the politician's suspicion of the military.[14] If, with Magsaysay's passing, any remaining young officers who shared his *élan* should find their goals consistently frustrated, a rationale for more drastic group political action would be created which could pose a threat to constitutional processes.

The press plays a more important political role in the Philippines than the military, but, like the army, insofar as it ever acts as a group its main group interest is the preservation of its own effectiveness. It is also an important avenue of entrance into the political elite. Both Carlos Romulo and Manuel Manahan were newspaper editors.

The politically significant segment of the Philippine press is primarily an English-language press and is concentrated in Manila. Manila dailies are larger in circulation and in number of pages than anywhere else in Southeast Asia. This in turn requires larger staffs and larger printing plants, and, since the publishing business is large-scale enterprise, sizable investment as well. Large investors in the publishing business have often accumulated their capital in other enterprises, such as sugar or shipping, and thus can speak, directly or indirectly, for those interests. The *Philippines Free Press*, with a uniquely national distribution, is politically the most important weekly; it speaks primarily for and to the middle class. The growing provincial press—more than twenty-five weeklies and dailies by 1958—operates with very little capital and is showing some of the proverbial political independence of American small-town newspapers. Unlike the setup in Indonesia, no newspapers are political party organs.

The political importance of the press has been primarily in its ex-

[14] *Manila Bulletin,* July 27, 28, and 30, 1956.

posure of and attack on governmental inefficiency and corruption, in which it has been more vigilant than the opposition party. Fortunately it has never been harassed by government censorship or the shutting down of presses. In fact even libel laws have not significantly restrained what has sometimes been called the "freest press in the world." In recent years, however, both legislative and executive officials have seen the importance of having press agents. Many newsmen play a dual role of reporter and "public relations officer." The financial arrangements involved in this relationship could substantially qualify the freedom and integrity of political journalism.

Public school teachers, more numerous than the members of the armed forces, are also counted among the most powerful pressure groups in the Philippines.[15] In 1955 the streams of letters and delegations to Congress urging passage of a bill raising teacher salaries prompted those Congressmen questioned to judge it the bill of the year with the greatest constituent support. Teachers do not usually lobby so vigorously for other types of legislation, however. The teachers' strength lies in their opinion leadership role at the local level and in the appointment of chairmen of boards of election inspectors from among their ranks.

The Church

The Catholic Church is the largest and best-organized noneconomic interest group in the Philippines and in recent years the most important political force outside the political parties. The ecclesiastical elite does not openly enter politics; some of the Church hierarchy, however, come from families within the political elite and move in the same social circles. During the Magsaysay administration archbishops participated behind the scenes in high-level decision making on several issues. Leadership in Catholic lay organizations, on the other hand, is an accepted entryway into politics. For example, the former chief legal counsel of Catholic Action, Francisco Rodrigo, is now a senator.

The interest which the Church is most determined to further is Catholic education.[16] This policy takes the form of trying to limit government control over Catholic schools, to which all financially able Catholic parents have a Church-defined obligation to send their chil-

[15] Carl Lande, "Politics in the Philippines" (unpublished Ph.D. thesis, Harvard University, 1958), pp. 288 ff.

[16] See Joint Pastoral Letters of the Philippine Hierarchy, *Manila Times*, Feb. 18, 1953, and April 12, 1955.

dren, and to push the implementation of the constitutional mandate for religious instruction in public schools on terms favorable to the Church. In 1953 a concerted campaign in the press and in Congress, spearheaded by Catholic Action, to remove the three top officials of the Department of Education for failure to take adequate measures for public school religious instruction did not succeed. The desirability of having more elective leaders willing to act on the hierarchy's suggestions became apparent; the Church, therefore, in the election campaign of 1953 moved more actively onto the political stage than before and has remained there. The Church has publicly announced support simply for "Catholic candidates," but lay leaders and many local priests translate this formula into specific endorsements. Indirectly the hierarchy's personal preferences also become known. Magsaysay and the Nacionalista Party were the chief beneficiaries of such endorsement and preferences in 1953 and 1955. Church influence in elections has produced the desired result. There is no need for a "Catholic party." The hierarchy now has a decisive voice in the selection of a Secretary of Education, who is at present also the grand knight of the Knights of Columbus.

There is also a countermovement to increased Catholic political power and to what many feel is a Church attempt to control the whole educational system. A majority of its leadership is composed of Protestants and Masons. The anticlerical element in Philippine nationalism, so strong during the revolution, is its most important source of strength.

Political Parties

Philippine political parties are of several types. They are sometimes closely identified with a single economic interest group. The Democratic Party, for instance, was well known as the political organization of the sugar planters. Its leadership was upper class, it served their interests, and it depended for mass support on connections with local political bosses. The Democratic Alliance, on the other hand, gained its main support from small rice farmers, mostly tenants. Its leadership, which included some Communists, was from the middle class and depended for support on direct mass appeals with some policy content, not on traditional local leaders. The anti-Communist Progressives, though also led by middle-class professionals and businessmen who make direct contact with small farmers, represents a somewhat wider range of interests than did the Alliance.

Parties may also be leadership groups, with or without an ideology. The Avelino Liberal Party, which had no ideology but "pork" and patronage, indicated its nature by its name. It was the creation of Senator Avelino. It rose and fell in 1949. The Citizens Party, founded in September 1949, was at the same time an organization of "good government" crusaders and "the men of Tañada." When Senator Tañada teamed up with Senator Recto in 1957 to form the Nationalist Citizens Party under the banner of nationalism, even the strong ideological emphasis did not alter the fact that the party's strength was found mainly in the home provinces of the two senators, where personal relationships meant more than ideas. None of the above parties —whether of the interest- or leadership-group type—has ever elected a candidate in the national constituency except when in coalition with one of the major parties.

The two major Philippine political parties, Liberals and Nacionalistas, are not dominated by either a single-interest or leadership group, but are complex and shifting coalitions of both. The core of leadership in the two has been fairly constant since 1947, but there is no permanent party bureaucracy in either, since headquarters are opened only during election campaigns. There is no persistent ideological differentiation between them. Until Magsaysay came to power, both parties relied almost entirely on provincial and municipal leaders to deliver the vote. No real issues were needed. The only conflict of interest between the two has been the identification of the sugar-mill owners with the Liberals and, since 1953, the presence of the sugar planters in the Nacionalista-Democratic coalition. But since the planters, as already noted, cannot afford to be on the losing side, they would probably return to the Liberal fold should it appear that the party was about to win an election. The real policy battles are fought within the administration, after the elections, not before. Although the two major parties are elite-led and largely serve upper-class interests, their competition is nevertheless developing free institutions which will increasingly force that leadership to go directly to the masses for support.

· XXIV ·

The Political Process

DESPITE continuing debate among the more erudite of the Philippines' too numerous lawyers, there has been no postwar change in the formal structure of Philippine government. The totality of Philippine political institutions, however, has not remained unchanged in this period; quite the contrary. Informal bodies, such as parties, have undergone considerable transformation. They have been able to cushion the impact of new social forces seeking political expression so that the formal structure has not needed to be altered. A constitution which has weathered war and foreign occupation, internal rebellion, and the death in office of three presidents has become a part of Philippine tradition. To a greater extent than in other parts of Southeast Asia, except perhaps in former British colonies, Philippine governmental practices actually conform to constitutional provisions.

The Constitution

The Philippine constitution was drafted in 1935 by a popularly elected constituent assembly. This was not the first Philippine constitutional convention; that had met at Malolos in 1898–1899. Two delegates to the first convention were present at the second, and the two constitutions they helped frame were not fundamentally different in their democratic and liberal concepts.

There were three legal mandates given the 1935 framers by the

Tydings-McDuffie Act: the constitution was to be "republican in form," was to contain a bill of rights, and was to ensure religious freedom, all of which had already been included in the Malolos constitution. But there was no political pressure, or even unsolicited advice, from American officials that was designed to influence the drafting. More important as a channel of American influence was political experience. Approximately half the delegates to the convention had been elected officials in the government established by the Jones Act and were familiar with its principles and its language, much of which was borrowed from the U.S. constitution. A few had sat in the U.S. House of Representatives as resident commissioners.[1]

American influence was not so strong, however, as to preclude the intrusion of several distinctive features in the Philippine constitution. For instance, individualism, a cornerstone of American constitutional theory, is less important in the Philippines. The Philippine constitution has a bill of rights which includes all the protections of individual freedom either stated or implied in the American document, except those peculiarly related to American colonial history or to the jury system. But because of the restrictions of a hierarchical society and the absence of a long constitutional tradition, it has proven difficult for persons outside the upper and middle class to assert the rights there enumerated. Furthermore, the appearance of other, seemingly contradictory, provisions in the constitution indicates that the framers did not intend that the bill of rights should be as important a restraint on government action as it is in the United States.

For example, socialism finds partial expression in the Philippine constitution. Article II, section 5, declares that "the promotion of social justice to insure the well-being and economic security of all the people should be the concern of the State." This concern was further elaborated in Articles XIII and XIV with provisions authorizing compensated expropriation by the government of private estates for subdivision and resale to individuals, government establishment and operation of industries, and government regulation of relations between capital and labor. Each of these provisions has been implemented by both legislative and administrative action. Nevertheless social justice programs have not meant a radical transformation of Philippines society, but at most have allowed the process of change to begin.

Amending procedures of the Philippine constitution were patterned

[1] J. Ralston Hayden, *The Philippines* (New York: Macmillan, 1947), pp. 32–54.

after those found in some state constitutions in the United States. An amendment can be proposed either by a three-fourths vote of the legislature or by a convention. It must then be validated by a majority of those voting when presented to the electorate in a referendum. This process was first used in 1939 and 1940, in accordance with the wishes of President Quezon, to create an independent Commission on Elections, to re-create a bicameral legislature, and to change the President's single term of six years to a four-year term allowing one re-election.

The Executive

The most powerful institution which this constitution created is the presidency. As now constituted it has its origins in all three eras of Philippine history and in the U.S. offices of President and of state governor. But it is even more powerful, in relation to the other agencies of government, than any of its prototypes. The most important influence in determining the character of the office was the personality of Quezon. He had established himself as chief of the Nacionalista Party and the national leader while still president of the Senate, but he saw the much greater potential for national leadership in the executive. Therefore, though not a delegate, he exercised strong indirect control to make sure that the constitutional convention created a powerful President.

The President, in whom is vested "the executive power," is chosen by direct popular vote for a four-year term and may not serve for more than eight consecutive years. Though the Philippine constitutional language is not different from the American, the Philippine President has assumed a much wider power to issue executive orders, with or without delegation by Congress, and has seldom been challenged in the courts. In only one instance, the controversy over emergency powers in 1948 and 1949, was the President checked by the Court and Congress, for attempting to enact the budget by executive order.[2] This was in essence a political struggle which occurred at a period of rising strength in the opposition. There is a danger that in the future a President more popular than Quirino might be able to ignore both Congress and the Court with impunity. The outcome of this episode, however, and the fact that it was fought on legal grounds augur well for future Philippine constitutional development.

[2] See John Romani, *The Philippine Presidency* (Manila: University of the Philippines, 1956), pp. 70–76.

For an effective handling of the real postwar emergency, the Huk rebellion, the "emergency powers" especially authorized by the constitution were not really needed. The President's powers as commander in chief of the armed forces, including his authority to suspend the operation of the writ of habeas corpus in case of rebellion "or imminent danger thereof," were sufficient.

The Administration

Besides the army, there are three levels of administrative control through which the President undertakes to govern: the Executive Office, the heterogeneous Office of the President (including the foregoing), and the ten departments.[3]

Four officials in the Office of the President—the Budget Commissioner, the Social Welfare Administrator (who has, up to now, always been a woman), the Executive Secretary, and the President's Press Secretary (raised to cabinet rank by Magsaysay in 1956)—and the Chairman of the National Economic Council, together with the ten department heads, make up the cabinet. Like its American counterpart, the Philippine cabinet is not a constitutional body, but merely a group of advisers designated by the President, generally from his own political party. The constitution makes it impossible for a cabinet responsible to the legislature to develop. Not only is the President specifically given power to control the executive departments, but in addition Article VI, section 15, prevents any Congressman from holding "any other office or employment in the government" without forfeiting his seat.

The Vice-President is usually a member of the cabinet, but his position is not ex-officio and depends entirely on the President's wishes. If the Vice-President belongs to a party different from that of the President, as under Garcia, or to a different faction within the same party, as in the latter part of the Quirino administration, he is, of course, not counted among the President's advisers. When outside the official family the Vice-President has no duty other than to succeed

[3] Departments of Foreign Affairs, Finance, Justice, Agriculture and Natural Resources, Public Works and Communications, Education, Labor, National Defense, Health, and Commerce and Industry. The Department of the Interior was abolished in 1950, and many of its functions were transferred to the technical assistant on local government in the Office of the President. See Romani, *op. cit.*, pp. 116–120, and also Edwin Stene, "National Administrative Structure," in *Public Administration in the Philippines* (Manila: University of the Philippines, 1955), pp. 21–30.

to the presidency in event of the President's death or other incapacity; three out of four Philippine vice-presidents have become President in this way.

Besides the cabinet there are two other loci of governmental decision making which are most important for economic policy, the Central Bank and the National Economic Council. The Central Bank, created in 1948, is both a policy-making and an administrative body. It holds a tight rein on government monetary policy and also controls foreign exchange allotment, after the National Economic Council has set the order of priorities.

The National Economic Council was reorganized by President Magsaysay in 1955. The Council has eleven members, including four members of Congress, and is headed by a full-time chairman with a salary of 25,000 pesos,[4] twice that of any other cabinet member, and a sizable staff. The two most important functions of the Council are economic planning and, in conjunction with the U.S. International Co-operation Administration, the programing and supervision of U.S. aid. Though it has no power to carry out its plans directly, it may require other governmental agencies to submit reports on their implementation.[5] The Council's representative composition generally assures widespread support for its plans, but it is not as powerful as the Burmese Economic and Social Board.

The Civil Service and Administrative Behavior

The Philippine constitution, which truly expresses national aspirations, provides that appointments to the civil service should be made according to merit alone, "to be determined as far as practicable by competitive examination." Civil service employees are prohibited from engaging directly or indirectly in partisan political activity and are protected from removal or suspension except "for cause." Furthermore, the Bureau of Civil Service administers the government personnel system under legislation and rules that could be called progressive in the American context.

But in no aspect of Philippine government "is the gulf between theory and practice, between formal arrangements and informal practices, more obvious than in public personnel administration." [6] Some

[4] Officially 1 peso equals 50 cents (U.S.), but on the black market the rate is more than 3 to 1.

[5] Government Survey and Reorganization Commission, *Reorganization Plan No. 10* (Manila: Bureau of Printing, 1955).

[6] Ferrel Heady, "The Philippine Administrative System—Fusion of East and

of the discrepancies are a result of manipulation of the rules, others flow from a complete disregard of them. For instance, within the classified service there has been such widespread violation of restrictions on "temporary" hiring that in 1954 nearly 60 per cent of all employees in classified posts were "temporary." [7] Many remain "temporary" indefinitely, thus avoiding the necessity of passing an examination, but gaining no seniority rights. When vacancies occur, appointing officers seldom ask for certification of the three eligibles with the highest examination grades, as the law requires.

What causes this great "gulf between theory and practice"? Budgetary deficiencies, cultural values, social organization, and political pressures all work to warp the operation of an imported administration system. Very important in determining the actualities of the system are three loyalties of most Filipino administrators which are stronger than their loyalty to the merit principle or to efficient administration. First, and most important, is loyalty to family. Kinship ties more than any other factor determine political loyalties. Public office is often viewed more as an opportunity for fulfilling family responsibilities than as one for meeting responsibilities to the nation. For an appointing officer to fill a vacancy with a well-qualified stranger when a relative is looking for a job would subject him to severe family criticism. Secondly, of only slightly less importance are ritual kinship ties.[8] Third, loyalty to one's locality usually results in preferential treatment for town or province mates. There are, however, many administrators who do not accept this value pattern.

West," in William J. Siffin, ed., *Toward a Comparative Study of Public Administration* (Bloomington: Indiana University, 1957), p. 272.

[7] About two-thirds of the 360,000 government employees are in the classified service. The majority of the other one-third are in the armed forces, and most of the rest are public works laborers. See Ferrel Heady and Jose Abueva, "Personnel Administration: History and Organization," in Edwin O. Stene and Associates, *Public Administration in the Philippines*, p. 102; see also Jose Abueva, "Personnel Administration: Selection, Classification, and Employee Benefits," in *ibid.*, p. 125.

[8] Obligations arising from the relationship between child and godfather or between a child's father and his godfather, known commonly as the *compadre* system, weigh heavily on the responsible Filipino. A complex network of social relationships exists between baptismal sponsor and parent as well as between sponsor and child, and in the cities especially there are usually more than two sponsors. Though the godparent is expected to give the child gifts on a number of special occasions and to assist him in pursuing his education or in finding a job, if the need arises, the more important relationship is between parent and sponsor, the *compadres,* usually a fraternal one (Fred Eggan and others, *Area Handbook on the Philippines* [New Haven: Human Relations Area Files, Inc., 1956], I, 415–430).

In addition to these social pressures, there are political ones. A witness to their power is the incessant swarm of job seekers who hover around the offices of Congressmen asking for recommendations for government appointment. Appointing officers, who "knoweth from whence cometh" their appropriations, find it difficult to ignore such recommendations. Despite the constitution civil servants are also sometimes given election campaign duties by the party in power, but do not themselves comprise an independent political force.

General administrative behavior and decision making in the Philippines are characterized by what some writers have called "centralism." [9] Centralism means not only the denuding of local governmental powers and the concentration of decision making in Manila, but also the passing of every important decision, and many unimportant ones, to the heads of bureaus and departments. Centralism of this kind is reinforced by a highly sensitive concern for self-esteem. The subordinate tends to avoid all decisions, because any decision, if countermanded, will damage his self-esteem. And because damaging another's is most unwise, he avoids all controversial decisions which might hurt someone.

This aspect of administrative behavior is to some extent inevitable in the social setting. Another aspect, corruption, should not be so regarded. A certain amount of corruption is a legacy of the Spanish period, but this does not help explain the fact that it is considerably more widespread since the Second World War. The war period, in which stealing from the occupier was patriotism, had a baneful effect on Philippine moral standards. The postwar inflation has had an even more important impact on civil servants. Whereas the cost of living in 1956 was about three and one-half times that of 1940, many salaries in the middle and almost all in the upper brackets have not changed and none have as much as doubled. Salaries in the lowest one-fourth were doubled as a result of the Minimum Wage Law in 1951. But as of 1954, of all government employees 48 per cent were receiving no more than the minimum 1,440 pesos per year.[10] In the process of narrowing the salary gap between top and low-level civil servants, the economic pressures that result as those on top try to maintain their same relative social position work against honest administration. President Magsaysay, assisted by a vigilant press, made a persistent attempt to root out corruption in Philippine government, and there is

[9] Heady, "The Philippine Administrative System," pp. 263–265.
[10] Abueva, *op. cit.*, p. 127.

no question that public morals were raised to some extent during his administration. But little headway was made toward alleviating these economic pressures on civil servants.

Party Leader and National Leader

The central importance of the President in Philippine political decision making, either within the executive branch, as already described, or in relationship to the legislative branch, to be described, is not based primarily on his legal or constitutional prerogatives or on the established patterns of administrative control, but on his position as national and party leader.

Party leadership is derived from the powers inherent in national and governmental leadership, but in turn also reinforces those powers. In Quezon's time it was hard to distinguish the party leader from the national leaders since, for all practical purposes, there was only one political party. But in the postwar trend toward a two-party system and in the elevation to the presidency of such differing personalities as Quirino and Magsaysay, the distinction has become clear. The Liberal Party in 1946 was the creation of Roxas, though, like his successors, he had no official position in the organization of the party he led. Two of the three presidents since Roxas have been creatures of their parties. Both Vice-Presidents Quirino and Garcia, shortly before they assumed the presidency, had been considered dispensable by party bosses looking forward to the next election. Magsaysay was already a popular leader when nominated, but it took him nearly two years after election to win a dominant voice in the regular Nacionalista Party organization. The power of Magsaysay's national leadership made it easier for him to do this without using the crasser tools of politics. But Quirino and Garcia, who were even more successful in dominating the majority party organization, were comparatively unknown and thus had to rely on patronage and "pork barrel" to gain ascendancy.[11]

Unlike his position as party leader, the President's position as national leader is an independent source of power. The Filipino concept of national leadership, the personification of government to a much greater extent than exists in the contemporary Western world, is rooted in Philippine history and society. In the pre-Spanish Philippines the *datu* was the government. He was "father of his people" in a very intimate sense and was often thought to be endowed with magical

[11] See Romani, *op. cit.*, ch. vii.

powers. Not only did he arbitrate all disputes, public and private, but
he was expected by his loyal followers to bestow material bounty, especially in emergencies. This concept of national leadership is also
embodied in the Philippine constitution. In addition to preserving and
defending the constitution, the President swears to "do justice to every
man and consecrate myself to the service of the nation" (Article VII,
section 7).

After his election as President, Quezon conceived of himself quite
consciously as "chosen leader of the nation." [12] Quezon's leadership affected the masses only indirectly, however. His personal dealings were
with the local political bosses. Ramon Magsaysay fulfilled the Filipino
expectation of national leadership more effectively than his predecessors. The crowds that gathered at the Cebu airport to see his coffin
placed in a plane for Manila were heard to cry out in their grief, "Who
will take care of us now?" He was as truly the "father" of 23 million
people as one man can be. But even more than that, the hero worship
of unsophisticated rural people sometimes attributed magical powers
to him. Indeed it seemed not far from magic to a poor farmer when
the President cut through the maze of administrative tradition and
lethargy to grant personally a long-sought request. The political advantages derived from giving first priority to meeting the needs of
the common man were enormous. More than once Magsaysay can-
celed a cabinet meeting to travel through dust or mud to answer a
complaint made by a tenant against an illegal act of his landlord.
When it became known that the door of Malacañang was open to
all, people traveled for days to bring requests or controversies, both
serious and trivial, to the President for solution.[13]

A paradox posed by the success of Magsaysay as a national leader
in the Filipino tradition is that, although he was trying to encourage
administrative responsiveness to the people's needs at the grass roots,

[12] Hayden, *op. cit.*, pp. 71–75, 439.
[13] The Executive Office spends a large part of its time hearing and acting on a
wide variety of requests: for medicine and hospitalization for a poor child having
a rare disease, for rectification of improper administrative action, for justice to a
farmer unjustly treated by a landlord, and for jobs, jobs, jobs—from judge to clerk-
typist. These requests were so much encouraged by Magsaysay, and thus so multiplied, that they could not be handled through existing channels. A special President's Complaints and Action Commission within the Executive Office was set up
in January 1954 to receive and initiate action on all requests not merely for political
favors; its first chairman was Manuel Manahan. In the first sixteen months of operation the PCAC received over 75,000 complaints; at the end of that period nearly
50 per cent had been acted upon by the agencies to which they were referred.

he more frequently reinforced the predilection of the masses to by-pass local officials and turn to the President for help. A second paradox is that in giving so much time to his personal expression of concern for the "little people" Magsaysay sometimes denied himself the hours necessary for wise decisions on top policy questions which could have had an even greater long-term beneficial effect on mass welfare. This kind of paternalism also presents a dilemma because, though it builds a mass popularity which cuts through the political power of the local bosses, it could likewise be the starting point on the road to dictator-ship. Fortunately for Philippine democracy, Magsaysay used his vast political and legal powers more sparingly than his predecessors.

Executive-Legislative Relations

The preponderant constitutional power held by the Philippine Presi-dent in comparison to his U.S. prototype is most clearly seen in his relationship to Congress. The Philippine government is based on the theory of separation of powers, but the separation has taken more from the legislature than did the American constitution.[14] In addition the President's political power and prestige have allowed him, on oc-casion, to encroach still further.

Presidential domination of the legislative process is presently no-where nearly so complete as it was under Quezon. Almost all the laws enacted by the First National Assembly contained the language of the original Malacañang draft. On the other hand, under Quirino and Magsaysay, many important administration bills suffered sub-

[14] In addition to the constitutional authorization to recommend measures to Congress, as in the United States, the Philippine President is given other tools for controlling the congressional agenda. Article VI, section 21(2), provides that neither house may pass a bill on third reading unless three days before it shall have been printed and copies thereof distributed to the members, "except when the President shall have certified to the necessity of its immediate enactment." Since the regular session is constitutionally limited to 100 days and since most important bills are not passed on second reading, and are thus unfit for printing, until the last three session days, the presidential power of certification is a useful weapon. It gives administration measures priority at a period when there is not time to consider all pending legislation. Not all bills certified are administration "musts," however. Some are pet measures of individual Congressmen, the result of the bargaining process by which the President gets support for more important matters.

Despite certification, the Congress seldom finishes its necessary business within a hundred days, and special sessions have been called almost every year since independence. Though the constitutional language is not absolutely clear, the Philippine President has been able to interpret it to mean that he has complete control over the agenda of special sessions.

stantial amendment before passage, and others were permanently side-tracked. There is also a tendency now for more cabinet secretaries and agency chiefs to present draft legislation directly to Congressmen. But Congress, with only a small Legislative Reference Service, is so understaffed that it can draft little important legislation itself.

Malacañang's veto power is stronger than that of the White House in two respects. First of all, two-thirds of the total membership of each house, rather than two-thirds of those voting, is required to override a veto in the Philippines. Secondly, the President has an item veto over revenue, appropriations, and tariff bills. No law has yet been passed over a presidential veto. This is, of course, as much attributable to the President's political leadership as it is to constitutional provisions.[15]

Appointment and Appropriations

Although presidential powers of appointment are constitutionally about the same in the Philippines and in the United States, Philippine congressional prerogatives of confirmation are exercised by a Commission on Appointments made up of twelve members from each house, elected by their respective bodies "on the basis of proportional representation of the political parties therein." Patronage is for the most part the subject matter of Philippine politics. It is, therefore, understandable that it is an important focus of executive-legislative conflict. In the two periods in which Congress has been most hostile to the President, during the short Osmeña administration and the latter part of the Quirino administration, the President had great difficulty in getting his appointments accepted by the commission. To avoid congressional obstinancy the President must, of necessity, consult Congressmen, and commission members in particular, about prospective appointments, especially if the would-be appointee comes from or is to be assigned to the Congressman's home province. But the personalization and fluidity of Philippine party politics have prevented this need for consultation from solidifying into a Philippine equivalent of "senatorial courtesy."

After an appointment has been made, perhaps even confirmed, the Philippine Congress has devised a method of removal not constitutionally feasible under the U.S. performance-type budget. In the

[15] Romani, *op. cit.*, pp. 129–134. For the first six years of independence approximately 10–12 per cent of bills which were passed were vetoed. See Congress of the Philippines, House of Representatives, *History of Bills*, 1954, 1956.

Philippine line-item budget Congress may simply abolish the position of the unwanted official. Even at the height of Magsaysay's popularity in 1954, Congress used this technique against his overly efficient collector of internal revenue.

Despite this congressional ingenuity, the President's constitutional power over appropriations is still greater than in the United States. The item veto has already been noted. This is a power used ten to fifteen times against each appropriation bill.[16] But the most important constitutional restriction on Congress is the one prohibiting it from increasing any appropriation item for the executive branch. Still the Philippine Congress appears to exercise greater budgetary control than any similar body in Southeast Asia. No significant portion of government revenue is expended without congressional authorization.

After the appropriation bill is enacted, the President has one very extraordinary power over its expenditure which is not mentioned in the constitution: he may transfer funds from one agency to another. During the Quezon administration this power was unlimited.[17] Not until 1950 did Congress assert its constitutional prerogative and, in a move motivated by hostility to Quirino, prohibit the President from augmenting any item by more than 50 per cent; by 1953 the ceiling was lowered to 25 per cent. It was only with some difficulty that the popular Magsaysay was able to persuade Congress in 1955 to return to a 50 per cent ceiling, and for 1956 it was trimmed again to 40 per cent.[18] This percentage is a good index of the power balance in executive-legislative relations.

An important segment of congressional appropriations are not included in the general appropriations measure. Public works are financed by a separate bill, with special political significance.[19] The "pork barrel," adapted from the American institution of the same name, accounts for 10–50 per cent of the public works appropriation —depending on the degree of political control over project allocation which defines "pork." But the "pork barrel" plays a much more im-

---

[16] Romani, *op. cit.*, pp. 97–99.

[17] See "Historical Analysis of the Presidential Power to Transfer Funds," in Odell Walby, *Philippine Public Fiscal Administration: Readings and Documents* (Manila: University of the Philippines, Institute of Public Administration, 1954), pp. 318–325.

[18] Section 8, Republic Act 1350. Under Garcia for the fiscal year 1959 the limitation was down to 30 per cent.

[19] Romani, *op. cit.*, pp. 104–105.

portant role in Philippine national politics than does its American forebear in Washington. Furthermore, in the Philippines the control over the distribution of "pork" is more blatantly political. A sum—which grew from 7 million pesos in 1953 to 31 million pesos in 1956 —is publicly announced as "pork" after long caucuses among Congressmen, as well as between them and the President, and divided among the legislators. In 1956 the congressional caucus allotted 100,000 pesos to representatives and 250,000 pesos to senators; the attempt to deny these benefits to minority members was unsuccessful, as it has been since 1952.[20] Finally, with the advice of their constituents and with an eye on the next campaign, each Congressman, in dividing his "pork," decides which village is to get a schoolhouse and which town a new road and enters the project by name in the line-item public works bill.

Although in the constitutional convention it was agreed that public works expenditures should not be considered "appropriations" for purposes of the restriction on congressional increase of items, this does not, in practice, greatly reduce presidential influence. It is traditional for public works appropriations to be taken "out of the general funds in the national treasury not otherwise appropriated." Thus even after the appropriation bill is passed, the availability of such funds is limited. In his ability to determine the order of priority by which funds will be released for the projects of individual Congressmen the President's political power is enhanced.[21]

Another large segment of the President's power derives from his sole discretion in disbursement of the "contingency fund." Under Magsaysay in 1955 the fund reached an all-time high of 10 million pesos to be spent for "rural improvement," relief and rehabilitation of victims of calamities, past or future, augmentation of appropriations already authorized, and creation of new positions. This gave the President ample opportunity to make good on his innumerable promises of artesian wells and village schoolhouses. It also enabled him to staff an agrarian reform agency, the Agricultural Tenancy Commission, without congressional authorization.[22] Congress, appalled at the political implications of such disbursements, in 1956 cut the amount

[20] *Manila Times*, June 24, 1956. See also L. O. Ty, "The Liberals Lost a Weapon," *Philippines Free Press*, July 26, 1952, pp. 5, 57.

[21] Edwin Stene and Odell Waldby, "Budget and Financial Control," in *Public Administration in the Philippines*, p. 176.

[22] See p. 491.

in half and limited its use to relief of suffering from recent or future natural calamities.

As shown in the course of describing the exercise of particular powers, Congress has been, in the broad trend, increasingly assertive in its relations with the executive. The real fear of executive dictatorship in the Quezon era is gone. The change is due in large part to the personality of the presidents and the congressional leaders and also to the progressive differentiation of interests within the political elite, expressing itself both in political parties and in executive-legislative conflict. The political power of Congress is now stronger than its constitutional position.

The Legislature

The Philippine Congress since 1940 has been bicameral in organization. The change was brought about on the instance of President Quezon without articulation of the basic cause of the change. Quezon's prime purpose seemed to have been to divide his potential opposition in the legislative branch.[23] Postwar experience has proved that the President may indeed be able to use House-Senate rivalries to his own advantage.

The opponents of bicameralism in 1940 declared that a Senate elected from a national constituency would be composed only of wealthy men and would thus "undermine democracy." This prediction has not been wholly correct. Though some men have been nominated for the Senate primarily because of what they could contribute to the party coffers, the Senate as a body has a more progressive legislative record than the House. In some instances it has proved to be representative of national interests which have not found an effective voice in the House. This is probably because senators are less dependent on the vagaries of local politics for their election and must campaign on a national platform, paying some attention to "the issues." The election of representatives, on the other hand, is determined almost entirely by the shifting alliances of personal factions and a skillful distribution of "pork" within the district, with national—or interest-group-oriented —issues playing relatively little part.

The twenty-four Senate members are elected from the nation at large for six-year terms, with eight members chosen every two years. Unlike his American counterpart, the Vice-President of the Philippines is not the presiding officer of the Senate. The Senate president

[23] See Hayden, *op. cit.*, pp. 229–237.

is elected; more than half the time since independence he has been concurrently president of the majority party. If this dual role were to become a firm tradition, stable Senate leadership would be assured. But it has not. In 1952, when Liberal and Nacionalista coalition strengths were evenly matched and both were racked by factionalism, no Senate president was chosen until after one-fourth of the regular session had been wasted in wrangling. Once elected, however, the Senate president's powers are nearly as great as those of the Speaker.

The House of Representatives at present has 102 members, but the constitutional maximum is 120. Each of the electoral districts elects a single member; there is at least one district to a province. Representatives are elected for four years, in the same year as the President. The House speakership has not been as unstable a position as the Senate presidency, because greater membership in the House makes shifts and maneuvers of blocs more difficult. During most of the Quirino administration Speaker Perez was president of the majority Liberal Party. Speaker Laurel, on the other hand, was one of the leaders of the opposition to President Magsaysay within the Nacionalista camp from 1954 to 1957. But in either case they gave strong direction to the legislative work of the House. The presiding officers of both houses derive considerable political strength, not possessed by their American prototypes, from their power to disburse large unitemized sums in the budget and to transfer funds from one item to another within the appropriations for their respective houses.[24]

The relative power of the two houses is approximately the same as the balance in the U.S. Congress. The Philippine Senate is weakened by the fact that it does not have the exclusive power to confirm appointments, but its election from a national constituency gives it added prestige and to the individual senators added political influence. The Senate is considered a steppingstone to the presidency. Eight out of fourteen active contenders for that office since the war have been senators or ex-senators; only Magsaysay among the four presidents of the Republic did not spend some time in the upper chamber.

The committee structure in the Philippine Congress is patterned after that in U.S. legislatures, that is, standing committees divided by subject matter to which bills are referred before being reported to the floor for debate. There are some important differences, however.

[24] For 1959 this lump sum in the House of Representatives amounted to nearly 5 Million pesos, an all-time high (Napoleon G. Rama, "Secret Salaries," *Philippines Free Press*, June 14, 1958, pp. 5, 37).

Committee chairmanships are not won by seniority, but are distributed by agreement within the majority caucus, accompanied by considerable conflict and delay. Furthermore, committees in the Philippine legislature meet very infrequently. Most hold no public hearings and meet in executive session only once or twice a year. Occasionally special committees are set up for the purpose of undertaking investigations. But investigations have not been a very effective means of legislative control over the executive.

The weakness of the committee system means that the locus of decision making in Congress is concentrated in the majority party caucus of each house, which is usually held in an informal atmosphere outside the Congress building. Within the caucus "the leadership," headed by the presiding officer of the house, is dominant.

The Judiciary

Philippine jurisprudence is an amalgam of its Spanish and American heritage. But as this heritage is interpreted by Filipinos, it is inevitably mingled with Filipino values. Thus in the reliance of judges on previous American and Philippine decisions a kind of Philippine-American common law is being developed. (Philippine Supreme Court decisions could be, and were, appealed to the U.S. Supreme Court up to the end of the Commonwealth.)

The administration of justice is centered in two national bodies, the Supreme Court and the Department of Justice. The Supreme Court is composed of eleven justices, appointed by the President to serve until retirement at 70. The Court's original jurisdiction is unimportant, but because of the Philippine unitary system and because of the great faith that Filipinos put in the wisdom and impartiality of the Supreme Court, its appellate jurisdiction is very broad indeed, including, among others, all cases in which an error or question of law is involved. The great respect for the Court in the Philippines is also manifest in the tendency of the minority party to take essentially political questions to the Supreme Court for resolution. When no mutually satisfactory compromise can be arranged, only the arbitration of the highest court is acceptable. The Philippine Supreme Court has been willing to decide on political questions framed in legal terms to a much greater extent than its American prototype.

According to the constitution, a two-thirds vote of all the members of the Court is required to declare a law or executive order unconstitutional. The Court has occasionally invalidated executive excesses, though in reviewing social legislation it has not been as conservative an influence as was the U.S. Supreme Court in the early 1930s. On the other hand, the Court itself has not escaped executive encroachment. The onslaught of a determined Quezon, in successful disregard of the constitution, reduced the Court's number from eleven to seven through Commonwealth Act no. 3 in 1936. Not until 1948 was the Court's membership restored to its constitutional number.

Above the municipal level, where justices of the peace are too often political pawns, the Philippines has one of the most independent judiciaries in Southeast Asia. Before 1954, when the Secretary of Justice could, at his discretion, transfer judges-at-large anywhere in the Philippines and thus assign particular judges to particular cases, the divergence from the principle of separation of powers was major and had been much abused. But in that year an amendment to the Judiciary Act abolished the position of judge-at-large and increased the number of district judges, with fixed jurisdictions. Now the administrative supervision of the Secretary over the statutory courts is very limited.[25]

Local Government

The Philippines is a unitary state with a highly centralized administration. These characteristics are especially evident in local government, as set forth in the Administrative Code. The country is divided into fifty-three provinces, most of which have existed within their present boundaries for more than fifty years. Since 1955 they have all been headed by popularly elected governors. The governor is chief executive of the province and chairman-member of the three-man provincial board. But he has almost no control over the heads of administrative departments in the province, who are all appointed by and responsible to department heads in Manila.[26] The provincial board may not issue ordinances or adopt a budget, nor does it have any taxing power. The province depends almost entirely on tax allotments and grants from the municipalities and the national government. But weak as the provincial government is administratively, the governor is politically very important. In the pyramid of leader-follower groups of which Philippine political parties are made, the provincial governor is usually

[25] Hayden, *op. cit.*, ch. x. See also Abelardo Samonte, "General Law Enforcement," in Stene, *Public Administration in the Philippines*, pp. 247–250.

[26] See John Romani and M. Ladd Thomas, *A Survey of Local Government in the Philippines* (Manila: University of the Philippines, 1954), ch. iii.

the link between municipal and national leaders. Useful in this role is the governor's power temporarily to suspend municipal officials. Sometimes a governor's political following may be so strong that he himself assumes a position in the national leadership.

The municipality, unlike the province of which it is the only subdivision, has its own law-enforcement officers, the power of ordinance making, and the power to tax, though 50 per cent of its funds still come in allotments from national taxes. It is governed by a mayor and council elected at large every four years. After election each councilman is assigned the supervision of a district which contains one or more barrios, or villages. (A municipality, like an American county, includes both urban and rural areas.) Until 1956 the only barrio official was the unpaid barrio lieutenant, usually appointed by the municipal councilor, but the Administrative Code now provides for the popular election of a lieutenant and a barrio council. This is the first village self-government since the establishment of Spanish control.

Both provinces and municipalities are subject to careful supervision by the Local Governments Office in Malacañang. Governors and mayors may be removed for cause and temporarily or, after a final decision on the administrative charges brought, permanently replaced. This supervision is thought to be a necessary check on the abuses of local officials, but they are now so "inoculated with the doctrine of central direction [that they] are almost unable to take independent action in local matters."[27] Chartered cities, not under provincial supervision, are even more directly under Malacañang's thumb.[28]

The Electoral System

Elections in the Philippines form a more important part of the real decision-making process than in most other Asian countries. Unless a deep and protracted socioeconomic crisis should occur, it seems safe to assume that they will continue to be the only recognized method for achieving political power. It will be a long time, however, before elections become a method for effective expression of public

[27] *Ibid.*, p. 124.

[28] There are now twenty-eight chartered cities (including almost all major population centers), nearly three times the number before the war. In almost half the President still appoints the mayor, and in seven all or part of the city council. But since 1954 one city has been restored to municipal status, and ten previously appointed mayors have been made elective. See *ibid.*, ch. iv, and also Roy Owsley and Associates, *Philippine City Charters* (Manila: University of the Philippines, Institute of Public Administration, 1956).

opinion on national issues; at present they are little more than a way of choosing political leadership. Only a small percentage of the electorate attempt to correlate issues and candidates, and they are given little assistance in this by the candidates themselves.

Elections are held throughout the Philippines every two years on the second Tuesday of November, a date which has a familiar ring to Americans but is rather inappropriate in the Philippines since it falls in the middle of the typhoon and rice-planting season. All literate citizens over 21 years of age, subject to residence requirements and certain minor disqualifications, are entitled to vote. The literacy requirement is unique in Southeast Asia. Although not strictly applied, it seems to have reduced the percentage of those voting to a figure below the average for other Asian countries with electoral experience. In the presidential election of 1957 about 50 per cent of the adult population voted, compared to 60 per cent in the United States in 1956 and over 80 per cent in Indonesia in 1955.

A board of election inspectors administers both registration and voting in each precinct. It is perhaps the most important link in the chain of command administering Philippine elections. Today its voting members include a chairman, usually a schoolteacher, appointed by the Commission on Elections, and two inspectors, appointed by the parties having the largest and next largest number of votes in the preceding presidential election. These boards can make or break honest elections, and they have done both. Before 1951 the boards were made up of two majority and one minority party inspector. Most inspectors worked only for partisan advantage; a single minority voice was a feeble defense against fraud. In 1951 a Liberal Congress, quarreling with President Quirino and sobered by the "rape of democracy" in the 1949 elections, made substantial changes in the election law, reducing majority representation to one inspector. As a result the boards have since fulfilled their duties more honestly.

Changes in the Election Code constitute an interesting example of how competition within a very restricted elite can produce legislation which will increase the chances for interest groups outside that elite to enter the political arena. In 1957 for the first time in history not one, but two, well-qualified men made a vigorous bid for the presidency without having their own election inspectors and together gained about 30 per cent of the vote. One of them got most of his support from the "underrepresented majority," the small farmers.

The performance of the two was based on a faith in the honesty of the electoral process which had not existed six years earlier.

Continued progress in election administration since the amendments to the law in 1951 must be credited largely to the Commission on Elections, practically a fourth branch of government. The chairman and two members are appointed to staggered nine-year terms by the President and are ineligible for reappointment; they are removable only by impeachment. The commission has exclusive charge of election-law enforcement and may deputize any governmental agency or officer to ensure free and honest polling. The commission may also suspend from the performance of duties relative to the conduct of elections any local officials "who shall fail to comply with its instructions . . . and appoint their temporary substitutes." Much of the commission's success depends on the respect shown its orders and instructions by administrative officers; since 1951 co-operation by national officers has been fairly good. Nevertheless, whatever has been done to ensure free elections has depended in large part on the leadership within the commission.

There have been three areas of election administration in which the commission has concentrated its reform efforts: maintaining a peaceful, orderly atmosphere for voting; eliminating fraudulent registration; and protecting the tabulation and reporting of returns from dishonest manipulation. The commission's commendable record in these areas would not have been possible without the co-operation of the armed forces, placed technically under the commission's command, and of an aroused middle-class citizenry, especially those organized in the National Movement for Free Elections and co-operating civic groups.

It has often been said that the Election Code provisions concerning a board of inspectors favors a two-party system in the Philippines. Actually, before 1951 the Code contributed to one-party dominance. Today an election inspector is no longer considered a prerequisite for successful candidacy, and thus a third party seems feasible. Furthermore, a 1951 change in the composition of the ballot delivered a forceful blow to party discipline and to the traditional overrepresentation of the majority, at the same time encouraging personal alliances and new parties. Before 1951 ballots provided not only a place to write in the name of candidates, but a space in which voters, by writing the party's name, could automatically vote for all the party's candidates, a procedure called "block voting." This provision was of primary importance for the Senate race where eight men are elected at large from the national constituency. It meant that nomination from a party clearly in the majority was tantamount to election, since the ease of writing one word instead of eight or more was, when strongly encouraged by party bosses, an irresistible convenience for most voters. But in the 1951 amendment to the Election Code "block voting" was abolished. If "constitution" is taken in its broadest sense, this was the most important constitutional change in the postwar Philippines. Recto's "guest candidacy" on the Liberal ticket in 1955, with his subsequent election, and Macapagal's election as Vice-President in 1957 could not have occurred without this change.

Since the eight senatorial candidates with the highest number of votes, regardless of party label, are elected, representation in the Senate of a third party with well-known candidates is now possible. This, coupled with the possibility of election to the presidency or to the House of Representatives with only a plurality, would seem to leave the way open for a permanent three-party system. There is an important factor militating against a stable third party, however. Politicians' hunger for patronage and "pork," which is distributed by the President, is so great in the Philippines—similar to other newly emergent party systems—that the existence of a single minority party has already been endangered. Since political allegiance can generally be held only so long as there is a reasonable expectation of wielding power and/or enjoying its material rewards, large numbers of minority men customarily join the majority party shortly after each election or, if the outcome seems certain, before the election. In such an atmosphere no third party could long survive unless it were to have a mainly ideological basis. Persistent ideological divisions are rare in the Philippines today.

Party Organization, Nominations, and Elections

Philippine political party organization is formally democratic, but actually highly centralized. It is more heavily official-dominated than its American counterparts. The organization of the two major parties is similar. Neither has deviated too radically from the prewar Nacionalista organization.

The biennial national convention held in Manila is formally the party's ruling body. Like American party conventions, however, few important decisions are made by the eight hundred or more hot, cheering (or booing) delegates. The pattern, until 1953, was for unanimous approval of the presidential candidate, already agreed upon by the top party leaders, ratification of the presidential candidate's choice for Vice-President, and a "vote of confidence" in the executive committee which was given the right to pick the Senate slate from among the seventy to eighty names presented in nomination on the floor. Since then, however, both parties' conventions have made some major decisions on the floor. When a party is without a single recognized leader, as was the minority Liberal Party in 1955 or the majority Nacionalista Party after Magsaysay's death in 1957, contending leaders are forced to seek out delegate support. But most crucial decisions are still made behind closed doors; it will be some time before the full convention is transformed into a real decision-making body.

It is the executive committee—composed of senators, representatives, governors, and nonofficials in roughly equal proportions and a few cabinet members—which runs the party. This committee is, in practice, chosen by co-option. It is generally representative of the regional and factional strengths within the party. The executive committee of the majority party to a considerable extent can be said to run the country. Under Quirino on at least one occasion the newspapers reported that the Liberal Party executive committee had "appointed" a cabinet member.[29]

In party affairs the executive committee drafts the biennial platform—to which few people pay any attention. In 1957 the Nacionalista committee was given the responsibility of choosing the vice-presidential candidate. The committee usually undertakes the selection of Senate candidates also, ostensibly the convention's prerogative. It does not always limit its consideration to the names presented at the convention and has even chosen candidates who were, at convention time, still members of the opposing party. There are several factors which restrict the executive committee's freedom of choice, however. An attempt is made to have one candidate from each of the old eight senatorial districts, since his personal political organization in his home territory is expected to carry the whole ticket there. Factional balance, also highly desirable, includes attention to interest groups and to personal and familial alliances.

The executive committee is considerably weakened by the fact that it has little power over the nomination of candidates for the House, who are usually nominated by party conventions within the districts and must be district residents. Many determined candidates do not

[29] *Manila Times*, April 26, 1953.

even accept defeat in the conventions. For example, in 1953 two-thirds of the congressional districts had more than one candidate calling himself "Nacionalista." [30] The party imposes no penalties on the maverick who wins, unless he maintains open opposition to party leadership.

In the traditional pattern of Philippine election campaigns there is a liberal sprinkling of florid oratory—in which the opposition attacks corruption and the incumbent extols his fine record—with rural folk waiting patiently for many hours to hear a nationally known figure. All-night election rallies in town plazas are interlarded with song-and-dance acts and are looked upon by the villager as the best free entertainment of the season.

But the ritual speechmaking is much less important than a skillful distribution of material inducements. For an incumbent, "pork barrel" expenditures, employing the largest possible number of laborers, are most significant. Other kinds of campaign expenditures are stringently restricted by the Election Code. For instance, a candidate is prohibited from spending more than an amount equal to a year's salary of the office he seeks. Vote buying, whether direct or indirect, and free food, drink, and transportation for voters during campaigns are specifically proscribed. But these prohibitions are dead letters and merely serve to describe what is actually common practice. Campaign expenses have risen in recent years. Now Congressmen generally spend from four to forty times their annual salary of 7,200 pesos.

Vote buying and lavish public banquets given by local political bosses, all designed to reinforce the followers' obligation to accept the leader's leadership, cannot be curtailed simply by legal fiat, but will fall gradually into disuse as they become ineffective. There are some signs that this is already beginning to happen.

Education and urbanization are reducing the usefulness of such election expenditures, though the effects of both are felt more in the national constituency than in most provinces. Voter "independence" is in part made possible by the fact that mass communications media with political content are reaching a large and growing percentage of the electorate. There are probably nearly half a million radio receiving sets in the Philippines, or one for every eight families.[31] More than half of these are in the Manila area, however. Most villages have no

[30] *Manila Times,* Nov. 9, 1953.

[31] Government figures are based on radios registered for tax purposes and thus grossly understate the actual total (Eggan, *op. cit.,* III, 1063–1074).

electricity and battery sets are expensive. The press is more important than the radio as a political tutor of the electorate. It gives a more adequate coverage of political news and reaches more people outside the Manila area. There is a national readership for the politically significant newspapers and magazines of something over 1,500,000, or nearly one-third of all voters in 1957. [32] A 1952 survey reported that about 20 per cent of village heads of households who vote were regular readers of newspapers with substantial political content.[33]

Contact with the communication media signifies a voter's advance from the mass of "followers" at the third level of participation in the electoral process to a new level at which he gets from outside his immediate social milieu a significant part of the information and opinion assisting him to decide how to vote. His decision is to this extent depersonalized, and he is, in part, removed from the three-step traditional hierarchy by which the national elite reaches the mass only through a network of local and provincial political leaders. The voter's "advance" is sometimes, but not always, simultaneous with movement into the middle class.

It is to this group of "independents" alone that candidates can speak of interests or issues, economic, religious, or otherwise, even though presented in gross oversimplification. But those involved in the mass media are still a minority. To win an election without relying on the traditional local intermediaries requires strong charismatic leadership capable of capturing the direct loyalty of the masses, and even this may not suffice. Magsaysay had charisma. He proved in 1953 that a superior political machine, buttressed by the power of incumbency, could be defeated by a marathon nation-wide handshaking campaign. But Magsaysay was also aided by a national party; he had the backing of most provincial governors. The experience of Manahan in 1957 showed that campaigning in the Magsaysay style, if openly opposed to the established parties and almost without organizational support, could not win against administration politicians.

Changes in campaign techniques are merely surface manifestations of basic changes in elite-mass relations. As has been noted in Chapter XXII, the politics of a colonial dependency focus on the struggle for independence. The elite which assumes the leadership in this struggle

[32] *Ibid.*, pp. 1014, 1019–1020. In 1954 the circulation of dailies, weeklies, and fortnightlies with substantial political content, in all languages except Chinese, was nearly 600,000.

[33] Generoso Rivera and Robert McMillan, *The Rural Philippines* (Manila: Mutual Security Agency, 1952), p. 157.

cannot be successfully challenged on other issues or dislodged by
competing interests. If independence is won easily, the political elite,
unlike that in Indonesia or in Vietnam, need not organize the masses.
With the transfer of sovereignty to the Philippine Republic, however,
the removal of the overriding issue of independence lifted the lid on
the political pot and allowed the conflicting interests within the elite
to boil openly. In a postindependence governmental structure which
necessitates mass acceptance of elite leadership through elections and
in a society in which, through education and urbanization, the masses
are becoming self-conscious about their own economic interests, two
or more parties compete and the system of hierarchical loyalties
which has determined Filipino voting behavior to date tends to break
down. Elite leadership is forced more and more to go directly to the
masses with a program to justify its continuance in power.

This process was interrupted in the early postwar period, however,
by two legacies of the war and enemy occupation, the Hukbalahap
movement and a rapid rise in governmental corruption. Suppression of
Huk-related organizations removed for a time from the arena of legal
political competition the two most alert segments of mass opinion,
independent labor and tenant unions. Within that arena public probity
replaced independence as the overriding issue, tending to eclipse urgent socioeconomic policy problems. For five years the electoral process was cynically discounted as a frustration of the popular will. One of
the great services of Magsaysay to his nation was that in his effort, as
he called it, "to restore the people's faith in the government," he dealt
strongly enough with the Huks and with corruption and election
fraud to allow other problems to engage the public mind and to allow
the resumption of peaceful political activity by tenants and laborers.
Economic conflicts within the elite became important public political
issues. Restoration of faith in the electoral process started again a
trend toward greater responsibility of the political elite to the masses.

The death of Magsaysay served to re-emphasize the importance
of his moral leadership while he was alive. Under his successor the
Philippines again slipped into wholesale corruption and political ir-
responsibility. Having once rescued itself from such a plight by
democratic means, however, the Philippine electorate may be able
to do so again. The new political techniques learned under Magsaysay
are not likely to be forgotten.

There is a group of industrial producers who, in need of exchange
controls to continue capital imports, are faced with an administra-

tion dominated by agricultural-export producers and incapable of or unwilling to make adequate foreign curriencies available. It would appear that these industrialists, still a small segment of the political elite, may in the long run join with an indignantly articulate middle class desirous of clean government and thereby provide leadership for the aroused small farmer seeking "land reform." Any such realignment would contribute to the growth of a mass-based two-party system clarified by a differentiation of economic interest. It must be remembered, however, that Philippine leadership has considerable capacity for meeting crises with makeshift solutions that do not upset the power structure. Any basic changes will probably come slowly. On the other hand, the possibility of violent "solutions," should unrest become acute, cannot be discounted altogether.

·XXV·

Major Problems

THE Philippines finds itself in the fortunate position of being able to take very much for granted its continued national existence and territorial integrity, barring, of course, global holocaust. Though the country has religious and linguistic diversity approximating that of Indonesia, it has no problem of political unity. It has experienced direct, centralized rule over almost all its territory for nearly two centuries, so that to regard Manila as the center of government is a Filipino's second nature. Politicians have come to have a vested interest in a centralized regime. Furthermore, there are no profound cultural divisions within the Christian population; the intense Western impact has bridged many that did exist. All educated Filipinos now have a common intellectual heritage, though with some religious variation. Linguistic-regional loyalties are meaningful, but contain no element of political separatism. Marriage across linguistic lines often occurs among the middle class and the elite. Regional balance is a political tradition and not only in a party's senatorial ticket; if the presidential nominee comes from Luzon, the vice-presidential candidate must come from the southern islands, and vice versa. The people's loyalty to the Philippine nation within its present geographical boundaries is a valid assumption of politics.

There are those within the Philippines, however, who do not have an active loyalty to the nation, that is, ethnic minorities, both indigenous and foreign. Their separateness creates social problems. Only the Chinese pose a major political problem, however, because of their number (over 1 per cent of the total population) and economic power and because a substantial percentage have an active political loyalty to another nation.[1] Diplomatic relations with the Nationalist government have been maintained by the Philippines. But though the two governments share an anti-Communist policy, the position of the Chinese in the Philippines has prevented relations from being cordial. Philippine strategy against Chinese residents, spurred by a rising tide of nationalism, has been a kind of pincers movement. New administrative and legal obstacles to naturalization are constructed, while at the same time the government takes other steps to make it more difficult for the Chinese to maintain their culture or their economic position as long as they remain aliens. In 1954 a law was passed providing for the gradual nationalization, that is, Filipinization, of retail trade. Chinese wholesaling in rice has been given severe competition by government agencies, and administrative policy has denied foreign exchange allocations to aliens. One result has been to drive Chinese capital into industry; another, less constructive, has been an increasing use of Filipino "dummies" by Chinese businessmen. The Chinese, without any legitimate avenue of political expression, find that the only way to avoid the application of restrictive measures is through bribery. Besides these economic measures, stringent rules have been adopted to regulate the operations of Chinese schools. Despite this harassment and the fact that there has been no quota for legal Chinese immigration since 1950, several hundred actually enter each year, as "temporary visitors" and otherwise. Compared with other places to which they might emigrate, the Philippines still holds promise of considerable opportunity for the much-harried Chinese.

Internal Security

National unity has been less of a problem in the Philippines than internal security. Until 1953 and reaching its peak of activity in 1950, there was a well-organized armed element attempting to overthrow the Philippine government, the Hukbalahap.[2] But Huk-led rebellion has now been reduced to scattered raids along the eastern and southern edge of Central Luzon. Two top Communist leaders remain "in the field"; two others have been killed. Luis Taruc and many other Communists less well known are serving prison terms of various durations.

[1] See above, p. 451.   [2] See above, pp. 441–443.

The Communist Party and its affiliates were outlawed by executive order in 1948, which was reinforced by congressional enactment in 1957. The army's Military Intelligence Service undertook a campaign to alert the people to the dangers of peaceful Communist infiltration, and since 1954 no labor or tenant union has been clearly shown to be Communist-dominated.

But no matter how successful, suppression of overt unrest is no substitute for solution of the problems that occasioned it. As long as the cause remains, unrest could flare again to dangerous proportions under the Communist leadership that is now under cover. The main cause in the Philippines was agrarian injustice coupled with widespread lack of faith in legal processes as the means of bringing justice. Magsaysay and his advisors saw the need for getting at the root of the evil. His administration did correct many injustices. But the restoration of tenants' faith in legal processes was achieved largely because Ramon Magsaysay was the prime mover of those processes and because the tenants had confidence in him personally as a leader. With his death they became painfully aware of the fact that much of what they had expected of him still remained to be accomplished.

Agrarian Problems and Policies

The Philippine agrarian problem derives from a large and growing tenant class which increasingly resents landlord dominance of tenancy relationships.[3] Almost all tenancy is share tenancy, and most share tenancy is on riceland. Since Central Luzon, the main rice-surplus area, accounts for about one-third of the Philippines' rice production, share tenancy is primarily a problem for that region. Besides usurious interest rates and onerous noneconomic landlord demands, the sharing system itself is very burdensome to the tenant. In 1948 over 58 per cent of rice share tenants in the Philippines paid 50 per cent or more of their crop as rent; in Central Luzon it was over 70 per cent. The Rice Share Tenancy Act,[4] on the other hand, required that when the tenant furnished work animals and farm implements and shared planting and harvesting costs with the landowner he should get 55 per cent of the crop. Many share tenants who were able to reduce their payments to the landlords after 1948 attributed the improvement to the Huk movement.

[3] See above, pp. 435, 452–453.
[4] Generoso Rivera and Robert McMillan, *Rural Philippines* (Manila: Mutual Security Agency, 1952), p. 60.

It was a desire to prevent a renewal of agrarian rebellion that spurred a landlord-dominated Congress into passing the Agricultural Tenancy Act of 1954, the first agrarian reform measure that Magsaysay had requested. This was by no means a radical law, but it did provide some increase in the rice tenants' share and in his security, preventing, for example, any ejectment by the landlord without a court order and limiting such court orders to "just causes" as set forth in the law. Furthermore, many of the law's benefits were extended to previously unprotected tenants producing crops other than rice.

Improvement of the law was not, however, Magsaysay's greatest contribution to agrarian relations. The old Rice Share Tenancy Act had existed mostly on paper, but the new act the Magsaysay administration undertook to enforce. Immediately after its passage the President set up an Agricultural Tenancy Commission by executive order. The commission sends information teams out to hold rallies in towns and villages, explain the meaning of the act, and distribute copies of the text. These are followed by mediation teams which hear complaints about nonenforcement of the act, usually from tenants, and initiate mediation to bring agreement between tenant and landlord in accordance with the law. Disputes that cannot be mediated must be taken to the Court of Agrarian Relations.

Another important government program designed to alleviate agrarian unrest by buttressing the economic security of small farmers is the providing of agricultural credit. The only way to drive the usurer out of business is to compete with him successfully. This the farmers' co-operative marketing associations have been doing in many areas, with financial assistance and administrative supervision from the government's Agricultural Credit and Co-operative Financing Administration. Repayment has been better than in any Philippine government-financed credit program in the past, membership participation in co-operative affairs has been wider, and administrative irregularities, though not unheard of, had not by 1957 assumed such proportions as to threaten the program's success.[5]

---

[5] The ACCFA lends money to over 400 co-operatives, which in turn lend to nearly 300,000 members, using the members' crops stored in the co-op warehouse as security.

Still another government program which was ostensibly designed to lift the poor tenant into independent prosperity was organized land settlement. Since one-eighth of the land area of the Philippines, mostly in Mindanao and Palawan, is arable public land available for homesteading or purchase, settlement of new areas has consistently been proposed in some quarters as the cheapest and most effective

To slow the movement of debt-ridden small farmers into tenancy and to make the tenancy relationship more just are essential aspects of any agrarian reform program. Considerable progress was made in these fields under Magsaysay. But essential also to true reform of the socioeconomic structure of Philippine rural life is land redistribution. Programs to this end have been abortive.

Land redistribution, when phrased as "government purchase of large landed estates," does not have a novel or radical sound in the Philippines. It is a policy which was initiated by the Americans and continued by Quezon. A re-examination of the landed estates policy was stimulated by the report of Robert Hardie, Mutual Security Agency economist, in 1952 which recommended a drastic reform similar to that instituted by U.S. occupation authorities in Japan. But his recommendations were not given sympathetic consideration by the Quirino administration. In fact, in the last three years of the Quirino regime there were not even any purchases of landed estates under the existing statutes.[6]

The Magsaysay administration, however, was inaugurated in an atmosphere of expectancy, especially of land reform. In a partial attempt to meet this expectation the chief executive had, by the end of 1954, initiated government purchase of two large estates, and the Bureau of Lands had amended the rules for redistribution of estates already held so as to provide greater protection for the rights of cultivators wishing to acquire title to their own plots. Before greatly expanding the land redistribution program, however, he felt the need of congressional assent. Landlord opposition to the bill which his advisers drafted was strong. Little was left of it when the legislative fight was over; in fact, the bill finally passed was considered by many to be weaker than the existing law. Unfortunately President Magsaysay underestimated his own power of legislative leadership in the situation. The land tenure reform bill became law in September 1955.

In the final analysis the President, though receiving an additional appropriation of 100 million pesos from bonds to be issued, was so seriously restricted in his powers of expropriation that a rapid reform

kind of land reform. The program has been effective primarily for providing relief of unemployment, increase of food production, and fulfillment of political promises, but has not reduced tenancy. Only a small percentage of settlers come from the highly tenanted areas of Central Luzon. See Wurfel, "Philippine Agrarian Reform under Magsaysay, I," *Far Eastern Survey*, XXVII (Jan. 1958), 7–13.

[6] See Wurfel, "Philippine Agarian Reform under Magsaysay, II," *Far Eastern Survey*, XXVII (Feb. 1958), 23–30.

program was practically impossible. The law is written in such a way —exempting from expropriation corporate landholdings up to 1,480 acres and individual landholdings up to 740 acres "of contiguous area" —that any owner who is determined to retain his land can find some legal loophole by which to do so. And the procedure for negotiated purchase is so cumbersome, taking several months at best, that the small staff of the Land Tenure Administration, established by the law, cannot handle very many estates at once. Though the law authorized the expenditure of 60 million pesos for estate purchase in the first year, less than 700,000 pesos was actually spent.[7] Whereas petitions from groups of tenants for government purchase of estates were filed in Manila at the rate of nearly one estate a day during the first six months of the Administration's life, by June 1957 actual acquisition of estates had averaged less than one a month. Even when estates were acquired, the price paid by the government—in order to get the owner's agreement—was often so high that resale to tenant cultivators at cost was beyond their means.

Land redistribution is designed to lay the groundwork for political stability by giving the largely disaffected tenant farmers a greater stake in the economy. In reducing the landlords' economic role in rural society it also weakens their political power there, and thus that balance of political forces necessary for democratic government is furthered. Since land redistribution in the Philippines does not apply to estates operated with wage labor, but only to tenant-farmed land, no adverse effect on agricultural production is likely. In fact, by raising the level of aspiration in new owners it could result in increased production per unit of cultivated area. These are goals that the present program is not achieving to any significant degree.

Economic Development Problems and Policies

The land redistribution program could have been designed to channel capital from land into industrial investment—by paying landlords in certificates useful only for that purpose—and thus have helped solve the basic Philippine economic problem, the accumulation of capital and its productive use. But it was not so designed, and the problem remains an acute one. As has been noted, the Philippines has accepted the private enterprise system more completely than most other Southeast Asian countries.[8] But its upper class does not have the

[7] Land Tenure Administration, *Annual Report, 1956* (mimeographed), pp. 41–42.
[8] See above, p. 455.

frugal spirit which was an important contributory factor to Japan's rapid capitalistic economic growth. Consequently a smaller percentage of upper-bracket incomes are saved and invested than in Japan or the United States. This low propensity to save has been one of the factors requiring the government to play an important role in economic development. Even with a comparatively large and vigorous private entrepreneurial class and an administration friendly to it, the Philippine National Economic Council published a Five Year Plan in January 1957 which called for an increased percentage of government investment. Like other such plans in Southeast Asia it emphasized industrialization.

In carrying out this plan, which is a modest one, merely projecting existing rates of investment and growth, the Philippines has both advantages and disadvantages in comparison with other Southeast Asian countries.[9] In the first place, intense Westernization has meant that the Philippine economy, even in rural areas, is more highly monetized than that of other Southeast Asian countries. Thus economic institutions, such as banks, which assume a money economy are established throughout the country and should substantially assist development. Furthermore, a friendly attitude toward Western nations, especially the United States, enables the Philippines to attract considerable amounts of much-needed foreign capital, both public and private. Readiness to accept foreign assistance whenever crisis threatens could, however, be a disadvantage if it should delay the hard thinking and realistic planning necessary to deal with economic problems domestically, as has sometimes happened in the Philippines.

One disadvantage for Philippine economic development may be overoptimism on the part of the planners, a chronic difficulty for planners everywhere but an error especially easy to fall into in a country where there was such regular and rapid growth—5 per cent annual increase of national income—from 1950 to 1955. Much of this, however, was merely delayed rehabilitation from the Second World War; it will be a rate difficult to sustain. The high rate of Philippine population growth, about 2.9 per cent per annum, aggravates the problem.

The fact that Philippine nationalism has not yet produced a spirit which accepts the national welfare as paramount is another disad-

[9] See Benjamin Higgins, "Development Problems in the Philippines: A Comparison with Indonesia," *Far Eastern Survey*, XXVI (Nov. 1957), *passim.*

vantage. Thus certain minimal economic controls essential for the success of a development plan are exceedingly difficult to enforce. Avoidance of customs and tax laws is commonplace. Filipinos occasionally refer to themselves as the "world's worst taxpayers." Only a small percentage of persons in the upper brackets pay the legally required income tax. Many politicians fail to register their land for taxation purposes. Widespread tax evasion seriously inhibits any noninflationary role of the government in economic development and prevents it from providing adequate services for the lower income groups.

In an economy in which taxation is haphazard and state enterprise is not dominant, foreign exchange controls, though also difficult to enforce (it is authoritatively estimated that illegal foreign trade transactions in 1957 caused the Central Bank to lose about 100 million pesos in badly needed foreign exchange), can become the most important tool for directing investment. Fabricating industries employing thousands of persons depend on a continuing flow of imports for operation. Maintaining an adequate foreign exchange balance and restricting its use are thus absolutely essential. Producers' efforts to gain unrestricted use of the foreign exchange generated by their exports are, therefore, resisted by the Central Bank. Tariffs, like exchange controls designed to encourage and protect "infant industry," will soon become a more important mechanism for channeling investment. Though full rates on U.S. goods cannot apply until 1974, Philippine tariffs already provide considerable protection. Foreign exchange controls will nevertheless retain their pre-eminence as a focus for political controversy, since any advantages given importers must work to the direct disadvantage of the equally articulate exporters, as long as the artificial exchange rate of two pesos to one dollar is retained. On the other hand, the costs of tariff protection, which are borne mainly by the consumer, and its immediate benefits, that is, government revenue from customs duties, are distributed more widely throughout the economy.

Industrialization has been popularized as a cure for unemployment, which is the most obvious manifestation of the nation's basic economic problems, and is widely thought of as the most serious. The labor force is now growing faster than new employment opportunities; by May 1956 about 12 per cent, or one million persons, were unsuccessfully seeking employment.[10] Because of the Filipino family system the human consequences of unemployment are not as dire as in the United

[10] *Philippine Survey of Households Bulletin* (May 1956), p. 10.

States, but are still unfortunate. The existence of large numbers of unemployed keeps wages down and seriously hampers the growth of the trade union movement.

Educational Problems and Policies

Though the Philippines has a higher percentage of literates and a better-developed educational system than elsewhere in Southeast Asia, it is nevertheless facing an educational crisis. One aspect of the crisis is the problem of language. The impracticability of English as the language of instruction in the primary grades has become increasingly evident to educational administrators. Instruction in a language which is almost totally unfamiliar to most children before entering school makes of reading a rote process with little comprehension and seriously hampers the child's grasp of other subjects.[11] Though a major portion of time is spent in the first four grades in learning English, an average fourth-grade graduate has by no means mastered the language. And only 34 per cent of the children who start the first grade ever reach the fifth.[12] To try to reduce this waste of time and effort by both teacher and pupil, in 1957 the vernacular was made the language of instruction in the first two grades, with English to be merely one subject. Thus, for example, in Cebu the second-grade teacher instructs in Cebuano; in Ilocos Sur, in Ilocano. There is now an acute lack of teaching materials in the vernacular, but the needs are being quickly met.

With English continuing to be the language of instruction for intermediate, secondary, and collegiate education, the problem of maintaining the quality of English remains. The English ability of the average high school graduate has declined sharply in the last decade, so much so that most are incapable of university level work in the English language. Filipino educators nevertheless have no plans for, or even expressed intentions of, abandoning English as the language of secondary and higher education. Though National Language (essentially Tagalog) is a required subject from the first grade, it is unpopular, and there has been no attempt to prepare Tagalog for a role as the language of instruction in higher education. Tagalog is gaining

[11] See Clifford Prator, *Language Teaching in the Philippines* (Manila: U.S. Educational Foundation, 1950).

[12] Napoleon G. Rama, "The School Crisis," *Philippines Free Press*, XLIX (June 7, 1958), 7. This is true mainly because most villages have no school beyond the fourth grade.

ground, but not primarily through the schools. It is the language of the movies and, increasingly, of the radio.

Another aspect of the educational crisis is financial. Like other Philippine governmental functions, public education is highly centralized; the national budget includes the great bulk of all educational expenditures. Education has always been the largest single item in the budget of the Republic. The absolute figure has increased by over 70 per cent since 1957,[13] during which time there has been no inflation. This does not look like evidence of a crisis, but one nevertheless exists. Teachers' salaries were increased in 1953, but in real purchasing power they are not yet to prewar levels. Finally, and most importantly, though teacher-pupil ratios have increased, facilities have not even begun to allow for enforcement of the compulsory education law. In 1958 the Secretary of Education estimated that only half of the school-age children were in schools of any type.

Inadequate funds have lowered the quality of public education and have forced more and more education-hungry youth into private schools. Private school enrollment has been growing faster than public, particularly at the secondary level. But as the cost to the parents goes up, the opportunities for upward social mobility are narrowed, thus threatening Philippine democratic development. The expansion of private schools, which now account for nearly 20 per cent of total enrollment, also contributes substantially to plummeting educational standards. About 60 per cent of private school enrollment is in "non-sectarian," in most cases profit-making, institutions. Many of these schools, in fact, distribute profits to stockholders so high that they would cause a successful Texas oilman to transfer his investments. With the profit motive predominant, the quality of education suffers. Every public-spirited citizen decries the schools that sell diplomas to persons who have not attended any classes. A greater danger, however, is the watering down of the educational process in a way not obvious to the student, who has never known anything better. Poorly trained college graduates, especially in academic and professional fields, now constitute a glut on the labor market. Too large a number have expectations of status and earning power far beyond either their capabilities or, if they are qualified, existing appropriate jobs.[14]

[13] Eggan, *op. cit.*, II, ch. x.

[14] Another aspect of the educational crisis is religious controversy, so intense in a few localities that it has been the cause of school boycotts. It is sparked by the determination of the Catholic Church to exercise more influence over the educational system. (See above, pp. 459–460.)

Foreign Policy Problems

The foreign policy of the Philippines takes an unswerving anti-Communist position and finds its closest ally in the United States. In fact the Philippine stand in international relations has been so close to that of the United States that it has been misunderstood by other Asian countries as mere parroting of a "line." Most Filipinos believe that the policy they are pursuing best serves their own national interests. At the same time they often have trouble understanding how a non-Communist can be a neutralist. This genuine mutual misunderstanding of roles, caused basically by the Philippines' cultural identification with Europe and the United States, has resulted in its ideological isolation from the rest of Southeast Asia, which is only beginning to be broken down. The postwar period has witnessed a series of events serving as a slow educational process for Filipino leaders. In this process they have come to desire closer identification with Asia, but at the same time they realize more fully how separate they really are in the minds of their Asian neighbors.[15]

The Philippines had had few significant contacts with Southeast Asia before the Magsaysay administration. Then in 1954 it helped to establish the Southeast Asia Treaty Organization and the following year had to defend this action at the Bandung Conference. During 1955 an increasing number of Filipino doctors and nurses joined "Operation Brotherhood" in South Vietnam to serve the refugees from the north, under the auspices of the Junior Chamber of Commerce. The year 1956 was a turning point. Bitter criticisms from Prince Norodom Sihanouk after his apparently cordial state visit came as a shock to Filipinos, again revealing basic misunderstandings. Throughout the year situations multiplied in which Filipinos abroad were called upon to declare their independence of U.S. policies. When they returned, nationalist feeling at home was thereby stimulated.

Even before 1956, however, a Philippine foreign policy independent of that of the United States was becoming evident. The Philippines has always been opposed to the U.S. rebuilding of Japan as its strongest Asian ally. Although the Philippine government finally signed a reparations agreement in 1955, on the basis of $550 million in cash, goods, and services and $250 million in long-term development loans, most Filipinos have shown little enthusiasm for the American-

[15] For a careful description of Philippine foreign relations see Russell Fifield, *The Diplomacy of Southeast Asia* (New York: Harpers, 1958).

supported plan to have Japan play an even greater part in Southeast Asian economic development programs. The Philippines' strong stand against colonialism, both within and without the UN Trusteeship Council, has also diverged from American policy on several occasions.

Philippine-American Relations

Philippine criticism of the United States has most frequently grown out of the nature of Philippine-American relations themselves, which both Americans and Filipinos have often called a "special relationship." Economic relations between them have been of two types, trade and aid.

Trade relations are determined by the Bell Act of 1946, as amended by the Laurel-Langley Agreement of 1955. The 1946 act provided that, after the end of duty-free trade in 1954,[16] each country would begin levying tariff on the imports of the other at 5 per cent of the total duty, with a 5 per cent increase each year until the full duty was reached in 1974. All important Philippine exports were given quotas in the U.S. market. The 1946 trade agreement was frequently criticized as retarding Philippine industrialization because it allowed free entry of American products. But Philippine interests wanted also to extend the duty-free privilege on Philippine exports to the United States. Therefore it was agreed that the speed at which U.S. tariff rates were increased could be slowed while Philippine tariffs were raised more rapidly. In reality the added protection to Philippine infant industries was not great, since exchange controls had already allowed the Philippines to exclude most nonessential and competing imports.[17] The "parity" provision in the Bell Act, giving U.S. citizens equal rights with Filipinos in exploitation of natural resources is another irritant in Philippine-American relations. In 1954 the United States agreed to make parity "mutual," that is, applicable to Filipino enterprises in the

[16] See above, p. 441.

[17] As Philippine sugar exporters are gradually forced to pay the U.S. duty, the sugar business will become somewhat less profitable. But since the U.S. price is still well above the world price, Philippine sugar equal to the quota will continue to go to the United States. Thus the absolute quota on Philippine sugar imports into the United States will continue to be important. The Philippine sugar producers were, therefore, understandably upset when the U.S. Congress in 1956 reallocated quotas in the expanded U.S. sugar market without increasing the Philippine share. Filipinos felt that this was retaliation for Philippine restrictions on the importation of leaf tobacco from the United States, and the fires of nationalism in 1956 were fed. See Frank Golay, *The Revised U.S.-Philippine Trade Agreement of 1955* (Southeast Asia Program, Cornell University, Data Paper no. 23; Ithaca, N.Y., Nov. 1956).

United States. This was a concession of little importance, however, as Filipinos were well aware.

United States aid to the Philippines falls into two categories and roughly two periods. The first category and period may be called rehabilitation aid. During the first five years after the war the United States expended about $2 billion in grants to the government and payments to individuals compensating for war damage and wartime military service.[18] Except for restoring prewar facilities, none of these funds could be said to have contributed to sustained economic growth.

The recommendations of the 1950 Economic Survey Mission [19] for social, economic, and administrative reform and for $250 million in additional aid introduced the second period, with emphasis on planned development. The United States insisted on adequate supervision of the aid subsequently given, so that a large American administrative and advisory staff was created.[20] In fact the presence of Americans in Philippine government offices influencing administrative decisions gradually developed as a source of Philippine-American friction and in 1956 contributed to the revival of nationalist feeling.

The path of Philippine-American military relations has been increasingly stony also. While Magsaysay was Secretary of National Defense, the relations between the U.S. military advisers in the Joint U.S. Military Advisory Group and the Philippine military leaders were generally cordial. United States training and equipment helped substantially to bring military victory over the Huks. The U.S. military's admiration for Magsaysay grew to such proportions that it was hard to conceal and became an issue in the 1953 presidential elections. In 1956, however, U.S. and Philippine generals exchanged public criticism.[21]

[18] See Garel Grunder and William Livezey, *The United States and the Philippines* (Norman: University of Oklahoma Press, 1951), ch. xv, and also Shirley Jenkins, *American Economic Policy towards the Philippines* (Stanford: Stanford University Press, 1954), p. 52. For detailed figures, 1945–1949, see Economic Survey Mission to the Philippines, *Report* (Washington: Government Printing Office, 1950), p. 36.

[19] See above, p. 444.

[20] Although the High Commissioner's office during the Commonwealth had a staff of about a hundred Americans, from 1951 to 1955 the total number of Americans employed by U.S. civilian agencies in the Philippines averaged approximately one thousand (George A. Malcolm, *American Colonial Careerist* [Boston: Christopher, 1957], p. 168).

[21] In answering JUSMAG charges that the Philippine government was not properly utilizing the large, but undisclosed, amount of U.S. equipment being given under the 1947 military assistance agreement (estimated at a cumulative total of $1 billion dollars in 1956), Defense Secretary Balao explained that this was be-

The Military Bases Agreement of 1947 has been the greatest single source of friction in postwar Philippine-American relations. Many Filipinos believe that the terms of this, as of other agreements signed in 1946 and 1947, were effectively dictated by the United States. The United States thereby acquired a 99-year lease over twenty-three bases large and small, active and inactive. It also acquired legal jurisdiction over its bases and its personnel roughly equivalent to the provisions of the subsequent status-of-forces agreement with Japan. Unlike the Japanese arrangement, however, the United States has jurisdiction over many kinds of offenses committed by Filipinos within its bases. Legal controversy over jurisdiction arose as early as 1948 and intensified in 1956–1957.

Ownership of base land was another focus of controversy, touched off by Attorney General Brownell's statement in 1953 that title, which had been acquired before independence, remained with the United States. Filipino critics of this decision consistently confused title to land with sovereignty over the territory of the bases. Little was done by U.S. spokesmen to clear up this confusion until Vice-President Nixon, during his visit to the Philippines in July 1956, reaffirmed U.S. recognition of Philippine sovereignty over the bases and promised to turn over the title papers to the Philippine government. This conciliatory move was designed to smooth the way for the opening of negotiations leading to expansion and "modernization" of the bases. But other aggravating incidents and a changing climate of opinion within the Filipino elite frustrated the progress of these negotiations.

In March 1956 Speaker Jose Laurel, Jr., had launched a move to "re-examine" Philippine-American relations, for which he found wide support. The upshot was the adoption by the House of a special committee report which demanded several revisions of the bases agreement, including reduction of the number and areas of bases to those absolutely necessary for military purposes and limitation of U.S. military criminal jurisdiction over U.S. military personnel and U.S. property.[22] With slight modification the Philippine panel in the bases negotiations, headed by Senator Emmanuel Pelaez, agreed. These demands seemed so extreme to the American negotiators and seemed to

---

cause the Philippines lacked funds for a huge build-up of man power. Balao added: "We are a poor country. The administration is more inclined to divert funds for more urgent projects such as the rural development program" (*Manila Times*, Sept. 12, 1956).

[22] *Manila Times*, Sept. 5, 1956.

stray so far from the original purposes of the negotiations that talks were broken off in December 1956. This marked the first time negotiations between the two countries had been broken off, an important milestone in the development of Philippine nationalism. Talks were not resumed for another two years.

Philippine nationalism has not been heated by the fire of recent revolution and thus remains moderate by Asian standards. But it has been affected in the last few years by a growing Filipino realization of what other Asians are thinking about them, with consequent newly felt needs for national cultural assertion. It has also been intensified by unfortunate incidents which have brought about Filipino disillusionment with the traditional "special relations" with the United States. The rural masses, who have never dealt with Americans in the role of equals, still look upon the United States with uncritical respect. Intensified nationalism is as yet largely an elite phenomenon. It is nevertheless something much broader and deeper than a short-term political movement with limited immediate goals, as it has sometimes been characterized in Washington.

Senator Claro Recto has played the leading role in the recent resurgence of nationalism. As early as 1952 he criticized the Philippine-American military assistance pact for not including the automatic guarantee of U.S. assistance that was written into the NATO alliance. In 1956 he called on Filipinos to be "realistic" and recognize that their country was a "military protectorate" and an "economic colony" of the United States. He has been persistent, but neither consistently logical nor accurate in his criticisms. Nevertheless no critique of Senator Recto can gainsay the fact that, in large part because of his very persistence, Philippine nationalism today extends far beyond his own followers.

Some Filipino leaders see this potent force as a necessary discipline for social and economic progress and are attempting to channel its power to such positive ends. That its spirit may also increase Philippine-American disagreements appears probable.

SUGGESTED READING

GENERAL WORKS

Eggan, Fred, Evett D. Hester, Norton S. Ginsburg, and Staff. *Area Handbook on the Philippines.* (Subcontractor's Monograph, University of Chicago.) 4 vols. New Haven: Human Relations Area Files, Inc., 1956. Although covering all aspects of Philippine life, this is a study of uneven usefulness. The sociological, anthropological, and geographical sections are particularly good, presenting new material clearly and with keen analysis. The section on education is a rich statistical source.

Hayden, J. Ralston. *The Philippines: A Study in National Development.* New York: Macmillan, 1947; first printed 1942. By far the most complete and perceptive account and analysis of the development of Philippine self-government and of the policy problems of the Commonwealth period. Hayden was for a time Vice-Governor-General.

Ravenholt, Albert J. "The Philippines: Where Did We Fail?" *Foreign Affairs,* XXIX (April 1951), 406–416. A critical, pessimistic analysis of the whole political, social, and economic scene, written at a time when only pessimism seemed realistic.

XXII: The Historical Background

Abaya, Hernando. *Betrayal in the Philippines.* New York: A. A. Wyn, 1946. An anti-Roxas interpretation of early postwar Philippine politics in which collaboration was a major issue; revealing, but often inaccurate.

Agoncillo, Teodoro. *Revolt of the Masses: The Story of Bonifacio and the Katipunan.* Quezon City: University of the Philippines, 1956. This prize-winning biography is at the same time a provocative analysis of the class character of the Philippine Revolution. It has been a most controversial book.

Bernstein, David. "America and Dr. Laurel," *Harper's Magazine,* CXCVII (Oct. 1948), 82–88. A well-written, but unfavorable, analysis of the ideology and political tactics of Jose P. Laurel, appearing at a time when he was about to run for the presidency.

———. *The Philippine Story.* New York: Farrar, Straus and Co., 1947. The best brief, interpretive history of the Philippines up to 1941. The last half of the book provides the most complete and accurate account of the war and immediate postwar years from a point of view critical of Roxas and MacArthur. Bernstein was political adviser to Quezon and Osmeña.

Buenafe, Manuel. *Wartime Philippines.* Manila: Philippine Education Foundation, Inc., 1950. A well-told story of Japan in the Philippines, starting many years before 1941; an ambivalent, and thus typical, treatment of collaboration. Although rich in detail, its usefulness is marred by lack of any reference footnotes.

Castillo, Teofilo and Jose del. *The Saga of Jose P. Laurel (His Brother's Keeper).* Manila: Associated Author's Co., 1949. A very favorable, and incomplete, biography written at a time when Laurel was a presidential candidate. It is important as an interpretation of the war period from the point of view of one who held the highest political office under the Japanese.

Chapman, Abraham. "Note on the Philippine Elections," *Pacific Affairs,* XIX (June 1946), 193–198. The most complete account of the 1946 elections readily available, written before one became suspect for speaking favorably of the Democratic Alliance.

Cunningham, Charles H. *The Audiencia in the Spanish Colonies, as Illustrated by the Audiencia of Manila.* Berkeley: University of California Press, 1919. The most detailed description in print of Spanish colonial government in the Philippines.

Curry, Roy W. *Woodrow Wilson and Far Eastern Policy, 1913–1921.* New York: Bookman Associates, 1957. Includes 35 pages of an intimate and revealing account of Wilson's role in Philippine policy of this period.

Elsbree, Willard. "The 1953 Philippine Presidential Elections," *Pacific Affairs,* XXVII (March 1954), 3–15.

Eyre, James K. *The Roosevelt-MacArthur Conflict.* Chambersburg, Pa.: privately printed for the author by Craft Press, 1950. A detailed account of the relationships of Quezon, Osmeña, Roosevelt, and MacArthur in the period 1941–1946. Although treating MacArthur's role quite critically, it provides a key to understanding his political activities in the immediate postwar period.

Forbes, W. Cameron. *The Philippine Islands.* Cambridge: Harvard University Press, 1945. (Condensation of 1928 two-volume edition.) Best general account of American administration in the Philippines by an important participant. Mr. Forbes was Governor-General from 1909 to 1913.

Grunder, Garel A., and William Livezey, *The Philippines and the United States.* Norman: University of Oklahoma Press, 1951. The best history of U.S. Philippine policy, emphasizing the role of the U.S. Congress, placed in its political context. It relies heavily on congressional documents.

Kalaw, Teodoro M. *The Philippine Revolution.* Manila: Manila Book Co., Inc., 1925. A detailed, but uncritical, account of the period 1892–1902.

Liang, Dapen. *The Development of Philippine Political Parties.* Hongkong: South China Morning Post, 1939. The most detailed account extant of Philippine parties prior to the establishment of the Commonwealth.

Majul, Cesar A. *The Political and Constitutional Ideas of the Philippine Revolution.* Quezon City: University of the Philippines, 1957. With introduction by Leopoldo Y. Yabes. An excellent analysis of the origins and implications of early Philippine thought.

Palma, Rafael. *The Pride of the Malay Race.* Trans. from the Spanish by Ramon Ozaeta. New York: Prentice-Hall, 1949. The biography of Rizal which won the Commonwealth prize in 1938. It gives the Masonic version of Rizal's last days and thus has been kept off the required reading list for Philippine high schools by Catholic Church pressure.

Quirino, Carlos. *Magsaysay of the Philippines.* Quezon City: Phoenix Press, Inc., 1958. The most complete biography so far of the late President. It consists mostly of anecdotes, selected to reveal a variety of facets of Magsaysay's character, and is a sympathetic, but not eulogistic, treatment.

Included is considerable general historical material. This is an important source on the politics of the Quirino and Magsaysay administrations.

Recto, Claro M. *Three Years of Enemy Occupation: The Issue of Political Collaboration in the Philippines.* Manila: People's Publishers, 1946. An effective apologia for those Filipinos who held political office under the Japanese.

Rizal, Jose. *Noli Me Tangere.* Trans. by Jorge Bocobo. Manila: R. Martinez and Sons, 1956. Also trans. by Charles Derbyshire under the title *The Social Cancer.* Written originally in Spanish, published in Berlin in 1887, this is the best and the most famous novel ever written by a Filipino. It played a major role in arousing nationalist feeling in the Philippines in the late nineteenth century because of its graphic portrayal of the evils of the Spanish colonial system.

Smith, Robert Aura. *Philippine Freedom.* New York: Columbia University Press, 1958. A very readable brief history of the postwar Philippines which avoids discussion of some of the most controversial, and thus important, issues. The constitution of the Philippines and the Philippine Trade Agreement Revision Act of 1955 are among the important documents in the appendices.

Worcester, Dean C. *The Philippines, Past and Present.* New York: Macmillan, 1930. (Revision, condensation, and expansion by J. Ralston Hayden of 1913 two-volume edition.) A detailed, critical, and at times partisan, account of the vicissitudes of American rule in the Philippines by a man who was a member of the Philippine Commission from 1900 to 1913. It contains six valuable appendices.

XXIII: The Contemporary Setting

Central Bank of the Philippines. *Statistical Bulletin.* The most complete ready source of trade, production, and labor statistics on the Philippines.

Economic Survey Mission to the Philippines. *Report to the President of the United States.* Washington: Government Printing Office, 1950. The "Bell Report."

Kroeber, Alfred L. *The Peoples of the Philippines.* New York: Anthropological Handbook Fund, 1943. A descriptive analysis of cultural-linguistic groups in the Philippines by a leading anthropologist, with heavy emphasis on non-Christians.

Pal, Agaton. "A Philippine Barrio: A Study of Social Organization in Relation to Planned Cultural Change," *Journal of East Asiatic Studies,* V (Oct. 1956), 333–486. The best available study in depth of a Christian village.

Rivera, Generoso, and Robert McMillan. *The Rural Philippines.* Manila: Mutual Security Agency, 1952. The first multicommunity sociological survey of Christian villages made in the Philippines. Based on nearly 4,000 interviews in 13 widely scattered barrios. Because of its revelation of government neglect of the barrios, it was the focus of political controversy at the time of its release.

Stephens, Robert P. "The Prospect for Social Progress in the Philippines," *Pacific Affairs*, XXIII (June 1950), 139–152. An assessment of the economic and social setting of politics.

XXIV: The Political Process

Coquia, Jorge. *The Philippine Presidential Election of 1953*. Manila: University Publishing Co., 1955. The best study of the Philippine electoral process to date, it includes a detailed description of nomination and election procedures and an assessment of the parties, the interests, and the issues.

Corpuz, Onofre D. *Bureaucracy in the Philippines*. Manila: University of the Philippines, Institute of Public Administration, 1957. A careful critical history of the Philippine Civil Service, both American and Filipino.

Dalton, James. "Ins and Outs in the Philippines," *Far Eastern Survey*, XXI (July 30, 1952), 117–123. The best available account and analysis of the 1951 elections.

Elsbree, Willard H. "The Philippines," in Rupert Emerson, *Representative Government in Southeast Asia*. Cambridge: Harvard University Press, 1955. Pages 92–117. A survey and analysis of Philippine government and politics.

Heady, Ferrel. "The Philippine Administrative System—Fusion of East and West," in William J. Siffin, ed., *Toward the Comparative Study of Public Administration*. Bloomington: Indiana University, Department of Government, 1957. Pages 253–277. An excellent treatment of administrative structure and behavior in its social and historical setting.

Lande, Carl H. "Local Politics and the Pork Barrel," *Sunday Times Magazine* (Manila), July 29, 1956, pp. 4–7. A convincing attempt to justify the great importance of "pork" in Philippine politics.

———. "Politics in the Philippines." Unpublished Ph.D. thesis, Harvard University, 1958. The best analysis to date of Philippine political behavior, relying very heavily on an anthropological approach.

Olson, Lawrence. "After Magsaysay, What?" *American Universities Field Staff Report*, Oct. 1957. A perceptive report on the 1957 election campaign.

Ravenholt, Albert. "The Peso Price of Politics," *American Universities Field Staff Report*, May 1958. By the most acute resident-observer of Philippine politics and society today.

Romani, John H. *The Philippine Presidency*. Manila: University of the Philippines, Institute of Public Administration, 1956. The best postwar work on Philippine national political institutions.

——, and M. Ladd Thomas. *A Survey of Local Government in the Philippines*. Manila: University of the Philippines, Institute of Public Administration, 1954. Includes description and analysis of all levels of local government. It is the best source available on the subject.

Stene, Edwin O., and Associates. *Public Administration in the Philippines*. Manila: University of the Philippines, Institute of Public Administration, 1955. The co-operative effort of seventeen Filipino and American authors, this descriptive analysis of the structure and techniques of administration is based on extensive research.

XXV: Major Problems

Bernstein, David. "Lessons from Luzon," *Yale Review*, XXXVIII (March 1949), 509–519. An assessment of the Huks and the agrarian situation shortly after the amnesty of 1948 had failed.

Golay, Frank. "Philippine Monetary Debate," *Pacific Affairs*, XXIX (Sept. 1956), 253–264. Penetrating assessment of the Philippines' most controversial economic policy.

Hahn, Walter F., Joseph A. Peters, and Edgar Rosenthal. "The United States and the Philippines," in Robert Strausz-Hupe, Alvin J. Cottrell, and James E. Dougherty, eds., *American-Asian Tensions*. New York: Praeger, 1956. Pages 123–147.

Jacobini, H. B., and Associates. *Governmental Services in the Philippines*. Manila: University of the Philippines, Institute of Public Administration, 1956. The most complete description available of the organization and the substance of the programs of Philippine governmental agencies.

Jenkins, Shirley. *American Economic Policy toward the Philippines*. Stanford: Stanford University Press, 1954. The most complete description of U.S.-Philippine economic relations and of Filipino attitudes on this subject.

McHale, Thomas. "Problems of Economic Development in the Philippines," *Pacific Affairs*, XXV (June 1952), 160–169. From an institutional approach. It includes important insights.

Pelzer, Karl J. *Pioneer Settlement in the Asiatic Tropics*. New York: Institute of Pacific Relations, 1945. Includes 80-page coverage of the history of land tenure and land policy in the Philippines, its contemporary patterns, and a detailed description of land settlement projects in Mindanao.

Prator, Clifford. *Language Teaching in the Philippines*. Manila: U.S. Educational Foundation, 1950. A keen analysis of the language crisis in Philippine education, including both the question of the language of instruction and that of teaching methods in English.

Ravenholt, Albert. "The Amir-Mindalano—Profile of a Filipino Mohammedan Leader," *American Universities Field Staff Report*, July 1956. Reveals the role of the educated Muslim leader in Philippine national life.

Recto, Claro M. *My Crusade*. Manila: Carag Publishers, 1955. A collection of speeches and open letters by the leading protagonist of President Magsaysay and proponent of Philippine nationalism.

Scaff, Alvin. *The Philippine Answer to Communism*. Stanford: Stanford University Press, 1955. A detailed account of the Philippine army's Economic Development Corps land settlement project in Mindanao, with sociological emphasis. Also included is the best summary history of the Philippine Communist movement.

Taruc, Luis. *Born of the People*. With foreword by Paul Robeson. New York: International Publishers, 1953. An "autobiography" of the Hukbalahap *supremo* which is reported to have been actually written by the Huk's American Communist adviser, William Pomeroy.

GENERAL READING LIST

INDEX

General Reading List

Ball, W. Macmahon. *Nationalism and Communism in East Asia.* Melbourne: Melbourne University Press, 1952. A good general discussion of the economic and social forces which lie behind political turbulence.

Benda, Harry J. "Communism in Southeast Asia," *Yale Review,* XLV (Spring 1956), 417–429. A theoretical essay on communism's bid for the social forces released by nationalism.

Braibanti, Ralph. "The Southeast Asia Collective Defense Treaty," *Pacific Affairs,* XXX (Dec. 1957), 321–341. One of the best analyses.

Chatham House Study Group. *Collective Defence in South East Asia.* London: Royal Institute of International Affairs, 1956. A careful examination of the implications of SEATO.

Dobby, E. H. G. *South East Asia.* London: University of London Press, 1950. A useful study for the physical geography of the area, but weak in its treatment of political aspects.

Du Bois, Cora. *Social Forces in Southeast Asia.* Minneapolis: University of Minnesota Press, 1949. An excellent general introduction to the cultural patterns of the area by one of the pioneers in anthropological research there.

Elsbree, Willard H. *Japan's Role in Southeast Asian Nationalist Movements.* Cambridge, Mass.: Harvard University Press, 1953. A useful short study based principally on Japanese materials.

Emerson, Rupert. "Paradoxes of Asian Nationalism," *Far Eastern Quarterly,* XIII (Feb. 1954), 131–142.

——. *Representative Government in Southeast Asia.* Cambridge, Mass.: Harvard University Press, 1955. A valuable assessment of the prospects of democratic institutions in the Southeast Asian countries.

Farley, Miriam S. *United States Relations with Southeast Asia, 1950–1955.* New York: Institute of Pacific Relations, 1956.

Fifield, Russell H. *The Diplomacy of Southeast Asia, 1945–1958.* New York: Harper, 1958. A unique and comprehensive coverage.

Furnivall, J. S. *Colonial Policy and Practice: A Comparative Study of Burma and Netherlands India.* New York: New York University Press, 1956. First published in 1948, this volume is a pioneering work in the field of comparative Southeast Asian studies. It contains a full exposition of the author's theory of plural economy.

Ginsberg, Norton, ed. *The Pattern of Asia.* Englewood Cliffs, N.J.: Prentice-Hall, 1958. Includes 167 pages on Southeast Asia. It is the best concise physical, economic, and social geography of the region and has excellent maps.

Hall, D. G. E. *A History of South East Asia.* London: Macmillan; New York: St. Martin's Press, 1955. Scholarly, well documented, and comprehensive. Emphasis is upon the precolonial period. It does not deal with the Philippines.

Harrison, Brian. *A Short History of South East Asia.* London: Macmillan; New York: St. Martin's Press, 1955. A much shorter survey than that by Hall, but nonetheless very useful.

Heine-Geldern, Robert. *Conceptions of State and Kingship in Southeast Asia.* (Southeast Asia Program, Cornell University, Data Paper no. 18.) Ithaca, N.Y., 1956. Useful to an understanding of the traditional, precolonial, political ethos.

Henderson, William. "The Development of Regionalism in Southeast Asia," *International Organization,* IX (Nov. 1955), 463–476. The best treatment available.

Holland, William L., ed. *Asian Nationalism and the West.* New York: Macmillan, 1953. Contains long and valuable papers on the postwar political situations in Vietnam, Malaya, and Indonesia.

Isaacs, Harold R. *No Peace for Asia.* New York: Macmillan, 1947. A valuable account of the situation in 1945–1946, particularly good on Indochina and Indonesia.

Jacoby, Erich. *Agrarian Unrest in Southeast Asia.* New York: Columbia University Press, 1949. A useful synthesis of much of the best literature relating to agrarian problems of the area.

Kahin, George McT. *The Asian-African Conference, Bandung, Indonesia, April 1955.* Ithaca, N.Y.: Cornell University Press, 1956. Includes a selection of the more important documents of the conference in their official version.

King, John Kerry. *Southeast Asia in Perspective.* New York: Macmillan, 1956. A good analysis of the development of United States foreign policy toward the countries of the area.

Landon, Kenneth P. *Southeast Asia: Crossroads of Religions.* Chicago: University of Chicago Press, 1947. A useful introduction. Some sections are marred by being rather superficial.

Mende, Tibor. *South East Asia between Two Worlds.* London: Turnstile Press, 1955. The observations of a political journalist on Burma, Indonesia, and Pakistan. His two worlds are China and India.

Mills, Lennox A., and Associates. *The New World of Southeast Asia.* Minneapolis: University of Minnesota Press, 1949. Now badly outdated, but containing several country surveys which are still of value.

Peaslee, Amos J. *Constitutions of Nations.* 2d ed. The Hague: Nijhoff, 1956. Valuable for texts of constitutions of the states.

Purcell, Victor. *The Chinese in South East Asia.* London: Oxford University Press, 1951. A full standard historical work. It contains a discussion of many of the social and economic tensions which are central to the position of the Chinese today. It is most useful and most comprehensive in its treatment of conditions prior to the Second World War.

Rosinger, Lawrence K., and Associates. *The State of Asia.* New York: Alfred Knopf, 1951. A valuable collection of country survey articles by specialists, but somewhat out of date.

Scalapino, Robert A. " 'Neutralism' in Asia," *American Political Science Review,* XLVIII (March 1954), 49–62. An excellent analysis.

"Southeast Asia in Transition," *Journal of International Affairs,* vol. X, no. 1 (1956). Nine short articles on the area. Some of them are of the country survey type; others treat problems in terms of the region as a whole.

Spencer, J. E. *Asia, East by South.* New York: Wiley, 1954. A geography of the area. It is stronger than Dobby's treatment with regard to social aspects.

Thayer, Philip W., ed. *Nationalism and Progress in Free Asia.* Baltimore: Johns Hopkins University Press, 1956. This and the following collection of papers were presented by leading Asian intellectuals and political figures to conferences held in Rangoon in 1952 and 1955 under the sponsorship of Johns Hopkins University. Both collections contain valuable material, though there is unevenness in the quality of the papers.

——. *South East Asia in the Coming World.* Baltimore: Johns Hopkins University Press, 1953.

Thompson, Virginia, and Richard Adloff. *The Left Wing in Southeast Asia.* New York: Sloane, 1950. Dated and somewhat uneven, but nevertheless useful.

——. *Minority Problems in Southeast Asia.* Stanford: Stanford University Press, 1955. This is one of the few treatments of the problems, but the coverage is of uneven quality and sometimes sketchy.

Trager, Frank N., and Associates. *Marxism in Southeast Asia: A Study of Four Countries.* Stanford: Stanford University Press. Forthcoming.

United Nations. *Economic Survey of Asia and the Far East.* Published annually. These reports of the Economic Commission for Asia and the Far East (ECAFE) contain reliable surveys of economic data, both for particular countries of the South and East Asian area and for the area as a whole.

Vandenbosch, Amry, and Richard A. Butwell. *Southeast Asia among the Powers.* Lexington, Ky.: University of Kentucky Press, 1957. A rather popular treatment; uneven in quality.

Wolf, Charles, Jr. "Soviet Economic Aid in Southeast Asia," *World Politics,* X (Oct. 1957), 91–101. A sophisticated discussion of some important new problems in the international relations of the area.

Zinkin, Maurice. *Asia and the West.* New York: Institute of Pacific Relations, International Secretariat, 1953. A stimulating discussion of central economic and social problems faced by the countries of Asia at the point of their emergence from colonial rule. Although concerned principally with the Indian subcontinent, the book is valuable also for its insights into Southeast Asian situations.

Index